LINGUISTIC SURVEY OF INDIA

VOL. V.

INDO-ARYAN FAMILY

EASTERN GROUP.

PART II

SPECIMENS OF THE BIHĀRĪ AND ORIYĀ LANGUAGES.

VOLUMES OF

THE LINGUISTIC SURVEY OF INDIA

VOL. I. PART I INTRODUCTORY.
PART II COMPARATIVE VOCABULARY.
VOL. II. MŌN-KHMĒR & SIAMESE-CHINESE FAMILIES (INCLUDING KHASSI & TAI).
VOL. III. TIBETO-BURMAN FAMILY
PART I GENERAL INTRODUCTION, TIBETAN DIALECTS, HIMALAYAN DIALECTS, & NORTH ASSAM GROUPS.
PART II BODO-NĀGĀ & KACHIN GROUPS.
PART III KUKI-CHIN & BURMA GROUPS.
VOL. IV. MUṆḌĀ & DRAVIDIAN LANGUAGES.
VOL. V. INDO-ARYAN FAMILY, (EASTERN GROUP).
PART I BENGALI & ASSAMESE.
PART II BIHĀRĪ & OṚIYĀ.
VOL. VI. INDO-ARYAN FAMILY, MEDIATE GROUP (EASTERN HINDI).
VOL. VII. INDO-ARYAN FAMILY, SOUTHERN GROUP (MARĀṬHI).
VOL. VIII. INDO-ARYAN FAMILY, NORTH-WESTERN GROUP.
PART I SINDHI & LAHNDĀ.
PART II DARDIC OR PIŚACHA LANGUAGES (INCLUDING KASHMĪRĪ).
VOL. IX. INDO-ARYAN FAMILY, CENTRAL GROUP.
PART I WESTERN HINDI & PANJĀBI.
PART II RAJASTHĀNĪ & GUJARĀTĪ.
PART III BHIL LANGUAGES INCLUDING KHANDESI, BANJARI OR LABHANI, BAHRUPIA ETC.
PART IV PAHARI LANGUAGES & GUJURI.
VOL. X. ERANIAN FAMILY.
VOL. XI. "GIPSY" LANGUAGES.

राष्ट्रपति भवन, नई दिल्ली-4.
RASHTRAPATI BHAVAN,
NEW DELHI-4.

October 20, 1966.

Dear Sri Sundarlal,

Thank you very much for undertaking the task of republication of Grierson's LINGUISTIC SURVEY OF INDIA. It is a pleasure to know that you were able to complete the republication of the 50 volumes of Max Muller's 'Sacred Books of the East' within 3 years. Your work, I may assure you, is of the greatest value to the intellectuals of the world.

With the best wishes,

Yours sincerely,

(S. Radhakrishnan)

Sri Sundarlal,
Motilal Banarsidass,
Post Box 1586,
Bungalow Road,
Jawaharnagar,
Delhi-7

CONTENTS.

OṚIYĀ.

MAPS.

LINGUISTIC SURVEY OF INDIA.

SYSTEM OF TRANSLITERATION ADOPTED.

A.—For the Dēva-nāgarī alphabet, and others related to it—

अ *a*, आ *ā*, इ *i*, ई *ī*, उ *u*, ऊ *ū*, ऋ *ṛi*, ए *e*, ए *ē*, ऐ *ai*, ओ *o*, ओ *ō*, औ *au*.

क *ka*	ख *kha*	ग *ga*	घ *gha*	ङ *ṅa*	च *cha*	छ *chha*	ज *ja*	झ *jha*	ञ *ña*
ट *ṭa*	ठ *ṭha*	ड *ḍa*	ढ *ḍha*	ण *ṇa*	त *ta*	थ *tha*	द *da*	ध *dha*	न *na*
प *pa*	फ *pha*	ब *ba*	भ *bha*	म *ma*	य *ya*	र *ra*	ल *la*	व *va* or *wa*	
श *śa*	ष *sha*	स *sa*	ह *ha*		ड़ *ṛa*	ढ़ *ṛha*	ळ *ḷa*	ळ्ह *ḷha*.	

Visarga (ः) is represented by *ḥ*, thus क्रमशः *kramaśaḥ*. *Anuswāra* (ं) is represented by *ṁ*, thus सिंह *siṁh*, वंश *vaṁś*. In Bengali and some other languages it is pronounced *ṅg*, and is then written *ṅg*.; thus বংশ *baṅgśa*. *Anunāsika* or *Chandra-bindu* is represented by the sign ~ over the letter nasalized, thus में *mẽ*.

B.—For the Arabic alphabet, as adapted to Hindūstānī—

ا	*a*, etc.	ج	*j*	د	*d*	ر	*r*	س	*s*	ع	ʻ
ب	*b*	چ	*ch*	ڈ	*ḍ*	ڑ	*ṛ*	ش	*sh*	غ	*gh*
پ	*p*	ح	*ḥ*	ذ	*z̤*	ز	*z*	ص	*ṣ*	ف	*f*
ت	*t*	خ	*kh*			ژ	*zh*	ض	*ẓ*	ق	*q*
ٹ	*ṭ*							ط	*t̤*	ک	*k*
ث	*s̤*							ظ	*z̤*	گ	*g*
										ل	*l*
										م	*m*
										ن	*n*
										ں	when representing *anunāsika* in Dēva-nāgarī, by ~ over nasalised vowel.
										و	*w* or *v*
										ہ	*h*
										ی	*y*, etc.

Tanwīn is represented by *n*, thus فوراً *fauran*. *Alif-i maqṣūra* is represented by *ā̦*;— thus, دعوی *da'wā̦*.

In the Arabic character, a final silent *h* is not transliterated,—thus بنده *banda*. When pronounced, it is written,—thus, گناه *gunāh*.

Vowels when not pronounced at the end of a word, are not written in transliteration. Thus, बन *ban*, not *bana*. When not pronounced in the middle of a word or only slightly pronounced in the middle or at the end of a word, they are written in small characters above the line. Thus (Hindī) देखता *dēkh^{a}tā*, pronounced *dēkhtā*; (Kāśmīrī) चुह् چھ *ts^{u}h*; कर् کر *kar^{u}*, pronounced *kor*; (Bihārī) देखथि *dēkhath^{i}*.

C.—Special letters peculiar to special languages will be dealt with under the head of the languages concerned. In the meantime the following more important instances may be noted :—

(*a*) The *ts* sound found in Marāṭhī (च), Puṣhtō (څ), Kāśmīrī (ڇ, च), Tibetan (ཙ), and elsewhere, is represented by *t͟s*. So, the aspirate of that sound is represented by *t͟sh*.

(*b*) The *dz* sound found in Marāṭhī (ज), Puṣhtō (ځ), and Tibetan (ཛ) is represented by *d͟z*, and its aspirate by *d͟zh*.

(*c*) Kāśmīrī ڽ (ञ) is represented by *ñ*.

(*d*) Ṣindhī ڻ, Western Panjābī (and elsewhere on the N.-W. Frontier) ݨ, and Puṣhtō ڼ or ں are represented by *ṇ*.

(*e*) The following are letters peculiar to Puṣhtō :—

ټ *ṭ* ; څ *t͟s* or *d͟z*, according to pronunciation ; ډ *ḍ*; ړ *ṛ* ; ږ *ẓh* or *g*, according to pronunciation ; ښ *ṣh* or *ḳh*, according to pronunciation ; ڼ or ں *ṇ*.

(*f*) The following are letters peculiar to Sindhī :—

ٻ *bb* ; ڀ *bh* ; ٿ *th* ; ٽ *ṭ* ; ٺ *ṭh* ; ڦ *ph* ; ڄ *jj* ; جھ *jh* ; ڇ *chh* ;

ڃ *ñ* ; ڌ *dh* ; ڊ *ḍ* ; ڏ *ḍḍ* ; ڍ *ḍh* ; ڪ *k* ; ک *kh* ; ڳ *gg* ; گھ *gh* ;
ڱ *ṅ* ; ڻ *ṇ*.

D.—Certain sounds, which are not provided for above, occur in transcribing languages which have no alphabet, or in writing phonetically (as distinct from transliterating) languages (such as Bengali) whose spelling does not represent the spoken sounds. The principal of these are the following :—

á,	represents	the sound	of the	*a* in *all*.
ă,	„	„	„	*a* in *hat*.
ĕ,	„	„	„	*e* in *met*.
ŏ,	„	„	„	*o* in *hot*.
e,	„	„	„	*é* in the French *était*.
o,	„	„	„	*o* in the first *o* in *promote*.
ö,	„	„	„	*ö* in the German *schön*.
ü,	„	„	„	*ü* in the „ *mühe*.
t͟h,	„	„	„	*th* in *think*.
d͟h,	„	„	„	*th* in *this*.

The semi-consonants peculiar to the Muṇḍā languages are indicated by an apostrophe. Thus *k'*, *t'*, *p'*, and so on.

E.—When it is necessary to mark an accented syllable, the acute accent is used. Thus in (K͟hōwār) *ássistai*, he was, the acute accent shows that the accent falls on the first, and not, as might be expected, on the second syllable.

BIHĀRĪ.

Bihārī means properly the language of Bihar, and is spoken over nearly the whole of that Province. It is spoken also outside its limits, but it is fitly called by the above name; for not only is it, as a matter of fact, specially the language of Bihar, but also the only one of its dialects which has received any literary culture is peculiar to the north of that province. On the west, Bihārī is spoken in the Eastern districts of the Province of Agra, and even in a small portion of Oudh. On the south it is spoken on the two plateaux of Chota Nagpur. Roughly it covers an area of 90,000 square miles, and is the language of 36,000,000 people. It extends from the lower ranges of the Himalayas on the North to Singhbhum on the South, and from Manbhum on the South-east to Basti on the North-west. Within the area in which it is spoken are the two great cities of Benares and Patna.

Where spoken.

Bihārī is bounded on the North by the Tibeto-Burman Languages of the Himalayas, on the East by Bengali, on the South by Oṛiyā, and on the West by the Chhattīsgaṛhī, Baghēlī, and Awadhī dialects of Eastern Hindī. It is the most Western of the languages which form the Eastern Group of the Indo-Aryan Vernaculars.

Language-boundaries.

Bihārī has hitherto been classed as belonging to the Mediate Group of these vernaculars, being thus brought into close relationship with Eastern Hindī, Baghēlī, and Chhattīsgaṛhī. Further investigation has, however, shown that this classification cannot be correct. It certainly belongs to the same group as Bengali, Oṛiyā, and Assamese. It is true that the nationalities who speak it are historically connected with the United Provinces and not with Bengal. All their family ties, all their traditions, point to the West and not to the East. But at present our affair is not with ethnic relations, but with the facts of grammar, and, taking grammar as the test, there can be no doubt either as to the origin or affiliation of Bihārī. Like Bengali, Oṛiyā, and Assamese, it is a direct descendant, perhaps the most direct of the descendants, of the old form of speech known as Māgadhī Prakrit, and has so much in common with them in its inflexional system that it would almost be possible to make one grammar for all the four languages.

Its Classification.

In order to show this, it will be necessary to give a brief comparative sketch of the grammars of Bihārī and of Bengali, its neighbour to the East. Bihārī, as we go westward, more and more departs from the standard of Bengali, and approaches that of the other languages of the United Provinces. I shall therefore take, for the purposes of comparison, the dialect, Maithilī, which is situated on the East of the Bihārī tract, and which is therefore most near to Bengali. I shall show, not only the principal points in which Maithilī agrees with Bengali, but also those in which it differs from it in favour of its Western neighbour Eastern Hindī.

Bihārī compared with Bengali.

In regard to pronunciation, Bihārī occupies a middle place between Bengali and Eastern Hindī. Nothing is so characteristic of Bengali as its pronunciation of the vowel *a* and of the consonant *s*. The first is sounded like the *o* in the English word *not*, and as it is of frequent

Pronunciation.

occurrence, this note gives the predominating tone-colour of a Bengali sentence. In Maithilī, the same vowel has also a broad sound, not so broad as in Bengali, but still distinctly broader than the sound which the vowel takes in Central Hindōstān. It is something between the *u* in *cub* and the *o* in *cob*. As we go westward, this broad pronunciation is gradually lost, till it entirely disappears in the most Westerly dialect of Bihārī,—Bhojpurī. As regards the letter *s*, the ancient Māgadhī was unable to use the sound, and substituted for it a sound approaching that of an English *sh*. On the other hand, the Prakrit-speaking tribes more to the West could not say this *sh*, and substituted for it *s*. Here Bengali and Eastern Hindī exactly represent the ancient state of affairs. The Bengalis, like the men of Gilead, say 'shibboleth,' while the inhabitants of Hindōstān, like the Ephraimites, can only say 'sibboleth.' Here Bihārī has thrown in its lot with the latter. The sound of the English *sh* is non-existent in all its dialects. I have said that Bengali turns every *s* into *sh*; but this is only true of the Standard form of speech. The line of distinction between the *s*-sound and the *sh*-sound is not quite coincident with the language-boundary. North-Western Bengali, where it marches with Bihārī, in Purnea and Malda, follows the Bihārī custom, and cannot pronounce *sh*. Taking these two points as the test, we may say that in pronunciation, Bihārī partakes partly of the characteristics of Bengali, and partly of those of the West; with a leaning towards the latter. Finally, in connection with this subject, the old Maithilī alphabet is nearly the same as that in use, at the present day, in Bengal.

Declension.

In the declension of a noun in the various Indo-Aryan vernaculars two processes are involved. There is first the preparation of the base to receive the appropriate postposition, and there is, secondly, the selection and suffixing of the latter in order to give the required meaning of case. Thus, if we wish to express in Hindī the idea contained in the English words 'of a horse,' we first take the word *ghōṛā*, meaning 'a horse.' We then prepare this word for the addition of its postposition by changing *ghōṛā* to *ghōṛē*. So prepared it is called the oblique form of the base. Then to this oblique form we add the genitive postposition *kā*, and obtain *ghōṛē-kā*, of a horse. In Hindī, the oblique form of the base is frequently the same as the nominative, or, as the latter is called, the direct form of the base, but, whenever it is different, it always, or nearly always, ends in *ē*. In Bihārī, the oblique form is common in the case of pronouns, and also occurs in the cases of certain nouns ending in *l*, *r*, and *b*. Save in a few exceptional cases, it ends in *ā*, not *ē*. Examples are *ham*ᵉ*r-ā-kē*, to me: *dekh*ᵃ*b-ā-saũ*, from seeing; *pah*ᵃ*r-ā-mẽ*, in a watch. In Bengali, it is the same, except that the oblique form in the case of nouns is more rare. Examples are *ām-ā-kē*, to me; *dekhib-ā-r*, of seeing. So in Hindī, the oblique form of the genitive postposition is *kē*, but in Bhojpurī, the only dialect of Bihārī in which it has an oblique form, it is *kā*, and this oblique form of the genitive is used to form the nominative plural, a peculiar construction quite unknown to Hindī. Thus *ham*ᵉ*nī-ke*, of us, oblique form, *ham*ᵉ*nī-kā*, used to mean 'we.' So also in Maithilī, we have *ham-ā-r*, of us, of me, and the nominative plural *ham*ᵉ*rā-sabh*, we all. The same construction occurs in Bengali. We have *santān-ēr*, of a son, and its oblique form, *santān-ēr-ā*, used as a nominative plural, to mean 'sons.' Again, *ām-ā-r*, of us, of me, and the nominative plural *ām-a-rā*. We thus see that in the formation of the oblique base of a noun or of a pronoun, Bihārī agrees with Bengali, and not with Eastern Hindī.

In the matter of postpositions, Bihārī takes a middle course. It has the same postposition for the Dative-Accusative, *kē*, as Bengali. For most of the other cases the postpositions, such as *mā̃*, in, are more closely connected with Eastern Hindī.

Adjectives.

As regards adjectives, the distinction of gender is very slightly observed in Bihārī and Bengali, while it is always remembered in the West.

Conjugation.

It is, however, in the conjugation of the verb that the most striking affinities with Bengali present themselves. Bihārī has three auxiliary verbs, two of which are found in Bengali and not in Hindī. The Bihārī for 'I am seeing' is *dekhait-chhī*, and in Bengali, the same phrase is translated *dekhitē-chhi*. In one dialect of Bihārī, the word for 'I am' is *bāṭī̃*, and in Bengali it may be *baṭi*. In Bihārī and Bengali, the sign of the future tense is the letter *b*. Thus, Bihārī *dekh-ab*, Bengali *dekh-iba*, I shall see. In Hindī, it is formed in an altogether different way. So in the same two languages the sign of the Past tense is *l*. Thus, Bihārī *dekh-ᵃlanhⁱ*, he saw, Bengali, *dekh-ilen*.

Both in Bihārī and Bengali, the sense of number has almost disappeared in the conjugation of the verb. The old numbers of each tense still remain in existence, but their forms are used to show respect or the reverse, instead of the distinction between plural and singular. In Hindī, there is an important rule regarding the conjugation of the past tense of verbs. In the case of intransitive verbs, the construction is active. We say, 'I went.' In the case of transitive verbs, the construction is passive. We cannot say 'I struck him.' We must say, 'he was struck by me.' In Bihārī and Bengali, this distinction has long since been obliterated, and so far as outward appearance goes, all verbs, both transitive and intransitive, are conjugated actively. For 'I struck,' we have the Bihārī *ham mārᵃlāhᵘ*, and the Bengali *āmi mārilām*, just as for 'I went,' we have *ham gelāhᵘ*, and *āmi gelām*. There is a further point in this connexion which will not be evident to anyone who only knows literary Bengali. In the Bengali spoken by the uneducated, the conjugation of the past tense of a transitive verb is always distinguished from that of the past tense of an intransitive verb. In both the construction is active, though the forms used are different. A Bengali villager says *gelō* for 'he went,' but '*mārilē*' for 'he struck.' The same distinction is observed in Bihārī, where 'he went' is *gēl*, and 'he struck' is *mārалᵃkai*. It is hardly necessary to point out that all this is quite different from the idiom of Eastern Hindī.

To sum up,—we observe that, taking grammatical forms as the test, Bihārī occupies a position intermediate between Bengali and Eastern Hindī. In pronunciation, it leans rather to the latter, although there are traces of Bengali influence. In declension, it partly follows Bengali and partly Eastern Hindī, but in the most important point, the preparation of the oblique form of the base, it follows the former and differs altogether from the latter. In conjugation, it differs altogether from Hindī, and closely follows Bengali. For the above reasons, we are compelled to consider that Bihārī and Bengali belong to one and the same group, that is to say, that the former belongs to the Eastern and not to the Mediate Group of Indo-Aryan languages, with which it has hitherto been classed.

Dialects.

Bihārī has three main dialects, Maithilī or Tirᵃhutiā, Magahī, and Bhojpurī. Each of these has several sub-dialects. The three dialects fall naturally into two groups, *viz.*, Maithilī and Magahī on the one hand, and Bhojpurī on the other. The speakers are also separated by ethnic peculiarities, but Magahī and Maithilī, and the speakers of these two dialects, are much more closely connected together than either of the pair is to Bhojpurī. Magahī, indeed, might very easily be classed as a sub-dialect of Maithilī, rather than as a separate dialect. The differences between the two groups of languages will be found fully dealt with under the head of Bhojpurī, on pp. 41 and ff., *post*. I shall here content myself with noting the most superficial differences between them, which strike the most casual observer.

In the declension of nouns, Bhojpurī has an oblique form of the genitive case, which is wanting in the substantives of the other dialects.

In pronouns, the honorific pronoun of the second person is *apane* in Maithilī and Magahī, but *raüre* in Bhojpurī.

The verb substantive in Maithilī is usually *chhai* or *achh'*, he is. In Magahī it is usually *hai*, and in Bhojpurī it is usually *bāṭē*, *bāṛē*, or *hāwē*. The three dialects all agree in forming the present tense definite by adding the verb substantive to the present participle. Thus, Maithilī *dekhait-achh'*, Magahī *dekhait-hai*, Bhojpurī *dēkhat-bāṭē*, he is seeing. But Magahī has also a special form of the present, *viz.*, *dēkha-hai*, he sees, and so has Bhojpurī, *dēkhe-lā*, he sees or will see. Finally, the whole system of verbal conjugation is amazingly complex in Maithilī and Magahī, but is as simple and straightforward in Bhojpurī as it is in Bengali or Hindī.

There are other minor differences between the three dialects, but the above are those which are most characteristic and striking. Each dialect will be dealt with separately in the following pages, where the fullest details will be found. Suffice it to say here that Maithilī and Magahī are the dialects of nationalities which have carried conservatism to the excess of uncouthness, while Bhojpurī is the practical language of an energetic race, which is ever ready to accommodate itself to circumstances, and which has made its influence felt all over India. The Bengali and the Bhojpurī are two of the great civilisers of Hindōstān, the former with his pen, and the latter with his cudgel.

Ethnic differences between speakers of Bhojpurī and of the other Bihārī dialects.

This last remark brings us to the consideration of the ethnic differences between the speakers of Maithilī and Magahī on the one hand, and those who speak Bhojpurī on the other. These are great. Mithilā, a country with an ancient history, traditions of which it retains to the present day, is a land under the domination of a sept of Brāhmaṇs extraordinarily devoted to the mint, anise, and cummin of the law. For centuries it has been a tract too proud to admit other nationalities to intercourse on equal terms, and has passed through conquest after conquest, from the north, from the east, and from the west, without changing its ancestral peculiarities. The story goes that, at the marriage of Rāma-chandra, the Brāhmaṇs of Mithilā showed the same uncivilised pride which is the characteristic of their descendants of the nineteenth century. This Brahmanical domination has left ineffaceable marks upon the nature of the rest of the population. Mithilā, or Tirhut, is one of the most congested parts of India. Its inhabitants increase and multiply and impoverish the earth, nor will they seek other means of life than agriculture, or other lands on which to practise the one art with which they are acquainted. Magadha, on the other hand, although it is intimately connected with the early history of Buddhism, was for too long a time a cockpit for contending Musalmān armies, and too long subject to the head-quarters of a Musalmān Province, to remember its former glories of the Hindū age. A great part of it is wild, barren, and sparsely cultivated, and over much of the remainder cultivation is only carried on with difficulty by the aid of great irrigation works widely spread over the country, and dating from prehistoric times. Its peasantry, oppressed for centuries, and even now, under British rule, poorer than that of any other neighbouring part of India, is uneducated and unenterprising. There is an expressive word current in Eastern Hindōstān which illustrates the national character. It is '*bhadēs*', and it has two meanings. One is 'uncouth, boorish,' and the other is 'an inhabitant of Magadha.' Which meaning is the original, and which the derivative, I do not know: but a whole history is contained in these two syllables.

The Bhojpurī-speaking country is inhabited by a people curiously different from the others who speak Bihārī dialects. They form the fighting nation of Hindōstān. An alert and active nationality, with few scruples, and considerable abilities, dearly loving a fight for fighting's sake, they have spread all over Aryan India, each man ready to carve his fortune out of any opportunity which may present itself to him. They furnish a rich mine of recruitment to the Hindōstānī army, and, on the other hand, they took a prominent part in the mutiny of 1857. As fond as an Irishman is of a stick, the long-boned, stalwart, Bhojpurī, with his staff in hand, is a familiar object striding over fields far from his home. Thousands of them have emigrated to British Colonies and have returned rich men; every year still larger numbers wander over Northern Bengal and seek employment, either honestly, as pālkī bearers, or otherwise, as dacoits. Every Bengal Zamindar keeps a posse of these men, euphemistically termed 'darwāns,' to keep his tenants in order. Calcutta, where they are employed, and feared, by the less heroic natives of Bengal, is full of them. Such are the people who speak Bhojpurī, and it can be understood that their language is a handy article made for current use, and not too much encumbered by grammatical subtilties.

The following are the figures showing the number of people estimated to speak each dialect in the area in which Bihārī is spoken:—

	Number of Speakers.
Maithilī	10,000,000
Magahī	6,239,967
Bhojpurī	20,000,000
TOTAL	36,239,967

For reasons which I shall explain when dealing with the Maithilī dialect, *vide post*, pp. 14 and ff., it is impossible to estimate the numbers of speakers of Bihārī in those parts of India which lie outside the Bihārī area. The only exception is that we are able to estimate the number of speakers of Bihārī in Assam, and in the non-Bihārī speaking districts of Bengal. These figures are as follows:—

	Maithilī.	Magahī.	Bhojpurī.	Total.
Number of speakers in Assam	66,575	33,365	65,730	165,670
„ in non-Bihārī Bengal	196,782	231,485	346,878	775,145
TOTAL	263,357	264,850	412,608	940,815

The total number of speakers of Bihārī, who are recorded above, is, therefore, 36,239,967+940,815, or altogether 37,180,782.

AUTHORITIES—

The authorities on each dialect will be found in the pages devoted to it. I shall content myself here with merely giving the names of those books which deal with Bihārī as a whole.

CAMPBELL, Sir G.,—*Specimens of Languages of India, including those of the Aboriginal Tribes of Bengal, the Central Provinces, and the Eastern Frontier.* Calcutta, 1874. Contains lists of words and sentences in all the Bihārī Dialects.

FALLON, S. W.,—*A new Hindustani-English Dictionary.* Benares and London, 1879. Contains much information regarding the various dialects.

HOERNLE, A. F. R., C.I.E.,—*A Grammar of the Eastern Hindī compared with the other Gauḍian Languages.* London, 1880. Describes Maithilī and Bhojpurī only.

GRIERSON, G. A., C.I.E.,—*A Handbook to the Kayathí Character.* Calcutta, 1881. 2nd Edition, 1899. In the title of the 2nd Edition, the word 'Kayathí' is altered to 'Kaithí.'.

GRIERSON, G. A., C.I.E.,—*Essays on Bihárí Declension and Conjugation. Journal* of the Asiatic Society of Bengal, Vol. lii, 1883, Pt. I, pp. 119 and ff.

GRIERSON, G. A., C.I.E.,—*Seven Grammars of the Dialects and Sub-dialects of the Bihárí Language.* Parts I—VIII. Calcutta, 1883—1887.

GRIERSON, G. A., C.I.E.,—*Bihar Peasant Life; Being a Discursive Catalogue of the Surroundings of the People of that Province.* Calcutta and London, 1885.

HOERNLE, A. F. R., and GRIERSON, G. A.,—*A Comparative Dictionary of the Bihārī Language.* Part I, Calcutta, London, and Leipzig, 1885. Part II. Calcutta, London, and Leipzig, 1889. Only two parts issued.

FALLON, S. W., TEMPLE, R. C., C.I.E., and LALA FAQIR CHAND,—*A Dictionary of Hindūstānī Proverbs.* Benares and London, 1886. Contains many Bihārī proverbs scattered through it, and has a special section for Bhojpurī ones.

CROOKE, B. A.,—*Rural and Agricultural Glossary for the N.-W. Provinces and Oudh.* Calcutta. 1888. Contains much information about Bihārī.

CHRISTIAN, JOHN,—*Behar Proverbs.* London, 1891.

KELLOGG, The Rev. S. H.,—*A Grammar of the Hindí Language, in which are treated .... the Colloquial Dialects of ...... Bhojpúr, Magadha, Maithila, etc., with copious philological Notes.* Second Edition, London, 1893.

Written character.

No less than five different characters are used in writing Bihārī, *viz.*, the Bengali, the Oṛiyā, the Maithilī, the Dēva-nāgarī, and the Kaithī. The Bengali and Oṛiyā characters are only employed in writing a form of Magahī current in Manbhum and the Native State of Mayūrbhanja, respectively. The Maithilī character is used by Brāhmaṇs in writing Maithilī, and will be described when dealing with that dialect. There remain the Dēva-nāgarī and the Kaithī.

The Dēva-nāgarī character is the alphabet used in books written for the educated, and, in writing, by the educated. The following account of it is given here, as this is the first time we meet with it in the Survey. The description will not be repeated with every language which uses it.

THE DĒVA-NĀGARĪ ALPHABET.[1]

VOWELS.

अ	*a*	आ	*ā*	इ	*i*	ई	*ī*	उ	*u*	ऊ	*ū*
ऋ	*ṛi*	ॠ	*ṛī*	ऌ	*lṛi*	ॡ	*lṛī*	ऎ	*e*	ए	*ē*
ऐ	*ăĭ*	ऐ	*ai*	ऒ	*o*	ओ	*ō*	औ	*ăŭ*	औ	*au*
अँ,	*ã,*	अं	*aṁ*	अः	*aḥ.*						

CONSONANTS.

Gutturals .	क	*ka*	ख	*kha*	ग	*ga*	घ	*gha*	ङ	*ṅa.*
Palatals .	च	*cha*	छ	*chha*	ज	*ja*	झ	*jha*	ञ	*ñ.*
Cerebrals .	ट	*ṭa*	ठ	*ṭha*	ड	*ḍa*	ढ	*ḍha*	ण	*ṇa.*
Dentals .	त	*ta*	थ	*tha*	द	*da*	ध	*dha*	न	*na.*
Labials .	प	*pa*	फ	*ph*	ब	*ba*	भ	*bha*	म	*ma.*
Semi-vowels	य	*ya*	र	*ra*	ल	*la*	व	*va.*		
Sibilants .	श	*śa*	ष	*sha*	स	*sa*	ह	*ha.*		

Although for the sake of completeness the vowel signs ॠ *ṛī*, ऌ *lṛi*, ॡ *lṛī* are included in the list of characters, they are not used at all in ordinary Hindī. They are, however, required in transcribing Sanskrit grammatical works into the Hindī language.

The forms of the vowels given above are the initials, and are used only at the beginning of a word; when subjoined to a consonant they take the following forms :—

a (not expressed), *ā* ा; *i* ि, *ī* ी; *u* ु, *ū* ू; *ṛi* ृ; *e* ॆ, *ē* े; *ăĭ* ॅ, *ai* ै; *o* ॊ, *ō* ो; *ăŭ* ौ, *au* ौ.[2]

Thus क *ka*, खा *khā*, गि *gi*, घी *ghī*, चु *chu*, छू *chhū*, जृ *jṛi*, झे *jhe*, टॆ *ṭè*, ठै *ṭhăĭ*, डै *ḍai*, ढो *ḍho*, तो *tō*, थौ *thăŭ*, दौ *dau*.

In the following cases the combination of consonant and vowel gives rise to peculiar forms :

र *r* with *u* is written रु.
र *r* „ *ū* „ „ रू.

When one consonant follows another with no vowel between, the two are combined into one compound letter. In most cases the elements of the compound are easily distinguishable, as in स्व *sva*, क्ल *kla*, and म्न *mna*; but there are some in which the elements are so altered as to be with difficulty recognised.

---

[1] Most of this is based partly on the corresponding portion of Mr. Beames' Bengali Grammar and partly on the corresponding portion of Mr. Kellogg's Hindī Grammar.

[2] The signs ऎ ॆ, ऐ ॅ, ऒ ॊ, and औ ौ have been introduced by European scholars in late years, and have been adopted by some of the best Benares Paṇḍits. These short vowels do not exist in Sanskrit, to which language the Dēva-nāgarī alphabet was originally confined, but do occur in the Modern Indian languages, and hence additional signs have had to be invented for them.

Consonants are compounded in three ways, *viz.*, 1stly, by writing one above the other, as क्क *kka*, ट्ट *ṭṭa*; 2ndly, by writing one after the other, omitting in all but the last the perpendicular stroke, and uniting the remainder of the character to that next following, as ब्द *bda*, त्थ *ttha*, य्य *yya*; 3rdly, some letters, when in combination, partially or wholly change their form, thus, क् *k* + ष *sha* becomes क्ष *ksha*, also written क्ष; ज् *j* + ञ *ña*, ज्ञ *jña*.

र *ra* takes two different forms, according as it is the first or last letter of a compound. Thus, when initial in a conjunct, it is written as a semi-circle (called *rēph*) above the second consonant, as in सर्प *sarp*[1]; but when non-initial it takes the form of a short stroke below the preceding consonant, as in ग्रहण *grahaṇ*.

When a conjunct of which र *ra* is the first member, consists of more than two consonants, the semi-circle *rēph* is written over the last letter, as in धर्म्म *dharmm*, सर्व्व *sarvv*. When a conjunct with र *ra* initial is vocalized by ि *i*, ी *ī*, े *e*, े *ē*, ै *ăi*, ै *ai*, ो *o*, ो *ō*, ौ *ău*, ौ *au*, or is followed by *anuswār*, then *rēph* is written to the right of them all; thus, धर्म्मी *dharmmī*, मूर्त्ति *mūrtti*, सर्व्वं *sarvvaṁ*, etc.

Conjuncts are classified as strong, weak, or mixed, according to the character of the letters composing them.[2] Conjuncts formed of strong letters only, are termed *strong*, and those formed of weak letters only, *weak* conjuncts. Combinations of strong and weak letters are called *mixed* conjuncts. The following list will be found to comprise all the more common combinations, arranged in three classes.

Strong Conjuncts.

क्क *kka*, क्ख *kkha*, क्त *kta*; ग्ध *gdha*, च्च *chch*, च्छ *chchha*, ज्ज *jja*, ज्झ *jjha*, ट्ट *ṭṭa*, ट्ठ *ṭṭha*; ड्ग *ḍga*, ड्ड *ḍḍa*; त्क *tka*, त्त *tta*, त्थ *ttha*, त्प *tpa*, द्ग *dga*, द्द *dda*, द्ध *ddha*, द्भ *dbha*, प्त *pta*, प्प *ppa*, प्फ *ppha*, ब्ज *bja*, ब्द *bda*, ब्ध *bdha*, ब्ब *bba*, ब्भ *bbha*.

Weak Conjuncts.

ण्ण, ण्ण *ṇṇa*, ण्य *ṇya*, न्न *nna*, न्म *nma*, न्य *nya*, न्र *nra*, न्व *nva*, न्स *nsa*, म्न *mna*, म्म *mma*, म्य *mya*, म्र *mra*, म्ल *mla*, म्ह *mha*, य्य *yya*, र्ण *rṇa*, र्म *rma*, र्य *rya*, र्व *rva*, र्श *rśa*, र्ष *rsha* र्ह *rha*, ल्म *lma*, ल्य *lya*, ल्ल *lla*, ल्ह *lha*, व्य *vya*, व्र *vra*, व्व, व्व *vva*, श्न *śna*, श्य *śya*, श्र *śra*, श्ल *śla*, श्व *śva*, श्न *śna*, ष्म *shma*, ष्य *shya*, ष्व *shva*, स्न *sna*, स्म *sma*, स्य *sya*, स्र *sra*, स्व *sva*, स्स *ssa*; ह्म *hma*, ह्य *hya*, ह्र *hra*, ह्ल *hla*, ह्व *hva*.

Mixed Conjuncts.

क्म *kma*, क्य *kya*, क्र *kra*, क्ल *kla*, क्व *kva*, क्ष *ksha*; ख्य *khya*; ग्न *gna*, ग्म *gma*, ग्य *gya*, ग्र *gra*, ग्ल *gla*, ग्व *gva*; घ्न *ghna*, घ्य *ghya*, घ्र *ghra*; ङ्क *ṅka*, ङ्क *ṅkka*, ङ्ग *ṅga*, ङ्घ *ṅgha*; च्य *chya*; छ्र *chhra*; ज्ञ *jña*, ज्म *jma*, ज्य *jya*, ज्र *jra*, ज्व *jva*; ञ्च *ñcha*, ञ्छ *ñchha*, ञ्ज *ñja*, ञ्झ *ñjha*; ड्र *ḍra*; ण्ट *ṇṭa*, ण्ठ *ṇṭha*, ण्ड *ṇḍa*, ण्ढ *ṇḍha*; त्न *tna*, त्म *tma*, त्य *tya*, त्र *tra*, त्व *tva*, त्स *tsa*; थ्य *thya*; द्न *dna*; ध्य *dhya*, ध्र *dhra*, ध्व *dhva*; न्त *nta*, न्थ *ntha*, न्द *nda*, न्ध *ndha*; प्न *pna*, प्म *pma*, प्य *pya*, प्र *pra*, प्ल *pla*, प्स *psa*; ब्य *bya*, ब्र *bra*; भ्य *bhya*, भ्र *bhra*; र्क *rka*, र्ख *rkha*, र्ग *rga*, र्घ *rgha*, र्च *rcha*, र्छ *rchha*, र्ज *rja*, र्त *rta*, र्थ *rtha*, र्द *rda*, र्ध *rdha*, र्प *rpa*, र्ब *rba*, र्भ *rbha*; ल्द *lda*, ल्प *lpa*, ल्ब *lba*; श्च *ścha*; ष्क *shka*, ष्ट *shṭa*, ष्ठ *shṭha*, ष्प *shpa*; स्क *ska*, स्त *sta*, स्थ *stha*, स्प *spa*, स्फ *spha*.

Anunāsik (अनुनासिक) ँ, simply denotes the nasalization of a preceding vowel, and

[1] In most modern Indian languages, the inherent *a* of the final consonant of a word is not pronounced, and is omitted in transliteration. Full explanations regarding this point will be found under the languages or dialects concerned.

[2] By the strong letters are intended all the five classes of mute letters, both smooth and aspirated; by weak letters, all other consonants.

can therefore never begin a syllable. It is written directly over or to the right of the vowel thus nasalized; thus कहाँ *kahā̃*, क्यों *kyō̃*. In books edited by foreigners, *Anuswār* (अनुस्वार) is commonly, but incorrectly, written instead of *Anunāsik* (अनुनासिक). It is represented in transliteration by the sign ˜ over the nasalized vowel. Thus बाँस *bā̃s*, में *mẽ*.

Anuswār (अनुस्वार) ं, which, in strict accuracy, denotes a stronger nasalization than the above, is written, like *Anunāsik*, over, or to the right of the preceding vowel; as, अंश *aṁś*, बंश *baṁś*. In Hindī, however, *anuswār* is generally used as a short way of writing a nasal when preceding another consonant of its class. Thus, लंका instead of लङ्का *laṅkā*; संच instead of सञ्च *sañch*; पंडित instead of पण्डित *paṇḍit*; अंत instead of अन्त *ant*; खंभा instead of खम्भा *khambhā*.

Visarg (विसर्ग), meaning 'emission of breath' indicates a weak aspiration, which has euphonically taken the place of a sibilant letter or *r*. It is only found in pure Sanskrit words, and even then, though occurring in the original, is commonly omitted in Hindī. It is written thus, :; *e.g.*, in दुःख *duḥkh*, usually written and pronounced दुख *dukh*, = दुस् + ख *dus* + *kha*; अन्तःकरण *antaḥ-karaṇ*.

Besides these, several other signs are used in Sanskrit, which, as they occasionally appear in Hindī, may here be explained:—

Virām (विराम), 'pause' is written under a consonant, thus क् *k*, and denotes the absence of the inherent *a* by which the consonant is vocalized. It is also called *hal*.

Avagrah (अवग्रह), ऽ, indicates the elision of an initial अ *a* after a final ए *ē* or ओ *ō*; as, त्रिंशोऽध्यायः *triṁśō 'dhyāyaḥ*, for त्रिंशो अध्यायः *triṁśō adhyāyaḥ*. It is, therefore, analogous to the English apostrophe. The half pause, । , is written at the end of the first line of a couplet of poetry; the full pause, ॥, at the end of the second. These marks are only prosodial, and, besides these, there are no other marks of punctuation. In prose they are used as equivalent to the ordinary full stop and the full stop at the end of a paragraph respectively. In most native works, indeed, punctuation is disregarded, and space is not even left between the words. The symbol २ between two words indicates that the former of the two is repeated; as, वह अपने २ घर गए *wah apᵃnē apᵃnē ghar gaē*.

The mark ॰ is used, like the period in English, to indicate the abbreviation of a word; as रामायन बा॰ *Rāmāyan Bā.*, for रामायन बालकाण्ड *Rāmāyan Bāl-kāṇḍ*.

The characters for the numerals are these:—

१	२	३	४	५	६	७	८	९	०
1	2	3	4	5	6	7	8	9	0

The leading feature in Indian arithmetic being the division by four, the signs for fractions are adapted thereto. The rupee is divided into $4 \times 4 = 16$, parts called *ānā*, which are thus designated (units of all kinds are also thus divided)—

1 *ānā* or $\frac{1}{16}$	/)	9 *ānās*	॥/)
2 *ānās*	//)	10 *ānās*	॥//)
3 *ānās*	///)	11 *ānās*	॥///)
4 *ānās*	।)	12 *ānās*	॥।)
5 *ānās*	।/)	13 *ānās*	॥।/)
6 *ānās*	।//)	14 *ānās*	॥।//)
7 *ānās*	।///)	15 *ānās*	॥।///)
8 *ānās*	॥)	One rupee	१).

Table showing the Kaithī alphabet, as written by Tirhutī, Bhojpurī & Magahī Scribes

Tirhutī	Bhojpurī	Magahī	English	Tirhutī	Bhojpurī	Magahī	English
[illegible]	[illegible]	[illegible]	a	[illegible]	[illegible]	[illegible]	ṇ
[illegible]	[illegible]	[illegible]	ā	[illegible]	[illegible]	[illegible]	t
[illegible]	[illegible]	[illegible]	i	[illegible]	[illegible]	[illegible]	th
[illegible]	[illegible]	[illegible]	u	[illegible]	[illegible]	[illegible]	d
[illegible]	[illegible]	[illegible]	ū	[illegible]	[illegible]	[illegible]	dh
[illegible]	[illegible]	[illegible]	ē	[illegible]	[illegible]	[illegible]	n
[illegible]	[illegible]	[illegible]	ai	[illegible]	[illegible]	[illegible]	p
[illegible]	[illegible]	[illegible]	ō	[illegible]	[illegible]	[illegible]	ph
[illegible]	[illegible]	[illegible]	au	[illegible]	[illegible]	[illegible]	b
[illegible]	[illegible]	[illegible]	k	[illegible]	[illegible]	[illegible]	bh
[illegible]	[illegible]	[illegible]	kh	[illegible]	[illegible]	[illegible]	m
[illegible]	[illegible]	[illegible]	g	[illegible]	[illegible]	[illegible]	y
[illegible]	[illegible]	[illegible]	gh	[illegible]	[illegible]	[illegible]	r
[illegible]	[illegible]	[illegible]	ṅ	[illegible]	[illegible]	[illegible]	l
[illegible]	[illegible]	[illegible]	ch	[illegible]	[illegible]	[illegible]	w
[illegible]	[illegible]	[illegible]	chh	[illegible]	[illegible]	[illegible]	s'
[illegible]	[illegible]	[illegible]	j	[illegible]	[illegible]	[illegible]	kh
[illegible]	[illegible]	[illegible]	jh	[illegible]	[illegible]	[illegible]	s
[illegible]	[illegible]	[illegible]	ñ	[illegible]	[illegible]	[illegible]	h
[illegible]	[illegible]	[illegible]	ṭ				
[illegible]	[illegible]	[illegible]	ṭh				
[illegible]	[illegible]	[illegible]	ḍ				
[illegible]	[illegible]	[illegible]	ḍh				

The Kaithī alphabet is, properly speaking, the alphabet used by the Kāyath or Kāyastha caste,—the writing caste of Northern India. While not so complete as the Dēva-nāgarī, for some of the rarer letters are altogether wanting, it bears to that alphabet much the same relation that the English current written hand does to the printed character. It is in general use all over the north of India, from the Gujerat coast to the river Kosi. Throughout this great tract it has of course many variations, some depending upon locality and others upon individual handwriting. Although primarily a cursive written hand, it has been raised to the dignity of type in Bihar and Gujerat. In Bihar, it is used for teaching the lower classes, to whom a knowledge of Dēva-nāgarī is an unnecessary luxury, the elements of a primary education. In Gujerat, it has been elevated to the position of a national character. The introduction of this printed character in Gujerat is a matter within the memory of the present generation. The oldest books published in the Gujarātī language were printed in the Dēva-nāgarī type.

In the following account of the Kaithī character, only the simple letters will be described. The compound letters are rare, and, when met, will be easily recognised. So far as Bihārī is concerned, the Kaithī used changes slightly according to locality, and three varieties are recognised, *viz.*, that of Mithilā, that of Magah, and that used in writing Bhojpurī. These three are shown on the plate opposite.

KAITHĪ OR KĀYATHĪ ALPHABET.

VOWELS.

અ *a* આ *ā* ઇ *i* ઈ *ī* ઉ *u* ઊ *ū*.
એ *ē* ઐ *ai* ઓ *ō* ઔ *au* અં *aṁ* અઃ *aḥ*.

CONSONANTS.

Gutturals.	ક	*ka*	ખ	*kha*	ગ	*ga*	ઘ	*gha*		
Palatals.	ચ	*cha*	છ	*chha*	જ	*ja*	ઝ	*jha*		
Cerebrals.	ટ	*ṭa*	ઠ	*ṭha*	ડ	*ḍa*	ઢ	*ḍha*		
Dentals.	ત	*ta*	થ	*tha*	દ	*da*	ધ	*dha*	ન	*na*
Labials.	પ	*pa*	ફ	*ph*	બ	*ba*	ભ	*bha*	મ	*ma*
Semi-Vowels.	ય	*ya*	ર	*ra*	લ	*la*	વ	*va*		
Sibilants.	શ	*śá*	ષ	*sha*	સ	*sa*				
Aspirate.	હ	*ha*								

અ *a*, being inherent in each consonant, is only written when initial in a word or syllable; thus, we write અપ *ap*, ટુઅ *tua*, but પ *pa*, ત *ta*. The other vowels, when following a consonant, are substituted for the inherent અ *a*, and, in this case, they take the following forms:—

અ *a* (not expressed); આ *ā* ા;
ઇ *i* િ; ઈ *ī* ી; ઉ *u* ુ; ઊ *ū* ૂ;
એ *ē* ે; ઐ *ai* ૈ; ઓ *ō* ો; ઔ *au* ૌ.

Thus, the several vowel sounds, when they follow consonants, are written as follows:—

ક *ka*, કા *kā*, કિ *ki*, કી *kī*, કુ *ku*, કૂ *kū*, કે *kē*, કૈ *kai*, કો *kō*, કૌ *kau*.

The vowel mark ं is called અનુસ્વાર *anuswār* as in Dēva-nāgarī. It denotes the nasalization of a preceding vowel, and can therefore never begin a syllable. It is written over, or to the right of the preceding vowel: as, અંસ *aṁs*, બાંહ *bā̃h*. It is used for both the *anunāsik* and the *anuswār* of Dēva-nāgarī. The mark ः is called બિસર્ગ *bisarg*, and indicates a weak aspiration. It is only found in pure Sanskrit words, and even then, though occurring in the original, is commonly omitted in Hindī; as, દુઃખ *duḥkh* written and pronounced દુખ *dukh*.

I now proceed to deal with each of the three dialects separately.

MAITHILĪ OR TIR'HUTIYA.

Grihē śūrā raṇē bhītāḥ, paraspara-virōdhinaḥ,
Kulā-'bhimāninō yūyaṁ Mithilāyāṁ bhavishyatha.

Heroes at home, cowards in the battle-field, ever quarrelling amongst yourselves, and inordinately full of family-pride, shall ye be in Mithilā.

Rāma-chandra's curse on the Mithilā Brāhmaṇas.

Where spoken.

Maithilī or Tir'hutiyā is, properly speaking, the language of Mithilā, or Tairabhukti (the ancient name of Tirhut). According to the *Mithilā-māhātmya*, a Sanskrit work of considerable repute in the territory which it describes, Mithilā is the country bounded on the north by the Himālaya Mountains, on the south by the Ganges, on the west by the River Gandak and on the east by the River Kōsī.[1] It thus includes the British Districts of Champaran, Muzaffarpur, and Darbhanga, as well as the strip of the Nepal Tarai which runs between these Districts and the lower ranges of the Himalayas. The Districts of Muzaffarpur and Darbhanga originally formed one District called Tirhut, and that name is still used as a convenient appellation for the country included in these two Districts. At the present day, the language of the greater portion of Champaran is a form of Bhojpurī and not Maithilī, but, with that exception, Maithilī is spoken over the whole of this tract. It has also extended east of the river Kōsī, and occupies the greater part of the District of Purnea, and has moreover crossed the Ganges, and is now spoken over the whole of the south-Gangetic portion of the Bhagalpur District, over the eastern portion of the south-Gangetic portion of the Monghyr District, and in the north and west of the Sonthal Parganas.

Sub-dialects.

Maithilī is spoken in its greatest purity by the Brāhmaṇs of the north of the Darbhanga and Bhagalpur Districts and by those of western Purnea. These men have a literature and traditions which have retarded the corruption of the dialect. It is also spoken with some purity, but with more signs of the wearing away of inflexions in the south of the Darbhanga District, and in those portions of the Monghyr and Bhagalpur Districts which lie on the northern bank of the Ganges. This may be called Southern Standard Maithilī. To the east, in Purnea, it becomes more and more infected with Bengali, till, in the east of that District it is superseded by the Siripuriā dialect of that language which is a border form of speech, Bengali in the main, but containing expressions borrowed from Maithilī, and written, not in the Bengali character, but in the Kaithī of Bihar. Siripuriā will be found described on pp. 139 and ff. of Vol. v, Pt. I, under the head of Bengali. The Maithilī spoken in Purnea may be called Eastern Maithilī.

South of the Ganges, Maithilī is influenced more or less by the Magahī spoken to its west, and partly also by Bengali. The result is a well-marked dialect, locally known as *Chhikā-chhikī bōlī*, from its frequent use of the syllable '*chhik*,' which is the base on which the conjugation of the Verb Substantive is conjugated.

---

[1] *Gaṅgā-himavatōr madhyē nadī-pañcadaśāntarē* |
Tairabhūktir iti khyātō dēśaḥ parama-pāvanaḥ ||
* * * * * * * * * * * *
Kauśikīṁ tu samārabhya Gaṇḍakīṁ adhigamya vai |
Yōjanāni chaturviṁśa vyāyāmaḥ parikīrttitaḥ ||

The Maithilī spoken in the Muzaffarpur District, and in a strip of country on the eastern side of Darbhanga is strongly infected by the neighbouring Bhojpurī spoken in various forms in the adjacent district of Saran and in the greater part of Champaran. So much is this the case, that, as spoken by some people, it is difficult to say where the dialect is Maithilī or Bhojpurī. It may be called Western Maithilī.

The Musalmāns of Mithilā do not all speak Maithilī. In Muzaffarpur and Champaran, they speak an altogether different dialect, closely allied to the language of Oudh. It is locally known as Shēkhaī or as Musalmānī, and is sometimes called Jolahā Bōlī, after the caste which forms one of the most numerous Musalmān tribes, according to popular opinion, of the locality. The true Jolahā Boli, however, is the language spoken by the Musalmāns of Darbhanga, which is a form of Maithilī, though somewhat corrupted by the admission of Persian and Arabic words to its vocabulary.

Number of speakers.

The details of the number of people who speak each form of Maithilī will be given subsequently, in dealing with each of the sub-dialects. The following are the totals :—

Name of Sub-dialect.	Number of Speakers.
Standard	1,946,800
Southern Standard	2,300,000
Eastern	1,302,300[1]
Chhikā-chhikī	1,719,781
Western	1,783,495
Jolahā	337,000
Total number of speakers of Maithilī in Maithilī-speaking districts	9,389,376

These figures do not include the speakers of Maithilī in the Nepal Tarai, concerning whom no figures are available. Under any circumstances, therefore, we shall be justified in assuming that at least ten million people speak Maithilī in the country of which it is the vernacular.

It is impossible to state how many speakers of Maithilī live outside the Maithilī tract proper, as no figures are available. In the census of 1891, Maithilī and the other Bihār dialects were grouped together with the various languages of Central and Western Hindōstān under the one head of 'Hindī.' We cannot now separate the figures. It is possible, in the case of the Provinces of Lower Bengal and Assam, to ascertain from the Census records, the number of people hailing from each District in Bihār, and also the total number of persons who come from all parts of India in which, according to the Census, 'Hindī' is spoken. With the aid of these figures we can, in the case of these two provinces, divide the number of people recorded in the Census as speaking 'Hindī,' proportionately to these two sets of figures, and the results may be expected to represent approximately the number of people in each District of these two Provinces speaking, respectively, the language of each District of Bihār. By totalling up the figures thus gained for the Maithilī-speaking Districts, we may expect to obtain the number of people speaking that dialect outside the Maithilī-speaking area. Unfortunately, the theory is not borne out by local experience. For instance, a calculation of this kind shows that there should be 6,900 speakers of Maithilī in Burdwan,

[1] Include 2,300 Thārūs of North Purnea, who, apparently, speak a corrupt form of Eastern Maithilī.

but the local authorities report, in answer to enquiries subsequently made, that as a matter of fact there are no speakers of the language in the District. In such a matter, even the experience of District Officers may be at fault, and though I do not offer the following figures relating to Bengal and Assam as certainly correct, I believe that they have a better foundation than any other assertion which can be made on the point, and give them for what they are worth.

Table showing the estimated number of speakers of Maithilī within the Lower Provinces of Bengal, but outside the area in which Maithilī is the Vernacular Language.

Name of District.	Number of Speakers.	Remarks.
Burdwan	6,900	The local authorities report that there are no speakers of Maithilī in the District.
Bankura	300	
Birbhum	3,900	
Midnapore	7,900	
Hooghly	2,400	
Howrah	4,000	
24-Parganas	8,800	
Calcutta	34,000	
Nadia	3,300	
Jessore	700	
Murshidabad	33,100	
Khulna	400	
Dinajpur	26,700	
Rajshahi	9,100	
Rangpur	5,000	
Bogra	4,000	
Pabna	3,500	
Darjeeling	13,900	
Kuch-Bihar (State)	3,200	
Dacca	10,800	
Faridpur	1,500	
Backergunge	1,000	
Mymensingh	5,000	
Chittagong	1,200	
Noakhali	32	
Tippera	800	
Malda	5,000	
Cuttack	100	
Puri	110	
Balasore	140	
Total	196,782	

Table showing the estimated number of speakers of Maithilī within the Province of Assam.

NAME OF DISTRICT.	Number of Speakers.	REMARKS.
Cachar Plains	20,400	
Sylhet	9,200	
Goalpara	3,700	
Kamrup	800	
Darrang	4,100	
Nowgong	2,250	
Sibsagar	15,600	
Lakhimpur	10,050	
Naga Hills	150	
Khasi and Jaintia Hills	300	
Lushai Hills	25	
TOTAL	66,575	

We cannot give similar figures for other Provinces of India, as in their Census Reports, the population figures for people whose home is Bihar are not given district by district. In most of them the number of people coming from the Province of Bihar as a whole is given, and it might be thought that it would be possible to ascertain from this the approximate number of people coming from the Maithilī-speaking tract by dividing that number in the proportion that the whole population of the Maithilī-speaking tract bears to the total population of Bihar; but any such attempt would be misleading. Of the three nationalities which occupy Bihar, the Maithilī, the Magahī, and the Bhojpurī, the first are a timid, home-staying people, who rarely leave their abodes for distant provinces of India, while, on the other hand, the Bhojpurīs are an enterprising tribe found in numbers all over the land, and even in distant countries, like Mauritius and Natal. Any proportional division would not take this important factor into consideration, and, as a result, would show a far greater number of inhabitants of Mithilā in foreign provinces than is really the case.

We must therefore content ourselves with recording the following figures for the Provinces of Bengal and Assam, and leave the question of the number of speakers of Maithilī in other provinces of India as an insoluble problem :—

Total number of people speaking Maithilī at home, say	10,000,000
Estimated number of people speaking Maithilī elsewhere in the Lower Provinces	196,782
Estimated number of people speaking Maithilī in Assam	66,575
TOTAL	10,263,357

Maithilī literature.

Maithilī is the only one of the Bihārī dialects which has a literary history. For centuries the Paṇḍits of Mithilā have been famous for their learning, and more than one Sanskrit work of authority has been written by them. One of the few learned women of India whose name has come down to us, was Lakhimā Ṭhakkurāṇī, who, according to tradition, lived at the middle of the 15th century A.D. Nor was the field of vernacular literature neglected by them. The earliest vernacular writer of whom we have any record was the celebrated Vidyāpati Ṭhakkura, who graced the court of Mahārāja Śiva Siṁha of Sugāonā, and who flourished about the same time. As a writer of Sanskrit works he was an author of considerable repute, and one of his works, translated into Bengali, is familiar as a text-book, under the name of the *Purusha-parīkshā*, to every student of that language. But it is upon his dainty songs in the vernacular that his fame chiefly rests. He was the first of the old master-singers whose short religious poems, dealing principally with Rādhā and Kṛishṇa, exercised such an important influence on the religious history of Eastern India. His songs were adopted and enthusiastically recited by the celebrated Hindū reformer Chaitanya who flourished at the beginning of the sixteenth century, and, through him, became the house-poetry of the Lower Provinces. Numbers of imitators sprung up, many of whom wrote in Vidyāpati's name, so that it is now difficult to separate the genuine from the imitations, especially as in the great collection of these Vaishnava songs, the *Pada-kalpa-taru*, which is the accepted authority in Bengal, the former have been altered in the course of generations to suit the Bengali idiom and metre. Up to nearly twenty years ago, the *Padā-kalpa-taru* was the only record which we had of the poet's works, but, in the year 1882, the present writer was enabled to publish, in his *Maithilī Chrestomathy*, a collection of songs attributed to him, which he collected in Mithilā itself, partly from the mouths of itinerant singers and partly from manuscript collections in the possession of local Paṇḍits. That all the songs in this collection are genuine, is not a matter capable of proof, but, there can be little doubt that most of them are so, although the language has been greatly modernised in the course of transition from mouth to mouth during the past five centuries.

Vidyāpati Ṭhakkura or, as he is called in the vernacular, Bidyāpat[i] Ṭhākur, had many imitators in Mithilā itself, of whom we know nothing except the names of the most popular, and a few stray verses. Amongst them may be mentioned Umāpati, Nandīpati, Mōda-nārāyaṇa, Rāmāpati, Mahīpati, Jayānanda, Chaturbhuja, Sarasa-rāma, Jayadēva, Kēśava, Bhañjana, Chakrapāṇi, Bhānunātha, and Harshanātha or, in the vernacular, Harakh-nāth. The last two were alive when the present writer was in Darbhanga twenty years ago.

Amongst other writers in Maithilī may be mentioned Man-bōdh Jhā, who died about the year 1788 A.D. He composed a *Haribans*, or Poetical Life of Kṛishṇa, of which ten cantos are still extant, and enjoy great popularity.

The drama has had several authors in Mithilā. The local custom has been to write the body of a play in Sanskrit, but the songs in the vernacular. The best-known of these plays are as follows. None of them has been published.

The *Pārijāta-haraṇa*, and the *Rukmiṇī-pariṇaya*, both by Vidyāpati Ṭhakkura.

The *Gaurī-pariṇaya* by Kavi-lāla.

The *Ushā-haraṇa* by Harshanātha above mentioned.

D

The *Prabhāvatī-haraṇa* by Bhānunātha above mentioned.

Under the enlightened guidance of the late Mahārāja of Darbhanga, there has been a remarkable revival of Maithilī literature during the past few years. At least one author deserving of special note has come to the front, Chandra Jhā, who has shown remarkable literary powers. He has written a *Mithilā-bhāshā Rāmāyaṇa*, and a translation, with an edition of the original Sanskrit text, of the *Purusha-parīksha* of Vidyāpati Ṭhakkura, both of which will well repay the student by their perusal.

Translations of the Scriptures into Maithilī.

No translation of any part of the Bible into Maithilī has been issued by the Bible Society, nor is that language included amongst those into which the Serampore Missionaries translated the Scriptures. At the same time, if an article in the *Calcutta Review* is to be believed, the first translation of any portion of the Bible made into any language of Northern India was that of the Gospels and Acts, made into the Chhikā-chhikī dialect of Maithilī by Father Antonio at the end of the eighteenth century. For further particulars reference may be made to the section on Chhikā-chhikī bōlī, on p. 96 *post*. The only other translations with which I am acquainted are versions of the Sermon on the Mount, and other short portions of Scripture, made about twenty years ago by Mr. John Christian, and lithographed and published at Monghyr.

AUTHORITIES—

I.—EARLY REFERENCES.—The earliest reference which I can find to Maithilī or Tirᵃhutiyā is in the Preface to the *Alphabetum Brammhanicum*, published in 1771, from which an extract has been quoted in dealing with the Bengali language in Vol. v, Pt. I, p. 23. In the list of languages mentioned on p. viii is 'Tourutiana.'

Colebrooke in his famous Essay on the Sanskrit and Prakrit languages written in the year 1801, is the first to describe Maithilī[1] as a distinct dialect. He points out its affinity with Bengali, discusses the written character used by the Brāhmaṇs, and adds, 'As the dialect of Mithilā has no extensive use, and does not appear to have been at any time cultivated by elegant poets, it is unnecessary to notice it any further in this place.' Since then,[2] like the other dialects of Bihar, Maithilī remained unnoticed and forgotten, till Mr. Fallon gave a few specimens of it in the *Indian Antiquary* in the year 1875.[3] In the preceding year, it is true, some examples of the dialect were given in Sir George Campbell's *Specimens*,[4] but they are there classed as some of many dialects of Hindī spoken in Bihar. Indeed, at this time, it was the general belief that, all over Bihar, the language spoken was a corrupt form of Hindī, whereas, as Colebrooke had long previously pointed out, it was much more nearly allied to Bengali than to the Hindī of the North-Western Provinces. Matters remained in this state, till the present writer published his Maithilī grammar in the year 1880-81.

---

[1] *Asiatic Researches*, Vol. VII, 1801, pp. 199 and ff. Reprinted in his Essays, Ed. 1873, p. 26.

[2] Note, however, Aimé-Martin's *Lettres édifiantes et curieuses*, Paris, 1840. In Vol. II, p. 295, when describing the languages of India, he says 'the *Marthila* (sic) se retrouve dans Neypal.'

[3] *Indian Antiquary*, Vol. IV 1875, p. 340.

[4] *Specimens of Languages of India, including those of the Aboriginal Tribes of Bengal, the Central Provinces and the Eastern Frontier*. Calcutta, 1874. The specimens given are headed, 'Vernacular of West Tirhoot'; 'Vernacular of East Tirhoot'; and 'Vernacular of West Purneah (Hindee),' respectively. They will be found on pp. 60 and following.

II.—GRAMMARS—

GRIERSON, G. A.,—*An Introduction to the Maithilī Language of North Bihár. Containing a Grammar, Chrestomathy and Vocabulary.* Part I, *Grammar.* Extra Number to *Journal,* Asiatic Society of Bengal, Part I, for 1880. Separate Reprint, Calcutta, 1881. Part II, *Chrestomathy and Vocabulary.* Extra Number to ditto for 1882. Separate Reprint, Calcutta, 1882.

GRIERSON, G. A.,—*Seven Grammars of the Dialects and Sub-Dialects of the Bihárí Language.* Part I, *Introductory.* Calcutta, 1883. Part IV, *Maithil-Bhojpurí Dialect of Central and South Muzaffarpúr,* 1884. Part V, *South Maithilí Dialect of South Darbhangá, North Munger, and the Madhepúrá Subdivision of Bhagalpúr.* Part VI, *South Maithil-Mágadhí Dialect of South Munger and the Bárh Subdivision of Patna.* Part VII, *South Maithilí-Bengálí Dialect of South Bhagalpúr.* Part VIII, *Maithil-Bangálí Dialect of Central and Western Puraniyá.*

HOERNLE, A. F. R.,—*A Grammar of the Eastern Hindí compared with the other Gaudian Languages.* London, 1880. In this Grammar, Dr. Hoernle was the first to recognise Maithilī as a dialect separate from Hindī. He was able to give some specimens of its grammatical forms, but no published materials were then available.

KELLOGG, The Revd. S. H.,—*A Grammar of the Hindí Language, in which are treated . . . . the colloquial dialects of Maithila, etc., with copious philological notes.* Second Edition, Revised and Enlarged. London, 1893. (The first edition does not deal with Maithilī.)

III.—DICTIONARIES—

GRIERSON, G. A.,—There are vocabularies attached to the Maithilī Chrestomathy, above mentioned, and to the edition of Manbōdh's Haribans mentioned below.

HOERNLE, A. F. R., and GRIERSON, G. A.,—*A Comparative Dictionary of the Bihārī Language.* Part I, Calcutta, 1885. Part II, 1889. Only two parts issued.

IV.—GENERAL LITERATURE—

Regarding Vidyāpati, see Beames, *The Early Vaishnava Poets of Bengal, Indian Antiquary* ii, 1873, p. 37, and the same author's *On the Age and Country of Bidyāpati,* ibid. iv, 1875, p. 299. See also, the Bengali Magazine, the *Baṅga-darśana,* Vol. iv, for Jyaishṭha, 1282, Bg. san, pp. 75 and ff. Also the present writer's *Vidyāpati and his Contemporaries, Indian Antiquary,* Vol. xiv, 1885, p. 182; Eggeling, *Catalogue* of Sanskrit MSS. in the India Office Library, Part iv, No. 2864; and the present writer in the *Proceedings* of the Asiatic Society of Bengal, for August, 1895. Also the present writer's *On some mediaeval Kings of Mithilā, Indian Antiquary,* Vol. xxviii, 1899, p. 57. The following contain editions of the Bengali recension of the poet's works. *Vidyāpati-krita-padāvali,* edited by Akshaya-chandra Sarkār. Chinsurah, 1285, Bg. s. *Vidyāpatir Pādavali,* Edited with an Introduction by Śaradā-charaṇ Maitra. Second Edition, Calcutta, 1285, Bg. s. *Prāchīna Kāvya Saṅgraha,* Part I, Edited by Akshaya-chandra Sarkār. Calcutta, 1291, Bg. s. The Mithilā recension is published in the present writer's Maithilī Chrestomathy.

For the benefit of those who wish to study Maithilī, the following is a list of the principal works which have been published in the language.

The present writer's Maithilī Chrestomathy referred to above under the head of Grammars, contains several other texts besides the poems of Vidyāpati.

Twenty-one Vaishṇava Hymns, Edited and translated by the present writer. *Journal* of the Asiatic Society of Bengal, Vol. liii, 1884, Special Number, pp. 76 and ff.

Manbodh's Háribans, Edited and translated by the same. Ibid. Vol. li, 1882, pp. 129 and ff., and Vol. liii, 1884, Special Number, pp. 1 and ff.

Selected Specimens of the Bihārī Language, Part I, The Maithilī Dialect. The Gīt Dīnā Bhadrik, and the Gīt Nebārak. Edited and translated by the same. *Zeitschrift* der deutschen morgenländischen Gesellschaft. Vol. xxxix, 1885, pp. 617 and ff.

Vidyāpati's *Purusha-parīkshā,* Edited and translated in prose and verse into Maithilī by Chandra Jhā, Darbhangā, Rāj Press, Śake 1810.

Mithilā-Bhāshā Rāmāyaṇa, by Chandra Jhā. A version of the story of the Rāmāyaṇa in Maithilī verse. Darbhangā, Union Press, San 1299 Faslī.

Table showing the various alphabets used in Mithilā.

Dēva-nāgarī.	Kaithī.	Maithili	English Translitera-tion	Deva-nāgarī	Kaithi	Maithili	English Translitera-tion
अ	𑂃	𑒁	*a*	ञ		𑒘	*ña*
आ	𑂄	𑒂	*ā*	ट	𑂗	𑒙	*ṭa*
इ	𑂅	𑒃	*i*	ठ	𑂘	𑒚	*ṭha*
ई	𑂆	𑒄	*ī*	ड	𑂙	𑒛	*ḍa*
उ	𑂇	𑒅	*u*	ढ	𑂛	𑒜	*ḍha*
ऊ	𑂈	𑒆	*ū*	ण	𑂝	𑒝	*ṇa*
ऋ		𑒇	*ṛi*	त	𑂞	𑒞	*ta*
ॠ		𑒈	*ṝi*	थ	𑂟	𑒟	*tha*
ऌ		𑒉	*lṛi*	द	𑂠	𑒠	*da*
ए	𑂉	𑒋	*ē*	ध	𑂡	𑒡	*dha*
ऐ	𑂊	𑒌	*ai*	न	𑂢	𑒢	*na*
ओ	𑂋	𑒍	*ō*	प	𑂣	𑒣	*pa*
औ	𑂌	𑒎	*au*	फ	𑂤	𑒤	*pha*
अं	𑂃𑂁	𑒁𑓀	*aṁ*	ब	𑂥	𑒥	*ba*
अः	𑂃𑂂	𑒁𑓁	*aḥ*	भ	𑂦	𑒦	*bha*
क	𑂍	𑒏	*ka*	म	𑂧	𑒧	*ma*
ख	𑂎	𑒐	*kha*	य		𑒨	*ya**
ग	𑂏	𑒑	*ga*	र	𑂩	𑒩	*ra*
घ	𑂐	𑒒	*gha*	ल	𑂪	𑒪	*la*
ङ	𑂑	𑒓	*ṅa*	व	𑂫	𑒫	*va* or *wa*
च	𑂒	𑒔	*cha*	श		𑒬	*śa*
छ	𑂓	𑒕	*chha*	ष		𑒭	*sha*
ज	𑂔	𑒖	*ja*	स	𑂮	𑒮	*sa*
झ	𑂕	𑒗	*jha*	ह	𑂯	𑒯	*ha*

* The semi-vowel य is not used by Kāyasths in writing Maithilī, the vowel इ being substituted for it.

No less than three different alphabets are in use in the tract in which Maithilī is spoken. The Maithilī character proper is that used by Maithil Brāhmaṇs, and is closely akin to the Bengali. It is not used by persons of the other castes. The character which is used by all the other castes, and which is generally employed, with a few local variations, over the whole of Northern India, from Bihar to Gujerat, is the Kaithī. It is not a complete alphabet, using only the long form of the vowel 'i' for both the short and the long vowels, and the short form of 'u' for similar purpose. A fount of Kaithī type is adopted by the Bengal Government for official publications in the vernacular, intended for publication in Bihar, in which this deficiency has been supplied, and books are now printed in Patna in the same type, so that gradually the written character is becoming more correct in this respect. The Dēva-nāgarī character is used by a few of the educated classes who have come under the literary influence of Benares, and it is understood and read by all persons who pretend to a liberal education.

Written Character.

The table opposite shows the three alphabets current in Mithilā in juxtaposition. Specimens will subsequently be given in all three. In transliterating those in Kaithī, the necessary correction of distinguishing between the long and short 'i' and 'u' will be made.

The pronunciation of the Maithilī language is not so broad as that of Bengali, nor so narrow as in the languages of the North-Western Provinces. This is principally noticeable in the sound given to the vowel अ *a*, which is neither so broad as the *o* in *hot*, nor is so close as that of the *a* in *America*, but is something between the two. Another point of resemblance with Bengali is the pronunciation of the compound consonant ह्य *hya*. In Bengali this is pronounced as if it were *jjh'a*. Thus ग्राह्य *grāhya* is pronounced *grājjh'o*. In Maithilī it is pronounced as if it were *zhjya*, and *grāhya* is pronounced *grăzhjya*. In other respects the pronunciation of the consonants is the same as in the country round Benares. Thus the letter ष *sh*, when not compounded with another consonant, is pronounced as if it were ख *kh*. In the Kaithī character there is even no peculiar character for *kh*, and that for *sh* is used instead. Thus the word षष्ठ *shashth*, sixth, is pronounced *khasht*, and in the Kaithī character the word *khēt*, a field, is written 𑂭𑂵𑂞 *shēt*. The compound ष्प *shp* is pronounced *hfp*. Thus पुष्प *pushp*, a flower, is pronounced *puhfp*. The letters स *s* and श *ś*, are both pronounced like the *s* in *sin*. Thus शेष *śesh*, remainder, is pronounced, and usually written, सेख *sêkh*. The letter श is usually reserved to represent the Persian ش. Thus شيخ, *shēkh* is written in Nāgarī शेख and in Kaithī 𑂬𑂵𑂭 *i.e.*, शेष.

Pronunciation.

As in other Bihārī dialects, the vowels *e* and *o*, and the diphthongs *ai* and *au* have each two sounds, a short and a long one. Accurate writers distinguish these when writing in the Dēva-nāgarī character, but no distinction is made between them in the Maithilī or in the Kaithī characters. In transliterating the following specimens the distinction will always be carefully shown. The following are the signs used in the Dēva-nāgarī character, together with the signs used in transliterating them:—

Dēva-nāgarī.		Transliteration.
Initial.	Non-initial.	
ए	े	*e*, as in एकरा *ek*ᵃ*rā*, तेकरा *tek*ᵃ*rā*.
ए	े	*ē*, as in एकर *ēkar*, तेकर *tēkar*.
ओ	ो	*o*, as in ओकरा *ok*ᵃ*rā*, होइए *hoiai*.
ओ	ो	*ō*, as in ओकर *ōkar*, लोक *lōk*.
ऐ	ै	*ăĭ*, as in ऐसनहिं *ăisanah*ⁱ, देखैतिऔ *dekhăitiau*.
ऐ	ै	*ai*, as in ऐसन *aisan*, देखैत *dekhait*.
औ	ौ	*ăŭ*, as in औतिए *ăŭtiai*, पौलहंक *păŭl*ᵃ*hák*.
औ	ौ	*au*, as in औतांह *autāh*, पौतांह *pautāh*.

Regarding the pronunciation of these vowels, it will be convenient to consider the long ones first, as they are those which are most familiar to students of Indian languages. The letter *ē* is pronounced like the *a* in *mate ; ō* as the second *o* in *promote ; ai* as the *i* in *might ;* and *au* as the *ou* in *house.*

As for the short vowels, each has the short sound of the corresponding long one Thus, *e* is pronounced as the *é* in the French word *était ; o* is the first *o* in the word *promote,* and is well represented by the *o* of the French word *votre,* while *ō* is represented by the *ô* of *vôtre.* It has *not* the sound of the *o* in *hot.* The diphthong *ăĭ* has no good representative in English. It is almost the first *i* in *mightily,* but is pronounced still shorter ; so *ăŭ* may be approximately represented by the *ou* in *householder,* when spoken quickly as compared with the *ou* in *house,* which is distinctly long.

The vowel *a* has four distinct sounds, which should be noted. They can be shown in Dēva-nāgarī writing, but not in the two other alphabets of Mithilā. They are as follows :—

Dēva-nāgarī.		Transcription.
Initial.	Non-initial.	
अ	...	*a*, as in अग्नि *agn*ⁱ, fire ; मरैछी *maraichhī*, I am dying.
अं	'	*á* as in देखबंह *dekh*ᵃ*báh*, you will see.
आ	ा	*ā*, as in आगू *āgū*, before ; मारब *mārab*, I shall beat.
आ	ा	*ă*, as in आगुआ *ăguā*, a preceder ; मारैछी *măraichhī*, I am beating.

Regarding the pronunciation of these vowels, that of *a* has been already described. It is something between that of the *a* in *America*, and that of the *o* in *hot*. The letter *á* is the long sound of this. It is nearly confined to the termination of the second person plural of verbs, and is pronounced like the *a* in *all*. It is not usually represented in native writing, but is commonly written as if it was merely *a*. When it is desired to show it in writing, it is sometimes represented by ' above the line, and sometimes by :, thus देखबॅह or देखब:ह. This sound, it should be noted, is not nearly so marked in Maithilī, as it is in Bhojpurī, in which dialect it is pronounced with a distinct drawl. The letter *ā* is the well-known *a* of *father*. The letter *ă* is the short sound of this. It is something like the *a* in *farrier*. In Bengali it is pronounced rather flatter, like the *a* in *hat*, but its pronunciation in Bihārī is somewhat broader than this. In native writing it is not customary to indicate it, an ordinary आ *ā* being usually written in its place. Sometimes, however, अ *a* is written for this sound, instead of आ *ā*. Thus we have both आगुआ and अगुआ for *ăguā*.

In Maithilī, the vowels *a*, *i*, and *u* are often so pronounced as to be hardly audible. They are then, in transliteration, written as small letters above the line,—thus, ᵃ, ⁱ, ᵘ The small ᵃ only occurs in the middle of words in unaccented syllables. It is often not pronounced at all by some speakers, but a quick ear will usually distinguish a faint breathing where it occurs like the Hebrew *shwa mobile*. It is found in most Indian languages. In Hindī, it is usually left unwritten, or, at most, is transliterated by an apostrophe. An example in that language is the word मारना which fully transliterated on the usual system would be written *māranā*, but which is commonly transliterated *mārnā* or *mār'nā*. Under the system adopted in this Survey it would be transcribed *mārᵃnā*. The reason which necessitates this is the requirements of other languages of India, such as Kāshmīrī, in which this imperfect ᵃ-sound occurs in positions in which it would be impossible to represent it either by omitting it or by an apostrophe. An example of its use in Maithilī occurs in the word देखलकै *dekhalᵃkai*, he saw, which is pronounced nearly, but not quite, as if it were *dekhalkai*.

The small ⁱ and the small ᵘ occur only at the end of a word. They are, as said above, hardly audible, and sound more like a weak aspirate coloured by the vowel than anything else. Examples of these two imperfect vowels occur in the words देखलन्हि *dekhᵃlánhⁱ*, he saw, and देखिअहु *dekhiáhᵘ*, let me see you. These imperfect vowels are frequently nasalised, as in, देखितहिँ *dekhitáhⁱ*, immediately on seeing, and in देखलहुँ *dekhᵃláhᵘ*, I saw. It should not be supposed that every *i* or *u* at the end of a word is pronounced in this imperfect way. Sometimes such a letter is fully pronounced, as in the word पानि *pāni*, water. Care will be taken to show the correct pronunciation in the transliteration.

As usual in most of the languages of Northern India, the letter *a* at the end of a word of more than one syllable, is not pronounced. Thus, the word फल is pronounced *phal*, and not *phala*. This pronunciation will be observed in transliteration, by not writing the final *a*. Thus, फल will be transliterated *phal*.

The remarks contained in the last three paragraphs refer only to prose. It should be carefully remembered that in poetry all the above-mentioned vowels are fully pronounced. Thus, in Hindī poetry, मारना is pronounced *māranā*, not *mārnā*. Hence, in transliterating poetry, all these small letters will be abandoned, and full sized letters on the line will be written in their places. So, the final *a* of a word, will be written in such circumstances. Thus, in poetry, the words quoted above as examples will be written *dekhalakai*, *dekhalánhi*, *dekhiáhu*, *dekhitáhī*, *dekhaláhū*, and *phala*.

As regards Accent, the general rule is to throw it back as far as possible, but there are exceptions, and in such case the accent will be indicated by a ´ on the accented vowel, as in *dekh'láhᵘ* quoted above. The accent cannot be thrown further back than the antepenultimate, and if the penultimate is long the accent falls on it. Thus, *dekhal'kaínhⁱ*, not *dekhalákainhⁱ*.

Rule of the Short Antepenultimate.

The following rule, known as the Rule of the Short Antepenultimate, is most important. It runs through the whole Bihārī language, and unless it is remembered, numerous difficulties will arise which would at once be cleared away by its application. It should be remembered that it only applies to *Tadbhava*[1] words.

Before coming to the rule itself, it should be noted that, in *Tadbhava* words, the diphthongs ऐ *ai* and औ *au* are always contractions of अ *a* (or आ *ā*)+इ *i* (or ए *ĕ*) and अ *a* (or आ *ā*)+उ *u* (or ओ *o*) respectively, and may be always, at option, written and pronounced अइ *aï*, अए *aĕ*, आइ *āï*, or आए *āĕ*, and अउ *aü*, अओ *aö*, आउ *āü*, or आओ *āö*, respectively according to their origin. Hence, in applying the Rule, ऐ *ai* and औ *au* should always be counted as consisting of two syllables.

a. Whenever the vowel आ *ā* finds itself in the antepenultimate syllable, *i.e.*, the third from the end of a word, it is shortened to अ *a*. Thus, the long form of *nāū*, a barber, is नाउआ *nāüā* or नौआ *nauā*; the long form of आगि *āgi*, fire, is आगिया *āgiyā*; and the instrumental case of पानि *pāni*, water, is पानिएँ *pāniẽ*. This आ *ā* is often written अ *a*, so that the above words would be written नउआ *naüā*, अगिया *agiyā*, and पनिएँ *paniẽ*, respectively.

b. Any other long vowel or diphthong finding itself in the antepenultimate syllable is shortened, provided a consonant, which is not a merely euphonic *y* or *w*, follows it. Thus, from सीखब *sīkhab*, to learn, सिखलक *sikh'lak*, he learned; नेना *nēnā*, a boy, long form, नेनवा *nen'wā*; but from चूअब *chūab*, to drip, चूअबह *chūabĕh*, you will drip, in which the ऊ *ū* is followed by a vowel, and from पीअब *piab*, to drink, पीयबह *pīy'bĕh*, you will drink, in which the ई *ī* is followed by euphonic *y*.

c. Any vowel or diphthong, whatever, finding itself removed more than three syllables from the end of a word, is shortened, whether it is followed by a consonant or not. Thus, from देखब *dēkhab*, to see, देखैतिऔ *dekhaitiau*, (if) I had seen; from सूतब *sūtab*, to sleep, सुतितथीन्हि *sutit'thīnh'*, (if) he had slept.

d. In counting syllables for the above rules, ऐ *ai* and औ *au*, as already stated, count as two, thus, देखै *dekhai*, he sees. The imperfect vowels इ *i* and उ *u*, at the end of a word, are not counted as syllables, nor is the silent अ *a* in the same position. Thus,

[1] The meaning of the words *Tatsama* and *Tadbhava* will be found fully explained in the General Introduction. Briefly stated, *Tatsamas* are words which are borrowed at the present day from Sanskrit, and which appear in their Sanskrit form while *Tadbhavas* are words derived from Sanskrit, but which have passed through a process of phonetic development, outside of Sanskrit, till they have arrived at the form which they bear at the present day. To quote a parallel example from French substituting Latin for Sanskrit, *angelus* is a *tatsama*, while *ange* is a *tadbhava*. So the English *fragile* is a *tatsama*, but *frail* is a *tadbhava*.

आओरि *āor'*, not अओरि *aōr'* and देखब *dēkhab*, not देखब *dekhab;* but लोकनि *lokani*, people, not लोकनि *lōkani*, because the final इ *i* is fully pronounced in this word. On the other hand, the imperfect अ *a* in the middle of a word *is* counted. Thus, देखबह *dekh'bāh*, not देखबह *dēkh'bāh*.

The principal difficulty to the beginner in the study of Maithilī, is the bewildering maze of verbal forms. For each person of each tense sometimes as many as seven or eight different forms may be used. This is due to the fact that the verb agrees not only with its subject, but with its object. Although the distinction of number has disappeared from the modern language, the distinction between superior, or honorific, and inferior, or non-honorific, forms is substituted. In order to simplify the comprehension of the verbal paradigms in the accompanying sketch of Maithilī Grammar, the following general rules are here laid down.

Maithilī Grammar.

General Rules to be observed in conjugating the Maithilī Verb.

Verbs do not change for number, but each person has several forms. There are four principal forms depending, each, upon the honour of the subject and of the object (direct or remote).

The four forms are:—

1. Subject non-honorific, Object non-honorific, *e.g.*, he (a slave) sees him a (slave).
2. Subject non-honorific, Object honorific, *e.g.*, he (a slave) sees him (a king).
3. Subject honorific, Object non-honorific, *e.g.*, he (a king) sees him (a slave).
4. Subject honorific, Object honorific, *e.g.*, he (a king) sees him (a king).

The second and fourth forms are usually made by lengthening the final vowel (when necessary), and adding *nh'*. Thus *dekh'láth'*, he (a king) saw him (a slave); and *dekhal'thīnh'*, he (a king) saw him (a king). In the third and fourth forms, in which the subject is honorific, the second person is the same as the first. Thus (third form) *dekh'lai*, I saw, or you saw; (fourth form) *dekh'lainh'*, I saw, or you saw.

The *Rule of Attraction* is as follows: If a verbal form ends in *ai* or *ainh'*, and the object (direct or remote) is in the second person, the *ai* is changed to *au* and the *ainh'* to *aunh'*. Thus, *Murtā nēnā-kē măral'kai*, Murtā beat the child; but, *Murtā toharā-kē măral'kau*, Murtā beat you. *Ok'rā gārī-mā̃ kōn māl chhai*, what goods are in this cart? but, *toh'rā gārī-mā̃ kōn māl chhau*, what is there in *your* cart (remote object). In the first person, *au* is often spelt *áh'*. Thus, *măraliau* or *măraliáh'*, I struck you.

The letter *k* may be added to any form in *ai* or *au* without changing the meaning. Thus, *măral'kai* or *măral'kaik: măral'kau* or *măral'kauk*.

Forms ending in *ai* or *aik*, or *au* or *auk*, always belong either to the first or third forms, and are hence only used when the object is non-honorific.

It is hoped that if these rules are borne in mind, no difficulty will be experienced in grasping the principles of Maithilī Grammar, as shown in the following sketch. In this sketch, verbal terminations formed by changing *ai* to *au*, or by adding *k*, are omitted, to save space. These are provided for by the above general rules.

MAITHILĪ SKELETON GRAMMAR.

I.—**Nouns.**—A noun has three forms. (1) Short, (2) Long, (3) Redundant. Thus—

	Short.		Long.	Redundant.
	ghōrā	a horse	*ghor*ᵉ*wā*	*ghorauā*
	ghar	a house	*ghar*ᵉ*wā*	*gharauā*
	māli	a gardener	*māliyā*	*mālīwā*
	nāū	a barber	*nauā*	*nauawā*
Adjectives	*mīṭhā*	sweet	{ *miṭh*ᵉ*kā* *miṭhákkā*	} *miṭhák*ᵉ*wā*
	mīṭhī (fem.)	sweet	{ *miṭh*ᵉ*kī* *miṭhákkī*	} *miṭhákiyā*

The short form may be weak or strong. Thus *ghōr* or *ghōrā*, a horse. Usually only one form is used, but sometimes both.

Number.—Plural is formed by adding a noun of multitude, such as *sabh* or *sabáhⁱ*, all; *lokani*, people. Thus, *nēnā*, a boy; *nēnā sabh*, *nēnā sabáhⁱ*, *nēnā lokani*, boys.

Case.—The only true case is the Instrumental formed by adding *ē̃*, before which a final *ā* is elided, ⁱ becomes *i*, and *ī* or *ū* shortened. Thus *nēnē̃*, by a boy, *nēnā sabáhiē̃*, by boys; *phal*, a fruit, *phalē̃*; *pāni*, water, *pāniē̃*; *nēnī*, a girl, *neniē̃*; *Raghū*, nom. prop., *Raghuē̃*. To these may be added a rare locative in *ē*, *hⁱ*, or *hⁱ*, as *gharē*, *gharáhⁱ*, or *gharáhⁱ*, in the house. Also a Genitive in *uk* or *k*, as in the following,—*nēnāk*, of a boy; *nēnā sabhak* or *sabáhik*, of boys; *phalak*, of a fruit; *pānik*, of water; *nēnīk*, of a girl; *Raghūk*, of *Raghū*.

Other cases are formed by postpositions, added to the form of the Nominative, or to the oblique form when such exists. Some of these are *kē̃*, to; *sā̃*, *saũ*, from or by; *kēr* or *kar*, of; *mē̃*, *mā̃*, in. Thus, *nēnā kē̃*, to a boy.

Gender.—*Tadbhava* nouns and adjectives in *ā*, form the feminine in *ī*. Thus, *nēnā*, fem. *nēnī*. Long forms in ᵉ*wā*, have fem. in *iyā*. Thus, *nen*ᵉ*wā*, *neniyā*. Redundant forms in *auā* have *īwā* in the fem. Thus, *nenauā*, *nenīwā*. *Tadbhava* adjectives ending in silent consonant form the fem. in ⁱ. Thus *baṛ*, great, fem. *baṛⁱ*; *adh*ᵉ*lāh*, bad, fem. *adh*ᵉ*lāhⁱ*. So also some *Tatsama* words, e.g., *sundar*, beautiful; fem. *sundarⁱ*.

Oblique form.—Certain nouns, principally ending in *b*, *r* and *l*, have an oblique form in *ā* used before postpositions. Thus, *pahar*, a guard; *pah*ᵉ*rā saũ*, from a guard. These are principally verbal nouns in *b* and *l*. Thus *dēkhab*, to see, *dekh*ᵉ*bā saũ*, from seeing; *dekh*ᵉ*bāk*, of seeing: *pachh*ᵉ*tāol*, regretting, *pachh*ᵉ*tāolā* (or *pachh*ᵉ*taulā*) *saũ*, from regretting. So also, the verbal noun in ⁱ has an oblique form in *a* or *ăi*. Thus *dēkhⁱ*, the act of seeing; *dēkha kē̃*, or *dēkhăi kē̃*, for seeing, and so on. Irregular are *dēb*, giving, obl. *dēmăi*; *lēb*, taking, obl. *lēmăi*.

II.—**Pronouns.**—

	I		Thou		Self	This	
	Obsolete.	Modern.	Obsolete.	Modern.		Non-honorific.	Honorific.
Sing.							
Nom.	*mē̃*	*ham*	*tō̃*	*tō̃h*, *tō̃*	*áp*ᵉ*nahⁱ*	*i*, *ī*	*i*, *ī*
Obl.	*mohⁱ*	...	*tohⁱ*	...	*ap*ᵉ*nā*, *áp*ᵉ*nahⁱ*	*ehⁱ*	...
Gen.	*mōr*	{ *hámar* *hamār*	*tua* *tōr*	} *tōhar*, *tohār*	*apan*, *appan*	*ē-kar*	*hinak*
Plur.							
Nom.	...	*ham sabh*	...	*tō̃h sabh*	*áp*ᵉ*nah*ᵉ *subh*	*i* or *ī sabh*	*i* or *ī sabh*

	That, he		Who		That, he		Who? (substantive)	
	Non-honorific.	Honorific.	Non-honorific.	Honorific.	Non-honorific.	Honorific.	Non-honorific.	Honorific.
Sing.								
Nom.	*ō*	*ō*	*jē*	*jē*	*sē*	*sē*	*kē*	*kē*
Obl.	*ohⁱ*	...	*jāhⁱ*	...	*tāhⁱ*	...	*kāhⁱ*	...
Gen.	*ō-kar*	*hunak*	*ja-kar*	*janik*	*ta-kar*	*tanik*	*ka-kar*	*kanik*
Plur.								
Nom.	*ō sabh*	*ō sabh*	*jē sabh*	*jē sabh*	*sē sabh*	*sē sabh*	*kē sabh*	*kē sabh*

Kī, what? (substantive); Obl. base, *kathī*, gen. *kathik*.

Kōn, who? or what? (adjective), does not change.

Keo, anyone, someone (substantive); obl. *kák*ᵉ*rahⁱ*; gen. *kak*ᵉ*rō*. Also obl. *kāhū*; gen. *kāhuk*.

Kōnō, any, some (adjective), does not change.

*Kichh*ᵘ, something; obl. *kathū*, gen. *kathūk*.

*Kichh*ᵘ, when it means anything, does not change. Thus *kathū kē̃*, to something; *kichhu kē̃*, to anything.

Honorific Pronoun, *ahā̃*, *ahaĩ*, *áp*ᵉ*nahⁱ* or *ápane*, your Honour; obl. *ahā̃*, *ahaĩ*, *apane*; gen. *ahā̃k*, *ahaĩk*, *ap*ᵉ*nek*.

All the above Genitives have an oblique form in *ā*, as follows :—

Direct.	Oblique.
mōr	*mōrā*
hamar	*ham^{a}rā*
tōr	*tōrā*
tōhar	*toh^{a}rā*
apan	*ap^{a}nā*
ē-kar	*ek^{a}rā*
hinak	*hin^{a}kā*
ō-kar	*ok^{a}rā*
hunak	*hun^{a}kā*
ja-kar	*jak^{a}rā*
janik	*janikā*
ta-kar	*tak^{a}rā*
tanik	*tanikā*
ka-kar	*kak^{a}rā*
kanik	*kanikā*

Each of these oblique genitives can all be used as a kind of secondary oblique base to which the postpositions can be attached. Thus besides *jāh^{i} kē*, to whom, we can have *jak^{a}rā kē*, and so on. For the modern forms of the first and second persons, and for the Honorific forms of the other pronouns, these are the only forms used. Thus accusative, *ham^{a}rā* ; dat., *ham'rā kē*, *toh^{a}rā kē*, *hin^{a}kā kē*, and so on. We even have nominative plural like *ham^{a}rā sabh*, *toh^{a}rā sabh*. The non-honorific oblique forms are also used as adjectives, and *eh^{i}* and *oh^{i}* are *only* used as adjectives, or as substantival pronouns referring to inanimate things. The secondary oblique bases are never used as adjectives. *Kī* is never used as an adjective. These oblique forms agree with nouns in oblique cases. Thus, *hamar ghar*, my house ; but *ham^{a}rā ghar sā̃*, from my house.

III.—Verbs.—

A.—Auxiliary Verb, and Verb Substantive.—Present Participle, *achhait*, existing.

Present, I am—

Form 1.	Form 2.	Form 3.	Form 4.
1. *chhī, chhiai* [1]	*chhiainh^{i}*	*chhī, chhiai* [1]	*chhiainh^{i}*
2. *chhăh* [2]	*chhahūnh^{i}*	*chhī, chhiai* [1]	*chhiainh^{i}*
3. *achh^{i}, chhai* [3]	*chhainh^{i}*	*chhath^{i}*	*chhathīnh^{i}* [4]

Optional forms, (1) *chhiăh^{u}* ; (2) *chhē, chhaī, chhahăk, chhahīk* ; fem. *chhah^{i}* ; (3) *chhik, chhah^{u}, ah^{i}, hai* ; (4) *chhathūnh^{i}*.

Alternative form, I am—

Form 1.	Form 2.	Form 3.	Form 4.
1. *thikăh^{u}, thikiai* [1]	*thikiainh^{i}*	*thikăh^{u}, thikiai* [1]	*thikiainh^{i}*
2. *thikăh* [2]	*thik^{a}hūnh*	*thikăh^{u}, thikiai* [1]	*thikiainh^{i}*
3. *thik, thikai* [3]	*thikainh^{i}*	*thikăh* [4]	*thik^{a}thīnh^{i}* [5]

Optional forms, (1) *thikiăh^{u}* ; (2) *thikē, thikaī, thik^{a}hăk, thik^{a}hīk* ; fem. *thikīh* or *thikīh^{i}* ; (3) *thik, thikăh^{u}* ; fem. *thik^{i}* ; (4) fem *thikih* or *thikīh^{i}* ; (5)*thik^{a}thūnh^{i}*.

Past, I was—

Form 1.	Form 2.	Form 3.	Form 4.
1. *chhalăh^{u}, chhaliai* [1]	*chhaliainh^{i}*	*chhalăh^{u}, chhaliai*	*chhaliainh^{i}*
2. *chhalăh* [2]	*chhal^{a}hūnh^{i}*	" "	"
3. *chhal, chhalai* [3]	*chhalainh^{i}*	*chhalăh* [4]	*chhal^{a}thīnh^{i}* [5]

Optional forms, (1), (2), (4), (5), as in *thikăh^{u}* ; (3) *chhalăh^{u}* ; fem. *chhal^{i}*.

Alternative form, I was—

Form 1.	Form 2.	Form 3.	Form 4.
1. *rahī, rahiai* [1]	*rahiainh^{i}*	*rahī, rahiai* [1]	*rahiainh^{i}* [1]
2. *rahăh* [2]	*rah^{a}hūnh^{i}*	" "	"
3. *rahai* [3]	*rahainh^{i}*	*rahath^{i}* [3]	*rah^{a}thīnh^{i}* [4]

Optional forms, (1) *rahiăh^{u}* ; (2) *rah, rah^{a}hăk, rah^{a}hīk* ; fem. *rahăh^{i}* ; (3) *rahai* is seldom used, *rahau* being generally employed instead ; (4) *rah^{a}thūnh^{i}*.

B.—Transitive Verb.—*dēkhab*, to see. Root, *dēkh*.

Verbal Nouns, (1) *dēkhab*, obl. *dekh^{a}bā*; (2) *dēkhal*, obl. *dekh^{a}lā*; (3) *dēkh^{i}*, obl. *dēkha* or *dēkhāi*.
Participles. Pres., *dekhait*. fem. *dekhait^{i}*; *Past*, *dēkhal*, fem. *dēkhal^{i}*.
Conjunctive Participle, *dēkh^{i} kā̃* (or *kaī*, or *kai-kā̃*), having seen.

Adverbial Participle, *dekhitahī̃*, on seeing.

Simple Present, I see; *Present Conditional*, (if) I see:

Form 1.	Form 2.	Form 3.	Form 4.
1. *dēkhī, dekhiai* 2. *dēkhāh* [1] 3. *dekhai* [2]	*dekhiainh^{i}* *dekh^{a}hūnh^{i}* *dekhainh^{i}* [3]	*dēkhī, dekhiai* " " *dēkhāth^{i}*	*dekhiainh^{i}* " *dekh^{a}thīnh^{i}* [4]

Optional forms, (1) *dekh^{a}hāk, dekh^{a}hīk*; fem. *dēkhāhī̃*; (2) *dekhai* is only used in the simple present, *dekhau* being generally employed instead in the Present Conditional; (3) so also, *dekhaunh^{i}* is generally employed in the Conditional; (4) *dekh^{a}thūnh^{i}* is more usual than *dekh^{a}thīnh^{i}*.

Future, I shall see. Three varieties:—

First variety, the same as the Simple Present, to which, however, the syllable *gā* is generally added. Thus, *dēkhī-gā*, I shall see.

Second Variety—

Form 1.	Form 2.	Form 3.	Form 4.
1. *dēkhab, dekh^{a}bai* 2. *dekh^{a}bāh* [1] 3. Wanting	*dekh^{a}bainh^{i}* *dekh^{a}bahūnh^{i}* wanting	*dēkhab, dekh^{a}bai* " " wanting	*dekh^{a}bainh^{i}* " wanting

Optional forms, (1) *dekh^{a}bẽ, dekh^{a}bahāk, dekh^{a}bahīk*; fem. *dekh^{a}bāhī̃*. The syllable *gā* may be added to any form. Thus, *dēkhab-gā*.

Third Variety—

Form 1.	Form 2.	Form 3.	Form 4.
1. *dekh^{a}tiai* [1] 2. wanting 3. *dēkhat*, [2] *dekh^{a}tai*	*dekh^{a}tiainh^{i}* wanting *dekh^{a}tainh^{i}*	*dekh^{a}tiai* [1] " *dekh^{a}tāh, dēkhāth^{a}* [3]	*dekh^{a}tiainh^{i}* " *dekh^{a}thūnh^{i}* [4]

Optional forms, (1) *dekhitāh$^{\bar{u}}$*; (2) fem. *dēkhat^{i}*; (3) fem. *dekh^{a}tīh, dekh^{a}tīk^{i}*; (4) *dekh^{a}thīnh^{i}*. The syllable *gā* may be added to any form. Thus *dekh^{a}tiai-gā*.

Imperative, Let me see—

Form 1.	Form 2.	Form 3.	Form 4.
1. *dēkhū, dekhiai* 2. *dēkh, dēkhāh* [1] 3. *dēkhau*	*dekhiainh^{i}* *dekh^{a}hūnh^{i}* *dēkhaunh^{i}*	*dēkhū, dekhiai* " " *dēkhuth^{a}*	*dekhiainh^{i}* " *dekh^{a}hūnh^{i}*

Optional forms, (1) *dākhẽ, dekh^{a}hāk, dākh^{a}hīk*; fem. *dēkhāhī̃*; Precative form, *dekhihā*, be good enough to see; *dēkhal jāh*, etc.

Past Conditional, (If) I had seen—

Form 1.	Form 2.	Form 3.	Form 4. [2]
1. *dekhitāh$^{\bar{u}}$, dekhitiai* [1] 2. *dekhitāh* [2] 3. *dekhait, dekhitai*	*dekhitiainh^{i}* *dekhit^{a}hūnh^{i}* *dekhitainh^{i}*	*dekhitāh$^{\bar{u}}$, dekhitiai* [1] " " *dekhitāth^{i}*	*dekhitiainh^{i}* " *dekhit^{a}thīnh^{i}* [3]

Optional forms, (1) *dekhiti*; (2) *dekhitẽ, dekhit^{a}hāk, dekhit^{a}hīk*; fem. *dekhitāhī̃*; (3) *dekhit^{a}thūnh^{i}*. Some people say *dekhaitāh$^{\bar{u}}$* instead of *dekhitāh$^{\bar{u}}$*, and so throughout.

Present Definite, I am seeing—
Masculine, *dekhait chhī*, or *dekhaichhī*, and so throughout.
The 3rd person singular is commonly *dekhaïchh^{i}*.
Feminine, *dekhait^{i} chhī* or *dekhaichhī*, and so throughout.
The verb *thikāh^{u}* may be substituted for *chhī* throughout.

Imperfect, I was seeing—
Masculine, *dekhait chhalāh$^{\bar{u}}$* or *dekhaichhalāh$^{\bar{u}}$*, and so throughout.
Feminine, *dekhait^{i} chhalāh$^{\bar{u}}$* or *dekhaichhalāh$^{\bar{u}}$*, and so throughout.
The verb *rahī* may be substituted for *chhalāh$^{\bar{u}}$* throughout.

Past, I saw—

	Form 1.	Form 2.	Form 3.	Form 4.
1.	*dēkhal, dekh^{e}lai* [1]	*dekh^{e}lainh^{i}* [3]	*dekhal, dekh^{e}lai* [1]	*dekh^{e}lainh^{i}* [3]
2.	*dekh^{e}lăh* [2]	*dekh^{e}lahūnh^{i}*	"	"
3.	*dekh^{e}lak, dekhal^{e}kai*	*dekh^{e}lakainh^{i}*	*dekh^{e}lánh^{i}, dekh^{e}láth^{i}*	*dekhul^{e}thīnh^{i}* [4]

Optional forms, (1) *dekh^{e}láh^{ū}, dekh^{e}li, dekh^{e}liai*, the fem. of *dēkhal* is *dēkhal^{i}*; (2) *dekh^{e}lẽ, dekh^{e}laï, dekh^{e}lahák, dekh^{e}lahīk*, fem. *dekh^{e}līh^{i}*, or *dekh^{e}līh^{i}*; (3) *dekh^{e}liainh^{i}*; (4) *dekhal^{e}hūnh^{i}*.

Perfect, I have seen. Two varieties :—

(1) Formed by adding *achh^{i}*, etc., throughout to all persons of the Past. Thus *dēkhal achh^{i}, dekh^{e}lai achh^{i}*, etc., I have seen.

(2) Formed by adding the present of the Auxiliary Verb to *dekh^{e}lẽ*, the Instrumental of the second verbal noun. Thus *dekh^{e}lẽ chhī*, I have seen, and so on.

Pluperfect, I had seen. *dekh^{e}lẽ chhaláh^{ū}* (or *rahī*), and so on.

C.—Neuter Verb.—*Sūtab*, to sleep.

The second and fourth forms are rarely used in Neuter Verbs.
Simple Present, and Present Conditional, I sleep, (if) I sleep; *sūtī*, as in the Transitive Verb.
Future, I shall sleep, *sūtab*, etc., as in the Transitive Verb.
Imperative, Let me sleep, *sūtū*, as in the Transitive Verb.
Past Conditional, (if) I had slept, *sutitáh^{ū}*, as in the Transitive Verb.
Present Definite, I am sleeping, *sutait chhī*, etc., as in the Transitive Verb.
Imperfect, I was sleeping, *sutait chhaláh^{ū}*, etc., as in the Transitive Verb.

Past, I slept.

	Form 1.	Form 2.
1.	*sut^{e}lī, sut^{e}liai* [1]	*sut^{e}lī, sut^{e}liai* [4]
2.	*sut^{e}lăh* [2]	" "
3.	*sūtal* [3]	*sut^{e}lăh* [4]

Optional forms, (1) *sut^{e}láh^{ū}* (2) *sut^{e}lẽ, sut^{e}laï, sut^{e}lahák, sut^{e}lahīk*; fem. *sut^{e}līh*, or *sut^{e}līh^{i}*; (3) *sut^{e}lai*; fem. *sūtai*; (4) *sut^{e}lanh^{i}*; fem. *sut^{e}līh, sūt^{e}līh^{i}*.

Pluperfect, I had slept, *sutal chhaláh^{ū}*, etc., as in the Perfect.

Perfect, I have slept.

First variety.

sut^{e}lī achh^{i}, etc., after the analogy of Transitive Verbs.

Second variety.

	Form 1.	Form 2.
1.	*sūtal chhī*	*sūtal chhī*.
2.	*sūtal chhăh*	" "
3.	*sūtal achh^{i}*	*sūtal chhath*

Feminine *sūtal^{i} chhī*, and so on. Any form of the Auxiliary may be used.

D.—Verbs whose roots end in *āb*; *pāeb*, to obtain; first and third forms only given. *Present Part.*, *păbait* or *pāit*; *Past Part.*, *pāol*; *Root*, *pāh*.

	Simple present.	Future.	Imperative.	Past Conditional.	Past.	Perfect.	Pluperfect.
1.	*pābī* or *pāi*	*pāeb, pāob*	*pāū*	*paitáh^{ū}*	*pāol, paulai*	*pāol achh^{i}* or *paulẽ chhī*.	*paulẽ chhaláh^{ū}*
2.	*pābăh*	*paibăh, paubăh*	*pābăh*	*paităh*	*paulăh*	...	...
3. I.	*pătau, păbau*	*pāet, pāot*	*pătau, păbau*	*păbait*	*paulak*	...	...
3. III.	*pābath^{i}*	*paităh, pautăh*	*pābath^{u}*	*paitáth^{i}*	*paulanh^{i}*	...	...

These include all causal verbs, the verbs *gāeb*, to sing, and *āeb*, to come, and all Transitive Verbs with infinitives in *āeb*, except *khāeb*, to eat. Other Intransitive Verbs whose infinitives end in *āeb* and *khāeb*, are conjugated as follows :—

	Simple Present.	Future.	Past Conditional.	Past.	E.—Irregular Verbs.
1.	*khāī*	*khāeb*	*khaitáh^{ū}*	*khāel*	*jāeb*, to go. Past Part., *gēl*. *karab*, to do. Past Part., *kail*. *dharab*, to seize, place. Past Part., *dhail*. *dēb*, to give. Past Part., *dēl*. *lēb*, to take. Past Part., *lēl*. *hoeb* or *haib*, to become. Past Part., *bhēl*. *marab*, to die. Past Part., *muil* or *moral*.
2.	*khāh*	*khaibăh*	*khaităh*	*khailăh*	
3. I.	*khāau*	*khāet*	*khāet*	*khailak*	
3. III.	*khāth^{i}*	*khaităh*	*khaitáth^{i}*	*khailanh*	

MAGAHĪ OR MĀGADHĪ.

Magaha dēsa hai kañchana purī,
Dēsa bhalā pai bhākhā burī.
Rahalū̃ Maggaha kahalū̃ 'rē',
Tekarā-lā kā marabē rē ?

Magah is a land of gold. The country is good, but the language is vile. I lived there and have got into the habit of saying '*rē*.' Why, '*rē*,' do you beat me for doing so?[1]

Name of Dialect.

Magahī or Māgadhī is, properly speaking, the language of the country of Magadha. The Sanskrit name of the dialect is hence Māgadhī, and this name is sometimes used by the educated; but the correct modern name is Magahī.

The ancient kingdom of Magadha.

The ancient country of Magadha (now often called Magah) corresponded to what is at the present day, roughly speaking, the District of Patna, together with the northern half of the District of Gayā. It contained at different times three famous capital cities. The oldest was Rāja-gṛiha, the modern village of Rajgir, situated in the heart of the low range of hills which at the present day separates the District of Patna from that of Gayā. The history of Rāja-gṛiha is enveloped in the mists of legend. Suffice it to say that, according to tradition, its most celebrated king was named Jarā-sandha, who was overlord of a great part of Central Hindōstān. In the middle of the sixth century B.C., it was ruled by king Bimbi-sāra, who is famous as the patron of the Buddha. Here that great reformer lived for many years, and the ruined site of the city teems with reminiscences of him. Bimbi-sāra's son and successor founded the city of Patna, which in after years became the capital of Magadha in supersession of Rāja-gṛiha. Here, in the latter half of the third century B.C. were the head-quarters of the great Aśōka, under whom Buddhism was finally adopted as the state religion. The whole of Northern India was directly subject to him, as far south as Orissa, and a great portion of what is now Afghanistan, and of the Deccan as far south of the River Krishna, were under kings who recognised his suzerainty.

Under the Musalmāns, the capital of the country was the town of Bihār, in the south of the Patna District, the name of which, a relic of ancient times, is a corruption of the Buddhist word *vihāra* or monastery. From this town, the whole *sūba* or Province of Bihār took its name.

During British supremacy, up to the year 1865, the greater part of the present Patna District and the north of the present Gayā District, an area which closely corresponded to that of the ancient Magadha, formed one District known as Zila' Bihār; the south of Gayā, together with a portion of the Hazaribagh District, being known as Zila' Rāmgaṛh. From that date, the two Districts of Patna and Gayā have been in existence.

---

[1] *Vide* p. 34 *post*. The unfortunate man has lived in Magah and has acquired the vulgar habit of ending every question with the word '*rē*', which, elsewhere in India, is the height of rudeness. He gets into a quarrel over this when he comes home, and earns a drabbing for insulting some one. Yet, so ingrained is the habit that while apologising he actually uses the objectionable word.

Area in which Magahī is spoken.

Magahī is, however, not confined to the old country of Magadha. It is also spoken all over the rest of Gayā and over the District of Hazaribagh; also, on the West, in a portion of the District of Palamau, and, on the East, in portions of the Districts of Monghyr and Bhagalpur. Over the whole of this area, it is practically one and the same dialect, with hardly any local variations. Only near the city of Patna is it infected with idioms belonging to the North-Western Provinces by the strong Musalmān element which inhabits that town, and which itself speaks more or less correct Urdū.

Eastern Magahī.

On its eastern border, Magahī meets Bengali. The two languages do not combine, but the meeting ground is a bilingual one, where they live side by side, each spoken by its own nationality. Each is, however, more or less affected by the other, and the Magahī so affected possesses distinct peculiarities, entitling it to be classed apart as a sub-dialect, which I have named Eastern Magahī. We find this dialect in South-East Hazaribagh, in Manbhum, in the South-East of the District of Ranchi, in the Native State of Kharsāwān, and even so far South as the Native States of Mayūrbhanja and Bamra which belong politically to Orissa and Chhattisgarh, respectively. It is also spoken as an isolated island of speech in the West of the District of Malda.

Pure Magahī has also found its way down South of the District of Ranchi, and appears in the North of the District of Singhbhum, and in the Native States of Sarai Kalā and Kharsāwān, where it is spoken side by side with Oṛiyā. It will be noticed that both Standard Magahī and Eastern Magahī are spoken in Kharsāwān. Here the dividing cause is not difference of locality, but difference of caste. For further particulars concerning Eastern Magahī, and for the various local names by which it is called, the reader is referred to pages 145 and ff.

Linguistic Boundaries.

Magahī is bounded on the North by the various forms of Maithilī spoken in Tirhut across the Ganges. On the West it is bounded by the Bhojpurī spoken in Shahabad and Palamau. On the North-East it is bounded by the Chhikā-chhikī Maithilī of Monghyr, Bhagalpur and the Sonthal Parganas, and on the South-East by the Bengali of Manbhum and East Singhbhum. Standard Magahī is bounded on the South by the Sadān form of Bhojpurī spoken in Ranchi. It then, in the form of Eastern Magahī, runs along the eastern base of the Ranchi plateau through the Bengali-speaking District of Manbhum, and finally curls round to the West, below the south face of the same plateau in the North of the Oṛiyā-speaking District of Singhbhum, reappearing here as Standard Magahī. It will thus be seen that a belt of Magahī-speaking population bounds the Ranchi plateau on three sides, the North, the East, and the South.

There are three *enclaves* of Eastern Magahī, one in the Native States of Mayūrbhanja and Bamra, where it is surrounded on all sides by Oṛiyā, and is known as Kuṛumālī, and the other in Western Malda, where it is called Khoṇṭāi, and is bounded on the North and West by Maithilī, and on the East and South by Bengali.

The area in which Magahī is spoken is illustrated in the map facing page 1, and the area of Eastern Magahī is shown in greater detail in the map facing page 147.

Number of speakers.

The following are the figures which show the number of people who speak Magahī in Districts in which it is a vernacular :—

Name of District.	Number of Speakers.	Total for each Sub-dialect.
A.—Standard Magahī—		
Patna	1,551,362	
Gaya	2,067,877	
Bhagalpur	7,195	
Monghyr	1,019,000	
Palamau	150,000	
Hazaribagh	1,069,000	
Singhbhum	25,867	
Sarai Kalā State	34,815	
Kharsāwān State	987	
TOTAL FOR STANDARD MAGAHĪ		5,926,103
B.—Eastern Magahī—		
Hazaribagh	7,333	
Ranchi	8,000	
Manbhum	111,100[1]	
Kharsāwān State	2,957	
Bamra State	4,194	
Mayūrbhanja State	280	
Malda	180,000	
TOTAL FOR EASTERN MAGAHĪ		313,864
GRAND TOTAL FOR MAGAHĪ		6,239,967

For the reasons stated when dealing with Maithilī, *vide ante*, pp. 14 and ff., it is impossible to ascertain the number of people whose native language is Magahī, but who live in parts of India where Magahī is not the vernacular. All that can be done is to give for the Provinces of Bengal and Assam, the following estimated figures. No figures of any kind are available for other parts of India :—

[1] The figures include some speakers of pure Magahī.

Table showing the estimated number of speakers of Magahī, within the Lower Provinces of Bengal, but outside the area in which Magahī is the vernacular language.

Name of District.	Number of Speakers.	REMARKS.
Burdwan	16,600	
Bankura	1,600	
Birbhum	3,900	
Midnapur	14,900	
Hooghly	5,000	
Howrah	7,900	
24-Parganas	19,300	
Calcutta	90,200	
Nadia	2,000	
Jessore	600	
Murshidabad	22,800	
Khulna	900	
Dinājpur	2,900	
Rajshahi	1,100	
Rangpur	900	
Bogra	1,100	
Pabna	1,800	
Darjeeling	700	
Jalpaiguri	2,300	
Kuch Bihar (State)	350	
Dacca	8,200	
Faridpur	1,300	
Backergunge	1,000	
Mymensingh	500	
Chittagong	1,100	
Noakhali	64	
Tippera	400	
Cuttack	80	
Puri	180	
Balasore	170	
Ranchi	20,141	Spoken in the North of the District by immigrants from Hazaribagh.
Jashpur State	1,500	
TOTAL	231,485	

Table showing the estimated number of speakers of Magahī within the Province of Assam.

Name of District.	Number of Speakers.	REMARKS.
Cachar Plains	10,200	
Sylhet	4,600	
Goalpara	1,800	
Kāmrūp	400	
Darrang	2,100	
Nowgong	1,100	
Sibsagar	7,900	
Lakhimpur	5,000	
Naga Hills	100	
Khasi and Jaintia Hills	150	
Lushai Hills	15	
TOTAL	33,365	

NOTE.—Nearly all those are tea-garden coolies.

The following is, therefore, the total number of speakers of Magahī recorded in the above tables:—

Number of people speaking Magahī at Home	6,239,967
" " " " elsewhere in the Lower Provinces	231,485
" " " " in Assam	33,365
TOTAL	6,504,817

Character of the language.

Magahī is condemned by speakers of other Indian languages as being rude and uncouth like the people who use it. In fact the principal difference between it and Maithilī is that the latter has been under the influence of learned Brāhmaṇs for centuries, while the former has been the language of a people who have been dubbed boors since Vedic times.[1] To a native of India, one of its most objectionable features is its habit of winding up every question, even when addressed to a person held in respect, with the word '*rē*'. In other parts of India this word is only used in addressing an inferior, or when speaking contemptuously. Hence a man of Magah has the reputation of rudeness, and is liable to earn an undeserved beating on that score, as has been illustrated in the little popular song which is prefixed to this section.

[1] Compare Atharva-vēda, v, xxii, 14.

Magahī Literature.

Magahī has no indigenous written literature. There are many popular songs current throughout the area in which the language is spoken, and strolling bards recite various long epic poems which are known more or less over the whole of Northern India. One of these, the Song of Gōpīchandra, has been published by the present writer, with an English translation, in the Journal of the Asiatic Society of Bengal, Vol. liv, Part I, 1885, pp. 35 and ff. Another very popular poem, which has not yet been edited, is the Song of Lōrik, of which an account will be found in the eighth volume of the reports of the Archæological Survey of India, and in the present writer's Notes on the District of Gayā.[1]

The only other printed specimens of the dialect with which I am acquainted are the fables at the end of the Grammars mentioned below, and a translation of the New Testament. The latter is a version in the 'Magadh' language, and was printed at Serampore in 1826. A revised version of the Gospel of St. Mark was issued by the Calcutta Branch of the Bible Society in the year 1890, and is still on sale.

AUTHORITIES—

CAMPBELL, Sir G.,—*Specimens of Languages of India. Including those of the Aboriginal Tribes of Bengal, the Central Provinces, and the Eastern Frontier.* Calcutta, 1874. Page 60. Lists of Words and Sentences in the 'Vernacular of Patna' and 'of Gaya.'

GRIERSON, G. A.,—*Seven Grammars of the Dialects and Sub-Dialects of the Bihárí Language. Part III. Mágadhí Dialect of South Patna and Gaya. Part VI. South-Maithil-Mágadhí Dialect of South Munger and the Báṛh Subdivision of Paṭná.* Calcutta, 1883 and 1886.

KELLOGG, the Rev. S. H.,—*A Grammar of the Hindí Language, in which are treated……the colloquial dialects of……Magadha……etc., with copious philological notes.* Second Edition, Revised and Enlarged. London, 1893. The first edition does not deal with Magahī.

HOERNLE, A. F. R., and GRIERSON, G. A.,—*A Comparative Dictionary of the Bihārī Language.* Part I, Calcutta, 1885. Part II, 1889. Only two parts issued.

Written Character.

The character in general use in writing Magahī is Kaithī, for the alphabet of which see the plate facing p. 11. The Dēva-nāgarī alphabet is also occasionally used. For Eastern Magahī, we find the Bengali, and even the Oṛiyā alphabet employed. Examples of the use of all these alphabets will be found in the following specimens.

Pronunciation.

The pronunciation of Magahī is not so broad as in Maithilī. The letter अ *a* is usually pronounced like the *u* in 'nut,' as in the North-Western Provinces. In the last syllable of the second person of a verb, it is, however, pronounced like the *a* in 'all.' It will then be transliterated *á*. Thus मार *mārá*, beat thou. There is the same confusion of ष *sh* and ख *kh* that we find in Maithilī. When not compounded with another consonant, both are pronounced *kh*. The letters श *ś* and स *s* are both pronounced like the *s* in 'sin.'[2] The vowel आ *ā* is sometimes pronounced like the *a* in 'mad.' It is then transliterated *ă*. Thus मारलकइ *măral°kaï*. Regarding this sound, and the other vowels, see the remarks under the head of Maithilī on page 22, which also apply to Magahī. See also the remarks on page 23 regarding the small ° in the middle of a word in unaccented syllables. The vowels इ *i* and उ *u* at the end of a word are fully pronounced in Magahī, and not as ' or " as in Maithilī. A final अ *a* is not usually[3] pronounced in

---

[1] Calcutta, 1893.

[2] *Vide ante*, p. 21, for further details.

[3] A final *a* is pronounced in the second person of verbs, as in मार *mārá* given above.

prose, but is pronounced in poetry. The pronunciation will be followed in the transliteration. Thus फल will be transliterated *phal* in prose, and *phala* in poetry.

The **Rule of the Short Antepenultimate** applies in Magahī, exactly as it does in Maithilī. The reader is referred to pages 24 and ff.

Magahī Grammar.

As in the case of Maithilī, the chief difficulty of Magahī Grammar is the number of verbal forms for each person. The verb, as in Maithilī, agrees both with its subject and with its object, and, while there is no distinction of number, there are the four forms of each person depending on the honour of the subject and the object.

As in Maithilī, the four forms are as follows :—

1. Subject non-honorific, Object non-honorific.
2. Subject non-honorific, Object honorific.
3. Subject honorific, Object non-honorific.
4. Subject honorific, Object honorific.

The second and fourth forms may be distinguished by the fact that they always end in *n*. The preceding vowel is generally, but not always, *i* or *u*, and, though this is not shown in the paradigms, these are often pronounced long. Thus, besides *dekhal°thin*, he (honorific) saw him (honorific), we may have *dekhal°thīn*.

The **Rule of Attraction** closely agrees with that which obtains in Maithilī. If a verbal form ends in *aï* (or *ai*) *ī* or *in*, and the Object, direct or remote, is in the second person, the *aï* (or *ai*) is changed to *aü* (or *au*), the *ī* to *ū*, and the *in* to *un*. This rule also applies when the *Subject* of the verb is connected indirectly with the second person. Thus, if the subject of a verb is '*his* brother', the termination would be *aï* or *ī*, but if it is '*your* brother,' the termination would be *aü* or *ū*. The letter *ō* is often substituted for *aü*. The following examples illustrate this rule :—

Rām lar°kā-kē māral°kaï, Ram beat the child.
Rām toh°rā lar°kā-kē māral°kaü, Ram beat *your* child.
Ok°rā gāṛī-mē kaün māl haï, What goods are there in his cart ?
Toh°rā gāṛī-mē kaün māl haü, What goods are there in *your* cart ?
Dekhal°thin, he has seen His Honour.
Dekhal°thun, he has seen *Your* Honour.
Ōkar bhāī āil°thī haï, his brother has come.
Tōhar bhāī āil°thū haï, *your* brother has come.

Note that in the last instance, the auxiliary has not changed its form.

The letter *k* may be added to any form in *aï* (or *ai*), *aü* (or *au*), or *ō*, without changing the meaning. Thus, *māral°kaï* or *māral°kaïk* ; *māral°kaü* or *māral°kaük*.

Besides the ordinary Present Definite and Imperfect formed as in other Aryan languages by adding the Auxiliary Verb to the Present Participle, Magahī has two tenses, which may be called the Present Indefinite, and the Past Indefinite, respectively. They are formed by adding the Auxiliary Verb to the root, to which the letter *a* has been appended. Thus *dēkha hā̃*, I see ; *dēkha halū̃*, I saw. These tenses are of very frequent occurrence.

On the whole, Magahī Grammar closely follows that of Maithilī. The two main distinguishing points are, first, the use of the two tenses just mentioned, and, second, the form of the Verb Substantive, which is *hī*, I am, instead of the very common Maithilī *chhī*.

It should be remembered that the rules of Magahī spelling are in no way fixed, and that forms will often be met which deviate from those now given, but it is hoped that if the above remarks are borne in mind, no difficulty will be experienced in grasping the principles of Magahī Grammar, as shown in the following sketch. In this sketch, verbal terminations formed by changing *aï* to *aü*, *ī* to *ū*, or *in* to *un*, or by adding *k*, are omitted, to save space. They are provided for by the above general rules.

MAGAHĪ SKELETON GRAMMAR.

I.—NOUNS—

Each has three forms as in Maithilī. Thus (short) *ghōrā*, (long) *ghor^{a}wā*, (redundant) *ghorauwā*, a horse.	The short form may be weak (as *ghōr*), or strong (as *ghōrā*).

Number.—Plural is formed by adding *n* and shortening a final long vowel. Thus, *ghorā*, horse, pl. *ghōran*; *ghar*, a house, pl. *gharan*. Plural may also be formed by adding nouns of multitude, such as *sab*, *lōg*. Thus *ghōrā sab*, the horses; *rājā lōg*, the kings.

Case.—The only two cases are the Instrumental and the Locative, formed, as in Maithilī by the addition of *ẽ* and *ē* respectively, before which a final *ā* is elided, and a final *ī* or *ū* is shortened. Thus, *ghōrẽ*, by a horse; *ghōrē*, in a horse: *phal*, a fruit; *phalẽ*, *phalē*: *mālī*, a gardener; *maliẽ*, *māliē*. These forms do not occur in the Plural.

Other cases are formed by postpositions added to the nominative, or (when that exists) to the oblique form (see below). Some of these are *kē*, to (also used as a sign of the Accusative); *sē*, *sẽ*, *satĩ*, from or by; *lā*, *lēl*, *khātir*, *lāgi*, for; *mē*, *mẽ*, *mō̃*, in; *k*, *ke*, *kēr*, of. Before the postposition *k*, a final long vowel is shortened. Thus *ghōrak*, of a horse. When the noun ends in a consonant, *a* is inserted. Thus *phal-ak*, of a fruit.

Gender.—Adjectives do not change for gender.

Oblique Form.—In all nouns ending in vowels, the oblique form is the same as the Nominative. In all nouns ending in consonants, it may either be the same as the nominative, or may add *e*. Thus *ghar ke* or *ghare ke*, of a house.

Verbal nouns in *l* have an oblique form in *lā*. Thus *dēkhal*, seeing; oblique form *dekh^{a}lā*. Other verbal nouns follow the ordinary rule about nouns ending in consonants.

II.—PRONOUNS—

	I		Thou		Self	This	That, He.
	Inferior form.	Superior form.	Inferior form.	Superior form.			
Sing.							
Nom.	—	*ham*	*tū̃*, *tō̃*		*ap^{a}ne*	*ī*	*ū*
Obl.	*mōrā*	*ham^{a}rā*	*tōrā*	*toh^{a}rā*	*ap^{a}ne*	*eh*	*oh*
Gen.	*mōr*, or *mōrā*, (f.) *mōrī*	*hammar*, *hamār*, *hamare*	*tōr*, *torā*, (f.), *tōrī*	*tōhar*, *tohār*, *tohare*	*ap^{a}ne-ke*, *apan*	*ē-kar*, *eh-ke*, etc.	*ō-kar*, *oh-ke*, etc.
Plur.							
Nom.	*hamanī*	*ham^{a}ranī*	*tohanī*	*toh^{a}ranī*	*ap^{a}ne sab*	*ī*	*ū*
Obl.	*hamanī*	*hamaranī*	*tohanī*	*toh^{a}ranī*	*ap^{a}ne sab*	*inh*	*unh*

	Who.	He, that.	Who?	What (thing).	Anyone, someone.
Sing.					
Nom.	*jē*, *jaun*	*sē*, *taun*	*kē*, *kō*, *kaun*	*kā*, *kī*, *kaũchī*	*keu*, *kōī*, *kāhū*
Obl.	*jeh*	*teh*	*keh*	*kāhe*	*kekaro*, *kaunō*
Gen.	*jē-kar*, *jeh-ke*, etc.	*tē-kar*, *teh-ke*, etc.	*kē-kar*, *keh-ke*, etc.		
Plur.					
Nom.	*jē*, *jinh^{a}kanī*	*sē*, *tinh^{a}kanī*	*kē*, *kinh^{a}kanī*	*kī* is peculiar to South-East Patna, *kaũchi* to Gaya.	Anything, something, is *kuchhu*, *kuchchho* or *kuchchha-o*, which has no oblique form.
Obl.	*jinh*	*tinh*	*kinh*		

NOTE.—In the above, the Oblique forms of the Plural are often used for the Nominative. There are many forms of the oblique plural. The following are those of the pronoun of the first person (the others can be formed from analogy), *ham^{a}ninh*, *ham^{a}ranhī*, *hamaranh*. The spelling of these fluctuates. Thus, we find *ham^{a}nin*, and so on. From *ī*, we have, *inhanh*, *inhanī*, *ikh^{a}nin*, *akh^{a}nī*, *ekh^{a}nī*, *inh^{a}kanhī*, *inh^{a}kā*. So also for *ū*, *jē*, *sē* and *kē*. The spelling of all these fluctuates.

Oblique Genitives.—All genitives in *kar* have an oblique form in *k^{a}rā*. Thus, *ē-kar*, *ek^{a}rā*; *ō-kar*, *ok^{a}rā*; *jē-kar*, *jek^a-rā* and so on. This can be used as a kind of secondary oblique Case of the pronoun, to which postpositions can be attached. Thus, Dat. sing., *ek^{a}rā kē*, and so on.

III.—VERBS—

A.—Auxiliary Verbs & Verbs Substantive.

	Present, I am, etc.				*Past*, I was, etc.			
	Form I	Form II	Form III	Form IV	Form I	Form II	Form III	Form IV
1	*hī* [1]	—	*hĩ* [2]	—	*halū̃* [1]	—	*halĩ* [2]	—
2	*hẽ* [3]	*hahin* [4]	*hā* [5]	*hahun* [6]	*halẽ* [3]	*hal^{a}hin*	*halā* [4]	*hal^{a}hun*
3	*hai* [7]	*hahin* [8]	*haĩ* [9]	*haĩn* [10]	*hal* [5]	*hal^{a}hin* [6]	*halan* [7]	*hal^{a}thin* [8]

Optional forms:—

[1] *Hahī*, *hikū̃*; [2] *hiai*; [3] *hā*, *hē*, *hai*, *hahĩ*, *hahĩ*; fem. *hī*, *hĩ*; [4] *hahin*; [5] *hahū*, *hahō*, *hahā̃*; [6] *hakhun*; [7] *hā*, *hē*. *hō*, *hā̃*, *has*, *hakai*, *hahĩ*; [8] *hakhin*; fem. *hakhīn*, *hakhinī*; [9] *hath*, *hathī*; [10] *hathin*; fem. *hathīn*, *hathinī*.

Optional forms:—

[1] *Halī*; [2] *haliai*; [3] *halā*, *halē*, *hal^{a}hĩ*, *halā̃*; fem. *halī*, *halĩ*; [4] *halōh*, *hal^{a}hū*, *hal^{a}hō*, *hal^{a}hā̃*; [5] *halai*, *hal^{a}hĩ*; fem. *halī*; [6] *hal^{a}khin*; fem. *hal^{a}khīn*, *hal^{a}khinī*; [7] *hal^{a}thī*; fem. *halin*; [8] fem. *hal^{a}thīn*, *hal^{a}thinī*.

B.—Transitive Verb.—*Dēkhab*, to see. Root, *dēkh*.

Verbal nouns, 1, *dēkhab*, obl. not used; 2, *dēkhal*, obl. *dekh^{a}lā*; 3, *dēkh*, obl. *dēkhe*.
Participles, *Pres*. *dēkhit*, *dēkhat*, *dekhait*; fem. -*tī*; obl. -*te*; *Past*. *dēkhal*; fem. -*lī*; obl. -*le*.
Conjunctive Participle, *dēkh ke* or *dekh kar*.

Simple Present. I see, etc. *Present Conditional*, (if) I see, etc. *Past*. I saw, etc.

	Form I	Form II	Form III	Form IV	Form I	Form II	Form III	Form IV
1	*dēkhū̃* [1]	——	*dēkhī̃* [2]	——	*dekh^{a}lū̃* [1]	——	*dekh^{a}lī̃* [3]	——
2	*dēkh* [3]	*dekh^{a}hin*	*dēkhá* [4]	*dekh^{a}hun*	*dekh^{a}lē* [2]	*dekhal^{a}hin*	*dekh^{a}lá* [4]	*dekhal^{a}hun*
3	*dekhai* [5]	*dekh^{a}hin* [6]	*dēkhath* [7]	*dekh^{a}thin* [8]	*dekh^{a}lak* [5]	*dekhal^{a}kan* [6]	*dekhal^{a}thī*	*dekhal^{a}thin* [7]

Optional forms:—

[1] *dēkhī*; [2] *dekhiai*; [3] *dēkhē̃*, *dēkhã*, *dēkhē*, *dēkh^{a}hī̃*; fem., *dēkhi*, *dēkhī̃*, *dēkhū*; [4] *dēkhāh*, *dekh^{a}hū*, *dekh^{a}hō*, *dekh^{a}hū̃*; [5] *dēkhē*, *dēkhas*; [6] *dekh^{a}khin*; fem. *dekh^{a}khīn*, *dekh^{a}khinī*; [7] *dēkhī̃*, *dekh^{a}thī*; [8] *dēkhin*, *dekh^{a}thin*; fem., *dekh^{a}thīn*, *dekh^{a}thinī*.

Optional forms:—

[1] *dekh^{a}lī*; [2] *dekh^{a}liai*; [3] *dekh^{a}lē*, *dekh^{a}lã*, *dekhal^{a}hī̃*; fem. *deklī*, *dekh^{a}lī̃*, *dekh^{a}lū*; [4] *dekh^{a}lāh*, *dekhal^{a}hū*, *dekhal^{a}hō*, *dekh^{a}hū̃*; [5] *dekh^{a}kai*, *dekhal^{a}kai*; fem. *dekh^{a}li*; [6] *dekh^{a}lan*, *dekhal^{a}khin*; fem., *dekh^{a}lin*, *dekhal^{a}kin*, *dekhal^{a}khin*, *dekhal^{a}khinī*; [7] *dekhal^{a}hin*, *dekhal^{a}kathin*; fem., *dekhal^{a}thīn*, *dekhal^{a}thinī*.

Future, I shall see.—Two varieties.

Variety I— / Variety II—

	Form I	Form II	Form III	Form IV	Form I	Form II	Form III	Form IV
1	*dēkhab* [1]	——	*dekh^{a}bai*	——	Wanting	Wanting	Wanting	Wanting
2	*dekh^{a}bē̃* [2]	*dekhab^{a}hin*	*dekh^{a}bá* [3]	*dekhab^{a}hun*	Wanting	Wanting	*dekhihá* [1]	Wanting
3	Wanting	Wanting	Wanting	Wanting	*dēkhī* / *dēkhat* [2]	*dekhat^{a}hin* [3]	*dekhihē* / *dekh^{a}tan* [4]	*dekhat^{a}thin* [5]

Optional forms:—

[1] *dekh^{a}bō̃*, *dekh^{a}baū*; fem. *dekh^{a}bī*; [2] *dekh^{a}bã*, *dekh^{a}bē*, *dekhabã*, *dekhab^{a}hī̃*; fem. *dekh^{a}bī*, *dekh^{a}bī̃*, *dekh^{a}bū*; [3] *dekh^{a}bāh*, *dekhab^{a}hū*, -*hō*, -*hū̃*;

Optional forms:—

[1] *dekhihāh*; [2] *dekh^{a}tai*; [3] *dekh^{a}hin*, *dekh^{a}khin*; fem. *dekh^{a}khīn*, *dekh^{a}khanī*, [4] *dekhat^{a}thī*; fem. *dekh^{a}tin*; [5] fem. *dekhat^{a}thīn*, *dekhat^{a}thinī*.

The *Imperative* is the same as the Simple Present. Precative Forms are *dekhab^{a}hū*, *dekhihá*, and *dēkhi*.

Past Conditional, (if) I have seen, etc.

	Form I	Form II	Form III	Form IV
1	*dekhaitū̃* [1]	——	*dekhaitī̃*	——
2	*dekhaitē̃*	*dekhait^{a}hin*	*dekhaitá*	*dekhait^{a}hun*.
3	*dekhait*	*dekhait^{a}hin*	*dekhaitan*	*dekhait^{a}thin*.

Or *dekh^{a}tū̃*, or *dekhitū̃*, and so throughout. The word *hal* may be added throughout. Thus *dekhaitū̃ hal*. Optional forms as in the Past of the Auxiliary.

Present Indefinite, I see; *dēkha hī* or *dēkhe hī*, and so throughout, conjugating the Auxiliary Verb.

Past Indefinite, I saw; *dēkha halū̃*, or *dēkhe halū̃*, and so throughout.

Present Definite, I am seeing; *dekhait* (*dēkhit* or *dēkhat*) *hī*, and so throughout.

Imperfect, I was seeing; *dekhait* (etc.) *halū̃* and so throughout.

Perfect, I have seen, formed by adding *hai*, *hē*, *ha*, or *hā̃* to the Past. Thus, *dekh^{a}lū̃ hai*, I have seen. *Pluperfect*, I had seen, similarly formed by adding *hal* or *halai*. Thus *dekh^{a}lī hal*, I had seen.

C.—Neuter Verbs.—These only differ in the conjugation of the Preterite, and of the tenses derived from it, which follow that of *halū̃* not that of *dekh^{a}lū̃*. Thus 3, Form I, *giral*, he fell. So *gir^{a}lū̃ hai*, I have fallen.

D.—Verbs whose roots end in *ā*; *pāeb*, to obtain. *Pres. Part.*, *pāwat*, *pāit*.

	Simple Pres.	Future.	Past.	Past Conditional.	
1	*pāī̃* or *pāwī̃*	*pāeb*	*paulū̃* or *pailū̃*	*pautū̃* or *paitū̃*	Forms containing *au*, like *paulū̃*, *pautū̃*, are only used in the case of transitive verbs, except *khāeb*, to eat, which does not use such forms. They are never used in the east of the Magahī tract.
2	*pāwá*	*paibá* or *pābá*	*paulá* or *pailá*	*pautá* or *paitá*	
3	*pāwath*	*pāī*, *pāit*	*paulak* or *pailak*	*pāwat* or *pāit*	

E.—Irregular Verbs.

Jāeb, to go; Past Part., *gēl*.
Karab, to do; „ *kail*.
Marab, to die; „ *muil* or *mūl*.
Dēb to give; „ *dēl* or *dihal*.
Lēb, to take; „ *lēl* or *lihal*.
Hōeb, to become; „ *hōl*, *hōil* to *bhēl*.

BHOJPURI.

Lāṭhi-mẽ guṇa bahuta haĩ, sadā rākhihā saṅga,
Naddī nāra-agāha jala, tahā̃ bachāwai aṅga.
Tahā̃ bachāwai aṅga, jhapaṭa kuttā-kē mārai :
Dushmana dāwāgira, hōe tina-hū̃-kē jhārai.
Kaha Giri-dhara Kabi-rāya, bāta bā̃dhā yaha gā̃ṭhī.
Saba hathyāra-kē chhāṛi hātha-mẽ rākhā lāṭhī.

The Bhojpuri National Anthem.

(Thus paraphrased by Mr. W. S. Meyer, I.O.S.)

Great the virtues of the Stick !
Keep a Stick with you alway—
Night and day, well or sick.

When a river you must cross,
If you'd save your life from loss,
Have a stout Stick in your hand,
It will guide you safe to land.

When the angry dogs assail,
Sturdy Stick will never fail.
Stick will stretch each yelping hound
On the ground.

If an enemy you see,
Stick will your protector be.
Sturdy Stick will fall like lead
On your foeman's wicked head.

Well doth poet Girdhar say
(Keep it carefully in mind)
'Other weapons leave behind,
Have a Stick with you alway.'

Name of the dialect.

Bhojpurī, or, if the word were strictly transliterated, Bhoj'purī,[1] is properly speaking the language of Bhojpur, the name of a Town and Pargana in the north-west of the District of Shahabad. It is a place of some importance in the modern history of India. The town is the original head-quarters of the Dumraon Raj, and the battle of Buxar was fought at Bagh'sar a few miles to its west. Politically, it belongs rather to the United Provinces than to Bihār, although it is at the present day included within the boundaries of the latter province. It was from its neighbourhood that the famous Bundelkhand heroes, Alhā and Ūdan, traced their origin, and all its associations and traditions point to the west and not to the east.

The Bhojpur Country.

Area covered by the dialect.

The language called after this locality has spread far beyond its limits. It reaches, on the north, across the Ganges, and even beyond the Nepal frontier, up to the lower ranges of the Himalayas, from Champaran to Basti. On the South, it has crossed the Sone, and covers the great

[1] The word Bhojpuri has obtained currency in English, and it would be an affectation of purism to spell the name 'Bhoj'purī.'

Ranchi plateau of Chota Nagpur, where it ultimately finds itself in contact with the Bengali of Manbhum, and with the Oṛiyā of Singhbhum.

The language boundaries.

Of the three Bihārī dialects, Maithilī, Magahī, and Bhojpurī, it is the most western. North of the Ganges, it lies to the west of the Maithilī of Muzaffarpur, and, south of that river, it lies to the west of the Magahī of Gaya and Hazaribagh. It then takes a south-easterly course, to the south of the Magahī of Hazaribagh, till it has covered the entire Ranchi Plateau, including the greater part of the Districts of Palamau and of Ranchi. Here, it is bounded on the east by the Magahī spoken in the sub-plateau parganas of Ranchi and by the Bengali of Manbhum. On the south it is here bounded by the Oṛiyā of Singhbhum and the Native State of Gangpur. The boundary then turns to the north, through the heart of the Jashpur State, to the western border of Palamau, along which line it marches with the form of Chhattīsgaṛhī spoken in Sargūjā and western Jashpur. After passing along the western side of Palamau, the boundary reaches the southern border of Mirzapur. It follows the southern and western borders of that District up to the river Ganges. Here it turns to the east, along the course of that stream, which it crosses near Benares, so as to take in only a small portion of the north Gangetic portion of Mirzapur. South of Mirzapur, it has still had Chhattīsgaṛhī for its neighbour, but on turning to the north, along the western confines of that District, it has been bounded on the west, first by the Baghēlī of Baghelkhand, and then by Awadhī. Having crossed the Ganges, its boundary line lies nearly due north to Tāṇḍā on the Gogra, in the District of Fyzabad. It has run along the western boundary of the Benares District, across Jaunpur, along the west of Azamgarh, and across Fyzabad. At Tāṇḍā, its course turns west along the Gogra and then north up to the lower ranges of the Himalayas, so as to include the District of Basti. Beside the area included in the above language frontier, Bhojpurī is also spoken by the members of the wild tribe of Thārūs, who inhabit the Districts of Gonda and Bahraich.

Bhojpurī compared with the other Bihārī dialects.

The area covered by Bhojpurī is, in round numbers, some fifty thousand square miles. At home, it is spoken by some 20,000,000 people as compared with the 6,235,782 who speak Magahī, and the 10,000,000 who speak Maithilī. So far, therefore, as regards the number of its speakers, it is much more important than the other two Bihārī dialects put together. This division of the dialects of Bihārī into two groups, an eastern, consisting of Maithilī and Magahī, and a western, Bhojpurī, commends itself on both linguistic and ethnic grounds. The two eastern dialects are much more closely connected with each other than either is connected with Bhojpurī. In grammatical forms, Maithilī and Magahī have much in common that is not shared by Bhojpurī, and, on the other hand, Bhojpurī has peculiarities of declension and conjugation which are unknown to the other two. There is a difference of intonation, too, between the east and the west, which is very marked to anyone who is familiar with the languages of Eastern Hindōstān. In Maithilī, the vowel *a* is pronounced with a broad sound approaching the '*o* in *hot*' colour which it possesses in Bengali. Bhojpurī, on the contrary, pronounces the vowel with the clear sharp-cut tone which we hear all over Central Hindōstān. Contrasted with this the dialect also possesses a long drawled vowel, which is written in many different ways,

Pronunciation compared.

but which is always pronounced like the *aw* in *awl*.[1] This last sound also occurs both in Maithilī and in Magahī, but not nearly to so great an extent, and moreover, when it does occur in these dialects, it is not so liable to be noticed owing to the broad sound of the frequently occurring vowel *a*, with which it is, as pronounced in the east, easily confounded. In Bhojpurī, on the contrary, the contrast between this drawled *á* and the clear-cut sound of the common *a* is so very marked, and the drawled *á* is of such frequent occurrence, that it gives a tone to the whole language which is recognised at once.

Declension and conjugation compared.

In the declension of nouns, the favourite Bhojpurī postposition of the genitive is *ke*, while in the Eastern dialects it is either *k* or *kar* or *kēr*. Besides this, the genitive of a Bhojpurī substantive has an oblique form, a thing unknown to Maithilī or Magahī. As regards pronouns, Bhojpurī has a word for 'your honour',—viz. *raure*,—which does not occur in the east. In the conjugation of verbs, the Bhojpurī verb substantive, *bāṭē*, he is, does not appear in the other two, while the form of the verb substantive which may be called common to the three dialects,—*hai*, he is,—is throughout its conjugation pronounced so differently in Bhojpurī that it can hardly be recognised as the same verb. In the conjugation of the finite verb, Bhojpurī has a present tense,—*dēkhī-lā*, I see,—which is peculiar to itself, and is not met in the other two dialects. Finally,—Bhojpurī has cast aside all that maze of verbal forms which appals the student when he first attempts to read Maithilī or Magahī. All those forms which depend upon the person of or the degree of respect to be shown to the object, which are so characteristic of these two dialects, are absent from Bhojpurī, and instead we have a simple conjugation, with rarely more than one form for each person.

Sub-dialects.

Bhojpurī has three main varieties,—the Standard, the Western, and Nagpuriā. It has also a border sub-dialect called Madhēsī, and a broken form called Thārū. Standard Bhojpurī is spoken mainly in the Districts of Shahabad, Ballia, and Ghazipur (Eastern half), and in the Doab of the Gogra and the Gandak. As its name implies, Western Bhojpurī is spoken in the Western Districts of Fyzabad, Azamgarh, Jaunpur, Benares, the western half of Ghazipur, and South-Gangetic Mirzapur, while Nagpuriā is spoken in Chota Nagpur. Madhēsī is spoken in Champaran, and Thārū Bhojpurī along the Nepal frontier from that district to Bahraich.

Standard Bhojpurī.

Standard Bhojpurī extends over a large area, and exhibits some local peculiarities. The most noticeable is the preference of the more southern Districts of Shahabad, Ballia and Ghazipur, and of the southern part of Saran, for the letter *ṛ* instead of *ṭ* in the conjugation of the auxiliary verb. Thus, while the Northern Standard Bhojpurī prefers to say '*bāṭē*' for 'he is,' the Southern prefers *bāṛē*. In the centre and north of Saran, there is a peculiar form of the Past tense of the verb, in which *u* is substituted for the *l* which is usually typical of Bihārī; but this anomaly does not go further north, and in Eastern Gorakhpur, the language differs but little from that of Shahabad. Still further to the north-west, in Western Gorakhpur and in Basti, there are a few other divergencies from the Standard, but they are not of importance, and are mainly due to the influence of the neighbouring western

[1] This is the sound which I transliterate by *á*.

variety of the dialect. Natives, who are quick to recognise any divergence of dialect, call the language of Eastern Gorakhpur Gorakhpurī, and the language of the west of that district and of Basti, Sarwariā.[1]

Western Bhojpurī also known as Pūrbī.

Western Bhojpurī is frequently called Pūrbī, or the Language of the East, *par excellence.* This is naturally the name given to it by the inhabitants of Western Hindōstān, but has the disadvantage of being indefinite. It is employed very loosely, and often includes languages which have nothing to do with Bhojpurī, but which are also spoken in Eastern Hindōstān. For instance, the language spoken in the east of the District of Allahabad is called Pūrbī, but the specimens of it which have been sent to me are clearly those of a form of Eastern Hindī. It altogether wants the characteristic features of Bhojpurī,—the present in *-lā* and the Past in *-al,*—and instead has the well-known Eastern Hindī Past in *-is.* I have hence decided to abandon the term Pūrbī altogether, and to use instead the term 'Western Bhojpurī,' which, while not so familiar to Natives, has the advantage of being definite, and of connoting exactly what it is wanted to express.

Standard Bhojpurī and Western Bhojpurī compared.

As compared with Standard Bhojpurī, the following are the principal points of difference in Grammar. In Standard Bhojpurī, the termination of the Genitive is *ke,* with oblique form *ka;* in the Western dialect it is *ka* or *kăĭ,* with an oblique form *kē.* The latter has also an Instrumental Case ending in *an,* which is altogether wanting in the Standard language. In Western Bhojpurī, the adjective is liable to change according to the gender and case of the noun which it qualifies. This is much rarer in the Standard form of the language. The use of the pronouns in the two forms of speech differs considerably. The forms of the demonstrative pronouns vary, and the word *tũh* can be used as an honorific pronoun of the second person in the West, which is not the case in the East. In the East the oblique form of nouns and pronouns usually ends in *ā,* while in the West, it always ends in *ē.* The Verb Substantive has two forms in both sub-dialects, but the *hăwĩ,* I am, of the East has become *hauĭ* in the West. As forms of this verb are of frequent occurrence, and as the difference of pronunciation is very marked, the result of this last point is that the 'tone-colour' of each of the two sub-dialects shows considerable diversity from that of the other. In the conjugation of the verb, there are two marked differences. Nothing is more marked in Standard Bhojpurī than the nasal tone which is given to the termination of the first person plural, which, being also used for the singular, is of frequent occurrence. Thus a man of Shahabad says *ham kailĩ* for 'I did'. In Western Bhojpurī this nasal is dropped in the plural, and we only have *ham kailī.* Moreover, in the latter, the first person plural is not nearly so often used for the Singular, as in the Standard. The termination of the third person plural also differs considerably in the two forms of speech. In the Standard it ends in *-an* or in *-ani,* and in the West it ends in *-aĩ.* The above are only the most noteworthy points of difference between the two main forms of Bhojpurī. There are many other minor ones, for which the reader is referred to the grammatical notes prefixed to the specimens. See, especially, pp. 249 and ff.

Nagpuriā.

The Nagpuriā of Chota Nagpur differs from the Standard type principally in the fact that it has borrowed grammatical forms from the neighbouring Chhattīsgaṛhī of the east of the Central Provinces.

[1] For an explanation of this last name, see pp. 238 and ff.

Instances are the use of the termination *-har*, to give definiteness to a noun, and the suffix *-man* to form the plural. There are other divergencies from the Standard which will be found described on pp. 280 and ff. It may be noted that Nagpuriā is sometimes known by the people who speak it as Sadān or Sadrī and is called by the Muṇḍa tribes of Chota Nagpur 'Dikkū Kājī.'

Madhēsī.

The Madhēsī of Champaran is the language of the '*Madhya-dēśa*,' or 'Middle country,' between the Maithilī of Tirhut and the Bhojpurī of Gorakhpur. As its name implies it is a border form of speech possessing some of the characteristics of each dialect. Its structure is, however, in the main that of Bhojpurī.

Thārū Bhojpurī.

The Thārūs who inhabit the Tarai along the Nepal frontier have no speech of their own. Wherever we find them they have adopted more or less completely the language of their Aryan neighbours. Those who are found in the British districts from Bahraich to Champaran speak a corrupt form of Bhojpurī, mixed here and there with aboriginal words which will repay the investigations of the ethnologist. It is worth noting that the Thārūs of Bahraich and Gonda speak Bhojpurī, although the local Aryan language is not that language, but is Eastern Hindī.

The area in which Bhojpurī is spoken is shown in the map facing page 1.

Number of speakers.

The following are the figures which show the number of speakers of Bhojpurī within the area in which it is a vernacular. The totals are given for each sub-dialect. For details, district by district, the reader is referred to the various sections dealing with each sub-dialect:—

Southern Standard		4,324,293
Northern Standard, *viz.*:—		
Dialect of Saran	1,504,500	
Gorakhpurī	1,307,500[1]	
Sarwariā	3,353,151[1]	
TOTAL		6,165,151
Western Dialect		3,939,500
Nagpuriā		594,257
Madhēsī		1,714,036
Thārū Bhojpurī		39,700
TOTAL		16,776,937

Besides the above, there is the population of the Nepal Tarai, which, of necessity, cannot be numbered. A moderate estimate would put the Bhojpurī speakers of that tract at three millions, so that we are justified in estimating the whole number of people who speak Bhojpurī at home, as in round numbers 20,000,000.

For the reasons stated when dealing with Maithilī, *vide ante* pp. 14 and ff., it is impossible to ascertain the number of people whose native language is Bhojpurī, but who live in parts of India where Bhojpurī is not the vernacular. All that can be done is to give for the Provinces of Bengal and Assam the following estimated figures. No figures of any kind are available for the rest of India.

[1] Include some speakers of Thārū Bhojpurī and Domrā.

Table showing the estimated number of speakers of Bhojpurī, within the Lower Provinces of Bengal, but outside the Area in which Bhojpurī is the Vernacular Language.

Name of District.	Number of Speakers.	Remarks.
Burdwan	12,800	
Bankura	1,600	
Birbhum	9,200	
Midnapur	40,600	
Hooghly	4,900	
Howrah	19,000	
24-Parganas	23,000	
Calcutta	71,600	
Nadia	3,600	
Jessore	1,500	
Murshidabad	40,900	
Khulna	1,690	
Dinajpur	7,300	
Rajshahi	4,000	
Rangpur	17,900	
Bogra	9,400	
Pabna	7,000	
Darjeeling	4,500	
Jalpaiguri	9,300	
Kuch-Bihar (State)	4,800	
Dacca	11,600	
Faridpur	2,300	
Backergunge	900	
Mymensingh	24,800	
Chittagong	1,200	
Noakhali	162	
Tippera	2,200	
Bhagalpur	7,406	
Cuttack	350	
Puri	340	
Balasore	920	
Jashpur State	200	
TOTAL	346,878	

Table showing the estimated number of speakers of Bhojpurī within the Province of Assam.

Name of District.	Number of Speakers.	REMARKS.
Cachar Plains	18,400	
Sylhet	18,500	
Goalpara	3,100	
Kamrup	900	
Darrang	3,200	
Nowgong	1,800	
Sibsagar	10,300	
Lakhimpur	9,000	
Naga Hills	130	
Khasi and Jaintia Hills	350	
Lushai Hills	50	
TOTAL	65,730*	* Nearly all these are tea-garden coolies.

The following is, therefore, the total number of speakers of Bhojpurī recorded in the above tables :—

Number of people speaking Bhojpurī at home	20,000,000
" " " " elsewhere in the Lower Provinces	346,878
" " " " in Assam	65,730
Total	20,412,608

Bhojpurī Literature.

Bhojpurī has hardly any indigenous literature. A few books have been printed in it. Those which I have met will be found mentioned in the list of Texts given under the head of Authorities. So far as I am aware, no portion of the Bible has been translated into the dialect. Numerous songs are current all over the Bhojpurī area, and the national epic of Lōrik, which is also current in the Magahī dialect, is everywhere known.

AUTHORITIES—

A.—EARLY REFERENCES.

I know of no early references to the Bhojpurī language. Bhojpur, itself, is frequently mentioned by Muhammadan historians, and its wild inhabitants are referred to in no complimentary terms. Nor is the word Pūrbī, so far as I am aware, met with in any early writer, as the name of a language. The following article, taken entire from Yule's 'Hobson Jobson,' illustrates the use of the word from the earliest times as a geographical and ethnical title.

Poorub, and Poorbeea, ss. Hind. *Pūrab, Pūrb,* 'the East,' from Skt. *pūrva* or *pūrba*, 'in front of,' as *paścha* (Hind. *pachham*) means 'behind' or 'westerly' and *dakshina*, 'right-hand' or 'southerly.' In Upper India the term usually means Oudh, the

Benares division, and Behar. Hence POORBEEA (*pūrbiyā*), a man of those countries, was, in the days of the old Bengal army, often used for a sepoy, the majority being recruited in those provinces.

1553. "Omaum (Humayun) Patxiah.........resolved to follow Xerchan (Sher Khan) and try his fortune against him...... and they met close to the river Ganges before it unites with the river Jamona, where on the West bank of the river there is a city called Canose, one of the Chief of the kingdom of Dely. Xerchan was beyond the River in the tract which the natives call PUREA. ...." *Barros*, IV. ix. 9.

1616. "Bengala, a most spacious and fruitful province, but more properly to be called a kingdom, which hath two very large provinces within it, PURB and Patan, the one lying on the East, the other on the West side of the river." *Terry*, Ed. 1665, p. 357.

1666. "La Province de Halabas s'appelloit autrefois PUROP ...." *Thevenot*, v. 197.

1881. "........My lands were taken away,
And the Company gave me a pension of just eight annas a day;
And the POORBEAHS swaggered about our streets as if they had done it all......... ".
Attar Singh loquitur, by '*Sowar*,' in an Indian paper, the name and date lost.

B.—GRAMMARS AND VOCABULARIES.

BEAMES, J.,—*Notes on the Bhojpurí dialect of Hindi spoken in Western Behar*. *Journal* of the Royal Asiatic Society, Vol. iii, N. S., 1868, pp. 483 and ff.

CAMPBELL, Sir G.,—*Specimens of Languages of India. Including those of the Aboriginal Tribes of Bengal, the Central Provinces, and the Eastern Frontier*. Calcutta, 1874. P. 60, Lists of Words and Sentences in the Vernacular of Champaran. P. 95, Ditto in the Kharwar of Shahabad.

HOERNLE, A. F. R., C.I.E.,—*A Grammar of the Eastern Hindí compared with the other Gauḍian Languages*. London, 1880. Contains a Grammar of Western Bhojpuri, under the name of 'Eastern Hindí.'

REID, J. R., I.C.S.,—*Report on the Settlement Operations in the District of Azamgarh*. Allahabad, 1881. Appendix II contains a full account of the Western Bhojpuri spoken in the District; Appendix III, which has been separately printed, consists of a full Vocabulary of the same.

ALEXANDER, E. B.,—*Statistical, Descriptive, and Historical Account of the North-Western Provinces of India*. Vol. vi, Cawnpore, Gorakhpur, and Basti. Allahabad, 1881. On p. 372 there is an account of the form of Bhojpuri spoken in Gorakhpur.

GRIERSON, G. A.,—*Seven Grammars of the Dialects and Sub-dialects of the Bihári Language. Part II,—Bhojpúrí Dialect of Sháhabád, Sáran, Champáran, North Muzaffarpur, and the Eastern Portion of the North-Western Provinces*. Calcutta, 1884.

HOERNLE, A. F. R., and GRIERSON, G. A.,—*A Comparative Dictionary of the Bihārī Language*, Part I, Calcutta, 1885. Part II, 1889. Only two parts issued.

KELLOGG, The Rev. S. H.,—*A Grammar of the Hindí Language, in which are treated ...... the Colloquial Dialects of.........Bhojpúr,.........etc., with copious philological notes*. Second Edition, Revised and Enlarged, London, 1893.

GIRINDRA-NĀTH DUTT,—*Notes on the Vernacular Dialects spoken in the District of Saran*. *Journal* of the Asiatic Society of Bengal, Vol. lxvi, 1897, Pt. I, pp. 194 and ff.

C.—TEXTS.

FRASER, H.,—*Folklore from Eastern Gorakhpur (N.-W. P.)*, *Journal* of the Asiatic Society of Bengal, Vol. lii, 1883, pp. 1 and ff. Contains a number of songs. Edited by the present writer.

GRIERSON, G. A.,—*Some Bihārī Folksongs*. *Journal* of the Royal Asiatic Society, Vol. xvi, 1884, Part I, pp. 196 and ff.

GRIERSON, G. A.,—*The Song of Alhā's Marriage*. *Indian Antiquary*, Vol. xiv, 1885, pp. 209 and ff.

GRIERSON, G. A.,—*Two versions of the Song of Gopīchand*. *Journal* of the Asiatic Society of Bengal, Vol. liv, 1885, Part I, pp. 35 and ff.

GRIERSON, G. A.,—*Some Bhoj'pūrī Folksongs*. *Journal* of the Royal Asiatic Society, Vol. xviii, 1886, pp. 207 and ff.

GRIERSON, G. A.,—*Selected Specimens of the Bihārī Language. Part II. The Bhoj'pūrī Dialect. The Gīt Naikā Banjar'wā*. *Zeitschrift* der deutschen Morgenländischen Gesellschaft. Vol. xliii, 1889, pp. 468 and ff.

LĀL KHAṚG BAHĀDUR MALL, MAHĀRĀJĀDHIRĀJ KUMĀR,—*Sudhābund*. A collection of sixty *Kajalī* Songs. Bankipur, 1884.

RAVI-DATTA ŚUKLA, Paṇḍit,—*Dēvākshara-charitra*, a drama. Contains scenes in Bhojpurī. Benares, 1884.

RAVI-DATTA ŚUKLA,—*Jaṅgal-mẽ Maṅgal or a short Account of some recent Doings in Ballia*. Benares, 1886.

RĀM-GARĪB CHAUBE, Paṇḍit,—*Nāgarī-bilāp*. Benares, 1886.

FALLON, S. W., TEMPLE, Capt. R. C., and LĀLĀ FAQĪR CHAND,—*A Dictionary of Hindustānī Proverbs*. Benares, 1886. On pp. 274 and ff. there is a collection of Bhojpurī Proverbs.

TEGH 'ALĪ,—*Badmāsh-darpaṇ*. Benares, 1889. A collection of songs in the language of Benares City.

Written Character.

The character in general use in writing Bhojpurī is the Kaithī, for the alphabet of which, see the plate facing p. 11. The Dēva-nāgarī is also used by the educated classes. Examples of both these alphabets will be found in the following specimens.

Pronunciation.

There is a marked difference between the pronunciation of Bhojpurī and that of the two eastern dialects of Bihārī. The sound of the latter, especially of Maithilī, more nearly approaches that of Bengali, owing to the frequent occurrence of the letter *a* which is pronounced rather broadly. In Bhojpurī, on the contrary, the letter *a* is usually pronounced in the clear-cut way which we find elsewhere in the North-Western Provinces, *i.e.*, like the *u* in *nut*.

The long, drawled *a* which I transliterate *á*, is especially common in Bhojpurī, and its contrast with the short clear-cut *a*, which is of frequent occurrence, gives a striking piquancy to the general tone-colour of the dialect. Usually, this drawled *á* is left unrepresented in writing but its existence is fully recognised, and various attempts are made by different people to portray it. Thus, some write the sign ' over the consonant containing this vowel. Others write ' after it. Others write : after it, and others repeat the letter अ *a* after it. For instance, the word *dēkhá-lá*, you see, is written by some देखॅलॅ; by others देखऽलऽ; by others देख:ल:; and by others देखअलअ. The first method is that adopted by the present writer.

The short vowel, which I transliterate *ă*, which is pronounced like the *a* in *mad*, and which is common in Maithilī and Magahī, does not occur in Bhojpurī. The clear-cut *a* pronounced like the *u* in *nut* is always substituted.

The **Rule of the Short Antepenultimate** occurs in Bhojpurī as in the other Bihārī dialects. The only difference is that a long *ā* is shortened to *a* and not to *ă*. Thus, the third person Past of *māral*, to strike, is *mar°las*, he beat, not *măr°las*. For further particulars regarding the shortening of the Antepenultimate, a fact which is continually observed in Bhojpurī, see pp. 24 and ff.

As customary, when the letter *a* in the middle of a word is silent, or is only very lightly heard, it is represented by a small ° above the line. As elsewhere, this is not done in poetry, in which every *a*, even the *a* at the end of a word is fully pronounced.

Bhojpurī Grammar.

Bhojpurī Grammar is much more simple than that of Maithilī or Magahī. Except in a few isolated instances, the form of the verb depends only on the subject. The Object has no effect upon it. In Standard Bhojpurī, the first person singular is very rarely used, the plural being used instead, but this is not the case in the Western sub-dialect.

Bhojpurī has a peculiar form of the Present Indicative, which closely corresponds to the Naipālī Future, and which is, itself, often used in the sense of the Future. It is formed by adding the suffix *-lā* to the Present Subjunctive. According to Dr. Hoernle, this suffix means 'gone,' and is used like the *-gā* of the Hindōstānī Future. Just as the Hindōstānī *dēkhū̃-gā*, mean literally 'I am gone that I may see,' hence 'I am going to see,' hence 'I shall see,' so do the Naipālī *dēkhū̃-lā*, and the Bhojpurī *dēkhī-lā*. In the last named instance the tense has come to be more often used as a present.

Bhojpurī has its own Verb Substantive. Just as *chhī*, I am, is typical of Maithilī, and *hī*, I am, is typical of Magahī, so *bāṭī̃*, *bāṛī̃*, or *bānī̃*, is typical of Bhojpurī.

It is hoped that, if the above remarks are borne in mind, no difficulty will be experienced in grasping the principles of Bhojpurī grammar, as shown in the following sketch :—

BHOJPURĪ SKELETON GRAMMAR.

I.—NOUNS—

Each has three *forms* as in Maithilī. Thus (short) *ghōṛā*, (long) *ghoṛ^{a}wā*, (redundant) *ghoṛauā*. The long form sometimes ends in *ē* instead of *ā*. Thus, *ghoṛ^{a}wē*. All these forms may have their termination nasalised. Thus *ghoṛ^{a}wā̃*. The short form may be weak (as *ghōṛ*) or strong (as *ghōṛā*).

Number.—Plural is formed by adding *ni*, *nh*, or *n*, and shortening a preceding long vowel. Thus *ghōṛā*, horse, *ghoṛani*, *ghōṛanh*, or *ghōṛan*, horses; *ghar*, a house, pl. *gharani*, *gharanh* or *gharan*. Plural may also be formed by adding nouns of multitude, such as *sabh*, all, *lōg*, people. Thus *ghōṛā sabh*; *rājā lōg*.

Case.—The only true cases are the Instrumental and Locative Singular, formed, as in Maithilī, by the addition of *ẽ* and *ē* respectively, before which a final *ā* is elided, and a final *ī* or *ū* is shortened. Thus, *ghōṛẽ*, by a horse; *ghōṛē*, on a horse: *phal*, a fruit, *phalẽ*, *phalē*: *mālī*, a gardener; *maliẽ*, *maliē*. These forms do not occur in the plural.

Other cases are formed by postpositions added to the nominative, or (when such exists) to the oblique form; see below. Some of these are *kē*, to (also used as a sign of the accusative); *sē*, *tē*, *santē* or *kar^{a}tē*, by; *khātir*, *lāg*, *lā*, for; *sē*, *lē*, from; *k*, *ke*, *kāi*, of; *mẽ*, *mō̃*, on.

Before the postposition *k*, a final long vowel is shortened, as in *ghōṛak*, of a horse; when the noun ends in a consonant, *a* is inserted, as in *gharak*, of a house. There is an oblique genitive postposition *kā*. Thus *rājā-ke mandir*, the king's palace; but *rājā-kā mandir-mẽ*, in the king's palace. The distinction is seldom observed by the uneducated.

Gender.—In Standard Bhojpurī, adjectives do not change for gender.

Oblique Form.—Verbal nouns in *al* have an oblique form in *lā*. Thus *dēkhal*, seeing; *dekh^{a}lā-mẽ*, in seeing. Verbal nouns in the form of the root have an oblique form in *e*. Thus, *dēkh*, seeing; *dekhe-lā*, for seeing. In all other nouns, the oblique form is the same as the nominative.

II.—PRONOUNS—

	I.		Thou.		Your Honour.	Self, Your Honour.	This.	That, He.
	Inferior form.	Superior form.	Inferior form.	Superior form.				
Sing. Nom.	*mẽ*	*ham*	*tū̃* or *tẽ*	*tū̃* or *tẽ*	*rauwā̃*, *rawā̃*, *raurā*	*ap^{a}ne*	*ī*, *ihe*, *ihā̃*	*ū*, *ō*
Obl.	*mohi* or *mō*	*ham^{a}rā*	*tohi* or *tō*	*toh^{a}rā*	as nom.	*ap^{a}nā*	*ehi*, *ehẽ*, *ihā̃*	*ohi*, *oh*, *ō*, *uhā̃*
Gen.	*mōr*, *mōre*	*hamār*, *ham^{a}re*	*tōr*, *tōre*	*tohār*, *toh^{a}re*	*rāur*, *raure*	*apan*, *appan*, or *ap^{a}ne*.	*eh-ke*	*oh-ke*
Plur. Nom.	*ham^{a}nī-kā*	*ham^{a}ran*	*toh^{a}nī-kā*	*toh^{a}ran*	*rauran*, *rawan*	*ap^{a}nan*	*inh-kā*	*unh-kā*
Obl.	*ham^{a}nī*	*ham^{a}ran*	*toh^{a}nī*	*toh^{a}ran*	Ditto.	*ap^{a}nan*	*inh*	*unh*

	Who.	He, that.	Who?	What (thing).	Any one, some one.
Sing. Nom.	*jē*, *jawan*, *jaun*	*sē*, *tē*, *tawan*, *taun*	*kē*, *kawan*, *kaun*	*kā*	*keū*, *kēhu*, *kaunō*
Obl.	*jeh*, *jaunā*	*teh*, *taunā*	*keh*, *kaunā*	*kā*, *kāhe*, *kethī*	*keū*, *kehū*, *kaunō*
Gen.	*jeh-ke*, *jē-kar*, *jek^{a}re*	*teh-ka*, *tē-kar*, *tek^{a}re*	*keh-ke*, *kē-kar*, *kek^{a}re*	*kā-ke*, *kāhe-ke*, *kethī-ke*	*kek^{a}ro*, *kathiyo*. *kek^{a}ro*
Plur. Nom.	*jinh-kā*, *jawan*, *jaun*	*tinh-kā*, *tawan*, *taun*	*kinh-kā*, *kawan*, *kaun*	Anything, something, is *kachhu*, *kuchchho* or *kuchhuo*. Declined like a substantive.	
Obl.	*jinh*	*tinh*	*kinh*		
Gen.	*jinh-ke*	*tinh-ke*	*kinh-ke*		

An optional form of the oblique singular of *ū*, is *wāhi*; of *jē*, *jāhi*; of *tē*, *tāhi*; of *kē*, *kāhi*. For *teh*, we can substitute *tehi* or *tẽ*; for *oh*, *ohi* or *ō*, and so on for the others.

There are many forms of the oblique plural in all the above. The following are those of *ī*. The others can be formed by analogy. *Ek^{a}ni inhan*, *inhanh*, *inh^{a}ni*; so *ok^{a}ni*, *unhan*, etc.; *jek^{a}ni*, etc. The spelling of all these fluctuates.

The genitives in *r* and *re* have a feminine form in *ī*, which is met in poetry. Thus *mōrī*, *ham^{a}rī*, and so on.

All these genitives have an oblique form in *ā*, viz. *mōrā*, *ham^{a}rā*, *tōrā*, *toh^{a}rā*; so also *ek^{a}rā*, *ok^{a}rā*, *jek^{a}rā*, *tek^{a}rā* and *kek^{a}rā*. These can be used as fresh oblique bases of the Pronoun. Thus *mōrā-sē*, from me; *ek^{a}rā-sē*, from this, and so on. In the plural they become *ham^{a}ran*, *toh^{a}ran*, *ek^{a}ran*, etc.; thus *ham^{a}ran-sē*, from us.

III.—VERBS—

General Note.—In all Verbs, the first person singular is hardly ever used except in poetry. The plural is used instead. The use of the second person singular is vulgar. The plural is here also used instead. The first person plural is commonly used instead of the second person when it is desired to show respect. The syllable *sá* may be added to the second or third person to show the plural number or respect. Thus *dēkhá-lá-sá*, your honour sees.

It is quite common to use Masculine forms instead of the Feminine.

A.—Auxiliary Verbs, and Verbs Substantive—

Present, I am, etc.

	Form I.				Form II.			
	Sing.		Plur.		Sing.		Plur.	
	Masc.	Fem.	Masc.	Fem.	Masc.	Fem.	Masc.	Fem.
1	(*baṛō̃*)	—	*baṛī̃* or *bāṛī̃*	*bāṛyū̃*	(*hắwō̃*)	—	*hắwī̃*, *hắī̃*	*hắwyū̃*
2	*bāṛ*, *bāṛē*, *baṛasi*, *bāṛas*	*bāṛis*	*bāṛá*, *bāṛáh*	*bāṛū*	*hắwē*, *hắwas*, etc.	*hắwis*	*hắwá*, *hắwáh*	*hắū*
3	*bā*, *bāṛē*, *bāṛa*, *bāṛō*, *baṛasi*, *baṛasu*, *bāṛas*	—	*bāṛan*	*bāṛin*	*hắ*, *hắwē*, *hắwasi*, *hắwas*	—	*hắwan*	*hắwin*

Past, I was, etc.

	Form I.				Form II.			
	Sing.		Plur.		Sing.		Plur.	
	Masc.	Fem.	Masc.	Fem.	Masc.	Fem.	Masc.	Fem.
1	(*rah^{a}lō̃*)	--	*rah^{a}lī̃*	*rah^{a}lyū̃*	(*rahō̃*)	—	*rahī̃*	*rahyū̃*
2	*rah^{a}lē*, *rah^{a}las*	*rah^{a}lī*, *rah^{a}lis*	*rah^{a}lá*, *rah^{a}láh*	*rah^{a}lū*	*rahē*, *rahas*	*rahī*, *rahis*	*rahá*, *raháh*	*rahū*
3	*rahal*, *rah^{a}lē*, *rah^{a}lasi*, *rah^{a}las*	*rah^{a}lī*	*rah^{a}lan*	*rah^{a}lin*	*rahē*, *rahasi*, *rahas*	*rahī*	*rahan*	*rahin*

Sometimes the *h^{a}* is dropped. Thus *ralī̃*, I was.

The Strong Verb Substantive is *hōkhal*, to become, conjugated regularly.

The Negative Verb Substantive is *nahī̃khī̃* or *naïkhī̃*, I am not, conjugated regularly, but only in the present tense.

B.—Finite Verb—

Verbal Nouns.—(1) *dēkh*, obl., *dēkhe*; (2) *dēkhal* (infinitive), obl., *dekh^{a}lā*; (3) *dēkhab*, no obl. form. All mean 'to see' 'the act of seeing.'

Participles.—Pres. *dēkhat, dēkhit, dekhait*; Fem., *dekh^{a}ti*, etc.; obl., *dekh^{a}tā*, etc.: Past, *dēkhal*; Fem., *dekh^{a}li*; obl. *dekh^{a}lā*.

Conjunctive Participle.—*dēkh-ke* or *dēkhi-ke*; *kā* may be used instead of *ke*.

Simple Present.—I see, etc.; and Present Conditional (if) I see, etc.

	Sing.		Plur.	
	Masc.	Fem.	Masc.	Fem.
1	(*dēkhō̃*)	—	*dēkhī̃*	*dēkhyū̃*
2	*dēkh, dēkhē* *dekhasi,* *dēkhas*	*dēkhis*	*dēkhā* *dēkhāh*	*dēkhū*
3	*dēkhē,* *dēkha, dēkhō,* *dekhasi,* *dekhasu,* *dēkhas*	—	*dēkhan* *dekhani*	*dēkhin*

Present Indicative, I see, etc., I shall see, etc.

	Sing.		Plur.	
	Masc.	Fem.	Masc.	Fem.
1	(*dēkhā-lō̃*)	—	*dēkhī-lī* *dēkhī-lē*	*dēkhā-lyū̃*
2	*dēkhō-lē* *dēkhe-lē*	*dēkhā-lisi*	*dēkhā-lā(h)* *dēkhe-lā(h)*	*dēkhā-lū*
3	*dēkhā-lī* *dēkhe-lī*	*dēkhā-li*	*dekhō-lē, -lan,* *-lani* *dēkhe-lē, -lan,* *-lani*	*dēkhā-lin*

Past, I saw, etc.

	Sing.		Plur.	
	Masc.	Fem.	Masc.	Fem.
1	(*dekh^{a}lō̃*)	—	*dekh^{a}lī̃*	*dekh^{a}lyū̃*
2	*dekh^{a}lē* *dekh^{a}las*	*dekh^{a}lī* *dekh^{a}lis*	*dekh^{a}lā(h)*	*dekh^{a}lū*
3	*dekh^{a}lē* *dekh^{a}las* *dekh^{a}lasi*	*dekh^{a}li*	*dekh^{a}lan* *dekh^{a}lani*	*dekh^{a}lin*

Future, I shall see, etc.

	Sing.		Plur.	
	Masc.	Fem.	Masc.	Fem.
1	(*dekh^{a}bō̃*) (*dekh^{a}baũ*)	—	*dēkhab, dekh^{a}bī* *dekhihā*	*dēkhib, dekhibi*
2	*dekh^{a}bē*	*dekh^{a}bi* *dekh^{a}bis*	*dekh^{a}bā(h)*	*dekh^{a}bū*
3	*dēkhī*	—	*dekhihē* *dekhihen*	—

Past Conditional, I had seen, etc.

	Sing.		Plur.	
	Masc.	Fem.	Masc.	Fem.
1	(*dekh^{a}tō̃*)	—	*dekh^{a}tī̃*[1]	*dekh^{a}tyū̃*
2	*dekh^{a}tē* *dekh^{a}tas*	*dekh^{a}tī* *dekh^{a}tis*	*dekh^{a}tā(h)*	*dekh^{a}tū*
3	*dēkhat, dēkhit* *dekh^{a}tē* *dekh^{a}tas* *dekh^{a}tasi*	*dekh^{a}ti*	*dekh^{a}tan* *dekh^{a}tani*	*dekh^{a}tin*

[1] or *dekhitī̃*, and so throughout.

The *Imperative* is the same as the Simple Present. *Precative Forms* are, singular, *dekhihē, dēkhū, dekh^{a}bē*; Plural, *dekhihā, dekhihau, dēkhī, dekh^{a}bā*.

Present Definite. I am seeing, *dēkhat bānī̃*, and so on. Contracted form *dekh^{a}tānī̃*, or *dekh^{a}tārī̃* and so on. The participle does not change for gender or number.

Imperfect, I was seeing, *dēkhat rah^{a}lī̃*, or *dēkhat rahī̃*, and so on. The participle does not change for gender or number.

Perfect, *I have seen*, formed by adding *hā̃* or *hā* to the *Past*. *hā̃* is used in the first and third persons plural, and *hā* in the second person, and in the third person singular. Thus *dekh^{a}lī̃ hā̃*, I have seen: *dekh^{a}lā hā*, you have seen. *Hā̃* may be substituted for *hā̃* *hā* for *hā*.

Another form of the Perfect is made by conjugating the locative of the Past Participle, with the Present tense of the auxiliary verb. Thus, *dekh'lē bānī̃*, I have seen, *dekh'lē bāṛā*, you have seen, and so on.

Pluperfect, I had seen, *dekh'lē rah'lī̃* or *rahī̃* and so on. The syllable *hā* may be added. Thus, *dekh'lē rah'lī̃ hā*. In the second person, and in the third person singular, *hā* is used instead of *hā̃*.

C.—Neuter Verbs—

In the third person singular masculine of the past, they may take the form of the Past Participle, without any suffix. Thus beside *gir'lē* and *gir'las*, we may have also *giral* (fem. *gir'lī*), meaning, 'he fell.'

In the second form of the Perfect, the nominative, and not the locative of the Past Participle is used. Thus, *giral bānī̃*, not *gir'lē bānī̃*, I have fallen. In the Pluperfect, the form is the same as in the Active Verb. Thus, *gir'lē rah'lī̃* or *rahī̃*, I had fallen.

D.—Verbs whose roots end in *āw* and *ā*—

Those in *āw* are all transitive verbs, except the neuter verb *gāw*, sing.

Example,—*pāwal*, to obtain ; Pres. Part., *pāwat*, *pāwit*, *pāit* ; Past Part., *pāwal*.

	Simple Pres.		Pres. Ind.		Past.		Future.		Past Conditional.	
	Sing. Masc.	Plur. Masc.	Sing. Masc.	Plur. Masc.	Sing. Masc.	Plur. Masc.	Sing. Masc.	Plur. Masc.	Sing. Masc.	Plur. Masc.
1	*pāū̃*	*pāī̃*	*pāwe-lō̃*	*pāī-lā*	*paulō̃*	*paulī̃*	*paibō̃*	*pāib*	*pautō̃*	*pautī̃*
2	*pāwē*	*pāwā*	*pāwe-lē*	*pāwe-lā*	*paulē*	*paulā*	*paibē*	*paibā*	*pautā*	*pautā*
3	*pāwas*	*pāwan*	*pāī-lā*	*pāwe-lē*	*paulas*	*paulan*	*pāī*	*paihē̃*	*pāit* or *pāwat*	*pautan*

Those in *ā* are all neuter verbs, except the active verb *khā*, eat.

Example,—*khāil*, to eat ; Pres. Part., *khāit* or *khāt* ; Past Part., *khāil*.

	Simple Pres.		Pres. Ind.		Past.		Future.		Past Conditional.	
	Sing. Masc.	Plur. Masc.	Sing. Masc.	Plur. Masc.	Sing. Masc.	Plur. Masc.	Sing. Masc.	Plur. Masc.	Sing. Masc.	Plur. Masc.
1	*khāū̃*	*khāī̃*	*khā-lō̃*	*khāi-lā*	*khailō̃*	*khailī̃*	*khaibō̃*	*khāīb*	*khaitō̃*	*khaitī̃*
2	*khāwē*	*khāwā*	*khā-lē*	*khā-lā*	*khailē*	*khailā*	*khaibē*	*khaibā*	*khaitē*	*khaitā*
3	*khāwas*	*khāwan*	*khā-lā*	*khā-lē*	*khailas*	*khailan*	*khāī*	*khaihē̃*	*khāit*	*khaitan*

A neuter verb, such as *aghā*, be satiated, would make its 3rd sg. past optionally *aghāil*. The verb *āw*, come, is treated as a verb in *āw* in the Present Indicative (*āwe-lā*), he comes, and the Preterite Conditional (*autī̃*, (if) I had come). In the other tenses, it is treated as a verb in *a*. Thus *ailī̃*, I came ; *āil*, he came.

E.—Irregular Verbs—

karal, to do ;	Past Part.	*karal* or *kail*, Conj. Part. *ke* or *kā*.
dharal, to place, seize ;	„	*dharal* or *dhail*, „ *dhai* or *dhā*.
mar, to die ;	„	*maral* or *mūal*, Pres. Part., *marat* or *mūat*.
jāil, to go ;	„	*gail*.
dēl, to give ;	„	*dihal* or *dēl*.
lēl, to take ;	„	*lihal* or *lēl*.
hōal, to become ;	„	*bhail*.

F.—Causal Voice, formed by adding *āw* to root. Thus *dekhāwi-lā*, I cause to see. The double causal adds *'wāw*.

G.—Potential Passive Voice, formed by adding *ā* to the root. Thus *dekhāī-lā*, I can be seen.

MAITHILĪ OR TIRᵃHUTIYĀ.

The standard dialect is the language which is specially called Tirᵃhutiyā by people in other parts of India. It is called Maithilī by its speakers. Its head-quarters are the North and Centre of the Darbhanga District, where the Maithil Brāhmaṇs muster in large numbers. In the South of Darbhanga it is spoken in the slightly corrupt form which I call Southern Standard Maithili. It is spoken in its greatest purity by Maithil Brāhmaṇs, and the other higher castes of its habitat. The lower castes have a habit of clipping their final syllables which will be abundantly shown in the specimens. The same peculiarity is observable in the Southern variety of the Standard Language.

Standard Maithilī is also spoken in that portion of the District of Monghyr (except in the southern portion of Gogri Thana), which lies north of the Ganges. As its geographical position would suggest, it is the Southern variety which is spoken here. The District of Bhagalpur is similarly divided into two portions, a northern and a southern by the Ganges. North Bhagalpur is a long narrow strip of country which runs from the Ganges right up to the Nepal frontier, and includes two sub-divisions, *viz.*, Supaul on the north, and Madhipura, south of Supaul, on the banks of the Ganges. Standard Maithilī is spoken over the whole of North Bhagalpur, the pure variety being spoken in Supaul, and the southern in Madhipura.

In the District of Purnea, which lies to the east of North Bhagalpur, the bulk of the population speak Eastern Maithilī, but the Brāhmans of that District, especially those living to the west on the Supaul border, speak pure Standard Maithilī.

The following is the estimated population speaking both varieties of Standard Maithilī :—

Name of District.	Number of Speakers.
Darbhanga	2,460,000
Monghyr	800,000
Bhagalpur	956,800
Purnea	30,000
TOTAL .	4,246,800

With reference to the above, it may be mentioned that the Magistrate of Monghyr has returned 1,000,000 people as speaking Maithilī in his District. On further inquiry it appears that it may be estimated that, of these, 800,000 speak Standard Maithilī, and the remaining 200,000 the Chhikā-chhikī Bōlī of the South of the Ganges. All the above figures are estimates made by the local officers, as the Census figures do not distinguish between Maithilī and the Hindī dialects of the North-Western Provinces.

No attempt has been made by the local officials to distinguish the populations speaking the true Standard Maithilī and its Southern variety. The matter is not of great importance, but the following estimates, based on my own experience, will not, I think, be found to be very incorrect :—

TRUE STANDARD MAITHILĪ.

Name of District.	Number of Speakers.
Darbhanga	1,460,000
Bhagalpur	456,800
Purnea Brāhmaṇs	30,000
TOTAL .	1,946,800

SOUTHERN STANDARD MAITHILĪ.

Name of District.	Number of Speakers.
Darbhanga	1,000,000
Monghyr	800,000
Bhagalpur	500,000
TOTAL .	2,300,000

The following specimen is in the pure Maithilī dialect used by the Tirhutiā Brāhmaṇs and other higher class people of the Darbhanga District, their head-quarters. It is written in the character which they use themselves,—the Maithilī, *par excellence.* This character is only used by these Brāhmaṇs, and accordingly I have also given the same specimen in the variety of the Kaithī character which is used in that District. Both specimens are in facsimile. Writers in this part of the country are very careless, and hence, there are minor differences, principally owing to slips of the pen, between the two copies. These are not sufficient to render separate transliterations necessary, and so I have given only one transliteration, following, as a rule, the copy in the Maithilī character, and silently correcting any mistakes as they occur. It should be remembered that the Maithilī character is used only by Brāhmaṇs, and that other higher class people use the Kaithī character :—

[No. I.]

INDO-ARYAN FAMILY. EASTERN GROUP.

BIHĀRĪ.

MAITHILĪ DIALECT (MAITHILĪ CHARACTER, AS USED BY BRĀHMAṆS).

(DARBHANGA DISTRICT.)

কোনো মনুষ্যকেঁ দুই বালক রহৈন্হি। ওহি মে সঁ ছোট বাপ সঁ কহলন্হি জে হে বাবু
বাবু ধন সম্পত্তি মে জে হমর হিস্সা হোয় সে হমরা দীয় ত ওহি ও অপন্ হা
অপন সম্পত্তি বাঁটি দেলথীন্হি। থোড়েক দীন বিতলা উত্তর ছোটকা বেটা
সভ কিছু কেঁ একট্ঠা কয় দূর দেশ চল গেলাহ আওর ওতহি লুচ্চপনী সঁ অপন সম্প
ত্তি উড়া দেলক। জখন ও সভ কিছু খর্চ কয় চুকল তখন ওহি দেশ
মে মহা অকাল পড়ল নৈক আওর ও কষ্ট কনে মে লাগল। এলা গ নৈক আওর জাকেঁ
ওহি দেশক নিবাসী সভ মে সঁ এক লোক হৌ কো তেঁ রহেঁ লাগলা জে ও কবা
অপনা খেত সভ মে সুগর চরাবনেঁ পঠৌলনি কৈঁ আওর ও ওহী ভূসি স
কেঁ সুগর খাইত ছল নৈক অপন পেট ভরবেঁ চাহৈত ছলাহ আওর কো ও কখান
হি কিছু দেওক আচর্জ সকল ন ও কবা জ্ঞান ভেল নৈক ও বিচার কৈলক জে
হমরা বাপ কেঁ বনিহার সভ কে খায় কম অধিক নহি পাকৈত ছৈন্হি আওর

হম ভূখ মরৈছী হম অপনা বাপ কনগ জাএব আ ওকরাসঁ কহবন্হি

জে বাবু হম ধর্ম্মক বিরুদ্ধ আ অপনেক সমক্ষ পাপ কয়

নছি হমকে বিশ্বপনেক বেটা কহাবেক যোগ্য নহি ছী হমরা অপন

বনিহার জেঁ কারা খন আ ওতখন ওউঠল আ অপনা বাপক সমী

প এলন পরন্তু জখনও ওকরাকাহি দূর নকীও করবাপ ও কহ্মাদ মকে দয়াক

লথী ন্হি আ ওকরা দৌড়িকেঁ ওকরা বোকারেঁ লগাই কেঁ ওকরা চুম্মা লেলথী ন্হি

বেটা ওকরা কহৈক ন্হি জে বাবু হম ধর্মক বিরুদ্ধ আ অপনেক সমক্ষ

পাপ কয়নছি হমকে বিশ্বপানক বেটা কহাবেক যোগ্য নহি ছী

পর ন্তু বাপ অপনা লোকরকে ডমক কহলথী ন্হি জে সভসঁ উত্তম বস্ত্র রহোব

কেঁ লেকআপহিরাবহ আ ওকরা হাথমে ঔঁঠী পাও বাম পন হীপ হিরারুৎ আ

অবহম সভ নাক নিখাউ আ আনন্দ করী কিএকত জেহমর বেটা মরি জাত দুন্ধ

জীবিত ভ নছি হেরাএল রহ নমোফ বিত ভইলন ছি আ ওতখন ও লোক

নিশ্বানন্দ করৈঁ লাগলাহ

ওকর জেঠ বেটা খেতমে ছলৈক জখনও ঘর কসমীপন্ধ বন জখনও বাজা

আ ওর নাচক শব্দ সুননক আ ও অপনা সেবক মধ্য সমতক কেঁ অপ

নাচগবজা কেঁ শব্দ সুনলকৈক জেঁ ডা কী থি কৈক ও হুনকা ম কঁহলকৈ

ন্হি জে অপান বাজাগ আএল বুঝি আও অপানক বাপ বড়ভসে

র কয়লন্হি অছি ঐ হেতু কী হুনকা বেজা নিরোগ পাওল অছি পরন্তু ও

ক্রোধ কেঁ ভীতর নহি গেলাহ ঐ হেতু হুনক বাপ বাহর আবি হুনকা

বুঝারেঁ লগলাহ ও বাপা কেঁ উত্তর দেলন্হি জে দেখু হম এতেক বরষ সঁ

অপানেক সেবা কাবৈ ছী আও কহিও অপানক আজ্ঞা উলঙ্ঘন নহিঁ

কেঁলন্হি আও অপানে হমরা কহিও বকরীক বাচ্চা নহি দেলন্হি জে হম অপনা

মিত্র সভ কসঙ্গ আনন্দ করিতহুঁ পরন্তু অপনেক ভারেঠ জের

হাঁড়বেশ্যা সভ কসঙ্গ অপনেক সম্পত্তি খা গেল অছি ও হিনকা

তনে অপনে ওকরা নিমিত্ত রসোঁসে বকয়ন অছি বাপ হুনকা ক

হলথীন্হি জে হে বাউনক তোঁ সদা হমরে সঙ্গ ছা আও জে কিছু

হমর অছি সে তোহর থিকহু পরন্তু আনন্দ করব হাস্কিত হৈঁ

ব উচিত ছল কিএক তোহর ভাই মরি গেল ছল সে ফেরি জীলন অ

ছি হেরা গেল ছল সে ফেরি ভেটল অছি =

[No. 1.]

INDO-ARYAN FAMILY. EASTERN GROUP.

BIHĀRĪ.

MAITHILĪ DIALECT, KAITHĪ CHARACTER. (DARBHANGA DISTRICT.)

(AS USED BY HINDŪS OF THE HIGHER CASTES, WHO ARE NOT BRĀHMAṆS.)

कौनो मनुष्य कें दुइ बेटा रहैन्हि। ओहि मे सँ छोटका — बाप सौं — कहलकैन्हि — हे
बाबु — धनसम्पति — मे सौं — जे हमर — हिस्सा होए — से हमरा दीअ — तखन — ओ उनका —
अपन — सम्पति — बांटि — देलथिन्ह। थोडेक — दीन — बितला — उपरा — छोटका — बेटा — सब
किछु ऐकट्ठा कै — दूर देश — चलि गेल — ओम — बात रे — व्ययनी में — अपन — सम्पति — उड़ा
देलक। जखन ओ सब — किछु खर्च कै चुकल — तखन — ओहि देश मे — महा अकाल — पड़लै — ओर
ओकरा — दुःख होइ लगलै — ओ ओहि — देशक — निवासी — कोनो सौं —
जा मिललै — ओ ओकरा — अपना खेत — सब मे — सुगर — चरबै ले — पठौलकै
ओर — ओहि — छिमाड़ — सौं जे सुगर — खाइत छलै — अपन पेट — भरै चाहैत छल — आ
कोनो — ओकरा — किछु देलकै — ओर — जखन ओकरा — ग्यान भेलै — तँ ओ बाजल
कि — हमरा — बाप के — कतेक नौकर चाकर — रोटी सौं — अघाइ — रहै छथि — ओर हम —
भूखें — मरै छी — हम अपना — बाप लग जाइ — आ ओकरा — कहबैन्हि — जे —
हे बाबु — हम धर्म के — विरुद्ध — ओर — अपने के — आगां — पाप कैलहुँ — हम फेरि — अपने के
बेटा कहबै के — जोग नहि छी — हमरा — अपन मजदूर — जकाँ राखु — तखन ओ उठल
आ ओ — अपना — बाप के — समीप — चलल — परन्तु — जखन ओ — दूरे छल — कि ओकर
बाप ओकरा देखलकै — दया उठलथिन्ह — ओर — दौड़ कै — ओकरा — गला मे — लपटि कै — ओ

उठातु आबि छथीन्ह — जे हारनता — उठौन्हि — जे — श्रीबाबू — हम धर्म्मविरुद्ध — औ अ
पनेक असम्यक् पाप कैल अछि — हम आब नि — अपनेक — पुत्र होबैक — योग्य नहि छी —
परन्तु बाप — अपना — नोकर — सबसँ — कहलथीन्ह जे — सबसँ उत्तम — वस्त्र — पहिरबै —
हिनका — पहिराउ — औ हिनका — हाथमे — औठी — औ जौन — पैरमे — पनही पहिराउ
आ जौन — हमरा सबौन्हि — खाई — औ आनन्द करी — किएक जी — ई हमर बेटा — मुइल
छल से जीवित — भेल — छथि — हेराएल छल — से भेटल अछि — आ जौन — तखन — आम
भेलन्हि आनन्द करैत छलाह — ओहि समय ओकर जेठ बेटा — खेतमे छलैक — ओ जखन — घरक — समीप
पहुँचल — तखन बाजा — और — नाचक शब्द सुनलक — आ जौन — अपना नोकर —
सबमेसँ — एकटाकेँ अपना लग — बजाऔलक — पुछलकैक — जे ई की थिकैक — ओ हुनका सँ कहलकैक
जे — अपनेक — भाई — आएल छथि — आ जौन — अपनेक — बाप — बड़ उत्सव कैने छथीन्ह
अछि — परन्तु ओ क्रोधसँ — भीतर — नहि गेलाह — एहि कारण — बापे आबि
हुनका — बुझाबए लगलाह — ओ बापकेँ — उत्तर देलथीन्ह — जे देखु — हमरा एते बरख
सँ — अपनेक — सेवा करैत छी — आ कहियो — अपनेक — आज्ञा — उल्लंघन — नहि कैल
आ जौन — अपने हमरा कहियो — छागरो नहि देल — जे हम अपना — मित्र सबक — संग आन
न्द करितहुँ — परन्तु अपनेक ई बेटा — जे वेश्या सबक संग — अपनेक — सम्पत्ति — खाए गेल
अछि, जे हिनि आएल — अपने — ओकरा — निमित्त — बड़ उत्सव कैने छी — अछि। बाप हुनका
कहलथीन्ह — बाउआ — सदा — हमरा — संग छह — आ जौन — जे किछु — हमर — अछि —
तोहर — थिकहु। परन्तु — आनन्द करब — हर्षित — होयब — उचित छल — किएक तँ —
ई तोहर — भाई — मुइल छल — से फेर जिउल — अछि — हेराएल छल — से भेटि गेल अछि

[No. 1.]

INDO-ARYAN FAMILY. EASTERN GROUP.

BIHĀRĪ.

MAITHILĪ DIALECT AS USED BY BRĀHMAṆS AND HIGHER CASTE HINDŪS.

(DARBHANGA DISTRICT.)

Kōnō manukhya-kẽ dui bēṭā rahainh[i]. Oh[i]-sã chhoṭ[a]kā
A-certain man-to two sons were. Them-from the-younger

bāp-sã kahal[a]kainh[i], jē, 'au bābū, dhan-sampatt[i]-mẽ-sã jē
the-father-to said, that, 'O Father, the-property-in-from which

hamar hissā hōy, sē ham[a]rā diyâ.' Takhan ō
my share may-be, that to-me be-good-enough-to-give.' Then he

hun[a]kā apan sampatt[i] bãṭ[i] del[a]thinh[i]. Thōṛek din
to-them his-own property having-divided gave. A-few days

bit[a]lā-uttar chhoṭ[a]kā bēṭā sabh-kichh[u]-kẽ (ekaṭṭhā kăī),
on-passing-after the-young son everything (together having-made),

katah[u] dūr dēs chal-gēl; āor ōtah[i] luch[a]panī-mẽ apan
somewhere far country departing-went; and there debauchery-in his-own

sampatt[i] uṛā-dēlak. Jakhan ō sabh-kichh[u] kharch kăī
property (he)-squandered. When he everything expenditure having-done

chukal, takhan oh[i] dēś-mẽ mahã akāl paṛ[a]laik, āor ok[a]rā
finished, then that country-in a-great famine fell, and to-him

kalēs hōe lag[a]laik, āor ō jāe-kã oh[i] dēśak nibāsī-
trouble to-be began, and he having-gone that country-of the-dwellers-

sabh-mẽ-sã ek-gōṭāk-otai rahăī lāgal, jē ok[a]rā
all-(sign of plur.)-in-from one-individual's-near to-dwell began, who him

ap[a]nā khēt-sabh-mẽ sūgar charāba-lăī paṭhaul[a]kai, āor ō oh[i]
his-own fields-(plur.)-in swine feeding-for sent, and he those

chhīmaṛ[i]-sã jē sūgar khāit-chhalaik apan pēṭ bharăī chāhait-chhal.
husks-with which the-swine eating-were his-own belly to-fill wishing-was,

āor keo ok[a]rā nah[i] kichh[u] dēik. Āor jakhan ok[a]rā jñ(gy)ān
and anyone to-him not anything gives. And when to-him sense

bhelaik, ō bichār-kailak jē, 'ham[a]rā bāp-kẽ banihār-sabhak
became, he considered that, 'my father's labourers-(plur.)-of

khāek-sã adhik rōṭi pakait-chhainh[i], āor ham bhūkh-sã
eating-of-than more loaves being-cooked-are, and I hunger-from

maraichhī. Ham ap[a]nā bāpak-lag jāeb,' āor hun[a]kā-sã kah[a]bainh[i]
am-dying. I my-own father's-near will-go, and him-to I-will-say

jē, "au bābū, ham dharmak biruddh āor ap^{a}nek **adhyaksh**
that, "O Father, I of-virtue against and of-your-Honour (in)-sight-of
pāp kail-achh^{i}. Ham phēr^{i} ap^{a}nek bēṭā kahābāïk y(j)ogy^{a}
sin have-done. I again your-Honour's son of-being-called fit
nah^{i} chhī. Ham^{a}rā apan banihār jakā̃ rākhal-jāo."' Takhan ō
not am. Me thine-own labourer like please-to-keep."' Then he
uṭhal, āor ap^{a}nā bāpak samīp chalal, parantu jakhan ō pharākah^{i}
arose, and his-own father-of near went, but when he at-a-distance
chhal, kī ōkar bāp ok^{a}rā dēkh^{i}-kăï dayā kăïl^{a}thīnh^{i}, āor
was, that his father him having-seen compassion made, and
dauṛi-kăï ok^{a}rā garā-mē̃ lapaṭ^{i}-kăï ok^{a}rā chumbā̃ lel^{a}thīnh^{i}.
having-run him on-the-neck having-embraced to-him a-kiss took.
Bēṭā hun^{a}kā kahal^{a}kainh^{i} jē 'au bābū, ham dharmak biruddh āor
The-son to-him said that 'O Father, I of-virtue against and
ap^{a}nek adhyaksh pāp kail-achh^{i}. Ham phēr^{i} ap^{a}nek bēṭā
of-your-Honour in-sight-of sin have-done. I again your-Honour's son
kahābāïk y(j)ogy^{a} nah^{i} chhī.' Parantu bāp ap^{a}nā nōkar-
of-being-called fit not am.' But the-father his-own servants-
sabh-sā̃ kahal^{a}thīnh^{i} jē, 'sabh-sā̃ uttam bastra bahār (bāhar) kăï
(plur.)-to said that, 'all-than excellent clothes out having-made
hin^{a}kā pahirābåh, āor hin^{a}kā hāth-mē̃ aũṭhī, paer-mē̃ pan^{a}hī
this-person clothe, and this-person's hand-on a-ring, feet-on shoes
pahirābå, āor ham^{a}rā-lokani khāī, āor ānand karī; kiek-tā̃ ī
put-on, and-(let) us-people eat, and rejoicing make; because this
hamar bēṭā muil chhal, sē phēr^{i} jīul achh^{i}; herāel chhal, sē phēr^{i}
my son dead was, he again alive is; lost was, he again
bhēṭal achh^{i}.' Āor takhan ō-lokani āna(nd) karăï lag^{a}lāh.
met is.' And then they-people rejoicing to-do began.

Ō-kar jēṭh bēṭā khēt-mē̃ chhalaik. Jakhan ō gharak samīp
His elder son field-in was. When he of-the-house near
pahũchal, takhan ō bājā āor nāchak śabd sun^{a}lak, āor ap^{a}nā
arrived, then he music and dancing-of the-sound heard, and his-own
sēbak-sabh-mē̃-sā̃ ek-kē̃ ap^{a}nā lag bajā-kăï, puchhal^{a}kaik
servants-(plur.)-in-from one-to of-himself near having-called, he-asked
jē, 'ī kī thikaik?' Ō hun^{a}kā-sā̃ kahal^{a}kainh^{i} jē, 'ap^{a}nek
that, 'this what is?' He him-to said that, 'your-Honour's
bhāī āel chhath^{i}, āor ap^{a}nek bāp baṛ utsab kailanh^{i}-
brother come is, and your-Honour's father a-great feast has-
achh^{i}: ē hēt^{u} kī hun^{a}kā bēś nirōg pāol-achh^{i}.'
made: (for)-this reason that him well safe-and-sound has-found.'
Parantu ō krōdh kăï bhitar nah^{i} gēlāh. Ē hēt^{u} hunak
But he anger having-made within not went. (For)-this reason his

bāp bāhar āb^{i} hun^{a}kā bujhābăĭ lag^{a}lāh. Ō
father outside having-come him to-remonstrate-with began. He

bāp-kẽ uttar dēlanh^{i} jē, 'dēkhū, ham etek barakh-sã
the-father-to answer gave that, 'look, I so-many years-from

ap^{a}nek sēbā karaichhī, āor kahiō ap^{a}nek ăjñ(gy)ā(k)
your-Honour's service am-doing, and ever your-Honour's orders

ullaṅghan nah^{i} kail, āor ap^{a}ne ham^{a}rā kahiō chhāgar-ō nah^{i}
disobedience not did, and your-Honour to-me ever a-goat-even not

dēl, jē ham ap^{a}nā mitra-sabhak saṅg ānand karitáh^{a}.
gave, that I (my)-own friends-(plur.)-of with rejoicing I-might-make.

Parantu ap^{a}nek ī bēṭā, jē bēśyā-sabhak saṅg ap^{a}nek
But your-Honour's this son, who harlots-(plur.)-of with your-Honour's

sampatt^{i} khā-gēl-achh^{i}, jēh^{i} āel, ap^{a}ne ok^{a}rā nimitt
property has-devoured, when he-came, your-Honour of-him for-the-sake

baṛ utsab kail-achh^{i}.' Bāp hun^{a}kā kahal^{a}thīnh^{i} jē, 'hē bālak,
a-great feast has-made.' The-father to-him said that, 'O child,

tõ sadā ham^{a}rē saṅg chhâ, āor jē-kichh^{u} hamar achh^{i}, sē tōhar
thou always of-me-even with art, and whatever mine is, that thine

thikáh^{u}. Parantu ānand karab, harkhit haib, uchit chhal, kiek-tã
is. But rejoicing to-make, rejoiced to-be, proper was, because

ī tōhar bhāī muil chhal, phēr^{i} jīul achh^{i}: herāel chhal, phēr^{i}
this thy brother dead was, again alive is: lost was, again

bhēṭal achh^{i}.'
met is.'

The next specimen is a letter in Standard Maithilī, which formed part of the record of a case tried by me in the Darbhanga District some twenty years ago. It was originally written in the Kaithī character, but is here given in the Dēva-nāgarī. It is in other respects given exactly as it was written, only names of persons and places being, for obvious reasons, changed.

[No. 2.]

INDO-ARYAN FAMILY. EASTERN GROUP.

BIHĀRĪ.

MAITHILĪ DIALECT. (DARBHANGA DISTRICT.)

॥ श्री चंपाबती निकट दुरमिल झा लिखित पत्र ॥

स्वस्ति चिरंजीबि चंपाबती कें आशीख, आगा लछुमनक जुबानी ओ चीठी सौं अहाँ सभक कुशल छेम बूझल, मन आनंद भेल। श्री लछमी देबि कें नेना छोट छैन्हि, जेहि सौं ओकर परबरश छोड़क से अबश्य कर्त्तव्य थीक। इनिका माता नहि; अहैं लोकनिक भरोस तेल कुँड़क निगाह रहैन्हि। एक बकस पठाओल अछि, से अहाँक हेतु, अहाँ राखब; बकस में छौ ६) टा रुपैया छैक, ओ मसाला सभ छैक; से बकस खोलि दुइटा रुपैआ ओ आधा २ सभ मसाला लछमी दाइ कें अपने चुप्पे देबैन्हि, दुइटा रुपैआ मसाला बकस अपने राखब; अहैं लै भेजाओल अछि। कोनो बातक मन में अंदेशा मति राखो; जे चीज बस्तु सभ अहाँक नोकसान भेल अछि से सभ पहुँचत, तखन हम निश्चिंत होइब॥

श्री समधी जी कें प्रनाम; आगा भोला साहु कें बहुत दिन भेलैन्हि अहाँ लोकनि तकाजा नहिं करैछिऐन्हि; हमार बेटा जेहन छथि से खूब जनैछी; जल्दी रुपैआ असूल करू, नहिँत पोछू पछताएब। बखारीक धान सभ बेंच लेलन्हि। एह बेकूफ कें कहाँ तक नीक अकिल होतैक॥

श्री बाबू गोबिंद कें आशीख।

	रुपैआ	अमोट धारा
रहिकाक पहुना	२)	२
श्री लछमी दाइ	२)	२
श्री छोटी जनी	२)	२

[No. 2.]

INDO-ARYAN FAMILY. EASTERN GROUP.

BIHĀRĪ.

MAITHILĪ DIALECT. (DARBHANGA DISTRICT.)

TRANSLITERATION AND TRANSLATION.

Śrī Champābatī nikaṭ Durmil Jhā likhit patra.
The-respected Champābatī near (to) Durmil Jhā written letter.

Swast^{i}.
It-is-well (i.e. may-good-luck-attend-you).

Chiraṁjīb^{i} Champābatī-kẽ āśīkh, āgā Lachhumanak
The-long-lived Champābatī-to blessings, moreover (from)-Lachhuman's

jubānī ō-chīṭhī-saũ ahā̃ sabhak kuśal-chhēm būjhal. Man ānand
words and-letter-from you all well-being I-learnt. Heart pleased

bhēl. Śrī Lachh^{a}mī-Dēb^{i}-kẽ nēnā chhōṭ chhainh^{i},
became. The-respected Lakshmī-Dēbī-to child little is,

jeh^{i}-saũ ōkar parbaraś hoik sē abaśya kartabya thīk. Hunikā
what-(means-) by his support may-be that surely to-be-done is. To-her

mātā nah^{i}; ahaĩ lokanik bharōs tēl kũṛak nigāh rahainh^{i}.
mother (is-)not; you people-of hope oil pot-of (let-the-)eye remain.

Ēk bakas pathāol-achh^{i}, sē ahā̃k hēt^{u}, ahā̃ rākhab;
One box I-have-sent, that you-of for, you will-keep-(it);

bakas mẽ chhau-ṭā rupaiyā chhaik ō masālā sabh chhaik; sē
box in six rupees are and spices all are; that

bakas khōl^{i} dui-ṭā rupaiā ō ādhā ādhā sabh masālā Lachh^{a}mī
box opening two rupees and half half all spices Lakshmī

Dā^{i}-kẽ ap^{a}ne chuppē debainh^{i}, dui-ṭā rupaiā masālā bakas
Dāi-to you silently will-give, two rupees spices box

ap^{a}ne rākhab; ahaĩ lai bhejāol-achh^{i}. Kōnō bātak man mẽ
you keep; you for I-have-sent. Any things-of heart in

andēśā mat^{i} rākhī; jē chīj bast^{u} sabh ahā̃k noksān
anxiety do-not keep; whatever things property all your injured

bhēl-achh^{i}, sē sabh pahũchat, takhan ham niśchint
has-been, that all will-reach-(you), then I easy-in-(my)-mind

baib. Śrī sam^{a}dhī-jī-kẽ pranām; āgā
will-be. The-respected father-in-law-to compliments; moreover

Bhōlā Sāh^{u}-kẽ bahut din bhelainh^{i}, ahā̃ lokani takājā nah^{i}
Bhōlā Sāhu-to many days passed, you people demand not

karaichhiainh^{i} ;	hamār	bēṭā	jēhan	chh ı',	sō	khūb	janaichhī ;
are-making ;	*my*	*son*	*what-sort,*	*is,*	*that*	*well*	*you-know ;*

jaldī	rupaiā	asūl	karū,	nah^{i}-ta	pīchhū	pachh^{a}tāeb.
soon	*rupees*	*realization*	*make,*	*otherwise*	*afterwards*	*you-will-repent.*

Bakhārīk	dhān	sabh	bēch-lēlanh^{i},	eh	bēkūph-kē̃	kahā̃-tak
Of-granary	*the-paddy*	*all*	*he-has-sold,*	*this*	*fool-to*	*till-when*

nīk	akil	haitaik.	Śrī	Bābū	Gōbind	kē̃	āśikh.
good	*sense*	*will-be.*	*The-respected*	*Bābū*	*Gōbind*	*to*	*blessings.*

	Rupaiā. *Rupees.*	Amōṭ dhārā. *Mango-conserve slabs.*
Rahikāk pahunā *Of-Rahikā bridegroom.*	2	2
Śrī Lachhamī Dāi. *Respected Lakshmī Dāi.*	2	2
Śrī chhōṭī janī *Respected little girl-folk.*	2	2

TRANSLATION OF A LETTER WRITTEN BY DURMIL JHĀ TO MUSAMMAT CHAMPĀBATĪ.

After compliments,—May you live for a long time. My good wishes to Champābatī. Moreover, I have learnt both from the mouth of Lakshmaṇ and from your letter that you are all well, and my heart has been pleased thereby. Lakshmī Dēbī has had a little child, and we must make arrangements for its support; she has no mother, and I hope that you will keep an eye on her, and see that she gets everything necessary (*lit.* oil and pots). I have sent you a box herewith; it is for you, keep it. In the box there are six rupees, and some Kābulī * fruits; open the box and give two rupees and half the fruit to Lakshmī Dāi, but give it privately. You will keep two rupees, the remainder of the fruit, and the box; I have sent them for you. Don't be unhappy about anything: all your property, which has been spoilt, will be recovered for you; and then only will I be easy in my mind.

My compliments to the father-in-law. Moreover, it is a long time since you have pressed Bhōlā Sāhu to pay the money he owes. You know what sort of temper my son has, so realize the money quickly, or you will repent afterwards. He has sold all the paddy in the granary. When will the fool get decent wisdom?

My good wishes to Gōbind Bābū.

	Rs.	Slabs of mango conserve.
For the Rahikā bridegroom	2	2
For Lakshmī Dāī .	2	2
For the little girl .	2	2

* The word *masālā* usually means spices. I am, however, assured that here it must be translated as above.

The next specimen is a short poem by the famous old Master-singer, Vidyāpati Ṭhākur, who flourished at the end of the 15th century. He was court poet to Rājā Śiva-siṁha of Sugāonā, a village still existing in the Darbhanga District. There is a tradition that this king was summoned by the Emperor to Delhi for some offence, and that Vidyāpati obtained his patron's release by an exhibition of clairvoyance. The Emperor locked him up in a wooden box and sent a number of the courtesans of the town to bathe in the river. When all was over he released him, and asked him to describe what had occurred. Vidyāpati immediately recited *impromptu* the poem which I now give as a specimen of his powers, describing a beautiful girl at her bath. Astonished at his power, the Emperor granted his petition to release King Śiva-siṁha.

The poem has been handed down by word of mouth for centuries, and the language is, no doubt, modernised; but there is little doubt that, whatever we may think of the legend, the ideas are those of the poet himself.

As customary, the poet inserts in the last verse his own name.

In poetry, all vowels, even a silent *a* at the end of a word, and those represented in prose by small letters above the line in the middle or at the end of a word, are fully pronounced.

[No. 3.]

INDO-ARYAN FAMILY. EASTERN GROUP.

BIHĀRĪ.

MAITHILĪ DIALECT. (DARBHANGA DISTRICT.)

A POEM BY VIDYĀPATI ṬHĀKŪR.

कामिनि करए सिनाने । हेरइते हृदय हरए पचबाने ॥
चिकुर गलए जल धारा । मुख-ससि डर जनि रोअए अँधारा ॥
तितल बसन तनु लागू । मुनि-हुँ-क मानस मन-मथ जागू ॥
कुच-जुग चारु चकेवा । निअ कुल आनि मिलाओल देवा ॥
ते सँकाए भुज पासे । बाँधि धरिअ घन उड़त अकासे ॥
भनहि बिद्यापति भाने । सुपुरुख कबहुँ न होए नदाने ॥

TRANSLITERATION AND TRANSLATION.

Kāmini karae sinānē,
A-fair-one does bathing,
heraïte hṛidaya harae pacha-bānē.
on-seeing the-heart seizes the-five-arrowed-one.
Chikura galae jala-dhārā,
Her-locks melt (in)-a-water-stream,
mukha-sasi ḍara jani roae ā̃dhārā.
moon-face (in-)fear as-though weeps darkness.
Titala basana tanu lāgū,
The-wet garments (to-)the-body cling,
muni-hũ-ka mānasa mana-matha jāgū.
hermits-even-of (in)-the-soul the-God-of-Love awakes.
Kucha-juga chāru chakēwā,
The-bosom-pair fair chakēwās,
nia kula āni milāola dēwā.
own family having-brought united the-God.
Tē sā̃kāe bhuja-pāsē,
Therefore in-fear in-the-arm-noose,
bā̃dhi dharia, ghana uṛata akāsē.
having-bound clasp, clouds they-will-fly into-the-sky.
Bhanahi Bidyāpati bhānē,
Saith Vidyāpati the-sun-(of-poets),
su-purukha kaba-hũ na hōe na-dānē.
a-wise-man ever not becomes a-fool.

FREE TRANSLATION OF THE FOREGOING.

1. The pretty one is bathing, and as I gaze, the five-arrowed (God of Love) seizes my heart.

2. Her locks melt in a cascade of water-drops, as though darkness were weeping in fear of the brightness of her moon-face.

3. Her garments, wet (and transparent), cling to her form, and so fair is the vision that (Cupid), the soul-disturber, awakes even in the hearts of hermits.

4. Her two fair bosoms are a pair of sweet *chakēwās*,[1] as though God had brought and united each to its mate.

5. Therefore, for fear that they will fly away to the clouds in the sky, bind them and hold them fast in the snare of thine arms.

6. Singeth Vidyāpati, the Sun among the Poets, 'a wise man never proves himself a fool.'[2]

The above is the straightforward meaning of the above lines. But, as is customary in Indian poetry, it is so arranged that altogether different senses can be obtained by dividing the words differently. Thus, if we divide the first line as follows, and slightly alter the spelling, we get,—

Kā Maïna kara e sinānē, hera ite hṛidaya Hara Pacha-bānē.

Which means, 'O Maina, God of Love, why art thou beckoning? See here, on her heart is seated Hara (*i.e.*, her bosom), (thine enemy,) O thou who hast five arrows.'

So the second line may be divided,—

Chikura galae jala-dhārā, mukha-sasi ḍara jani ro, ae ãdhārā.

Which means, 'Weep not (*jani ro*), O darkness, in fear of her moon-face, for her locks are clouds, which will soon overshadow (its brightness).

Again, the third verse,—

Tita lava sanatana lāgū, muni-hũ-ka mānasa Mana-matha jāgū.

Which means, 'There (on her bosom, or Hara,[3]) the pious have fixed their devotion, for thou, O Cupid, hast awoken even in the hearts of hermits.

The next specimen is a short extract from the *Hari bans*, a poetical life of Kṛishṇa, written by Man-bōdh Jhā in the latter half of the eighteenth century.

---

[1] The Brahminy duck, a snow-white bird. Under ordinary circumstances, they are cursed never to pass the night together.

[2] *I.e.*, *verb. sap. sat.*

[3] In the first verse, her bosom was compared to the God Hara, who was the destroyer of the Indian Cupid. Hence, when the latter attacks the saints, they fix their minds on the former in self-protection. But, alas for their good intentions, Hara, himself, has taken the form of her bosom.

FREE TRANSLATION OF THE FOREGOING.

When some time had passed, (the babe) Hari soon began to be able to use his hands and feet.

What place was there, where he did not go? How often did he go outside even the court-yard of the house?

Gleefully used Madam Jasōdā to laugh, as she ever and again caught him up, and brought him back from the outer doorway.

Sharp as a little needle would he strut about, till he became the worry of her life.

How often did she snatch burning coals out of his very hand! and how often did he burn (his fingers) when she was not looking!

The next specimen is a short poem written in the middle of the last century by Bhānu-nāth Jhā. It describes the pangs suffered by a Herdmaiden who has been deserted by Krishṇa. According to custom, the poet enters his own name, and that of his patron, the father of the present Mahārāja of Darbhanga in the last verse.

[No. 5.]

INDO-ARYAN FAMILY. EASTERN GROUP.

BIHĀRĪ.

MAITHILĪ DIALECT. (DARBHANGA DISTRICT.)

A POEM BY BHĀNU-NĀTH JHĀ.

जदुपति बुझिअ बिचारी । अभिनब बिरह बेआकुलि नारी ॥
नलिन सयन नहिँ भाबे । तनि पथ हेरइति दिबस गमाबे ॥
केओ चानन कर लेपे । केअओ कहइ जिउ रहल सँछेपे ॥
कोन परि करति निबाहे । सित-कर किरन सतत करु दाहे ॥
तप जनि करइ सकामे । निस दिन जपइति रह तसु नामे ॥
भानु-नाथ कबि भाने । रस बुझ महेसुर सिंघ सुजाने ॥

TRANSLITERATION AND TRANSLATION.

Jadupati bujhia bichārī,
O-Krishṇa understand having-considered,
abhinaba biraha beākuli nārī.
fresh severance distraught the-lady.
Nalina sayana nahĩ bhābē,
Lotus bed not pleases,
tani patha heraïti dibasa gamābē.
his path watching the-day she-passes.
Keo chānana kara lēpē,
Some sandal do anointing,
keao kahai jiu rahala sãchhēpē.
some say life was in-danger.
Kona pari karati nibāhē ?
What on will-she-make recourse?
Sita-kara kirana satata karu dāhē.
Moon rays continually do burning.
Tapa jani karai sakāmē,
Austerities as-it-were she-does zealously,
nisa dina japaïti raha tasu nāmē.
night day muttering she-remains his name.
Bhānu-nātha kabi bhānē,
Bhānu-nāth poet sings,
rasa bujha Mahesura Siṅgha sujānē.
sentiment understands Mahēśvara Siṁha the-wise.

FREE TRANSLATION OF THE FOREGOING.

O Kṛishṇa, learn and understand. Distraught is the lady by the fresh severance.

Even a bed of lotuses pleases her not. On his (*i.e.*, thy) path gazing does she pass the day.

Some are anointing her body with cooling sandal-paste, while others stand by and say she cannot live.

To what can she have recourse? Even the cool rays of the moon continually burn her.

She is, as it were, performing austerities with but one fixed desire, and night and day she prays, murmuring but his[1] name in her prayers.

Saith the Poet Bhānu-nāth, The wise Mahēśvara Siṁha understands the sentiment.

The next specimen is a translation of the Parable of the Prodigal Son into the form of Maithilī which is used by the lower caste Hindūs of the Darbhanga District. It will be noticed that the principal differences are that in the first place the vocabulary is not so sanskritised, and, in the second place, that the forms of the verb which end in *nh'*, and which denote that respect is shown to the object are not used.

It is printed in Kaithī type.

[1] *Tasu* is an old or poetical form of the genitive, equivalent to *takar*.

[No. 6.]

INDO-ARYAN FAMILY. EASTERN GROUP.

BIHĀRĪ.

MAITHILĪ DIALECT (AS USED BY HINDŪS OF THE LOWER CASTES).

(DARBHANGA DISTRICT.)

એક ગોટા કે દુઇ વેટા રહૈક। છોટકા વેટા વાપ સોં કહલકૈક જ વાપ હમર હિસ્સા સભ ધન દૈ દહ। વાપ ઓકરા હિસ્સા ધન વાટિ દેલકૈક। થોડેક દિન પર છોટકા વેટા અપન સભ ધન એકટ્ઠા કૈ વડ઼ી દૂર દેસ ચલિ ગેલ। ઓત અપન સભટા ધન કુકરમ મેં ઓહા દેલક। ઓકર સભ ધન જખન ઓહા ગેલૈક, ઓહી દેસ મેં વડ઼ ભારી અકાલ પડ઼લૈ। તખન ઓ ઓહી દેસ મેં એક ગોટાક ઓહી ડામ સુગર ચરૈવા પર નોકર રહલ। ઓકરા સુગરક ખૈવાક ભૂસો ને ખૈવા લૈ મેટૈ। જખન ઓકરા હોસ મેલૈક મોન પડ઼લૈ જે હમરા વાપક ઓહી ડામ કતેક નોકર અછિ જકરા ખા પી કે અધિક ધન વચૈછૈક। હમ એત ભૂખેં મરૈછી। હમ વાપક ઓત જાએવ કહવૈ જે હમ તોહર ઓ ભગવાનક વડ઼ અપરાધ કૈલ। હમ તોહર વેટા કહૈવાક જોગ નહિ છિઓ। હમરા તોં અપના ઓહિ ડામ નોકર રાખ। ઈ સભ વાત મન મેં ભાજિ વાપક ઓત ચલલ। વાપક લગ પહુચલ। લેકિન જખન અરકૈહિ છલ ઓકર વાપ દેખિતહિ મમતક લેલ ઓકરા દિસ જલદી ચલલૈ. ઓકરા ગરદનિ મેં લગા કે ચુમુવા લેલકૈક। વેટા કહલકૈ જે વાપ હમ તોહર ભગવાનક વડ઼ અપરાધ કૈલહુ તૈં હમ તોહર વેટા કહૈવા જોગ નહિ છી। ઓકર વાપ અહિ પર અપના નોકર કે કહલકૈ જે ખૂવ નીક ર ઙુઆ લા, એકરા પહરા, ઔંઠી હાથ મેં દહી, પનહી સે પહરા દહી। મોટાએલ વાછા લા કે માર જે હમ સભ ખા પી કે ખુસી કરી। કિએક તો હમર વેટા મરિ કે જી ઐલૈ। ઈ વેટા હેરા ગેલ છલ સે ભેંર મેટલ। ઈ કહિ સભ ખુસી કર લાગલ।

જખન ઓકર વડ઼કા વેટા ખેતસોં ઘર અવૈત રહૈ, ઘરક નગ઼ીચ નાચ ઓ ગાન સુનલક। અપના નોકર સોં પુછલકૈ જે આઈ કો છિએક જે નાચ ગાન હોઇછૈક। ઓ સભ કહલકૈક જે તોહર ભાઈ આએલ અછિ નીકે જેકા ઐલૈ હૈ તૈં તોહર વાપ એક મોટાએલ વાછા મરલક હૈ। તાહિ પર ઓ તમસાએ ગેલૈ, ભીતર નહીં ગેલ। તખન ઓકર વાપ વાહર આવિ ઓકરા નેહોરા કર લાગલૈ। ઓ અપના વાપ સોં કહલક જે એતેક દિન સોં હમ તોહર સેવા કૈલિઔ તોહરા કહલા સોં કોનો કાજ વાહર નહીં

𑂍𑂶𑂪, 𑂞𑂶𑂋 𑂞𑂷𑂁 𑂯𑂧𑂩𑂰 𑂍𑂯𑂱𑂋 𑂥𑂍𑂩𑂲𑂍 𑂥𑂒𑂹𑂒𑂷 𑂢𑂵 𑂎𑂰𑂉 𑂪𑂶 𑂠𑂵𑂯𑂪 𑂔𑂵 𑂯𑂧 𑂃𑂣𑂢𑂰 𑂠𑂷𑂮𑂹𑂞 𑂮𑂦𑂍 𑂮𑂁𑂏𑂵 𑂎𑂳𑂮𑂲 𑂍𑂩𑂱𑂞𑂯𑂳𑂁𑃀 𑂪𑂵𑂍𑂱𑂢 𑂞𑂷𑂯𑂩 𑂆 𑂥𑂵𑂗𑂰 𑂔𑂵 𑂃𑂣𑂢 𑂮𑂦 𑂡𑂢 𑂩𑂝𑂹𑂙𑂲𑂥𑂰𑂔𑂲𑂧𑂵𑂁 𑂋𑂯𑂰 𑂍𑂵𑂁 𑂄𑂉𑂪 𑂃𑂓𑂱 𑂞𑂍𑂩𑂰 𑂪𑂶 𑂞𑂷𑂁 𑂧𑂷𑂗𑂰𑂉𑂪 𑂥𑂰𑂓𑂰 𑂧𑂰𑂩𑂪 𑂃𑂓𑂱, 𑂥𑂰𑂣 𑂍𑂯𑂪𑂍𑂶, 𑂥𑂵𑂗𑂰 𑂞𑂷𑂁 𑂯𑂩𑂠𑂧 𑂯𑂧𑂩𑂰 𑂮𑂁𑂏 𑂩𑂯𑂶𑂓𑂶, 𑂔𑂵 𑂍𑂱𑂓𑂳 𑂡𑂢 𑂯𑂧𑂩𑂰 𑂃𑂓𑂱 𑂮𑂵 𑂮𑂦 𑂞𑂷𑂯𑂩𑂵 𑂓𑂱𑂌𑂍𑃀 𑂯𑂧𑂩𑂰 𑂮𑂦𑂍𑂵 𑂎𑂴𑂥 𑂎𑂳𑂮𑂲 𑂍𑂩𑂥 𑂥𑂴𑂕 𑂔𑂵 𑂞𑂷𑂯𑂩 𑂦𑂰𑂅 𑂧𑂩𑂱 𑂍𑂵𑂁 𑂔𑂲𑂥 𑂔𑂷 𑂉𑂪𑂸 𑂃𑂓𑂱𑃀

[No. 6.]

INDO-ARYAN FAMILY. EASTERN GROUP.

BIHĀRĪ.

MAITHILĪ DIALECT (AS USED BY HINDŪS OF THE LOWER CASTES).

(DARBHANGA DISTRICT.)

TRANSLITERATION AND TRANSLATION.

Ek gōṭā-kẽ dui bēṭā rahaik. Chhoṭ^{a}kā bēṭā bāp-saũ
One person-to two sons were. The-younger son father-to

kahal^{a}kaik jē, 'bāp, hamar hissā sabh dhan dăī dâh.' Bāp
said that, 'Father, my share all wealth having-given give.' Father

ō-kar hissā dhan bāṭ^{i} del^{a}kaik. Thōrek din par chhoṭ^{a}kā bēṭā
his share wealth dividing gave. A-few days on the-younger son

apan sabh dhan ekaṭṭhā kăī baṛī dūr dēs chal^{i} gēl.
his-own all wealth together making very distant country going went.

Ōt apan sabh-ṭā dhan ku-karam-mẽ ohā-dēlak. Ō-kar
There his-own entire wealth bad-deeds-in he-wasted. His

sabh dhan jakhan ohā-gelaik, oh^{i} dēs-mẽ baṛ bhārī
all wealth when was-wasted, that country-in a-great heavy

akāl paṛ^{a}lai. Takhan ō oh^{i} dēs-mẽ ēk gōṭāk oh^{i}-ṭhām
famine fell. Then he that country-in a person's near

sūgar charaibā-par nōkar rahal. Ok^{a}rā sugarak khaibāk
swine feeding-on servant remained. By-him of-swine of-feeding

bhūs-ō nē khaibā-lăī bhēṭai. Jakhan ok^{a}rā hōs bhelaik, mōn
chaff-even not eating-for was-got. When to-him senses became, consideration

paṛ^{a}lai jē, 'ham^{a}rā bāpak oh^{i}-ṭhām katek nōkar achh^{i}, jak^{a}rā
happened that, 'my father's near how-many servants are, to-whom

khā-pī-kẵ adhik dhan bachai-chhaik; ham ēta bhūkhẽ
having-eaten-(and)-drunk much wealth remains-over; I here by-hunger

marai-chhī. Ham bāpak ōta jāeb, kah^{a}bai jē, "ham tōhar ō
am-dying. I father's there will-go, I-will-say that, "I of-thee and

Bhag^{a}bānak baṛ ap^{a}rādh kail. Ham tōhar bēṭā kahaibāk jōg
of-God great sin did. I thy son of-being-called worthy

nah^{i} chhiau. Ham^{a}rā tõ ap^{a}nā oh^{i}-ṭhām nōkar rākhâ." '
not am-by-thee. Me thou thine-own near a-servant keep." '

Ī-sabh bāt man-mẽ ṭhān^{i}, bāpak ōta chalal. Bāpak
These words mind-in having-resolved, father's there he-went. Father's

lag pahũchal. Lēkin jakhan pharakẵ-h^{i} chhal, ō-kar bāp
near he-arrived. But when at-a-distance-even he-was, his father

dekhitáh[i] mam[a]tak lēl; ok[a]rā dis jal[a]dī chal[a]lai; ok[a]rā gar[a]dan[i]-mẽ
on-seeing compassion took; his direction quickly he-went; his neck-on

lagā-kã chumbā lel[a]kaik. Bēṭā kahal[a]kai jē, 'bāp, ham
having-stuck kiss took. The-son said that, 'Father, I

tōhar Bhag[a]bānak baṛ ap[a]rādh kailáh[u]. Taĩ ham tōhar bēṭā
of-thee of-God great sin did-for-thee. Therefore I thy son

kahaibā jōg nah[i] chhī.' Ō-kar bāp eh[i]-par ap[a]nā nōkar-kẽ
(of)-being-called fit not am.' His father this-on his-own servants-to

kahal[a]kai jē, 'khūb nīk nīk nuā lā, ek[a]rā pahirā;
said that, 'very good good garment bring, on-this-(person) put-on;

aũṭhī hāth-mẽ dahī; pan[a]hī-sē pahirā-dahī; moṭāel bāchhā lā-kã
a-ring hand-on put; shoes-with clothe; the-fatted calf having-brought

mārâ, jē ham-sabh khā-pī-kã khusī karī.
kill, that we having-eaten-(and)-drunk happiness may-make.

Kiyăik-tau hamar bēṭā mar[i]-kã jī-ailai; ī bēṭā herā-gēl-
Because my son having-died has-come-to-life; this son had-been-

chhal, sē phēr bhēṭal.' Ī kah[i] sabh khusī
lost, he again has-been-got.' This saying all happiness

kara lāgal.
for-making began.

Jakhan ō-kar baṛ[a]kā bēṭā khēt-saũ ghar abait-rahai, gharak
When his elder son the-field-from home was-coming, of-the-house

naj[a]dīk nāch ō gān sun[a]lak. Ap[a]nā nōkar-saũ puchhal[a]kai je,
near dancing and singing he-heard. His-own servant-from he-asked that,

'āī kī chhiaik, jē nāch gān hoi-chhaik?' Ō-sabh kahal[a]kaik
this what is, that dancing singing is-occurring?' They said

jē, 'tōhar bhāī āel achh[i]; nīkē jekã̃ ailai-hai, taĩ tōhar
that, 'thy brother come is; well because he-is-come, therefore thy

bāp ēk moṭāel bāchhā măr[a]lak-hai.' Tāh[i]-par ō tam[a]sāe-gelai,
father a fatted calf has-killed.' That-on he became-angry,

ã̃gan nah[i] gēl Tal[?]hun ō-kar bāp bāhar āb[i] ok[a]rā
to-the-inner-court not went. Then his father outside having-come to-him

nehōrā kara lag[a]lai. Ō ap[a]nā bāp-saũ kah[a]lak jē, 'etek
entreaty to-make began. He his-own father-to said that, 'so-many

din-saũ ham tōhar sēbā kailiau. Toh[a]rā kah[a]lā-saũ kōnō kāj
days-from I thy service did-for-thee. Thy saying-from any action

bāhar nah[i] kail, taiō tõ ham[a]rā kahiō bak[a]rīk
outside not I-did, nevertheless thou to-me ever of-a-goat

bachch-ō nē khāe-lăī dēlâh, jē ham ap[a]ṇā dōst-sabhak
the-young-one-even not eating-for gavest, that I my-own friends-of

saṅgē khusī karitáhũ. Lēkin tōhar ī bēṭā, jē apan
with happiness might-have-made. But thy this son, who his-own

sabh dhan raṇḍī-bājī-mẽ ohā-kā̃ āel achhⁱ, takªrā-lāl tõ
all wealth harlotry-in having-squandered come is, him-for thou
moṭāel bāchhā mārªlā-achhⁱ.' Bāp kahalªkai, 'bēṭā, tõ har-dam
the-fatted calf hast-killed.' The-father said, 'son, thou always
hamªrā saṅg rahai-chhaī. Jē-kichhª dhan hamªrā achhⁱ, sē sabh tohar-ē
me with remainest. Whatever wealth to-me is, that all thine-even
chhiauk. Hamªrā-sabh-kẽ khūb khusī-kar būjh, jē tōhar
is-to-thee. To-us much happiness-of (there-is)-propriety, for thy
bhāī marⁱ-kā̃ phēr jī-ailau-achhⁱ.'
brother having-died again has-come-to-life-for-thee.'

SOUTHERN STANDARD MAITHILĪ.

Between the District of Darbhanga, and those Districts of Bengal proper in which the Bengali language is spoken, lie the northern portions of the Districts of Monghyr and Bhagalpur, and the entire Districts of Purnea and Malda, all of which lie north, or, in the case of Malda, north-east of the River Ganges. Purnea and Malda may be left out of consideration for the present. Northern Bhagalpur consists of two subdivisions, Supaul and Madhipura. The former is the northern of the two, and is bounded on the west by the Darbhanga District and on the east by the low country which contains the shifting bed of the River Kusi, and which separates it from the District of Purnea. The language and people of Supaul are the same as that of Northern and Central Darbhanga, and the specimens previously given for that area, will also do for the dialect spoken in it. Going from west to east in order, the Samastipur subdivision of Darbhanga, North Monghyr, and the Madhipura subdivision of Bhagalpur form a belt of land on the northern bank of the Ganges, in which also Maithilī is spoken, but not quite so purely as in the true Standard Maithilī tract of Central and North Darbhanga. A grammar of the form of the dialect here spoken will be found in part V of the *Seven Grammars of the Dialects and Sub-dialects of the Bihārī Language*, written by the present author. The following are the chief points of difference between it and Standard Maithilī :—

A. PRONUNCIATION—

The principal difference is that the rule of shortening the antepenultimate vowel is not followed in the case of the Simple Present of a verb. Thus, 'he sees,' is *dēkhai*, not *dekhai* as in Standard Maithilī.

B. NOUNS—

Anotner termination of the Genitive is *ke*. Before the Genitive termination *k*, a final long vowel is shortened. Thus, from *nēnā*, a boy, one form of the Genitive is *nēnak*, not *nēnāk*, as in Standard Maithilī. The Locative in *ē*, which is rare in Standard Maithilī, is much more common in this southern form of the dialect.

C. PRONOUNS—

The Genitives of the Personal Pronouns are as follows,—*mōr*, *mōre*, or *mōra* ; *hamar*, *ham*ᵉ*re*, or *ham*ᵉ*ra* ; *tōr*, *tōre*, or *tōra* ; *tōhar*, *toh*ᵉ*re*, or *toh*ᵉ*ra*. The Honorific pronoun of the second person is *āis*, *ahā̃*, or *ap*ᵉ*ne*. The Genitives of *jē*, who ; *sē*, he ; and *kī*, who? ; are *jē-kar*, *tē-kar*, and *kē-kar*, respectively. The corresponding oblique forms are *jek*ᵉ*rā*, *tek*ᵉ*rā*, and *kek*ᵉ*rā*. The oblique form of *kī*, what?, is *kathī*, *kethī*, *kāhe*, *kah'*, or *kiyē*.

D. VERBS—

The following are the terminations used in the Simple Present, and in the Past, Indicative and Conditional. The four Forms have the same power as in Standard Maithilī :—

Person.	Form I.	Form II.	Form III.	Form IV.
1	*ū̃*, *ō̃*, or *aū*	Same as Form IV	*ī*, *iai* (Fem. *ī̃*)	*iainh*.
2	*ē* (Fem. *ī*), *ē̃*, *ai*, *aī̃*, *hī̃*, or *hīk*.	Same as Form IV	*āh*, *ā*, *hau*, or *hauk*	*hunh*.
3	*ai* or *aik*	Same as Form IV	*ath*, *ath'*, *ā* (Fem. *ī*), or *anh* (Fem. *inh*.)	*thinh*, *hinh*.

The Past tense Indicative of transitive verbs has the following terminations in the third person :—

Forms I and II.—*ak*, *kaik*. Form III.—*kā*, *ē̃*, *anh*, *āt*. Fem. *kī*, *inh*, *īt*. Form IV.—*hinh*, *khinh*.

In the case of intransitive verbs, the second person has the following terminations:—

Form I.—*ā*, *haĩ*, *hā*.

In the third person, Form I either drops all terminations, or else take one of the following,—*ē*, *ai*, and, in North Monghyr, *a*. The terminations of Forms III and IV are those given above in the table, with, in addition, *ē*, *āt* ; fem. *īt*.

In addition to the above, the following terminations may be used in the Past tense of any verb, whether transitive or intransitive:—

Form I.—1st person, *ā̃* (only in North Monghyr); 3rd person, *kai*.

Form III.—1st person, *ianh*, *ihanh*; 2nd person, *hā*.

The following are the terminations of the Future:—

Person.	Form I.	Form III.	Forms II and IV.
1	*bō̃*, *bai*, *baik*	*ab*	*bainh*.
2	*bē*, *bẽ*, *bai*, *baĩ*, *bhẽ*, *bhaĩ*, *bhĩ*, *bhik*	*bāh*, *bā*, *bhau*, *bhauk* . . .	*bhunh*.
3	*at*, *tai*, *taik*; (Fem.) *aiti* . .	*tanh* (Fem. *tinh*), *tā* (Fem. *tī*), *tāt* (Fem. *tīt*), *tath'*.	*thinh*, *thanī*.

As in Standard Maithilī, the object influences the form of the verb which should be used. The following rules illustrate this:—

Forms I and II are used when the subject is non-honorific. Forms III and IV when it is honorific.

Forms II and IV are used when the object, direct or remote, is mentioned with respect.

When the object, direct or remote, is in the second person, an *ai* or *aik* in any termination of the first or third person is changed to *au* or *auk*, respectively. The terminations *hĩ*, *ai*, and *aik*, are only used when the object, direct or remote, is inferior to the subject. So also *au* and *auk*, except that, when they are pronounced with a kind of drawl, the object is mentioned with some, though not great, respect.

AUXILIARY VERBS—

Instead of *hai*, he is, the following forms are also used:—*ah'*, *ah*, *eh*, *yeh*, *ya*, *ha*, *ehai*.

Besides the base '*chha*' which we meet in Standard Maithilī, there is also a base *chhika*. Thus, *chhikai*, he is. A common form of the 3rd singular of the simple verb is *achh*, or *chha*, instead of *achh'*.

In Madhipura, the Past Participle of the verb *hōeb*, to become, is *hōl*, as well as the *bhēl* of Standard Maithilī.

AUTHORITY—

GRIERSON, G. A.,—*Seven Grammars of the Dialects and Sub-dialects of the Bihārī Language*. Part V. *South Maithilī*. *Dialect of South Darbhangā, North Munger, and the Madhepūrā subdivision of Bhagalpūr*. Calcutta, 1885.

The first of the following specimens is a portion of the Parable of the Prodigal Son, in the form of the dialect spoken in Madhipura. As the dialect so closely resembles Standard Maithilī, and as other specimens will be given, it is unnecessary to give the entire Parable.

Note the tendency to throw a final short *i*, by epenthesis, into the preceding syllable. Thus *chail*, for *chal'*, having gone; *paiṛ* for *paṛ'*, having fallen, and *bā̃eṭ*, i.e., *bā̃iṭ*, for *bā̃ṭ'*, having divided. Note, also, the form *kar'-kāi-kō̃*, having done.

[No. 7.]

INDO-ARYAN FAMILY. EASTERN GROUP.

BIHĀRĪ.

MAITHILĪ DIALECT (SOUTHERN VARIETY). (MADHIPURA, BHAGALPUR.)

SPECIMEN I.

કોઇ આદમી કે દુઇ વેટા છલૈ। છોટકા વેટા અપના વાપ કે કહલકૈ કિ
હમ્મર હિસ્સા ધન વાંટ દેઅ। ઓકર વાપ દૂનો ભાઇ કે ધન વાંટ દેલકૈ।
કુછુ દિનક વાદ છોટકા વેટા ધન સવ જમા કરિ કૈ કોં કોનો આઉર મુલુક
કે ચૈલ દેલકૈ। તવ આપન ધન સવ ઔખીનિક પાછાં વેરવાદ કૈ દેલકૈ
જખન ઊ સવ ખરચ કૈ દેલકૈ તવ ઓને વૈડ અકાલ પૈડ ગેલૈ। તવ ઊ આદમી
ગરીવ હોવૈ લાગલ। તવ સહર મેં કોનો આદમી કોતે ઊ નોકર રહિ ગેલ॥

TRANSLITERATION AND TRANSLATION.

Kōe ādᵃmī-kē dui bēṭā chhalai. Chhoṭᵃkā bēṭā apᵃnā bāp-kē
A-certain man-to two sons were. The-younger son his-own father-to

kahalᵃkai ki, 'hammar hissā dhan bā̃eṭ dēā.' Ōkar bāp dūnō
said that, 'my share wealth having-divided give.' His father the-two

bhāī-kē dhan bā̃eṭ delᵃkai. Kuchhᵘ dinak bād chhoṭᵃkā bēṭā dhan
brothers-to wealth having-divided gave. Some of-days after the-younger son wealth

sab jamā karⁱ-kăī-kō̃, kōno āur muluk-kē chail-delᵃkai. Tab āpan dhan
all collected having-made, some other country-to went-away. Then his-own wealth

sab aukhinik pāchhā̃ berᵃbād kăī-delᵃkai. Jakhan ū sab kharach kăī-delᵃkai, tab
all revelry-of after wasted he-made. When he all spent had-made, then

ōnē baiṛ akāl paiṛ gelai. Tab ū ādᵃmī garīb hōwăī lāgal.
there a-great famine having-fallen went. Then that man poor to-be began.

Tab sahar-mē̃ kōno ādᵃmī kōtē ū nōkar rahⁱ-gēl.
Then the-city-in a-certain man near he a-servant remained.

The next specimen comes from the Begusarai Subdivision of North Monghyr. It is a folk-tale, illustrating the proverbial folly of a Jolahā, or man of the weaver caste. The Jolahās are the wise men of Gotham of Bihār folk-tales.

The original is given in facsimile, as it is a good specimen of the Kaithī character of North Monghyr.

[No. 8.]

INDO-ARYAN FAMILY.

EASTERN GROUP.

BIHĀRĪ.

MAITHILĪ DIALECT (SOUTHERN VARIETY). (BEGUSARAI, NORTHERN MONGHYR.)

SPECIMEN II.

A FOLK-TALE.

[illegible]

[illegible]

[illegible]

[illegible]

[illegible]

[illegible]

[illegible]

[illegible]

[illegible]

[illegible]

[illegible]

[illegible]

[illegible]

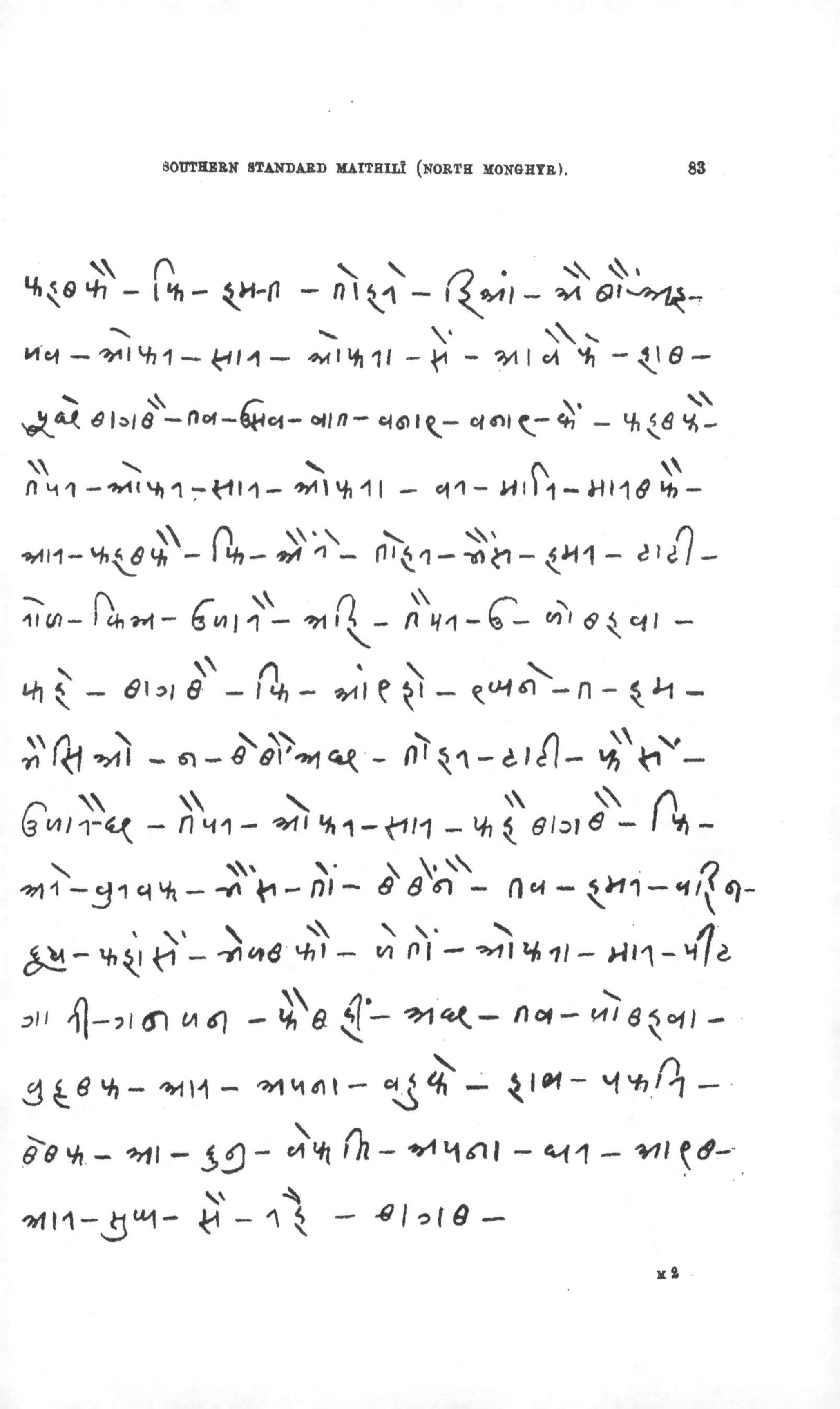

[illegible]

[No. 8.]

INDO-ARYAN FAMILY. EASTERN GROUP.

BIHĀRĪ.

MAITHILĪ DIALECT (SOUTHERN VARIETY). (BEGUSARAI, NORTHERN MONGHYR.)

SPECIMEN II.

A FOLK-TALE.

TRANSLITERATION AND TRANSLATION.

Kōi gā̃w-mē̃ ēgō jol^{a}hā rahai. Jab ō kamāet kamāet
A-certain village-in a weaver was. When he labouring labouring
das pand^{r}ah rupaiā jaur kailak, tab ap^{n}ā maugī-sē̃ kah^{a}lak ki,
ten fifteen rupees collected made, then his-own wife-to he-said that,
'ai rupaiā-sē̃ ham bhaĩs mōl-lēb, ār ō-kar dūdh dahī khāeb.'
'these rupees-with I a-buffalo will-buy, and its milk (and) tyre will-eat.'
Oi-par jolah^{a}niā̃ kahal^{a}kai ki, 'ham-hū̃ dūdh dahī laihar
That-on the-weaver's wife said that, 'I-also milk (and) tyre to-my-father's-house
paṭhāel karab.' Ī bāt sun^{i}-kē̃ jolah^{a}wā khisiāe-kē̃ ok^{a}rā
sending will-do.' This word having-heard the-weaver having-become-angry her
bar mār^{i} mǎral^{a}kai, ār kahal^{a}kai ki, ' 'ham-ta dūdh dahī
a-great beating beat, and said that, 'I-on-my-part milk (and) tyre
khaibē na kailī-ah, ī laih^{a}rē paṭhaitī.' Tai-par
eating-even not have-done, this-(woman) to-her-father's-house will-send.' That-on
ōkar maugī rūs^{i}-kē̃ lahirā chal^{a}lai. Tab jolah^{a}wā
his wife having-been-huffed to-her-father's-house went. Then the-weaver
ok^{a}rā pāchh^{u} pāchh^{u} phirābāī-lēl chalal. Jāet jāet apan
her behind behind causing-her-to-return-for went. Going going his-own
sasurār gēl. Tab ō-kar sār ok^{a}rā-sē̃ puchhal^{a}kai
father-in-law's-house he-reached. Then his brother-in-law him-from asked
ki, 'Tō̃ kahā̃ ailē̃-achh?' Tai-par ō jolah^{a}wā kahal^{a}kai ki, 'ham-ta
that, 'You where have-come?' That-on that weaver said that, 'I-on-the-one-hand
toh^{a}rē hiā̃ ailaũ-ah.' Jab ō-kar sār ok^{a}rā-sē̃ ābāī-ke
to-you only-here have-come.' When his brother-in-law him-from coming-of
hāl pūchhe lāg^{a}lai, tab ō sab bāt banāe-banāe-kē̃
the-reason asking began, then he the-whole affair constructing-constructing
kahal^{a}kai. Tai-par ō-kar sār ok^{a}rā bar mār^{i} māral^{a}kai, ār kahal^{a}kai
told. That-on his brother-in-law him a-great beating beat, and said
ki, 'aī-rē! tōhar bhaĩs hamar ṭāṭī rōj kia ujārai-ah^{i}?' Tai-par
that, 'Ah! your buffalo my mat-fence every-day why destroys?' That-on

ō jolah^{a}wā kahe lăg^{a}lai ki, 'ā̃e-hō, ekh^{a}nē-ta ham bhăĭsi-ō
that weaver saying began that, 'Oh! oh! now-even-on-the-one-hand I a-buffalo-even

na lelaũ-achh. Tōhar ṭāṭī kaisẽ ujārai-chha?' Tai-par ō-kar sār
not have-got. Your mat-fence how is-it-destroying?' That-on his brother-in-law

kahăĭ lăg^{a}lai ki, 'arē bur^{a}bak, bhaĩs tõ lēlẽ nai, tab hamar bahin dūdh
saying began that, 'O fool! a-buffalo you did-get not, then my sister milk

kahā̃-sẽ bhejhal^{a}kau jē tõ ok^{a}rā mār pīṭ gāri gañjan
where-from sent-of-thine that you her beating striking abuse distress

kail^{a}hī-achh?' Tab jolah^{a}wā bujh^{a}lak, ār ap^{a}nā bah^{u}-ke hāth pakar^{i}
have-done?' Then the-weaver understood, and his-own wife's hand seizing

lēlak, ā dun^{u} bēkat^{i} ap^{a}nā ghar āel, ār sukh-sẽ rahăĭ
took, and the-two persons their-own house came, and happiness-with to-remain

lāgal.
began.

FREE TRANSLATION OF THE FOREGOING.

In a certain village there dwelt a weaver. When he had saved some ten or fifteen rupees by honest labour, he said to his wife, 'I'll buy a buffalo with this money, and drink the milk and tyre which I get from it.' His wife replied, 'and I'll send some milk and tyre regularly to my own people.' This reply angered the weaver, and he gave her a sound drubbing, saying, 'before I've eaten my milk and tyre, this creature wants to send it to her father's house.' Then up got his wife, and went off in a huff to her own people. The weaver followed her in the hope of bringing her back, and at length reached his father-in-law's. There he met his brother-in-law, who asked him why he had come, 'O, as for me,' he said, 'I've only come to see *you*.' The brother-in-law, however cross-questioned him, and the weaver told him the whole story in detail. Thereon the brother-in-law gave *him* a sound drubbing, crying, as he did so, 'Ah, then, so it's your buffalo that breaks down my fence every day!' The weaver cried between the blows, 'Oh! Oh! Why I don't even own a buffalo, so how can it have broken down your fence.' Then said the brother-in-law, 'You fool! If you had not a buffalo, how did my sister send the milk here about which you gave her all that beating and abuse?' Then the weaver understood, and took his wife by the hand and brought her home, and there they lived happy ever afterwards.

EASTERN MAITHILĪ OR GAŌWĀRĪ.

The language of the greater part of Purnea District closely resembles the South Maithilī with which we have just been dealing. East of the Mahananda, however, the bulk of the population speaks a form of Northern Bengali, which has already been described, under the head of that language. We may, therefore, say that Maithilī is the language of Central and Western Purnea, as contrasted with the Bengali of the East of the District. Over this tract, and especially in the West, people of the Brāhmaṇ caste speak pure Standard Maithilī similar to what is spoken in North Darbhanga, and in the Supaul Subdivision of Bhagalpur. The number of speakers of this Standard dialect in the District is estimated at 30,000. The corrupt Maithilī which is illustrated by the following specimens is spoken by the illiterate classes throughout the centre and west of the District, and, even to the east of the River Mahananda by Hindūs. The Bengali of the east of the District is principally spoken by Muhammadans. This corrupt form of Maithilī is locally known as Gāōwārī, or the village dialect. If it is desired to give it a more definite name, we may call it Eastern Maithilī. It is estimated that it is spoken by 1,300,000 speakers.

To the above, 1,300,000 speakers of Eastern Maithilī, should be added the 2,300 Thārūs who inhabit the northern part of the District, who, so far as I can gather, speak a corrupt form of the dialect.

Full particulars regarding the Thārūs will be found on pp. 311 and ff, under the head of Bhojpurī. Unfortunately, in Purnea, they are so wild that it has been found impossible to procure any specimens of their language.

The total number of speakers of Eastern Maithilī is therefore 1,302,300.

The principal points of difference between it and Standard Maithilī are the following:—

I. PRONUNCIATION.—As in Southern Maithilī, in the Simple Present, a long vowel is not shortened before *ai* or *au*. Thus, *dēkhai*, not *dekhai*, he sees.

II. NOUNS.—The termination of the Genitive is *k*, *ke*, *kar* or *kŏr*.

III. PRONOUNS.—One form of the nominative of the pronoun of the first person is *hammẽ*, and of the second person, *tōhẽ*. The genitive singular sometimes ends in *e*; thus, *tōhar* or *toh*ᵃ*re*, thy. The Honorific Pronoun of the second person is *ap'ne*, *ihā̃*, or *ahā̃*. The Demonstrative pronouns are *i*, *ī*, *ẽ*, *ihāy*, *ethī*, or *ithī*, this, and *ū*, *wẽ*, *wahāy*, or *uthī*, that. The genitives of *jē*, who; *sē*, he; and *kē*, who? are *jakar* or *jē-kar*; *takar* or *tēkar*; and *kakar* or *kē-kar*, respectively. The corresponding oblique forms are *jak*ᵃ*rā* or *jek*ᵃ*rā*; *tak*ᵃ*rā* or *tek*ᵃ*rā*; and *kak*ᵃ*rā* or *kek*ᵃ*rā*. 'What?' is *kī* or *kā*, oblique, *kathī* or *kithī*. Anyone, someone, is *kōi*, oblique, *kathū*, *kōnō*, *kak*ᵃ*ro*, *kek*ᵃ*ro*, or *kek*ᵃ*rahau*. Anything, something, is *kuchh* or *kuchh*ᵘ, oblique, *kuchh*, *kuchh*ᵘ, or *kethī*. The plural of all pronouns is formed by adding *sab*, *sibī*, *sī*, or *ār*.

IV. VERBS.—In Standard Maithilī, there are four sets of forms to each person, depending on the respect shown both to the subject and the object. In the first form, the subject is non-honorific, and the object also non-honorific. In the second, the subject is non-honorific, but the object is honorific. In the third, the subject is honorific, and the object non-honorific. In the fourth, both are honorific. In Eastern Maithilī, the forms in which special honour is shown to the object have almost disappeared, that is to say, only the first and third forms are in common use. A few isolated instances of the fourth form will be mentioned subsequently.

As in Standard Maithilī, the plural is the same as the singular. The first person is often used honorifically instead of the second.

The following are the terminations used in the Simple Present, the Past, and the Past Conditional:—

Person.	Form I.	Form III.
1	*ū̃̄, ō, aū̃, āū̃,* or *ā̃̄*	*ī, iai.*
2	*ā, ē, ē̃,* or *aĩ*	*ā̂, hâk, hauk.*
3	*ai, aik*	*at.*

In the Past tense, the third person singular also may end in *kai* or *kaik*, and, in the case of transitive verbs, in *ak*. In the case of intransitive verbs, we may also have, for the same person, the termination *kā*.

For the Future, we have the following terminations:—

Person.	Form I.	Form III.
1	*bai, bō̃* or *baū̃*	*ah, bī.*
2	*bā, bē, bē̃, baĩ, bhē̃,* or *mē̃*	*bâ, bᵃhâk, bhauk.*
3	*at, tai, it, itai, tah, itah*	...

ibai, ibō̃, etc., may be substituted for *bai, bō̃,* etc., thus resembling the Bengali form. Eastern Maithilī *dekhibō̃,* is equivalent to the Bengali *dēkhiba,* pronounced *dekhibō,* I will see.

Regarding the use of these persons, it may be said that, as a rule, forms ending in *ai* or *aik* are used when the direct or remote object of the sentence is inferior to the subject. Moreover, when such terminations have the object, direct or remote, in the second person, they are changed, as in Standard Maithilī, to *au* and *auk,* respectively.

In the second and third persons, we sometimes find a termination *ain* used when special respect is shown to the object, direct or remote. If it is in the second person, this *ain* becomes *aun.* These are the only relics of the second and fourth forms of Standard Maithilī.

AUXILIARY VERBS—

The initial *h* of the Standard Maithilī *hai,* he is, is dropped, and we have *ai.* This verb forms a future, *haibai,* I shall be, which is conjugated throughout.

Besides the base '*chha,*' we have also a strengthened base '*chhika.*' Thus, *chhai, achh,* or *chhikai,* he is.

The Past tense of the verb *hōeb,* to become, is *hōl,* not *bhēl,* as in Standard Maithilī. In this, also, we see an approach to Bengali. *Bhēl* is, however, also used. 'Having become,' is *bhē-ke.*

FINITE VERBS—

The Past Participle in Standard Maithilī ends in *al,* thus, *dēkhal,* seen. In Eastern Maithilī it may also end in *il.* Thus, *dēkhil.* This is specially the case in Central

Purnea, on the Bengali Frontier. The same termination may also optionally be preserved in the tenses derived from that participle. Thus, Past, *dekhᵃlai* or *dekhilai*, he saw. Here again, we see the shading off into Bengali, which has *dekhilen.* Sometimes *in* is substituted for *l*, as in *kainē-chhaun*, for *kailē-chhaun*, (thy father) has made.

AUTHORITY—

GRIERSON, G. A.,—*Seven Grammars of the Dialects and Sub-dialects of the Bihárí Language.* Part VIII.—*Maithil-Bangálí Dialect of Central and Western Puraniyá.* Calcutta, 1887.

The first specimen is the Parable of the Prodigal Son. It is printed in the Kaithī character, and as the copy sent by the Collector is an excellent example of the way in which that character is written in Purnea, it is printed in facsimile. With it is given a transliteration into the Roman character. It has not been thought necessary to give an interlinear translation.

The second specimen is a popular song. It is printed in Kaithī type, and is accompanied by a transliteration and an interlinear and a free translation.

As usual, in written Kaithī, the spelling is capricious. The mistakes have been silently corrected in the transliteration of the first specimen.

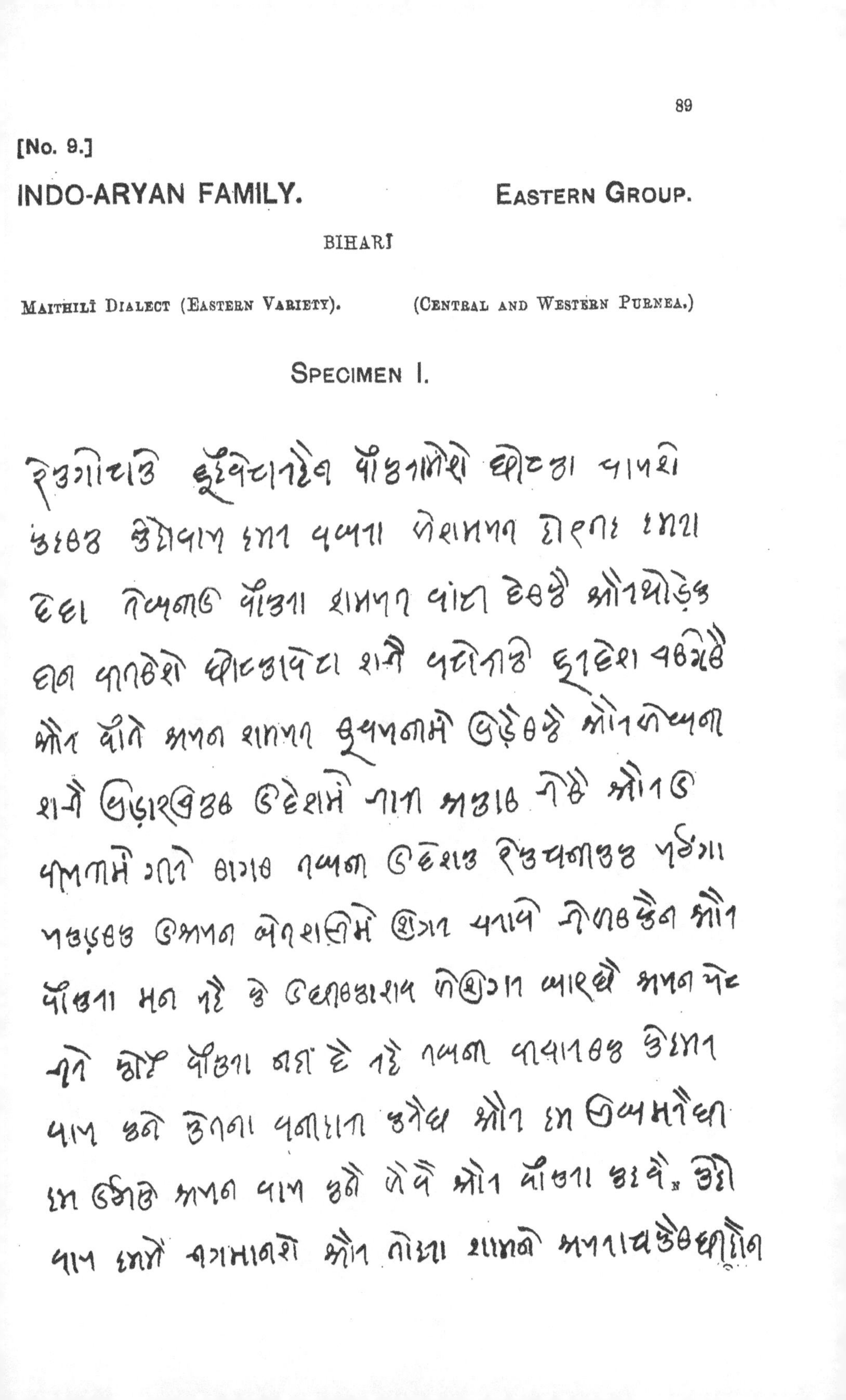

[No. 9.]

INDO-ARYAN FAMILY. EASTERN GROUP.

BIHARĪ

MAITHILĪ DIALECT (EASTERN VARIETY). (CENTRAL AND WESTERN PURNEA.)

SPECIMEN I.

[illegible]

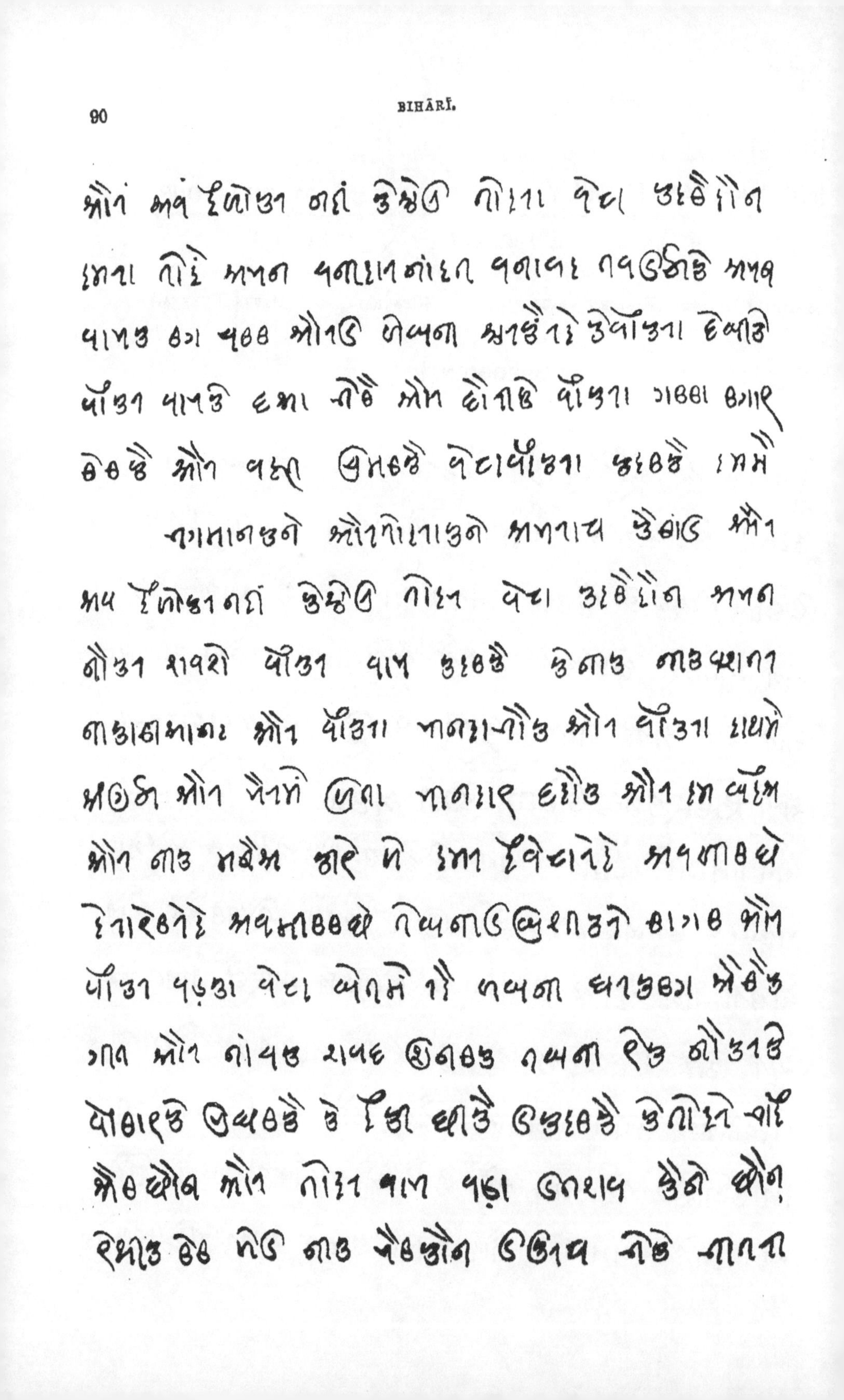

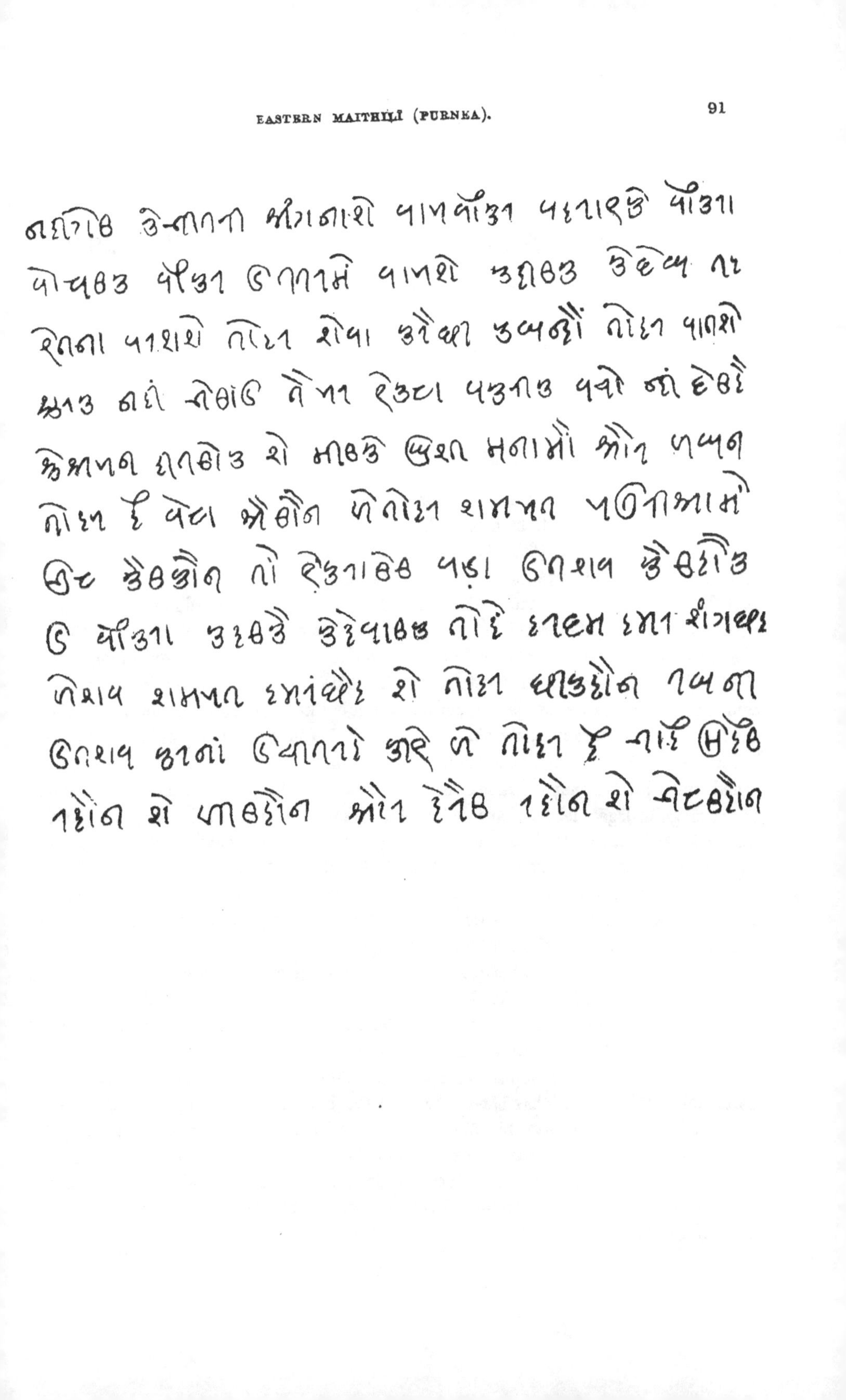

[illegible]

[No. 9.]

INDO-ARYAN FAMILY. EASTERN GROUP.

BIHĀRĪ.

MAITHILĪ DIALECT (EASTERN VARIETY). (CENTRAL AND WESTERN PURNEA.)

SPECIMEN I.

TRANSLITERATION.

Ek gōṭā-kē dui bēṭā rahain. Ok^{a}rā-mẽ-sē chhoṭ^{a}kā bāp-sē kah^{a}lak ke, 'hō bāp, hamar bakh^{a}rā jē sampat hōetah ha^{a}mrā dē-dā.' Tekh^{a}nī ū ok^{a}rā sampat bā̃ṭ^{i} del^{a}kai. Aur thōṛek din bit^{a}lē-sē chhoṭ^{a}kā bēṭā sabhai baṭōr^{i}-ke dūr dēs chal gelai, aur ōtē apan sampat luch^{a}panī-mẽ buṛail^{a}kai. Aur jekh^{a}nī sabhai buṛāe chukal ū dēs-mẽ bhārī akāl bhelai, aur ū bip^{a}ti-mẽ gire lāgal. Takh^{a}nī ū dēsak ēk dhanikak paṭhaṅgā[1] pakaṛ^{a}lak. Ū apan khēt sabh^{a}-mẽ sūgar charābe bhejal^{a}kain, aur ok^{a}rā man rahai ke ū chhil^{a}kā sab jē sūgar khāe-chhai apan pēṭ bharē. Kōi ok^{a}rā nahī̃ dai-rahai, takh^{a}nī bichār^{a}lak ke, 'hamar bāp kanē ket^{a}nā banihārī karaichh, aur ham bhūkh marai-chhī, ham uṭhi-ke apan bāp kanai jaibai, aur ok^{a}rā kah^{a}bai ke, "hō bāp, hammẽ Bhag^{a}mān-sē aur toh^{a}rā sām^{a}nē ap^{a}rādh kail-chhihaun, aur ab ī jōkar nahī̃ ke phēr^{a} toh^{a}rā bēṭā kah^{a}lai-haun. Ham^{a}rā tōhẽ apan banihār nā̃hat banābâh."' Tab uṭh^{i}-ke apan bāpak lag chalal, aur ū jekh^{a}nī phar^{a}kaī̃ rahē ke ok^{a}rā dekh^{i}-ke ōkar bāp-kē dayā bhelai; aur dauṛ^{i}-ke ok^{a}rā gallā lagāe lel^{a}kai; aur bahut chumalkai. Bēṭā ok^{a}rā kahal^{a}kai, 'hammai Bhag^{a}mān kanē aur toh^{a}rā kanē ap^{a}rādh kailāũ, aur ab ī jōkar nahī̃ ke phēr^{a} tōhar bēṭā kah^{a}lai-haun.' Apan naukar sab-sē ōkar bāp kahal^{a}kai ke, 'nīk nīk bastar nikāl[1] ānâh, aur ok^{a}rā pinhābhauk; aur ok^{a}rā hāth mẽ ā̃guṭhī, aur pair-mẽ jutā pinhāē dahauk, aur ham khaïa, aur nīk manaia, kiē jē hamar ī bēṭā (muil) rahe, ab jīl chhē; herāel-rahē ab milal-chhē.' Tekh^{a}nī ū khusī kare lāgal.

Aur ōkar baṛ^{a}kā bēṭā khēt-mẽ rahai. Jakh^{a}nī gharak lag ailaik gīt āur nā̃chak sabad sun^{a}lak. Takh^{a}nī ēk naukar-kē bolāe-ke puchhal^{a}kai ke, 'ī kī chhikai?' Ū kahal^{a}kai ke, 'toh^{a}re bhāī ail-chhaun, aur tōhar bāp baṛā utsab kaine-chhaun, ethik lēl jē ū nīk pail^{a}kaun.' Ū kur^{a}dh bhē-ke bhit^{a}rī nahī̃ gēl; ke bhit^{a}rī ā̃g^{a}nā-sē bap ōkar bah^{a}rāe-ke ok^{a}rā bodh^{a}lak. Ōkar uttar-mẽ bāp-sē kahilak ke, 'dēkhâ tah, et^{a}nā baras-sē tōhar sēbā karaichhī; kakhan^{a} haũ tōhar bāt-sē pharak nahī̃ bhelāũ; tai par ēk-ṭā bak^{a}rīk bach-chō nahī̃ delâ-hai, ke apan hit-lōk-sē mil-ke khusī manāmaũ; aur jakhan tōhar ī bēṭā ailaun, jē tōhar sampat paturiā-mẽ bhuṭ-kail^{a}kaun tõ ek^{a}rā lēl baṛā utsab kail^{a}hauk.' Ū ok^{a}rā kahal^{a}kai, ke, 'hē bālak, tōhẽ har-dam hamar saṅg chhâh; jē sab sampat hamar chhaih, sē tōhar chhik^{a}haun. Takh^{a}nī utsab kar^{a}nā̃ uchit rahe, kiē jē tōhar ī bhāī muil rahaun sē jīl^{a}haun; aur heraũ-rahaun sē bhēṭ^{a}l^{a}haun.'

---

[1] Protection.

[No. 10.]

INDO-ARYAN FAMILY. EASTERN GROUP.

BIHĀRĪ.

MAITHILĪ DIALECT (EASTERN VARIETY). (CENTRAL AND WESTERN PURNEA.)

SPECIMEN II.

A FOLK-SONG.

કથી વિનુ મુહમાં મલિન ભેલ સખિઆ હે। કથી વિનુ દેહિઆરે ઝમરી ગેલનાં।
પાન વિનુ મુહમાંરે મલિન ભેલ સખિઆ હે। પિઆ વિનુ દેહિઆરે ઝમરી ગેલનાં।
ગરજી ઉઠલ ઘન ઘોર સખિઆ હે। સેહો દેખિ ડરલ જિવ મોર સખિઆ હે।
ધરવૈ જોગિનિ કર ભેસ મેં સખિઆ હે। કરવૈ મેં પિઆ કે ઉદેસ સખિઆ હે।

TRANSLITERATION AND TRANSLATION.

Kathi binu muhamā̃ malina bhela, Sakhiā hē,
What without face pale became, Friend O,

Kathi binu dehiā, re, jhamari gela nā̃?
What without body, ah, emaciated went O?

Pāna binu muhamā̃, re, malina bhela, Sakhiā hē,
Betel without face, ah, pale become, Friend O,

Piā binu dehiā, re, jhamari gela nā̃.
Beloved without body, ah, emaciated went O.

Garaji uṭhala ghana ghōra, Sakhiā hē,
Roaring rose clouds terrible, Friend O,

Sē-hō dēkhi ḍarala jība mōra, Sakhiā hē.
That-also seeing feared life my, Friend O.

Dharabai jōgini-kara bhēsa mē̃, Sakhiā hē,
I-will-take ascetic-of guise I, Friend O,

Karabai mē̃ piā-ke udēsa, Sakhiā hē.
Will-do I beloved-of search, Friend O.

FREE TRANSLATION OF THE FOREGOING

For want of what has your face become pale, O Friend ?
For want of what has your body become emaciated ?
For want of betel, my face has become pale, O Friend,
For want of my Beloved, has my body become emaciated.
The clouds have risen with a sound of thunder, O Friend,
When I see that also, my soul is terrified, O Friend.
I will assume the garb of an ascetic, O Friend,
And will search for my beloved, O Friend.

CHHIKĀ-CHHIKĪ BŌLĪ.

This dialect is almost confined to the south of the Ganges. The only exception is a small tract on the north of the Ganges, in the south of the Gogri Thana of the Monghyr District, in which Chhikā-chhikī has intruded into the territory which properly belongs to Southern Standard Maithilī. It is spoken in the eastern part of South Monghyr, in South Bhagalpur, except in a small tract in the west of the Banka Subdivision, and in the north and west of the Sonthal Parganas, where it is separated from Bengali, by the range of hills running from the north-east to the south-west through the centre of that District. This mountain chain forms a natural barrier which precludes the existence of an intermediate form of speech between the two languages. Only in the south-west of the District, in the Subdivision of Deoghur (Dēogaṛh) is there a small tract, south and east of the town of Deoghur, where the two languages overlap without combining, Maithilī being spoken by people from Bihār, and Bengali by those of Bengal. The state of affairs is illustrated in the map opposite. It will, of course, be understood that this description takes no account of the Muṇḍā and Dravidian languages which are spoken in the Sonthal Parganas and the neighbouring Districts. Here the aborigines live more or less side by side with the speakers of Aryan languages, and in some parts of the Sonthal Parganas, as many as four languages are spoken by different tribes of people living in the same locality.

The following is the estimated number of people speaking Chhikā-chhikī Bōlī.

Name of District.	Number of Speakers.
Monghyr	200,000
Bhagalpur	920,000
Sonthal Parganas . . .	599,781
TOTAL .	1,719,781

The name 'Chhikā-chhikī' is that given to the dialect in Bhagalpur. In Monghyr, it is simply called Maithilī, which is misleading. In the Sonthal Parganas, it appears to have been considered to be a kind of Magahī, but this, as will be subsequently shown, is incorrect. It is called 'Chhikā-chhikī Bōlī,' owing to the frequence with which the word *chhikai*, meaning 'he is,' and its congeners is used. It is unnecessary to describe the grammar of this form of the dialect in detail. It closely resembles the language spoken north of the river in Madhipura and Purnea. Suffice it to draw attention to two peculiarities which it shares with the dialect spoken in Monghyr. The first is the fondness which it has for adding the sound of 'o' in the English word 'hot' to the end of words. This sound it represents by the letter ऑ, which is represented in transliteration by ŏ. It should be remembered that, in the following specimen, every ŏ at the end of a word is pronounced ŏ, like the 'o' in the word 'hot.' Thus, what in Standard Maithilī would be *apan*, own, becomes in South Bhagalpur *apᵃnŏ,* pronounced *ap'nŏ*. The other peculiarity is the tendency there is to lengthen a final short *i*. Thus, instead of the Standard Maithilī *karⁱ*, having done, South Bhagalpur has *karī*. The local dialect has other peculiarities which are not illustrated in the specimen. These can be learnt from the grammar mentioned below.

The language of Bhagalpur is partly influenced by the Bengali spoken in the neighbouring districts of Bengal. Excluding the Sonthal Parganas, it is the most eastern of the South-Gangetic Districts in which Bihārī in any form is spoken. It is of some special interest, because, so far as I know, the first translation of any portion of the Bible into a vernacular language of Northern India of which we have any record was made into it. Some time at the end of the 18th century 'Antonio, a Roman Catholic Missionary at Boglipur on the Ganges, translated the Gospels and the Acts into the dialect of the people of that District.'[1] It is to be regretted that no trace of this translation can now be found.

AUTHORITY—

GRIERSON, G. A.,—*Seven Grammars of the Dialects and Sub-dialects of the Bihārī Language.* Calcutta, 1887. Part VII.—*South Maithilī-Baṅgālī Dialect of South Bhagalpūr.* Calcutta, 1887.

The following specimen of the dialect is a translation of the Parable of the Prodigal Son. It is printed in the Dēva-nāgarī character, and is accompanied by a transliteration into the Roman character. The dialect so closely resembles that of the country across the Ganges, that an interlinear translation is unnecessary. Although printed in the Dēva-nāgarī character, it should be understood that the usual character employed in Bhagalpur, as in other parts of Bihār, is the Kaithī.

[1] *Calcutta Review*, Vol. v, June, 1846, p. 722. Also *Journal* of the Bengal Asiatic Society, Vol. lxii, 1893, pp. 41 and ff.

[No. II.]

INDO-ARYAN FAMILY. EASTERN GROUP.

BIHĀRĪ.

MAITHILĪ (CHHIKĀ-CHHIKĪ BŌLĪ) DIALECT. (SOUTH BHAGALPUR.)

एक आदमी के दू बेटा रहै। ओकरा में से छोटका अपनो बाप से कहलकै कि बाबू जे धन हमरा बखरा में होय ऊ हमरा दै दे। एकरा पर ऊ अपनो धन ओकरा बाँटी देलकै। आरो थोड़ी दिन भी नय बितलै कि ओकरो छोटका बेटा सब अपनो धन इकट्ठा करि के कोइ दोसरो देश घूमै लै चली गेलै आरो वहाँ अपनो सब धन के ऐश जैश में खरच करी देलकै। तबे वो मुलुक में बड़ी अकाल पड़लै आरू ऊ कंगाल होय गेलै। ऊ वो देश के नगर बासी के यहाँ गेलै आरो वहाँ रहै लगलै। ऊ ओकरा अपनो खेत में सूअर चरावै लै भेजी देलकै। ऊ ओकरा खावै लै नय देतियै। तबे ऊ हरख होई के अपनो पेट भूसा सें भरी लेतियै जे सूअर के खाय लै देल जाय रहै। जबे ओकरा होस भेलै तबे ऊ अपनो मनो में कहे लगलै कि हमरो बाप के एतना धन छै कि केतै नौकर खाय रहलो छै आरु बचै भी छै। जबे हमे भूख से मरी रहल छी। तबे हमे बाबू के यहाँ जायछी आरो बाबू के कहभैन कि हमे भगवान के उलटा काम करले छी। एकरै सें दुखी छी आरो तोरो लिगचाँ भी तोरो बेटा कहलावै लायक नय रहलाँ। हमरो भी नौकर रक्ख। जबे ऊ अपनो बाप कन गेलै हो बहुत दूर पर रहै कि ओकरो बाप ओकरा देखलकै आरु ओकरा बहुत दया भेलै। तबे ऊ दौड़ी के बेटा के गला में लगाय लेलकै आरु चुम्मा लेलकै। तबे ओकरो बेटा बोलै लगलै कि बाबू हमे भगवान के उलटा काम करी के पापी भेल छी आरो तोरो लगीच में भी तोरो बेटा कहलावै के जोग नय रहलाँ। तब ओकरो बाप अपनो नौकर से कहलकै कि बढ़ियाँ २ कपड़ा लत्ता लै लानो आरो ओकरा पिनाभैं आरु एक औंगठी भी हाथ में पिन्हाय दहौं आरु गोड़ में जुत्ता पिन्हाय दहौं आरो एक मोटो हैनो बछेड़ा के लानो के मारैं आरु हमरा सब मिली के खाओं पीओं आरो खुसी करौं॥

तखनो ओकरो बड़का बेटा खेत में छेलै। जखनी ऊ घर लिगचाँ ऐलै ऊ नाच गीत सुनी के नौकर सें पुछलकै कि ई सब कि होय छै। तबे हुनक नौकर बोललहैन कि तोरो छोटका भाई ऐल छौन। तोरो बाबू मोटो हैनो बछेड़ा मारले छौन। हुनी अपनो गेल लड़का के पैलकात जैहनो रहैन तैहनो। ऊ इ बात सुनि के खिसियाय गेलै आरो घर जावै में रुसी गेलै। तबे ओकरो बाप बाहर चललो ऐलै आरो ओकरा सें बहुत निहोरा बिनती करलकै। तबे ओकरो बेटा बाप से कहलकै कि इतना दिन से हमे तोरो सेबा करलिहौन आरो तोरो बात कभी नय टारलिहौन तबे तौं एको पाठा भी नय देलहै कि हमे यार दोस्त के संग खुशी करताँ। जब कि हमरो भाय कसबी पतुरिया के साथ अपनो सबटा धन लुटा पटाय चलल ऐलहौन तौं ओकरा लै मोटा हैनो बछेड़ा मारलहै। तबे ओकरो बाप बोललै कि तौंह तो सब दिन संग रहै छ अब जे कुछ हमरा पास छै ऊ सब तोरे छेकौं। अब ई बात मुनासिब छेकौं कि हमरा सब मिली जुली के खुसी करौं आरो ऊ तोरो भाय छेकौं जे मरी गेल रहौन से फेरु जिल-हौं आरो जे हेराय गेल रहौन से फेरु पैलो गेलहौन॥

[No. 11.]

INDO-ARYAN FAMILY. EASTERN GROUP.

BIHĀRĪ.

MAITHILĪ (CHHIKĀ-CHHIKĪ BŌLĪ) DIALECT. (SOUTH BHAGALPUR.)

TRANSLITERATION.

Ēk ād[a]mī kē dū bēṭā rahai. Ok[a]rā mē̃ sē chhoṭ[a]kā ap[a]nō bāp sē kahal[a]kai k[i], 'bābū, jē dhan ham[a]rā bakh[a]rā mē̃ hōy ū ham[a]rā dai dē.' Ek[a]rā par ū ap[a]nō dhan ok[a]rā bā̃ṭī dēl[a]kai. Āro thōṛō din bhī nay bit[a]lai k[i] ok[a]rō chhoṭ[a]kā bēṭā sab ap[a]nō dhan ikaṭṭhā kar[i] ke kō[i] dos[a]rō dēś ghūmāï lāï chal[a]lō gēlai āro wahā̃ ap[a]nō sab dhan kē aiś jaiś mē̃ khar[a]ch karī del[a]kai. Tabē hau muluk mē̃ baṛī akāl paṛ[a]lai, ār[u] ū kaṅgāl hōy gēlai. Ū hau dēś ke nagar-bāsī ke yahā̃ gēlai āro wahā̃ rahe lag[a]lai. Ū ok[a]rā ap[a]nō khēt mē̃ sūar charāwāï le bhējī del[a]kai. Ū ok[a]rā khāwāï le nay detiyai. Tabē ū har[a]kh hōï ke ap[a]nō pēṭ bhūsā sē̃ bharī letiyai jē sūar ke khāy lāï dēl jāy rahai. Jabē ok[a]rā hōs bhēlai tabē ū ap[a]nō manō mē̃ kahe lag[a]lai k[i], 'ham[a]rō bāp ke et[a]nā dhan chhai k[i] ketai naukar khāy rah[a]lō chhai ār[u] bachai bhī chhai. Jabē hamē bhūkh sē marī rahal chhī. Tabē hamē bābū ke yahā̃ jāy-chhī, āro bābū kē kah[a]bhain k[i], "hamē Bhag[a]wān ke ul[a]ṭā kām kar[a]le chhī. Ek[a]rai sē̃ dukhī chhī, āro tōrō lig[a]chā̃ bhī tōrō bēṭā kah[a]lāwe lāyak nay rah[a]lā̃. Ham[a]rō bhī naukar rakkh."' Jabē ū ap[a]nō bāp kan gelai hau, bahut dūr par rahai k[i] ok[a]rō bāp ok[a]rā dekhal[a]kai ār[u] ok[a]rā bahut dayā bhelai. Tabē ū dauṛī ke bēṭā ke galā mē̃ lagāy lel[a]kaī ār[u] chummā lel[a]kai. Tabē ok[a]rō bēṭā bōle lag[a]lai k[i], 'bābū hamē Bhagwān ke ul[a]ṭā kām karī ke pāpī bhēl chhī, āro tōrō lagich mē̃ bhī tōrō bēṭā kah[a]lāwāï ke jōg nay rah[a]lā̃.' Tab ok[a]rō bāp ap[a]nō naukar sē kahal[a]-kai k[i], 'baṛhiyā̃ baṛhiyā̃ kap[a]ṛā lattā lāï lānē āro ok[a]rā pinābhaī; ār[u] ēk õg[a]ṭhī bhī hāth mē̃ pinhāy dahī̃; ār[u] gōṛ mē̃ juttā pinhāy dahī̃; āro ēk mōṭō hēnō bachhēṛā kē lān[i] ke mārē̃ ār[u] ham[a]rā sab milī ke khāõ pīõ āro khusī karō̃.'

Takh[a]ni ok[a]rō baṛ[a]kā bēṭā khēt mē̃ chhelai. Jakh[a]ni ū ghar lig[a]chā̃ āïlai ū nāch gīt sunī ke naukar sē̃ puchhal[a]kai k[i], 'ī sab k[i] hōychhai?' Tabē hunak naukar bolal[a]hain k[i] 'tōrō chhoṭ[a]kā bhāī ail chhaun. Tōrō bābū mōṭō hēnō bachhēṛā mār[a]lē chhaun. Hunō ap[a]nō gēl laṛ[a]kā kē pail[a]kāt jāïh[a]nō rahain tāïh[a]nō.' Ū i bāt sun[i] ke khisiyāy gelai āro ghar jāwāï mē̃ rusi gelai. Tabē ok[a]rō bāp bāhar chal[a]lō āïlai āro ok[a]rā sē̃ bahut nihōrā bin[a]ti karal[a]kai. Tabē ok[a]rō bēṭā bāp sē kahal[a]kai k[i], 'it[a]nā din sē hamē tōrō sēbā kar[a]lihaun āro tōrō bāt kabhī nay tār[a]lihaun, tabē tō̃ ēkō pāṭhā bhī nay dēl[a]hē, ki hamē yār dōst ke saṅg khusī kar[a]tā̃. Jab k[i] ham[a]rō bhāy kas[a]bī paturiyā ke sāth ap[a]nō sab[a]tā dhan luṭā paṭāy chalal āïl[a]haun, tō̃ ok[a]rā le mōṭā hēnō bachhēṛā māral[a]hai?' Tabē ok[a]rō bāp bol[a]lai k[i], 'tō̃h tō sab din saṅg rahai chhâ, ab jē kuchh ham[a]rā pās chhai ū sab tōre chhekaũ. Ab ī bāt munāsib chhekaũ k[i] ham[a]rā sab milī julī-ke khusī karaũ, āro ū tōrō bhāy chhekaũ jē marī gēl rahaun sē phēr[u] jil[a]haũ āro jē herāy gēl rahaun sē phēr[u] pāïlau gel[a]haun.'

The District of Monghyr, like that of Bhagalpur, is divided into two tracts, a northern and a southern, by the river Ganges. Northern Monghyr consists of the Begusarai Subdivision, and of a portion of the Head-quarters Subdivision. South Monghyr consists of the rest of the Head-quarters Subdivision and of the Subdivision of Jamuī. The main language of the District is Bihārī which is spoken in two dialects. In Begusarai Subdivision, and in the greater part of that portion of the Head-quarters Subdivision which is north of the Ganges, Southern Standard Maithilī is spoken, in the form which has been already illustrated. In the south of Gogri Thana, which is in the Head-quarters Subdivision north of the Ganges, and in the eastern portion of the same Subdivision which is south of the Ganges, in what is known as the Kharagpur country, a variety of Maithilī is spoken, which closely resemble the '*Chhikā-chhikī*' dialect of Bhagalpur. In the rest of the District, the main language of the people is the Magahī dialect of Bihārī, with which we have nothing to do at present.

The following version of the Parable of the Prodigal Son is in the form of Maithilī which is spoken in the south of Gogri Thana, and in the Kharagpur country. It is spoken, approximately, by 200,000 people.

As it so closely resembles the dialect of Bhagalpur, it is unnecessary to discuss the grammar of the specimen. The following are the main peculiarities of the dialect.

It is very fond of adding a sound resembling the 'ŏ' in the English word 'hot' at the end of a word. It represents this sound sometimes by the letter *o* as in 'ham'ro', my, and sometimes by 'a', as in 'chal'la', he went. There is no rule observed in this 'o' or 'a' being used according to the fancy of the writer. In the specimen, sometimes one and sometimes the other is used, and I have followed this in the transliteration. All that is to be remembered is that every final 'o' and every final 'a' is to be pronounced like the 'ŏ' in 'hot'.

The vowels *e* and *i* are freely interchanged. Thus, in the same sentence, we have both *chhilai*, and *chhelai*, he was.

Words, which in Standard Maithilī, as well as in the Southern Standard Maithilī of Begusarai end in a short ', above the line, which is hardly pronounced, in this dialect end in a long *ī*. Thus, *karī*, having done, which corresponds to the *kar'* of Standard Maithilī and of Begusarai.

Note the forms *ham-ār*, we, and *ap'nok*, your-Honour.

[No. 12.]

INDO-ARYAN FAMILY. EASTERN GROUP.

BIHĀRĪ.

MAITHILĪ (CHHIKĀ-CHHIKĪ BŌLĪ) DIALECT. (EAST MONGHYR.)

कोई आदमी के दू बेटा छेलै ओकरा में से छोटका बाप से कहलकै कि हो बाप जे कुछ धन संपत छौ ओइ में जे हमरो हिस्सा होए छ से हमरा दे द तब ऊ धन संपत के बांटी देलकै बहुत दिन नो नै भेलै कि ओकर छोटका बेटा सब चीज क इकट्ठा करो धरो क बहुत दूर मुलुक चलल गेलै और उहां कुचालपनी में दिन रात रही क सबे धन संपत खोए देलकै जब कि सब धन संपत चलल गेलै तब ऊ गांव में अकाल भेलै आरो ऊ बिलल्ला हो गेलो आरो तब ऊ एक वह गांव के रहवैया कर रह लागल जे ओकरा सुअर चरावे लेल अपना खेत में भेजलकै आरो ऊ सुअर के खावे क जे बोकला छेलै सेहे खाएके अपना पेट भर चाहैछेल और ओकरा कोए कुछु न दै तब ओकरा चेत भेलै कि हमरो बाप के नौकर सब क भूख से बेसी रोटी मिलैछै और हमे भूख मरौं हमे उठी क अपन बापो के पास जैब आरो कहबैन कि हो बाप हमें भगवानों सोझा और तोहरो सोझा पाप कैल छी अब हमे तोहर बेटा कहावे के जोकर नइखी अब हमरा अपन नोकर राखो भाव तवे ऊ उठी के अपन बापो के पास चलल जब ऊ दूरे में छेलो कि ओकरो बाप ओकरा पर माया करलकर और दौरी क ओकरा गला में लपटो के चुम्मा लेलकै बेटा कहलकै हो बाप हमे तोरो और परमेसरवों सोझा पाप करलों अब हम तोरो बेटा कहावे के जोग नइ छी तब बाप अपना नौकर के कहलकै कि सबे से अच्छा कपड़ा निकालो क एकरा पहनाए दहीं आरो हाथ में अंगुठी और गोड़ में जुत्ता पहनाए दहीं आरो हम आर खांव और मौज उड़ावौं कहब कि हमर भई बेटा मरी गेल छेल फिनु जील हेराए गेल छिल फिनु मिलल तवे ऊ सब मौज उड़ावे लागल।

ओकर बड़का बेटा खेत में छेल और जब घरो लग अइलै तब नाचो के आनु बाजा के अवाज सुनलकै आरो ऊ अपन नौकर सबे में से एकठा अपना लग बोलाए के पुछलकै की छिकइ ऊ कहलकइ कि अपनोक के भाई ऐलो छोत आरो अपनोक के बाप अच्छा भोज कैल छैत कहिने कि अपनो बेटा क देहतन समंगत पैलका तब ओकरा गोस्सा भेलै और भीतर नइ जावे चाह एह लेल ओकर बाप बाहर आए

𑂍𑂵 𑂋𑂍𑂩𑂰 𑂧𑂢𑂰𑂫𑂵 𑂪𑂏𑂪𑂶 𑂇 𑂃𑂣𑂢𑂰 𑂥𑂰𑂣 𑂍𑂵 𑂔𑂫𑂰𑂥 𑂠𑂵𑂪𑂍𑂶 𑂍𑂱 𑂉𑂞𑂵 𑂠𑂱𑂢 𑂮𑂵 𑂯𑂧 𑂃𑂣𑂢𑂳𑂍𑂰 𑂍𑂵 𑂮𑂵𑂫𑂰 𑂍𑂩𑂷 𑂩𑂯𑂪 𑂓𑂲 𑂄𑂩𑂳 𑂍𑂦𑂲 𑂃𑂣𑂢𑂷𑂍𑂰 𑂍𑂵 𑂥𑂰𑂞 𑂢 𑂗𑂩𑂪𑂲𑂁 𑂞𑂶𑂨𑂷 𑂃𑂣𑂢𑂵 𑂉𑂍𑂗𑂰 𑂧𑂵𑂧𑂢𑂰 𑂦𑂲 𑂢 𑂠𑂵𑂪𑂲𑂁 𑂍𑂱 𑂋𑂍𑂩𑂰 𑂪𑂵 𑂍𑂵 𑂯𑂧𑂵 𑂠𑂷𑂮𑂹𑂞 𑂧𑂷𑂯𑂱𑂧 𑂍𑂵 𑂮𑂁𑂏𑂵 𑂄𑂢𑂢𑂹𑂠 𑂍𑂩𑂞𑂲𑂁 𑂄𑂩𑂷 𑂆 𑂥𑂵𑂗𑂰 𑂔𑂵 𑂞𑂷𑂩 𑂍𑂳𑂪 𑂡𑂢 𑂮𑂁𑂣𑂞 𑂍𑂵 𑂍𑂮𑂥𑂲 𑂣𑂰𑂓𑂳 𑂇𑂚𑂶𑂪𑂍𑂶 𑂋𑂍𑂩𑂰 𑂉𑂪𑂯𑂵 𑂮𑂵 𑂃𑂣𑂢𑂵 𑂥𑂚𑂍𑂰 𑂦𑂷𑂔 𑂍𑂶𑂪𑂷𑂁 𑂥𑂰𑂣 𑂍𑂯𑂪𑂍𑂶 𑂍𑂱 𑂩𑂵 𑂥𑂵𑂗𑂰 𑂞𑂷𑂁 𑂮𑂥𑂵 𑂠𑂱𑂢 𑂯𑂧𑂩𑂰 𑂮𑂰𑂧𑂢𑂵 𑂓𑂵𑂀 𑂄𑂩𑂷 𑂔𑂵 𑂍𑂳𑂓 𑂯𑂧𑂩 𑂓𑂲𑂍 𑂮𑂵 𑂞𑂷𑂩𑂵 𑂓𑂱𑂍𑂷 𑂧𑂏𑂩 𑂔𑂥𑂵 𑂞𑂷𑂩 𑂦𑂰𑂆 𑂧𑂩𑂪 𑂦𑂵𑂪 𑂔𑂲𑂪𑂷 𑂯𑂵𑂩𑂰𑂪 𑂦𑂵𑂪 𑂧𑂱𑂪𑂪 𑂓𑂸 𑂞𑂥 𑂞𑂷𑂯𑂩𑂰 𑂄𑂢𑂢𑂹𑂠 𑂯𑂷𑂫𑂵 𑂒𑂰𑂯𑂷𑃀

INDO-ARYAN FAMILY. EASTERN GROUP.

BIHĀRĪ.

MAITHILĪ (CHHIKĀ-CHHIKĪ BŌLĪ) DIALECT. (EAST MONGHYR.)

TRANSLITERATION AND TRANSLATION.

Kōi ād'mī-kē dū bēṭā chhelai. Ok'rā-mẽ-sē chhoṭ'kā bāp-sē

A-certain man-to two sons were. Them-in-from the-younger the-father-to

kahal'kai ki, 'hō bāp, jē kuchh dhan sampat chau, ō-ē-mẽ

said that, 'O father, what any wealth property is-to-you, it-indeed-in

jē ham'ro hissā hōechha, sē ham'rā dăī dâ.' Tab ū dhan

what my share becomes, that to-me giving give.' Then he the-wealth

sampat-kē bā̃ṭi del'kai. Bahut din bhī nai bhelai, ki ok'ra chhoṭ'kā

property dividing gave. Many days also not were, that his younger

bēṭā sab chīj-ka ekaṭṭhā karī dharī-ka, bahut dūr muluk

son all things together having-made having-taken, a-very far country

chal'la gelai, aur uhā̃ luchāpanī-mẽ din rāt rahī-ka sabhē dhan

going went, and there debauchery-in days nights remaining all wealth

sampat khōe del'kai. Jab ki sab dhan sampat chal'la gelai, tab

property losing gave. When that all wealth property going went, then

ū gā̃w-mẽ akāl bhelai, āro ū bilal'lā hō gelo, âro tab

that village-in a-famine happened, and he miserable becoming went, and then

ū ēk wah gā̃w-ke rah'waiyā kan raha lăg'la, jē ok'rā sūar

he a that village-of a-dweller near to-remain began, who him swine

charābăī lēl ap'nā khēta-mẽ bhejal'kai. Āro ū sūar-ke khābăī-ka jē

feeding for his-own field-in sent. And he swine-of eating-for what

bokh'lā chhelai, sē-hē khāe-ke ap'nā pēṭ bhara chāhaichhela,

husks were, those-even having-eaten his-own belly to-fill he-was-wishing,

aur ok'rā kōe kuchh' na dai. Tab ok'rā chēt bhelai ki,

and to-him anyone anything not gives. Then to-him senses became that,

'ham'ro bāp-ke naukar sabh-ka bhūkh-sē bēsī rōṭī milaichhai, aur

'my father's servants all-to hunger-than more bread is-got, and

hamē bhūkha maraũ. Hamẽ uṭhī-ka ap'na bāpo-ke pās jaiba,

I (of)-hunger die. I having-risen my-own father-of near will-go,

āro kah'bain ki, "hō bāp, hamẽ Bhag'wānõ sōjhā, aur toh'rō

and will-say that, "O father, I God-also before, and thee-also

sōjhā pāp kaila-chhī. Ab hamē toh'ra bēṭā kahābe-ke jōkar naī

before sin have-done. Now I thy son being-called-of worthy not

chhī. Ab ham^{a}rā ap^{a}na nōkar nākhī mānā."' Tabē ū uṭhī-ke
am. Now me thine-own servant like keep."' Then he rising

ap^{a}na bāpo-ke pās chal^{a}la. Jab ū dūrē-mẽ chhalo, ki
his-own father-of near went. When he distance-even-in was, that

ok^{a}ro bāp ok^{a}rā-par māyā karal^{a}kaï, aur daurī-ka ok^{a}rā galla-mẽ lap^{a}ṭī-ke
his father him-on pity made, and running him neck-in clasping

chummā lel^{a}kai. Bēṭā kahal^{a}kai, 'hō bāp, hamē tōro aur Paramēśwarõ
kisses took. The-son said, 'O father, I thy and God

sōjhā pāp kar^{a}lõ; āb ham tōro bēṭā kahābe-ke jōg naï chhī.'
before sin did; now I thy son being-called-of fit not am.'

Tab bāp ap^{a}nā naukar-kē kahal^{a}kai ki, 'sabhē-sē achchhā kap^{a}ṛā
Then the-father his-own servants-to said that, 'all-than good clothes

nikārī-ka ek^{a}rā pah^{a}nāe dahī̃; āro hātha-mẽ ā̃guṭhī,
having-brought-out this-person having-clothed give; and hand-in a-ring,

aur gōṛa-mẽ juttā pah^{a}nāe dahī̃; āro ham-ār khā̃w, aur mauj
and leg-in shoes having-clothed give; and we let-eat, and merriment

uṛāwaū; kahana ki ham^{a}ra ī bēṭā marī gēla chhela, phin^{a}
let-us-rouse; because that my this son having-died gone was, again

jīla; harāe gēla chhila, phin^{a} mil^{a}la.' Tabē ū sab mauj
lived; having-been-lost gone was, again was-got.' Then they all merriment

uṛābe lag^{a}la.
to-rouse began.

Ok^{a}ra baṛ^{a}kā bēṭā khēta-mẽ chhela, aur jab gharo lag ailai,
His elder son field-in was, and when the-house near he-came,

tab nācho-ke ār^{a} bājā-ke abāj sunal^{a}kai, āro ū ap^{a}na naukar
then dancing-of and music-of noise he-heard, and he his-own servants

sabhē-mẽ-sē ēk-ṭā ap^{a}nā lag bolāe-ka puchhal^{a}kai, 'kī chhikai?'
all-in-from one himself near having-called asked, 'what is?'

Ū kahal^{a}kai ki, 'ap^{a}nok-ke bhāī ailo chhōt, āro ap^{a}nok-ke
He said that, 'Your-Honour's brother come is-for-thee, and Your-Honour's

bāp achchhā bhōj kaila-chhait, kahinē ki ap^{a}no bēṭā-ka deh^{a}gar
father good feast has-made, because that his-own son well

samaṅgar pail^{a}kā.' Tab ok^{a}rā rōkh bhelai, aur bhītar nai jābe
prosperous he-got.' Then to-him anger happened, and inside not to-go

chāha. Eh lēl ok^{a}ra bāp bāhar āe-ke ok^{a}rā manābaï
he-wishes. This for his father outside having-come him to-entreat

lag^{a}lai. Ū ap^{a}nā bāp-ka jabāb del^{a}kai ki, 'ētē din-sē ham
began. He his-own father-to answer gave that, 'so-many days-from I

ap^{a}nukā-ke sēwā karī rahala chhī, ār^{a} kabhī ap^{a}nokā-ke bāto
Your-Honour's service doing remained am, and ever Your-Honour's word

na uṭhailaũ. Tai-o ap'ne ēk-ṭū mem'nā bhī na delā̃,
not disobeyed. Nevertheless Your-Honour one kid even not gave,

ki jek'rā lē-ka hamē dōst mōhim-ke jaurē ānand kar'taũ.
that which having-taken I friends acquaintances with joy I-might-make.

Āro ī bēṭā jē tōra kul dhan sampat-kē kas'bī pāchh"
And this son who thy whole wealth property harlots after

phek'lak, ok'rā ail'hē-sē ap'ne baṛ'kā bhōj kailō̃.' Bāp,
threw-away, his coming-on Your-Honour a-great feast made.' The-father

kahal'kai ki, 'rē bēṭā, tō̃ sabhē din ham'rā sām'lē chhaĩ; āro
said that, 'O son, thou all days me with art; and

jē kuchh ham'ra chhika, sē tōre chhiko. Magar jabē tōra
what anything mine is, that thine is. But when thy

bhāe mar'la bhēl, jīlau; heraila bhēl, mil'la chau,
brother dead became, lived-for-thee; lost became, got is-for-thee,

tab toh'rā ānand hōbe chāhi.'
then to-thee joy to-become is-proper.'

A dialect very similar to that of South Bhagalpur is spoken in the North and West of the Sonthal Parganas, the country of which is a continuation to the south and east of that of the former district. It is, as previously stated, separated from Bengali by the mountain range which runs down the centre of the Sonthal Parganas from north-east to south-west. Only in the Deoghur Subdivision do the two languages meet, and here speakers of Bihārī and of Bengali dwell side by side, each speaking his own language. The dialect in question has hitherto been classed as a form of Magahī, but the specimen shows that it is clearly a variety of Maithilī. As in South Bhagalpur, a final *i*, which in Standard Maithilī would be short, is here lengthened to *ī*, but no trace appears in the specimen of the preference for adding an 'ŏ' sounding like the 'o' in the word 'hot' to the end of words, which is so common in Monghyr and South Bhagalpur. It is unnecessary to give any lengthy specimen of the dialect spoken in the Sonthal Parganas. A few lines of the Parable of the Prodigal Son in a version which comes from Deoghur will be sufficient.

[No. 13.]

INDO-ARYAN FAMILY. EASTERN GROUP.

BIHĀRĪ.

MAITHILĪ DIALECT (SOUTHERN VARIETY). (DEOGHUR SUB-DIVISION OF THE SONTHAL PARGANAS.)

Ēk ād*mī-kē dū bēṭā chhalai. Ok*rā-mē̃-sē chhoṭ*kā ap*nā bāp-kē
One man-to two sons were. Them-in-from the-younger his-own father-to
kahal*kai, 'hō bābū, ham*rā hisā-mē̃ jē māl-jāl hōt sē bā̃ṭī
said, 'O father, my share-in what property will-be that having-divided
dē.' Tab bāp sabhē māl-jāl bā̃ṭī del*kan.
give.' Then the-father all property having-divided gave.

WESTERN MAITHILĪ.

This is the language of the Hindūs of the Muzaffarpur District. It is also spoken in the east of the District of Champaran, which lies immediately to the north-west of Muzaffarpur. The tract in Champaran is a strip of land about twelve miles long and two miles wide running along the eastern border of the District in Dhākā Thana. As already stated, the language is much infected by the dialects of Bhojpurī spoken in Saran and Champaran. It is estimated that Western Maithilī is spoken by the following number of people :—

Name of District.	Number of Speakers.
Muzaffarpur	1,754,695
Champaran	28,800
TOTAL .	1,783,495

The language spoken in the north of the District of Muzaffarpur differs somewhat from that spoken in the south, and hence specimens will be given of both varieties.

WESTERN MAITHILĪ OF NORTH MUZAFFARPUR.

The language of North Muzaffarpur is peculiar. Immediately to its west is the form of the Bhojpurī dialect, locally known as Madhēsī, which is spoken in the district of Champaran. In North Muzaffarpur, the language is in a transition stage, and is partly Maithilī, and partly Bhojpurī. It might with equal propriety be classed as a form of either language, and in the Grammar mentioned below, it is classed as a form of Bhojpurī. In the present Survey, I class it as a dialect of Maithilī because the country where it is spoken belongs historically to the ancient kingdom of Mithilā. The Brahmans of this part of the country speak a purer form of Maithilī than other castes, and still use the Maithilī alphabet.

The two following specimens are in the form of speech used by the lower castes. It is unnecessary to do more than draw attention to the numerous Bhojpurī forms which occur. Examples are the words *hā*, and *hāwē*, both meaning 'is'.

AUTHORITY—

Grierson, G. A.,—*Seven Grammars of the Dialects and Sub-dialects of the Bihārī Language.*—Part II.—*Bhojpūrī Dialect of Shāhābād, Sāran, Champāran, North Muzaffarpur, and the Eastern Portion of the North-Western Provinces.* Calcutta, 1884.

[No. 14.]

INDO-ARYAN FAMILY. EASTERN GROUP.

BIHĀRĪ.

MAITHILĪ (MAITHILĪ-BHOJPURĪ) DIALECT. (NORTH MUZAFFARPUR.)

SPECIMEN I.

एक केहु आदमी कें दू लड़िका रहै। ओह में से छोटका बाप से कहलक, हो बाबू, धन सबंस में से जे हम्मर हिस्सा/बखरा होय से हमरा के दे-द। त ऊ ओकरा कें अप्पन धन बाँट देलक। बहुत दिन न भेलैक कि छोटका लड़िका सब किछिओ जमा कर के दूर देस चल गेल और उहाँ लम्पटै में दिन गमबैत अप्पन सबंस गमा देलक। और जब ऊ अप्पन सब किछिओ उड़ा देलक; तब ओ देस में भारी अकाल परलैक, और ऊ कंगाल हो गेल। और ऊ जा के ओही देस के एक लमहर आदमी कने रहे लागल। ऊ ओकरा के अपना खेत में सूगर चरावे ला भेजलक। और ऊ अप्पन पेट छिलका से जे सूगर खाये भरे चाहलक; और केउ ओकरा के कुछ देइक न। तब ऊ चेतलक और कहलक, कि हमरा बाप के त कतेक जना फालतू नौकर के खाये से रोटो उबर जाइअ, और हम भूखें मरै! हम उठ के अपना बाप किहाँ जाएब और हुनका से कहबैन कि हो बाबू, हम लोक परलोक दुनू बिगाड़लो। हम अब अपने के बेटा कहावे जोग न छो, हमरो के एक जन बना के राखू। और ऊ उठ के अपना बाप किहाँ आएल। जब ऊ दूर रहे तब-हो ओकर बाप ओकरा देख क छोह कलकै, और हबस क गरा लगा लेलकै, और चुम्मा चाटो लेलकै। और बेटा बाप से कहलक, कि हो बाबू, हम परलोको बिगाड़लो और अपने के सोझा में भी पाप कैलो ह, और अब अपने के बेटा कहावे जोग न छो। ओकर बाप अपना नौकर सब से कहलन कि सब से बढ़िआँ कपड़ा निकाल के लेआव, और हिनका के पहिराव, और हिनका हाथ में औंठी, और गोड़ में पनही पहिरवहुन; और हम सब कचरी और गाजी, काहे कि हम्मर मरल बेटा जीअल ह; हेरा गेल रहे से फेन भेंटल ह। और ऊ सब आनन्द बधावा करे लगलन॥

ओकर जेठका बेटा खेत में रहे; और जब ऊ अपना घरे आएल और लगीच पहुँचल, तब बाजा और नाच होइत सुनलक। और ऊ नौकर सब में से एक नौकर के बोला के पुछलक, कि ई की होइत है। नौकर कहलकैन कि अपने के भाई ऐलन हँ और अपने के बाबूजी भोज कैलन हँ, एह लेल कि हुनका के ऊ नीमन और निरोग पैलन हँ। और ऊ खिसिआ गेल, और भितरो घर में न गेल। एह लेल हुनकर बाप बाहर अलथिन और हुनका के मनावे लगलथिन। और ऊ अपना बाप के उतारा देलन, कि देखू, हम अतेक बरस से अपने के सेवा करैछी और कहिओ अपने के कहल न टारलो; और तैयो अपने हमरा के कहिओ एको पठरुओ न देली कि हम अपना इआर दोस के संगे खुसी करतो; मगर अपने के ई बेटा, जे पतुरिआ सब के संगे अपने के धन उड़ा देलक, जौने बेर आएल तौने बेर अपने ओकरा लेल भोज कैली ह। बाप बेटा से कहलन कि, हो बबुआ, त सब दिन हमरा संगे छ, और जे कुछ हम्मर हवे से सब तोहरे छो। आनन्द बधावा करे के उचित है, काहे कि ई तोहर भाई मर गेल रहलो से जीलो ह; हेरा गेल रहलो से मिललो ह॥

[No. 14.]

INDO-ARYAN FAMILY. EASTERN GROUP.

BIHĀRĪ.

MAITHILĪ (MAITHILĪ-BHOJPURĪ) DIALECT. (NORTH MUZAFFARPUR.)

SPECIMEN I.

TRANSLITERATION AND TRANSLATION.

Ēk keh^{u} ād^{a}mī-kẽ dū laṛikā rahai. Oh-mẽ-sē chhoṭ^{a}kā bāp-sē
A certain man-to two sons were. Them-in-from the-younger the-father-to
kah^{a}lak, 'hō bābū, dhan-sarbas-mẽ-sē jē hammar hissā bakh^{a}rā hōy,
said, 'O father, wealth-property-in-from what my share portion may-be,
sē ham^{a}rā-kē dē dâ.' Ta ū ok^{a}rā-kẽ appan dhan bā̃ṭ
that me-to having-given give.' Then he him-to his-own wealth having-divided
dēlak. Bahut din na bhelaik k^{i} chhoṭ^{a}kā laṛikā sab kichhiō jamā
gave. Many days not were that the-younger son all everything collected
kar-ke dūr dēs chal gēl, aur uhā̃ lampaṭai-mẽ din
having-made a-far country having-gone went, and there debauchery-in days
gam^{a}wait appan sarbas gamā dēlak. Aur jab ū appan sab kichhiō
passing his-own property wasting gave. And when he his-own all anything
urā dēlak, tab ō dēs-mẽ bhārī akāl par^{a}laik, aur ū kaṅgāl
dissipating gave, then that country-in a-heavy famine fell, and he poor
hō-gēl. Aur ū jā-ke ōhī dēs-ke ēk lam^{a}har ād^{a}mī kanē rahe lāgal.
became. And he going that-very country-of a rich man near to-remain began.
Ū ok^{a}rā-kē ap^{a}nā khēt-mẽ sūgar charāwe-lā bhej^{a}lak. Aur ū appan pēṭ
He him his-own field-in swine feeding-for sent. And he his-own belly
chil^{a}kā-sē, jē sūgar khāyē, bhare chāh^{a}lak; aur keu ok^{a}rā-kē kuchh
husks-with, which the-swine eat, to-fill wished; and anyone him-to anything
dēik na. Tab ū chet^{a}lak aur kah^{a}lak ki, 'ham^{a}rā bāp-ke ta katek
gives not. Then he thought and said that, 'my father-of indeed how-many
janā phāl^{a}tū naukar-ke khāye-sē rōṭī ubar jāia, aur ham
men superfluous servants-of eating-from bread over-and-above goes, and I
bhūkhẽ marai-chhī. Ham uṭh-ke ap^{a}nā bāp kihā̃ jāeb, aur hun^{a}kā-
by-hunger am-dying. I having-arisen my-own father near will-go, and him-
sē kah^{a}bain k^{i}, "hō bābū, ham lōk par^{a}-lōk dunū bigāṛ^{a}lī. Ham
to I-will-say that, "O father, I this-world the-next-world both spoiled. I
ab ap^{a}ne-ke bēṭā kahāwe jōg na chhī; ham^{a}rō-kē ēk jan banā-ke
now Your-Honour-of son to-be-called fit not am; me-also a servant making

rākhū."' Aur ū uṭh-ke ap^{a}nā bāp kihā̃ āel. Jab ū dūı rahē,
keep."' And he having-risen his-own father near came. When he at-a-distance was,

tab-hī ōkar bāp ok^{a}rā dēkh-ka chhōh kal^{a}kai, aur habas-ka garā
then-even his father him having-seen compassion made, and having-run on-the-neck

lagā-lel^{a}kai, aur chummā chāṭī lel^{a}kai. Aur bēṭā bāp-sē kah^{a}lak ki,
applied-himself, and kiss licking took. And the-son the-father-to said that,

'hō bābū, ham par^{a}lōkō bigāṛ^{a}lī aur ap^{a}ne-ke sōjhā-mē̃ bhī pāp kailī-
'O father, I the-other-world-also spoiled and Your-Honour-of before also sin have-

hâ, aur ab ap^{a}ne-ke bēṭā kahāwe jōg na chhī.' Ō-kar bāp ap^{a}nā
done, and now Your-Honour-of son to-be-called fit not am.' His father his-own

naukar-sab-sē kah^{a}lan k^{i}, 'sab-sē baṛhiā̃ kap^{a}ṛā nikāl-ke lē-āwâ; aur
servants-to said that, 'all-than excellent clothes having-taken-out bring; and

hin^{a}kā-kē pahirāwâ; aur hin^{a}kā hāth-mē̃ aũṭhī, aur gōṛ-mē̃ pan^{a}hī
this-person-to put-on; and this-person's hand-on a-ring, and leg-on shoes

pahiraw^{a}hun; aur ham sab kach^{a}rī aur gājī; kāhe k^{i} hammar maral
put-on; and (let) us all eat and be-merry; because that my dead

bēṭā jīal hâ; hērā gēl rahē, sē phen bhẽṭal hâ.' Aur ū sab ānand
son alive is; lost gone was, he again found is.' And then all joy

badhāwā kare lag^{a}lan.
merriment to-make began.

Ō-kar jeṭh^{a}kā bēṭā khēt-mē̃ rahē, aur jab ū ap^{a}nā gharē āel aur lagīch
His elder son field-in was, and when he his-own house-in came and near

pahũchal tab bājā aur nāch hōit sun^{a}lak. Aur ū naukar-sab-mē̃-sē ēk
arrived then music and dancing being he-heard. And he his-servants-in-from one

naukar-kē bolā-ke puchh^{a}lak k^{i}, 'ī kī hōit bai?' Naukar kahal^{a}kain
servant having-called asked that, 'this what being is?' The-servant said

k^{i}, 'ap^{a}ne-ke bhāī ailan-hā̃, aur ap^{a}ne-ke bābū-ji bhōj kailan-hā̃;
that, 'Your-Honour's brother has-come, and Your-Honour's father feast has-made;

eh lēl k^{i} hun^{a}kā-kē ū nīman aur nirōg pailan-hā̃.' Aur ū khisiā-gēl
this for that him he good and healthy has-got.' And he became-angry

aur bhit^{a}rī ghar-mē̃ na gēl. Eh lēl hun-kar bāp bāhar al^{a}thin, aur hun^{a}kā-kē
and inner house-in not went. This for his father outside came, and him

manāwe lagal^{a}thin. Aur ū ap^{a}nā bāp-kē utārā dēlan k^{i}, 'dēkhū, ham
to-remonstrate-with began. And he his-own father-to answer gave that, 'see, I

atek baras-sē ap^{a}ne-ke sēwā karaichhī, aur kahiō ap^{a}ne-ke kahal
so-many years-from Your-Honour's service doing-am, and ever Your-Honour's saying

na ṭār^{a}lī, aur taiyō ap^{a}nē ham^{a}rā-kē kahiō ēkō paṭharu-ō na dēlī,
not disobeyed, and nevertheless Your-Honour me-to ever one-even kid not gave,

k^{i} ham ap^{a}nā iār dōs-ke sangē khusī kar^{a}tī; magar ap^{a}ne-ke
that I my-own lovers friends-of with merriment might-make; but Your-Honour's

ī bēṭā jē paturiyā-sab-ke saṅgē ap^{a}ne-ke dhan uṛā dēlak,
this son who harlots-of with Your-Honour's wealth dissipating gave,

jaune bĕr āel taune bĕr ap^{a}ne ok^{a}rā lēl bhōj kailī-hâ.'
at-what-very time he-came at-that-very time Your-Honour him for feast has-made.'

Bāp bēṭā-sē kah^{a}lan k^{i}, 'hō babuā, tū sab din ham^{a}rā saṅgē chhâ, aur
The-father the-son-to said that, 'O son, thou all days me with art, and

jē kuchh hammar hâwē sē sab tōh^{a}rē chhau. Ānand badhāwā kare-ke
what anything mine is that all thine is-to-thee. Joy merriment having-made

uchit hai, kāhe k^{i} ī tōhar bhāī mar-gēl rah^{a}lau, sē
proper is, because that this thy brother having-died-gone was-for-thee, he

jīlau-hâ; hērā-gēl rah^{a}lau, sē mil^{a}lau-hâ.'
has-lived-for-thee; lost-gone was-for-thee, he has-been-got-for-thee.'

MAITHILĪ-BHOJPURĪ OF SOUTH MUZAFFARPUR.

The form of Maithilī spoken in Central and South Muzaffarpur is still more strongly infected with Bhojpurī than that of the North of the District. This will be manifest from the following translation of the Parable of the Prodigal Son for which I am indebted to the kindness of Mr. A. Christian, Sub-Deputy Opium Agent of Tirhut. It was recorded in the Hajipur subdivision, situated in the south of the Muzaffarpur District.

AUTHORITY—

Grierson, G. A.,—*Seven Grammars of the Dialects and Sub-dialects of the Bihārī Language.* Part IV.—*Maithil-Bhojpurī Dialect of Central and South Muzaffarpūr.* Calcutta, 1884.

[No. 16.]

INDO-ARYAN FAMILY. EASTERN GROUP.

BIHĀRĪ.

MAITHILĪ (MAITHILĪ-BHOJPURĪ) DIALECT. (CENTRAL AND SOUTH MUZAFFARPUR.)

(A. Christian, Esq., 1898.)

एक जना के दुगो बेटा रहलइन। ओकरा मे से छोटका अपना बाबू से कहलकइन हो बाबू धन के बखरा जे कुछ हमर हो से द। तो ऊ ओकनी के बाँट देलकइन। तो कुछ दिन बितला पर छोटका बेटा सब जमा कलकइन तेकरा बाद बड़ा दूर परदेस चल गेलइन। उहाँ जा के सब धन कुकर्म मे निघटा देलकइन। पीछे सब निघटला पर ऊ देस मे बड़ा अकाल पड़लइ। ओकरा खाए पीए के दुक्ख होए लगलइ। तब ऊ गाँव मे कोई बरियार के इहाँ जा के गिरलइन। तो ओकरा अपना खेत मे सूअर चरावे ला भेज देलकइन। ओकरा मन मे छलइ के सूअर जे खोइया खाइत रहे से ऊ हमरा मिलइत ता खा के पेट भर लेती। सेहु कोउ न देइत रहइ। तब सोचलक कि हमरा बाप कने बहुत जन के खिया के बच जालैं और हम इहाँ भूख से मरीलि। हम उठ के अपना बाप कने जैती ओ कहिती कि हो बाबू के हम ईसर के इहाँ ओ तोहरा इहाँ पाप कैलो। हम अब ऐसन नहो कि तोहर लड़िका कहाईं। हमरो एगो जन जकित रखल। तब उठ के अपन बाप के इहाँ चललन। फरके से ओते देखलकइन तब बाप का ममत लगलइन दौर के गला में लपटा लेलकइन ओ बहुत मिलाजुली कलकइन। बेटा कहल-कइन हो बाबू ईसर के इहाँ ओ तोहरा इहाँ पाप कैलो। अब ऐसन नहो के तोहर बेटा कहाईं। बाप अपना जन से कहलकइन के निमन से निमन कपरा लाव ओ हिनका के पहिना देहुन ओ हाँथ में अउँठी ओ गोर मे जुता पहिना देहुन ओ पोसल पालल भरि के बचा लाव ओ मार हमनीका खाईं ओ अनन्द मनाईं। कि हमर ई बेटा जे मर गेल रहे से अब जी गेल ओ भुतला गेल रहे से अब मिल गेल। तब ऊ अनन्द मनावे लगलन॥

ओ घड़ी उनकर बड़का बेटा खेत मे रहलइन। जब घर के नगीच अलइन तो बाजा ओ नाचे के सबद सुनलकइन। तब एक जन के बोला के पुछलकइन के कोथी है। तब ऊ कहलकइन के तोहर भाई अलथुन है उन का देहे आँगी से नीक पलकथुन ओकरा लेल लोग के तोहर बाप खिअवइत हथुन। तो ऊ खिसिया के भितरी जाए न चहलथिन तो उनकर बाप मिकस के अलथिन ओ मनावे लगल-थिन। तब ऊ अपना बाप से जवाब कैलन देख तो प्रतेक दिन से तोहर सेवा कैलो ओ कबहूं तोहर कहल न टरलो ओ तूँ एगो पठरू भी न देल के हम अपना यारन के संग खुसी करती। जखनी तोहर ई बेटा अलथुन जे तोहर धन कसबिन संग उड़ा देलकथुन तेकरा ला जेवनार करौल। तब बाप कहलकइन के तूँ तो नित हमरा जोड़ हे और जे कुछ हमर है से तोहर है। बाकी खुसी मनावेके चाही काहे कि ई तोहर भाई जे मर गेल रहथुन से जी गेलथुन ओ भुला गेल रहथुन से मिल गेलथुन॥

[No. 16.]

INDO-ARYAN FAMILY. EASTERN GROUP.

BIHARĪ.

MAITHILĪ (MAITHILĪ-BHOJPURĪ) DIALECT. (SOUTH MUZAFFARPUR.)

TRANSLITERATION AND TRANSLATION.

(*A. Christian, Esq., 1898.*)

Ēk janā-kē dugō bēṭā rah^{a}laïn. Ok^{a}rā-mē-sē chhoṭ^{a}kā ap^{a}nā
One person-to two sons were. Them-in-from the-younger his-own

bābū-sē kahal^{a}kaïn, 'hō bābū, dhan-ke bakh^{a}rā jē kuchh hamar hō,
father-to said, 'O father, wealth-of share what any mine may-be,

sē dā.' Tō ū ok^{a}ni-kē bā̃ṭ del^{a}kaïn. Tō kuchh din bit^{a}lā-par
that give.' Then he them-to dividing gave. Then some days passing-on

chhoṭ^{a}kā bēṭā sab jamā kal^{a}kaïn. Tek^{a}rā bād baṛā dūr par^{a}dēs
the-younger son all collected made. That after very distant foreign-land

chal gelaïn. Uhā̃ jā-ke sab dhan kukarm-mē nighaṭā del^{a}kaïn.
having-gone went. There having-gone all wealth bad-deeds-in wasted he-gave.

Pīchhē, sab nighaṭ^{a}lā-par, ū dēs-mē baṛā akāl paṛ^{a}laï. Ok^{a}rā
Afterwards, all wasting-on, that land-in a-great famine fell. His

khāe pie-ke dukkh hōe lag^{a}laï. Tab ū gā̃w-mē kōī
eating drinking-of trouble being began. Then he the-village-in a-certain

bariyār-ke ihā̃ jā-ke gir^{a}laïn. Tō ok^{a}rā ap^{a}nā khēt-mē sūar
rich-man-of near having-gone he-fell. Then him his-own field-in swine

charāwe lā bhēj del^{a}kaïn. Ok^{a}rā man-mē chhalaï ke sūar jē
feeding for sending he-gave. His mind-in it-was that the-swine what

khōiyā khāit-rahē, sē-ū ham^{a}rā milaït, tō khā-ke peṭ
husks were-eating, those-also to-me might-be-got, then having-eaten my-belly

bhar-lētī. Sē-hū keu na dēit-rahaï. Tab soch^{a}lak ki, 'ham^{a}rā
I-might-fill. That-even anyone not was-giving. Then he-thought that, 'my

bāp kanē bahut jan-ke khiyā-ke bach jā-lē, aur ham
father near many servants-of having-fed remaining-over goes, and I

ihā̃ bhūkh-sē marī-lē. Ham uṭh-ke ap^{a}nā bāp kanē jaitī
here hunger-from am-dying. I having-arisen my-own father near would-go

ō kahitī ki, "hō bābū, ke ham Īsar-ke ihā̃ ō toh^{a}rā ihā̃
and would-say that, "O father, that I God-of near and thy near

pāp kailī. Ham ab aisan nahī ki tōhar laṛikā kahāī. Ham^{a}rō
sin did. I now such am-not that thy son I-may-be-called. Me-also

ēgō jan jakit rakhal."' Tab uṭh-ke apan bāp-ke ihā̃ chal^{a}lan.
a servant like keep."' Then having-arisen his-own father-of near he-went.

Phar^{a}kē-sē autē dekhal^{a}kaïn, tab bāp-kā mamat lag^{a}laïn,
Distance-from on-coming he-saw, then the-father-to compassion arrived,

daur-ke galā-mē lap^{a}tā lel^{a}kaïn, ō bahut milājuli kal^{a}kaïn. Bēṭā
running neck-on embracing he-took, and much greeting made. The-son

kahal^{a}kaïn, 'hō bābū, Īsar-ke ihā̃ ō toh^{a}rā ihā̃ pāp kailī. Ab
said, 'O father, God-of near and thy near sin I-did. Now

aisan nahī ke tōhar bēṭā kahāī.' Bāp ap^{a}nā jan-sē
such I-am-not that thy son I-may-be-called.' The-father his-own servants-to

kahal^{a}kaïn ke niman-sē niman kap^{a}rā lāwâ; ō hin^{a}kā-kē pahinā dēhun;
said that good-than good clothes bring; and this-person clothing give;

ō hā̃th-mē aũṭhī, ō gōr-mē jutā pahinā dēhun; ō pōsal pālal
and hand-on a-ring, and legs-on shoes clothing give; and fatted nourished

bhar^{i}-ke bachā lāwâ, ō mārâ, ham^{a}nīkā khāī ō anand manāī; ki
having-filled calf bring, and kill, let-us eat and rejoicing make; that

hamar ī bēṭā jē mar gēl rahē, sē ab jī gēl; ō bhut^{a}lā gēl
my this son who dead gone was, he now living went; and lost gone

rahē, sē ab mil gēl.' Tab ū anand manāwe lag^{a}lan.
was, he now found went.' Then they rejoicing making began.

Ō gharī un-kar baṛ^{a}kā bēṭā khēt-mē rah^{a}laïn. Jab ghar-ke
That hour his elder son field-in was. When the-house-of

nagīch alaïn, tō bājā ō nāche-ke sabad sunal^{a}kaïn. Tab ēk jan-kē
near he-came, then music and dancing-of noise he-heard. Then one servant-to

bolā-ke puchhal^{a}kaïn ke, 'kethī hai?' Tab ū kahal^{a}kaïn ke, 'tōhar
having-called he-asked that, 'for-what is-this?' Then he said that, 'thy

bhāī al^{a}thun-hai. Un^{a}kā dēhē ā̃gē-sē nīk palak^{a}thun, ok^{a}rā lēl
brother has-come-for-thee.[1] *His in-body limb-from well he-has-got, that for*

lōg-kē tōhar bāp khiawaït hathun.' Tō ū khisiyā-ke bhit^{a}rī jāe
people-to thy father feeding is-for-thee.' Then he having-become-angry within to-go

na chahal^{a}thin. Tō un-kar bāp nikas-ke al^{a}thin, ō manāwe
not wished. Then his father having-come-out came, and to-remonstrate

lagal^{a}thin. Tab ū ap^{a}nā bāp-sē jawāb kailan, 'dēkhâ tō etek din-sē
began. Then he his-own father-to answer made, 'see then so-many days-from

tōhar sēbā kailī, ō kab^{a}hū̃ tōhar kahal na ṭar^{a}lī, au tū̃ ēgō
thy service I-did, and ever thy saying not disobeyed, and thou a

paṭh^{a}rū bhī na dēlâ ke ham ap^{a}nā yāran-ke saṅg khusī kar^{a}tī.
kid even not gavest that I my-own friends-of with happiness might-have-made.

Jakh^{a}nī tōhar ī bēṭā al^{a}thun, jē tōhar dhan kas^{a}bin saṅg uṛā
When thy this son came-for-thee, who thy wealth harlots with having-wasted

dēlak^{a}thun, tek^{a}rā lā jew^{a}nār karaulâ.' Tab bāp kahal^{a}kaïn ke,
gave-for-thee, him for a-feast thou-madest.' Then the-father said that,

'Tū̃ tō nit ham^{a}rā jauṛ hē, aur jē kuchh hamar hai, sē
'Thou indeed always me with art, and what anything mine is, that

[1] Here, and elsewhere the termination *thun* (not *thin*) is used because the subject of the verb is connected with the person addressed. It is *thy* brother who has come, and *thy* father who is giving the feast. Had it been any one else's brother or father, the termination (a respectful one) would have been *thin*. I have attempted to indicate this by adding the words '*for thee*' to the translation of the verb, as a kind of *dativus commodi*. So also lower down.

tōhar hai. Bākī khusī manāwe-kē chāhī kāhe ki ī tōhar bhāī
thine is. But happiness making-for is-proper because that this thy brother
jē mar gēl rah^{a}thun, sē jī gel^{a}thun; ō bhulā gēl rah^{a}thun,
who dead gone was-for-thee, he living went-for-thee; and lost gone was-for-thee,
sē mil gel^{a}thun.'
he found went-for-thee.'

JOLAHĀ BOLĪ.

The Musalmāns of North-Gangetic Bihār do not all speak Maithilī. Those of the Western Districts, Champaran, Saran, and Muzaffarpur speak a dialect akin to the Awadhī of the North-Western Provinces, which will be discussed when dealing with that form of speech. In Darbhanga most of the followers of Islām do speak the Maithilī of their Hindū neighbours, in a corrupt form, mixed up with Arabic and Persian words. The upper classes, as well as the more highly educated Hindūs of that District, speak Urdū or Hindōstānī, the number of speakers of this language being returned as about 4,000. The census shows 338,667 Musalmāns in the Darbhanga District, and, of these, the local officials return 337,000 as speaking this corrupt Maithilī, or, as it is called from the name of the caste of Muhammadan weavers, who are numerous in the District, Jolahā Bōlī[1].

Specimens of this dialect will be found in the writer's *Introduction to the Maithilī Language*, and, as a further example, the following version of the Parable of the Prodigal Son is appended.

---

[1] In Bihār, this caste is called *Jolahā*, with the two first vowels short. Further west they are called *Jōlāhā*.

[No. 17.]

INDO-ARYAN FAMILY. EASTERN GROUP.

BIHĀRĪ.

MAITHILĪ (JOLAHĀ BŌLĪ) DIALECT. (DARBHANGA.)

कोनो आदमी के दो बेटा छलैन। ओई में से छोटका बेटा अपना बाप से कहलन हे बाप धन में से जे हम्मर हिस्सा होय से हमरा बाँट दए। तब ऊ उनका अप्पन धन बाँट देलखिन। बहुत दिन ने भेलैन की छोटका बेटा सब कुछ एक जगह क के बहुत दूर देस चल गेल और उहाँ लुचपन में थोरा दिन में अप्पन धन उड़ा देलक। जब ऊ सब कुछ उड़ा देलक तब ओई देस में मेहँगी पड़लैक और उह गेरीब हो गेल। और ऊ जा के ओ देस के रहवैया में से एक के इहाँ रहे लागल। ऊ घरवाला ओकरा खेत में सूअर चरावे भेजलकै। तब ऊ खेत के छीमड़ि से जे सूअर खाए अप्पन पेट भरे चाहलक और कोए ने ओकरा कुछ दईक। तय ओकरा होस भेलैक तब ऊ अपना जी में कहलक की हमरा बाप कने बनिहार के खाएक से बेसी रोटी पकइअ और हम भूख से मरैछी। हम उठ के अपना बाप कने जाएब और उनका से कहबैन की हे बाप हम खोदा कने और तोहरा कने गुनाहगार छी हम फेरो तोहर बेटा कहावे जोकर नहि छिओ। अप्पन बनिहार में से एक हमरो रक्ख। तब उहाँ से उठ कर ऊ अपना बाप कने चलल। लेकिन जब ऊ फटकिए रहे ओकर बाप ओकरा ऊपर माया कलकैन और दौड़ क ओकरा गला में लगा लेलकै और चुम्मा लेलकै। बेटा उनका कहलथीन जे औ बाबू हम खोदा कने और तोहरा कने गुनाहगार छी हम फेर तोहर बेटा कहावे जोकर नहि छिओ। लेकिन बाप अपना नौकर से कहलन की सब से नीक जूआ जे है से इनका पहनाहून और इनका हाथ में औंगूठी और गोड़ में जूता पहिन ला दहून, और सब कोइ मिल के खाएन और खूशी करेन। किअक की ए बेटा हम्मर मरल छल फेर जोअल है। हेराएल छल से मिलल है। तब ऊ सब खूशी करे लगलन॥

ओकर बड़का बेटा खेत में रहे। खेत से जब घर के लग आएल तब अपना घर में ढोल और नाच के आवाज सुनलक। और अप्पन नौकर में से एकठो के बोला के पुछलक, ई की छई। ऊ ओकरा कहलकै तोहर भाई ऐलौ ह, और तोहर बाप खूब बढ़ियाँ भोज कलकौ ह एई लेल की ऊ ओकरा तनदुरुस्त पलकौ ह। तब ऊ बड़ा गुस्सा भेल और घर ने गेल। एई लेल ओकर बाप अपना बड़का बेटा के मनावे लागल। तब ऊ अपना बाप के जवाब देलक की देख हम एत्ता बरस से तोहर सेवा कैलिओ ह और कहिओ ने तोहर बात काटलिओ ह और तू हमरा कहिओ एकठो पाठी भी ने देल की हम अप्पन दोस्त मोहीब ल क खैतोन। लेकिन ई बेटा तोहर धन से क कसबी पतुरिआ के संग उड़ा देलकौ ह और ऊ जखनिआ आएल तखनिआ ओकरा ला बेस खाइक कैल ह। बाप ओकरा से कहलकै बेटा तों सदा हमरा संग छ और जे कुछ हम्मर है से सब तोहर छौ। मगर खूशी करना वाजिब है किअक के ई तोहर भाई मरल छलौ से फेर जीलौ ह हेरा गेल छलौ से फेर मिललौ ह॥

[No. 17.]

INDO-ARYAN FAMILY. EASTERN GROUP.

BIHĀRĪ.

MAITHILĪ (JOLAHĀ BŌLĪ) DIALECT. (DARBHANGA.)

Kōno ād^{a}mī-kē dō bēṭā chhalain. Ōī-mẽ-sē chhoṭ^{a}kā bēṭā
A certain man-to two sons were. Them-in-from the-younger son

ap^{a}nā bāp-sō kah^{a}lan, 'hē bāp, dhan-mẽ-sē jē hammar hissā
his father-to said, 'O father, goods-in-from whatever my share

hōy, sē ham^{a}rā bā̃ṭ dae.' Tab ū un^{a}kā appan dhan
may-be, that me dividing give.' Then he to-them his-own property

bā̃ṭ-del^{a}khin. Bahut din ne bhelain ki chhoṭ^{a}kā bēṭā sab-
divided. Many days not had-passed that the-younger son every-

kuchh ēk-jagah-ka-ke bahut dūr dēs chal-gēl, ăŭr uhā̃
thing putting-together (to-)very distant country went-away, and there

luch^{a}pan-mẽ thōrā din-mẽ appan dhan uṛā-dēlak. Jab ū sab-
riotous-living-in a-few days-in his fortune squandered. When he every-

kuchh uṛā-dēlak, tab ōī dēs-mẽ mehā̃gī paṛ^{a}laik, ăŭr uh gerīb
thing had-wasted, then that country-in famine fell, and he poor

hō-gēl. Aŭr ū jā-ke ō dēs-ke rah^{a}waiyā-mẽ sō ēk-ke
became. And he having-gone that country-of inhabitants-in from one-of

ihā̃ rahăĩ lāgal. Ū ghar-wālā ok^{a}rā khēt-mẽ sūar charābe
near to-live began. That owner-of-the-house him field-in swine to-feed

bhejal^{a}kai. Tab ū khēt-ke chhīmaṛi-sō jē sūar khāē, appan
sent. Then he the-field-of the-husk-with which swine used-to-eat, his-own

pēṭ bhare chāh^{a}lak, ăŭr kōe ne ok^{a}rā kuchh daīk. Tab
belly to-fill wished, and any-body not to-him any-thing used-to-give. Then

ok^{a}rā hōs bhelaik, tab ū ap^{a}nā jī-mẽ kah^{a}lak ki, 'ham^{a}rā bāp
to-him senses became, then he his-own mind-in thought that, 'my father

kane banihār-ke khāek sō bēśī rōṭī pakaïa, ăŭr ham
near labourers-of required-for-the-food than more bread is-cooked, and I

bhūkh-sē maraichhī. Ham uṭh-ke ap^{a}nā bāp-kane jāeb, ăŭr un^{a}kā-sē
hunger-with am-dying. I arising my father-to will-go, and him-to

kah^{a}bain ki, "hē bāp, ham Khōdā kane ăŭr toh^{a}rā kane gunāh-gār
will-say that, "O father, I God before and thee before a-sinner

chhī. Ham pherō tōhar bēṭā kahābe jōkar nah^{i} chhiau. Appan
am. I again-also thy son to-be-called fit not am-for-thee. Thy

banihār-mẽ-sē ēk ham^{a}rō rakkhā."' Tab uhā̃-sē uṭh-kar ū
hired-servants-in-from one me-also keep."' Then there-from arising he

ap^anā bāp kane chalal. Lēkin jab ū phaṭ^akiē rahē, ōkar bāp
his-own father to went. But when he at-a-distance was, his father
ok^arā ûpar māyā kal^akain, ăŭr dauṛ-ka ok^arā galā-mẽ lagā-lel^akai
him upon compassion made, and running him the-neck-by embraced,
ăŭr chummā lel^akai. Bēṭā un^akā kahal^athīn jē, 'au bābū, ham Khōdā
and kiss took. Son to-him said that, 'O father, I God
kane ăŭr toh^arā kane gunāh-gār chhi, ham pher tōhar bēṭā kahābe
before and thee before a-sinner am, I again thy son to-be-called
jōkar nah[1] chhiau.' Lēkin bāp ap^anā naukar-sē kah^alan ki, 'sab-
fit not am-for-thee.' But father his-own servants-to said that, 'all-
sē nīk nūā jē hai sē in^akā pah^anāhūn, ăŭr in^akā
than good dress that may-be that to-this-person put-on, and this-person's
bāth-mẽ ăŭgūṭhī ăŭr gōṛ-mẽ jūtā pahin lā dahūn, ăŭr sab-keh^u
hand-on ring and feet-on shoes putting on give, and (let)-us-all
mil-ke khāen ăŭr khūśī karen. Kiak kī ē bēṭā hammar maral
uniting eat and merriment make. Because that this son my dead
chhal, pher jīal hai; herāel chhal, sē milal hai.' Tab ū sab
was, again alive is; lost was, he found is.' Then they all
khūśī kare lag^alan.
merriment to-make began.

Ōkar baṛ^akā bēṭā khēt-mẽ rahē. Khēt-sē jab ghar-ke lag
His elder son the-field-in was. The-field-from when house-of near
āel, tab ap^anā ghar-mẽ ḍhōl ăŭr nāch-ke āwāj sun^alak, ăŭr appan
came, then his house-in drum and dancing-of sound heard, and his
naukar-mẽ-sē ēk-ṭhō-kē bolā-ke puchh^alak, 'ī kī hai?' Ū ok^arā
servants-in-from one-to calling asked, 'this what is?' He to-him
kahal^akai, 'tōhar bhāī ailau-hâ, ăŭr tōhar bāp khūb baṛhiyā̃
said, 'thy brother has-come-for-thee and thy father very excellent
bhōj kal^akau-hâ; ēī lēl kī ū ok^arā tan-durust pal^akau-hâ.'
feast has-made-for-thee[1]; this for that he him healthy has-found-for-thee.'
Tab ū baṛā gussā bhēl ăŭr ghar ne gēl. Ēī lēl ōkar
Then he very angry became and in-the-house not did-go. This for his
bāp ap^anā baṛ^akā bēṭā-kē manābe lāgal. Tab ū ap^anā bāp-kē
father his elder son-to to-entreat began. Then he his father-to
jawāb dēlak kī, 'dēkhâ, ham ettā baras-sē tōhar sēbā kai-
answer gave that, 'see, I so-many years-from thy service have-
liau-hâ, ăŭr kahiau ne tōhar bāt kaṭ^aliau-hâ, ăŭr tū
rendered-to-thee, and ever not thy order disobeyed-to-thee, and thou
ham^arā kahiau ēk-ṭhō pāṭhī bhī ne dēlâ, kī ham appan
to-me at-any-time a-single kid even not didst-give, that I my
dōst-mōhib la-ka khaitaun. Lēkin i bēṭā tōhar dhan lē-ka
friends having-taken might-eat-for-thee. But this son thy wealth taking

[1] *I.e.*, a kind of *dativus commodi*. The meaning of the termination *au* is 'the feast was given to *thy* brother.'

kas^{a}bī-paturiā-ke saṅg uṛā-del^{a}kau-hâ ā̃ŭr ū jakh^{a}niā āel takh^{a}niā
harlots-of with has-wasted-for-thee and he even-when came even-then
ok^{a}rā-lā bēs khāik kailâ-hâ.' Bāp ok^{a}rā-sē kahal^{a}kai, 'bēṭā
him-for excellent feast thou-hast-made.' Father him-to said, 'O son
tõ sadā ham^{a}rā-saṅg chhâ, ā̃ŭr jē-kuchh hammar hai, sē sab tōhar
thou ever me-with art, and what-ever mine is, that all thine
hau. Magar khŭśī-kar^{a}nā wājib hai, kiak-ke ī tōhar bhāī
is-to-thee. But merry-making proper is, because-that this thy brother
maral chhalau, sē pher jīlau-hâ; herā-gēl chhalau, sē
dead was-for-thee, he again alive-is-for-thee; lost was-for-thee, he
pher mil^{a}lau-hâ.'
gain found-is-for-thee.'

STANDARD MAGAHĪ.

The following specimen comes from the District of Gaya, where it is acknowledged that the purest form of Magahī is spoken. It is a translation of the Parable of the Prodigal Son, and is printed in Kaithī type, in which character it was originally written. It has been set up in type, exactly as written, so as to show the inaccuracies of spelling, such as the substitution of *ī* for *i* and of *u* for *ū*, which are common in the written character. These inaccuracies have been silently corrected in the transliteration. Note that an initial *ō* is written *wō*, and that *s* is always written *ś*.

[No. 18.]

INDO-ARYAN FAMILY. EASTERN GROUP.

BIHĀRĪ.

MAGAHĪ DIALECT. (GAYA DISTRICT.)

SPECIMEN I.

એક આદમી કે દુ ગો બેટા હલથીન। ઉનકન્હીં મેં સે છોટકા અપન બાપ સે કહલક કે એ બાબુજી તોહર ચીજ બતુસ મેં સે જે હમર બખરા હો હૈ સે હમરા દે દ। તબ ઊ અપન સબ ચીજ બતુસ ઉનકન્હીં દુનોં મેં બાંટ દેલક। ઢેર દીન બીતે ના પૌલક કે છોટકા બેટવા અપન સબ ચીજ બટોર સટોર કે કોઈ બડ઼ી દુર દેસ મેં ચલલ ગેલ। હુઆં જા કે અપન સબ પુંજી કુચાલી મેં ઓઆન કર દેલક। આઉ જબ સબ ગલાં ચુકલ તબ ઊ દેસ મેં બડ઼ી ભારી અકાલ પડલ આઉ ઓકરા હોકસીક હોએ લગલર। તબ હુઆં કે એગો રહવઇઆ હીંઆં જા કે રહે લગલ। ઊ ઓકરા અપન બાચ મેં સુઅર ચરાવે લ પેઠીલકર। આઉ ઊ સુઅનીઅન કે ખાએ વાલા ભુસા સે અપન પેટ ભરે લ મી લહલક હલ બાકો કોઈ ઓકરા ના દે હલર। જબ ઓકરા બુઝાએ લગલર તબ કહલક કે હમર બાપ કે કૈગો નૌકર ચાકર હથ જીનકા હંડુઆમન ખાએ કે હરન જે અનકા અનકા કે દે હથ। આઉ હમ ભુખેં મર હી। અબ ઉઠ કે અપન બાપ હીં જાએબ આઉ ઉનકા સે કહબ કે એ બાબુજી હમ ભગવાન ભીનો આઉ તોહરા ભીનો બડ઼ા પાપ કૈલી। આઉ અબ હમ તોહર બેટા કહાવે જુકુર ના હી। તું હમરા અપન એગો મજુરા નીઅર રખ। બસ ઊ ઉઠલ આઉ અપન બાપ હીંઆં ગેલ। અખની ઓકરા પહુંચે લ કુછ દુર બાકીએ હલર કે ઓકર બપવા ઓકરા દેખલકર। ઊ દેખ કે ઓકરા બડ઼ા મોહ લગલર। આઉ દઉડ઼ કે ઓકરા ગલા સે ભાલલર આઉ ચુમે ચાટે લગલર। તબ બેટવા ઓકરા સે કહલકર કે એ બાબુજી હમ ભગવાન ભીનો આઉ તોહરા ભીનો બડ઼ા પાપ કૈલી આઉ હમ તોહર બેટા કહાવે જુકુર ના હી। બાકો ઓકર બપવા અપન નૌકરવન સે કહલકર કે ખુબ બેસ બેસ ઝુગા લાલો આઉ એકરા પેન્હાવહીં આઉ એકરા હાથ મેં અંગુઠી પેન્હા દેહીં આઉ ગોડ઼ મેં જુતા દેહીં આઉ હમન્હીં ખુબ ખાતે પીતે જાર આઉ ખુસી કરી કાહે કે ર બેટા હમર મર ચુકલ હલ આઉ ફેન કે જીઅલ હૈ ઈ ભુલા ગેલ હલ આઉ અબ ફેન કે મીલલ હૈ। આઉ ઊ સબ ખુસી મચાવે લગલન॥

ઓકર બડ઼કા બેટવા બાધ મેં હલર આઉ જબ હુઆં સે આ કે ઘર ભીનો પહુચલ તબ ગીત આઉ નાચ સુનલક। તબ એગો નૌકર કે બોલા કે પુછલક કે

𑂆 𑂮𑂥 𑂍𑂰 𑂯𑂷𑂅𑂞 𑂯𑂶 𑃀 𑂈 𑂍𑂯𑂪𑂍𑂅 𑂍𑂵 𑂞𑂷𑂯𑂩 𑂦𑂰𑂅 𑂊𑂪𑂟𑂳 𑂯𑂶 𑂮𑂵𑂅 𑂮𑂵 𑂞𑂷𑂯𑂩 𑂥𑂰𑂣 𑂎𑂰𑂥 𑂣𑂲𑂥 𑂍𑂩𑂅𑂞 𑂯𑂟𑂳 𑂍𑂰𑂯𑂵 𑂍𑂵 𑂥𑂵𑂗𑂰 𑂞𑂷𑂍𑂵 𑂮𑂳𑂎𑂹𑂎𑂵 𑂐𑂩 𑂃𑂶𑂪𑂟𑂲𑂢 𑂯𑂶 𑃀 𑂞𑂥 𑂈 𑂎𑂲𑂮𑂲𑂄 𑂏𑂵𑂪 𑂄𑂇 𑂦𑂲𑂞𑂩𑂵 𑂢𑂰 𑂏𑂵𑂪 𑃀 𑂞𑂥 𑂋𑂍𑂩 𑂥𑂣𑂹𑂣𑂵 𑂥𑂰𑂯𑂩 𑂢𑂱𑂍𑂪 𑂃𑂶𑂪𑂅 𑂄𑂇 𑂮𑂧𑂕𑂰𑂥𑂵 𑂥𑂳𑂕𑂰𑂥𑂵 𑂪𑂏𑂪𑂅 𑃀 𑂞𑂥 𑂈 𑂃𑂣𑂢 𑂥𑂰𑂣 𑂮𑂵 𑂥𑂷𑂪𑂪 𑂍𑂵 𑂉𑂞𑂵 𑂥𑂩𑂲𑂮 𑂮𑂵 𑂯𑂧 𑂞𑂷𑂯𑂩 𑂮𑂵𑂫𑂰 𑂍𑂩𑂅𑂞 𑂯𑂲 𑂄𑂇 𑂍𑂯𑂲𑂥𑂷 𑂞𑂷𑂯𑂩 𑂍𑂯𑂢𑂰 𑂮𑂵 𑂥𑂰𑂯𑂩 𑂢𑂰 𑂩𑂯𑂪𑂲 𑃀 𑂞𑂅𑂥𑂷 𑂉𑂏𑂷 𑂣𑂘𑂩𑂳 𑂦𑂲 𑂢𑂰 𑂠𑂵𑂪 𑂍𑂵 𑂃𑂣𑂢 𑂅𑂄𑂩 𑂠𑂷𑂮𑂞 𑂔𑂷𑂏𑂵 𑂎𑂳𑂮𑂲 𑂧𑂢𑂸𑂞𑂲 𑂯𑂪 𑃀 𑂥𑂰𑂍𑂲 𑂔𑂅𑂮𑂯𑂲𑂁 𑂞𑂷𑂯𑂩 𑂆 𑂥𑂵𑂗𑂰 𑂃𑂅𑂪𑂸 𑂔𑂵 𑂞𑂷𑂯𑂩 𑂮𑂥 𑂧𑂰𑂪-𑂔𑂰𑂪 𑂣𑂞𑂳𑂩𑂲𑂃𑂢 𑂧𑂵𑂁 𑂔𑂲𑂄𑂢 𑂍𑂩 𑂠𑂵𑂪𑂍𑂸 𑂞𑂳𑂁 𑂋𑂍𑂩𑂰 𑂪𑂰 𑂎𑂰𑂢 𑂣𑂲𑂃𑂢 𑂍𑂶𑂪 𑃀 𑂞𑂥 𑂋𑂍𑂩𑂰 𑂮𑂵 𑂈 𑂍𑂯𑂪𑂍𑂅 𑂍𑂵 𑂉 𑂥𑂵𑂗𑂰 𑂞𑂳𑂁 𑂞𑂷 𑂯𑂧𑂩𑂰 𑂮𑂰𑂧𑂢𑂵 𑂯𑂩𑂠𑂧 𑂧𑂵𑂁 𑂩𑂯 𑂯𑂶 𑂄𑂇 𑂔𑂵 𑂍𑂳𑂓 𑂯𑂧𑂩 𑂯𑂶 𑂮𑂵 𑂮𑂥 𑂞𑂷 𑂞𑂷𑂩𑂵 𑂯𑂇 𑃀 𑂯𑂧𑂢𑂲𑂯𑂷𑂁 𑂍𑂵 𑂇𑂒𑂲𑂞 𑂯𑂶 𑂍𑂵 𑂎𑂳𑂮𑂲 𑂧𑂢𑂰𑂥𑂷𑂁 𑂄𑂇 𑂄𑂢𑂢𑂹𑂠 𑂍𑂩𑂷𑂁 𑂍𑂰𑂯𑂵 𑂍𑂵 𑂞𑂷𑂩 𑂆 𑂦𑂰𑂅 𑂧𑂩 𑂏𑂵𑂪𑂇 𑂯𑂪 𑂔𑂲𑂪𑂇 𑂯𑂶 𑂦𑂳𑂪𑂪 𑂏𑂵𑂪𑂇 𑂯𑂪 𑂧𑂱𑂪𑂪𑂇 𑂯𑂶 𑃁

[No. 18.]

INDO-ARYAN FAMILY. EASTERN GROUP.

BIHĀRĪ.

MAGAHĪ DIALECT. (GAYA DISTRICT.)

SPECIMEN I.

TRANSLITERATION AND TRANSLATION.

Ek ād^{a}mī-kē dugō bēṭā hal^{a}thin. Un^{a}kanhī̃-mē̃-sē chhoṭ^{a}kā apan
One man-of two sons were. Them-in-from the-younger his-own

bāp-sē kah^{a}lak ke, 'ē bābū-jī! tōhar chīj-batus-mē̃-sē jē hamar
father-to said that, 'O father! thy property-in-from which my

bakh^{a}rā hō-hai sē ham^{a}rā dē-dâ.' Tab ū apan sab chīj-batus un^{a}kanhī̃
share may-be that me-to give.' Then he his-own all goods them

dūnō̃-mē̃ bā̃ṭ-dēlak. Ḍhēr din bīte nā paulak ke chhoṭ^{a}kā
both-between dividing-gave. Many days to-pass not were-allowed that the-younger

beṭ^{a}wā apan sab chīj baṭōr-saṭōr-ke kōī baṛī dūr dēs-mē̃ chalal-gēl.
son his-own all things collecting a-certain very far country-into went-away.

Huā̃ jā-ke apan sab pū̃jī kuchāli-mē̃ jiān-kar-dēlak. Āu jab sab
There going his-own all fortune misconduct-in he-wasted-away. And when all

gawā̃-chukal tab ū dēs-mē̃ baṛī bhārī akāl paṛal; āu ok^{a}rā dik-sik
he-had-lost then that country-in very heavy famine fell; and him-to trouble

hōāī lag^{a}lai. Tab huā̃-ke ẹgō rah^{a}waiyā hī̃ā̃ jā-ke rahe lagal. Ū ok^{a}rā
to-be began. Then there-of one inhabitant near going to-live he-began. He him

apan bādh-mē̃ sūar charāwe-lā peṭhaul^{a}kai. Āu ū suarian-ke khāe-wālā
his-own field-in swine feeding-for sent. And he swine-of eatable

bhūsā-sē apan pēṭ bhare-lā bhī lilhka-hal; bākī kōī ok^{a}rā nā dē-halai.
husks-with his-own belly to-fill also covet-did; but any-one him not was-giving.

Jab ok^{a}rā bujhāe lag^{a}lai tab kah^{a}lak ke, 'hamar bāp-ke kai-gō
When to-him understanding began then he-said that, 'my father-of several

naukar-chākar hath, jin^{a}kā hā̃ṭhuā-man khāe-kē haïn jē an^{a}kā an^{a}kā-kē
servants are, with-whom abundant food-for-eating is which others others-to

dē-hath; āu ham bhūkhē̃ marà-hī. Ab uṭh-ke apan bāp hī̃
giving-are; and I hunger-from dying-am. Now arising my-own father near

jāeb āu un^{a}kā-sē kahab ke, "ē bābū-jī, ham Bhag^{a}wān bhīrī
I-will-go and him-to I-will-say that, "O father, I God before

āu toh^{a}rā bhīrī baṛā pāp kailī, āu ab ham tōhar bēṭā kahāwe
and thee before great sin did, and now I thy son to-be-called

jukur nā̃ hī. Tū̃ ham^{a}rā apan ēgō majūrā nīar rakhâ."' Bas, ū
fit not am. Thou me thy-own one labourer like keep."' Enough, he
uṭhal āu apan bāp hīā̃ gēl. Jakhanō ok^{a}rā pahū̃che-lā kuchh dūr
arose and his-own father near went. When to-him to-reach some distance
bāki-ai halai ke ōkar bappā ok^{a}rā dekhal^{a}kai. Ū dēkh-ke ok^{a}rā
remaining-even was that his father him saw. He seeing him
baṛā mōh lag^{a}lai. Āu dauṛ-ke ok^{a}rā galā-sē mil^{a}lai, āu chūme chāṭe
great pity felt. And running his neck-with met, and to-kiss (and) lick
lag^{a}lai. Tab beṭ^{a}wā ok^{a}rā-sē kahal^{a}kai ke, 'ē bābū-jī, ham Bhag^{a}wān
began. Then the-son him-to said that, 'O father, I God
bhīrī āu toh^{a}rā bhīrī baṛā pāp kailī, āu ham tōhar bēṭā kahāwe
before and thee before great sin have-done, and I thy son to-be-called
jukur nā̃ hī.' Bākī ōkar bappā apan nokar^{a}wan-sē kahal^{a}kai ke, 'khūb
fit not am.' But his father his-own servants-to said that, 'very
bēs bēs lūgā lāō āu ek^{a}rā penhāwahī̃; āu ek^{a}rā hāth-mē̃ ā̃guṭhī
good good cloth bring and him put-on; and this-one hand-on ring
penhā-dēhī̃, āu gōṛ-mē̃ jūtā dēhī̃; āu ham^{a}nhī̃ khūb khātē-pītē-jāī̃, āu
put-on, and feet-on shoes give; and we well may-eat-and-drink, and
khusī karī̃; kāhe-kē ī bēṭā hamar mar chukal-hal, āu phen-ke jīal
merriment make; because this son my dead been-had, and again alive
hai; ī bhulā-gēl-hal, āu ab phen-ke milal-hai.' Au ū sab
is; this-one lost-had-been, and now again found-is.' And they all
khusī machāwe lag^{a}lan.
merriment to-make began.

Ōkar baṛ^{a}kā beṭ^{a}wā bādh-mē̃ halai. Āu jab huā̃-sē ā-ke ghar
His elder son field-in was. And when there-from coming house
bhīrī pahū̃chal tab gīt āu nāch sun^{a}lak. Tab ēgō naukar-kē bolā-ke
near reached then song and dance he-heard. Then one servant calling
puchh^{a}lak ke, 'ī sab kā hōit hai?' Ū kahal^{a}kai ke tōhar bhāī
asked that, 'this all what being is?' He said that thy brother
ā̃il^{a}thū hai, sēī-se tōhar bāp khān-pian karait-hathū; kāhe-ke
came(-for-thee)[1] *is, therefore thy father a-feast doing-is(-for-thee)*[1]*; because*
bēṭā nīkē sukhē ghar ā̃il^{a}thin-hai.' Tab ū khisiā gēl āu
the-son well (and) happy the-house-to come-is.' Then he angry became and
bhit^{a}rē nā gēl. Tab ōkar bappē bāhar nikal-ā̃llai āu sam^{a}jhāwe-bujhāwe
inside not went. Then his father outside came-out and to-conciliate
lag^{a}lai. Tab ū apan bāp-sē bōlal ke, 'ētē bachhar-sē ham tōhar
began. Then he his-own father-to spoke that, 'so-many years-since I thy
sēwā karait-hī āu kahiō tōhar kah^{a}nā-sē bāhar nā rah^{a}lī, taiō
service am-doing and ever-even thy saying-from out not lived, nevertheless

[1] This is to represent the force of the termination *thū*, instead of *thī*. It does not mean that the brother has come 'to thee,' but is a kind of *dativus commodi*, impossible to give accurately in English. The form in *thū* is used because it is '*thy* brother,' who is come. So later on, the feast is not given 'in thy honour' but it is '*thy* father' who has given it.

ēgō paṭh^{a}rū bhī nā dēlā ke apan iār-dōst jōre khusī
one kid even not thou-gavest that my-own friends with merriment

machautī-hal. Bākī jais^{a}hī̃ tōhar ī bēṭā āïlau jē tōhar sab māl-jāl
I-might-have-made. But as (even) thy this son came-for-thee who thy all property

paturian-mẽ jiān-kar-del^{a}kau tū̃ ok^{a}rā-lā khāu-piau kailā.' Tab ok^{a}rā-sē
harlots-in wasted-for-thee thou him-for a-feast hast-done.' Then him-to

ū kahal^{a}kai ke, 'ē bēṭā, tū̃ tō ham^{a}rā sām^{a}nē har dammẽ
he said that, 'O son, thou to-be-sure me before every moment-even

raha-hai, āu jē-kuchh hamar hai sē sab tō tōrē hau.
livest, and whatever mine is that all to-be-sure thine-even is-to-thee.

Ham^{a}nhī̃-kē uchit hai ke khusī machāwī̃ āu ānand
Us-to proper is that merriment we-may-raise and rejoicing

karī̃; kāhe-ke, tōr ī bhāī mar gelau-hal, jīlau
we-may-make; because, thy this brother dead(-for-thee)[1] became, alive

hai; bhūlal-gelau-hal, mil^{a}lau hai.'
is(-for-thee); had-been-lost(-for-thee), found is(-for-thee).'

The next specimen is also from Gaya. The remarks prefixed to the preceding specimen apply also to this. The subject is a folk-tale.

---

[1] These terminations are *au*, not *ai* because it is *thy* brother who was dead, etc.

[No. 19.]

INDO-ARYAN FAMILY. EASTERN GROUP.

BIHĀRĪ.

MAGAHĪ DIALECT. (GAYA DISTRICT.)

SPECIMEN II.

𑂍𑂷𑂆 𑂔𑂁𑂏𑂪 𑂧𑂵𑂁 𑂉𑂏𑂷 𑂮𑂰𑂡𑂳 𑂩𑂯 𑂯𑂪𑂢, 𑂇𑂢 𑂍𑂰 𑂦𑂲𑂩𑂲 𑂉𑂏𑂷 𑂩𑂰𑂔𑂰 𑂐𑂳𑂧𑂞𑂵 𑂐𑂳𑂧𑂞𑂵 𑂔𑂰 𑂣𑂯𑂳𑂀𑂒𑂪𑂢, 𑂄𑂇 𑂮𑂰𑂡𑂳 𑂍𑂵 𑂠𑂵𑂎 𑂍𑂵 𑂣𑂰𑂋𑂁 𑂪𑂰𑂏𑂍𑂵 𑂥𑂅𑂘 𑂏𑂵𑂪𑂢𑃀 𑂮𑂰𑂡𑂳 𑂇𑂢𑂍𑂰 𑂣𑂱𑂄𑂮𑂪 𑂔𑂰𑂢 𑂍𑂵 𑂟𑂷𑂚𑂰 𑂊𑂮𑂢 𑂔𑂁𑂏𑂪 𑂍𑂵 𑂍𑂳𑂓 𑂎𑂰𑂉 𑂪𑂰 𑂠𑂵𑂪𑂟𑂲𑂢, 𑂄𑂇 𑂣𑂰𑂢𑂲 𑂣𑂲𑂪𑂰 𑂠𑂵𑂪𑂟𑂲𑂢𑃀 𑂩𑂰𑂔𑂰 𑂎𑂰 𑂍𑂵 𑂄𑂇 𑂣𑂰𑂢𑂲 𑂣𑂲 𑂍𑂵 𑂥𑂯𑂳𑂞 𑂎𑂳𑂮 𑂦𑂵𑂪𑂢, 𑂄𑂇 𑂘𑂝𑂹𑂛𑂰 𑂯𑂫𑂰 𑂧𑂵𑂁 𑂟𑂷𑂚𑂵 𑂠𑂵𑂩 𑂥𑂶𑂘𑂪𑂰 𑂮𑂵 𑂟𑂍𑂶𑂢𑂲 𑂧𑂵𑂗 𑂏𑂵𑂪𑂅𑂢𑃀 𑂞𑂥 𑂩𑂰𑂔𑂰 𑂮𑂰𑂡𑂳 𑂔𑂲 𑂮𑂵 𑂯𑂰𑂟 𑂔𑂷𑂚 𑂍𑂵 𑂣𑂳𑂓𑂪𑂢 𑂍𑂵 𑂧𑂯𑂰𑂩𑂰𑂔 𑂯𑂧𑂩𑂰 𑂍𑂳𑂓 𑂮𑂱𑂎𑂰𑂫𑂢 𑂍𑂵 𑂥𑂰𑂞 𑂍𑂯𑂲𑂁 𑂍𑂵 𑂔𑂵𑂍𑂩𑂰 𑂮𑂵 𑂯𑂧𑂩 𑂍𑂪𑂹𑂨𑂰𑂢 𑂯𑂷𑂉𑃀 𑂮𑂰𑂡𑂳 𑂔𑂲 𑂥𑂷𑂪𑂪𑂢 𑂍𑂵 𑂆 𑂒𑂰𑂩𑂷 𑂥𑂰𑂞 𑂍𑂵 𑂎𑂵𑂄𑂪 𑂩𑂎, 𑂣𑂯𑂱𑂪𑂰 𑂆 𑂍𑂵 𑂢𑂰𑂩𑂰𑂨𑂢 𑂮𑂹𑂫𑂰𑂧𑂲 𑂍𑂵 𑂢𑂰𑂧 𑂯𑂩 𑂠𑂧 𑂔𑂣𑂢𑂰, 𑂠𑂳𑂮𑂩 𑂆 𑂍𑂵 𑂮𑂥 𑂔𑂲𑂫 𑂣𑂩 𑂠𑂨𑂰 𑂩𑂎𑂢𑂰, 𑂞𑂲𑂮𑂩 𑂆 𑂍𑂵 𑂃𑂣𑂢𑂰 𑂏𑂳𑂩𑂳 𑂍𑂵 𑂮𑂵𑂫𑂰 𑂍𑂩𑂢𑂰, 𑂄𑂇 𑂒𑂇𑂘𑂰 𑂆 𑂍𑂵 𑂍𑂦𑂲 𑂍𑂷𑂆 𑂥𑂰𑂞 𑂍𑂵 𑂐𑂧𑂝𑂹𑂙 𑂢𑂰 𑂍𑂩𑂢𑂰𑃀 𑂆 𑂒𑂰𑂩𑂷 𑂥𑂰𑂞 𑂍𑂵 𑂔𑂵 𑂍𑂵𑂇 𑂮𑂰𑂡𑂢 𑂍𑂩 𑂯𑂶 𑂋𑂍𑂩𑂰 𑂣𑂩 𑂦𑂏𑂫𑂰𑂢 𑂮𑂠𑂰 𑂎𑂳𑂮 𑂩𑂯 𑂯𑂟 𑂄𑂇 𑂃𑂢𑂹𑂞 𑂧𑂵𑂁 𑂋𑂍𑂩𑂰 𑂥𑂶𑂍𑂳𑂝𑂹𑂘 𑂧𑂲𑂪𑂞 𑂯𑂶𑃀 𑂉𑂍𑂩𑂰 𑂮𑂵𑂫𑂰𑂉 𑂉𑂍 𑂥𑂰𑂞 𑂩𑂰𑂔𑂰 𑂪𑂷𑂏 𑂍𑂵 𑂄𑂇 𑂦𑂲 𑂯𑂶𑃀 𑂈 𑂆 𑂯𑂶 𑂍𑂵 𑂢𑂹𑂨𑂰𑂫 𑂧𑂵𑂁 𑂣𑂍𑂹𑂍𑂰 𑂩𑂯𑂵 𑂍𑂵 𑂒𑂰𑂯𑂲𑃀 𑂍𑂦𑂲 𑂍𑂵𑂍𑂩𑂷 𑂎𑂰𑂞𑂲𑂩 𑂮𑂵 𑂍𑂵𑂍𑂩𑂷 𑂥𑂲𑂏𑂰𑂚𑂵 𑂦𑂰 𑂥𑂢𑂰𑂫𑂵 𑂍𑂵 𑂢𑂰 𑂒𑂰𑂯𑂲𑃀 𑂆 𑂮𑂥 𑂥𑂰𑂞 𑂩𑂰𑂔𑂰 𑂮𑂳𑂢 𑂍𑂵 𑂮𑂰𑂡𑂳 𑂔𑂲 𑂍𑂵 𑂣𑂰𑂋𑂁 𑂣𑂩 𑂏𑂲𑂩 𑂣𑂩𑂪𑂢 𑂄𑂇 𑂍𑂯𑂪𑂢 𑂍𑂵 𑂯𑂧𑂩𑂰 𑂞𑂴𑂁 𑂃𑂣𑂢 𑂒𑂵𑂪𑂰 𑂥𑂢𑂰 𑂪𑃀 𑂞𑂥 𑂮𑂰𑂡𑂳 𑂔𑂲 𑂍𑂯𑂪𑂢 𑂍𑂵 𑂔𑂰 𑂞𑂴𑂁 𑂢𑂹𑂨𑂰𑂫 𑂮𑂵 𑂩𑂰𑂔 𑂍𑂩 𑂪𑃀 𑂢𑂹𑂨𑂰𑂫 𑂮𑂵 𑂩𑂰𑂔 𑂍𑂩𑂢𑂰 𑂔𑂁𑂏𑂪 𑂧𑂵𑂁 𑂥𑂶𑂘 𑂍𑂵 𑂞𑂣𑂮𑂵𑂄 𑂍𑂩𑂢𑂰 𑂮𑂵 𑂦𑂲 𑂥𑂵𑂮 𑂯𑂶𑃀 𑂉𑂞𑂢𑂰 𑂧𑂵𑂁 𑂩𑂰𑂔𑂰 𑂍𑂵 𑂮𑂲𑂣𑂰𑂯𑂲 𑂣𑂇𑂔𑂲 𑂩𑂰𑂔𑂰 𑂍𑂵 𑂎𑂷𑂔𑂞𑂵 𑂎𑂷𑂔𑂞𑂵 𑂯𑂳𑂄𑂀 𑂣𑂯𑂳𑂀𑂒 𑂏𑂵𑂪𑂢𑃀 𑂞𑂥 𑂮𑂰𑂡𑂳 𑂔𑂲 𑂍𑂵 𑂣𑂩𑂢𑂰𑂧 𑂍𑂩 𑂍𑂵 𑂩𑂰𑂔𑂰 𑂃𑂣𑂢 𑂏𑂰𑂀𑂫 𑂧𑂵𑂁 𑂐𑂳𑂩 𑂊𑂪𑂢𑃁

[No. 19.]

INDO-ARYAN FAMILY. EASTERN GROUP.

BIHĀRĪ.

MAGAHĪ DIALECT. (GAYA DISTRICT.)

SPECIMEN II.

TRANSLITERATION AND TRANSLATION.

Kōī jaṅgal-mẽ ēgō sādhū raha-halan. Un'kā bhīrī ēgō Rājā
A-certain forest-in one saint used-to-live. Him near one king
bhulātē-bhulātē jā-pahũch'lan āu sādhū-kē dēkh-ke pāõ lāg-ke baiṭh-gēlan.
losing-(his)-way went-up-to and saint seeing (his)-feet touching sat-down.
Sādhū un'kā piāsal jān-ke thōṛā-aisan jaṅgal-ke phar khāe-lā del'thin,
The-saint him thirsty knowing a-little-like forest-of fruit to-eat gave,
āu pānī pilā del'thin. Rājā khā-ke āu pānī pī-ke bahut khus
and water to-drink gave. The-king eating and water drinking very glad
bhēlan, āu ṭhanḍhā hawā-mẽ thōṛē bēr baiṭh'lā-sē thakainī
became, and cool air-in some time-(for) sitting-by weariness
nikal-gelain. Tab Rājā sādhū-jī-sē hāth jōr-ke puchh'lan
went-out (was-removed). Then the-king the-saint-to hand clasping asked
ke, 'Mahārāj! ham'rā kuchh sikhāwan-ke bāt kahī̃, ke jek'rā-sē hamar
that, 'O-great-king! me some advice-of things say, that which-by my
kaleān hōy.' Sādhū-jī bol'lan ke, 'ī chārō bāṭ-ke iād rakhā.
welfare may-be.' The-saint spoke that, 'these four things memory keep.
Pahilā ī ke, Narāyan sāmī-ke nām har dam jap'nā.
The-first this that, God lord-of name every moment should-be-muttered.
Dūsar ī ke, sab jīu par dayā rakh'nā. Tīsar ī
The-second this that, all lives on compassion should-be-kept. The-third this
ke, an-kar chūk-ke chhamā kar'nā. Āu chauṭhā ī ke, kabhī
that, others mistake-of mercy is-to-be-made. And the-fourth this that, ever
kōī bāt-ke ghamanḍ nā-kar'nā. Ī chārō bāt-kē jē-keu sādhan-
any thing-of pride not-to-be-made. These four things who-ever brings-
kara-hai, ok'rā par Bhag'wān sadā khus raha-hath. Āu ant-mẽ
into-practice, him on God always pleased is. And the-end-in
ok'rā baikunṭh mila-hai. Ek'rā sewāy ēk bāt rājā-lōg-kē āu bhī hai.
him Heaven is-given. This besides one thing kings-for more also is.
Ū ī hai ke, neāw-mẽ pakkā rahe-kē chāhī. Kabhī kek'rō
That this is that, justice-in firm to-remain is-proper. Ever anybody-of

khātir sē kek^{a}rō bigāṛe yā banāwe-kē nā' chāhī.' Ī sab
favour for anybody-of to-unmake or to-make not is-proper.' These all

bāt Rājā sun-ke sādhū-jī-ke pā̃o-par gir-par^{a}lan, āu kah^{a}lan ke,
things the-king hearing the-saint-of feet-on fell-down, and said that,

'ham^{a}rā tū̃ apan chēlā banā-lā.' Tab sādhū-jī kah^{a}lan ke, 'jā
'me thou thine-own disciple make.' Then the-saint said that, 'go

tū̃, neāw-sē rāj-kara-gā. Neāw-sē rāj-kar^{a}nā, jaṅgal-mē̃
thou, justice-with govern. Justice-with it-is-proper-to-rule, forest-in

baiṭh-ke tapaseā-kar^{a}nā-sē bhī bēs hai.' Et^{a}nā-mē̃ Rājā-ke
sitting to-practise-austerities-than even better is.' In-the-meantime the-king-of

sipāhī patukī Rājā-kē khōj^{a}tē-khōj^{a}tē huā̃ pahũch-gēlan. Tab sādhū-jī-kē
sepoys followers the-king-for searching there arrived. Then the-saint-to

par^{a}nām-kar-ke Rājā apan gā̃w-mē̃ ghur-ailan.
bowing-down the-king his-own village-into returned.

FREE TRANSLATION OF THE FOREGOING.

In a certain forest there dwelt a saint. One day a king lost his way and approached him. When the king saw him he paid him reverence and sat down. The saint seeing that he was thirsty gave him some wild fruit to eat and some water to drink. When he ate the fruit and drank the water, the king became glad in heart, and, after sitting for a short time in the cool air, his weariness left him. Then reverently clasping his hands before the holy man he said to him, 'Reverend Sir, deign to tell me some words of advice, by which my welfare may be assured.' The saint replied, 'Keep in thy remembrance these four things: First, to ever keep repeating the name of God; Second, to show compassion to all living creatures; Third, to be tolerant to the errors of others; and Fourthly, never to be vain-glorious for any cause. He who practiseth these four things, with him God is well-pleased, and, in the end, he findeth eternal bliss. Besides these, there is one thing more to be observed by kings, and it is this:—Ever remain firm in justice, and never promote or degrade anyone out of partiality.' When the king had made an end of hearing these words, he fell at the feet of the holy man crying, 'Take thou me as thy disciple.' But the saint in answer said, 'Go thou, and rule thy kingdom justly. To rule with justice is better than sitting in the forest and practising austerities.' In the meantime, the soldiers and followers of the king, who had been seeking him, arrived, and the king bowed down before the saint and returned to his own village.

The dialect of the Patna District is practically the same as that of Gaya. It is not however so pure, being influenced, on the one hand, by the Musalmān element of the City of Patna, and, on the other hand, by the Maithilī spoken north of the Ganges in the Mozaffarpur District.

To the first may be attributed the use of the genitive postposition *kērā*, with a feminine *kērī*, instead of *kēr* which is an obvious imitation of the Urdū *kā*, feminine *kī*. We may also, in the same connexion note a common form of the third person singular of the Past tense, ending in *is;* thus, *dēkhis*, which is used by Musalmāns, as it is across the Ganges, and which is borrowed from the language current in Oudh.

To the influence of Maithilī may be attributed the use of the word *gelain*, he went, in the first of the two following specimens.

The first specimen from Patna is a little scene in a zamīndārī cutchery. In which a peon, named Gūhan Singh, brings a complaint against a tenant named Jag Mōhan Singh. It is printed in facsimile, exactly as it was written, thus giving an example of Kaithī hand-writing as current in Patna.

[No. 20.]

INDO-ARYAN FAMILY. EASTERN GROUP.

BIHĀRĪ.

MAGAHĪ DIALECT. (PATNA DISTRICT.)

SPECIMEN I.

[illegible]

[illegible]

[illegible]

[illegible]

[illegible]

[illegible]

[illegible]

[illegible]

[illegible]

[illegible]

[illegible]

[illegible]

[illegible]

[No. 20.]

INDO-ARYAN FAMILY. EASTERN GROUP.

BIHARĪ.

MAGAHĪ DIALECT. (PATNA DISTRICT.)

SPECIMEN I.

TRANSLITERATION AND TRANSLATION.

Gūhan Siṁh,—Ē Gumāstā-jī, ap'ne-sē ham kā kahī̃? Jag-Mōhan Siṁh,
Gūhan Siṅh,—O Agent-sir, you-to I what may-say? Jag-Mōhan Singh,
Mōhan Rāy Gaṅgā Lāl āur Pōkhan-ke khēt-ke pānī kāṭ-ke appan khēt-
Mōhan Rāy Gaṅgā Lāl and Pōkhan-of field-of water having-cut his-own field-
mē̃ lē-gēlan. Sē hiahī̃ sām'nē hathū.[1] Pūchh-lēhun. Ū-par gā̃ṛāṛī bhī
in took-away. He here before is(-for-you.) Ask-(him). That-on bund also
bā̃dh-del'thī, āur nich'lā khēt sabh paṭā-lel'thī. Ab pānī āwe-kē daur
he-constructed, and lower fields all levelled. Now water coming-for way
na-haï. Ūpar-kā[2] sabh khēṭē ṭā̃ṛ hō-gelai.
not-is. Up-of all fields barren become-have.

Gumāsta—Jag-Mōhan Siṁh, ī kā bāt haï?
The-Agent—Jag-Mōhan Singh, this what thing is?

Jag-Mōhan Siṁh,—Gūhan-Siṁh-sē ēk chilim gā̃jā-lā jhag'rā
Jag-Mōhan Singh,—Gūhan-Singh-with one pipe-bowl (-of) gānjā-for quarrel
hō-gēl-hal, ap'ne chal-ke dēkh-lâ. Ham kahā̃ gā̃ṛāṛī bā̃dh'lī-hē? Gā̃ṛāṛī
has-become, yourself going see. I where bund have-constructed? Bund
bā̃dh-ke tō Bhat'nī Kahārin sabh pānī le-gelain.[3]
having-constructed to-be-sure Bhat'nī water-bearer's-wife all water took-away.

Gumāstā.—Gūhan Siṁh chalâ; khēt tō dek'lāwâ.
The-Agent.—Gūhan Singh come-along; the-field now show (me).

The next specimen also comes from Patna, and is a village folksong describing how a young wife rebels against the harsh language of her mother-in-law. As it is in verse, the vowel *a* which is at the end of every word, but which is not pronounced in prose, is here fully pronounced. So also, the silent *a* in the middle of a word, which, in prose, is written as a small ' above the line. Hence, in both these cases, the *a* will be found fully written in the lines below. As in the case of the last specimen, it is printed in facsimile.

---

[1] Note the force of *hathū*, instead of *hathī*.
[2] *kā* is an oblique form of *ke*, borrowed from Bhojpurī.
[3] This is a Maithilī form.

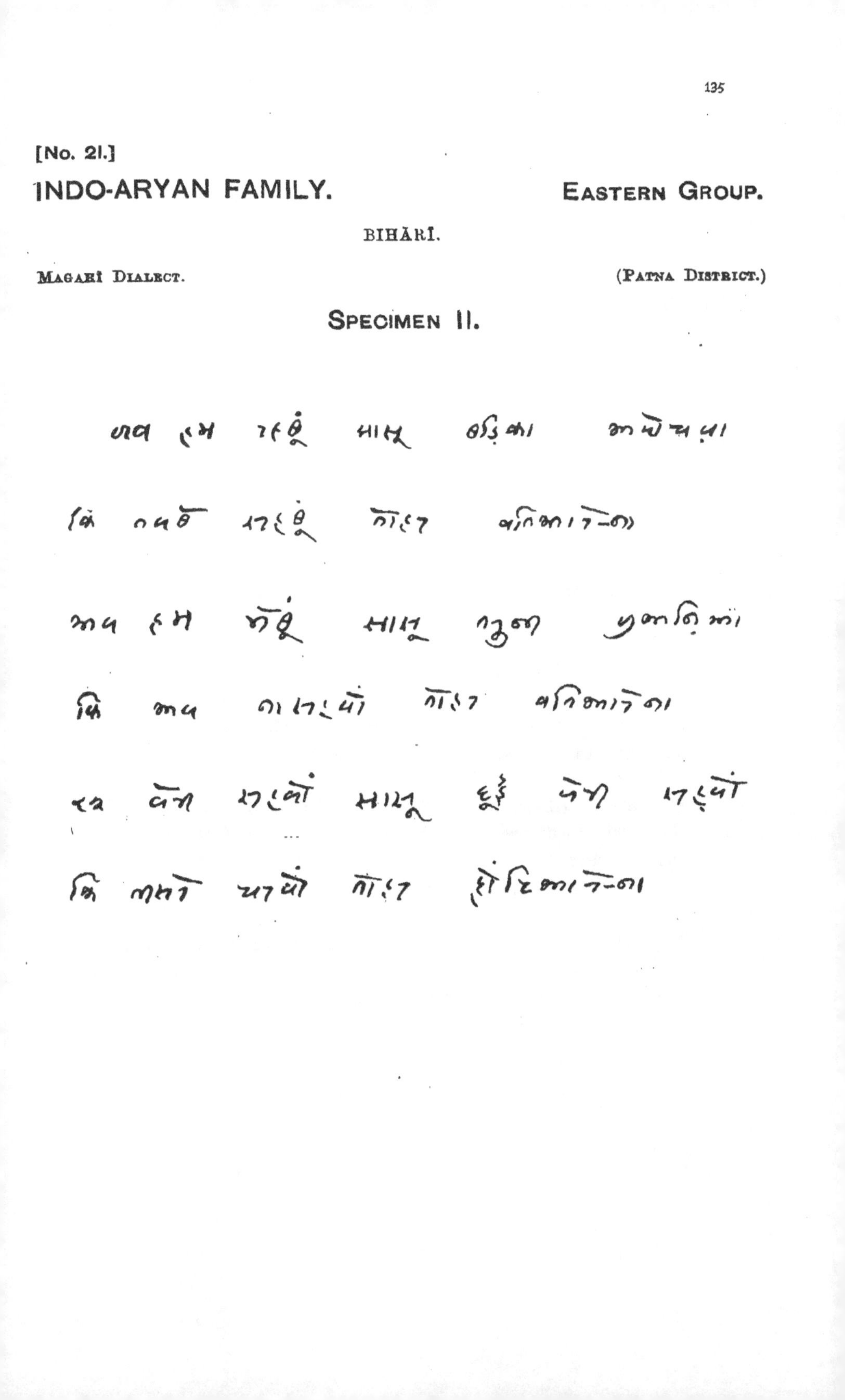

[No. 21.]

INDO-ARYAN FAMILY. EASTERN GROUP.

BIHĀRĪ.

MAGAHĪ DIALECT. (PATNA DISTRICT.)

SPECIMEN II.

[illegible]

[illegible]

[illegible]

[illegible]

[illegible]

[illegible]

[No. 21.]

INDO-ARYAN FAMILY. EASTERN GROUP.

BIHĀRĪ.

MAGAHĪ DIALECT. (PATNA DISTRICT.)

SPECIMEN II.

TRANSLITERATION AND TRANSLATION.

Jaba hama rahalū̃, Sāsū, laṛikā abodhawā,
When I was, O mother-in-law, a-girl without-sense,

Ki taba-lē sahalū̃ tōhara batiā-rē-nā!
That so-long I-brooked thy words!

Aba hama bhēlū̃, Sāsū, tarunī juaniā.
Now I have-become, O mother-in-law, tender youthful.

Ki aba nā sahabō̃ tōhara batiā-rē-nā!
That now not I-will-bear thy words!

Ēka bērī sahabō̃, Sāsū, dūi bērī sahabō̃.
One time I-will-bear, O mother-in-law, two times I-will-bear.

Ki tīsarē dharabō̃ tōhara jhō̃ṭiā-rē-nā!
That the-third-time I-will-catch-hold-of thy hair-topknot!

Magahī is also spoken by 150,060 people in the north-east of the Palamau District where it borders on Gaya and Hazaribagh. The following is a specimen. It is printed (as written) in the Dēva-nāgarī character:—

[No. 22.]

INDO-ARYAN FAMILY. EASTERN GROUP.

BIHĀRĪ.

MAGAHĪ DIALECT. (PALAMAU DISTRICT.)

हे भाई हम का कहियौ । झूठ डर के मारे अइसन डरइत हली कि जेकर हाल हम न कह सकियौ । का भेल कि काल्ह जब हम सब पहार के किनारे किनारे बजार से अवइत हली तब पहार के उपरे बाघ बहुत जोर से गरजइत हल । हमनी सब ढेर आदमी हली कुछ डर न लगल । लेकिन आज ओही रास्ता से हम अपन मामा के गाँव में ठीक दू पहर के बेर अकेले गेली हल, जब पहार के जरी तर नद्दी आरा पहुँचली हेअ तब एक दम बड़ा खड़बड़ाहट बन में नदी तरफ सुनली हेअ जेह से मेजाज हमर सुध में न रहल । हम बुझली कि बाघ आएल और हमरा के धएलक । हमर हाथ में तरवार हल लेकिन अवसर न मिलल कि मेआन से बाहर निकाली । करेजा थरथराए लगल, डर के मारे हम काठुआ गेली । बाघ के बिना देखली बघथेंड़ी लग गेल । लेकिन थोरे देर के बाद जब हम ओने देखली तो का देखली कि एक बूढ़ा सौंताल नदी के पानी जे पहार के उपरे से गिरइत हल मछरी मारे के बन्हइत हले । उहाँ से जे पथर नीचे बिगइत हले, सेई बोसो हाथ नीचे खड़बड़ाइते अवइत हलइ । जब ई देखली तब जीव में साहस भेल । हम अपने से ई बात खेआल कर के अपन साहस पर हसइत ही ॥

[No. 22.]

INDO-ARYAN FAMILY. EASTERN GROUP.

BIHĀRĪ.

MAGAHĪ DIALECT. (PALAMAU DISTRICT.)

TRANSLITERATION AND TRANSLATION.

Hē bhāī, ham kā kahiyō. Jhūṭh ḍar-ke-mārē aisan ḍaraït
O brother, I what may-say-(to-you). False fear-through so afraid
halī ki jēkar hāl ham na kah sakiyō.
I-was that of-which the-account I not say can-(to-you).

Kā bhēl ki kalh jab ham sab pahār-ke kinārē-kinārē
What was that yesterday when we all the-hill-of side-by-side
bajār-sē awaït halī tab pahār-ke up^{a}rē bāgh bahut jōr-sē
the-market-from coming were then the-hill-of on a-tiger great force-with
gar^{a}jaït hal. Ham^{a}nī sab ḍhēr ād^{a}mī halī kuchh ḍar na lagal, lēkin
roaring was. We all many men were any fear not was-felt, but
āj ōhī rāstā-sē ham apan māmā-ke gā̃o-mē̃ ṭhīk
to-day that-very way-by I my-own maternal-uncle-of village-in just
dū-pahar-ke bēr akēlē gēl-hal. Jab pahār-ke jarī tar nadī-ārā
noon-of at-the-time alone had-gone. When the-hill-of foot below the-river-bank
pahūch^{a}lī-hēa, tab ēk-dam baṛā khaṛ^{a}baṛāhaṭ ban-mē̃ nadī taraph
I-reached, then all-at-once great crash the-forest-in the-river toward
sun^{a}lī-hēa, jeh-sē mijāj hamar sudh-mē̃ na rahal. Ham bujh^{a}lī
I-heard, whereby temper my proper-state-in not remained. I thought
ki bāgh āel aur ham^{a}rā-kē dhaelak. Hamar hāth-mē̃ tar^{a}wār hal.
that the-tiger came and me caught. My hand-in a-sword was.
Lēkin aw^{a}sar na milal ki mēān-sē bāhar nikālī.
But opportunity not was-got-by-me that sheath-out-of outside I-may-take-(it)-out.
Karējā thar^{a}tharāē lagal, ḍar-ke-mārē ham kaṭhuā-gēlī.
The-heart to-tremble began, fear-through I like-a-wooden-block-became.

Bāgh-kē binā dekh^{a}lē bagh-chē̃ṛī lag-gēl. Lēkin thōrē dēr-ke
The-tiger without seeing motionlessness seized (me). But little while-of
bād jab ham ōne dekh^{a}lī tō kā dekh^{a}lī, ki ēk būṛhā Saūtāl
after when I that-side saw then what I-saw, that one old Santal
nadī-ke pānī jē pahār ke up^{a}rē-sē giraït-hal machh^{a}rī māre-kē
the-river-of water which the-hill of top-from falling-was fish killing-for
banhaït halai. Uhā̃ sē jē pathar nīchē bigaït halai sēī
damming was. There from what stones downward throwing he-was those-very

bīsō	hāth	nīchē	khaṛ'baṛāitē	awaīt	halaī.	Jab	ī
scores-of	*cubits*	*downwards*	*crashing*	*coming*	*were.*	*When*	*this*

ḍekh'lī	tab	jīw-mẽ	sāhas	bhēl.	Ham	ap'ne-sē	i	bāt
I-saw	*then*	*mind-in*	*courage*	*become.*	*I*	*in-my-own-mind*	*this*	*thing*

kheāl-kar-ke	apan	sāhas	par	hasaīt-hī.
thinking	*my-own*	*courage*	*on*	*am-laughing.*

Magahī is also spoken in the western portion of South-Gangetic Monghyr and in a small tract in the South-West corner of Bhagalpur. The language is the same as that spoken in Patna and Gayā, and it is quite unnecessary to give examples. Along the banks of the Ganges some Maithilī forms have intruded, but they are easily recognised.

AUTHORITY—

Grierson, G. A.,—*Seven Grammars of the Dialects and Sub-dialects of the Bihárí Language, Part VI. South-Maithil-Mágadhí Dialect, of South Munger and the Báṛh Subdivision of Patna.* Calcutta, 1886.

Ascending the plateau to the South and South-East of Gaya, we come to the District of Hazaribagh. Here, also, the language is the same as that of Gaya, and further examples are unnecessary. No monograph has been written regarding the Aryan Dialect spoken in this District. It will, of course, be understood that there are Dravidian and Muṇḍā tribes in the District who speak their own languages, which will be treated of in the proper place.

West of Hazaribagh, lies the District of Palamau, on the Eastern border of which, as already shown, Magahī is also spoken. On the South, Hazaribagh is separated from the Chota Nagpur plateau of the District of Ranchi by the valley of the Damuda and its affluents. The dialect of this latter plateau is not Magahī, but is a form of Bhojpurī, although in the North of the area Magahī is spoken by 20,141 settlers who have immigrated from Hazaribagh. We may, therefore, state as general facts, that, of the two plateaux in the Chota Nagpur Division, the Aryan language of the Northern, or Hazaribagh, plateau, is Magahī, and that of the Southern, or Ranchi, plateau, a form of Bhojpurī.

On the East of Hazaribagh, we drop down from the plateau into the Southern portion of the Sonthal Parganas and the North of the District of Manbhum. Bengali is the language of that portion of the Sonthal Parganas which adjoins Hazaribagh, and of the whole of the District of Manbhum. The latter District runs down the East side of the District of Ranchi, and both are bounded on the South by the District of Singhbhum, including the two Native States of Sarai Kala and Kharsawan. These also are below the Ranchi plateau, so also are the five Parganas of Silli, Bundu, Rahe, Baranda, and Tamar, which belong to Ranchi, and are situated in the extreme East of that District, bordering on Manbhum.

Manbhum is a Bengali-speaking District, and the same language is spoken in that part of Singhbhum, known as Dhalbhum, which is South of Manbhum. The State of Sarai Kala consists of two portions, an Eastern and a Western. In the Eastern, both Bengali and Oṛiyā are spoken by different nationalities. In the rest of Singhbhum, in the State of Kharsawan, and in the Western portion of the State of Sarai Kalā, the main language is Oṛiyā.

In all these sub-plateau tracts, however, there is a strong element speaking, not the main language of the locality, but some form of Magahī. We find pure Magahī spoken in the Chakradharpur Thana in the North of Singhbhum, just below the plateau, and also in the States of Sarai Kala and Kharsawan. So also, in Manbhum, and, again in Kharsawan, we find a corrupt Magahī spoken principally by Kuṛmīs, which, among other names, is usually called Kuṛmālī, a form of speech which we shall deal with presently. In the same District pure Magahī is spoken locally by some of the higher castes. In the five sub-plateau Parganas of Ranchi, besides the non-Aryan Muṇḍārī, there are spoken both Bengali and a dialect of Magahī, locally known as Pā̃ch Parganiā or Tamariā, which more nearly approaches the pure form of the language, and which is not so much mixed with Bengali as the dialect of the Manbhum Kuṛmīs. To conclude, as will be shortly explained, the same corrupt Bengali-Magahī language is also spoken in the South-East of the Hazaribagh District, on the border of Manbhum, in the thānās of Gola and Kashmar, and in a part of the Thana of Ramgarh, and, it may be added, in the distant District of Malda. All this will be subsequently dealt with. Suffice it to say that, at present, the Ranchi plateau is surrounded on three sides by a belt of speaker of Magahī, on the North and South, in its pure form, and on the East, mainly in a form corrupted by the neighbouring Bengali.

It must be noted that in this belt, Magahī is not the language of any locality. It is essentially a tribal language. In Manbhum, speakers of Kuṛmālī live side by side with speakers of Bengali, and in Singhbhum and its Native States, side by side with speakers of Oṛiyā, or, in the case of Eastern Sarai Kala, with some speakers of Oṛiyā, and with other speakers of Bengali.

This state of affairs is illustrated in the accompanying map.

The following tables show the relative importance of the various Aryan languages in these bilingual Districts:—

HAZARIBAGH.

	NUMBER OF SPEAKERS.
Magahī	1,069,000
Kuṛmālī	7,333
Muṇḍā and Dravidian Languages	87,550
Other Languages	438
TOTAL	1,164,321

MANBHUM.

Bengali including Khoṛiā Ṭhār	907,690
Kuṛmālī and Magahī[1]	111,100
Muṇḍā and Dravidian Languages	171,727
Other Languages	2,811
TOTAL	1,193,328

[1] Pure Magahī is spoken by Zamīndārs and Magahiyā Brāhmaṇs of Jharia, Katras, and Nowagarh, but separate figures are not available

RANCHI.

Magahī	20,141	
Pãch Parganiā	8,000	
Nagpuriā Bhojpurī	297,585	
Bengali	54,860	(principally spoken by Jains).
Muṇḍā and Dravidian Languages	731,946	
Other Languages	16,353	
TOTAL	1,128,885	

SINGHBHUM.

Magahī	25,867	
Bengali	106,686	(in Dhalbhum).
Oṛiyā	114,402	
Muṇḍā and Dravidian Languages	297,878	
Other Languages	655	
TOTAL	545,488	

SARAI KALA.

Magahī	34,815	
Bengali	4,115	(immigrants from Dhalbhum).
Oṛiyā	21,219	
Muṇḍā Languages	33,690	
TOTAL	93,839	

KHARSAWAN.

Magahī	987
Kuṛmālī	2,957
Oṛiyā	8,867
Muṇḍā Languages	22,659
TOTAL	35,470

Before dealing with Kuṛmālī, I shall describe the purer form of Magahī, which is current South of the Ranchi Plateau. The two following specimens come from Singhbhum, and may be taken to represent the Magahī of that District, and of Sarai Kala and Kharsawan. It will be seen that it is practically the same as that of Gaya and Hazaribagh. There is some carelessness shown in the use of the oblique genitive, as in *ōkar* for *ok*ᵃ*rā* in the first line of the first specimen, but no other peculiarity is presented. The first specimen is a short passage from the Parable of the Prodigal Son. It is quite unnecessary to give the whole, or to give an interlinear translation. The second specimen is a little fable. Here an interlinear translation has been given.

[No. 23.]

INDO-ARYAN FAMILY. EASTERN GROUP.

BIHĀRĪ.

MAGAHĪ DIALECT. (SINGHBHUM DISTRICT.)

SPECIMEN I.

कोई अदमी के दू बेटा हलइ। ओकर में से छोटका अपन बाप से कहलइ कि ए बाप धन-दौलत के जे हमर बखरा होव हइ से हमरा दे दे। तब ऊ अपन धन-दौलत बाँट देलइ। ढेर दिन नइ बितलइ कि छोटका बेटा सब जमा करलइ अवर दूर देश चल गेलइ अवर ऊ हुआँ धन-दौलत लुचइ में उड़ा देलइ। अवर जब ऊ सब उड़ा चुकलइ तब हुआँ बड़ी अकाल पड़लइ अवर ओकर दुक्ख होवे सुरू होलइ। अवरउ ऊ देश के एक अदमी के इहाँ जा के रहे लगलइ। अवर ऊ ओकरा सूअर चरावे ला अपन खेत में पेठैलइ। अवर ऊ सुअरवन के खाल छिलकवन से अपन पेट भरे खोजलइ। से उ ओकरा केउ नइ देलथीन। तब ओकर होश भेलइ अवर ऊ कहलइ कि हमर बाप के केतना मजूरा के खा के भी उब्र हइ, अवर हम भूखे मर ही। हम उठब अवर अपन बाप भीरी जैबइ, अवर ओकरा कहबइ बप्पा परमेशर भीरी अवर तोर भीरू पाप करेली हे। अब हम तोर बेटा कहावे लाइक नखी। हमरा तोर मजुरवन में से एक मजूर निअर रख ॥

TRANSLITERATION.

Kōī adªmī kē dū bēṭā halaï. Ōkar-mẽ-sē chhoṭªkā apan bāp-sē kahªlaï ki, 'ē bāp, dhan-daulat ke jē hamar bakhªrā hōwa haï sē hamªrā dē dē.' Tab ū apan dhan-daulat bā̃ṭ delaï. Ḍher din naï bitªlaï ki chhoṭªkā bēṭā sab jamā karªlaï awar dūr dēś chal gelaï. Awar ū huā̃ dhan-daulat luchaï-mẽ uṛā delaï. Awar jab ū sab uṛā chukªlaï tab huā̃ baṛī akāl parªlaï, awar ōkar dukkh hōwe surū holaï. Awar-u ū dēś-ke ēk adªmī-ke ihā̃ jā-ke rahe lagªlaï. Awar ū okªrā sūar charāwe-lā apan khet-mẽ peṭhailaï. Awar ū suarªwan-ke khāl chhilakªwan sē apan pēṭ bhare khojªlaï. Sē-u okªrā keu naï delªthīn. Tab ōkar hōś bhelaï, awar ū kahªlaï ki, 'hamar bāp kē ketªnā majūrā-kē khā ke bhī ubra haï, awar ham bhūkhe mara hī. Ham uṭhab awar apan bāp bhīrī jaibaï, awar okªrā kahªbaï, "bappā Paramēśar bhīrī awar tōr bhīrū pāp karªlī hē; ab ham tor bēṭā kahāwe lāik nakhi, hamªrā tōr majurªwan-mẽ-sē ēk majūr niar rakh."'

[No. 24.]

INDO-ARYAN FAMILY. EASTERN GROUP.

BIHĀRĪ.

MAGAHĪ DIALECT. (SINGHBHUM DISTRICT.)

SPECIMEN II.

A FABLE.

एगो सूम अपन सब धन-सम्पत् बेच के सोना किनलइ, अवर ओकरा ऊ गला के ईंटा नियर बना के धरती में गाड़ के रोज ओकर पहरा दे हलइ। ओकर कोई पड़ोसिया ई भेद अटकर से बूझे पइलइ, अवर ओकर घर सुन्ना पा के गड़ल सोनवा निकाल लेलइ। केतना रोज पीछे ऊ सूम ऊ ठाँव कोड़लइ। अवर खाली देख के रोए लगलइ। ओकर रोआई सुन के ओकर दोस्त मोहीम अइलथीन अवर ओकरा बुझा के कहे लगलथीन, ए-भाई, तू काहे खातिर सोच हें। जब लग सोनवा तोर पास हलउ, तब लग तू ओकर पहरादार छोड़ अवर कुछ तो नइ हले। एइ से तू ऊ गड़हा-ठो में एगो पथर रख ले अवर ओकरे भुलाएल सोनवा बुझ लेहीँ।

जे अदमी अपन धन के केकरो दुख बिपद में नइ लगाव हइ, अवर न अपन जीव में खा हइ, ओकर धन अकारथ हइ, अवर ऊ धन अइसने उड़ जा हइ॥

TRANSLITERATION AND TRANSLATION.

Egō sūm apan sab dhan-sampat bēch-ke sōnā kin^alaï, awar
A-certain miser his-own all wealth-property having-sold gold bought, and

ok^arā ū galā-ke ĩṭā niyar banā-ke dhar^atī-mẽ gāṛ-ke
it he having-melted a-brick like having-made the-ground-in having-buried

rōj ōkar pah^arā dē-halaï. Ōkar kōī paṛosiyā ī bhēd
(every)-day of-it guarding used-to-give. Of-him a-certain neighbour this secret

aṭ^akar-sē bujhe païlaï, awar ōkar ghar sunnā pā-ke gaṛal son^awā
guess-by to-discover got, and his house empty having-found the-buried gold

nikāl lelaï. Ket^anā rōj pichhē ū sūm ū ṭhā̃w koṛ^alaï awar khālī
having-extracted took. Some days after that miser that place dug and empty

dēkh-ke rōe lag^alaï. Ōkar rōāī sun-ke ōkar dōst-mōhīm aïl^athīn,
having-seen to-weep began. His weeping having-heard his friends came,

awar ok^arā bujhā-ke kahe lagal^athīn, 'ē bhāī, tū kāhe khātir sōcha-hẽ?
and him having-advised to-say began, 'O brother, thou what for art-grieving?

Jab-lag son^awā tōr pās halaū tab-lag tū ōkar pah^arādār chhōṛ
As-long-as the-gold of-thee near was-(to-thee), so-long thou of-it a-watchman except

awar kuchh tō naï halē. Ēi-sē tū ū gaṛ^ahā-ṭhō-mẽ egō pathar
other anything indeed not wast. This-from thou that hole-indeed-in a stone

rakh-lē, awar ok^arē bhulāel son^awā bujh-lēhī̃.'
place-for-thyself, and it-indeed the-lost gold imagine.'

Jē	ad^a^mī	apan	dhan-kē	kek^a^ro	dukh	bipad-mẽ	naï	lagāwa-haï,
What	*man*	*his-own*	*wealth*	*anyone's*	*grief*	*affliction-in*	*not*	*does-apply,*

awar	na	apan	jīw-mẽ	khā-haï,	ōkar	dhan	akārath	haï,	awar	ū	dhan
and	*not*	*his-own*	*life-in*	*does-eat,*	*his*	*wealth*	*useless*	*is,*	*and*	*that*	*wealth*

aïsanē	uṛ-jā-haï.
in-this-very-way	*flies-away.*

FREE TRANSLATION OF THE FOREGOING.

A certain miser sold all that he had, and bought some gold, which he melted and fashioned into a brick. He then buried it in the ground, and kept watch over it day-by-day. One of his neighbours guessed the secret, and, finding his house one day vacant, took out the gold and carried it off. Some days after, the miser dug the place up, and, finding nothing there, began to cry. His friends hearing his lamentations came to him, and began to console him, saying 'brother, why art thou grieving? As long as the gold was with thee thou wast nothing but its watchman; now, therefore, put a stone into the same hole, and imagine it to be thy lost gold.'

The riches of a man who neither uses them for the calamities or distresses of others, nor enjoys them himself, are of no use, and fly away just like the miser's gold.

EASTERN MAGAHĪ.

It has been already pointed out that in the localities where Bihārī meets Bengali, we find one of two conditions in existence. North of the Ganges, as a rule, the two languages gradually merge into each other, and we notice an intermediate dialect, such as, for instance, the Siripuriā of Eastern Purnea, which it is difficult to define either as the one or as the other language. The District of Malda presents an exception, for, here, we see two, and even three, nationalities living side by side, each adhering to its own form of speech. Thus, in one and the same village, there will be found speakers of Bihārī, Santālī, and Bengali, according to the respective origins of the speakers.

South of the Ganges, we come upon the same state of affairs as in Malda. For instance, as has already been shown,[1] there is a tract in the Deogarh Sub-division of the Sonthal Parganas, in which both Maithilī and Bengali, besides various Muṇḍā languages, are spoken side by side, without uniting into one general, composite speech. Going further south into Manbhum, we find that Bengali extends on the west up to the foot of the Ranchi and the Hazaribagh Plateaux. There it suddenly stops, face to face with the various forms of Bihārī which compose the Aryan speech of the highlands of Chota Nagpur.

There are, however, emigrants from these highlands into the Bengali-speaking area. These have retained their own language, though, as could only be expected of a small people living for generations in contact with a great people, they have not resisted the temptation of borrowing words and grammatical forms from those amongst whom they live. The result is a kind of mixed dialect essentially Bihārī in its nature, but with a curious Bengali colouring. It is the same with the speakers of Bihārī in Malda. It must be remembered that in each case, the dialect is not a local one. It is not, as in the case of Siripuriā, the language of a border tract between a country whose language is Bengali, and a country whose language is Bihārī. In each case this dialect is the language of a strange people in a strange land. All round them, and usually in a great majority, live the true people of the country, who speak a Bengali of considerable purity, and quite distinct from the mixed Bihārī spoken by these immigrants.[2]

In Manbhum this language is principally spoken by people of the Kuṛmī caste, who are numerous in the Districts of Chota Nagpur, and in the Orissa Tributary State of Mayurbhanja. They are an aboriginal tribe of Dravidian stock and should be distinguished from the Kurmīs of Bihar who spell their name differently, with a smooth,

---

[1] *Vide* ante, p. 95.

[2] To avoid misapprehension, I wish it to be clearly understood that the above remarks are in no way to be taken as deciding any ethnological problems, and that in talking of the Bengali speakers as the true people of the country, I do not mean that they necessarily are the autochthones of Manbhum. I am simply writing from the point of view of actual existing linguistic facts, and, from that point of view, Bengali speakers are, amongst the speakers of Aryan languages, the people who are in possession of the district at the present day.

instead of a hard, *r*.[1] The two quite distinct tribes have been mixed up in the Census, but as their habitats are also distinct, the following figures may be taken as showing with considerable accuracy the number of Kuṛmīs in the area under consideration :—

Name of District or State.	Number of Kuṛmīs.
Manbhum	226,034
Hazaribagh	71,065
Ranchi and Palamau	60,382
Singhbhum	12,400
Orissa Tributary States	39,989
Chota Nagpur Tributary States	27,944
TOTAL .	437,814

These Kuṛmīs do not all speak corrupted Bihārī. Many of them speak Bengali and Oṛiyā. On the other hand, in Manbhum, it is not confined to this one caste, but is also spoken by people of other tribes. The same dialect is spoken by aborigines in the Chhattisgarh Feudatory State of Bamra, where it is known as Sadrī Kōl. In the Orissa Tributary States, the Kuṛmīs nearly all talk Bengali, although living in an Oṛiyā-speaking country, and only very few have been returned as speaking the mixed dialect. It will thus be understood that the figures for the people speaking it will not agree with those given above for the tribe. The corrupted dialect has been returned under various names, but in every case it is essentially the same form of speech. The following table shows the number of its speakers, and the name under which, in each case, it was returned :—

Name of District or State.	Name under which originally returned.	Number of speakers.
Manbhum[2]	Magahī, Magahiā, Korthā, Kuṛmālī Ṭhār, Khaṭṭā, or Khaṭṭāhī.	111,100
Kharsawan State	Kuṛmālī	2,957
Hazaribagh	Bengali	7,333
Ranchi	Pā̃ch Parganiā or Tamariā .	8,000
Bamra State	Sadrī Kōl	4,194
Mayurbhanja State . . .	Kuṛmālī	280
Malda	Hindī	180,000
	TOTAL .	313,864

[1] See Journal of the Asiatic Society of Bengal, Vol. lxvii, 1898, Part III, pp. 110 and ff.

[2] These figures, however, include speakers of pure Magahī, who are Zamindars and Magahiyā Brāhmaṇs of Jharia, Katras, and Nawagarh. Separate figures for these are not available. The original figures received from Manbhum were 120,798, but these include some 9,700 speakers of the Kārmālī dialect of Santālī, which is quite distinct.

It will be most convenient to call this form of speech 'Eastern Magahī' for none of the local names applies sufficiently to all the speakers.

In Manbhum and Kharsawan this corrupt Magahī is spoken principally by Kurmīs, and is locally known as Kurmālī Ṭhār. The word 'Ṭhār' means literally fashion, and the name means the Aryan language as spoken in the Kurmālī fashion. It is also known as Korthā, or, in the north-west of Manbhum as Khaṭṭā, or, in the west of the same district, as Khaṭṭāhī. It is spoken all over the district, but most generally in the west and south-west. It is, in Manbhum, written in the Bengali character, and this has led to its having been described by some as a dialect of that language.

The following are the principal peculiarities of the dialect, as exhibited in the specimens received from Manbhum:—

Pronunciation.—A long *ō* becomes *a* (pronounced in the Bengali fashion like the *o* in 'hot') thus for *lōkēr*, of a man, we find *lakēr;* for *ō-kar* of him, (a Bihārī form), *a-kar;* we find in the same sentence both *gōrᵒkhiyā* and *garᵃkhiyā*, a shepherd; for *kōna*, anything, we have *kanha;* for *mōr*, my, and *tōr*, thy, *mar* and *tar;* and for *bhōj*, a feast, *bhaj*. So many others. The word *chhōṭō* (for *chhōṭa* in standard Bengali) is, however, pronounced *chhuṭu*.

An *i* or *e* is apt to change a preceding *a* to *e*. Thus Bengali *kahilek*, he said, becomes *kehalāk;* *kahi-ke*, having said, *kehi-ke;* *besi-ke* having sat, for *basi-ke;* *kerᵉlē āhā̃*, I have done; *keri-ke*, having done; *khʸenē*, at a time. So also *maīdhē* for *madhyē*, in.

In the word *hīchhā*, for *ichchā*, a wish, *h* has been prefixed.

Nouns.—The pleonastic suffix, *ṭā*, *ṭāi* or *ṭāy* is very common. Sometimes, it has the force of the English definite article. Thus *chhāwā-ṭā*, *the* child; *bēṭā-ṭāy*, *the* son. Its genitive case is *ṭek*, as in *ghaṛi-ṭek bādē*, after a space of twenty minutes. Here it gives the sense of 'about.'

The syllable *ek* is added in the sense of the English indefinite article. Thus, *thar-ek*, a little. *Ek-ṭā*, is used in the same sense, as in *ek-ṭā muniś-kē ḍāki-ke*, having called a servant.

In the declension of nouns, the sign for the Accusative-Dative is *kē*, which belongs both to Bihārī and Bengali. Thus *bāp-kē*, to the father. The Bihārī termination *lāy* or *lāi* is also used for the Dative, as in *chārāo-lāi*, for feeding.

The Genitive has several terminations, *viz.*—

(1) *ēr*. This is the regular Bengali termination, as in *lakēr*, of a man.

(2) *ē-kar*. This occurs only in *Bhagamānē-kar*, of God.

(3) *kar*. This is a Bihārī termination. It occurs in *daulat-kar*, of the wealth.

(4) *kēr*. This is also Bihārī. It occurs in *muluk-kēr*, of the country; *śūar-kēr*, of the hogs; *miṭhāi-kēr*, of the sweetmeats.

(5) *ek*. This is the commonest termination of all. It is a corruption of the Bihārī *ak*. It occurs in *dhanin-ek*, of a rich man; *bāp-ek*, of the father; *Bhagamān-ek*, of God; *muniś-ek*, of a servant. If a noun ends in *ā* there are irregularities. Thus, we have *ghaṛi-ṭ-ek*, of about twenty minutes; *bēṭā-k*, of a son; *lā-h-ek*, of a boat (*lā*, for *nā*).

The Instrumental and Locative, are formed by adding *ē*. Thus, *bādē*, afterwards; *ghārē*, in the house; *hā̃thē*, on the hand; *dakānē*, in the shop; *bhū̃khē*, by hunger.

The Plural is usually the same as the Singular, but in the case of human beings *gulā* is added. Thus *muniś-gulā-kē*, to the servants; *bābu-gulā-k*, of the Bābūs.

Pronouns.—The following forms occur:—

1st Person, *mãy*, I; *ma-kē*, to me; *mar*, my, but *hāmar pash*, near me; *hām*ᵃ*rā*, we; *hām*ᵃ*rā-kē*, to us; *hām*ᵃ*rā-kar*, of us.

2nd Person, *tãy*, thou; *tar*, thy, but *tah*ᵃ*rē*, or *tarē*, *ēsan*, like thee.

3rd Person, *ū*, he; *a-kē*, *ak*ᵃ*rā-ke*, him; *akar*, *ak*ᵃ*rā*, his (the latter only once, agreeing with a nominative plural).

Tē̃y, *sē*, he; *tā-khē* (sic) to him; *tā-kar*, of him. *Tāk*ᵃ*rē* (*hā̃tē*), (for the reason) of that. Similarly *ek*ᵃ*rē* (*hā̃tē*), (for the reason) of this; *tārādēr*, of them.

The Relative and Correlative Pronouns are *j̃ē*, and *sē*.

Adjectival pronouns are *ahē* and *sēi*, that, and *ehē*, this. *Kea* is anyone, and *kanha* is anything.

The Verb.—Singular and Plural are, as a rule, the same.

Auxiliary Verbs, and Verbs Substantive.

Present—

(1) *āhã*, I am: (2) *āhis*, thou art; *āhē*, *āhek*, he is. Once, as an auxiliary, *āihōk*, he is; *nēkhē*, *nēkhekh* (sic), *nēkhat*, he is not. *Hek*, *hekek*, *hetek*, he becomes, he is going on.

Past—

(1) *Helaō̃*, I was.

(3) *Hel*, *helek*, he was.

Also, (1) *rahã*, I was.

(3) *rahē*, *rehek*, he was.

Other forms—

Haï-ke, having become.

Hēlēi, *heli*, on becoming.

*Ah*ᵃ*bē keris*, thou doest existing, thou existest.

Finite Verbs.

Present Tense.

1st Person, *lāgaō̃*, I seem; *khāṭahã*, I labour.

2nd Person, *keris*, thou doest.

Imperative.

1st Person, *chālē̂*, let us come.

2nd Person, *dē*, give thou; respectful, *rākhē̃*, keep; inferior, *pindhāohāk*, put on; *dehāk*, give.

Present Definite.

Only one instance occurs, in the curious form, *khāwāis-āhē*, he is feeding.

IMPERFECT.

Only one instance, *bĕche-helaõ*, I was selling.

HABITUAL PAST.

Pāotāk, he (they) used to get; *pārᵃtāk*, he (they) used to be able.

FUTURE.

Pāyam, I shall get; *kaham*, I shall say; *kerbẽi*, we shall do; *debẽi*, we shall give.

PAST—

1st Person.—This occurs under three forms; *viz.*:—

(*a*) *Pāolaõ*, I obtained; *kehᵃlaõ*, I said; *khujᵃlaõ*, I demanded; *dekhᵃlaõ*, I saw; *lāgᵃlaõ*, I began; *ṭekᵃlaõ*, I obstructed.

(*b*) *Pāolẽi*, I obtained; *delẽi*, I gave.

(*c*) *Aṭāolāhan*, I reached; *śudhāolāhan*, I enquired.

2nd Person.—Only one instance, *lāgāolē*, thou didst commence.

3rd Person.—This usually ends in *āk*, as in *kehᵃlāk*, he said; *delāk*, he gave; *guchāolāk*, he lost; *sirāolāk*, he finished; *rahᵃlāk*, he stayed; *kerᵃlāk*, he made; *pāolāk*, he obtained; *khāolāk*, he ate; *bãchᵃlāk*, he survived; *lāgᵃlāk*, they began; *śudhālāk*, he (they) enquired; *bujhāolāk*, he entreated; *uṛāolāk*, he wasted.

In the case of Intransitive verbs sometimes the Bihārī custom of dropping all terminations is followed, as in *gēl*, he went.

Sometimes almost pure Bengali forms are used, as in *kehᵃlek*, he said; *kahᵃlen*, he said.

PERFECT.—This is built on the Bihārī system.

1st Person.—(*a*) Transitive verbs, *kerᵃlē-āhã*, I have done; *kāṭᵃlē-āhã*, I have disobeyed.

(*b*) Intransitive verbs, *maral-āhã*, I have died.

2nd Person.—Transitive verb, *delē-āhis*, thou hast given.

3rd Person.—(*a*) Transitive verb, *ṭhānᵃlē-āhē*, he has considered; *ānᵃlē-āhē*, he has brought. Also *pāolē-āïhōk*, he has got.

(*b*) Intransitive verb, *āol-āhek*, he has come; *gēl-āhek*, he has gone.

PLUPERFECT.—*Rākhᵃlē-rahē*, he appointed (a long time ago); another form is *mari rahē*, or *mari rehek*, he died (a long time ago). Before the auxiliary the final *l* of the Past Participle of an intransitive verb, becomes *r*. Thus *gēr* (for *gēl*) *rahã*, I had gone; *gēr rahē*, he had gone.

PAST CONJUNCTIVE.—The following appears to belong to this tense: *keretēlia*, (that) they might have made.

CONJUNCTIVE PARTICIPLE.—This is pure Bihārī. Thus,—*bãṭi-ke*, having divided; *lēi-ke*, having taken; *jāi-ke*, having gone; *keri-ke*, having made; *kehi-ke*, having said, and many others.

As examples of Compound Verbs, we have *dēi-delāk*, he gave; *dauṛi jāi-ke*, having run, and others.

THE CONDITIONAL PARTICIPLE—*delẽi*, on giving; *hẽlēi*, *heli*, on becoming.

OTHER FORMS are *ghurek bērā*, the hour of returning; *khābāṛ*, of eating.

Idiom—

The Negative is *nehi* or *niki.*

Example of a Potential Verb,—*sirāolē pār'tāk,* they used to be able to finish.

Example of an Inceptive Verb,—*kere lāg'lāk,* they began to make.

Note the form *richek,* a little, a corruption of the Bihārī *rachi-ke,* or *achik.*

The following specimens come from Manbhum, and are in the Bengali character. They may also be taken as illustrating the Kuṛmālī of Kharsāwān. They have been written down for the purposes of the Survey by Babu Sital Chandra Chattérjia, Sub-Inspector of Schools :—

[No. 25.]

INDO-ARYAN FAMILY. EASTERN GROUP.

BIHĀRĪ.

EASTERN MAGAHĪ DIALECT.

SPECIMEN I.

KUṚMĀLĪ ṬHĀR. (MANBHUM DISTRICT.)

এক লকের ছুটা বেটা ছালিয়া রেহেক। তারাদের মইধে ছুটু বেটাটায় অকর্ বাপ্‌কে কেহলাক্ যে বাপ্-হে হামরাকর্ দৌলতকর যে মঁয় হিঁসা পায়ম্ সে মকে দে। তখন তাকর বাপ্ আপন দৌলত বাঁটিকে অকর হিঁসা দেঁই দেলাক্। থড়েক দিন বাদে ছুটু বেটা ছাওয়াটা আপন ধন দরিব লেইকে বিদেশ গেল্। সে ঠিনে যাইকে উজবক্ হইকে সভে ঘুচাওলাক্। যভে খর্‌চা কেরিকে সভে শিরাওলাক তভে অহে মুলুককের বেড়ি আকাল হেলেক। তাক্‌রে খাতির অকর দুখ হেঁলেই ক্ষেণে সেই মুলুককের এক বেড়ে ধানিনেক্ ঘারে রহলাক্। অহে ধনিনটা অকরাকে টাঁইড়ে শূয়র চারাওলাই গোরখিয়া রাখলে-রহে। অহেলায় গরখিয়া শূয়রকের খাবার চকা খাইকে আপন পেট ভরায়েক িহঁছা কেরলাক। বিচকম তাখে কেয় কন্‌হ নেহি দেলেঁই। মনে মনে ঠানলে আহে মর বাপেক্ ঘারে কেতেক বেরহুনিয়া আহেক। অকরা মান্‌ষি এতিক বেরহুন্ পাওতাক যে খাইকে নেহি শিরাওলে পারতাক্। আর মঁয় ভূঁখে মরল্ আহঁ। মঁয় বাপেক্ ঠাই যাইকে কহম্ বাপ্-হে মঁয় ভগমানেকর ঠাঁই আর তর্ ঠাঁই দষ কেরলে আহঁ। তর বেটাক লাক মঁয় না লাগঁও। তঁয় মকে মুনিশ রাখেঁ। তাকর বাদে উ আপন বাপেক্ ঘার গেল্। অকর বাপ অকে ফারাকলে দেখিকে বেড়ি দুখ্ পাওলাক্। অকর বাপ্ আপন্ ছাওয়াটাকে দেখিকে দৌড়ি যাইকে ঘেঁচায় ধরিকে চুমা খাওলাক। তখন অকর ছাওয়াটায় কেহলাক্, বাপ্‌হে তর্ ঠিনে আর ভগমানেক ঠিনে মঁয় গুণহাঁ কেরলে আহঁ। তর বেটাক্ লাক্ মঁয় না লাগঁও। অকর বাপে মুনিশগুলাকে কহলেন যে অকে বেশ লুগা আনিকে পিঁধাওহাক্ আর অকর হাঁথে অংঠি দেহাক্, গড়ে জুতা দেহাক। আর চালেঁ হামরা খাই পিকে মজা কেরবেঁই। মর এহে বেটাটা মরি রেহেক আর বাঁচলাক্; হারাঁই গের রহে আর পাওলেঁই। এতনাটা কেহিকে মজা কেরে লাগলাক্॥

অহে লক্‌টার্ বড় বেটাটা খেত গের রহে। সে ঘুরেক বেরা যখন ঘার পঁহুচাপঁহুচি হেল তেখ্‌নে নাচ্ বাজনাকর জাঁক শুনিকে একটা মুনিশকে ডাকিকে শুধাওলাক কিনা লায় এতেক নাচ বাজনা হেহেক রে। মুনিশটাই কেহলেক তর্ ভাই আওল আহেক্, তাকরে হঁতে কুটুম্‌কে খাওয়াইসাহে কেসে ন অকে ভালঁই ভালঁই পাওলে আই-হোক। একরে হঁতে অকর রাগ হেলেক, ঘারে নিহি গেল্। অকর বাপ্ তখন্ বাহরায় আসিকে আনেক আনেক বুঝাওলাক। তখন তেঁয় কেহলাক মঁয় এতনাদিন তর্ মুনিশেক লেথে খাটহঁ কখ্‌ন মঁয় তর কাথা নেহি কাটলে আহঁ মনেক তঁয় মকে একটা ছাগেছোয়া নিহি দেলে আহিস যে পাঁচ ভাই মজা কেরেতেলিয়। তর যে বেটাটাই তহরে এসন্ নাচনি লেঁইকে তরে এসন ধন দরিব উড়াওলাক্ সে ঘুরিকে পঁহচৎ না পঁহচতে তঁয় ভজ লাগাওলে। তখন অকর বাপ্ কেহলাক সভে দিনত তঁয় হামর পষ অহবে কেরিস। সভে ধন দরিব তরে হেকেক। কিন্তুক এখন রিচেক মজা কেরে হেভেক কেসেন তব এহে ভাইটা মরি রহে ঘুরিকে বাঁচল হারাঁই গের রহে ঘুরিকে পাওলাঁও॥

[No. 25.]

INDO-ARYAN FAMILY. EASTERN GROUP.

BIHĀRĪ.

EASTERN MAGAHĪ DIALECT.

SPECIMEN I.

KUṚMĀLĪ ṬHĀR. (MANBHUM DISTRICT.)

Ek lakēr du-ṭā bēṭā chhāliā rehek. Tārādēr maïdhē chhuṭu bēṭā-ṭāy
One man-of two son children were. Of-them among (the)-younger son
a-kar bāp-kē keh^alāk jē, 'bāp-hē, hām^arā-kar daulat-kar jē mãy hĩsā
his father-to said that, 'father-O, our property-of what I share
pāyam sē ma-kē dē.' Takhan tā-kar bāp āpan daulat bā̃ṭi-ke
shall-get that me-to give.' Then his father own property dividing
akar hĩsā dē̃i-delāk. Thaṛek din bādē chhuṭu bēṭā chhāwā-ṭā āpan
his share made-over. A-few days after younger son child own
dhan-darib lēi-ke bidēś gēl. Sē ṭhinē jāi-ke
property-(and)-things taking foreign-land went. (To)-that place going
uj^abak haï-ke sabhē ghuchāolāk. Jabhē kharchā keri-ke sabhē
(a)-fool being all-(his-property) he-lost. When expenses making all
śirāolāk, tabhē ahē muluk-kēr bēṛi ākāl helek. Tāk^arē khātir a-kar
he-finished, then that land-of great famine was. This for his
dukh hēlēi kh^enē, sēi muluk-kēr ek bēṛē
distress of-being at-the-time, that land-of one great
dhaninek ghārē rah^alāk. Ahē dhanin-ṭā ak^arā-kē ṭā̃iṛē śūar
wealthy-man's house-in he-stayed. That rich-man him in-the-fields swine
chārāo-lāi gor^akhiyā rākh^alē-rahē. Ahē-lāy gar^akhiyā śūar-kēr
feeding-for shepherd appointed. That-for (so-that) the-shepherd the-hogs-of
khābār chakā khāi-ke āpan pēṭ bharāyek hĩchhā ker^alāk. Bich^akam
(the)-food-of husks eating own stomach filling-of wish he-made. But
tā-khē kēa kanha nohi delē̃i manē-manē ṭhān^alē-āhē, 'mar
him-to any-one anything not on-giving in-(his)-mind he-thought, 'my
bāpek ghārē ketek bēr^ahuniyā āhek. Ak^arā mānshi
father's house-in how-many wages-earning-labourers are. His men
etik bēr^ahun pāotāk jē khāi-ke nehi śirāolē
so-much wages-(in-food) used-to-get that eating not to-finish
pār^aṭāk, ār mãy bhū̃khē maral āhā. Mãy bāpek ṭhāi jāi-ke
they-used-to-be-able, and I (by)-hunger dying am. I father's near going

kaham, "bāp-hē, mā̃y Bhagamānē-kar ṭhā̃i ār tar
will-say, "father-O, I God-of in-the-presence and of-thee

ṭhā̃i dash kerᵃlē-āhā̃. Tar bēṭāk lāk mā̃y nā
in-the-presence sin committed-have. Thy son-of like I not

lāgaō̃ ; tā̃y ma-kē muniś rākhē̃."' Tā-kar bādē ū āpan
do-appear ; thou me (thy)-servant keep."' This after he own

bāpek ghār gēl. A-kar bāp a-kē phārāk-lē dēkhi-ke bēṛi
father's house went. His father him a-distance-from seeing great

dukh pāolāk ; a-kar bāp āpan chhāwāṭā-kē dēkhi-ke dauṛi jāi-ke
sorrow felt ; his father own child seeing running coming

ghē̃chāy dhaṛi-ke chumā khāolāk. Takhan a-kar chhāwā-ṭy kehᵃlāk,
neck holding kisses gave. Then his child said,

'bāp-hē, tar ṭhinē ār Bhagamānek ṭhinē mā̃y gunᵃhā̃
'father-O, thy presence-in and God-of the-presence-in I sin

kerᵃlē-āhā. Tar bēṭāk lāk mā̃y nā lāgaō̃.' A-kar bāpē
committed-have. Thy son-of like I not do-appear.' His father

muniś-gulā-kē kahᵃlen jē, 'a-kē bēś lugā āni-ke pindhāohāk, ār
servants-to said that, 'him-to good cloth bringing cause-to-put-on, and

a-kar hā̃thē angṭhi dēhāk, gaṛē jutā dēhāk, ār chālē̃ hāmᵃrā
his hands-on rings give, legs-on shoes give, and come we

khāi pi-ke majā kerᵃbē̃i ; mar ehē bēṭā-ṭā mari-rehek,
eating drinking merriment will-make ; my this son died-had,

ār bā̃chᵃlāk ; hārā̃i gēr-rahē, ār pāolē̃i.' Etᵃnā-ṭā kehi-ke
and revived ; lost gone-had, and I-regained.' This-much saying

majā kere lāgᵃlāk.
merriment doing they-began.

Ahē lak-ṭār baṛa bēṭā-ṭā khēt gēr rahē. Sē ghurek
That man's elder son field gone had. He returning-of

bērā jakhan ghār pā̃huchā-pā̃huchi hel tekhᵃnē nāch-bājᵃnā-kar
at-the-time when house almost-reached was then dancing-and-music-of

jā̃k śuni-ke, ek-ṭā muniś-kē ḍāki-ke śudhāolāk, 'kinā-lāy etek
splendour hearing, one servant calling asked, 'what-for this-much

nāch bājᵃnā hehek-rē?' Muniś-ṭā-i kehᵃlek, 'tar bhāi
dance (and) play is-going-on-eh?' The-servant said, 'thy brother

āol āhek. Tākᵃrē hātē kuṭum-kē khāwāis-āhē, kese na
come has. Of-that for relations he-is-feeding, why because

a-kē bhālā̃i-bhālā̃i pāolē-āihōk.' Ekᵃrē hātē a-kar rāg
him in-good-condition he-got-has.' This for his anger

helek, ghārē nihi gēl. A-kar bāp takhan bāhᵃrāy āsi-ke,
rose, house-in not did-go. His father then out coming,

ānek-ānek bujhāolāk. Takhan tē̃y kehᵃlāk, 'mā̃y etᵃnā-din tar muniśek
a-good-deal entreated. Then he said, 'I so-many-days thy servant-of

X

lĕkhē khāṭ-ahā̃. Kakhna mā̃y tar kāthā nehi kăṭ'lē-āhā̃, manek
like labour. Ever I thy words not disobeyed-have, even-then
tā̃y ma-kē ek-ṭā chhāgē-chhōwā nihi delē-āhis jē pā̃ch
thou me-to one goat-young not given-thou-hast that five
bhāi majā keretēlia. Tar jē bēṭā-ṭā-i tah'rē ēsan,
brethren merriment would-have-made. Thy what the-son of-thee like,
nāch'ni lẽi-ke, tarē ēsan dhan-darib uṛāolāk, sē
dancing-girls taking, of-thee like property-(and)-things wasted, that
ghuri-ke, pāh'chat-nā-pāhach'tē, tā̃y bhaj lāgāolē.'
returning, immediately-on-reaching-(home), thou feast commencedest.'
Takhan a-kar bāp keh'lāk, 'sabhē din-ta tā̃y hāmar pash
Then his father said, 'all days-while thou me with
ah'bē keris. Sabhē dhan-darib tarē hekek; kintuk ekhan
living doest. The-whole property-(and)-things thine are; but now
richek majā kere hetek, kēsen tar ehē bhāi-ṭā mari rahē,
some merriment do should, why (because) thy this brother died had,
ghuri-ke bā̃chal; hārā̃i gēr-rahē, ghuri-ke pāolā̃.'
again (has)-lived; lost gone-had, again I-got.'

[No. 26.]

INDO-ARYAN FAMILY. EASTERN GROUP.

BIHĀRĪ.

EASTERN MAGAHĪ DIALECT.

SPECIMEN II.

KUṚMĀLĪ ṬHĀR. (MANBHUM DISTRICT.)

STATEMENT OF A PERSON ACCUSED IN A CRIMINAL COURT.

হজুর মঁয় দকানে বেসিকে মিঠাই বেচে হেলঁও। চারটা বাবু আইকে মিঠাইকের কেতেক দর শুধাওলাক। মঁয় কেহলঁও সব জিনিসেক ত একদর নেখেখ। অহে বাবুগুলাঁয় শুনিকে কেহলাক সভে দরিব মিলাঁয়কে এক সের হামরাকে দেহাক। মঁয় এক সের মিঠাই দেলেঁই আর আঠ আনা দাম খুজলঁও। তখন বাবুগুলাইঁ কেহলাক্ যে হামরাকর সঁগে পয়সা নেখৎ। অহে লদি লা আছেক। উঁহা যাইকে দাম দেবেঁই। মঁয় ভদরান মানুষ দেখিকে মঁয় কন্‌হ নিহি কেহলঁও। ঢের খেন হেলি পয়সা নিহি দেলাক্ দেখিকে মঁয় লদীতক্ গের রহুঁ। যাইকে দেখলঁও লাটা সেঠিন্ নেখেই। ঢের্ ধুরলে থানাঁই থানাঁই দেখলঁও লাটা ঢের ধুর্ গেল আছেক্। তেখনে মঁয় পেছাঁই পেছাঁই দৌড়ে লাগলঁও। ঘড়িটেক্ বাদে মঁয় লাটাকে আঁটাওলাহন্। আঁটাইকে লাহেক্ মাঁঝিটাকে বাবুগুলাক্ কাথা শুধাওলাহন। লা মাঁঝি কন্‌হ নিহি কেহলাক। মঁয়্ তখন্ পানী নাভিকে লাটাকে টেকলঁও। তখন বাবু গুলাঁয় লাহেক্ ভিতর্‌লে বাহরায়কে মকেই চর কেরি্কে গুল্ কের্‌লাক্ আর দুইটা বাবুইঁ ফাঁড়ি যার্‌লে একটা সিপাহি ডাকা কারাইকে আনলাক্। মঁয় সিপাহিকে সব কাথা খুলিকে কহি দেলেঁই। সিপাহি মর কাথা নেহি শুনিকে গিরিপ্তান কেরিকে আঁনলে আছে। দহাই ধরমা অতার মঁয় নিহি চরি কেরলে আইঁ। মঁয় বড়ি গরিব লক। মর কেউ নেখৎ বাবা সত্ বিচার্ করি দে। মর্ কন্‌হ দষ নেখে॥

INDO-ARYAN FAMILY. EASTERN GROUP.

BIHĀRĪ.

EASTERN MAGAHĪ DIALECT.

SPECIMEN II.

KUṚMĀLĪ ṬHĀR. (MANBHUM DISTRICT.)

STATEMENT OF A PERSON ACCUSED IN A CRIMINAL COURT.

Hajur, mãy dakānē besi-ke miṭhāi bēche helaõ. Chār-ṭā
Sir, I the-shop-in sitting sweetmeats selling was. Four

Bābu āi-ke miṭhāi-kēr ketek dar śudhāolāk. Mãy keh^{a}laõ, 'sab
Babus coming sweetmeats-of how-much price asked. I said, 'all

jinisek ta ek-dar nēkhekh.' Ahē Bābu-gulãy śuni-ke keh^{a}lāk,
things-of indeed same-price is-not.' Those Babus hearing said,

'sabhē darib milãy-ke, ek sēr hām^{a}rā-kē dehāk.' Mãy ek sēr miṭhāi
'all things mixing, one seer us-to give.' I one seer sweetmeats

delẽi, ār āṭh ānā dām khuj^{a}laõ. Takhan Bābu-gulãi keh^{a}lāk jē,
gave, and eight annas price asked. Then the-Babus said that,

'hām^{a}rā-kar sãgē pay^{a}sā nēkhat. Ahē ladi lā āhek. Ũhā jāi-ke
'of-us with pice is-not. In-that river (a)-boat is. There going

dām debẽi.' Mãy bhad^{a}rān-mānush dēkhi-ke mãy kanha nihi
price we-shall-give.' I gentlemen seeing I anything not

keh^{a}laõ. Ḍhēr khen heli pay^{a}sā nihi delāk dēkhi-ke mãy ladi-tak
said. Long time having-been pice not gave seeing I the-river-up-to

gēr-rahũ; jāi-ke dekh^{a}laõ lā-ṭā sē-ṭhin nēkhēi. Ḍhēr dhur-lē thānãi
went; going I-saw the-boat there is-not. Great distance-from discerning

thānãi dekh^{a}laõ lā-ṭā ḍhēr dhur gēl āhek. Tekh^{a}nē mãy
discerning saw the-boat great distance gone has. Then I

pechhãi pechhãi dauṛe lāg^{a}laõ. Ghaṛi-ṭek bādē mãy lā-ṭā-kē
after after-(the-boat) running began. Twenty-minutes-of after I the-boat

ãṭāo-lāhan. Āṭāi-ke lāhek mãjhiṭā-kē Bābu-gulāk kāthā śudhāolāhan
reached. Reaching the-boat-of the-boatman the-Babus-of news I-asked.

Lā-mãjhi kanha nihi keh^{a}lāk. Mãy takhan pānī nābhi-ke
The-boatman anything not said. I then (in-the)-water plunging

lā-ṭā-kē ṭek^{a}laõ. Takhan Bābu-gulãy lāhek bhitar-lē bāh^{a}rāy-ke,
the-boat obstructed. Then the-Babus the-boat-of inside-from coming-out,

ma-kē-i char keri-ke gul ker^{a}lāk, ār dui-ṭā Bābu-ī phãṛi-ghār-lē
me-even thief calling noise made, and two Babus-also the-(police)-outpost-from

ek-ṭā sipāhi ḍākā-kārāi-ke ān^{a}lāk. Mãy sipāhi-kē sab kāthā khuli-ke
a constable sending-for brought. I the-constable-to every word openly
kahi-delẽi. Sipāhi mar kāthā nehi śuni-ke giriptān-keri-ke ān^{a}lē-āhē.
told. The-constable my words not listening-to arresting has-brought.

Da-hāi, dharmā-atār, mãy nihi chari keṛ^{a}lē-āhã. Mãy baṛi
Two-alases, incarnation-of-justice, I not theft have-committed. I-(am) very
garib lak; mar kēü nēkhat, Bābā, sat bichār kari-dē, mar
poor man; mine anyone there-is-not, O-father, true justice do, mine
kanha dash nēkhē.
any guilt (there)-is-not.

SADRĪ KŌL.

The main Aryan language of the Feudatory State of Bamra, which lies to the West of the Keonjhar State, is Oṛiyā. Most of the aborigines speak Muṇḍā languages, but some of them use a corrupt Aryan language, which is locally known as Sadrī, or more correctly Sadᵃrī Kōl. As in the case of the Sadrī Korwā sub-dialect of Chhattīsgaṛhī, the word 'Sadrī' is used when an aboriginal tribe abandons its own language and takes to an Aryan one. Sadrī Kōl is reported to be spoken by 4,194 people. It is not, as might be expected, a dialect of the surrounding Oṛiyā, but is a form of the Eastern Magahī dialect. Immediately to its East, in the States of Keonjhar and Mayurbhanja, a form of Eastern Magahī is also spoken, called Kuṛmālī, but Sadrī Kōl does not agree so closely with this as it does with the Kuṛmālī Ṭhār of Manbhum and Kharsawan, with which it is practically identical. The pronunciation, too, is the same, the vowel *a* being sounded as in Oṛiyā, *viz.*, like the *o* in 'hot.'

Two specimens are given of this dialect. The first is a short extract from the Parable of the Prodigal Son, and the other a folk-tale. A few instances of the influence of Oṛiyā will be noticed. Such are the genitive *māl-jālar*, of property, and plurals like *suar-mānē*, swine ; *hāmᵃrē-mān*, we.

[No. 27.]

INDO-ARYAN FAMILY. EASTERN GROUP.

BIHĀRĪ.

EASTERN MAGAHĪ DIALECT.

SPECIMEN I.

SADRĪ KŌL. (STATE BAMRA.)

Gōṭē ād'mī-kēr dui-ṭhur bēṭā rahin. Unhā-lē chhōṭ bēṭā ō-kar
One man-of two sons were. Them-from the-younger son his
bāp-kē kah'läk, 'ē ābā, māl-jālar jin bhāg mōr bhāg-mē
father-to said, 'O father, of-the-property what share my share-in
giri, sē-kē mō-kē dē.' Sē ō-kar māl-jāl bhāg-kar dēlāk. Purē
will-fall, that me-to give.' He his property having-divided gave. Many
din nai jāilā chhōṭ bēṭā māl-jāl sōb-kē ek-ṭhin jamā-kar-khan
days not went the-younger son the-property all in-one-place having-collected
bidēs gelāk. Ō-ṭhānē kherāp kām-mē sab māl-jāl kharach
a-foreign-country went. There bad conduct-in all the-property spent
kar-delāk: sab māl-jāl kharach kar-ke serāi-khan, ō dēs-mē
he-made: all the-property spent having-made having-completed, that country-in
maharg holāk, āur ō bahūt dukh pālāk. Tāhān utar-mē ō ō
a-famine became, and he much distress got. There after-in he that
dēs-kar ek ād'mī-kar ghar-mē āsh'rā lelāk, āur ō ād'mī ō-kē
country-of a man-of house-in shelter took, and that man him
dōin-mē suar charāi pāiṭhālā. Sē suar-mānē jōn tasu
fields-in swine to-feed sent. He the-swine (plural) what husks
khāt-rahin, ō-kē khāi-kōr pēṭ purāi-kē man kar'lāk. Ō-kē
used-to-eat, those having-eaten his-belly filling-for mind made. Him-to
ō kēhū delāin nāhin khāi-kē.
those anyone gave not eating-for.

[No. 28.]

INDO-ARYAN FAMILY. EASTERN GROUP.

BIHARĪ.

EASTERN MAGAHĪ DIALECT.

SADRĪ KŌL. (STATE BAMRA.)

SPECIMEN II.

Ek gāũ-mē buḍhā buḍhī dui jhan rah^{a}len. Bahũt
One village-in an-old-man an-old-woman two persons were. Many
ād^{a}mī par-dēs jāi-ke kāmāi-khan lānat-hen. Sē-khanē
men foreign-country having-gone having-earned bringing-are. Then
buḍhiā-kē hĩsgā lāg^{a}lāk. Tōb-lē buḍhī kah^{a}lāk,
the-old-woman-to envy became-attached. Then the-old-woman said,
'ō buḍhā, sabē-tō kamāi-khan lānat-hen, hām^{a}rē-man
'O old-man, all-indeed having-earned bringing-are, we
jāb.' Kāudhē sab din sarag-kēr ek hātī dhān khāt-rahē, jē
will-go.' Where all day heaven-of an elephant paddy used-to-eat, there
buḍhā ogār^{a}lāk. Hātī ālāk. Hātī khāt-rahē. Dhān
the-old-man watched. The-elephant came. The-elephant eating-was. Paddy
khāi-khan jāāt-rahē sarag-pur. Tōb-lē buḍhā põchh-mē
having-eaten going-he-was (to)-the-heaven-city. Then the-old-man the-tail-on
dhar^{a}lāk. Hātī buḍhā-kē lē-gelāk sarag-pur. Ũhā̃
seized-hold. The-elephant the-old-man took-away (to)-the-heaven-city. There
buḍhā bahũt kamāi khālāk. Tōb-lē ō hāti-kēr põchh-kē
the-old-man much having-earned ate. Then he the-elephant-of the-tail
dhar^{a}lāk, āu nichē ālāk, āur buḍhiā-kē kah^{a}lāk, 'Buḍhiā
seized, and down came, and the-old-woman-to said, 'Old-woman
dēkh, et^{a}rā kamāi-khan lāin-han.' Tōb-lē buḍhiā dekh^{a}lāk,
see, so-much having-earned I-have-brought.' Then the-old-woman saw,
aur ō-kar jiu bahũt ānand holāk. Buḍhiā kah^{a}lāk, 'mō-hõ
and her soul very rejoiced became. The-old-woman said, 'I-too
jābõ.' Tōb-lē dōnō jhan gelāin, hātir põchh dhaĩr-khan,
will-go.' Then both persons went, the-elephant's tail having-seized,
sarag-pur. Ō-mānē ũhā̃ khōb kamāilāin khālāin. Tōb-lē
(to)-the-heaven-city. They there well earned ate. Then
buḍhā bichār kar^{a}lāk. Buḍhiā-kē kah^{a}lāk. Tōb phēr
the-old-man consideration made. The-old-woman-to he-spoke. Then again
buḍhā hāti-kēr põchh-kē dhar-kēr gāũ-kēr ād^{a}mī-kē
the-old-man the-elephant-of the-tail having-seized the-village-of men

lēgek lāgin ālāk. Tōb gāũ-kēr ād'mī-kē põchh'lāk, 'kāhō,
bringing-of for came. When the-village-of men he-asked, 'well,
ĩhā̃ bhūkē marat-hān. Chalā, sarag-pur-mē bahũt dhān chāul
here in-hunger you-are-dying. Come, the-heaven-city-in much paddy rice
milat-hē. Ũhā̃-kēr tāmbi bahũt baḍā hāi.' Tōb-lē sab gāũ-kēr ād'mī
is-found. There-of the-seer very big is.' Then all the-village-of men
bichār kar'lāin, āur buḍhā kē 'chalā, bhāi, jāba,' kah'lāin.
consideration made, and the-old-man-to 'come, brother, we-will-go,' said.

Tōb-gē āur ō hāti-kē ogār'lāin, āur ō hāti-kēr
Then and that elephant they-watched, and that elephant-of
põchh-mē buḍhā dhar'lāk. Phēr buḍhā-kēr piṭh-mē āur
the-tail-on the-old-man seized-hold. Again the-old-man-of the-back-on another
ek jhan potār'lāk. Ō-kar piṭh-mē āur ek jhan potār'lāk. Phēr
one person embraced. His back-on another one person embraced. Again
āur ek jhan potār'lāk. Āesan gāũ-kēr sab ād'mī pot'rā-pot'rī
another one person embraced. Thus the-village-of all the-men embracing-on-embracing
halāin. Tōb-lē hāti upar-kē chal'lāk. Sarag-pur-kēr ādhā bāṭ
became. Then the-elephant above-to started. The-heaven-city-of half way
haĩ-khan, ek jhan pāchhē-kēr ād'mī puchh'lāk, 'haĩ-hō, buḍhā,
having-become, one person behind-of a-man asked, 'well, old-man,
et'rā dhūr lē-jāāt-hī, jē ũhā̃ ket'nā baḍ tāmbi āhē?'
so-much distance you-are-taking-(us), what there how big the-seer is?'
Tōb-lē buḍhā ēk hāt-mē hāti-kēr põchh-kē dhaĩr-khan ek
Then the-old-man one hand-in the-elephant-of the-tail having-held one
hāt-mē tāmbi-kē batālāk, 'et'nā baḍ tāmbi hē.' Tōb-lē phēr ek ād'mī
hand-in the-seer explained, 'so big the-seer is.' Then again one man
puchh'lāk, 'nāi sun'lī-hō; ket'nā baḍ tāmbi āhe-jē.' Tōb-lē buḍhā
asked, 'not I-have-heard-you; how big the-seer is-what.' Then the-old-man
dōnō hāt-kē chhōḍ-kar, 'et'nā baḍ tāmbi āhē,' bol'lāk. Tōb-lē hātī
both hand letting-go, 'so big the-seer is,' said. Then the-elephant
sarag-pur chaĩl-gelāk; ād'mī sab paiḍ-kar mar-gelāin.
to-the-heaven-city went-away; the-men all having-fallen died.

FREE TRANSLATION OF THE FOREGOING.

Once upon a time there lived an old couple in a certain village. A number of the villagers used to go abroad to earn money, and would return rich men. This roused the old woman's envy, and said she, 'see how much these people bring home from their earnings. Let us go too to try our luck.' So the old man went and watched at a place where an elephant of Heaven used to come down and graze all day on paddy. According to his custom he came down and ate his fill, and was returning to the City of

Heaven, when the oldster caught hold of his tail and was carried up with him. He arrived there safely, and found plenty of work at high wages; so when he had earned a great deal, he again caught hold of the elephant's tail, and was carried down home again. 'See,' said he to his wife, 'how much I have earned.' When the old woman saw it, her soul was filled with joy, and she replied, 'I'll go too.' So they both set out, and both caught hold of the elephant's tail and in due course arrived at the City of Heaven. There they earned plenty and ate well, till one day the old man thought over things, and, after telling his better half, caught hold of the elephant's tail and went down home to fetch up his fellow-villagers. When he got there he asked them all to come back with him. 'Why,' said he, 'are you all dying here of hunger, when there is plenty of paddy and rice to be got in the City of Heaven. Moreover, the seer[1] up there is a very big one.' Then the villagers thought over the matter and agreed to go with the oldster. So they went out and watched for the elephant, and when he was starting home the old man caught hold of his tail. Another fellow caught him round the back. Then another caught the second round the back, and another the third, and so on till all were hanging like the tail of a kite from the elephant's tail, each one clasping the waist of the one above him. They had got half way to the City of Heaven when one of the rear men called out to the oldster, 'hulloa, old man, you are taking us a very long way. How big is the seer up there?' The oldster held on to the elephant's tail with one hand, and motioned with the other saying, 'it is so big.' Then another fellow shouted, 'I couldn't hear what you said. How big is the seer?' The oldster let go with both hands, saying, 'it is so big.' So the elephant went on his way to the City of Heaven alone, and all the men fell down to the earth and were killed.

Eastern Magahī is also spoken in the south-east of the Hazaribagh District, on the border of Manbhum, in the Thanas of Gola and Kashmar, and in a portion of Thana Ramgarh. Although still more closely based on standard Magahī than the Kuṛmālī Ṭhār of Manbhum, it possesses the remarkable peculiarity of being what might be called a bi-lingual language. I mean that while in the main it is Magahī, it adopts into its texture Bengali words and phrases, nay, even entire sentences, as they stand, without any alteration. For instance, in the specimen which follows, the first sentence is pure Bengali, while the second is Magahī. The two languages, as elsewhere south of the Ganges, are mechanically mixed, and are not chemically combined. This presence of a very evident Bengali element, and the fact that it is, like Kuṛmālī Ṭhār, written in the Bengali character, has led the dialect to be incorrectly called Bengali, and, as such, it has been returned by the local officials. A perusal of the specimen will, however, show, that it is really Magahī, and that the Bengali element has been introduced much as some English people introduce French phrases into their language.

The following specimen is the Parable of the Prodigal Son. It is in the Bengali character, and awkward attempts have been made to represent the Bihārī sounds, to which that alphabet and system of pronouncing it, are not adapted. These attempts have been altered to the normal Bihārī system of spelling in the transliteration.

[1] In India, the weight known as a *seer* varies from place to place. Of course, the rate of sale being the same, the larger the seer, the better for the purchaser.

[No. 29.]

INDO-ARYAN FAMILY. EASTERN GROUP.

BIHĀRĪ.

EASTERN MAGAHĪ DIALECT.

SO-CALLED 'BENGALI' OF HAZARIBAGH. (HAZARIBAGH DISTRICT.)

এক লোকের দু বেটা ছিল। তকরমে ছোট বেটা আপন বাপসে কহলই, এ বাপ চিজকে যে বখরা হাম্ পায়েব সে হামরা দেই দে। তকরমেসে চিজ ভাগ কর দেলেন। থোরনা দিনমে ছোট বেটা সমস্ত একসঙ্গ করকে দূর দেশ চলি গেলা আর সে জগন মে নাহক খরচ করকে সব চিজ আপন খোয় দেলক। সে সব চিজ খরচ করনে বাদ সে মুলুক মে ভারি আকাল ভেল ও সে দুখমে পড়ে লাগলা। তব সে ধায়কে সে দেশের এক লোকের আশ্রয় লেলক। সে লোক তকরা আপন ক্ষেতে শুয়র চরনে পাঠাই দেলেন। পরে শুয়র যে ভুষা খাইতলথি সেই দেই সে পেট ভরতে খায়েস করলেক কিন্তু কেউ তক্‌রা দিলেক না। পরে হোস ভেলে সে বাজকালক হামীর বাপকে কতে মাহিনাওয়ালা নকর খাহৎ ও বাঁচত হৎ আর হাম ইহাঁ ভুখে মরহি। হাম উঠকে আপন বাপ ইহাঁ যায়েব, তকরা কহবন বাপ হাম ভগবান ইহাঁ পাপ করলেহি ও তোহার হুজুর মে হাম তোহার বেটা যোগ্য নহি, হামরা এগো নকর বরাবর রাখ। তব উঠকে আপন বাপকে নজিক গেল। কিন্তু দূরসে তকরা বাপ দেখে পাওলক আর মায়া করকে দৌড়কে ঘেঁটামে ধরকে চুমা লেলক। বেটা তকরা কহলক এ বাপ হাম ভগবান ইহাঁ পাপ করলেহি ও তোহর হুজুর মে হাম তোহর বেটা যোগ্য নহি। মগর বাপ আপন নকর লোককে কহলক জলদি সবসে বেশ লুগা আনকে এনকো পিনহন, এসকা হাতমে আঙ্গটী ও গোড়মে জুতা পিনহায় দেহন; আর হামরিন খায় ও আনন্দ রহি; কারণ হামার এ বেটা মর গেল রহে বাঁচল হ্যায়, হেরাএল গেল রহে, মিলল হ্যায়। পরে সে সব আঁনন্দ করে লাগল॥

আর তকর বড় বেটা ক্ষেতমে হোলক, সে আয়কে ঘরকে নজিক নাচ ও বাজনা শুনে পায়লক তখন সে এক নকরকে বোলায়কে পুছলক এ সব কি। সে তকরা কহলক তোহর ভাই আএল হো আর তোহর বাপ ভোজ তৈয়ার করলে হ্যায়, কাহেনা সে তকরা নিরোগ দেহীমে পাওলক। কিন্তু সে খিসি-অয়লা, ভিতর যায় খুজলা না। তকর বাদমে ওকর বাপ বাহার আয়কে পরবোধ করে লাগলথিন। মগর সে জবাব করকে আপন বাপকে কহলই দেখ এতনা বচ্ছর ধরকে হাম তোহর সেবা করলেহি তোহর কোন বাত কখনি লঙ্ঘন না করলি। তকরমে তোঁএ কখন হামরা এগো ছাগরীকে বাচ্ছা নেহি দেলক যে হামার দোস্ত লোককে সঙ্গে আনন্দ করি। মগর তোহর এ বেটা যে পাতুরিয়াকে সঙ্গ তোহর সম্পত বরবাদ করলেক সে যখন আয়লক তখন তকর লাগকে বড়া ভোজ তৈয়ার করলেক। মগর সে তকরা কহলক বেটা তুই সব দিন হামার সঙ্গ হ্যায় আর হামার যে কুছ হ্যায় সে সব তোহর। মগর খুসি ও আনন্দ করনা উচিত কারণ তোহর ই ভাই মর গেল রহে বাঁচল হ্যায় হেরাএল গেল রহে মিলল হ্যায়॥

[No. 29.]

INDO-ARYAN FAMILY. EASTERN GROUP.

BIHĀRĪ.

EASTERN MAGAHĪ DIALECT.

SO-CALLED 'BENGALI' OF HAZARIBAGH. (HAZARIBAGH DISTRICT.)

Ek lōkēr du bēṭā chhila. Takar-mē chhōṭ bēṭā āpan
One of-person two sons were. Them-of-among the-younger son his-own

bāp-sē kah^{a}laï, 'ē bāp, chij-ke jē bakh^{a}rā hām pāeb, sē
father-to said, 'O father, property-of what share I will-get, that

hām^{a}rā dēi-dē.' Takar-mē sē chij bhāg kar-delen. Thor^{a}nā din-mē
to-me give.' Thereupon he property division made. A-few days-in

chhōṭ bēṭā samasta ēk-saṅg kar-ke dūr dēś chali-gēlā,
younger son whole together collected-having a-distant country went-away,

ār sē-jagan-mē nāhak kharach kar-ke sab chij āpan
and that-place-in wanton expenses having-done all property his-own

khōy-dēlak: sē sab chij kharach-kar^{a}nē bād sē-muluk-mē bhāri
wasted: he all property expending after that-country-in a-severe

ākāl bhēl, ō sē dukh-mē paṛe lāg^{a}lā. Tab sē jāy-ke sē
famine occurred, and he distress-in to-fall began. Then he having-gone that

dēśēr ēk lōkēr āśray lēlak. Sē lōk tak^{a}rā āpan khētē
of-country a-certain of-man shelter took. That man him his-own on-field

śūar char^{a}nē pāṭhāi-delen. Parē śūar jē bhushā khāital^{a}thi sēi
swine to-feed sent-off. Then swine which husks did-eat that

dēi sē pēṭ bhar^{a}tē khāes kar^{a}lek, kintu keu tak^{a}rā dilek nā.
with he belly to-fill wish did, but any-body to-him gave not.

Parē hōs bhēlē, sē bāj-kālak, 'hāmār bāp-ke katē
Afterwards senses having-returned, he said, 'my father-of how-many

māhināwālā nakar khā-hat ō bā̃cha-ō-hat ār hām ihā̃
hired servants eating-are and sparing-also-are and I here

bhukhē mara-hi. Hām uṭh-ke āpan bāp-ihā̃ jāeb.
with-hunger am-dying. I having-arisen my-own father-near will-go.

Tak^{a}rā kah^{a}ban, "bāp, hām Bhag^{a}wān ihā̃ pāp kār^{a}lē-hi, ō
To-him I-will-say, "father, I God near sin have-done, and

tohār hujūr-mē. Hām tohār bēṭā jogg'a na-hi; hām^{a}rā ēgō nakar
thy presence-in. I thy son worthy am-not; me one servant

barābar rākh."' Tab uṭh-ke āpan bāp-ke najīk gēl. Kintu
like keep."' Then having-arisen own father-of near went. But

dūr-sē tak^{a}ra bāp dēkhe pāolak, ār māyā kar-ke dauṛ-ke
distance-from him father to-see got, and compassion having-made running

ghēchā-mē dhar-ke, chumā lēlak. Bēṭā tak'rā kah'lak, 'ē bāp, hām
neck-on holding, a-kiss took. The-son to-him said, 'O father, I
Bhag'wān ihā̃ pāp kar'lē-hi, ō tōhar hujur-mē. Hām tōhar bēṭā
God near sin have-done, and thy presence-in. I thy son
jogg'a na-hi.' Magar bāp āpan nakar-lōk-kē kah'lak, 'jal'di
worthy am-not.' But the-father his-own servant-people-to said, 'quickly
sab-sē beś lugā ān-ke en-kō pin'han; es-kā hāt-mē āngṭī
all-than good clothes bringing this-(person)-to put-on; his hand-on ring
ō gōṛ-mē jutā pinhāy-dehan; ār hām'rin khāy ō ānand rahi;
and foot-on shoes put-on; and let-us feast and merry be;
kāran hāmār ē bēṭā mar-gēl-rahē, bā̃chal-hai; herāel-gēl-rahē,
because my this son had-died, revived-is; had-been-lost,
milal-hai.' Parē sē-sab ānand kare lāgal.
found-is.' Afterwards they-all rejoicing to-do began.

Ār takar baṛa bēṭā khēt-mē hōlak. Sē āy-ke ghar-ke najik,
And his eldest son the-field-in was. He coming the-house-of near,
nāch ō bāj'nā śune pāelak. Takhan sē ēk nakar-kē bolāy-ke
dancing and music to-hear got. Then he one a-servant-to calling
puchh'lak, 'ē sab ki?' sē tak'rā kah'lak, 'tōhar bhāi
asked, 'this all what?' he to-him said, 'thy brother
āel-hō ār tōhar bāp bhōj taiyār-kar'lē-hai, kāhenā sē
come-is-(for-thee) and thy father a-feast has-made-ready, because he
tak'rā nirōg dēhī-mē pāolak.' Kintu sē khisiailā, bhitar jāy khuj'lā
him sound body-in found.' But he got-angry, inside to-go sought
nā. Takaṛ bād-mē ō-kar bāp bāhār āy-ke par'bōdh kare
not. Of-that after his father out coming remonstrating to-make
lāgal'thin, magar sē jawāb kar-ke, āpan bāp-kē kah'lai, 'dēkh,
began, but he answer making, his-own father-to said, 'see,
et'nā bachchhar dhar-ke hām tōhar sēbā kar'lē-hī; tōhar kōna
these-many years during I thy service have-done; thy any
bāt kakh'ni langhan nā-kar'li; takar-mē tõe kakhan hām'rā ēgō
word never disobedience I-did-not; but-still thou ever to-me one
chhāg'rī-ke bāchchhā nēhi dēlak jē hāmār dōst-lōk-ke saṅgē ānand
goat-of young-one not gavest that my friends-of with rejoicing
kari. Magar tōhar ē bēṭā jē pāturiyā-ke saṅg tōhar
I-may-make. But thy this son who harlots-of with thy
sampat bar'bād kar'lek, sē jakhan ailak, takhan takar lāg-ke baṛā
property wasting made, he when came, then him for great
bhōj taiyār kar'lek.' Magar sē tak'rā kah'lak, 'bēṭā, tũi sab-din
feast ready thou-madest.' But he to-him said, 'son, thou all-days
hāmār sang hai, ār hāmār jē kuchh hai, sē sab tōhar.
of-me with are, and my what anything is, that all (is)-thine.

Magar	khusi	ō	ānand	kar^anā	uchit,	kāran	tōhar	i	bhāi
But	*happiness*	*and*	*rejoicing*	*making*	*(is-)meet,*	*because*	*thy*	*this*	*brother*

mar-gēl-rahē,	bā̃chal-hai ;	herāel-gēl-rahē,	milal	hai.'
had-died,	*revived-is ;*	*had-been-lost,*	*found*	*is.'*

In the extreme east of the Ranchi District, on the border of Manbhum, are the five sub-plateau Parganas of Silli, Baranda, Rahe, Bundu, and Tamar. A reference to the map facing p. 140 will show that the east and south-east of Ranchi is a meeting place of three overlapping forms of Aryan speech. In the south-east, the main language is the Nagpuriā Bhojpurī, which is the Aryan form of speech used in the rest of the District, but here the Jain Mā̃jhīs and the well-to-do cultivating and trading castes speak the Sarākī form of Bengali. In the five Parganas above-mentioned, the main Aryan language is a form of Eastern Magahī, but, here also, the Bengali Sarākī overlaps in Pargana Tamar. It may be added that, in the five Parganas, Nagpuriā is also spoken by some people, though, for the sake of clearness, this is not shown in the map. Finally, over the whole of both the South-east and the East, the general language is the non-Aryan Muṇḍārī, with which we are not at present concerned, and which is not shown in the map, as it only deals with Aryan languages.

The form of Eastern-Magahī spoken in the five Parganas is known as Pā̃ch Parganiā. As it is strongest in Pargana Tamar, it is also called Tamariā. It closely resembles the Kuṛmālī Ṭhār of Manbhum. The principal apparent difference is the result of the characters employed in writing. In Manbhum, the character adopted is the Bengali, and the language is looked at, so to speak, through Bengali spectacles. Hence words are spelled as a Bengali would spell them, and, more especially, an ō-sound is represented as elsewhere in Manbhum, by the letter অ *a*. In the five Parganas, on the other hand, the Kaithī alphabet is used, and the language is looked at through Hindī spectacles, and an ō-sound is represented by the letter ओ *ō*.

We also see signs of the influence of Sarākī Bengali[1] in the aspiration of words like *jhan* for *jan*, a person.

Instances of the representation of the ō-sound of the letter *a* occur on almost every line. The spelling is capricious, and this is retained, as illustrating how the pronunciation, affected by the Western Bengali, can only be represented with difficulty in the Kaithī character. Thus, we have *rōhē* for *rahē*, he was; *kōhal* and *kahal*, to say; *kot^anā*, for *kat^anā*, how many ?

The Declension of nouns follows Magahī, the only exception being the Dative Plural of *chākar*, a servant, which is *chākar-gulā-gē*.

As regards Pronouns, the word for 'I' is *mōẽ* or *maẽ*. The word for 'Your Honour' is *rāur*, which is borrowed from Nagpuriā.

As to Verbs, we have *hekō̃* for 'I am,' which is a corruption of the Magahī *hikũ*. We have also the form which was noted in Kuṛmālī Ṭhār, viz., *āhō̃*, I am; *āhis*, thou art; *āhē*, he is, and so on. We have, moreover, forms like *dētō̃-ē* he used to give; *mōrōtō-hō̃*, I am dying. The first person singular of the Future ends in *mũ*, as in *kah^amũ*, I will say. A final short *i* is pronounced in the preceding syllable, as in so many Bengali dialects and as in Nagpuriā. Thus, we have *kaïr*, having done, and

---

[1] *Vide ante*, Vol. V, Part I., pp. 86 and ff.

many others. Similarly there is *saüb* for *sabu*, all. The Conjunctive Participle is formed by the addition of *kōhan*, or *kahan* as in *uiṭh-kōhan* or *uiṭh-kahan*, having arisen. It will be remembered that in Sadrī Kōl we had *khan*.

This dialect is classed as a form of Magahī, but it varies so greatly in the mouths of different people, that it might sometimes be classed as a form, not of Magahī, but of Nagpuriā Bhojpurī. The following specimen is, as a glance will show, clearly Magahī and not Nagpuriā, but the list of words and sentences given subsequently on pp. 327 and following, are equally clearly Nagpuriā. In classifying the dialect, I have followed the specimen, as being less liable to be affected by the personal equation than a list of disconnected words and grammatical forms.

[No. 30.]

INDO-ARYAN FAMILY. EASTERN GROUP.

BIHĀRĪ.

EASTERN MAGAHĪ DIALECT.

PĀCH PARGANIĀ OR TAMARIĀ. (RANCHI DISTRICT.)

કોનોં એક આદમી કેર દુઇઠો છુઆ રોહે। તેકર માંહને છોટ છુઆઠા આપન વાપ કે કોહલક, વાપ મહં ધન કેર જે હિસા પામું સે મોકે દેઉ। તેકર માંહને ઓકર વાપ સે ધન હિસા કરી દેલક। વહુત દિન ના હોત કેર છોટ છુઆઠા સઉવ ધન જમા કોરી લેલક, આર દૂર ગાંવ કે ચરલ ગેલક। આર સે ધન કે તાહાં કુકામ માંહને ઉડાય દેલક। આર જખન સે સઉવ ખરચ કરી ચુકલક, ગાંવેં ખૂબ આકાલ હોલક, આર સે વહુત કસ્ટ પાએ લાગલક। તખન સે સેઇ ગાંવ કેર નહરઅઠ આદમી કેર પાસે રહલક। આર સે આદમી તેકે આપન ટાંઇડ઼ે સુઅરી ચરાયકે પઠાય દેલક। તેકર વાદ સે આદમી સુઅરી જે ઘાંસ ખાત રહે સેઇ ઘાંસ ખાયકહન પેટ ભરામું રજ્ઞા કરલક। આર કેઉ તેકે દેતોંએ નાહીં। તેકર વાદ જેવિ વુહે પારલક, સે કહલક મોર વાપકેર કોતના તલપ લેવૈઆ ચાકર જતના ખાય કેર દરકાર તેકર લેક વેશી પાએલા આર મોએં રહાં ભૂખે મોરોતો હોં। મોએં ઉઠી કોહન રહીં લેક મોર વાપકેર પાસ જામું, આર તેકે કહમું। વાપ, મએં ભગવાન કેર પાસે આર તાઉરકેર પાસેક પાપ કરી આહોં, આર મએં તાઉર છુઆ હેકોં કોઇ કોહન કહલ વેસ ના લાગે। મોકે તાઉરકેર તલપ પાવૈઆ ચાકર નકમ રાખૂ। તેકર વાદ સે ઉઠી કહન આપન વાપકેર પાસ ગેલક। કિન્તુ સે આતાકે રહત કેર તેકર વાપ તેકે દેખે પાએ કહને કુરદ જાય કહન ટોટાય ધરી કહન ચૂમ ખાલક। આર છુઆ તેકે કહલક વાપ મએં ભગવાનકેર પાસે આર તોર પાસેક પાપ કરી આહોં, આર મએં તાઉરકેર છુઆ હેકોં કોઇ કહન કોહલ વેસ ના લાગે। કિન્તુ વાપ આપન ચાકરગુલાગે કહલક જે સઉવ લેક વેસ લુગા લારી કહન એકે પિનધાવા, આર ઇકર હાથે અંગ઼ઠી આર ગોડ઼ે જૂતા પિનધાય દેવા આર ખાય કહન હામને ખુસી હોઇ। કાહન મોર એહે છુઆઠા મોરી જાય રહે, સે આઉરી વાંચય ઉઠલક હેજાય જાય રહે, પાવલક। આર સે સઉવ કોઇ ખુસી હોય લાગલક॥

સેખન તેકર વડ઼ વેટા ટાંઇડ઼ે રહે। સે આય કહન ઘરકેર પાસ પહુંચલક, આર નાચ આર વાજના સુને કે પાલક। કિ એક હન ચાકર કે ડાકી કહન પુછલક ઇ સઉવ કા। સે તેકે કહલક તોર ભાઇ આય આહે આર તોર વાપ વહુત આદમીકેર ખાય

केर चीज खामा करल आहे। कारन तेके वेसे पालक। किन्तु से खिसालक; भीतर जायके नाहीं मानलक। से तेहें तेकर बाप बाहिरे आय कहल तेके बुझायके लागलक। से जवाब दे कहल आपन बाप के कहलक देखिन एतिक बछर हेके मोएं तोर सेवा करोतोहों; तोर हुकुम कोखनो नाईं काटल नोहों तबहुं नाउर संगिनकेर छूआउ नाईं देली, जे मोन आपुस के ले कहल खुसी करो। किन्तु तोर एहे छुआटा आय आहे जे छुआटा! कसबीकेर संगे तोर सउब धन खाय गुचाय आहे तखन नउने तेकर लागिक बहुत आदमीकेर खाएकेर चीज खामा करल आहो। किन्तु से तेके कहलक बेटा तें सउब दिनेर मोर संगे आहिस आर मोर जे आहे से सउब तोर। किन्तु नोहे करनेके उचित, आर खुसी होइ कारन तोर एहे भाई मोरल जाय रहे फेर बांच्या हे हेराय जाय रहे पावलक॥

[No. 30.]

INDO-ARYAN FAMILY. EASTERN GROUP.

BIHĀRĪ.

EASTERN MAGAHĪ DIALECT.

PĀCH PARGANIĀ OR TAMARIĀ. (RANCHI DISTRICT.)

Kōnō ēk ādªmī-kēr dui-ṭā chhuā rōhē. Tēkar mā̃hªnē chhōṭ chhuā-ṭā
Certain a man-of two sons were. Them among the-younger son

āpan bāp-kē kōhªlak, 'bāp, maẽ dhan-kēr jē hisā pāmū̃ sē
his-own father-to said, 'father, I property-of which share will-get that

mō-kē dēu.' Tēkar mā̃hªnē ōkar bāp sē dhan hisā-kaïr dēlak. Bahut
me-to give.' Them-of among his father that property dividing gave. Many

din nā hōt, këi chhōṭ chhuā-ṭā saüb dhan jāmā-kōir-lēlak, ār
days not being, that the-younger son all property collected, and

dhūr gā̃w-kē chaïl-gēlak. Ār sē dhan-kē tā̃hā̃ kukām mā̃hªnē
distant village-to went-away. And that property there evil-deeds in

uṛāy-dēlak. Ār jakhan sē saüb kharach-kaïr-chukªlak, gā̃wẽ khūb
wasted-away. And when that all he-had-spent, the-village-in great

ākāl hōlak; ār sē bahut kasṭ pāe lāgªlak. Takhan sē sēi
famine took-place; and he much trouble to-get began. Then he that-very

gā̃w-kēr rahaïaṭ ādªmī-kēr pāsē rahªlak. Ār sē ādªmī tē-kē āpan
village-of inhabitant man-of near lived. And that man him his-own

ṭā̃ïṛē suaïr chārāy-kē paiṭhāy-dēlak. Tēkar bād sē ādªmī, suaïr
fields-in swine feeding-for sent-away. That after that man, swine

jē ghā̃s khāt-rahē, 'sēi ghā̃s khāy-kahan pēṭ bharāmū̃,'
which grass used-to-eat, 'that-very grass having-eaten belly I-will-fill,'

ichchhā karªlak. Ār keu tē-kē dētō̃-ē nāhī̃. Tēkar bād jēbi
a-wish made. And any-one him-to used-to-give not. That after when

būjhe-pārªlak, sē kahªlak, 'mōr bāp-kēr kotªnā talap-lewaiïā chākar
he-came-to-senses, he said, 'my father-of how-many pay-taking servants

jatªnā khāy-kēr darªkār tēkar lēk bēśi pāẽ-lā ār
as-much eating-for (is)-necessary that than more get and

mōẽ ihā̃ bhūkhē mōrōtō-hō̃. Mōẽ uiṭh-kōhan
I here from-hunger am-dying. I arising

ihā̃ lēk mōr bāp-kēr pās jāmū̃, ār tē-kē kahªmū̃, "bāp,
here from my father-of near will-go, and him-to will-say, "father,

maẽ Bhōgªwān-kēr pāsē ār rāur-kēr pāsē-ū pāp kaïr-āhō̃
I God-of near and you-of near-also sin have-done

ār maẽ rāur chhuā hekō̃ kōi-kōhan kahal bēs nā lāgē.
and I your son am anyone-to to-say good not does-appear.

Mō-kē rāur-kēr talap-pāwaïā chā̈kar rakam rākhū."' Tēkar
Me you-of pay-getting servant like keep."' That

bād sē uiṭh-kahan āpan bāp-kēr pās gēlak. Kintu sē
after he arising his-own father-of near went. But he

phārākē rahat, kēi tē-kar bāp tē-kē dēkhe-pāe-kah^{a}nē
a-long-way-off was, that his father him having-been-able-to-see

kuid-jāy-kahan ṭōṭāy dhaïr-kahan chūm khālak. Ār chhuā tē-kē
running neck taking-hold-of a-kiss ate. And son him-to

kah^{a}lak, 'bāp, maẽ Bhag^{a}wān-kēr pāse ār tōr pāsē-ū pāp
said, 'father, I God-of near and thy near-too sin

kaïr-āhõ, ār mōẽ rāur-kēr chhuā hekõ kōī-kahan kōhal bēs
have-done, and I you-of son am any-one-to to-say good

nā lāgē.' Kintu bāp āpan chākar-gulā-gē kah^{a}lak jē, 'saüb-lēk
not does-appear.' But the-father his-own servants-to said that, 'good-than

bēs lugā lāin-kahan ē-kē pindhāwā, ār īkar hāthē ā̃g^{a}ṭhī
good cloth bringing this-one put-on, and this-one's hand-on ring

ār gōṛē jūtā pindhāy-dēwā; ār khāy-kahan hām^{a}rē khusī
and feet-on shoes put-on; and eating we happy

hōī; kāran mōr ēhē chhuā-ṭā mōïr-jāy-rahē, sē āur bā̃ich-ghuṛ^{a}lak;
be; because my this son dead-was, he again returned-safe;

hejāy jāy-rahē, pāw^{a}lak.' Ār sē saüb^{a} kōī khusī hōy lāg^{a}lak.
lost was, is-found.' And that all men merry to-be began.

Sēkhan tēkar baṛ bēṭā tā̃ïṛē rahē. Sē āy-kahan ghar-kēr
At-that-time his elder son field-in was. He coming house-of

pās pahũch^{a}lak, ār nāch ār bāj^{a}nā sune-kē pālak. Kī ēk
near approached, and dancing and music hear-to got. Then one

jhan chākar-kē ḍāik-kahan puchh^{a}lak, 'I saüb kā?' Sē tē-kē
man servant calling he-asked, 'This all what(is)?' He him-to

kah^{a}lak, 'Tōr bhāī āy-āhē, ār tōr bāp bahut ād^{a}mī-kēr
said, 'Thy brother is-come, and thy father many men-of

khāy-kēr chīj jāmā-kaïr-āhē. Kāran tē-kē bēsē pālak.' Kintu
eating-for things has-collected. The-reason-(is) him well he-found.' But

sē khisālak; bhītar jāy-kē nāhĩ mān^{a}lak. Sē-tēhẽ tēkar bāp
he grew-angry; inside to-go not wished. Therefore his father

bāhirē āy-kahan tē-kē bujhāy-kē lāg^{a}lak. Sē jawāb dē-kahan āpan bāp-kē
outside coming him to-conciliate began. He answer giving his-own father-to

kah^{a}lak, 'dēkhīn, ētik bachhar-lēk mōẽ tōr sēwā kārōtō-hõ. Tōr hukum
said, 'see, so-many years-from I thy service am-doing. Thy orders

kōkh^{a}nō nāī kāiṭ-rōhõ. Tahā̃ī rāur chhīgir-kēr chhuā-ū
never not I-transgressed. Nevertheless Your-Honour goat-of young-one-even

nāī dēlĩ, jē mōr āpus-kē lē-kahan khusī karī. Kintu tōr ēhē chhuā-ṭā
not gave, that my friends having-taken merry I-may-make. But thy this son

āy-āhē, jē chhuā-ṭā kas^{a}bī-kēr saṅgē tōr saüb dhan khāy-guchāy-āhē,
has-come, which son harlots-of company-in thy all fortune has-wasted,

takhan raürē tēkar lāgin bahut ād^{a}mī-kēr khāe-kēr chīj
at-that-time Your-Honour him for many men-of eating-of things

jāmā-kaīr-ābī.' Kintu sē tē-kē kah^{a}lak, 'bēṭā, taī saüb dinē-i mōr saṅgē
has-collected.' But he him-to said, 'son, thou all days-even me with

āhis, ār mōr jē āhē sē saüb tōr. Kintu rījhē kare-kē uchit,
art, and mine whatever is that all thine. But merry to-make (is) proper,

ār khusī hoī, kāran tōr ēhē bhāī mōir jāy-rahē, phēir bā̃ich-āhe;
and glad let-us-be, because thy this brother dead was, again saved-is;

hejāy jāy-rahe, pāw^{a}lak.'
lost was, is-found.'

It has been already pointed out[1] that nearly all the 40,000 Kuṛmīs who inhabit the Orissa Tributary States, speak a form of Western Bengali, though the other Aryan-speaking inhabitants of that area have Oṛiyā for their mother tongue. In the States of Mayurbhanja and Keonjhar, however, 280 Kuṛmīs have been returned as speaking a dialect named Kuṛumālī, which, on examination, turns out to be another instance of Eastern Magahī. Here, the corrupting element is more Oṛiyā than Bengali, and, moreover, the specimens received being written in the Oṛiyā character, they have necessarily acquired a further resemblance in orthography to that language, which probably does not properly belong to them. Instances of borrowing from Oṛiyā abound, but even some of these are curious distortions. For instance, the word for 'was,' *helēk*, is evidently a corruption of the Magahī *halaik*, but the *a* of the first syllable has been changed to *e*, under the influence of the Oṛiyā *helā*, while Bengali has possibly had a share in changing the final *aik* to *ēk*. On the whole the dialect agrees very closely with the Kuṛmālī Ṭhār of Manbhum. We have the same representation of an *o*-sound by *a* and the same base, *ah*, for the auxiliary verb.

It will be sufficient to give one specimen. It is the statement in a criminal court of a person accused of murder. It is written in the Oṛiyā running hand and is printed in facsimile.

---

[1] Vide *ante*, p. 146.

[No. 31.]

INDO-ARYAN FAMILY. EASTERN GROUP.

BIHĀRĪ.

EASTERN MAGAHĪ DIALECT.

KUṚUMĀLĪ SUB-DIALECT. (MAYURBHANJA STATE.)

[illegible] ?

[illegible] ।

[illegible] ?

[illegible]

[illegible] ।

[illegible] ?

[illegible]

[illegible] ।

[illegible] ?

[illegible] ।

[illegible] ?

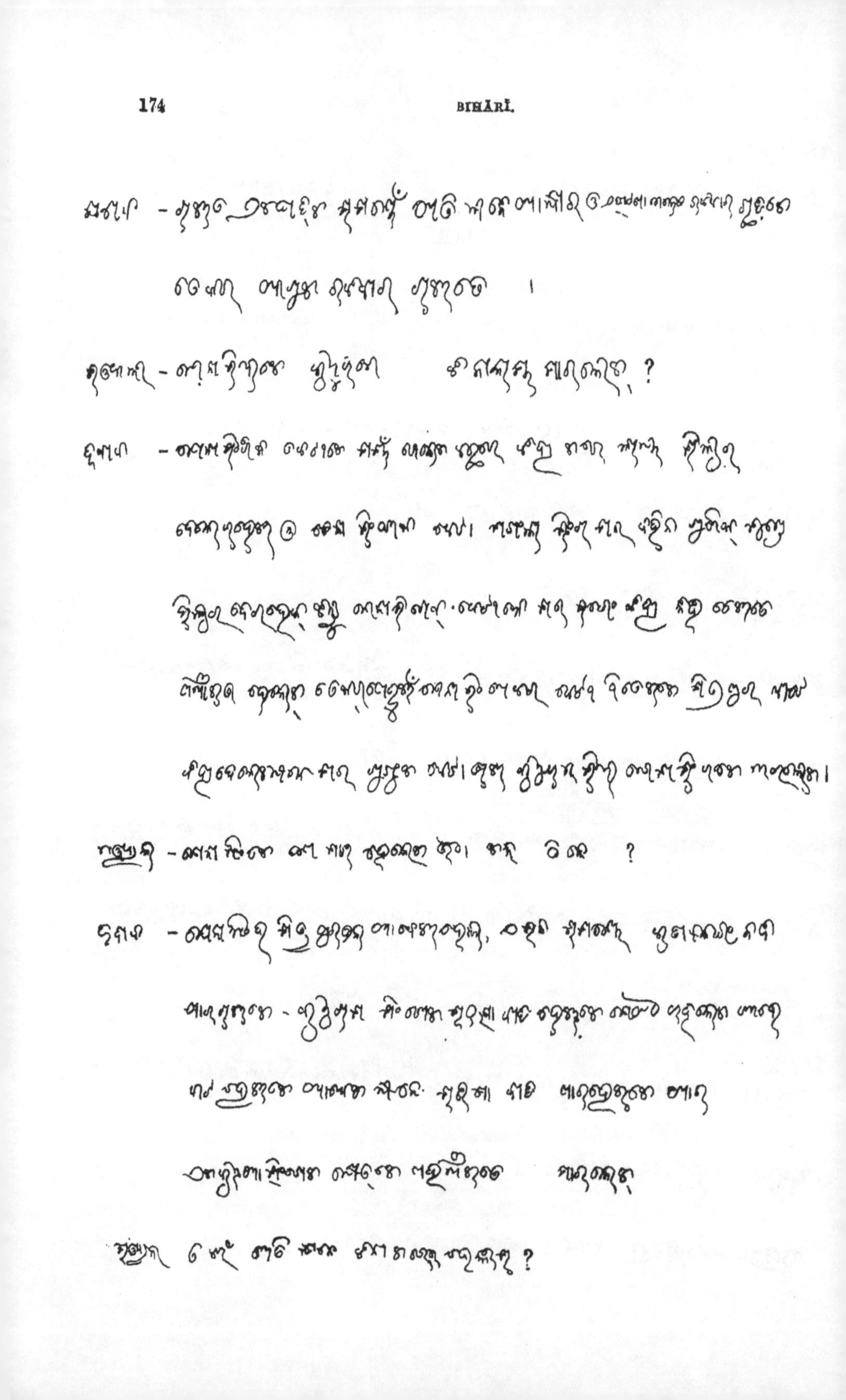

[illegible] — [illegible]

[illegible] — [illegible]?

[illegible] — [illegible] (1) [illegible] (2) [illegible]

(3) [illegible] (4) [illegible]! [illegible]

[illegible]

[illegible]।

[illegible] — [illegible]?

[illegible] — [illegible]।

[illegible] — [illegible] (3) [illegible]?

[illegible] — [illegible] (3) [illegible]।

[illegible] — [illegible]?

[illegible] — [illegible]।

[No. 31.]

INDO-ARYAN FAMILY. EASTERN GROUP.

BIHĀRĪ.

EASTERN MAGAHĪ DIALECT.

KUṚUMĀLĪ SUB-DIALECT. (MAYURBHANJA STATE.)

Saōyāl (Sawāl),—Kurāḍiā Pra. Panḍupāl gā̃w-ēk Jēnā Singh ekhyan kāhā̃ āhē?
Question,— Kurāḍihā Parganā Panḍupāl village-of Jēnā Singh now where is?

Jawāb,— U ekhyan mari-gēlā-hē.
Answer,—He now dead-gone-is.

Sawāl,—Kēsan kari-ke marªlā?
Question,—How doing did-he-die?

Jawāb,— Kurāḍiā Praganā Āsªkanda gā̃w-ēk Budhu-rām Singh Jēnā Singh-kē
Answer,—Kurāḍihā Parganā Āskanda village-of Budhu-rām Singh Jēnā Singh
marāwªlē-āhēk akar ṭhēṅgāy kari-ke.
has-caused-to-die his by-club doing.

Sawāl,— Ketek ṭhēṅgāy mārªlēk, ō kan-ṭhinē ṭhēṅgāy
Question,—How-many-(times) by-club did-he-strike, and in-what-place with-the-club
māri mārªlēk?
striking did-he-kill (-him)?

Jawāb,—Jēnā Singh-ēk dehinā dhāri-k kān jaṛiī̃, ēk ṭhēṅgā māraïtē-ī.
Answer,—Jēnā Singh's right side's ear at-the-root, one club-blow on-striking-merely.
Ahē-māïrē-i ahē-ṭhinē jhaṛi-khasªlā.
On-that-striking-merely in-that-place he-fell-down..

Sawāl,—A-kē māri-hel-ēk khyanē tā̃y ā̃ikhē dekhªlē-āhas ki nihī̃?
Question,—Him of-being-beaten at-the-time you with-eye have-seen or not?

Jawāb,— Hā̃, dekhªlē-āhā̃.
Answer,—Yes, I-have-seen.

Sawāl,— Ē ghaṭªnā kabē helēk, ō kati-khyanē?
Question,— This occurrence when did-it-occur, and at-what-time?

Jawāb,— Rāït ēk-ghaṛī-k samayē̃. Ati-khyanē āndhār. Ō ē
Answer,—At-night of-one-hour at-the-time. At-that-time (it was-)dark. And this
ghaṭªnā gel-ēk Rabi-bār chhāṛi-ke tēkar āgu-k Rabi-bār
occurrence of-the-passed Sunday not-counting of-it the-preceding-of Sunday
rāïtē.
at-night.

Sawāl,—Jēnā Singh-kē Budhu-rāmē kinā-lāy mārªlēk?
Question,—Jēnā Singh Budhu-rām for-what killed?

Jawāb,—Jēnā Singh-ēk bēṭī-kē mā̃y gel-ēk bachharē bihā kare-lāy sindur
Answer,—Jēnā Singh's daughter-to I of-last in-year marriage for-making vermilion
delē-rahēï. Ō Jēnā Singh-ēk bēṭā Maṅg*lā Singh mar bahin Guni-k muṇḍā
had-given. And Jēnā Singh's son Manglā Singh my sister Guni's head
sindur dē-rahēk. Kintu, Jēnā Singh-ēk bēṭī-kē mar saṅgē bihā
vermilion had-given. But, Jēnā Singh's daughter of-me with (in)-marriage
nihi dēïtē, pañchāit helēk. Tēkar pechhaī̃, Jēnā Si. akar
not giving, a-caste-assembly took-place. Of-that after, Jēnā Singh his
bēṭī Pitēi-kē, Mitrapur bāṭē bihā dēl-ēk-khyanē mar
daughter Pitēi-to, Mitrapur on-road (in)-marriage at-the-time-of-giving my
guṅgu-k bēṭā-bhāi Budhu-rām Singh Jēnā Singh-kē mār*lēk.
elder-uncle's son-brother Budhu-rām Singh Jēnā Singh killed.

Sawāl,—Jēnā Sing-kē jē māri-helēk, ulā kan-ṭhinē?
Question,—Jēnā Singh when he-had-killed, that in-what-place?

Jawāb,—Jēnā Singh Mitrapur-lē awēi-helā, ēsan-samayē Buṛhā-balaṅg nadī
Answer,—Jēnā Singh Mitrapur-from was-coming, at-such-time the-Buṛhā-balaṅg river
pār-hei-ke, Budhu-rām Singh-ēk sarisā bāṛi heï-ke, jē bāṭ rah*lēk,
having-crossed, Budhu-rām Singh's mustard field through, what path was,
ahē bāṭ hei-ke āw-ēk khyanē sarishā bāṛi pār-hei-ke,
that path along of-coming at-the-time the-mustard field having-crossed,
ār ēk Budhiā Singh-ēk khēt-kē pahā̃chaïtē mār*lēk.
another one Budhiā Singh's field-to on-arriving he-struck(-him).

Sawāl,—Taī̃ ati-khyanē kinā karēi-helis?
Question,—You at-that-time what were-doing?

Jawāb,—Mā̃y ati-khyanē-kuhiī̃ ḍāṇḍāi-rahā̃.
Answer,— I at-that-time was-standing.

Sawāl,—Ār uṭhinē keu rah*lā ki nihī̃?
Question,—Other there any-one was or not?

Jawāb,— Ahē-ṭhinē ēhē hājirā āsāmi: (1) Nachhaman Sing:
Answer,— At-that-place these present accused: (1) Lakshman Singh:
(2) Ruhiā Sing: (3) Bānu Sing: (4) Pāṇḍu Sing: ēhē
(2) Ruhiā Singh: (3) Bānu Singh: (4) Pāṇḍu Singh: these
sab rah*lā. Kintu Khushāli Mājhī uṭhinē nihi rah*lā. Hamar
all were. But Khushāli Mājhī there not was. Me
ṭhikalē duī kuṛi das hāt dhūri āsāmi Budhiā Singh-ēk
from two score ten cubits in-distance accused Budhiā Singh's
sarisha bāṛiī̃ rah*lā.
mustard field-in he-was.

Sawāl,—Taī̃ ki ār keu Jēnā Singh-kē mār*lē āki nihi?
Question,—You or other any-one Jēnā Singh beat or not?

Jawāb,—Maī̃ ki ār hājirā āsāmiraī̃ kēha-ī nihī̃ mār*lē-āhēk.
Answer,—I or other present accused-persons any-one-even not have-beaten.

Sawāl,—Ēhē (ka)-chihnē-dēl ṭhēṅga kākar?
Question,—This ka-marked club whose?

Jawāb,— Ēhē (ka) chihnē-dēl ṭhēṅgā Budhu-rām Singh-ēk. Ēhē-ṭhēṅgāi
Answer,—This ka-marked club Budhu-rām Singh's. With-this-club
mār^a^lē-rahēk.
he-had-beaten.

Sawāl,—Ēhē maral muṇḍā ō maṭā chādar ō mālā kākar hekēk?
Question,—This dead head and coarse sheet and garland whose are?

Jawāb,— Ēhē sab Jēnā Singh-ēk hekēk.
Answer,—These all Jēnā Singh's are.

FREE TRANSLATION OF THE FOREGOING.

Question.—Where is now Jēnā Singh of the village of Paṇḍupāl, Parganā Kurāḍihā?

Answer.—He is now dead.

Q.—How did he die?

A.—Budhu-rām Singh, of Āsk anda in Parganā Kurāḍihā, clubbed him to death.

Q.—How many times did he strike him, and in what part of his body?

A.—He gave Jēnā Singh only one blow under the right ear. Immediately on receiving the blow he fell down there and then.

Q.—When he was struck, did you see it with your own eyes?

A.—Yes. I saw it.

Q.—When did this take place, and at what hour?

A.—At one hour of the night. It was then dark. This was on the night of the Sunday before last.

Q.—Why did Budhu-rām kill Jēnā Singh?

A.—Last year, I applied vermilion to the forehead of Jēnā Singh's daughter, as a preliminary to marrying her. Moreover, his son, Manglā Singh, had similarly put vermilion on the head of my sister, Guni. But when afterwards Jēnā Singh refused to give his daughter to me in marriage, there was held a caste-assembly to settle the dispute. After that, Budhu-rām, who is my cousin and the son of my elder uncle, killed Jēnā Singh on the Mitrapur road, when he was giving his daughter to Pitēi.

Q.—Where did he kill Jēnā Singh?

A.—Jēnā Singh was coming from Mitrapur. On the way, after crossing the Burhā-balang river, and after passing along the path which led through Budhu-rām's mustard-field, and entering another field belonging to Budhiā Singh, then it was that Budhu-rām struck him.

Q.—What were you doing at the time?

A.—I was standing there.

Q.—Was anyone else there at the time?

A.—The present accused persons were there, *viz.*, Lakshmaṇ Singh, Ruhiā Singh, Bānu Singh, and Pāṇḍu Singh. But Khushālī Mājhī was not there. He was some fifty cubits away from me, in a mustard-field.

Q.—Did you or anyone else also strike Jēnā Singh?

A.—Neither I nor any of the other accused persons struck him.

Q.—Whose is this club which is marked for identification with the letter 'Ka'?

A.—It belongs to Budhu-rām Singh. It is with it that he struck the blow.

Q.—Whose are this severed head, and this coarse sheet, and this wooden chaplet?

A.—They all belong to Jēnā Singh.

It will be observed that the last District named in the list given on p. 146 is the North-Gangetic one of Malda. Here the dialect is not spoken by Kurmīs, but by other castes of South-Bihar nationality, who have crossed the Ganges and settled in that district. As in the other localities, it is distinctly a form of Magahī, and it is not clear how this form of speech has come to be spoken there. The dialect of Bihārī which is spoken to the north, in Purnea, and, to the west, in Bhagalpur and the Sonthal Parganās, is Maithilī, and the main language of Eastern Malda is a form of Bengali. So also to the south of the District. One explanation, which is ingenious, but which, so far as I know, is unsupported by any admitted facts, is found in a tradition that there was a wave of conquering inhabitants of Gaya and Patna, which occupied the Districts, in order, of Monghyr, Bhagalpur, the Sonthal Parganās, and Malda. In the two first Districts, they became absorbed into the allied Maithilī-speaking race which then occupied the country, and adopted their language. So also in the North-western half of the Sonthal Parganās, where they were separated from the Bengalis, who encroached from the south and east, by the mountains in the centre of that District. In Malda, however, they came into contact with an alien, Bengali-speaking race, with whom they did not mix, and whose language they declined to adopt; although, in process of time, their own tongue gradually adopted some of its more striking forms.

The dialect is locally known as Hindī or as Khoṇṭāi, and is principally spoken by people of the Chain, Nāgar, and other similar castes in West Malda. The language of each caste differs slightly. Indeed all over Malda District, we find a curious mixture of language, different nationalities and tribes in one and the same village each speaking its own language, which may be Santālī, Bihārī, or Bengali. Even each of these three languages varies according to the caste of the speaker. Khoṇṭāi is reported as being spoken by 180,000 people.

Both the following specimens are written in the Bengali character. Hence it must be remembered that we are looking at Magahī through Bengali spectacles. The spelling is therefore eccentric from the point of view of one accustomed to the same language written in the Dēva-nāgarī character.

The only form which need be noticed is the word *hōyᵉchhi*, it is, which is borrowed from the neighbouring Maithilī of Purnea.

The first specimen is the Parable of the Prodigal Son, and the second, a short folk-tale. Both have been most carefully written by Babu Radhesh Chandra Set.

[No. 32.]

INDO-ARYAN FAMILY. EASTERN GROUP.

BIHĀRĪ.

EASTERN MAGAHĪ DIALECT.

KHONṬĀI SUB-DIALECT. (WEST OF DISTRICT MALDA.)

SPECIMEN I.

(Babu Radhesh Chandra Set, 1898.)

এক জনাকে দু বেটা হলই। ছোটা লড়কা আপ্নন্ বাপ্কে কহল্কই, বাবা, হাম্রা হিস্সাকে গিরস্তি হাম্রা দে। তো বাপ্ দোনকে আপন্ গিরস্তি বাঁটি দেলকই। তো থোরা দিন্ বাদ্ ছোটো বেটা আপন্ জেতনা হলই সব হাত করিকে কোই দুর দেস চলি গেলই। তাঁহামে লুচ্চাপানা করিকে সব তহস্নস্ করি দেলকই। তব যব এক্দম্ ওকর হাত খালি হোলই তো ওই দেস্মে বড্ডা আকাল পর্লই। আর উ বড়া মুস্কিল মে গিরলই। তব উ যাকর ওই দেস্কে কোই সহোরিয়াকে মিললই। তো ওই সহোরিয়া বিথান্মে ওকরা আপন্ সুয়র্ চড়াওলা ভেজকই। উঁহা উ সুয়র্ খোয়কী ভুঁসিসে বড়া খুসী হোকে পেট্ ভরতিয়ই। ঔর ওকরা কোই কুচ্ছু নহি দেতিয়ই। যব্ ওকর্ গেয়ান্ ভেলই তো আপনা আপনি বোলে লাগলই, হামর্ বাপ্কে ঘর্কে কেত্তা চাকর পাইট আপনে খাতিয়াই আর্ পর্কে বিলাতিয়াই, আর হাম্মা ভুক্খে মরেহি। হাম্মা উঠিকে বাপ্কে ভিরা যাকে ওকরা বোলো,—বাপ, হাম্মা সরগ ভিরা ও তোরা ভিরা পাপ্ করলিউ। আর্ হাম্মা তোরা বেটা কাহালানে লায়ক নহি হই। হাম্মা আপন রাখনি চাকর্ করি লে। তব্ উ উঠ্ঠিকে আপন্ বাপ্ ভিরা আলই। লকিন উ বহুৎ দূর রহতই, বাপ ওকরা দেখে পায়্কে দৌড়্কে লড়কাকে গলা ধরিকে চুম্মা খাবে লগলই। তব্ লড়কা বাপ্কে কহলকই—বাপ হাম্মা স্বরগ ভিরা ও তোর সামনে পাপ করলিয়ই, আর হাম্মা তোর্ লড়কা কহনে লায়ক নই হাই। লকিন্ বাপ্ আপন চাকর্কে কহলকই, আচ্ছা পোসাক্ আন্ ও একরা পরা দে। চল্ সব্কোই খানাপিনা করি ও আনন্দ করি। কাহে কি হামরা এহি লড়কা মরি গেলা হলই, আর্ ফের বাচলই। এ হেঁরা গেলা হলই, আব পালিয়ই। তব্ সব্ কোই রং তামাসা করনে লগলই ॥

ইধর্ তো বড়া লড়কা খেৎমে হলই। যব ঘর্ আবে লগলই তো ঘর্কে লগিজ্ আতে নাচনা গাওনা সুনে পালকই। তো এক্ চাকর্কে ডাকিকে পুছকই ই সব্ কাহে হোয়ছি। চাকর্ কহলকই তোরা ভাই আলা হই। লড়কা ভালা ভালইসে আলই সোই, আপনা বাপ্ এক্ ভোজ্ দেলকেই। তো বড়া লড়কা বড়া রাগলই ও ঘর্ নাই সানালকই। তো বাপ্ বাহার্ আকর্ ওকরা বড়া ঘিংগটী করনে লগলই। তো বড়া লড়কা বাপ্কে জবাব্ দেলকই—কি তাজ্জব, এতনা বচ্ছর হাম্মা তুমরা ঘরে খটলি ও কভি তুমরা হুকুম্ বাহার্ কাম্ না করলি, ও তব্ভি আপনে হামরা কব্ভি একঠো পাঁঠা ভি নহি দেলন্ যো হাম্মা আপনা সাগা কুটুম্ লেকে আন্দ্ করতিয়ই। আর্ তোর্ এই লড়কা তোর গরহস্তি খানগী কসবীসে তহস্নস করকও, লকিন্ উ আতেহি ওকর্ বাস্তে তু এক্ ভোজ্ দেয়লে। তব্ বাপ্ ওকরা কহলকই বেটা তু বরাবর্ হামরা সাঁত হাঁয়, হাম্মর যো কুছ্ সব্ তোর্হি হউ। ই মোনাসিব হয়্ যো হামরা আন্দ হোঁ ও হাঁসিখুসি করোঁ। যো তোর্ ভাইম্মা যো মর্ গেলা হলও, সো ফের বঁচলও; যো হেঁরা গেলা হলও, ফের্ মিললও ॥

[No. 32.]

INDO-ARYAN FAMILY. EASTERN GROUP.

BIHĀRĪ.

EASTERN MAGAHĪ.

KHOṆṬĀI SUB-DIALECT. (WEST OF DISTRICT MALDA.)

SPECIMEN I.

(Babu Radhesh Chandra Set, 1898.)

Ēk janā-kē du bēṭā halaï. Chhōṭā laṛ^{a}kā āppan bāp-kē
One man-to two sons were. The-younger child his-own father-to

kahal^{a}kaï, 'bābā, hām^{a}rā hissā-ke girasti hām^{a}rā dē.' Tō
said, 'father, my share-of household-property me give.' Then

bāp dōna-kē āpan girasti bā̃ṭi del^{a}kaï. Tō thōrā din
father both-to his-own household-property dividing gave. Then a-few days

bād chhōṭō bēṭā āpan jet^{a}nā halaï, sab hāt kari-ke
after the-younger son his-own what-ever was, all hand-(in) making

kōi dur dēs chali-gelaï. Tā̃hā-mē luchchā-pānā kari-ke sab
some distant country went. There licentiousness making all

tahasnas kari-del^{a}kaï. Tab jab ēk-dam ōkar hāt khāli hōlaï tō
waste he-made-complete. Then when completely his hand empty was then

ōi dēs-mē baḍḍā ākāl par^{a}laï, ār u baṛā muskil-mē gir^{a}laï.
that country-in a-great famine fell, and he great difficulty-in fell.

Tab u jā-kar ōi dēs-ke kōi sahoriyā-kē mil^{a}laï. Tō ōi
Then he going that country-of a-certain townsman-to met. Then that

sahoriyā bithān-mē ok^{a}rā āpan suyar charāolā bhej^{a}kaï. Ũhā u suyar
townsman field-in him his swine to-tend sent. Then he swine's

khōy^{a}kī bhũsi-sē baṛā khusī hō-ke pēṭ bhar^{a}tiyaï; aur
food husk-with very glad being (his-)belly he-would-have-filled; and

ok^{a}rā kōi kuchchhu nahi detiyaï. Jab ōkar geyān bhelaï,
him-to any-one anything not used-to-give. When his senses became,

tō āp^{a}nā-āp^{a}ni bōle lāg^{a}laï, 'hāmar bāp-ke ghar-ke kettā
then himself-to to-say he-begun, 'my father's house-of how-many

chākar-pāïṭ āp^{a}ne khātiyāi ār par-kē bilātiyāi, ār
servants themselves used-to-eat and others-to used-to-distribute, and

hāmmā bhukkhē mare-hi. Hāmmā uṭhi-ke bāp-ke bhirā jā-ke ok^{a}rā
I with-hunger am-dying. I rising father's near going him

bōlō, "bāp, hāmmā sarag bhirā ō tōrā bhirā pāp
will-say, "Father, I heaven near and of-thee near sin

kar^{a}liu. Ār hāmmā tōrā bēṭā kāhālānē lāyak nahi haï.
committed-for-thee. Any-more I thy son of-being-called fit not I-am.
Hāmmā āpan rākh^{a}ni chākar karí-lē.'' Tab u uṭṭhi-ke
Me thy retained servant having-made-keep.'' Then he rising
āpan bāp bhirā ālai. Lakin u bahut dūr rah^{a}taï, bāp
his-own father near came. But he very far remaining-even, the-father
ok^{a}rā dēkhe pāy-ke daur-ke lar^{a}kā-ke galā dhari-ke chummā khābe
him to-see obtaining running the-son's neck seizing kiss to-eat
lag^{a}laï. Tab lar^{a}kā bāp-kē kahal^{a}kaï, 'bāp, hāmmā swarag bhirā
began. Then the-son the-father-to said, 'father, I heaven near
ō tōr sām^{a}nē pāp kar^{a}liyaï, ār hāmmā tōr lar^{a}kā kah^{a}nē
and of-thee before sin committed, any-more I thy son of-calling
lāyak naï hā.' Lakin bāp āpan chākar-kē kahal^{a}kaï, 'āchchhā pōsāk ān
fit not am.' But the-father his-own servants-to said, 'good clothes bring
ō ek^{a}rā parā dē. Chal, sab-kōi khānā-pinā-kari, ō ânand kari.
and this-(person) putting-on give. Come, let-all-(of-us) eat-and-drink, and joy make.
Kāhe-ki hām^{a}rā ehi lar^{a}kā mari gelā-halaï, āb pher bāch^{a}laï; ē hērā gelā-halaï,
Because my this son dying had-gone, now again survived; he lost had-been,
āb pāliyaï.' Tab sab-kōi rang-tāmāsā kar^{a}nē lag^{a}laï.
now I-recovered-him.' Then all merriment to-make began.

Idhar tō barā lar^{a}kā khēt-mē halaï. Jab ghar ābe lag^{a}laï,
On-this-side indeed the-elder son field-in was. When house-(to) to-come he-begun,
tō ghar-ke lagij ātē nāch^{a}nā gāonā sune pāl^{a}kaï. Tō ēk chākar-kē ḍāki-ke
then house-of near coming dancing singing to-hear he-got. Then one servant calling
puchh^{a}kaï, 'i sab kāhe hōy^{a}chhi?' Chākar kahal^{a}kaï, 'tōrā bhāi ālā-haï.
he-asked, 'this all why is-being-(done)?' The-servant said, 'thy brother has-come.
Lar^{a}kā bhālā-bhālaï-sē ālaï, sōi āp^{a}nā bāp ēk bhōj del^{a}kaï.' Tō
His-son well-and-safely returned, therefore Your-Honour's father one feast gave.' Then
barā lar^{a}kā barā rāg^{a}laï, ō ghar nāi sānāl^{a}kaï. Tō bāp bāhār ā-kar
the-elder son very angry-was, and house not entered. Then the-father out coming
ok^{a}rā barā ghing^{a}ṭī kar^{a}nē lag^{a}laï. Tō barā lar^{a}kā bāp-kē jawāb del^{a}kaï,
him much entreaty to-make began. Then the-elder son the-father-to reply gave,
'Ki tājjab! et^{a}nā bachchhar hāmmā tum^{a}rā gharē khaṭ^{a}li, ō kabhi tum^{a}rā
'How wonderful! so-many years I your house-in served, and ever thy
hukum bāhār kām nā kar^{a}li, ō tabbhi āp^{a}ne hām^{a}rā kabbhi ēk-ṭhō pāṭhā bhi
order beyond work not did, and still Your-Honour me ever one kid even
nahi dēlan, jō hāmmā āp^{a}nā sāgā kuṭum lē-ke ānd kar^{a}tiyaï. Ār tōr ēi
not gave, that I my friends relations taking joy might-make. And thy this
lar^{a}kā tōr gar^{a}hasti khān^{a}gi kas^{a}bi-sē tahasnas kar^{a}kao, lakin
son thy household-property harlots strumpets-with waste made-for-thee, but
u ātē-hi ōkar wāstē tu ēk bhōj dey^{a}lē.' Tab bap ok^{a}rā
he immediately-on-arriving his sake-for thou one feast gavest.' Then the-father him

kahalᵃkaī, 'bēṭā, tu barābar hāmᵃrā sā̃t hā̃y, hāmmar jō kuchh sab
said, 'son, thou always my company-in art, my which anything-(is) all
tōr-hi haü. Ī monāsib hay jō hāmᵃrā ānd hō̃ ō hā̃si-khusi karō̃.
thine-only is-to-thee. It proper is that we joyful become and merriment make.
Jō tōr bhāiyā jō mar gelā-halaö, sō pher bā̃chᵃlaö; jō hērā
Because thy brother who dying had-gone-for-thee, he again survived-for-thee; who lost
gelā-halaö, pher milᵃlaö.'
had-been-for-thee, again was-recovered-for-thee.'

[No. 33.]

INDO-ARYAN FAMILY. EASTERN GROUP.

BIHĀRĪ.

EASTERN MAGAHĪ DIALECT.

KHOṆṬĀI SUB-DIALECT. (WEST OF DISTRICT MALDA.)

SPECIMEN II.

(Babu Radhesh Chandra Set, 1898.)

এক বদ্‌রাগী গির্‌হস্ত বড়া মাস্ পিয়ার্ করতিয়ই। এক্ দিন্ পাঁঠাকে মাস্ কিনি আনিকে আপ্পন বহুকে ওই মাস রাঁধনে কহিকে বাহার্ গেলই। বহু ওকর্ বাত মানিকে মাস্ রাঁধিকে ভানসা ঘর্‌মে কোই বাসন্‌মে করিকে ঢাঁপিকে রক্‌খকই। লকিন্ দইবিসে এক কুত্তা ভানসা ঘর্ যাকর্, ওই বাসন্‌কে মাস খা গেলই, থোরা সা রহলই। বহু ওই জানিকে হাকাবাকি কুত্তাকে তো হাঁকা দেলকই। লকিন্ পুরুস্ আকর্ কি কহতই, এই ডরমে কাঁপনে লগলই। আর্ কোই উপায় না দেখ্ কর্ নিটঠুর পুরুস্‌কে হাত সে বঁচনেকে বাস্তে ওকরা কুত্তাকে জুট্‌ঠা মাসহি খাবে দেলকই। পুরুস্ মাস্ কাহে থোরা হোলই যব্ এই বাত পুছকই তো বহু জবাব দেলকই,—বাঁকি মাস্ লড়কা বালা খা গেলই। লড়কা বালা খা গেলই শুনিকে গির্‌হস্ত্ আর্ ভালা বুরা কুছ্ নহি কহলকই॥

লকিন্ ওই ঘর্‌মে এক্ চালাক্ বেটী লড়কা হালাই। উ স্বরুসে সব্ বাত্ জানতিয়াই। মা বাপ্‌কে বোলি চালি সুনিকে উ মনে মনেই সোচতে লগলাই আর্ কি করিয়াই। কুত্তা মাস্ খা লেলকই ই বাত্ কহনা মুস্‌কিল, না কহলা ভি বেমোনাসিব। বোললেসে মা মার্ খাতয়াই, না কহলে সে বাপ্ জুট্‌ঠা খাতয়ই॥

[No. 33.]

INDO-ARYAN FAMILY. EASTERN GROUP.

BIHĀRĪ.

EASTERN MAGAHĪ DIALECT.

KHOṆṬĀI SUB-DIALECT. (WEST OF DISTRICT MALDA.)

SPECIMEN II.

(Babu Radhesh Chandra Set, 1898.)

Ēk bad-rāgi gir^{a}hast baṛā mās piyār-kar^{a}tiyaï. Ēk din pā̃ṭhā-ke
One violent-tempered householder much meat liked. One day kid's

mās kini āni-ke āppan bahu-kē ōi mās rā̃dh^{a}nē kahi-ke bābār gelaï. Bahu
meat buying bringing his-own wife-to that meat to-cook saying out he-went. Wife

ōkar bāt māni-ke, mās rā̃dhi-ke bhānsā-ghar-mē kōi bāsan-mē kari-ke ḍhā̃pi-ke
his word respecting, meat cooking cook-room-in some dish-in placing covering

rakkh^{a}kai. Lakin daïbi-sē ēk kuttā bhānsā-ghar jā-kar, ōi bāsan-ke mās
put. But fate-by one dog cook-room entering, that dish-of meat

khā-gelaï, thōrā sā rah^{a}laï. Bahu ōi jāni-ke hākābāki kuttā-kē tō hā̃kā-
ate-up, little only remained. The-wife that perceiving quickly the-dog then drove-

del^{a}kaï. Lakin purus ā-kar ki kah^{a}taï, ēi ḍar-mē kā̃p^{a}nē lag^{a}laï.
away. But husband having-come what shall-she-say, this fear-at to-tremble she-begun.

Ār kōi upāy nā dēkh-kar niṭṭhur purus-ke hāt-sē bā̃ch^{a}nē-ke wāstē, ok^{a}rā
Other any means not having-found cruel husband's hand-from to-be-saved for, him

kuttā-ke juṭṭhā mās-hi khābē del^{a}kaï. Purus mās kāhe thōrā holaï
the-dog's leavings meat-actually to-eat she-gave. The-husband meat why short became

jab ēi bāt puchh^{a}kai, tō bahu jawāb del^{a}kai, 'bā̃ki mās laṛ^{a}kā-bālā
when this word asked, then the-wife reply gave, 'the-remaining meat the-children

khā-gelaï.' Laṛ^{a}kā-bālā khā-gelaï suni-ke gir^{a}hast ār bhālā burā kuchh nahi
ate-up.' Children ate-up hearing householder any-more good bad anything not

kahal^{a}kaï.
said.

Lakin ōi ghar-mē ēk chālāk bēṭī-laṛ^{a}kā hālāi. U suru-sē sab
But that house-in one intelligent girl-child was. She the-beginning-from all

bāt jān^{a}tiyāi. Mā-bāp-ke bōli-chāli suni-ke, u manē manē-i
words knew. The-mother-(and)-father's talk hearing, she mind-in mind-in

sōch^{a}tē lag^{a}lāi, 'āb ki kariyāi? Kuttā mās khā-lel^{a}kaï. I bāt kah^{a}nā
to-think begun, 'now what shall-I-do? Dog meat ate-up. This word to-tell

muskil; nā kah^{a}lā-bhi bē-monāsib. Bol^{a}lē-sē mā mār khāt^{a}yāi,
(is)-difficult; not to-tell-also is-improper. From-telling (my)-mother beating will-eat,

na kah^{a}lē-sē bāp juṭṭhā khāt^{a}yaï.'
not from-telling (my)-father leavings will-eat.'

STANDARD BHOJPURĪ.

Standard Bhojpurī centres round the town of Bhojpur, which is situated on the bank of the Ganges in the North-West of the Shahabad District. From this it extends to the east and south over the whole of that district, and is bounded in the first of these directions by the river Sone, which, however, it crosses at the south, reaching for a few miles into the District of Palamau. To the west, it crosses the frontier between the Lower Provinces and those of the north-west, and covers the whole of the south Gangetic portion of Ghazipur.

Standard Bhojpurī is also spoken north of the Ganges in the districts which border on the Ganges and are opposite Shahabad, *viz.*, Saran, Ballia, and Ghazipur. It is spoken over the whole of Ballia, over the south and the eastern half of Ghazipur (it should be remembered that this district lies on both sides of the Ganges), Western Bhojpurī similar to that spoken in Benares District being spoken in Western Ghazipur. In Saran, it is confined to the more southern parganas. As we go north, the language gradually changes to what may be called Northern Bhojpurī, which is spoken in various forms over Northern and Central Saran, and in the eastern parts of Gorakhpur. No figures are available to show the number of people in Saran, who speak each form of the dialect, nor would it be easy to do so under any circumstances, for the two forms of speech differ so slightly, and merge so gradually into each other, that there is a large area which might very properly be claimed by both. We shall not, however, be far wrong, if, subject to certain explanations to be made later on, we say that, of the 2,404,500[1] people returned from that district as speaking Bhojpurī, about a million speak the Standard form of the dialect. We may, therefore, put down the number of speakers of standard Bhojpurī as follows :—

Name of District.	Number of people speaking Standard Bhojpurī.
Shahabad	1,901,353
Palamau	50,000
Saran	1,000,000
Ballia	903,940
Ghazipur (half)	469,000
TOTAL	4,324,293

The Town and Pargana of Bhojpur, from which the Bhojpurī dialect takes its name, are situated in the Shahabad District, hence the form of the dialect which is current in that district may be considered to be the purest. The two following specimens come from Shahabad, and the language is that illustrated in the preceding grammatical sketch. Besides Bhojpurī, the local authorities reported a separate sub-dialect spoken by 171 Kharwārs, a wild tribe inhabiting the south of the district. An examination, however, of the specimen sent of the Kharwār language shows that it is the same as the ordinary Bhojpurī of the District. It is not sufficiently corrupt to entitle it to be classed as a broken dialect. The total Bhojpurī-speaking population of Shahabad is therefore 1,901,182+171 or 1,901,353.

The first specimen is a translation of the Parable of the Prodigal Son. It is printed in the Dēva-nāgarī character, in which character the specimens, as received, were written. It has the advantage of distinguishing between short and long *e* and *o*.

[1] Revised figures.

[No. 34.]

INDO-ARYAN FAMILY. EASTERN GROUP.

BIHĀRĪ.

SPECIMEN I.

BHOJPURĪ DIALECT. (DISTRICT SHAHABAD.)

एक अदमी का दू बेटा रहे। छोटका अपना बाप से कहलस की ए बाबू-जो धन में जे हमार हिस्सा होखे से बाँट दीँ। तब ऊ दूनो के बाँट देलस। थोड़-ही दिन में छोटका बेटा सभ धन बटोर के दूर देस चल गइल। उहाँ सभ धन कुचाल में उड़ा देलस। जब सभ खरच कं देलस तब ओह देस में बड़ा अकाल पड़ल। ओकरा बड़ा दुख होखे लागल। तब ऊ ओह देस का एक अदमी इहाँ आ के रहे लागल जे ओकरा के अपना खेत में सूअर चरावे खातिर भेज देलस। आउर ऊ आनन्द से ओही भूसी से आपन पेट भरित जे सूअर खात रहस। आउर ओकरा के केहु कुछ देत ना रहे। आउर जब ओकरा अपना बिचार मे आइल त सूझल की कतना हमरा बाप का नोकर चाकर का रोटी खेला से बाँच जाला आ हम भूखे मूअत बानीँ। हम उठब अपना बाप किहाँ जाइब आ कहब की ए बाबू-जी हम परमेसर का सोझा पाप कइलीँ आ रौरो सोझा। हम एइ जोग नेखीँ जे राउर बेटा कहाईँ। हमरा के अपना नोकरन में राखीँ। ऊ उठल अपना बाप किहाँ आइल। बाकी अबहीँ थोड़े दूर रस्ता में अवते रहे की ओकर बाप देखलस। त छोहा के दौरल ओकरा के गला में लगा के चूमा लेवे लागल। लड़िका अपना बाप से कहलस की बाबू-जी हम इसवर का सनमुख पाप कइलीँ आउर रौरो सोझा आउर अब फेर राउर बेटा कहावे जोग नेखीँ। ओकर बाप अपना नोकरन से कहलस नीमन लूगा ले आवं इनका के पेन्हावं आ एक अँगुठी हाथ में आउर पनहो गोड़ में पेन्हावं हमनीका साथे खात जाईँ आनन्द करीँ। काहे की हमार बेटा मू गइल रहे आ फेर जीअल भूलाइल रहे आ मिल गइल। आउर उन्हनीका आनन्द करे-लगले सं॥

ओकर बड़का भाई खेत में रहे। जैसे घर का नगीच आइल नाच राग सुनलस। एगो नोकर के बोला के पुछलस कि ई का होत बा। जबाब देलस की राउर भाई अइले हा। राउर बाप उनका के भोज देत बाड़े काहे की जोअत जागत आँगी देहो नीके पहुँचले हा। ई सुन के खिसिआ गइल। भीतर ना गइल। ओकर बाप बाहर आइल आ मिनती करे लागल। त जबाब में अपना बाप से कहलस की हाए अतना दिन राउर सेवा कैलीँ ना रौरा बात के उलघने कैलीँ। तेहू पर रौआँ एगो पठरूओ ना देलीँ जे अपना हितन का साथे आनन्द मनैतीँ। बाको जसहीँ ई लड़िका राउर आइल जे सभ धन राउर पतुरिआ में उड़ा देलस रौरा ओकरा के भोज देलीँ। तेह पर ओकरा के जबाब देलस की बेटा, तूँ सदई हमरा साथ बाड़ आउर जे कुछ हमरा पास बा से तोहरे हं। उचित हं की हमनीका आनन्द करीँ आ खुस होईं एइ खातिर की तोहार भाई मर गइल रहे आउर फेर जी गइल भुला गइल रहे आ फेर मिल गइल॥

[No. 34.]

INDO-ARYAN FAMILY. EASTERN GROUP.

BIHĀRĪ

BHOJPURĪ DIALECT. (DISTRICT SHAHABAD.).

TRANSLITERATION AND TRANSLATION.

Ēk ad^{a}mī-kā[1] dū bēṭā rahē. Chhoṭ^{a}kā ap^{a}nā bāp-sē kah^{a}las kī, 'ē
One man-of two sons were. The-younger his-own father-to said that, 'O

bābū-jī, dhan-mẽ jē hamār hissā hōkhē sē bā̃ṭ-dī̃.' Tab ū dūnō-
father, property-in which my share may-be that dividing-give.' Then he both-

kē bā̃ṭ-dēlas. Thōṛ-hī din-mẽ chhoṭ^{a}kā bēṭā sabh dhan baṭōr-ke
to dividing-gave. A-few-even days-in the-younger son all property collecting

dūr dēs chal-gaïl. Uhā̃ sabh dhan kuchāl-mẽ uṛā-dēlas. Jab
distant country-to went-away. There all fortune evil-conduct-in he-wasted-away. When

sabh khar^{a}ch-kâ-dēlas, tab oh dēs-mẽ baṛā akāl paṛal. Ok^{a}rā baṛā dukh
all he-had-spent, then that country-in great famine fell. To-him great trouble

hōkhe lāgal. Tab ū oh dēs-kā ēk ad^{a}mī ihā̃ jā-ke rahe lāgal, jē
to-be began. Then he that country-of one man near going to-live began, who

ok^{a}rā-kē ap^{a}nā khēt-mẽ sūar charāwe khātir bhēj-dēlas, āur ū ānand-sē
him his-own field-in swine feeding for sent-away, and he pleasure-with

ōhī bhūsī-sē āpan pēṭ bharit jē sūar khāt-rahas,
those-very husks-with his-own belly would-have-filled which the-swine used-to-eat,

āur ok^{a}rā-kē kēhu kuchh dēt-nā-rahē. Āur jab ok^{a}rā ap^{a}nā
and him-to any-body any-thing giving-not-was. And when to-him his-own

bichār-mē āil ta sūjhal kī, 'kat^{a}nā ham^{a}rā bāp-kā nōkar
consideration-in it-came then he-considered that, 'how-much my father-of servants

chākar-kā rōṭī-khailā-sē bā̃ch-jā-lā, ā ham bhūkhē mūat-banī̃. Ham uṭhab
servants-of bread-eating-after remains, and I hunger-from dying-am. I will-arise

ap^{a}nā bāp kihā̃ jāib ā kahab kī, "ē bābū-jī, ham Par^{a}mēsar-kā
my-own father near will-go and will-say that, "O father; I God-of

sōjhā pāp kaïlī̃ ā raur-ō sōjhā. Ham eh jōg naikhī̃
before sin did and of-Your-Honour-too before. I of-this worth not-am

jē rāur bēṭā kahāī̃, ham^{a}rā-kē ap^{a}nā nok^{a}ran-mẽ
that Your-Honour's son I-may-be-called, me thy-own servants-among

rākhī̃."' Ū uṭhal ap^{a}nā bāp kihā̃ āil; bākī ab^{a}hī̃ thōṛē-dūr
keep."' He arose his-own father near came; but yet a-little-distance-off

rastā-mẽ aw^{a}te-rahē kī ōkar bāp dekh^{a}las. Ta chhohā-ke
way-in (he)-coming-was that his father saw-(him). Then being-compassionate

---

[1] Here the signs of the genitive is in the oblique form because *bēṭā* is in the plural.

daural, ok'rā-kē galā-mē̃ lagā-kē chūmā lēwe lagal. Larikā ap'nā
he-ran, him neck-in enfolding kisses to-take began. The-son his-own
bāp-sē kah'las ki, 'bābū-jī, ham Is'war-kā san'mukh pāp kaïlī̃ āur
father-to said that, 'father, I God-of before sin did and
raur-ō sōjhā, āur ab pher rāur bēṭā kahāwe jōg
Your-Honour-too before, and now again Your-Honour's son to-be-called fit
naikhī̃.' Ōkar bāp ap'nā nok'ran-sē kah'las, 'nīman lūgā lē-āwā,
I-am-not.' His father his-own servants-to said, 'good clothes bring-out,
in'kā-kē penhāwā, ā ēk ā̃guṭhī hāth-mē̃ āur pan'hī gōṛ-mē̃ penhāwā;
him put-on, and one ring hand-on and shoes feet-on put;
ham'nī-kā sāthē khāt-jāī̃, ānand karī̃, kāhe-kī hamār bēṭā
(let-)us together eat, merry make, because-that my son
mū-gaïl-rahē ā pher jīal; bhulāil-rahē, ā mil-gaïl.' Aur
had-been-dead and again alive-became; had-been lost, and found-is.' And
unh'ni-kā ānand karē lag'lē-sā.
they merry to-make began.

Ōkar baṛ'kā bhāī khēt-mē̃ rahē. Jaisē ghar-kā nagich āil nāch
His elder brother field-in was. As house-of near he-came dancing
rāg sun'las. Ēgō nōkar-kē bolā-ke puchh'las ki, 'ī kā hōt-bā?'
music he-heard. One servant calling he-asked that, 'this what is-being?'
Jabāb dēlas ki, 'rāur bhāī āilē-bā. Rāur bāp un'kā-
Answer he-gave that, 'Your-Honour's brother is-come. Your-Honour's father him-
kē bhōj dēt-bāṛē kāhe-kī jīat jāgat ā̃gē-dēhī
to feast is-giving because-that alive (and)-awake in-good-health
nīkē pahũch'lē-hā.' Ī sun-ke khisiā-gaïl, bhītar nā gaïl.
safely he-has-arrived.' This hearing he-angry-became, inside not went.
Ōkar bāp bāhar āil ā min'tī kare-lāgal. Ta jabāb-mē̃
His father outside came and to-entreat-(him) began. Then answer-in
ap'nā bāp-sē kah'las ki, 'hāe, at'nā din rāur sēwā
his-own father-to he-said that, 'alas, so-many days Your-Honour's service
kailī̃; nā raurā bāt-ke ulagh'nē kailī̃, tēhū par
I-did; not Your-Honour's words transgression-even I-did, that-too on
rauā̃ ēgō paṭh'ru-ō nā dēlī̃ jē ap'nā hitan-kā sāthē
Your-Honour one kid-even not gave that my-own friends-of with
ānand-manaitī̃. Bākī jas'hī̃ ī laṛikā rāur āil jē
I-might-have-rejoiced. But when-even this son of-Your-Honour came who
sabh dhan rāur paturiā-mē̃ uṛā-dēlas raurā ok'rā-kē
all fortune thy harlot-among squandered Your-Honour him-to
bhōj dēlī̃.' Teh-par ok'rā-kē jabāb dēlas ki, 'bēṭā, tū̃ sadaī
feast gave.' There-upon him-to answer he-gave that, 'son, thou always
ham'rā-sāth bāṛā, āur jē kuchh ham'rā pās bā sē tohar-ē hā.
me-with art, and what even me with is that thine-even is.

Uchit hâ kī ham'nīkā ānand karī̃ ā khus hōī̃, eh khātir ki
Proper is that we merry make and pleased be, this for that
tohār bhāī mar-gaïl-rahē, āur pher jī-gaïl; bhulā-gaïl-rahē, ā
thy brother had-died, and again alive-became; had-been-lost, and
pher mil-gaïl.'
again found-is.'

[No. 35.]

INDO-ARYAN FAMILY. EASTERN GROUP.

BIHĀRĪ.

SPECIMEN II.

BHOJPURĪ DIALECT. (DISTRICT SHAHABAD.)

DEPOSITION OF A WITNESS.

इजहार अजोध्या राय सा: नवादा बेन प्र: आरे।

हम नवादा में मालिक हईं। मुदई मुदालेह के चिन्हीं-ले। साबिक में मकान हमरे पट्टी में रहल हा। बटवारा भइला पर हमरे पट्टी में बा॥

(सवाल)। उस मकान से मुदई को कुछ सरोकार है॥

(जवाब) कुछुओ ना। मुतरफा अगाड़ी ढोढ़ा के पावत रलीं हाँ। अब मुदई के पाईं-ले। ढोढ़ा दू भाई रहे। एक के नाम ढोढ़ा दोसरा के दसई। अन्दू अगाड़ियो से नोकरी चाकरी करे जात रहे हा। अबहूँ जा ले। बरिस दिन से बहरे रहे हा। घर में दसई बहु के छोड़ गइल रहे हा। अठारह सोनइस दिन भइल मकान पर गइल रहे हा। मुदई गोबरी राय आ हम गोबरधन राय की हाँ गइलीं। कहलीं की एकर मकान ई छोड दीं। मुदालेह कहलस की ना छोड़ब। ओह मकान में मुदालेह के गोरू बँधा-ला। हमनीका कहला पर कहलस की जा जे मन में आवे, से करीं। हम ना छोड़ब॥

INDO-ARYAN FAMILY. EASTERN GROUP.

BIHĀRĪ.

BHOJPURĪ DIALECT. (DISTRICT SHAHABAD.)

SPECIMEN II.

TRANSLITERATION AND TRANSLATION.

Ij'hār Ajōdhyā Rāy sā(kin) Nawādā Bēn Pra(ganā)
Deposition(-of) Ajodhyā Rāy resident-of Nawādā Bēn Parganā
Ārē.
Arrah.

Ham Nawādā-mē̃ mālik haī̃. Mudaī mudāleh-kē chinhī-lē.
I Nawādā-in owner am. The-petitioner accused I-know.
Sābik-mē̃ makān ham'r-ē paṭṭi-mē̃ rahal-hā. Baṭ'wārā bhailā-par
Formerly house my-indeed share-in was. Partition occurring-on
ham'rē paṭṭi-mē̃ bā.
my-even share-in it-is.

(Swāl[1]).— Us makān-sē mudaī-kō kuchh sarōkār hai?
(Question).— That house-with the-petitioner-to any connection is?

(Jawāb).— Kuchhu-ō nā. Mutar'phā agāṛi Ḍhōṛhā-sē
(Answer).— Any-even not. Ground-rent formerly Ḍhōṛhā-from
pāwat rahī̃-hā̃. Ab mudaī-sē pāī-lē. Ḍhōṛhā dū
getting I-was. Now the-petitioner-from I-get. Ḍhoṛhā two
bhāī rahē, ēk-ke nām Ḍhōṛhā, dos'rā-ke Dasaī. Bhandū
brothers were, one-of name Ḍhōṛhā, the-other-of Dasaī. Bhandū
agāṛiy-ō-sē nok'rī-chāk'rī kare jāt ralē-hā. Ab'hū̃ jā-lē.
before-too-from service to-do going had-been. Now-too he-goes.
Baris din-sē bah'rē ralē-hā. Ghar-mē̃ Dasaī-bahu-kē
A-year days-from out he-has-been. House-in Dasaī's-wife
chhōṛ-gail-ralē-hā. Aṭhārah onaïs din bhaïl makān-par gaïl-ralē-hā.
he-had-left. Eighteen nineteen days ago house-to he-had-gone.
Mudaī Gob'rī Rāy ā ham Gōbardhan Rāy kihā̃
The-petitioner Gobrī Rāy and I Gōbardhan Rāy near
gaïlī̃; kah'lī̃ ki, 'ēkar makān hâ, chhōṛ-dī̃.' Mudāleh
went; we-said that, 'this-one's house is, give-up.' The-accused

---

[1] The questions put by the Court are in the Court-language,—Hindōstānī.

kah^{a}las	kī,	'nā	chhōṛab.'	Oh	makān-mẽ	mudāleh-ke
said	*that,*	*'not*	*I-will-give-up.'*	*That*	*house-in*	*accused's*

gōrū	bā̃dhā-lā.	Ham^{a}nī-kā	kah^{a}lā-par	kah^{a}las	kī,	'jā,	jē
cattle	*is-tethered.*	*Our*	*saying-on*	*he-said*	*that,*	*'go,*	*which*

man-mẽ	āwē	sē	karibâ;	ham	nā	chhōṛab.'
mind-in	*comes*	*that*	*you-may-do;*	*I*	*not*	*will-give-up.'*

FREE TRANSLATION OF THE FOREGOING.

Deposition of Ajōdhyā Rāy, of Nawādā Bēn, Pargana Ārē.

I am an owner of Nawādā, and am acquainted with both the Complainant and with the Accused Person. Formerly the house (in dispute) was in my share of the village, and, when subsequently, there was a formal partition of the property, it also fell in my share.

Question.—Has the Complainant anything to do with that house?

Answer.—Nothing whatever. I used formerly to get the ground-rent for it from Ḍhōṛhā Singh. Now I get it from the Complainant. Ḍhōṛhā had a brother named Dasaī. Bhandū used for long to be absent from home on service. He still does this, and, this time, had been away for a year. He had left Dasaī's wife in his home. Eighteen or nineteen days ago he went to the house. The Complainant, Gobrī Rāy, and I went to Gōbardhan Rāy, and we said to him that the house was Bhandū's, and that he (Gōbardhan) should give it up. The accused said he would do no such thing. His cattle are still tethered there. When we spoke to him, he said we might do whatever came into our heads, but he would not give up the house.

It may be stated as a broad fact that, south of the Ganges, Standard Bhojpurī is bounded on the east and south by the left bank of the River Sone. Similarly the District of Shahabad is bounded on the east and south by the same river. On the south, however, the language has crossed the Sone and occupies a small strip of ground about eight miles wide on its right bank in the district of Palamau where it is spoken by about 50,000 people. Beyond this it becomes the impure Nagpuriā Bhojpurī which extends across the Ranchi Plateau of Chota Nagpur.

Although the language spoken in this small strip is standard Bhojpurī, it has a few divergencies from the examples which have just been dealt with. For this reason I give the two following specimens of the language of this tract. The first is a version of the Parable of the Prodigal Son, and the second is a villager's account of his adventures in the jungle. The principal divergencies from Standard Bhojpurī are the following.

In the pronouns, the direct form of the Genitive is sometimes used instead of the oblique. Thus, we have *ham āpan* (instead of *ap^{a}nā*) *bābū-jī kihā̃ jāī̃*, I will go to my father. Instead of *kichhu*, we have *kichh*, anything. For 'he,' we have *uhā̃-kā*, with a plural *unhi*.

In verbs, we may note the use of the Simple Present in the sense of the Future, thus, *jāī̃*, I will go, and *kahī̃*, I will say, instead of *jāib*, *kahab*. The verb *hāwī̃*, I am, becomes *haüwī*. So also *haüwā*, you are, and *haüwē*, it is. These, however, are hardly more than differences of spelling.

The most noteworthy peculiarities occur in the conjugation of the past tense. In Standard Bhojpuri, as in all other dialects and languages of the Eastern Indo-Aryan Group, the characteristic letter of this tense is *l*. Thus, Bengali *dēkhilām*, Maithili *dekhᵃlāhᵃ*, Bhojpuri *dekhᵃlī*, all meaning 'I saw'. In Palamau, however, instead of *l* the characteristic letter is frequently *u*. Examples are *kaüī*, I committed; *pahũchuī*, I arrived; *bujhuī*, I understood; *takuī*, I looked; *dekhuī*, I saw; *rahuē*, he was, they were; *bhaüē*, it became; *gaüē*, he went. The following are third persons plural, mostly in the sense of the singular; *dihuan*, they gave; *laguan*, they began; *uṭhuan*, they rose; *rahuan*, they were; *dekhuan*, they saw; *kahuan*, they said; *puchhuan*, they asked; *chahuan*, they wished. It will subsequently be seen that this form of the past is also used in Saran.

It should be observed that the past with *l* is also freely used. Thus, *dihᵃlī*, he, honorific, gave, and so on. In the following examples, the plural is used, in most cases, instead of the singular, *chahᵃlani*, they wished; *kahᵃlani*, they said; *chalᵃlani*, they went; *kaïlani*, they did; *lagᵃlani*, they began; *gaïlani*, they went; *aïlani*, they came.

[No. 36.]

INDO-ARYAN FAMILY. EASTERN GROUP.

BIHĀRĪ.

BHOJPURĪ DIALECT. (DISTRICT PALAMAU.)

SPECIMEN I.

कउनो अदिमी के दुइठे लरिका रहुए। उन्हि में से छोटका बाबू-जी से कहलसि की ए बाबू-जी धन में से जे किछ हमार बखरा होई से हमरा के बाँट दीं। तब उन्हाँका आपन धन बाँट दिहलीं। बहुत दिन ना बीतल की छोटका आपन कुल धन ले के परदेस में चल गउए और उहाँ लुचई में आपन धन उड़ा दिहलसि। जब उन्हि आपन कुल धन ओड़ा दिहुअन तब ऊ देसे बड़ा सुखार परलि और उन्हि गरीब भ गउए। तब उन्हि जा के ऊ देस के एक अदिमी कीहाँ रहे लगुअन। ऊ अदिमी उनका के अपना खेते सूअर चरावे के भेजलसि और जे बोकला सूअर खात रहुए ओही से ऊ आपन पेट भरे चहलनि। केहु उनका के किछ ना देत रहुए। जब उनका अकिल भउए तब कहलनि की हमरा बाबू-जी का कतना नोकर के खइला से रोटी बाँचत-होई और हम भूखे मरतानी। हम उठ के आपन बाबू-जी कीहाँ जाइँ और उन्ह से कहीँ की हे बाबू-जी हम सरग के उलटे और रावाँ निअरे पाप कउइँ एह से अब राउर लरिका कहावे जुकुर नइखीं। मो के अपना नोकरनि में से एकठे के बरोबर करीं। उन्हि उठुअन और अपना बाबू-जी का पास चललनि। मगर जब ऊ फरके रहुअन तबे उन्ह कर बाबू-जी उनका देखुअन और माया कइलनि और दौर के गला में लगाइ के चुमे लगलनि। लरिका उनका से कहलसि की ए बाबू-जी सरग के उलटे और रावाँ निअरे पाप कइ चुकलीं और अब राउर लरिका कहावे जुकुर नइखीं। मगर उन कर बाबू-जी आपन नोकर में से एक-ठे से कहुअन की सब से बढ़ियाँ लूगा ले आवं इनका के पहिरावं। और हाथ में अँगूठी और गोड़ में जूता पहिरावं। सभे खाईं और आनन करीँ काहे की हमार ई लरिका मर गइल रहुअन अब जी गइलनि। और भुला गइल रहुए फिन मिल गइल। तब चैन करे लगुअन॥

उ-बेला उन्ह कर बड़ भाई खेते रहुअन। और जब ऊ घर के पँजरा अइलनि तब बाजा और नाच के होरा सुनलनि। और आपन नोकरन में से एक के बलाइ के पुछुअन की ई का हं। तब नोकर उन्ह से कहलसि की राउर भाई अइले हा और राउर बाबू-जी नीक भोजन खिअउले हा। काहे की राउर बाबू-जो उन्हका के कुसल अनन से पउले हा। मगर ऊ खोस कइले और घर में जाय ना चहुअन। एही से उन कर बाबू-जी बाहर अउअन और उनका के मनावे लगुअन। तब ऊ बाबू-जी के जवाब दिहले की रावाँ देखीं हम रावाँ के ढेर दिन से टहल करतानी और राउर हुकुम कबहीं ना टरलीं हाँ। रावाँ हमरा-के कबहीं एगुड़ो पठरू भी ना दिहलीं की अपना इआर लोग के संगे चैन करीं। मगर ई राउर बेटा जे कसबी के संगे कुल धन ओरा दिहले जबे घरे अइले तबे रावाँ उनका खातिर नीक भोजन खिअउली हाँ। बाबू-जी कहुअन की ए बेटा तूँ तो सब दिन हमरा संगे रहत हउअं और जे किछ हमार हउए से सभ तोहरे हउए। मगर अबहीं अनन करे के और खुसी होखे के चाहत रहत हा काहे की तोहार ई भाई मर गइल रहल हा फिन जिअल हा। और भुला गइल रहल हा से मिलल हा॥

[No. 36.]

INDO-ARYAN FAMILY. EASTERN GROUP.

BIHĀRĪ.

BHOJPURĪ DIALECT. (DISTRICT PALAMAU.)

SPECIMEN I.

TRANSLITERATION AND TRANSLATION.

Kaūnō adimī-ke dui-ṭbē larikā rahuē. Unhi-mẽ-sē chhoṭ^{a}kā
A-certain man-of two sons were. Them-in-from the-younger
bābū-jī-sē kah^{a}lasi kī, 'ē bābū-jī, dhan-mẽ-sē jē-kichh hamār
father-to said that, 'O father, property-in-from what-ever my
bakh^{a}rā hōī sē ham^{a}rā-kē bā̃ṭ-dī̃.' Tab uhā̃-kā āpan
share will-be that me-to dividing-give.' Then he his-own
dhan bā̃ṭ-dih^{a}lī̃. Bahut din nā bītal kī chhoṭ^{a}kā
property dividing-gave-(them). Many days not passed that the-younger
āpan kul dhan lē-ke par^{a}dēs-mẽ chal gaüē, ăūr uhā̃
his-own all property taking foreign-country-into went away, and there
luchai-mẽ āpan dhan uṛā-dih^{a}lasi. Jab unhi āpan kul dhan
evil-deeds-in his-own fortune squandered. When he his-own all fortune
oṛā-dihuan, tab ū dēsē baṛā sukhār parali ăūr unhi
had-squandered-away; then that country-in great dryness fell and he
garīb bha-gaüē. Tab unhi jā-ke ū dēs-ke ēk adimī kīhā̃ rahe
poor became. Then he going that country-of one man near to-live
laguan. Ū adimī un^{a}kā-kē ap^{a}nā khēte sūar charāwe-kē bhej^{a}lasi,
began. That man him his-own in-fields swine to-feed sent,
ăūr jē bok^{a}lā sūar khāt-rahuē, ōhī-sē ū āpan pēṭ bhare
and what husks swine used-to-eat, those-even-with he his-own belly to-fill
chah^{a}lani. Kēhu un^{a}kā-kē kichh nā dēt-rahuē. Jab un-kā
wished. Anybody him-to anything not used-to-give. When him-to
akil bhaüē tab kah^{a}lani kī, 'ham^{a}rā bābū-jī-kā kat^{a}nā nōkar-ke
wisdom became then he-said that, 'my father-of how-many servants-of
khaïlā-sē rōṭī bā̃chat-hōī, ăūr ham bhūkhē mar^{a}tānī. Ham
eating-after bread might-be-saved, and I hunger-from am-dying. I
uṭh-ke āpan bābū-jī kīhā̃ jāī̃, ăūr unh-sē kahī̃ kī, "hē
arising my-own father of-near will-go, and him-to I-will-say that, "O
bābū-jī, ham Sar^{a}g-ke ul^{a}ṭē ăūr rāwā̃ niarē pāp kaūī̃;
father, I Heaven-of opposite and of-Your-Honour near sin have-done;

eh-sē ab rāur larikā kahāwe jukur naïkhī̃. Mō-kē
this-for now Your-Honour's son to-be-called fit I-not-am. Me

ap^{a}nā nok^{a}rani-mẽ-sē ēk-ṭhē ke barōbar karī̃."' Unhi uṭhuan ăūr
thine-own servants-in-from one of-(to) equal make."' He arose and

ap^{a}nā bābū-jī-kā pās chal^{a}lani. Magar jab ū phar^{a}kē rahuan tabē
his-own father-of near started. But when he far-off was then-even

unh-kar bābū-jī un-kā dekhuan ăūr māyā kaïlani, ăūr daur-ke galā-mẽ
his father him saw and pity did, and running neck-in

lagāi-ke chume lag^{a}lani. Larikā un^{a}kā-sē kah^{a}lasi kī, 'ē bābū-jī,
applying to-kiss began. The-son him-to said that, 'O father,

Sar^{a}g-ke ul^{a}ṭē ăūr rāwā̃ niarē pāp kaï-chuk^{a}lī̃, ăūr ab
Heaven-of opposite and of-Your-Honour near sin I-have-done, and now

rāur larikā kahāwe jukur naïkhī̃.' Magar un-kar bābū-jī
Your-Honour's son to-be-called fit I-not-am.' But his father

āpan nōkar-mẽ-sē ēk-ṭhē-sē kahuan kī, 'sab-sē baṛhiā̃ lūgā
his-own servants-in-from one-to said that, 'all-than good clothes

lē-āwâ, in^{a}kā-kē pahirāwâ, ăūr hāth-mẽ ãgūṭhī ăūr gōṛ-mẽ jūtā
bring, him-on put, and hand-in ring and feet-in shoes

pahirāwâ. Sabhē khāī̃, ăūr ānan karī̃; kāhe-kī hamār ī
put. (Let-us)-all eat, and rejoicing make; because my this

larikā mar gaïl-rahuan, ab jī gaïlani, ăūr bhulā gaïl-rahuē, phin mil-
son dead had-been, now alive became, and lost had-been, again found-

gaïl.' Tab chain kare laguan.
became.' Then merriment to-do they-began.

Ū-bēlā unh-kar baṛ bhāī khētē rahuan. Ăūr jab ū
That-time his elder brother in-field was. And when he

ghar-ke pāj^{a}rā aïlani tab bājā ăūr nāch-ke haurā sun^{a}lani, ăūr
house-of near came then music and dancing-of noise he-heard, and

āpan nokaran-mẽ-sē ēk-kē balāi-ke puchhuan kī, 'ī kā
his-own servants-in-from one-to calling asked that, 'this what

hâ?' Tab nōkar unh-sē kah^{a}lasi kī, 'rāur bhāī aïlē
is?' Then servant him-to said that, 'Your-Honour's brother come

hā, ăūr rāur bābū-jī nīk bhōjan khiaūlē-hā
is, and Your-Honour's father a-good dinner has-caused-to-eat

kāhe-kī rāur bābū-jī unh^{a}kā-kē kusal-anan-sē paūlē-hā.
because Your-Honour's father him health-joy-with found-has.

Magar ū khīs kaïlē, ăūr ghar-mẽ jāy nā chahuan.
But he anger did, and house-into to-go not wished.

Ehī-sē un-kar bābū-jī bāhar aūan ăūr un-kā-kē
This-indeed-because his father outside came and him

manāwe laguan. Tab ū bābū-jī-kē jawāb dih^{a}lē kī,
to-appease began. Then he father-to answer gave that,

'rāwā̃, dēkhī̃, ham rāwā̃-kē ḍhēr din-sē ṭahal
'Your-Honour, look, I Your-Honour-to many days-since service

kar^a^tānī, ăūr rāur hukum kab^a^hī̃ nā ṭar^a^lī̃-hā̃.
am-doing, and Your-Honour's orders ever-even not have-transgressed.

Rāwā̃ ham^a^rā-kē kab^a^hī̃ egurō paṭh^a^rū bhī nā dih^a^lī̃ kī
Your-Honour me-to ever-even one-even kid even not gave that

ap^a^nā iār lōg-ke saṅgē chain karī̃. Magar ī
my-own friend's people-of with rejoicing I-may-make. But this

rāur bēṭā jē kas^a^bī-ke saṅgē kul dhan oṛā-dih^a^lē,
Your-Honour's son who harlots-of with all fortune squandered-away,

jabē gharē aïlē, tabē rāwā̃ un-kā-khātir nīk bhōjan
just-as house-to came, just-then Your-Honour him-for a-good dinner

khiaülī-hā̃. Bābū-jī kahuan kī, 'ē bēṭā, tū̃ tō sab din
has-caused-to-eat. Father said that, 'O son, thou indeed all days

ham^a^rā saṅgē rahat-haüā, ăūr jē-kichh hamār haūwē sē sabh
me with remaining-art, and whatever mine is that all

toharē haüwē. Magar ab^a^hī̃ anan kare-kē ăūr khusī
thine-indeed is. But now rejoicing making-for and joy

hōkhe-kē chāhat-rahat-hā, kāhe-kī tohār ī bhāī mar-gaïl-rahal-hā,
being-for it-is-proper, because thy this brother had-died,

phin jial-hā; ăūr bhulā-gaïl-rahal-hā, sē milal-hā.'
again alive-is; and lost-had-been, he has-been-found.'

[No. 37.]

INDO-ARYAN FAMILY. EASTERN GROUP.

BIHĀRĪ.

BHOJPURĪ DIALECT. (DISTRICT PALAMAU.)

SPECIMEN II.

ए भाया हम का कहीँ। झूठे डर से अइसन डेरात रहईं की जे कर हाल हम ना कहि सकीँ। का भउए की काल्हि जब हमनिका पहार के पँजरे पँजरे पेठिया से आवत रहुईं तब पहार के उपरौँ बाघ बड़े जोर से गरजत रहुए। हमनिका ढेर अदिमी रहलीँ किछ डर ना लागल। मगर आजु ओही रह ते हम आपन मामा का गाँवे ठीक दू-पहरे अकेले गइल रहुईं। जब पहार के तरे नदो अरे पहुँचुईं। तब अचक्के बड़ो हड़हड़ी बन में नदी ओरे सुनाइलि जेहि से हमार जीव सुध में ना रहल। हम बुझुईं की बाघ आइल और हमरा के धइलस। हमरा हाथ में तरुआर रहल मगर जून ना मिलल की मिआन से बहरे निकालीँ। करेजा काँपे लागल, डर का मारे हम सूख गइलीँ। बाघ के बे-देखले टकटको लाग गइलि। मगर थोरिका देरो में जब हम ओह ओर तकुईं तो का देखुईं की प्रगुड़ा बूढ़ सौँताल नदो के पानो जे पहार के उपरे से गिरत रहुए, मछरो मारे के बान्हत रहुए, ओहर से जे पथल निचवाँ फेंकत रहुए सेई ओसोँ-हाँ हाथ निचवाँ खरबराते आवत रहुए। जब ई तकुईं तो जीव में साहस भउए और देह में फुरती भउए। हम अपने ई बात इआद करि के आपन साहस पर हंसत बानीँ॥

[No. 37.]

INDO-ARYAN FAMILY. EASTERN GROUP.

BIHARĪ.

BHOJPURĪ DIALECT. (DISTRICT PALAMAU.)

SPECIMEN II.

TRANSLITERATION AND TRANSLATION.

E bhāyā, ham kā kahī̃; jhūṭhē ḍar-sē aïsan ḍerāt
O brother, I what may-say; false-even fear-with so afraid

rahuī̃ ki jē-kar hāl ham nā kahi sakī̃. Kā
I-was that of-which the-condition I not to-say am-able. What

bhaüē ki kālhi jab ham^{a}ni-kā pahār-ke pā̃j^{a}rē pā̃j^{a}rē
became that yesterday when we hill-of near near

peṭhiyā-sē āwat rahuī̃, tab pahār-ke up^{a}rā̃ bāgh baṛē jōr-sē
market-from coming were, then hill-of on tiger great force-with

gar^{a}jat rahuē. Ham^{a}ni-kā ḍhēr adimī rah^{a}lī̃, kichh ḍar
roaring was. We many men were, any fear

nā lāgal. Magar āju ōhī rah-tē ham āpan māmā-kā
not seized(-us). But to-day that-very road-by I my-own maternal-uncle-of

gā̃wē ṭhīk dū-pah^{a}rē akēlē gaïl-rahuī̃. Jab pahār-ke tarē
to-village just at-noon alone gone-was. When hill-of below

nadi-arē pahũchuī̃, tab achakkē baṛī haṛ^{a}haṛī ban-mē̃ nadī
on-this-river-side I-reached then suddenly great disturbance forest-in river

ōrē sunāili, jehi-sē hamār jīw sudh-mē̃ nā rahal. Ham
towards was-heard, which-from my mind sense-in not remained. I

bujhuī̃ ki bāgh āil āür ham^{a}rā-kē dhaïlas. Ham^{a}rā hāth-mē̃ taruār
thought that tiger came and me caught. My hand-in sword

rahal, magar jūn nā milal ki miān-sē bah^{a}rē nikālī̃.
was, but opportunity not was-found that sheath-of out I-may-take-it-out.

Karējā kā̃pe lāgal, ḍar-kā mārē ham sūkh gaïlī̃, bāgh-kē
Liver to-shudder began, fear-of through I dried-up I-went, tiger

bē-dekh^{a}ḷē ṭak^{a}takī lāg gaïli. Magar thorikā dērī-mē̃ jab ham
without-seeing motionlessness seized me. But little time-in when I

oh ōr takuī̃, tō kā dekhuī̃ ki eguṛā būṛh Saũtāl nadī-ke
that side looked, then what did-I-see that one old Santāl river-of

pānī jē pahār-ke up^{a}rē-sē girat rahuē machh^{a}ri-māre-kē bānhat
water which hill-of above-from falling was fish-to-kill embanking

rahuē. Ohar-sē jē pathal nich^{a}wā̃ phē̃kat rahuē, sēi
was. That-side-from which stone downward throwing was-(he), they-(very)

bīsõhã	hāth	nich*wã	khar*barātē	āwat	rahuē.
for-scores	*(of)-cubits*	*downward*	*crashing*	*coming*	*were.*

Jab	ī	taku-ī̃	tō	jīw-mẽ	sāhas	bhaüwē	ăūr	dēh-mẽ
When	*this*	*I-saw-(I)*	*then*	*heart-in*	*courage*	*became*	*and*	*body-into*

phurutī	aüē.	Ham	ap*nē	ī	bāt	iād-kari-ke	āpan	sāhas-par
agility	*came.*	*I*	*my-self*	*this*	*thing*	*remembering*	*my-own*	*courage-at*

hãsat-bānī.
laughing-am.

FREE TRANSLATION OF THE FOREGOING.

Brother, what can I say? I was so terrified by an imaginary fear that it is impossible for me to describe it. It so happened that yesterday, when we were returning from market along the hill-side, we heard a tiger roaring very loudly above us. As we were a large company, none of us felt any fear. But, to-day, I was going alone along that very road to my uncle's village, and had reached the foot of the hill by the river, when, all at once, I heard a tremendous noise in the forest, which altogether turned my soul out of its senses. I thought to myself that the tiger had come, and had already caught me. I had a sword in my hand, but I had no time to draw it out of its sheath. My heart began to tremble, and I dried up through fear. Although I had not seen the tiger, I became motionless and fascinated by his supposed presence. A little while after, when I looked in that direction, what should I see, but an old Santal, who had been damming up the water which fell from the upper part of the hill, in order to catch fish. He had been throwing down stones from there, and they had come crashing down for scores of cubits. When I saw that, my heart was again filled with courage, and my limbs regained their wonted activity. When I remember this, I keep laughing at my own courageousness.

The dialect of the eastern half of Ghazipur, both north and south of the Ganges, is practically the same as that of Shahabad. This will be evident from the following version of the Parable of the Prodigal Son. The only special points which require notice are the forms of the Relative Pronoun and of its Correlative, which are *jewan* and *tewan*, instead of *jawan* and *tawan* respectively. We may also note the third person singular of the Verb Substantive, which is *bāi* instead of *bā*. These distinctions do not entitle us to class the language of eastern Ghazipur as a dialect separate from that of Shahabad. Ghazipur is a border district between the Standard Bhojpurī spoken in Ballia and the western form of the dialect spoken in Benares District. In the eastern Parganas of Muhammadabad and Gadha the dialect is the same as that of Ballia, while in the west, in Pargana Mahraich, it is the same as that of Benares District. The total number of speakers of Bhojpurī in Ghazipur is 938,000, of whom half, or 469,000, may be estimated as speaking the Standard, and half as speaking the western Sub-dialect.

[No. 38.]

INDO-ARYAN FAMILY. EASTERN GROUP.

BIHĀRĪ.

BHOJPURĪ DIALECT. (DISTRICT GHAZIPUR.)

(Babu Bholanath Ray, 1898.)

એગો આદિમી કા દુર વેટા નહલે। ઓ મેં સે છોટકા બેટવા અપના વાપ સે કહલસિ કી એ વાપ ધન ધન મેં જેત્તન હમાન વખ્રના હોખે તેત્તન વાંટિ દ। તવ ઊ ધન મેં વખ્રના વિઠગાર દિહલસિ। થોડિક દિન મેં છોટકા વેટવા કુલહિ ધન વો દ્દદ્વ વટોરિ કે પરદેસ ચલિ ગરલ। ઓહિજા જાર કે આપન કુલહિ ધન વો દ્દદ્વ શ્રજડી મેં ફૂંકિ દિહલસિં। જવ કુલહિ ઓનાર ગરલ, તવ ઓ દેસ મેં વડા સૂખા પડલ તવ કંગાલ હો ગરલ તવ ઓહિજા કે ઠાકુર કોહેં ગરલન। ઊ અપના ખેત મેં સૂઅર ચરાવે ખાતિર ભેજલસિ। જેત્તન વોકલ સૂઅર ખાતિ નહલીં તેત્તના સે પેટ ભરે કે ઓકર મન કરત રહે। કેહૂ ઓકરા કિછુ ના દેત રહે। તવ ઓકર આંખી ખુલલિ ઔર સોચલસિ કી હમના વાપ કોહેં કેતના મજુરા ખાર કે ફેંકત વાડેસ ઔર હમ કે દાના નરખે જૂરત। અવ હમ અપના વાપ કોહાં જારવો ઔર ઉન સે કહવી કિ, ઓ વાપૂ હમ તોહાર ઔર ભગવાન કે વડ પાપ કરલે વાડીં અવ યહ લાયક નરખીં કિ તોહાર વેટા કહાઈ હમના કે અપના મજૂરન મેં જાન। તવ ઉઠિ કે અપના વાપ કોહેં ચલલસિ અવહીં શ્રરલે નહલસિ કી તવે ઉન કર વાપ ઉન કે દેખલસિ। વાપકા છોહ લાગલ ઔર દૌડિ કે ઉઠા લિહલસિ ઔર ચૂમા દિહલસિ। તવ ઊ વેટા વાપ સે કહલસિ એ વાપ હમ ભગવાન ઔર તોહરા સામને પાપ કરલે વાડીં ઔર અવ હમ તોહાર વેટા કહાવે લાયક નરખીં। તવ ઓકર વાપ અપના નોકર સે કહલસિ કી નીમન લુગા લે આવ ઔર રવજા કે પહિનાવ ઔર ચલ હમ સભ કેહુ ખાઈ ઔર પીહીં ઔર મૌજ કરીં। કાહેકો ઈ હમાર વેટા મરિ ગરલ નહલસિ હૈ સો ફેર જી ગરલસિ હૈ, ભુલા ગરલ નહલસિ હૈ ફેર મિલિ ગરલસિ હૈ। ઔર તવ ઊ વધાવ વજાવે લાગલસિ॥

ઓકર વડકા વેટા તવ ખેત મેં રહે। જવ ઉહાં સે ચલિ કે ઘર કે ગોઇડ આરલ તવ ઊ વાજા ઔર નાચ કે શોર સુનલસિ। ઔર તવ અપના એક નોકર કે વલાર કે પુછલસિ કી ઈ સભ કા હોત વાર। તવ ઊ ઓકરા સે કહલસિ કી તોહાર ભાઈ અરલન હૈ ઔર તોહાર વાપ મૌજ કરત વાડસિ કાહે કી ઊ ઉનકરા કે ભલા ચંગા પવલન હૈ। તવ ઊ ખિસિઆર ગરલ, ઔર ઘર ના જાઈ।

𑂞𑂥 𑂋𑂍𑂩 𑂥𑂰𑂣 𑂥𑂰𑂯𑂩 𑂢𑂱𑂍𑂪𑂱 𑂄𑂅𑂪 𑂌𑂩 𑂋𑂍𑂩𑂰 𑂍𑂵 𑂒𑂵𑂩𑂇𑂩𑂲 𑂍𑂩𑂪𑂢𑃀 𑂞𑂥 𑂈
𑂃𑂣𑂢𑂰 𑂥𑂰𑂣 𑂮𑂵 𑂍𑂯𑂪𑂢𑂱 𑂠𑂵𑂎𑂲𑂁 𑂯𑂧 𑂉𑂞𑂢𑂰 𑂥𑂩𑂱𑂮 𑂩𑂰𑂇𑂩 𑂮𑂵𑂫𑂰 𑂍𑂩𑂞𑂲𑂁 𑂍𑂥𑂯𑂲𑂁 𑂩𑂰𑂇𑂩
𑂄𑂔𑂹𑂖𑂰 𑂢𑂰 𑂗𑂩𑂪𑂲𑂁 𑂞𑂥𑂯𑂴𑂀 𑂩𑂇𑂄𑂀 𑂯𑂧𑂩𑂰 𑂍𑂵 𑂉𑂍𑂷 𑂥𑂍𑂩𑂰 𑂢𑂰 𑂠𑂱𑂯𑂪𑂲𑂁 𑂍𑂱 𑂯𑂧 𑂃𑂣𑂢𑂰
𑂅𑂨𑂰𑂩𑂢 𑂍𑂵 𑂮𑂰𑂟 𑂧𑂸𑂔 𑂍𑂩𑂲𑂁 𑂪𑂵𑂍𑂱𑂢 𑂔𑂥𑂯𑂲𑂁 𑂩𑂰𑂇𑂩 𑂆 𑂥𑂵𑂗𑂰 𑂃𑂅𑂪𑂢𑂱 𑂔𑂵 𑂩𑂰𑂇𑂩
𑂮𑂥 𑂡𑂢 𑂥𑂵𑂮𑂰 𑂍𑂵 𑂮𑂰𑂟 𑂇𑂚𑂰 𑂠𑂱𑂯𑂪𑂢 𑂞𑂵𑂯𑂴 𑂣𑂩 𑂩𑂇𑂄𑂀 𑂇𑂢𑂍𑂰 𑂎𑂰𑂞𑂱𑂩 𑂦𑂷𑂔
𑂠𑂱𑂯𑂪𑂲𑂁𑃀 𑂞𑂥 𑂈 𑂋𑂍𑂩𑂰 𑂮𑂵 𑂍𑂯𑂪𑂢 𑂍𑂱 𑂯𑂵 𑂥𑂵𑂗𑂰 𑂞𑂴𑂀 𑂯𑂧𑂩𑂰 𑂮𑂰𑂟 𑂥𑂩𑂰𑂥𑂩 𑂥𑂰𑂚
𑂌𑂩 𑂔𑂵 𑂍𑂳𑂓 𑂯𑂧𑂰𑂩 𑂥𑂰𑂗𑂵 𑂮𑂵 𑂞𑂷𑂯𑂩𑂵 𑂯𑃀 𑂌𑂩 𑂆 𑂯𑂧𑂢𑂲𑂍𑂰 𑂒𑂰𑂯𑂲𑂁 𑂍𑂱 𑂯𑂧𑂢𑂲𑂍𑂰
𑂎𑂳𑂮 𑂯𑂷𑂆𑂁 𑂌𑂩 𑂄𑂢𑂢𑂹𑂠 𑂍𑂩𑂲𑂁 𑂍𑂰𑂯𑂵 𑂍𑂱 𑂆 𑂞𑂷𑂯𑂰𑂩 𑂦𑂰𑂆 𑂧𑂩𑂱 𑂏𑂅𑂪 𑂩𑂯𑂪𑂢𑂱 𑂯𑂶
𑂌𑂩 𑂤𑂵𑂩 𑂔𑂱𑂃𑂪𑂢𑂱 𑂦𑂳𑂪𑂰𑂅 𑂏𑂅𑂪 𑂩𑂯𑂪𑂢𑂱 𑂯𑂶 𑂌𑂩 𑂤𑂵𑂩 𑂧𑂱𑂪𑂪𑂢𑂱𑃁

[No. 38.]

INDO-ARYAN FAMILY. EASTERN GROUP.

BIHĀRĪ.

BHOJPURĪ DIALECT.

(DISTRICT GHAZIPUR.)

TRANSLITERATION.

(Babu Bholanath Ray, 1898.)

Egō adimī-kā dui bēṭā rah^a^lē. Ō-mẽ-sē chhoṭ^a^kā larikā ap^a^nā bāp sē kah^a^lasi kī, 'ē bāp an-dhan[1]-mẽ jewan hamār bakh^a^rā hōkhē tewan bẫṭi-dâ.' Tab ū dhan-mẽ bakh^a^rā bil^a^gāi dih^a^lani. Thorik din-mẽ chhoṭ^a^kā beṭ^a^wā kulhi dhan o daulat baṭōri-ke par^a^dēs chali gaïl. Ohi-jā jāi-ke āpan kulhi dhan o daulat phakaṛī-mẽ phũki dih^a^lasi. Jab kulhi orāi gaïl, tab ō dēs-mẽ baṛā sūkhā paṛal. Tab kaṅgāl hō-gaïl. Tab ohi-jā-ke ṭhākur kihẽ gaïlan. Ū ap^a^nā khēt-mẽ sūar charāwe khātir bhej^a^lani. Jewan bok^a^lā sūar khāti-rah^a^lī̃ tewanā-sē pēṭ bhaie-kē ō-kar man karat-rahē. Kēhu ok^a^rā-kē kichhu nā dēt-rahē. Tab ō-kar ẫkhi khulali ăūr soch^a^lasi kī, 'ham^a^rā bāp kihẽ ket^a^nā majūrā khāi-ke jīat bāṛē-sâ ăūr ham-kē dānā naikhē jūrat.[2] Ab ham ap^a^nā bāp kihẫ jāibī ăūr un-sē kah^a^bī kī, "Ō bāpu, ham tohār ăūr Bhāg^a^wān-ke baṛā pāp kailē-bāṛī̃. Ab eh lāek naïkhī̃ kī tohār bēṭā kahāī̃. Ham^a^rā-kē ap^a^nā majūran-mẽ jānâ."' Tab uṭhi-ke ap^a^nā bāp kihẽ chal^a^lani. Ab-hī̃ phailawē rah^a^lani kī tabbai un-kar bāp un-kē dekh^a^lani. Bāp-kā chhōh lāgal, ăūr dauṛi ke uṭhā lih^a^lani, ăūr chūmā dih^a^lani. Tab ū bēṭā bāp-sē kah^a^lasi, 'ē bāp, ham Bhag^a^wān ăūr toh^a^rā sām^a^nē pāp kaïlē-bāṛī̃, ăūr ab ham tohār bēṭā kahāwe lāek naïkhī̃.' Tab ō-kar bāp ap^a^nā nōkar-sē kah^a^lasi kī, 'nīman lūgā lē-āwâ ăūr in^a^kā-kē pahināwâ, ăūr chalâ, ham sabh kēhu khāī̃ ăūr pīhī̃, ăūr mauj karī̃, kāhe-kī ī hamār bēṭā mari gaïl rah^a^lani haī̃, au phēr jī gaïlani haī̃; bhulā-gaïl-rah^a^lani haī̃, phēr mili-gaïlani-haī̃. Ăūr tab ū badhāw bajāwe lag^a^lani.

Ō-kar baṛ^a^kā bēṭā tab khēt-mẽ rahē. Jab uhẫ-sē chali-ke ghar-ke goērā āili, tab ū bājā ăūr nāchi ke sōr sun^a^lasi; ăūr tab ap^a^nā ēk nōkar-kē balāi-ke puchh^a^lasi kī, 'ī sabh kā hōt bāi?' Tab ū ok^a^rā-sē kah^a^lasi kī, 'tohār bhāī ailan haī̃ ăūr tohār bāp mauj karat bāṛani, kāhe-kī un-k^a^rā-kē bhalā chaṅgā paūlan haī̃.' Tab ū khisiāi gaïl, ăūr ghar nā jāē. Tab ō-kar bāp bāhar nik^a^li āil, ăūr ok^a^rā-kē cheraūrī kaïlan. Tab ū ap^a^nā bāp-sē kah^a^lani, 'ḍekhī̃, ham et^a^nā baris rāur sēwā kaïlī̃, kab^a^hī̃ rāur āgyẫ nā ṭar^a^lī̃; tab-hũ rauẫ ham^a^rā-kē ēkō bak^a^rā nā dih^a^lī̃ kī ham ap^a^nā iāran-ke sāth mauj karī̃. Lēkin-jab-hī̃ rāur ī bēṭā ailani, jē rāur sabh dhan bēsā-ke sāth uṛā dih^a^lan, tēhū-par rauẫ un-k^a^rā khātir bhōj dih^a^lī̃.' Tab ū ok^a^rā-sē kah^a^lan kī, 'hē bēṭā, tũ ham^a^rā sāth barābar bāṛâ, ăūr jē kuchh hamār bāi sē toh^a^r-ē hâ. Ăūr ī ham^a^nī-kā chāhī kī ham^a^nī-kā khus hōī̃ ăūr ānand karī̃; kāhe-kī ī tohār bhāī mari gaïl rah^a^lani haī̃, ăūr phēr jialani; bhulāi gaïl rah^a^lani haī̃, ăūr phēr mil^a^lani.'

---

[1] Grain and wealth.

[2] To me grain (*i.e.* food) is not available.

BHOJPURĪ OF BALLIA.

Opposite Shahabad, on the north bank of the River Ganges, lies the North Western Provinces District of Ballia. It is closely connected with the Bhojpur Pargana by many ties, historical and traditional, and the language spoken in it is practically the same as that of Shahabad. This will be manifest from the following specimens, which are in the Dēva-nāgarī character.

Here and there, we see traces of the form of Bhojpurī which is common over the rest of the north Gangetic area. For instance, while the servant says to the elder brother *rāur bhāī āil bāṛē* quite correctly after the Shahabad fashion, the father uses the Sāran idiom, *bāṭē* instead of *bāṛē* in addressing the elder son.

[No. 39.]

INDO-ARYAN FAMILY. EASTERN GROUP.

BIHARĪ.

BHOJPURĪ DIALECT. (DISTRICT BALLIA.)

SPECIMEN I.

कवनों अदिमी-के दुइगो बेटा रहे। उन्हनी में से छोटका अपना बाप से कहलसि जे ए बाबू-जी धन में से जे हमार बखरा होखे से हमरा के दे दं। तब ऊ आपन धन उन्हनी के बाँटि दिहले। बहुत दिन ना बीते पावल की छोटका बेटा सभ कुछ जवर कइ के दूर देस आपन राह पकड़लसि। उहाँ लुचई में आपन दिन बितावत आपन धन उड़ा दिहलसि। अवर जब ऊ सभ उड़ा चूकल तब ओह देस में बड़ा अकाल पड़ल अवर ऊ कंगाल हो गइल। अवर उहाँ के रहनिहारन में से एगो कीहाँ रहे लागल। ऊ अपना खेत में सूअर चरावे के ओ के भेजि दिहलसि। ऊ ओही छीमी से जे सूअर खात रहले सं आपन पेट भरे चहलसि अवर दोसर केहु किछु ना दे। तब ओकरा चेत भइल की हमरा बाप का बहुत नोकरन का अधिक रोटी हो-ला अवर हम भूख से मरत बानीं। हम ऊठि के अपना बाप के पास जाइबि अवर उनिकरा से कहबि की ए बाबू हम सरग के उलिटा अवर रउरा सामने पाप कइले बानीं। अब हम राउर लरिका कहावे जोग नइखीं। हम के अपना नोकरन में से एगो के बराबर मानीं। तब ऊ उठि के अपना बाप के पास गइल। लेकिन जब तक ऊ दूरे रहे ओकर बाप ओकरा पर दया कइलसि अवर दौरि के ओकरा के अपना गला में लागि के चुमलसि। लरिका ओकरा से कह-लसि ए बाबू हम सरग के उलिटा अवर रउरा सामने पाप कइले बानीं। अवर अब राउर लरिका कहावे जोग नइखीं। बाकी ओकर बाप अपना अदिमिन से कहले की सब से अच्छा कपड़ा निकालि के ओ-करा-के पहिनावं अवर ओकरा अँगुरी में अँगुठी ओ गोड़ में जूता पहिनावं अवर हमनीका खाईं पोईं चैन करीं। काहे की ई हमार बेटा मरल रहल हा फिरि जीअल। भूलि गइल रहल हा फिरि मिलल हा। तब ऊ लोग खुसी करे लागल॥

ओकर जेठका लरिका खेत में रहे। और जब ऊ आवत खाँ घर के निअरा पहुँचल तब नाच ओ बाजा के भनक ओकरा कान में पहुँचल। और ऊ अपना अदिमिन में से एगो के अपना निअरा बोलाइ के पुछलसि की ई का हवे। ऊ नोकर उनिकरा से कहलसि की राउर भाई आइल बाड़े। अवर राउर बाप नीमन भोज कइले हा एह खातिर की ऊ उनिकरा के भला चंगा पउले हा। लेकिन ऊ खीसि कइलसि अवर भीतर ना जाए चहलसि। तब ओकर बाप बाहर आइ के मनावे लागल। ऊ अपना बाप के कहलसि की देखीं हम एतना बरिस से राउर सेवा करत बानीं और रउरा बात के कबहीं ना टरलीं और रउवाँ एको पठियो ना कबहीं दिहलीं की हम अपना संगिन के साथ खुसी करीं। लेकिन ई राउर लरिकी जे कसबी के साथ राउर धन खोइ घललसि जबे आइल तबहीं रउवाँ ओकरा खातिर अच्छा भोज कइलीं। बाप ओकरा से कहलसि की ए बेटा तूँ हमरा साथ हरदम रहं-लं और जे किछु हमार हं से तोहार हं। लेकिन हमनी के खुसी कइल ओ आराम कइल भल बाटे काहे की ई तोहार भाई सुअल रहल हा फिरि जीअल हा। भलल रहल हा फिरि मिलल हा॥

[No. 39.]

INDO-ARYAN FAMILY. EASTERN GROUP.

BIHĀRĪ.

BHOJPURĪ DIALECT. (DISTRICT BALLIA.)

SPECIMEN I.

TRANSLITERATION AND TRANSLATION.

Kaw'nõ adimī-kē dui-gō bēṭā rahē. Unh'nī-mẽ-sē chhoṭ'kā
A-certain man-to two sons were. Them-in-from the-younger
ap'nā bāp-sē kah'lasi jē, 'ē bābū-jī, dhan-mẽ-sē jē hamār
his-own father-to said that, 'O father, property-in-from what my
bakh'rā hōkhē sē ham'rā-kē dē-dā.' Tab ū āpan dhan unh'nī-
share may-be that me-to give.' Then he his-own property them-
kē bā̃ṭi-dih'lē. Bahut din nā bīte pāwal ki chhoṭ'kā beṭā
to dividing-gave. Many days not to-pass got that the-younger son
sabh-kuchh jawar-kaī-ke dūr dēs āpan rāh pakaṛ'lasi. Uhā̃
all-things collecting a-distant country-to his-own way took. There
luchai-mẽ āpan din bitāwat āpan dhan uṛā-dih'lasi. Awar
evil-conduct-in his-own days causing-to-pass his-own fortune he-squandered. And
jab ū sabh uṛā-chūkal tab oh dēs-mẽ baṛā akāl paṛal,
when he all had-spent then that country-in a-great famine fell,
awar ū kaṅgāl hō-gaïl. Awar ubā̃-ke rah'nihāran-mẽ-sē ēgō kihā̃
and he poor became. And there-of inhabitants-in-from one near
rahe lāgal. Ū ap'nā khēt-mẽ sūar charāwe-kē ō-kē bhēji-
to-live he-began. He his-own fields-in swine feeding-for him sent-
dih'lasi. Ū ōh-ī chhīmī-sē jē sūar khāt-rah'lē-sā āpan
away. He those-very husks-with which swine used-to-eat his-own
pēṭ bhare chah'lasi, awar dōsar kēhu kichhu nā
belly to-fill wished, and other any-one anything not
dē. Tab ok'rā chēt-bhaïl ki, 'ham'rā bāp-kā
used-to-give-(him). Then him senses-became that, 'my father-of
bahut nok'ran-kā adhik rōṭi hō-lā awar ham bhūkh-sē
many servants much bread is and I hunger-from
marat-bānī. Ham ūṭhi-ke ap'nā bāp-ke pās jāïbi, awar
am-dying. I arising my-own father-of near will-go, and
unik'rā-sē kahabi ki, "ē Bābū, ham sarag-ke ulṭā
him-to I-will-say that, "O Father, I heaven-of against

awar raürā sām'nē pāp kaïlē-bānī̃. Ab ham rāur
and of-Your-Honour before sin have-done. Now I Your-Honour's
larikā kahāwe jōg naïkhī̃. Ham-kē ap'nā nok'ran-mē̃-sē
son to-be-called worthy am-not. Me thine-own servants-among-from
ēgō-ke barābar mānī̃."' Tab ū uṭhi-ke ap'nā bāp-ke pās
one-of equal-to consider."' Then he having-arisen his-own father-of near
gaïl. Lēkin jab-tak ū dūrē rahē ōkar bāp ok'rā-par dayā
went. But while he at-a-distance was his father him-on compassion
kaïlasi, awar dauri-ke ok'rā-kē ap'nā galā-mē̃ lāgi-kē chum'lasi.
made, and having-run him his-own neck-on having-applied kissed.
Larikā ok'rā-sē kah'lasi, 'ē Bābū, ham sarag-ke uliṭā awar
The-son him-to said, 'O Father, I heaven-of against and
raürà sām'nê pāp kaïlē-bānī̃, awar ab rāur larikā kahāwe jōg
of-Your-Honour before sin have-done, and now Your-Honour's son to-be-called worthy
naïkhī̃.' Bākī ōkar bāp ap'nā adimin-sē kah'lē kī, 'sab-sē achchhā kap'rā nikāli-
not-am.' But his father his-own men-to said that, 'all-than good clothes taking-
ke ok'rā-kē pahināwâ, awar ok'rā ã̄gurī mē̃ ã̄guṭhī ō goṛ-mē̃ jūtā
out him put-on, and his finger-in (on) a-ring and feet-on shoes
pahināwâ, awar ham'nī-kā khāī̃ pīī̃ chain karī̃, kāhe kī ī hamār
put-on, and (let)-us eat drink (and) merriment make, because that this my
bēṭā maral rahal-hā, phiri jīal; bhūli gaïl-rahal-hā, milal-hā.' Tab ū lōg
son dead had-been, again became-alive; lost had-been, found-is.' Then those people
khusī kare lāgal.
rejoicing to-make began.

Ōkar jeṭh'kā larikā khēt-mē̃ rahē. Āür jab ū āwat-khā̃
His elder son field-in was. And when he coming-in
ghar-ke niarā pahũchal tab nāch ō bājā-ke bhanak ok'rā kān-mē̃
house-of near approached then dancing and music-of faint-sound his ear-into
pahũchal; ãür ū ap'nā adimin-mē̃-sē ēgō-kē ap'nā niarā bolāi-ke puchh'lasi kī,
arrived; and he his-own men-in-from one himself near calling asked that,
'ī kā hāwē?' Ū nōkar unik'rā-sē kah'lasi kī, 'rāur bhāī āil bāṛē
'this what is?' That servant him-to said that, 'Your-Honour's brother come is
awar rāur bāp nīman bhōj kaïlē-hā, eh khātir kī ū unik'rā-kē
and Your-Honour's father good feast has-made, this for that he him
bhalā-changā paülē-hā.' Lēkin ū khīsi kaïlasi awar bhitar nā jāe chah'lasi. Tab
in-good-health has-found.' But he anger made and inside not to-go wished. Then
okar bāp bāhar āï-ke manāwe lāgal. Ū ap'nā bāp-kē kah'lasi kī,
his father outside coming to-appease began. He his-own father-to said that,
'dēkh, ham et'nā baris-sē rāur sēwā karat-bānī̃ ãür raürā
'see, I so-many years-since Your-Honour's service am-doing and Your-Honour's
bāt-kē kah'hī̃ nā ṭar'lī̃ ãür raüwā̃ ēkō paṭhiyō nā kab'hī̃
words ever-even not transgressed and Your-Honour one-even kid-even not ever

dih*lī̃ kī ham ap'na saṅgin-ke sāth khusī karī̃. Lēkin ī rāūr
gave that I my-own friends-of with merriment might-make. But this Your-Honour's

larikā jē kas*bī-ke sāth rāūr dhan khōi-ghal*lasi, jabē
son who harlots-of with Your-Honour's wealth has-lost, when-even

āil tab*hī̃ raūwā̃ ok*rā khātir achchhā bhōj kaïlī̃. Bāp ok*rā-sē
he-came then-even Your-Honour him for good feast made. The-father him-to

kah*lasi kī, 'ē bēṭā, tū̃ ham*rā sāth har dam rahålå, ā̆ūr jē kichhu hamār
said that, 'O Son, thou me with every moment livest, and what thing mine

hå sē tohār hå. Lēkin ham*nī-kē khusī-kaïl ō ārām kaïl bhal bāṭē
is that thine is. But for-us merriment-making and pleasure making good is

kāhe-kī ī tohār bhāī mual rahal-hā, phiri jīal-hā; bhūlal rahal-hā, phiri
because this thy brother dead had-been, again alive-is; lost had-been, again

milal-hā.'
found-is.'

The next specimen, also from Ballia, is a villager's wail over hard times.

[No. 40.]

INDO-ARYAN FAMILY. EASTERN GROUP.

BIHĀRĪ.

BHOJPURĪ DIALECT. (DISTRICT BALLIA.)

SPECIMEN II.

कपिल-देव आजु तोहरा के ढेर दिन पर हम देखत बानीं। अतना दिन तूँ काँहाँ रहलं हा। अब तब हम तोहरा बारे में तोहरा गाँव के लोगन से पूछत रहलीं हाँ मगर केहु हाल साफ ना बतावत रहल हा। अब कई तोहरा घर के सभ बेकति अच्छी तरे बाड़ीं नूँ॥

ओबीध भइया तूँ का पूछत बाड़। जब हमरा हाल के सुनबं त तोहरो दुख बिआपी ओ आँखिन में से लोर गिरावे लगबं। जब हम एठाँ से घरे गइलीं तब से गिरहती के काम में बझलीं। राति दिन एहि काम में हम बानीं। दोसर केहु हमरा घर में अइसन नइखे जेकरा से हम के एको लेहजा के आराम मिली। काहे से की हमरा बाप के अँखिये जवाब दे दिहलेस ओ हमरा जेठ जना भाई हमरा पहुँचला का पहिले-ही परदेस चलि गइले अवर तब से एको चिठियो न भेजले हा। हमार महतारो ओ अउरी बेकति उनिकरा हाल चाल का ना पाउला से बेहाल बाड़ीं। हमार काका जी अपना लरिका बाला समेत अलगें रहे ले। एही सब ओजह से हम राति दिन फिकिरि ओ तरदुत से पिसाइल रही-ले। अबकीं दुइ दिन बीतल हा की हम राति खाँ कपरबथी का मारे खेत में अगोरे ना गइलीं। चारिगो बोझा लागल गोहूँ के हमरा खेत में से चोर काटि ले गइले हा सं। महराज के तहसीलदार मालगुजारी खातिर दुइ पियादा तनात कइले बाड़े। एको कउड़ी हमरा पासें नइखे की उनि के दीआव। मामा भी परसों अइले ओ उनिकरा से जब हम कुछ रुपया मँगलीं त उ साफे इनकार कइले। खोसा ई की घर के मारल बन में गइलीं। बन में लागलि आगि॥

[No. 40.]

INDO-ARYAN FAMILY. EASTERN GROUP.

BIHĀRĪ.

BHOJPURĪ DIALECT. (DISTRICT BALLIA.)

SPECIMEN II.

TRANSLITERATION AND TRANSLATION.

Kapil Dēv ! āju toh'rā-kē ḍhēr din par ham dēkhat-bānī.
Kapil Dēw ! to-day you many days after I seeing-am.
At'nā din tū̃ kāhā̃ rah'lā-hā ? Jab-tab ham toh'rā bārē-mē̃
So-many days you where were ? Some-times I you about
toh'rā gā̃w-ke lōgan-sē pūchhat rah'lī-hā̃, magar kēhu hāl sāph
your village-of people-from asking was, but any-body news plainly
nā batāwat-rahal-hā. Ab kahā, toh'rā ghar-ke sabh bekati achchhī tarē
not telling-was. Now say, your house-of all persons good ways-in
bāṛī, nū̃ ?
are, (or) not ?

Jībōdh bhaīyā, tū̃ kā pūchhat bārā ?[1] Jab ham'rā hāl-kē
Jībōdh brother, you what asking are ? When my accounts
sun'bā ta toh'rō dukh biāpī, ō ā̃khin-mē̃-sē lōr
you-will-hear then your-also anxiety will-fill(-you), and eyes-in-from tears
girāwe lag'bā. Jab ham eṭhā̃-sē gharē gaïlī
to-cause-to-drop you-will-begin. When I here-from home-to went,
tab-sē gir'hatī-ke kām-mē̃ bajh'lī. Rāti din ehi kām-mē̃
then-from household-of work-in was-I-entangled. Night (and) day this work-in
ham bānī. Dōsar kēhu ham'rā ghar-mē̃ aïsan naïkhē jek'rā-sē
I am. Another anyone my house-in such is-not whom-from
ham-kē ēkō leh'jā-ke ārām milī ; kāhe-sē-ki ham'rā bāp-ke ā̃khiyē
me-to one-even moment-of ease will-be-got ; because my father-of eyes-even
jawāb dē-dih'lis, ō ham'rā jēṭh janā bhāī ham'rā pahũch'lā-kā
replies gave[2], and my elder man brother my reaching-of
pahilē-hī par'dēs chalī-gaïlē, awar tab-sē ēkō chiṭhiyō
before-even foreign-land-to went-away, and that-time-since one-even letter-even
nā bhej'lē hā. Hamār mah'tārī ō aürī bekati unik'rā hāl-chāl-kā
not he-sent-has. My mother and other female-persons his news
nā paülā-sē bēhāl bāṛī. Hamār kākā-jī ap'nā larikā
not getting-from uneasy are. My uncle his-own children

[1] *Kā pūchhat bārā* means 'what you are enquiring about is so bad that the less said about it the better.'
[2] *I.e.* have become useless.

bālā samēt al'gē̃ rahē-lē. Ēhī sab ojah-sē ham rāti-din
wife with separate lives. These all causes-from I night-day

phikiri ō tar'dut-sē pisāïl rahī-lē. Ab'hī̃ dui din bītal-
anxiety and trouble-with crushed remain. Now-only two days passed-

hā kī ham rāti-khā̃ kapar-bathī-kā-mārē khēt-mē̃ agōre nā
have that I night-at headache-from field-in to-look-after not

gaïlī̃. Chāri-gō bōjhā lāgal gōhū̃-ke ham'rā khēt-mē̃-sē chōr kāṭi
went. Four bundles standing wheat-of my field-in-from thieves cutting

lē-gaïlē-hā-sâ. Mah'rāj-ke Tah'sīldār māl'gujārī khātir
taken-away-have. The-Mahārāja-of rent-collector rent for

dui piyādā tanāt kaïlē-bāṛē. Ēkō kaüṛī ham'rā pasē̃ naïkhē kī
two peons quartered has. One-even cowry me with not-is that

uni-kē diāu. Māmā bhī par'sō̃ aïlē ō unik'-
him-to may-be-given. The-paternal-uncle also the-day-before came and him-

rā-sē jab ham kuchh rup'yā mā̃g'lī̃ ta ū sāphē in'kār-kaïlē. Khīsā
from when I some money asked then he plainly refused. The-proverb

hâ kī, 'ghar-ke māral ban-mē̃ gaïlī̃; ban-mē̃ lāgali āgi."[1]
is that, 'home-of beaten forest-in I-went; forest-in was-set fire.'

FREE TRANSLATION OF THE FOREGOING.

To-day I see you, Kapil-dēo, after a long time. Where have you been so long? I now and then asked about you from your fellow-villagers, but no one gave a clear account. Tell me whether all your family is well.

Brother Jibōdh, what do you ask me! When you know about me, grief will overcome you also, and you will drop tears from your eyes. When I went home from this place, I became entangled myself in agriculture. By day and night I worked at it. There is no one in my family to relieve me for a moment from the toil; for my father's eyes have become useless, and my elder brother went off elsewhere, before I reached home, and has sent no letter since then. My mother and the rest of the family are unhappy because they hear no news from him. My uncle with his wife and children lives separately. For these reasons care and trouble crush me both day and night. Only two days ago I could not go to watch my field in the night on account of a headache. Thieves therefore cut away four bundles from my standing wheat crop. The rent-collector of the Mahārāja has quartered two peons on me to realize the rent, but I have not a cowry to pay them. My maternal uncle also came the day before yesterday and when I asked him for some money he flatly refused. Mine is only an instance of the saying, 'I was beaten at home and went to the jungle. When I got there the jungle took fire.'

[1] Out of the frying-pan into the fire.

The District of Saran lies on the north of the Ganges, opposite the east side of Shahabad, and the west side of Patna. I have already stated, *ante*, p. 186, that the language of the portion of Saran which borders on the Ganges is Standard Bhojpurī. This statement, however, requires a certain amount of modification.

A reference to the map will show that the language of Muzaffarpur, which lies to the east of Saran, across the river Gandak, is western Maithilī, which, as has been shown, is largely infected with Bhojpurī, and is in fact, a border form of speech between the two dialects. Again, the language of Ṗatna, opposite the south-east corner of Saran, is Magahī. Hence, as might be expected, the language of the east of Saran is tinged with Maithilī peculiarities, and that of the south-east with Magahī ones. To give specimens of all such mixed forms of speech would extend the volumes of the Survey beyond reasonable limits It must suffice, in the case of Saran, to deal, in detail, with the two main forms of speech, that of the south, and that of the north. For a more minute account of the various forms of speech current in the District, see *Notes on the Vernacular Dialects spoken in the District of Saran*, by Babu Girīndra-nāth Dutt, in the *Journal* of the Asiatic Society of Bengal, Vol. lxvi, 1897, Part I, pp. 194 and ff. It is to this gentleman that I am indebted for the specimens here given, which represent the Standard Bhojpurī spoken in the south of the district, over against Shahabad.

INDO-ARYAN FAMILY. EASTERN GROUP.

BIHARĪ.

BHOJPURĪ DIALECT. (DISTRICT SARAN.)

SPECIMEN I.

(Babu Girindra-nath Dutt, 1898.)

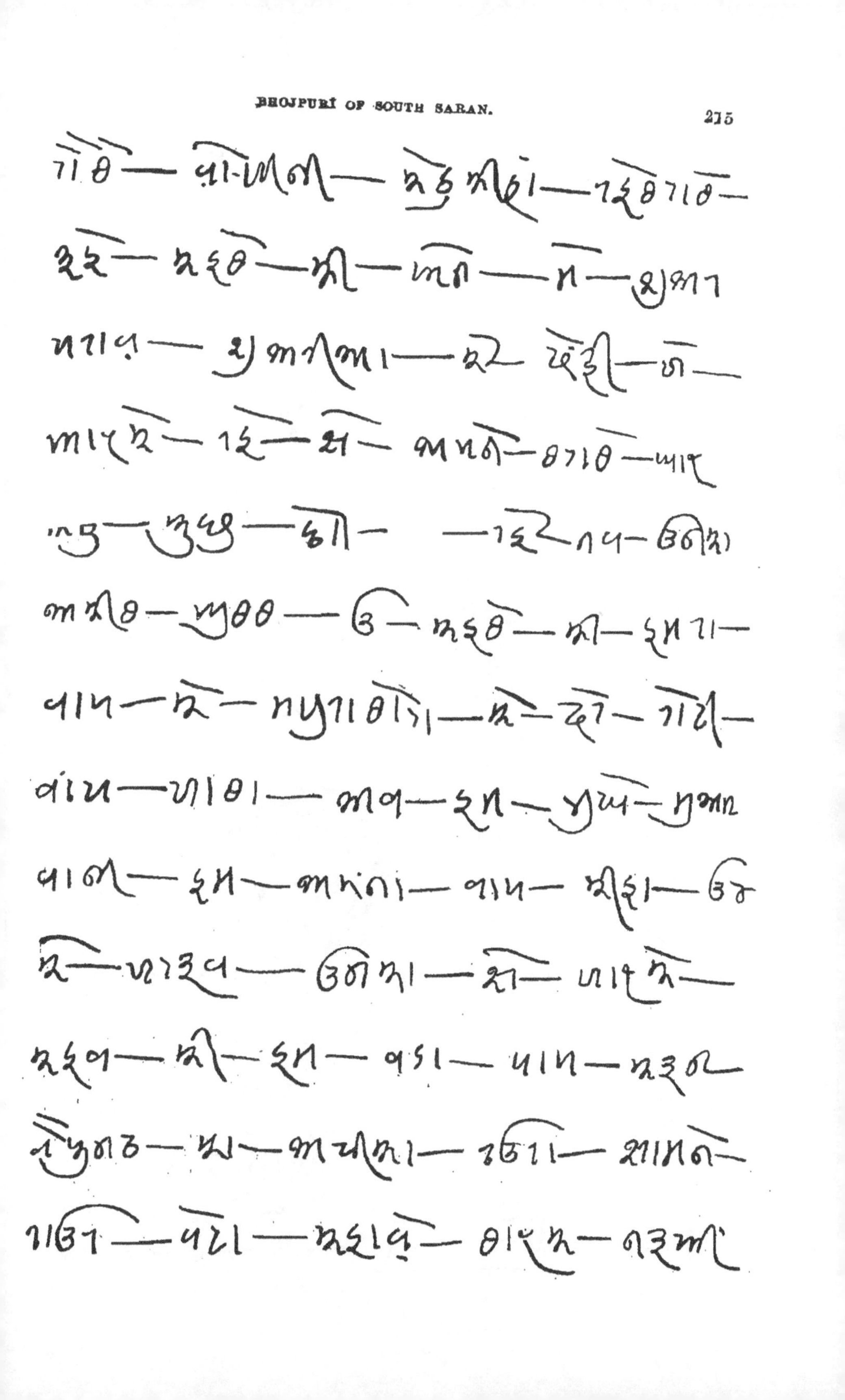

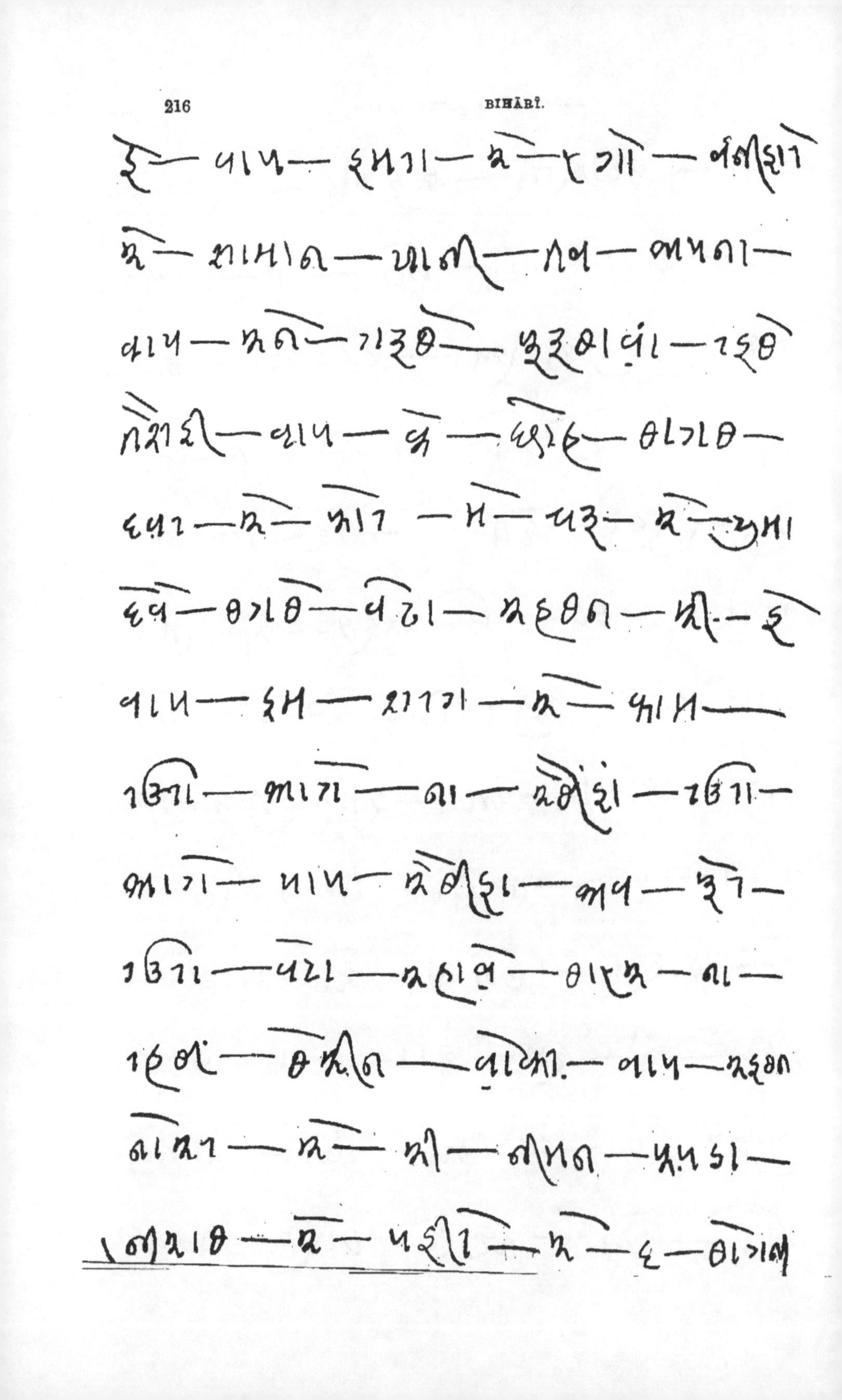

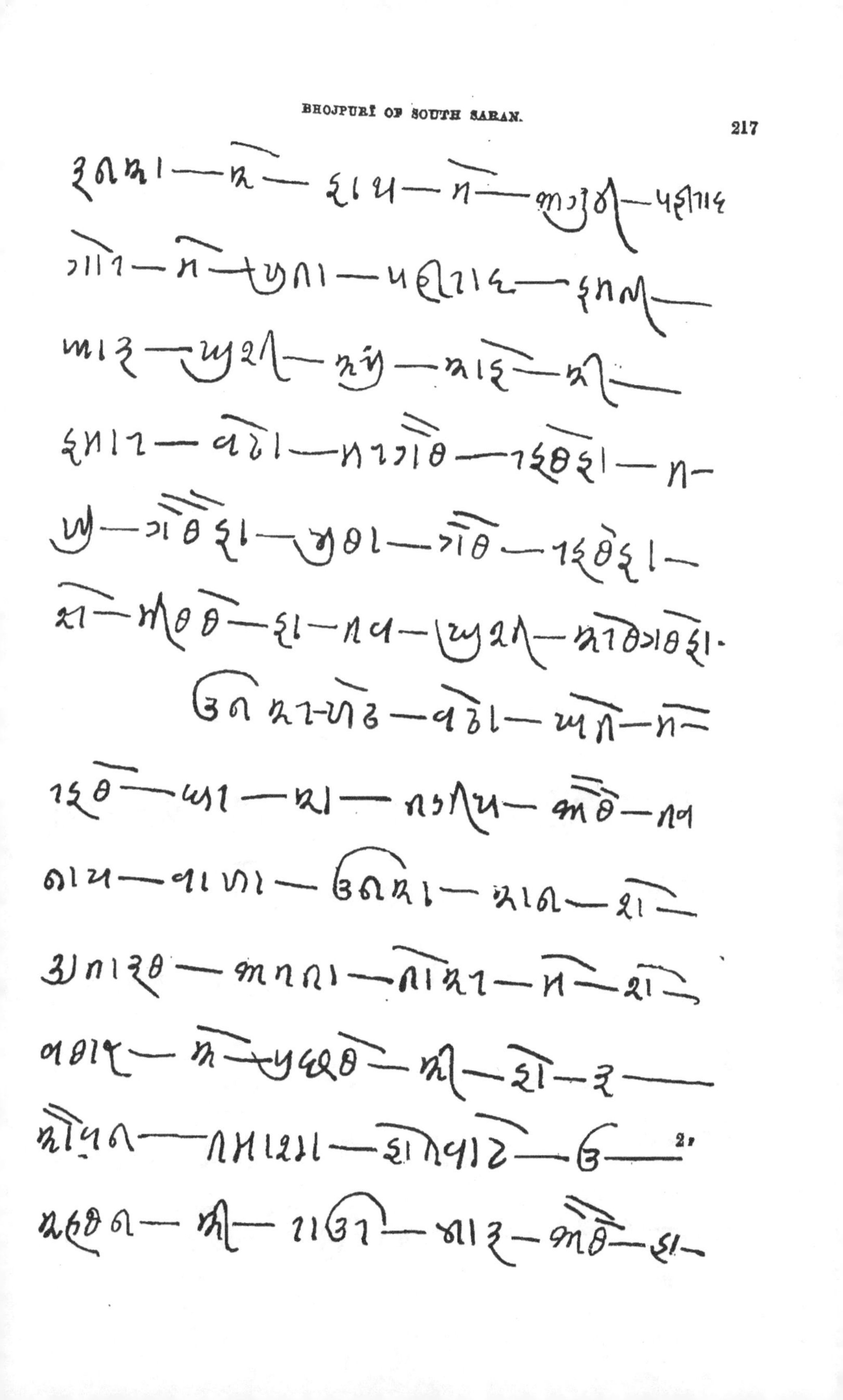

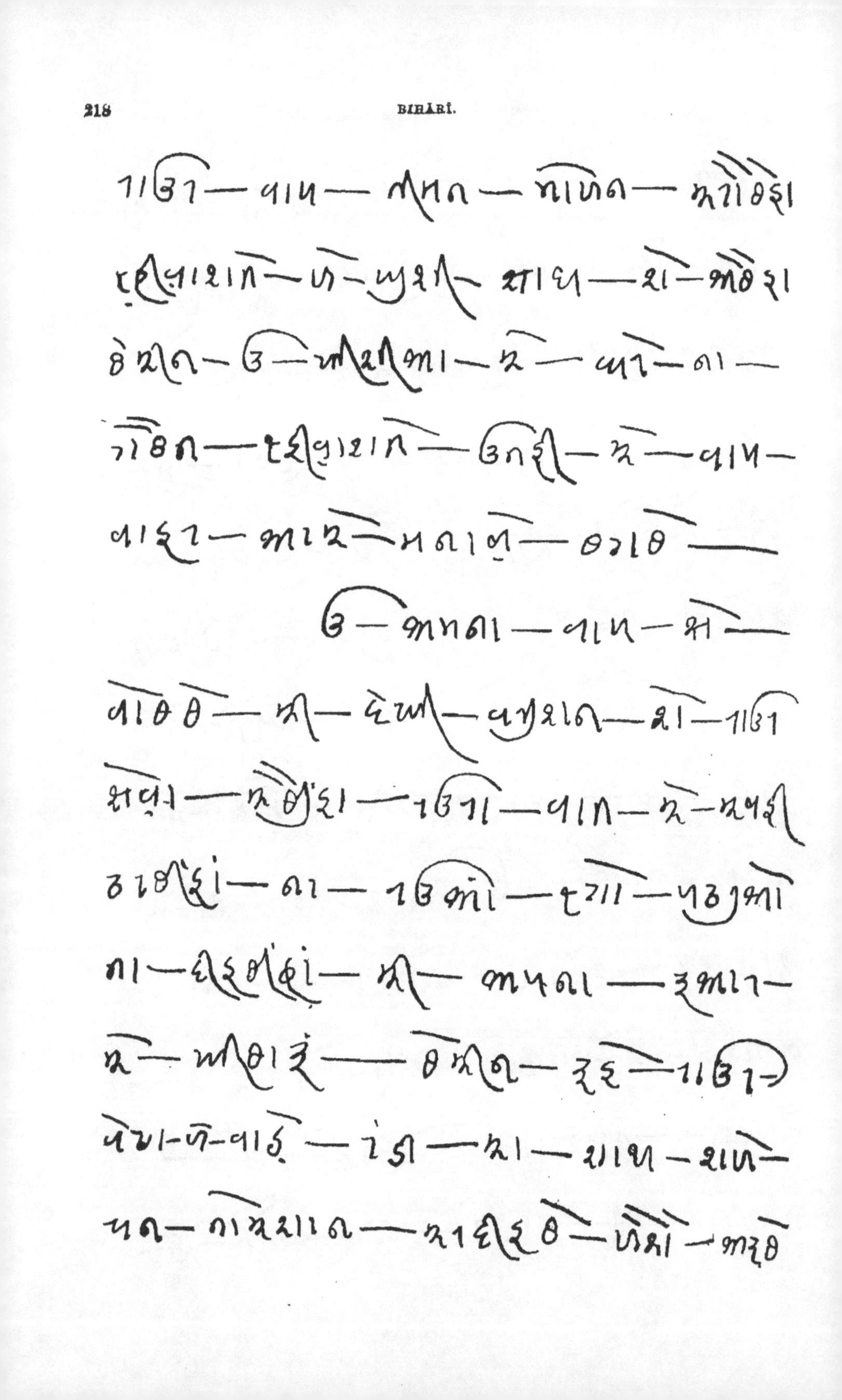

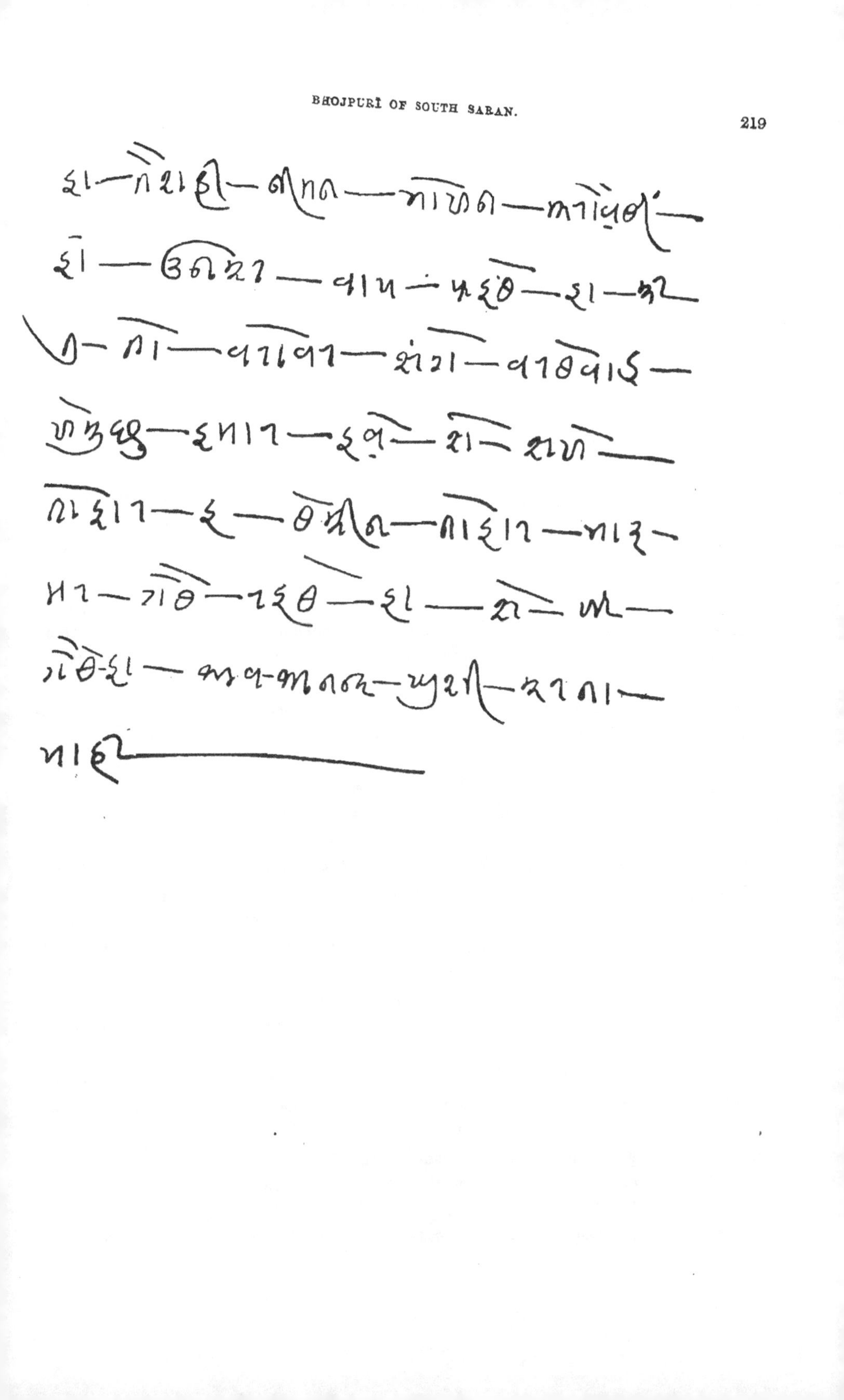

[No. 41.]

INDO-ARYAN FAMILY. EASTERN GROUP.

BIHARĪ.

BHOJPURĪ DIALECT. (DISTRICT SARAN.)

SPECIMEN I.

TRANSLITERATION AND TRANSLATION.

(*Babu Girindra-nāth Dutt, 1898.*)

Ek ad'mī kōī rahē. Ok'rā dui-gō bēṭā rahē. Choṭ'kā bāp-sē ap'nā
A man certain was. To-him two sons were. The-younger the-father-to his-own
kah'las kī, 'dhan hamār ādhā bā̃ṭ-dā.' Ōkar bāp dhan
said that, 'the-wealth my half dividing-give.' His father the-wealth
bā̃ṭ-dīhal. Thōrē din-mē chhoṭ'kā babuā dhan ekaṭṭhā kar-ke
dividing-gave. A-few days-in the-younger son the-wealth together having-made
bah'rā chal-gailē. Ohā̃ gailē luchābājī-mē sajē dhan
forth went-away. There he-went in-riotous-living the-entire wealth
uṛāe-dih'lē. Sajē dhan un-kar sadh-gail, tab baṛā
he-squandered. The-entire wealth his spent-was, then a-great
akāl paral oh dēs-mō. Garīb hōe-gailē, ō jini-kēhu kīhā̃
famine fell that country-in. Poor he-became, and somebody near
rahe lag'lē. Ihē kah'lē kī, 'khēt-mē sūar charāwā.' Suariā-ke
to-dwell began. This-one said that, 'the-field-in swine feed.' The-swine-of
ḍhẽṛhī jē khāe-kē rahē, sē ap'ne lag'lē khāe.
the-husks which eating-for were, those he-himself began to-eat.
Kēhu kuchhu dēt nā rahē. Tab un-kā akil khulal, ū kah'lē
Anyone anything giving not was. Then his senses opened, he said
kī, 'ham'rā bāp-ke majūrā-lōg-ke ḍhēr rōṭī bā̃ch jā-lā. Ab ham
that, 'my father's servant-people-of much bread surplus goes. Now I
bhūkhē muat-bānī. Ham ap'nā bāp kīhā̃ uṭh-ke jāib. Un-kā-sē
of-hunger dying-am. I my-own father near having-risen will-go. Him-to
jāe-ke kahab kī, "ham baṛā pāp kailī̃ Baikunṭh-kā, adhikā raūrā
having-gone I-will-say that, "I great sin did Heaven-of, moreover Your-Honour
sām'nē. Rāur bēṭā kahāwe lāek naīkhī̃. Hē bāp,
before. Your-Honour's son to-be-called fit I-am-not. O father,
ham'rā-kē ē-gō banihārē-kē sāmān jānī̃." ' Tab ap'nā bāp-kanē
me one servant-to equal consider." ' Then his-own father-near
gailē. Phailāwā̃ rah'lē tāīs-hī bāp-kē chhōh lāgal.
he-went. At-a-distance he-was then-even the-father-to compassion was-attached.

Dawar-ke kōrā-mē dhaï-ke chūmā dēwe lag^{a}lē. Bēṭā kah^{a}lan kī, 'hē bāp, ham
Running lap-in seizing kisses to-give he-began. The-son said that, 'O father, I
sar^{a}g-ke kām raürā āgē nā kailī̃-hā̃, raürā āgē
heaven-of duty Your-Honour's before not have-done, Your-Honour's before
pāp kailī̃-hā̃. Ab pher raürā bēṭā kahāwe lāek nā rah^{a}lī̃.'
sin have-done. Now again Your-Honour's son to-be-called fit not I-was.'
Lēkin ō-kar bāp kah^{a}lan nōkar-kē kī, 'nīman kap^{a}ṛā
But his father said the-servants-to that, 'excellent clothes
nikāl-ke pahire-kē dâ: log^{a}ni in-kā-ke hāth-mē ãguṭhī
having-brought-out wearing-for give: you-people his hand-on a-ring
pahirā-dâ, gōr-mē jutā pahirā-dâ. Ham^{a}nī khāī̃, khusī karī̃. Kāhe
put-on, feet-on shoe put-on. (Let) us eat, happiness make. Because
kī hamār bēṭā mar-gail-rah^{a}lē-hā, tâ jī-gailē-hā; bhulā-gail-rah^{a}lē-hā,
that my son had-died, indeed has-lived; had-been-lost,
sē milal-hā.' Tab khusī kare lag^{a}lē-hā.
he has-been-found.' Then happiness to-make they-began.

Un-kar jēṭh bēṭā khēt-mē rah^{a}lē. Ghar-kā nagich ailē, tab
His elder son field-in was. The-house-of near he-came, then
nāch bājā un-kā kān-sē sunāil. Ap^{a}nā nōkar-mē-sē
dancing music his ears-by were-heard. His-own servants-in-from
balāe-ke puchh^{a}lē kī, 'hō, ī kawan tamāsā hōt-bāṭē?' Ū
having-called he-asked that, 'ho, this what strange-thing is-occurring?' He
kah^{a}lan kī, 'rāur bhāī ailē-hā. Rāur bāp nīman
said that, 'Your-Honour's brother has-come. Your-Honour's father excellent
bhōjan karaulē-hā, ehi-wāstē jē khusī sāth sē ailē-
dinner has-caused-to-be-made, this-on-account-of that happiness with he has-
hā.' Lēkin ū khisiā-ke gharē nā gailan. Ehi-wāstē
come.' But he being-angry in-the-house not went. This-on-account-of
unhi-ke bāp bāhar ā-ke manāwe lag^{a}lē. Ū ap^{a}nā bāp-sē
his father outside having-come to-appease began. He his-own father-to
bol^{a}lē kī, 'dēkhī̃, barisan-sē rāur sēwā kailī̃-hā̃; raürā
said that, 'see, years-from Your-Honour's service I-have-done; Your-Honour's
bāt-kē kab^{a}hī ṭar^{a}lī̃-hā̃ nā. Raüā̃ ē-gō paṭharu-ō nā dih^{a}lī̃-
word ever I-have-disobeyed not. Your-Honour a-single kid-even not has-
hā̃, kī ap^{a}nā iār-kē khilāī̃. Lēkin ihē rāur
given, that my-own friends-to I-may-give-to-eat. But this Your-Honour's
bēṭā jē bāṛē, raṇḍi-kā sāth sajē dhan nok^{a}sān kar-dih^{a}lē, jaisē
son who is, harlots-of with the-entire wealth destruction has-made, just-as
ailē-hā täis^{a}hī nīman bhōjan karaulī̃-hā̃.'
he-has-come at-that-very-time an-excellent dinner thou-hast-caused-to-be-made.'
Un-kar bāp kah^{a}lē-hā kī, 'tū tō barōbar sangē bar^{a}lē-bāṛâ;
His father said that, 'thou indeed always with-(me) remainest;

jē-kuchhu hamār hâwē, sē sajē tohâr hâ. Lēkin tohār
whatever mine is, that entire thine is. But thy
bhāī mar-gail-rah[a]lē-hā, sē jī-gailē-hā, ab anand khusī kar[a]nā
brother had-died, he has-lived, now rejoicing happiness making
chāhī.'
is-proper.'

INDO-ARYAN FAMILY. EASTERN GROUP.

BIHĀRĪ

BHOJPURĪ DIALECT. (DISTRICT SARAN.)

SPECIMEN II.

(*Babu Girindra-nāth Dutt, 1898.*)

એગો સિઆર રહલે, એગો ગાએ રખલે રહલે । ત ઉનકર જાત લોગ પુછલ એ ભાઈ કૈસે મોટાઇલ બાડ़, કહલન કી હમ ફજિરે કા બેરા મુંહ ધોઈલે, એક ગાલ રોજો આંકર ચબાઈલે, ગંગાજી કે પાની એક ચિરુઆ પીલે, દાંત ભહરાગૈલ । સિઆર લોગ કહલે કી દાંત હમાર તુર દિહલન । ચલ ચોદનીકરો કે મારીં । ગૈલ લોગ તો ના ભેટાઇલ । ઓકર જાતિઆ ગૈઇએ કે મુઆ દિહલે ।

TRANSLITERATION AND TRANSLATION.

Ē-gō siār rah^ə^lē. Ē-gō gāe rakh^ə^lē-rah^ə^lē. Tâ un-kar
A jackal there-was. A cow he-used-to-keep. Then his

jāt-lōg puchhal, 'ē bhāī, kaisē moṭāil bāṛâ?' Kah^ə^lan kī, 'ham
caste-people asked, 'o brother, how fattened are-you?' He-said that, 'I

phajire-kā bērā mũh dhōī-lē, ēk gāl rōj-ō ā̃kar chabāī-lē,
morning-of at-the-hour face wash, one mouthful daily-also gravel I-chew,

Gaṅgā-jī ke pānī ēk chiruā pī-lē, dā̃t bhah^ə^rā-gail.' Siār-lōg kah^ə^lē
Ganges of water one handful I-drink, teeth have-fallen-out.' The-jackal-people said

kī, 'dā̃t hamār tūr-dih^ə^lan. Chalâ chodanikarō-kē mārī̃.' Gail lōg. Tō
that, 'teeth of-us he-broke. Come the-vile-one let-us-kill.' Went the-people. Then

nā bhēṭāil. Ō-kar jatiā gaiiē-kē muā-dih^ə^lē.
not they-found-him. His caste-fellows the-cow killed.

FREE TRANSLATION OF THE FOREGOING.

There was once upon a time a jackal who kept a cow (and lived upon its milk). Then the other jackals, his caste-fellows, asked him, saying, 'O brother, how have you got so fat?' He replied, 'every morning I wash my face. Every day I also chew a mouthful of gravel, and drink a handful of Ganges water. The result is that my teeth have all dropped out.'[1] The other jackals said, 'this fellow has broken our teeth.[2] Come, let us kill the base one.' They went (to look for him), but could not find him. So the jackals, his caste-fellows, killed the cow.

---

[1] The jackal is chaffing them. His tribe is notorious for impiety. He pretends that he has got so fat, not by drinking the milk of the cow, but by pious practices. He lives upon the purest food, and as he no longer requires to eat flesh, his teeth have dropped out as useless incumbrances. The absence of his teeth he puts forth as an additional proof of his piety.

[2] *Anglice*, he has pulled our legs.

NORTHERN STANDARD BHOJPURĪ.

This form of speech slightly differs from the true Standard Bhojpurī with which we have just been dealing. It may be called the speech of the Doab of the Gandak and the Gogra, omitting the tract of country immediately opposite Shahabad. This Doab includes the Districts of Saran, Gorakhpur and Basti, and the language varies slightly as we go north-west. The language of Central and North Saran, and of a portion of Tahsil Deoria in Gorakhpur, may be considered the model of the south-eastern part of this tract.

It has well-marked peculiarities which deserve notice. As we go further north, into Gorakhpur, we find two distinct sub-dialects, that to the east being commonly known as Gorakhpurī; and that to the west as Sarwariā. The latter extends still further to the west, and covers the whole of the Basti District, being, if we except the Thārū dialects of Gonda and Bahraich, the extreme north-western outpost of Bihārī. The eastern dialect of Gorakhpur, or Gorakhpurī, differs only slightly from that of Central and Northern Saran. All these various forms of speech will be found on the map facing page 1.

The following are the approximate figures for the population speaking the various forms of Northern Standard Bhojpurī :—

Name of District.	Approximate population speaking Northern Standard Bhojpurī.
Saran	1,404,500
Gorakhpur, Northern Standard Bhojpurī of Deoria, about .	100,000
„ Gorakhpurī	1,307,500
„ Sarwariā	1,569,307
Basti, Sarwariā	1,783,844
Total .	6,165,151

The dialect spoken in Central and North Saran is fully explained in the Bhojpurī Grammar of the present writer. It will suffice to mention a few of the principal points in which it differs from the Standard Bhojpurī of Shahabad.

I.—NOUNS—

The plural is sometimes formed by adding the syllable *sá*. Thus *ghōṛā-sá*, horses. In Standard Bhojpurī it is more usual to employ this suffix with verbs than with nouns.

II.—PRONOUNS—

Besides *ham*, I, *hamē* is also used. Besides the standard forms for 'this', Saran has also *haī*, genitive *hē-kar*, oblique form *hē* or *hek*ᵉ*rā*. Similarly, for 'that', we find *haū*, *heū*, *haūē*, *heuhē*, or *ūhē*, with a genitive, *hō-kar*, and an oblique form *hō* or *hok*ᵉ*rā*. For 'anyone', we sometimes meet *kōī*, and for the adjective 'what' *kauan*.

III.—VERBS—

A.—Auxiliary Verbs.

The Verb Substantive *bāṛē*, he is, often takes the form *bāṭē* in all districts north of the Ganges, though the form *bāṛē* is also used. We thus get forms like *bāṭī̃*, or *bānī̃*, I am; *bāṭá*, you are, and so on.

B.—Finite Verbs.

Simple Present.—Optional forms used in Saran are, 2nd Sing., *dekhuē, dekhues*; 3rd Sing., *dēkhuē, dēkhai*; 3rd Plur., *dēkhen*.

Past.—This, as has been remarked in the case of the Palamau specimens, besides having a form whose characteristic letter is *l*, has also a form whose characteristic letter is *u*. The following are the optional forms of this tense in use in Saran. 2nd Sing., *dekhᵃles, dekhuē*; 3rd Sing., *dekhuē*; 1st Plur., *dekhuī̃*; 2nd Plur., *dekhuāh, dekhuā*; 3rd Plur., *dekhᵃlen, dekhuan*.

The following forms in use in Saran are due to the influence of the Maithilī spoken to the east of the Gaṇḍak.

1st person,—ham dekhᵃliyaīn. Only used when the object of the verb is in the third person and special respect is shown to it. Thus, *ham rājā-kē dekhᵃliyaīn*, I saw His Majesty the King.

Ham dekhᵃliyāwā. Only used when the object of the verb is in the second person, and special respect is shown to it. Thus, *ham raūrā-kē dekhᵃliyāwā*, I saw your Honour.

2nd person, tū̃ dekhᵃlahus. Only used when contempt is shown to the object in the third person. Thus, *tū̃ maliyā-kē dekhᵃlahus*, you saw the wretched gardener.

Tū̃ dekhᵃlahun. Only used when respect is shown to the object in the third person. Thus, *tū̃ rājā-kē dekhᵃlahun*, you saw His Majesty.

Past Conditional.—2nd Sing., *dekhᵃtes*. 3rd Plur., *dekhᵃten*.

Generally speaking, Saran uses the suffixes *hā*, *hā*, *hā̃*, *hā̃*, etc., much more freely than Shahabad. They appear in all the Past tenses, and not only in the Perfect and Pluperfect. Thus, the Imperfect may be *ham-dēkhat rahᵃlī̃ hā̃*, I was seeing.

The characteristic feature of the Saran dialect is the use of the Past Tense with *u*, instead of that with *l*. This peculiarity extends to the Deoria Tahsil of Gorakhpur, but is not met with elsewhere in that district.

The following specimen comes from Deoria; note the frequent use of this *u*-Past. One or two forms may also be noted which properly belong to the Western Bhojpurī spoken across the Gogra. Such are the Instrumental in *an* as in *bhūkhan*, by hunger, and the third person in *aī̃*, as in *rahuaī̃*, they were. It has not been thought necessary to give an interlinear translation.

[No. 43.]

INDO-ARYAN FAMILY. EASTERN GROUP.

BIHĀRĪ.

BHOJPURĪ DIALECT. (DEORIA, GORAKHPUR DISTRICT.)

(Pandit Murli-dhar Nāgar, 1898.)

एक अदिमी के दुइ क्वँवड़ रहुऐं। उन्हन में से लहुरका कहुए की ए काका घर के धन में जवन हमरा बखरा होखे तवन दे दीं। ऊ आपन सगरी धन उन्हन कें बाँटि दिहुए। थोरै दिन भउए की लहुरका क्वँवड़ा सगरी धन अपने पाले लि-के बड़े लम्मे बहरा चलि गउए। उहवाँ सगरी धन बदमासी में लुटा दिहुए। जब सगरी धन ओरा गउए तं ओ देस में अकाल परुए। गरीब हो गउए। तं ओ देस के एगो बसिन्ना केहाँ रंहे लगुए। ऊ ओकरा के सूअरि चरावे के अपना खेत में भेजि दिहुए। ओकरा मन में अउए की सूअरि जवन छाल खातारीं ओही से आपन पेट भरतीं। अवर केहु ओकरा के खाये के ना देत रहुए। तं ऊ होस करुए आ कहुए की हमरा बाप कीहाँ दुकेतना बनिहार के खाये से अधिक रोटी मिलतारें आ हम भूखन मरतानी। हम अपना बाप के लगे उठि के जाब आ उनका से कहबि की हे बाप हम भगवान आगी आ तोहरी हजूर में बाउर काम कइले बानीं। हम तोहरा क्वँवड़ कहावे लायक ना बानीं। हमरा के अपने बनिहारन में एक के तरे राखीं। तब उठि के अपने बाप के लगें चलुए। अबहीं फरकहीं रहुए की उन के बाप के उनका देखि के छोह लगुए। आ दवरि के गर में गर मिला लिहुए। चुमुए चटुए। तं क्वँवड़ा कहुए की हे बाप हम अपने भगवान के उलटा आ तोहरा अगाड़ी बाउर काम कइले बानीं। अब ए लायक ना बानीं की तोहरा क्वँवड़ कहाईं। लेकिन बाप अपने नोकर चाकर से कहुए की खूब बढ़ियाँ कपड़ा निकारि इनकरा के पहिरावं आ हाथ में अँगूठी और गोड़ में जूता पहिरावं अवर सुख से खाईं। काहे से की हमरा बेटा मूअल रहुए अब जी गउए। भुलाइल रहुए मिलि गउए। तब सब केहु खुसी करे लगुऐं।

उन के वड़का क्वँवड़ा खेत में रहुए। जब घर के लग अउए तं बाजा आ नाँच के अवाज सुनुए। आ ऊ अपने नोकर में से एगो कें बुला के पुछुए, ई का है। तं लोग बतउलें की तोहरा भाई अइलें हँ। तोहरा बाप आछा २ खियउलें हउअनि। काहे की उनका सब तरे आछा पउलें। लेकिन ऊ खिसिया गउए आ भीतर ना आवे चहुए। तं उनका बाप बहरा हो के मनावे लगुए। ऊ बाप के जबाब दिहुए की देखं हम एतना दिन से तोहार खिजमति करतानी आ कवनो तोहरा हुकुम ना टरईं। बाकी तूँ कवहीं एको भेंरी के बाचा ना दिहुअ की अपने सँघातियन के संगी खुसी खइतीं पियतीं। लेकिन तोहरा बेटा जे हरजाइन में तोहरा धन माटी मिला दिहुए जवना घरी ऊ अउए ओही घरी रवाँ आछा भोजन कइईं। बाप कहलनि कीं तूँ सब दिना हमरा लगें बाड़ आ जवन हमरा है तवन तोहरा है। लेकिन खुसी करे के अवर खुस होखे के जरूर चाही काहे से की ई तोहार भाई मूअल रहुए से जी गउए भुलाइल रहुए से मिलि गउए ॥

[No. 43.]

INDO-ARYAN FAMILY. EASTERN GROUP.

BIHĀRĪ.

BHOJPURĪ DIALECT. (DEORIA, GORAKHPUR DISTRICT.)

TRANSLITERATION.

(Pandit Murli-dhar Nāgar, 1898.)

Ēk adimī-kē dui chhā̃waṛ rahuaī̃. Unhan-mē̃-sē lahurᵃkā kahuē kī 'ē kākā, ghar-ke dhan-mē̃ jawan hamār bakhᵃrā hōkhai tawan dē-dī̃.' Ū āpan sagᵃrī dhan unhan-kē̃ bā̃ṭi dihuē. Thōrai din bhaüē kī lahurᵃkā chhā̃wᵃṛā sagᵃrī dhan apᵃne pālē lē-ke baṛē lammē bahᵃrā chali gaüē. Uhᵃwā̃ sagᵃrī dhan badᵃmāsī-mē̃ luṭā dihuē. Jab sagᵃrī dhan orā gaüē, tâ ō dēs-mē̃ akāl paruē; garīb hō gaüē. Tâ ō dēs ke ēgō basinnā kehā̃ rahe laguē. Ū okᵃrā-kē sūari charāwe-kē apᵃnā khēt-mē̃ bhēji dihuē. Okᵃrā man-mē̃ aüē kī 'sūari jawan chhāl khātārī̃ ōhī-sē āpan pēṭ bharᵃtī̃.' Awar kēhu okᵃrā-kē khāye-kē nā dēt rahuē. Tâ ū hōs karuē, ā kahuē kī 'hamᵃrā bāp kihā̃ duketᵃnā banihār-kē khāye-sē adhik rōṭī milᵃtāraī̃ ā ham bhūkhan marᵃtānī. Ham apᵃnā bāp-ke lagē uṭhi-ke jāb ā unᵃkā-sē kahabi kī, "hē bāp ham Bhagᵃwān āgē ā tohᵃrī hajūr-mē̃-bāur kām kaïlē-bānī̃. Ham tohᵃrā chhā̃waṛ kahāwe lāyak nā bānī̃. Hamᵃrā-kē apᵃne banihāran-mē̃ ēk-ke-tarē rākhī̃."' Tab uṭhi-ke apᵃne bāp-kē lagē̃ chaluē. Abᵃhī̃ pharᵃkahī̃ rahuē kī un-ke bāp-kē un-kā dēkhi-ke chhōh laguē. Ā dawaṛi-ke gar-mē̃ gar milā lihuē, chumuē chaṭuē. Tâ chhā̃wᵃṛā kahuē kī, 'hē bāp ham apᵃne Bhagᵃwān-ke ulᵃṭā ā tohᵃrā agāṛī bāur kām kailē bānī̃. Ab ē lāyak nā-bānī̃ kī tohᵃra chhā̃waṛ kahāī̃.' Lēkin bāp apᵃne nōkar chākar-sē kahuē kī 'khūb baṛhiyā̃ kapᵃṛā nikāri in-karā-kē pahirāwâ ā hāth-mē̃ ā̃gūṭhī̃ aur gōṛ-mē̃ jūtā pahirāwâ, awar sukh-sē khāī̃ kāhe-sē kī hamᵃrā bēṭā mūal rahuē, ab jī gaüē; bhulāil rahuē, mili gaüē.' Tab sab kēhu khusī kare laguaī̃.

Un-ke baṛᵃkā chhā̃wᵃṛā khēt-mē̃ rahuē. Jab ghar ke lag aüē tâ bājā ā nā̃ch ke awāj sunuē ā ū apᵃne nōkar-mē̃ sē ēgō-kē̃ bulā-ke puchhuē, 'ī kā hai?' Tâ lōg bataülaī̃ kī 'tohᵃrā bhāī aïlaī̃-hā̃. Tohᵃrā bāp āchhā āchhā khiyaülaī̃ haüani kāhe-kī un-kā sab tarē āchhā paülaī̃.' Lēkin ū khisiyā gaüē ā bhītar nā āwe chahuē. Tâ unᵃkā bāp bahᵃrā hō-ke manāwe laguē. Ū bāp-kē jabāb dihuē kī 'dēkhâ ham etᵃnā din-sē tohār khijᵃmati karᵃtānī ā kawᵃnō tohᵃrā hukum nā ṭaruī̃. Bākī tū̃ kabᵃhī̃ ēkō bhē̃rī-ke bāchā nā dihuà kī apᵃne sā̃ghᵃtiyan ke saṅgē khusī khaïtī̃ piyatī̃. Lēkin tohᵃrā bēṭā jē harᵃjāin-mē̃ tohᵃrā dhan māṭī milā dihuē, jawᵃnā gharī ū aüē, ōhī gharī rawā̃ āchhā bhōjan karuī̃.' Bāp kahᵃlani kī 'tū̃ sab dinā hamᵃrā lagē̃ bāṛâ, ā jawan hamᵃrā hai tawan tohᵃrā hai. Lēkin khusī kare-kē awar khus hōkhe-kē jarūr chāhī kāhe-sē kī ī tohār bhāī mūal rahuē, sē jī gaüē; bhulāil rahuē, sē mili gaüē.'

GORAKHPURĪ.

Although the preceding specimen comes from the Gorakhpur District, it should not be taken as a sample of its language. It is only spoken in the south-east corner, in a small portion of Tahsīl Deoria, and is really an example of the dialect of the north-west of Saran. As we go north and west from this point, the use of the letter *u* in the Past Tense of verbs is abandoned, and we find a return to the letter *l* as in the South Saran and Shahabad. Omitting from consideration this small overflow of dialect from Saran, we find two kinds of Bhojpurī spoken in Gorakhpur, separated by a line running nearly north and south through the centre of the District. To the east of that line, the language is the ordinary Bhojpurī of North-West Bihar, except that the *u*-form of the Past Tense is not used. To the west of that line, the local dialect is that known elsewhere as Sarwariā which is also spoken in the adjoining District of Basti, and which will be dealt with later on.

As regards the Bhojpurī of the east of the District, it is, to speak more definitely, the language of the two Tahsīls of Padrauna and of Deoria and of about two-thirds of the Tahsīl of Hata. The language of the rest of the District is Sarwariā. The population figures of the District may be estimated as follows :—

Northern Standard Bhojpurī . . .	1,407,500	(including about 100,000 speakers of the Saran Dialect.)
Sarwariā	1,569,307	
Eastern Hindi (spoken by middle class Musalmans)	9,989	
Urdū (spoken by educated Musalmans) . .	6,204	
Other languages	1,057	
TOTAL .	2,994,057	

These figures take no account of the secret languages spoken by wandering tribes of Ḍōms and Naṭs, which have not been separated out in the local return. The languages spoken by Ḍōms and Naṭs are not of importance, and specimens will be given from other Districts.

AUTHORITIES—

A brief sketch of the local form of Bhojpurī will be found on p. 372 of the District Gazetteer. The language is generally described by Dr. Buchanan Hamilton, in vol. II of Montgomery Martin's *Eastern Indian* on p. 429.

Two specimens of the dialect spoken in Eastern Gorakhpur are here given. The first is a version of the Parable of the Prodigal Son. It is printed in the Kaithī character, and is a facsimile of the writing in current use in the District. A transliteration has also been given, but, after the other translated specimens, it has been considered useless to give an interlinear translation. The second specimen is a piece of folk-lore showing how the jackal outwitted the alligator. It is interesting to note that the incidents closely correspond to the adventures of 'Brer Tarpin' and of 'Brer Rabbit and Brer Wolf' in the Negro stories of Uncle Remus. In this case an interlinear translation as well as a free paraphrase has been given.

As might be expected, there are a few local peculiarities in the dialect. The one which most prominently strikes the eye is the method adopted for writing the broad *á*-sound, which is so marked a feature of Bhojpurī. It is represented by writing the letter *a* twice. Thus *aa*. Examples are *daa* for *dá*, *laa* for *lá*, *pahirāwaa* for *pahirāwá*, and many others. The only other point regarding pronunciation which is worthy of note is that the letter *r* is preferred to *ṛ*. Thus we have *paral*, it fell, instead of *paṛal*.

Instead of *tekªrā*, the oblique form of *sē*, he, we find *sekªra*. Instead of *kuchhu*, we find *kuchh*.

As usual in the North-Gangetic Districts, forms like *bāṭē* and the like are preferred to the southern *bāṛē*, he is. The form with *ṛ*, is, however, also used. There is a third person plural *bānẽ*, they are, or, honorifically, he is, which is based on the optional form of the first person, *bānī̃*.

There is a third person plural in *ẽ*, which has been borrowed from the trans-Gogra *aĩ* previously alluded to, see p. 225. Thus, *rahªlẽ*, they were. It has a feminine in *ī̃*, as in *kahªlī̃*, she said, used honorifically. It should be noted that, in the second specimen, *nāki*, the word translated 'alligator,' is feminine. Hence the verbs which it governs are in the feminine gender.

Another instance of borrowing from the trans-Gogra dialect is the use of the Instrumental case in *an*, in *bhūkhan*, by hunger.

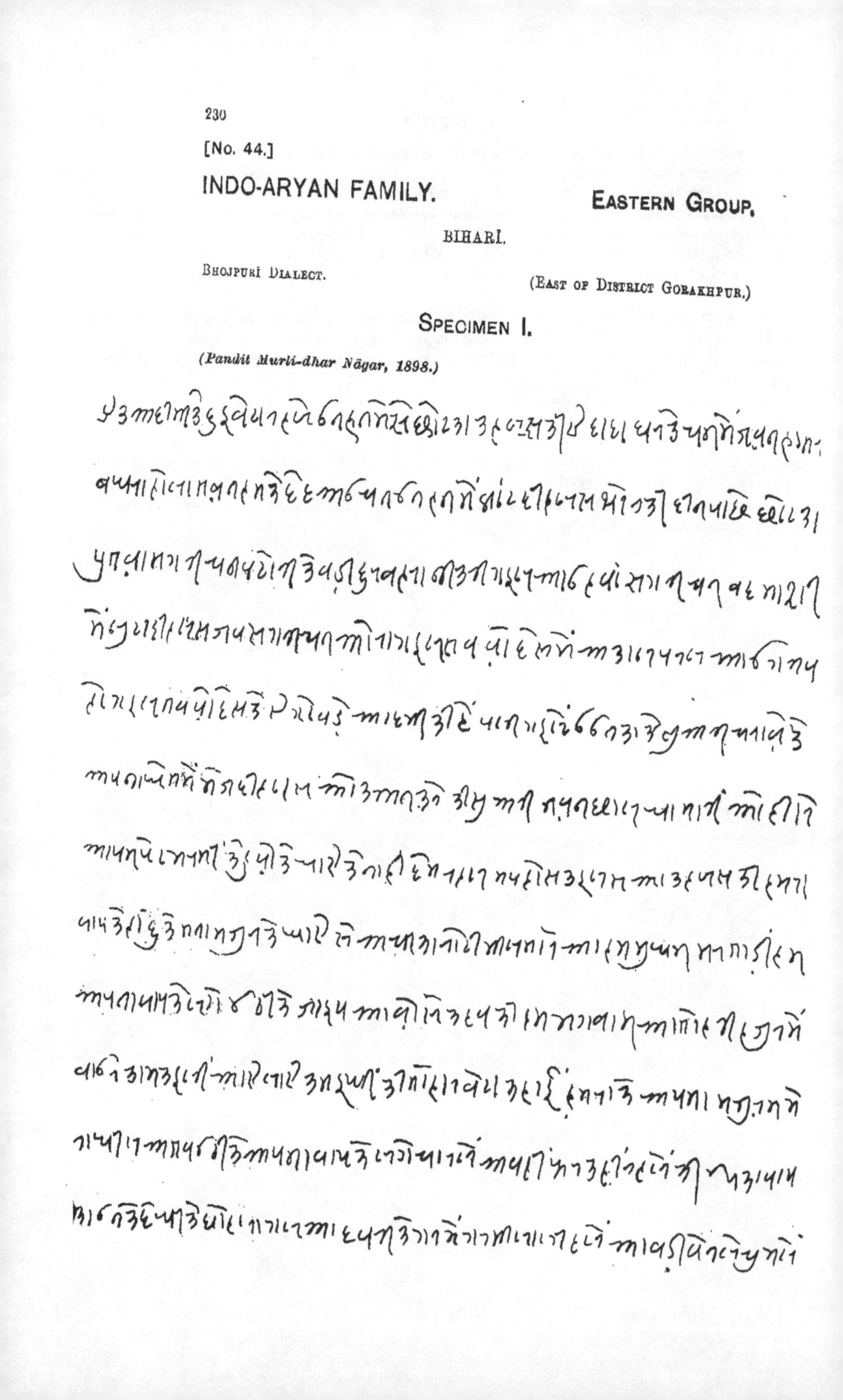

[No. 44.]

INDO-ARYAN FAMILY.

EASTERN GROUP.

BIHARI.

BHOJPURI DIALECT.

(EAST OF DISTRICT GORAKHPUR.)

SPECIMEN I.

(Pandit Murli-dhar Nāgar, 1898.)

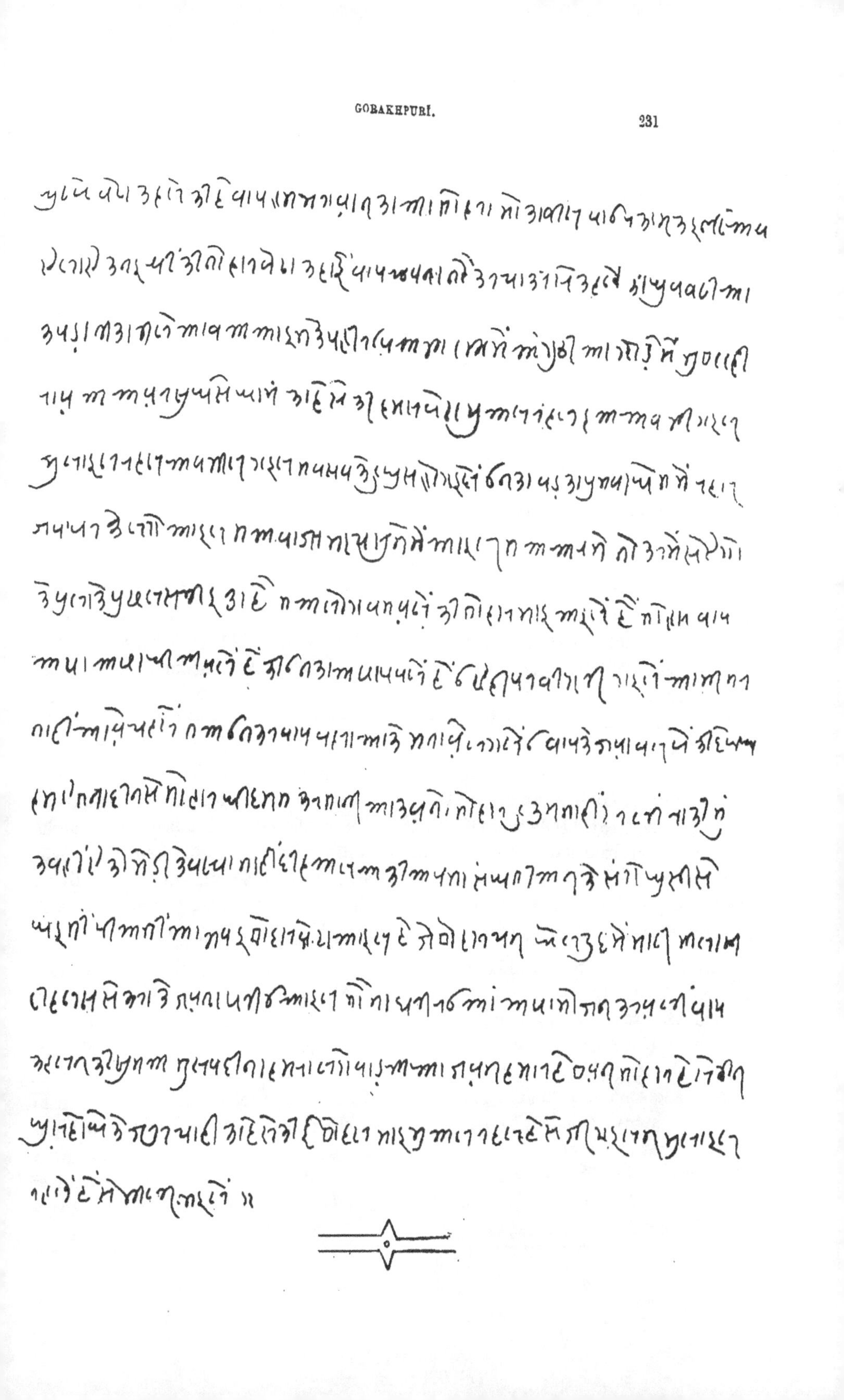

[No. 44.]

INDO-ARYAN FAMILY. EASTERN GROUP.

BIHĀRĪ.

BHOJPURĪ DIALECT. (EAST OF DISTRICT GORAKHPUR.)

SPECIMEN I.

TRANSLITERATION.

(Paṇḍit Murli-dhar Nāgar, 1898.)

Ēk adimī-kē dui bēṭā rahᵃlẽ. Unhan-mẽ-sē chhoṭᵃkā kahᵃlas kī, 'ē dādā ghar-ke dhan-mẽ jawan hamār bakhᵃrā hō-lā tawan ham-kē dē-dâ.' Ū dhan unhan-mẽ bā̃ṭ dihᵃlas. Thorᵃkī din pāchhē chhoṭᵃkā putᵃwā sagᵃrī dhan baṭōri-ke baṛī dūr bahᵃrā nikari gaïl. Ā uhᵃwā̃ sagarī dhan badᵃmāsī-mẽ luṭā dihᵃlas. Jab sagᵃrī dhan orā gaïl tab ō dēs-mẽ akāl paral ā ū garīb hō-gaïl. Tab ō dēs-ke ēgō baṛē adimī kīhẽ chali gaïlẽ. Ū unkā-kē sūari charāwe-kē apᵃnā khēt-mẽ bhēj dihᵃlas. Ōkar man karē kī sūari jawan chhāl khātārī̃ ōhī-sē āpan pēṭ bharᵃtī̃.' Kēhū ō-kē khāe-kē nāhī̃ dēt rahal. Tab hōs kaïlas, ā kahᵃlas kī, 'hamᵃrā bāp kehā̃ du-ketᵃnā majūr-kē khāe-sē adhikā rōṭī milᵃtārē̃ ā ham bhūkhan marᵃtāṛī̃. Ham apᵃnā bāp-ke lagē uṭhi-ke jāïb ā ō-sē kahab kī "ham Bhagᵃwān ā toharī hajūr-mẽ bāur kām kaïlī̃, ā ē lāek naïkhī̃ kī tohār bēṭā kahāī̃. Hamᵃrā-kē apᵃnā majūran-mẽ rākhi-lâ."' Tab uṭhi-ke apᵃnā bāp-ke lagē chalᵃlẽ. Ab-hī̃ pharᵃkahī̃ rahᵃlẽ kī un-kā bāp-kā un-kē dēkhi-ke chhōh lāgal ā dauri-ke gar-mẽ gar milā lihᵃlẽ, ā baṛī bēr lē chumᵃlẽ chuṭᵃlẽ. Bēṭā kahᵃlẽ kī, 'hē bāp ham Bhagᵃwān kā ā tohᵃrā mokābil bāur kām kailī̃ ab ē lāek naïkhī̃ kī tohār bēṭā kahāī̃.' Bāp apᵃnā nōkar chākar-sē kahᵃlẽ kī, 'khūb baṛhiā kapᵃṛā nikāri lē-āwâ ā inᵃkē pahirāwâ. Jā hāth-mẽ ā̃guṭhī ā gōṛē-mẽ jūtā pahirāwâ, awar sukh-sē khāī̃. Kāhe-sē kī hamār bēṭā mūal rahal hâ, ab jī gaïl; bhulāil rahal, ab mil gaïl.' Tab sab kēhū khus hō gaïlẽ.

Un-kā[1] baṛᵃkā putᵃwā khēt-mẽ rahal. Jab ghar-ke lagē āil tâ bājā nāch sune-mẽ āil. Tâ apᵃnē nokar-mẽ-sē ēgō-kē bulā-ke puchhᵃlas kī 'ī kā hai?' Tâ lōg bataülẽ kī, 'tohār bhāī ailẽ haī̃. Tohār bāp achhā achhā khiaülẽ-hẽ, kī un-kā achhā paülẽ-hẽ.' Ū ehi par bigari gaïlẽ ā bhītar nāhī̃ āwe chahᵃlẽ. Tâ un-kā bāp bahᵃrā ā-ke manāwe lagᵃlẽ. Ū bāp-kē jabāb la(gaü)lẽ kī, 'dēkhâ, ham etᵃnā din-sē tohār khidᵃmat karᵃtānī ā kawᵃnō tohār hukum nāhī̃ ṭarᵃlī̃, bāki tū̃ kabᵃhī̃ ēkō bhẽṛī-ke bāchā nāhī̃ dihâ-lâ kī apᵃnā sā̃ghatian-ke saṅgē khusī-sē khaïtī̃ piatī̃. Ā jab ī tohār bēṭa āil-hē jē tohār dhan khēl kūd-mẽ māṭī milāy dihᵃlas sekᵃrā-kē jawᵃnā gharī ū āil taunā gharī raüā̃ achhā bhōjan karaülī̃.' Bāp kahᵃlan kī, 'sunâ, tū̃ sab dinā hamᵃrā lagē bāṛâ ā jawan hamār-hẹ tawan tohār-hē. Lēkin khus hōkhe-kē jarūr chāhī, kāhe-sē kī ī tohār bhāī mūal rahal-hē, sē jī gaïlan; bhulāil rahᵃlẽ-hẽ, sē mili-gaïlẽ.'

---

[1] Mistake for *un-ke*.

[No. 45.]

INDO-ARYAN FAMILY. EASTERN GROUP.

BIHĀRĪ.

BHOJPURĪ DIALECT. (EAST OF DISTRICT GORAKHPUR.)

SPECIMEN II.

(Pandit Murli-dhar Nāgar, 1898.)

एगो सियार आ एगो नाकि में बड़ी संघत रहल। रात दिन बरब्बर एक संगे लोग रहें। ना उन के ऊ बिसारें ना उन के ऊ छाड़ें। कुछ दिन एही तरे बीत गइल। एक बेर कवनो बात में बिगार हो गइल, आ बिगारो अइसन भइल की एक के देखे में एक नत्र। नाकि कहलीं की हे सियार तूँ हम से का लपटियाइल बाड़अ, तोहरे अइसन हम बीस जने के ठाढ़े लील जाईलें। सियार भरना दिहलें की तूँ का हअऊ। हम बड़े बड़े के देख लेइब। तोहरा देहिँ के जोर बा हमरा अकिल के बा। तोहरा से जवन बने तवन करिहअ। हम तोहरा के मना नइखीँ करत। हमरा के राम बानें। फिर एही तरे दूनो जने कलह कइ के आपन आपन राह लिहलें। नाकि नद्दी में चलि गइलीँ सियार बन में॥

नद्दी के तीरे एगो पीपर के पेड़ रहे। ओकर सोरि कुछ दूरि ले पानी में चलि गइल रहल आ कुछ ऊपर रहे। एक दिन सियार राम ओही सोरि पर बइठ के पानी पीयत रहलें। तब लेक नाकि देख लिहलस आ डुबलि डुबल आ के उन के गोड़ धइलस। सियार अपने मन में कहलस की नाकि तअ आपन दाँव लिहलसि अब कवन उपाय करीँ। फेर कहलें की, हे नाकि तूँ भल बाड़ू। धरे के गोड़ तअ धइलू हअ सोरि। बस नाकि गोड़ छोड़ि के सोरि हउहा के धइ लिहलीँ। सियार मुँह रिगावत भागि गइलें आ नाकि हाथ मलि के रहि गइलीँ॥

अब बयर अउरी बढ़ि गइल। एक दिन नाकि सियार के मानि में जा के बइठि गइलीँ। सियार अवते मह्ँकि से बूझि गइलें की नाकि बइठल बाड़ीँ। कहलें की हे भया हमार मानि गुँगुआत रहलि हअ। आजु काहे नइखीँ गुँगुआत। तब लेक नाकि गुँगुअइलीँ। सियार कहलें की अब हमार मानो लेहलू। अच्छा एही में रहअ आ ई कहि के चालि दिहलें आ मानि में के रहल छाँड़ि दिहलें॥

तब एगो पतई के गाँज में जे गोड़ बटोरेलन से रहे लगलें। नाकि जोह लगा के गाँजो में पहुँचलि। पीछे सियार अइलें। तअ गाँज के पतई खड़बड़ देखि के बूझि गइलें की एह में नाकि आ गइल बाटीँ। कहलें की हे भया आगे तअ हमार गाँज खरखरात रहल। आजु काहे नइखीँ खरखरात। तब ले नाकि पत्ता खरखरइबे तअ कइलीँ। सियार कहलें, अच्छा तअ बूझि गइलीँ। बस करअ, दउरल चलि-गइल। तनिकी एक आगि ले आ के गाँज फूँक दिहलें। नाकि ओही में भसम हो गइलीँ॥

अकिल के आगे जोर कुछ ना काम करेला॥

[No. 45.]

INDO-ARYAN FAMILY. EASTERN GROUP.

BIHĀRĪ.

BHOJPURĪ DIALECT. (EAST OF DISTRICT GORAKHPUR.)

SPECIMEN II.

TRANSLITERATION AND TRANSLATION.

(Pandit Murli-dhar Nāgar, 1898.)

Ēgō siyār ā ēgō nāki-mẽ baṛī saṅghat rahal. Rāt din barabbar
One jackal and one alligator-in great friendship was. Night day always
ēk-saṅgē lōg rahẽ. Nā un-kē ū bisārẽ nā un-kē ū chhāṛẽ. Kuchh
together (these-)people lived. Not her he forgets not him she leaves. Some
din ēhī tarē bīt-gail. Ēk bēr kaw̃ᵃnō bāt-mẽ bigār
days in-this-very way passed. One time some thing-in enmity
hō-gail. Ā bigār-ō aïsan bhail ki ēk-kē
took-place. And the-enmity-also of-such-a-nature became that one
dēkhe-mẽ ēk nâ. Nāki kahᵃlī̃ ki, 'hē siyār, tū̃
seeing-in the-other not.[1] The-alligator said that, 'O jackal, you
ham-sē kā lapᵃṭiyāil bāṛâ? Tohᵃr-ē aïsan ham bīs janē-kē ṭhāṛhē
me-with why entangled are?[2] Thee like I twenty individuals standing
līl-jāī-lẽ.' Siyār bharᵃnā-dihᵃlẽ ki, 'tū̃ kā
(i.e. entirely) am-accustomed to-eat-up.' The-jackal staked-the-word that, 'you what
hâū? Ham baṛē baṛē-kē dēkh-lēib.[3] Tohᵃrā dẽhi-ke jōr bā, hamᵃrā akil-
are? I great-men great-men will-see. Thine body-of strength is, mine wisdom-
ke bā. Tohᵃrā-sē jawan banē tawan karihâ. Ham tohᵃrā-kē manā
of is. You-by what can-be-done that you-may-do. I you-to forbidding
naikhī̃ karat. Hamᵃrā-kē Rām bānẽ.' Phir ēhī tarē dūnō janē
not am-doing. Me-to Rām is.' Again in-this-very way both-even people
kallah-kaï-ke āpan āpan rāh lihᵃlẽ. Nāki naddī-mẽ chali gailī̃,
quarrelling their-own their-own way took. The-alligator river-into went away,
siyār ban-mẽ.
the-jackal forest-in.

---

[1] This means 'one could not brook the sight of the other', *i.e.*, each desired the annihilation of the other.

[2] *Lapᵃṭiyāil bāṛá* is spoken when one bears a long grudge against another on account of imaginary wrongs. The other sense in which it is used is 'when one lies in wait for the other to do wrong or injury to him.' Here the phrase has been used in the latter sense. The sentence therefore means, 'It is of no avail to you to lie in wait for me.'

[3] *Tū̃ kā*, etc.—*dēkh lēib*, you are nothing to me. I can face those who are really great in cunning and power.

Naddī-ke tīrē ēgō pīpar-ke pēṛ rahē. Ō-kar sōri kuchh dūri-lē
River-of bank-on one pipal-of tree was. Its root some distance-to
pānī-mẽ chali-gaïl-rahal, ā kuchh ūpar rahē. Ēk din siyār-Rām[1] ōhī
water-into had-gone, and some above was. One day jackal that-very
sōri-par baiṭh-ke pānī pīyat rah'lẽ. Tab-lek nāki dēkh-
root-on sitting water drinking was. In-the-meantime the-alligator happened-
lih'las ā ḍub'lē-ḍubal ā-ke un-ke gōṛ dhaïlas. Siyār ap'ne
to-see (him) and diving coming his foot caught. The-jackal his-own
man-mẽ kah'las kī, 'nāki tâ āpan dā̃w lih'lasi, ab kawan
mind-in said that, 'the-alligator to-be-sure her-own turn[2] took, now what
upāy karī̃?' Pher kah'lẽ kī, 'hē nāki, tū̃ bhal[3] bāṛū; dhare-kē
device may-I-do?' Again he-said that, 'O alligator, you good are; holding-for
goṛ tâ dhailū-hâ sōri.' Bas[4] nāki gōṛ chhōṛi-ke sōri
feet to-be-sure you-have-caught the-root.' Enough the-alligator feet letting-go the-root
haũhā-ke dhaï-lih'lī̃. Siyār mũh rigāwat bhāgi-gaïlẽ, ā
eagerly[5] caught. The-jackal with-face making-(him)-angry ran-away, and
nāki hāth mali-ke rahi-gaïlī̃.
the-alligator hand rubbing remained.

Ab bayar aür-ī baṛhi-gaïl. Ēk din nāki siyār-ke māni-mẽ
Now the-enmity more-even increased. One day the-alligator the-jackal-of den-in
jā-ke baïṭhi-gaïlī̃. Siyār aw'tē mahā̃ki-sē būjhi-gaïlẽ kī nāki
going sat-down. The-jackal on-coming the-scent-from understood that the-alligator
baïṭhal-bāṛī̃. Kah'lẽ kī, 'hē bhayā, hamār māni gũguāt-rahali-hâ,
is-seated. Said-he that, 'O brother, my den was-making-a-sound-like-gũ-gũ,
āju kāhe naïkhī̃ gũguāt?' Tab-lek nāki
to-day why is-not making-a-sound-like-gũ-gũ?' In-the-meantime the-alligator
gũguaïlī̃. Siyār kah'lẽ kī, 'ab hamār mān-ō leh'lū.
made-a-sound-like-gũ-gũ. The-jackal said that, 'now my den-also you-took.
Achchhā, ēhī-mẽ rahâ.' Ā ī kahi-ke chāli-dih'lẽ, ā māni-mẽ-ke
All-right, this-very-in live.' And this saying he-went-away, and den-in-of
rahal chhā̃ṛi-dih'lẽ.
living gave-up.

Tab ēgō pataï-ke gā̃j-mẽ jē Gōṛ baṭōre-lan sē rahe lag'lẽ.
Then one leaves-of pile-in which Gonds collect he to-live began.
Nāki jōh-lagā-ke gā̃jō-mẽ pahũchali. Pīchhē siyār
The-alligator search-applying the-pile-also-into went. Afterwards the-jackal

[1] In relating a tale the heroes of it are sometimes jokingly given the title of *Rām*, especially when they are cunning animals of the pattern of a jackal or a fox. But *Rām* is only added to the name of a male hero. To the name of a heroine *Rānī* is added, or sometimes *Dē*.

[2] *Dā̃w lēb*, to take revenge upon.

[3] *Tū̃ bhal bāṛū* means 'you are a great fool.'

[4] *Bas*=thereupon suddenly.

[5] *Haũhā ke* is used when one makes a mess of a thing by too great haste.

aïlẽ ; tá gā̃j-ke patai khar[a]baṛ dēkhi-ke būjhi-gaïlẽ ki
came ; then pile-of leaves upset seeing understood that

ēn-ū-mẽ nāki ā-gaïl-bāṭī, Kah[a]lẽ ki, 'hē bhayā,' āgē tâ
this-also-in the-alligator has-come., He-said that, 'O brother, formerly to-be-sure

hamār gā̃j khar[a]kharāt-rabal. Āju kāhe naïkhī khar[a]kharāt ?' Tab-lē
my pile was-rustling. To-day why not-is rustling ?' In-the-meantime

nāki pattā khar[a]kharaibē tâ kaïlī. Siyār kah[a]lẽ,
the-alligator leaves to-rustle actually made. The-jackal said,

'achchhā, tâ būjhi-gaïlī. Bas-karâ.' Daüral chali-gaïl tani-ki-ēk
'well, then I-have-understood. Put-a-stop-to-it.' Running he-went a-little

āgi lē-ā-ke gā̃j phū̃k-dih[a]lē. Nāki ōhī-mẽ bhasam hō-gaïlī.
fire bringing the-pile set-fire-to. The-alligator that-very-in ashes became.

Akil-ke āgē jōr kuchh nā kâm kare-lā.
Wisdom-of before brute-force any not work does.

FREE TRANSLATION OF THE FOREGOING.

Once upon a time there lived a jackal and a she-alligator in great friendship. Night and day lived they together; neither did he forget her, nor she leave him. In this way they lived for some time, till all of a sudden they quarrelled. So hot became the strife between them, that one could not bear the sight of the other. Said the alligator, 'O jackal, what is the use of your lying in wait for me? Why, my regular meal is twenty people like you.' Said the jackal, 'what are you? I am not afraid of any big animal. Your body may be strong, but it is I who have the brains. Do what you please. I don't ask you to stop. God will take care of me.' So wrangling in this way each went off on his own way. The alligator took to the river, and the jackal to the forest.

Now, on the bank of the river there was a fig-tree, with a root which projected over the stream, partly in the water, and partly out. One day master jackal was sitting on this root having a drink, when the alligator caught sight of him, and with a dive seized hold of his foot. Then said the jackal to himself, 'I' faith, the alligator has got her revenge now. What is the best thing for me to do?' Then he added aloud 'hulloa, alligator, you're a genius, you are. You thought you were going to catch my foot, and you have only caught hold of the root of the tree.' That was enough for the alligator. She let go his foot and grabbed at the root, while the jackal marched away making faces at her. All that she could do was to rub her hands together in disgust at the trick.

So the enmity increased more and more, and one day the alligator set out, and sat down in the jackal's den. When he came home, he perceived her scent, and guessed that she was sitting inside. To make sure, he said, 'well, upon my word. My den alway said '*gū̃ gū̃*,' and to-day it says nothing at all.' Then the alligator cried out '*gū̃ gū̃*,' and the jackal knew she was there. Said he, 'so you've taken my den too,' and went off and gave up living in it.

Then he made a home in a heap of dry leaves which had been collected by the Gōṇḍs. Here, too, the alligator traced him out, and one day hid herself in the pile to wait for him. When he came home, he found the leaves all upset, and guessed that she was there. Said he, 'I' faith, my heap of leaves always rustled before. Why it is not rustling to-day?' So the alligator made the leaves rustle, and the jackal said to himself, 'all right, now I know what's up. This must be stopped.' So off he ran, and fetched a little fire, with which he lit the pile of leaves, so that the alligator was burnt to ashes.

The moral of this is that brute force is of no avail against mother-wit.

SARWARIĀ.

Sarwariā, properly means the language of the Saruār country, but the name is not quite accurate, for the dialect which it connotes is not spoken over the whole of the Saruār tract, and is, moreover, spoken in parts of the country to which the name Saruār does not properly apply. Sarwariā is, however, a name sanctioned by the Census Report, and is a convenient one. I hence use it with the above explanation.

The word 'Saruār' is a corruption of *Sarayū-pāra*, or Trans-Sarayū; that is to say, the tract of country on the far side of the Sarayū or Gōgrā River, looking from the city of Ajudhiā, the ancient Ayōdhyā, near the modern town of Fyzabad. Strictly speaking, it therefore includes the whole of the districts of Bahraich, Gonda, Basti, Gorakhpur, and Saran, but, owing to a local tradition, it now-a-days only means the country on the left bank of the Gogra between Ajudhiā in Fyzabad, and Majhaulī in Gorakhpur. The story runs that when Rāma-chandra returned to Ayōdhyā from his exile the local Brāhmaṇs refused to sacrifice for him, on the ground that he was guilty of killing Rāvaṇa who was himself a member of their caste. He then imported some Brāhmaṇs from Kanauj, who performed the sacrifice, but who were promptly put out of caste for doing so by their brethren. They appealed to Rāma, who stood on the bank of the Gōgrā at Ayōdhyā, and shot an arrow across the river towards the east. It fell near Majhaulī in the south-east of the Gorakhpur District, and he declared that all the land from the Sarayū, *i.e.*, the modern Gōgrā, to the place where the arrow fell should belong to these Brāhmaṇs and their heirs for ever. Hence arose the well-known caste of Sarwariā Brāhmans, and the country held by them is considered the true Saruār country to the present day.

The Sarwariā sub-dialect of Bhojpurī is spoken all over the district of Basti, and over the western half of Gorakhpur. A glance at the map will show that only a small portion of the Basti district falls within the traditional Saruār tract, while on the other hand, the latter extends, in Gorakhpur, beyond the limits of the Sarwariā sub-dialect, and into the area in which the Northern Bhojpurī of Eastern Gorakhpur is spoken.

The population speaking Sarwariā is estimated as follows:—

Name of District.	Number of persons estimated as speaking Sarwariā.
Basti	1,783,844
Gorakhpur	1,569,307
TOTAL .	3,353,151

Taking the form of the dialect spoken in Basti, as the most extreme variety, we find that it differs from the Bhojpurī of East Gorakhpur principally in vocabulary. The words for things in common use frequently differ considerably. This will be observed in the two following specimens, and it is not necessary to draw attention to specific instances.

There are also, however, some differences of Grammar. The principal are the following. With them, I shall also mention the points in which the Basti dialect differs from Standard Bhojpurī.

We see the same reluctance to use the cerebral *ṛ* in Bastī that we observed in Gorakhpur. Thus, we find *paral*, it fell, used instead of *paṛal*. The termination of the genitive is *kăĭ*, with an oblique form *kē*. This is borrowed from Western Bhojpurī. Thus, *daïu-kai*, of God, but *bāp-kē lagẽ*, near the father. As in Gorakhpur, the instrumental singular ends in *an*, as in *bhūkhan*, by hunger. Adjectives sometimes change for gender. Thus, we have *fasil achchhī-hai*, the harvest is good.

There are several peculiarities in the declension of pronouns. The oblique form of the genitive always ends in *ē* instead of *ā*. Thus *hamᵃrē bāp-kē ihā̃*, near my father. So, *tuhᵃrē*, *okᵃrē*, *in-kē*, *apᵃnē*; and similarly, *taunē-sē*, from this. For the second personal pronoun honorific, instead of *rawā̃*, etc., Sarwariā has *tū̃*, genitive *tuhār*, obl., *tuhẽ* or *tuhᵃrē*. The third personal pronoun is *ū*, with an oblique form *ō* or *wah* instead of *oh*. The relative and correlative pronouns are *jaun* and *taun*, instead of *jē* and *sē*. Their oblique forms are *jaunē* and *taunē*. *Kāw* is 'what?', *kuchh* is 'anything', and *kitᵃnā* is 'how many.' Most of these pronominal peculiarities are also shared in common with Western Bhojpurī.

In verbs, the most noteworthy peculiarity of the Basti dialect is that the third person singular of the Past ends in *is* instead of in *as*. Thus, *kahᵃlis*, he said; so also, *dihᵃlis*, *lihᵃlis*, *pūchhᵃlis*, *kaïlis*, and others. In one instance, we have the Eastern Hindi *uṛāis*, he squandered, instead of *uṛaulis*. The Respectful Imperative ends in *au* as in *rākhau*. The Past Conditional may be the same in form as the present participle, here, too, following Eastern Hindi. Thus, we have *manāit*, for *manaitī̃*, might have made. The termination of the Conjunctive Participle may be *ke*, as in *jāy-ke*, having gone, or *kăĭ*, as in *dēkhi-kăĭ*, having seen. The oblique case of the verbal noun ends in *ăĭ*, instead of in *e*. Thus, *charāwăĭ-kẽ*, for feeding.

It is important to notice that the Potential Passive is formed by adding *'wā* and not *ā* to the root of the verb; thus, *kahᵃwāī̃*, I may be called, instead of the standard Bhojpurī *kahāī̃*.

The form of the Verb Substantive with *ṭ* is, as usual north of the Ganges, preferred to that with *ṛ*. Thus, *bāṭē*, he is, and so on.

Of the two following specimens of the Sarwariā of the Basti District, the first is a version of the Parable of the Prodigal Son, and the second a letter written by one native of the district to another.

[No. 46.]

INDO-ARYAN FAMILY. EASTERN GROUP.

BIHARĪ.

BHOJPURĪ DIALECT.

SARWARIĀ SUB-DIALECT. (DISTRICT BASTI.)

SPECIMEN I.

एक मनई के दुइ बेटवा रहलैं। वह में से छोटका बेटवा बाप से कहलिस कि बाप धन में जौन हमार बखरा होय तौन हम के मिलै। तब बाप ओ कें बाँटि दिहलिस। और थोरिक दिन बितलें छोटका बेटवा सब जौन कुछ रहल तौन लै के एक दूर देस में गइल और उहाँ आपन माल सब बदमाशी में उड़ाय दिहलिस। जब सब ओराय गइल तब वह देस में अकाल परल और ऊ गरीब हो गइल। तब ऊ एक बड़ मनई के इहाँ गइल। तब ऊ बड़ मनई ओ कें सूअर चरावे कें कहि दिहलैं। और ओकरे मन में रहल कि जौन बोकला सूअरि खाति बाय तौने से आपन पेट भरल करीं कि केहु ओ कें कुछ नाहीं देत रहल। तब ऊ होस में आय गइल कि हमरे बाप के इहाँ कितना मजूर जीअत खात बाटैं और हम भूखन मरत बाटीं। हम अपनं बाप के लगें जाय के कहब कि हम दइउ के ओ तुहार कौन कसूर कइलीं। अब अइसन नाहीं बाटीं कि तुहार बेटवा कहवाईं। अब तूं हम कें अपने मजूरन में राखौ। तब ऊ अपने बाप के पास गइल और ऊ इतने लामें रहल तब्बइ ओकर बाप देखि के मोह में आय के गटईं लगाय लिहलिस ओ चुम्मा-लिहलिस। और बेटवा बाप से कहलिस कि हम दइउ के ओ तुहरे कसूर कइलीं और एहि जोग नाहीं बाटीं कि तुहार बेटवा कहवाईं। तब बाप अपनं मनई से कहलिस कि नीक से नीक कपड़ा निकासि के इन कें पहिरावं और इन के हाथ में मुनरी गोड़ में जूता पहिरावं जौने में हम खाईं ओ खुस होईं। काहें कि हमार ई बेटवा मनों मरल रहल जीअल ओ हेराइल रहल मिलल। ऊ सब खुस भइल॥

तब बड़का बेटवा जौन खेत में रहल ऊ जब घर के लगें आइल और गाइब बजाइब सुनि के एक मनई कें बोलाय के पुंछलिस कि ई काव होत बाय। तब ऊ कहलिस कि तुहार भाई आइल है और तुहार बाप बहुत खातिर कइलैं हैं काहें से कि भला चंगा पउलैं हैं। तब ऊ रिसिआय के घर में नाहीं गइल। तब ओकर बाप बहराँ आय के मनुहार कइलिस। तब ऊ बाप से कहलिस कि देखौं इतने दिन से हम तुहार खिदमत करत बाटीं और कब्बौं तुहरे मन के बाहर नाहीं चललीं। तौन कब्बौं एको छेगड़ी कै बच्चो हम के नाहीं दिहलं कि अपने बेओहरिकन के साथें खुसी मनाइत और जब तुहार ई बेटवा आइल जौन तुहार धन दौलत पतुरिअन में उड़ाइस तेकर बहुत खातिर कइलं। तब ऊ कहलिस कि ए बेटवा तूं सदाँ हमरे साथ बाटं। और जौन हमार है तौन सब तुहार होय। और खुसी मनावे ओ खुस होवे के चाही काहें कि तुहार छोट भाई मरल रहल जीअल है और हेराय गइल रहल और मिलल है॥

[No. 46.]

INDO-ARYAN FAMILY. EASTERN GROUP.

BIHĀRĪ.

BHOJPURĪ DIALECT.

SARWARIĀ SUB-DIALECT. (DISTRICT BASTI.)

SPECIMEN I.

TRANSLITERATION AND TRANSLATION.

Ek manaī-kē dui beṭᵃwā rahᵃlaī. Wah-mẽ-sē chhoṭᵃkā beṭᵃwā
One man-to two sons were. Them-in-from the-younger son

bāp-sē kahᵃlis ki, 'bāp, dhan-mẽ jaun hamār bakhᵃrā hōy, taun
the-father-to said that, 'father, the-wealth-in what my share may-be, that

ham-kē milai.' Tab bāp ō-kẽ bā̃ṭi dihᵃlis. Ăūr thōrik
me-to be-given.' Then the-father him-to having-divided gave. And a-few

din bitᵃlẽ chhoṭᵃkā beṭᵃwā sab jaun kuchh rahal, taun
days on-passing the-younger son all what any-thing was, that

lāī-ke ēk dūr dēs-mẽ gaïl, ăūr uhā̃ āpan māl sab
having-taken a far country-in went, and there his-own property all

badᵃmāśī-mẽ uṛāy-dihᵃlis. Jab sab oṛāy-gaïl tab wah dēs-mẽ akāl
debauchery-in squandered. When all was-squandered then that country-in a-famine

paral, ăūr ū garīb hō-gaïl. Tab ū ēk baṛ-manaī-ke ihā̃ gaïl. Tab ū
fell, and he poor became. Then he a rich-man-of near went. Then that

baṛ-manaī ō-kẽ sūar charāwāī-kẽ kahi-dihᵃlaī, ăūr okᵃrē man-mẽ rahal ki,
rich-man him swine feeding-for told, and his mind-in it-was that,

'jā̃un bokᵃlā sūari khāti-bāy, taunē-sē āpan pēṭ bharal karī̃,'
'what husks the-swine are-eating, those-with my-own belly filled I-may-make,'

ki kēhū ō-kẽ kuchh nāhī̃ dēt-rahal. Tab ū hōs-mẽ āy-gaïl ki,
for any-one him-to any-thing not giving-was. Then he sense-in came that,

'hamᵃrē bāp-kē ihā̃ kitᵃnā majūr jīat khāt bāṭaī, ăūr ham
'my father's near how-many servants living eating are, and I

bhūkhan marat bāṭī̃. Ham apᵃnē bāp-kē lagẽ jāy-ke kahab ki,
by-hunger dying am. I my-own father-of near having-gone will-say that,

"ham daïu-kāī o tuhār kaun kasūr kaïlī̃. Ab aïsan nāhī̃ bāṭī̃ ki
"I God-of and of-thee what fault did. Now such not I-am that

tuhār beṭᵃwā kahᵃwāī. Ab tū̃ ham-kẽ apᵃnē majūran-mẽ rākhau."'
thy son I-may-be-called. Now thou me thine-own servants-among keep."'

Tab ū apᵃnē bāp-kē pās gaïl ăūr ū itᵃnē lāmẽ rahal tabbaī ō-kar
Then he his-own father-of near went and he when far was then-even his

bāp dēkhi-kăī mōh-mẽ āy-ke gaṭaĩ lagāy lihalis,
father having-seen pity-in having-come embracing having-applied took,

o chummā lihalis. Ăūr beṭawā bāp-sē kahalis ki, 'ham Daïu kăī o
and kisses took. And the-son the-father-to said that, 'I God of and

tuharē kasūr kaïlĩ, ăūr ehi jōg nāhĩ bāṭĩ ki tuhār beṭawā
of-thee fault did, and this worthy not I-am that thy son

kahawāĩ.' Tab bāp apanē manaī-sē kahalis ki, 'nīk-sē nīk
I-may-be-called.' Then the-father his-own men-to said that, 'good-than good

kapaṛā nikāsi-ke in-kẽ pahirāwâ, ăūr in-kē hāth-mẽ
clothes having-brought-out this-person-to put-on, and this-person's hand-on

munarī, gōṛ-mẽ jūtā pahirāwâ, jaunē-mẽ ham khāĩ o khus hōĩ;
a-ring, feet-on shoes put-on, so-that we may-eat and happy be;

kāhẽ ki hamār ī beṭawā manõ maral-rahal, jīal; o herāïl-rahal,
because that my this son as-it-were had-died, lived; he had-been-lost,

milal.' Ū sab khus bhaïl.
was-found.' They all happy became.

Tab baṛakā beṭawā jaun khēt-mẽ rahal, ū jab ghar-
Then the-elder son who the-field-in was, he when the-house-

kē lagẽ āïl, ăūr gāïb bajāïb suni-ke, ēk manaī-kẽ
of near came, and singing music having-heard, one man-to

bolāy-ke pūchhalis ki, 'ī kāw hōt-bāy?' Tab ū kahalis ki,
having-called he-asked that, 'this what is-being?' Then he said that,

'tuhār bhāī āïl-hai, ăūr tuhār bāp bahut khātir kaïlaī-haĩ;
'thy brother come-is, and thy father much affection has-made;

kāhẽ-sē ki bhalā chaṅgā paūlaī-haĩ.' Tab ū risiāy-ke
because that good healthy he-has-found-(him).' Then he having-become-angry

ghar-mẽ nāhĩ gaïl. Tab ō-kar bāp baharā̃ āy-ke manuhār
the-house-in not went. Then his father outside having-come remonstrating

kaïlis. Tab ū bāp-sē kahalis ki, 'dēkhĩ, itanē din-sē
did. Then he the-father-to said that, 'see, so-many days-from

ham tuhār khidamat karat-bāṭĩ, ăūr kabbõ tuharē man-kē bāhar
I thy service doing-am, and ever thy mind-of outside

nāhĩ chalalĩ; taun kabbõ ekkō chhegaṛī-kăī bachch-ō
not went; still ever a-single she-goat's young-one-even

ham-kē nāhĩ dihalâ ki apanē beoharikan-kē sāthẽ khusī
me-to not thou-gavest that my-own friends-of with happiness

manāit. Ăūr jab tuhār ī beṭawā āïl, jaun tuhār
I-might-have-made. And when thy this son came, who thy

dhan daulat paturian-mẽ uṛāis, tē-kar bahut khātir
wealth property harlots-on has-squandered, his much affection

kaïlâ.' Tab ū kahalis ki, 'ē beṭawā, tũ sadā̃ hamarē
you-made.' Then he said that, 'O son, thou always me

sāth bāṭâ, ăŭr jaun hamār hai, taun sab tuhār hōy.
with art, and what mine is, that all thine is.

Ăŭr khusī manāwăī o khus hōwăī-kē chāhī,
And happiness making and happy being-for is-to-be-wished,

kāhẽ-ki tuhār chhōṭ bhāī maral-rahal, jīal-hai ;
because-that thy younger brother had-died, has-lived ;

ăŭr herāy-gaïl-rahal, ăŭr milal-hai.'
and had-been-lost, and has-been-found.'

[No. 47.]

INDO-ARYAN FAMILY. EASTERN GROUP.

BIHĀRĪ.

BHOJPURĪ DIALECT.

SARWARIĀ SUB-DIALECT. (DISTRICT BASTI.)

SPECIMEN II.

स्वस्ति श्री शिवकुमार लाल जीव के लि॰ जगत नरायन लाल कै सलाम। कुसल आराम दोनोँ तरफ़ कै नेक चाही। आगे इहाँ कै हाल अस है कि खेत बारी सब बोइ गइल ओ फ़सिल अच्छी है ओ कटै कै जून आय गइल। से देखत चिट्ठी के तूँ दुइ हरवाह ले के इहाँ तक आइ जाव, जौने से सब खेत कटि जाय। ओ असोँ जवन पत्थर गिरल है तवने से भगवान हमार गाँव बँचाय दिहलैँ ओ फ़सिल मेँ कवनो रोग दोख नाहीँ लगल है। ओ और हाल सब अच्छा है। जियादे शुभ। मि॰ फागुन सुदी १३ सन १३०५ साल ॥

TRANSLITERATION AND TRANSLATION.

Swasti. Śrī Śiv-kumār Lāljīw-kē li(khitaṁ[1]) Jagat-narāyan
It-is-well. Śrī Śiv-kumār Lālji-to are-written Jagat-narāyan

Lāl-kăĭ salām. Kusal ārām dōnõ taraf-kăĭ nēk chāhī.
Lal's compliments. Welfare comfort both sides-of good are-to-be-wished.

Āgē, ihā̃-kăĭ hāl as hai ki khēt bārī sab bōi-gaïl,
Moreover, here-of affairs such are that fields farms all are-sown,

o fasil achchhī hai, o kaṭăĭ-kăĭ jūn āy-gaïl.
and the-harvest good is, and cutting-for the-time has-come.

Sē dēkhat chiṭṭhī-kē tū̃ dui har'wāh lĕĭ-ke ihā̃ tak
Therefore seeing the-letter you two labourers taking here to

āi-jāw, jaunē-sē sab khēt kaṭi-jāy. O asõ jawan
come, so-that all fields may-be-cut. And this-year what

patthar giral-hai taw'nē-sē Bhag'wān hamār gā̃w bā̃chāy-dih'laĭ.
hail has-fallen from-that God my village has-preserved.

O fasil-mē̃ kaw'nō rōg dōkh nāhĩ lagal-hai. O
And the-harvest-in any disease defect not has-attached. And

ăŭr hāl sab achchhā hai. Jiyādē śubh. Mi(tī) Phāgun
other affairs all good are. Further blessings. Date Phāgun

sudī 13, san 1305 sāl.
light-half 13, Faslī-year 1305 year.

FREE TRANSLATION OF THE FOREGOING.

It is well. The compliments of Jagat-nārāyan Lāl to Śiv-kumār Lāl. May both the writer and the recipient of this letter be prosperous. Moreover, the state of affairs

[1] A Sanskrit Past Participle Neuter, commonly used at the beginning of letters.

here is that all the fields have been sown, and have borne a fine harvest, which is now ready for reaping. Therefore, immediately on receipt of this letter, come here with two labouring men, so that all the fields may be cut. God Almighty has protected my village from the hail which fell this year, and there is no disease or defect in the crop. Everything else is prospering. Further blessings. Dated the 13th of the bright half of Phāgun, 1305 F. S.

The following version of the Parable of the Prodigal Son is in the dialect spoken in South-West Gorakhpur, which forms a portion of the true Saruār tract. It has been made by Pandit Rām-gharīb Chaubē, who is a native of that part of the country. As might be expected, while in the main closely corresponding with the dialect of Basti, it has some points of resemblance with the language of Eastern Gorakhpur. The most striking point of difference from the language of Basti, is that the third person singular of the Past Tense of Transitive verbs, ends in *as*, as in Standard Bhojpurī, and not in *is*, as in the dialect of that district. Thus, *kah*ᵉ*las*, not *kah*ᵉ*lis*, he said. Among minor points, we may notice the occasional use of *rāūr*, instead of *tuhār*, for the genitive of the second personal pronoun honorific, the latter being the Sarwariā, and the former, the Standard Bhojpurī form. Instead of *un*, the usual plural oblique form of the third personal pronoun, we have the slightly different *on*, while the singular oblique form is *ohi*, and not *wah*, as in Basti. The only other point worthy of special note is that the Potential Passive is formed, as in Standard Bhojpurī, by the addition of *ā* to the root, and not, as in Basti, by the addition of ᵉ*wā*. Thus, *kahāī̃*, not *kah*ᵉ*wāī̃*, I may be called.

The specimen is printed in the Dēva-nāgarī character, and a transliteration is given of it.

[No. 48.]

INDO-ARYAN FAMILY. EASTERN GROUP.

BIHĀRĪ.

BHOJPURĪ DIALECT.

SARWARIĀ SUB-DIALECT. (SOUTH-WESTERN GORAKHPUR.)

(Pandit Rām-gharīb Chaubē, 1899.)

एक जने के दुइठौं बेटा रहैं। ओहि में से छोटका अपने बाप से कहलस, की हे बाबू जी घर के धन दौलति में जवन हमार बखरा होय तवन हम कें बाँटि दं। तब ओकर बाप ओकर बखरा ओ-कें बाँटि दिहलस। थोरिक दिन में छोटका बेटा आपन कुलि धन एकट्ठा कै के परदेस निकसि गइल, और उहाँ आपन कुलि धन कुकरम में उड़ा दिहलस। जब ऊ आपन सर्बस उड़ा चुकल तब ओहि देस में बड़ा अकाल पड़ल। तब ऊ बड़ा दलिद्दर हो गइल। तब ऊ ओहि देस के एक धनी अदिमी के इहाँ जा के रहे लागल। ऊ धनी अदिमी ओ कें अपने खेतें सूअरि चरावे के भेजि दिहलस। उहाँ ओकर मन ओहि घास पात के देखि के जवन सूअरि खाति रहलीं डोलि गइल और मन में कहे लागल की हम कें जो ईहो मिलत तं खातीं। लेकिन ओ कें केइ किछु नाहीं देत रहल। तब ओकरे सूझल और ऊ अपने मन में कहलस की देखं हमरे बाप के केतना मजूरन कें एतना खाये कें मिलत बा की ऊ भरि पेट खइबो करै-लैं अवर बचइबो करै-लैं। अवर हम इहाँ भुक्खन मरत बाटीं। आवं चलीं अब अपने बापे किहाँ आ उन सें कहीं की हे बाबू जी हम भगवान के परतिकूल अवर तोहरे अगाड़ीं पाप कै चुकलीं, अब हम एह लायक नाहीं बाटीं की तोहार बेटवा कहाईं। से अब तूँ हम कें अपने एक चकरिहा के तरें राखं। एइसन सोचि के ऊ अपने बाप के लगें चलल। जब लामहीं रहल तब्बे ओकर बाप ओ के देखि के मारे छोह के दौरि के ओकरे लगें गइल और भेंट अँकवारि लिहलस और चुम्मे चाटै लागल। तब बेटा कहे लागल की हे बाबू जी हम भगवान के परतिकूल अवर तोहरे अगाड़ीं पाप कै चुकलीं अवर अब एह लायक नाहीं बाटीं की तोहार बेटा कहाईं। से अब हम कें अपने एक मजूर के तरें राखं। ओकर बाप ई सुनि के अपने एक नोकर से कहलस की सब से नीक कपड़ा निकारि लै आवं और इन कें पहिरावं। अवर इन के हाथ में अँगुठी अवर गोड़े में पनहीं पहिरावं। अवर चलं सभें खाईं पीईं अवर खुसी करीं। तब सब जनें खुसी मनावै लगलैं॥

ओकर बड़का बेटा खेत में रहल। जब घर के लगें आइल तं नाचि अवर बाजा कै भनक ओकरे कानें पड़लि। तब ऊ अपने एक नोकर कें बुलाय के पुछलस की ई का होत हवै। नोकर कहलस की राउर भाई जी अइलैं हैं अवर राउर बाबू जी ओन के निमित्तिक भोज करत बाटैं। काहे से की ओन कें आँगें देहें अवर कुसल अनन्द से पउलैं हैं। ऊ ई सुनि के रिसिया गइलैं अवर घर के भित्तर जाये कै मन नाहीं कइलैं। तब ओन के बाप बहरा अइलैं अवर ओन के मनावै लगलैं। तब ऊ अपने बाप से कहलैं हे बाबू जी देखं हम एतना दिन से तोहार सेवा सुबित करत चलि आवत हईं और कब्बों तोहार एक्को हुकुम नाहीं टरलीं। तब्बो तूँ हम कें एक्को भेंड़ी कै बच्चा नाहीं दिहलं की हम अपने सँघतिन के साथें आनन्द करीं। बाकी ज्योंहीं तोहार ई बेटा आइल त्योंहीं तूँ ओन के खातिर भोज कइलं हं। ई नाहीं सोचलं की ई तोहार उहे बेटउआ हउअँ जे तोहार धन कुकरम में नष्ट कै दिहलैं। तब बाप बोलल

की हे बेटा तूँ हमरे संगे सदाँ से बाटं अवर जवन कुछ हमार है तवन तुहार हैं । और ई तोहार भाई मानोँ मरि के जीअल है अवर भुला के मिलल है ए सेँ हमरन केँ चाही की खुसी करीँ अवर आनन्द मनाईँ ॥

TRANSLITERATION.

Ēk janē-kē dui-ṭhõ bēṭā rahaĩ. Ohi-mẽ-sē chhoṭ'kā ap'nē bāp-sē kah'las kī 'hē bābū-jī ghar-kē dhan daulati-mẽ jawan hamār bakh'rā hōy tawan ham-kẽ bãṭi dâ.' Tab ō-kar bāp ō-kar bakh'rā ō-kẽ bãṭi dih'las. Thōrik din-mẽ chhoṭ'kā bēṭā āpan kuli dhan ekaṭṭhā kăĩ-ke par'dēs nikasi-gaïl, ăūr uhã āpan kuli dhan kukaram-mẽ uṛā dih'las. Jab ū āpan sarbas uṛā chukal tab ohi dēs-mẽ baṛā akāl paṛal. Tab ū baṛā daliddar hō-gaïl. Tab ū ohi dēs-kē ēk dhanī adimī-kē ihã jā-ke rahăĩ lāgal. Ū dhanī adimī ō-kē ap'nē khētẽ sūari charawăĩ-kē bhēji dih'las. Uhã ō-kar man ohi ghās pāt-kē dēkhi-ke jawan sūari khāti-rah'lĩ ḍōli gaïl, ăūr man-mẽ kahăĩ lāgal kī ham-kẽ jō īhō milat tâ khātī̃. Lēkin ō-kẽ kēhū kichhu nāhī̃ dēt rahal. Tab ok'rē sūjhal ăūr ū ap'nē man-mẽ kah'las kī, 'dēkhâ, ham'rē bāp-kē ket'nā majūran-kẽ et'nā khāye-kẽ milat bā, kī ū bhari pēṭ khaïbō karăĩ-laĩ awar bachaïbō karăĩ-laĩ. Awar ham ihã bhukkhan marat bāṭī̃. Āwâ chalī̃ ab ap'nē bāpai kihã ā un-sẽ kahī̃ kī, "hē bābū-jī ham Bhag'wān-kē paratikūl awar toh'rē agāṛī̃ pāp kăĩ chuk'lī̃, ab ham eh lāyak nāhī̃ bāṭī̃ kī tohār beṭ'wā kahāī̃. Sē ab tũ ham-kẽ ap'nē ēk chakarihā-kē tarẽ rākhâ."' Eisan sōchi-ke ū ap'nē bāp-kē lagẽ chalal. Jab lām'hī̃ rahal tabbai ō-kar bāp ō-kē dēkhi-ke mārē chhōh-kē dauri-ke ok'rē lagẽ gaïl ăūr bhẽṭ ãk'wāri lih'las ăūr chummăĩ chāṭăĩ lāgal. Tab bēṭā kahăĩ lāgal kī, 'hē bābū-jī, ham Bhag'wān kē paraṭikūl awar toh'rē agārī̃ pāp kăĩ chuk'lī̃ awar ab eh lāyak nāhī̃ bāṭī̃ kī tohār bēṭā kahāī̃. Sē ab ham-kẽ ap'nē ēk majūr-kē tarẽ rākhâ.' Ō-kar bāp ī suni-ke ap'nē ēk nōkar-sē kah'las kī, 'sab-sē nīk kap'ṛā nikāri lăĩ āwâ ăūr in-kẽ pahirāwâ. Awar in-kē hāth-mẽ ãguṭhī awar gōṛē-mẽ pan'hī pahirāwâ. Awar chalâ, sabhẽ khāī̃ pīī̃ awar khusī karī̃.' Tab sab janẽ khusī manāwăĩ lag'laĩ.

Ō-kar baṛ'kā bēṭā khēt-mẽ rahal. Jab ghar-kē lagẽ āil tâ nāchi awar bājā kăĩ bhanak ok'rē kānẽ paṛali. Tab ā ap'nē ēk nōkar-kẽ bulāy-ke puchh'las kī 'ī kā hōt hâwai?' Nōkar kah'las kī 'rāur bhāī-jī aïlaĩ-haĩ, awar rāur bābū-jī on-kē nimittik bhōj karat bāṭaĩ. Kāhē-sē-kī on-kẽ ãgẽ dēhẽ awar kusal anand sē paülaĩ-haĩ.' Ū ī suni-ke risiyā gaïlaĩ awar ghar-kē bhittar jāye-kăĩ man nāhī̃ kailaĩ. Tab on-kăĩ bāp bah'rā aïlaĩ awar on-kẽ manāwăĩ lag'laĩ. Tab ū ap'nē bāp-sē kah'laĩ, 'hē bābū-jī, dēkhâ, ham et'nā din-sē tohār sēwā subit karat challi āwat hâĩ, ăūr kabbõ tohār ekkō hukum nāhī̃ ṭar'lī̃. Tabbō tũ ham-kẽ ekkō bhẽṛī kăĩ bachch-ō nāhī̃ dih'lâ kī ham ap'nē sãgh'tin-kē sāthẽ ānand karī̃. Bākī jyõ-hī̃ tohār ī bēṭā āil tyõ-hī̃ tũ on-kē khātir bhōj kailâ-hâ. Ī nāhī̃ soch'-lâ kī ī tohār uhai beṭ'wā haüaĩ jē tohār dhan kukaram-mẽ nashṭ kăĩ dih'laĩ. Tab bāp bōlal kī, 'hē bēṭā, tũ ham'rē saṅgē sadã-sē bāṭâ awar jawan kuchh hamār hai, tawan tuhār hai. Ăūr ī tohār bhāī mānõ mari-ke jīal hai; awar bhulā-ke milal hai; ē-sẽ ham'ran-kẽ chāhī kī khusī karī̃ awar ānand manāī̃.'

WESTERN BHOJPURĪ OR PŪRBĪ.

The Bhojpurī spoken in the Districts of Fyzabad, Jaunpur, Azamgarh, and Benares, in the centre of Mirzapur, and the West of Ghazipur differs in many particulars from the Standard Bhojpurī of Shahabad. The most striking point is the abandonment of the oblique form of nouns and pronouns which ends in *ā*, and which is so characteristic of all the dialects of Bihārī, and the substitution of an oblique form in *ē*, such as we meet in Standard Hindī. Western Bhojpurī is, in fact, the most Western outpost of the Eastern group of the Indo-Aryan family of languages, and possesses some of the features of its cousins to its West.

Western Bhojpurī has been admirably and most fully illustrated by Mr. J. R. Reid, and also forms the foundation of Dr. Hoernle's Gaudian Grammar. We thus possess more full information regarding it than we have about any form of the Bihārī language except, perhaps, Maithilī. It is a pity that Mr. Reid's grammar should be buried in a comparatively inaccessible settlement report.

The following is the estimated number of speakers of Western Bhojpurī :—

Name of District.	Number of Speakers.
Azamgarh	1,594,500
Fyzabad	250,000
Jaunpur	80,000
Benares	736,000
Ghazipur	469,000
Mirzapur	810,000
TOTAL .	3,939,500

AUTHORITIES—

HOERNLE, A. F. R., C.I.E.,—*A Comparative Grammar of the Gaudian Languages.* London, 1880. Contains a grammar of Western Bhojpurī, under the name of 'Eastern Hindī.'

REID, J. R., I.C.S.,—*Report on the Settlement Operations in the District of Azamgarh.* Allahabad, 1881. Appendix II contains a complete account of the dialect of the District. Appendix III, which has been separately printed, consists of a full Vocabulary of the same.

In Jaunpur and Fyzabad the dialect is spoken only in the extreme east of the District. In the rest of these two districts a form of Eastern Hindī is spoken. Regarding Ghazipur, *vide ante*, p. 201, and regarding Mirzapur, *post*, p. 264.

The following are the principal points in which Western Bhojpurī differs from the Standard form of the dialect. For further particulars, the student is referred to Mr. Reid's grammar from which most of these notes are taken.

I.—NOUNS—

The Plural is usually the same as the Singular, the typical termination *an*, being seldom used.

The postposition for the genitive is *ka* or *kaĭ* (instead of *kē*) with an oblique form *kē* (instead of *kā*). It may be stated as a general rule that, while in Standard Bhojpurī the oblique form of many nouns and pronouns ends in *ā*, in Western Bhojpurī it ends in *ē*.

Thus—

Standard Bhojpurī—

*Kap*ᵃ*ṭī kā mar*ᵃ*lā-ke kuchhu-ō dōkh nāhī;*

Western Bhojpurī—

*Kap*ᵃ*ṭī kē mar*ᵃ*lē-kaĭ kichha-ū dōkh nāhī*, there is no sin in (*lit.* of) slaying a deceiver.

Standard Bhojpurī—

*Ap*ᵃ*nā bāp-sē kah*ᵃ*lan;*

Western Bhojpurī—

*Ap*ᵃ*nē bāp-sē kah*ᵃ*laĭ*, he said to his father.

Standard Bhojpurī—

*Oh dēs-kā ēk sahar-kā rah*ᵃ*waiyā-kā pās;*

Western Bhojpurī—

*Oh dēs-kē ēk sahar-kē rah*ᵃ*waiyā-kē pās*, near an inhabitant of a city of that country.

Nouns have the usual Locative Singular in *ē*, as *gharē*, in a house, and also an Instrumental Singular in *an*, as *bhūkhan*, by hunger. Both the long and the redundant form of the noun are frequently used. Thus, *beṭ*ᵃ*wā* or *beṭauā*, the son. The redundant form sometimes ends (in the west of the District) in *aunā* or *īwā*. Thus, *ghoṛaunā*, the horse; *panīwā*, the water. The long and redundant forms usually give the force of the definite article, as above translated. For instance, *ēk nōkar-kē bulā-ke*, having called *a* servant; *nokar*ᵃ*wā kah*ᵃ*las*, *the* servant said.

II.—ADJECTIVES—

Adjectives change for gender and case as in Standard Hindī. Thus, *baṛē bēṭē kaĭ ghar*, the house of the elder son; *baṛī bēṭī*, an elder daughter; *bīs baṛē baṛē ghar*, twenty very big houses.

III.—PRONOUNS—

	I		Thou		Your Honour.	He, she (near).	He, she (remote).	It (near).	It (remote).
	Inferior.	Superior.	Inferior.	Superior.					
Sing.									
Nom.	*maĩ, mõ*	*ham, hamẽ*	*taĩ,*	*tũh, tũ*	*raurē, raurā, rauā*	*ī*	*ū*	*itthū, ithuā*	*otthū, othuī.*
Obl.	*mō, mõ*	*ham, hamẽ, hammaĩ*	*tō,*	*tũh, tōh*	*raurē, raurā, rauā*	*ē, ehi, in, inhaĩ*	*ō, ohi, un*.[1] *unhaĩ*	*itthū, ithuā*	*otthū, othuā.*
Gen.	*mōr,*	*hamār*	*tōr,*	*tuhār, tohār*	*raurē-kāi,* etc.	*ē-kar, in-kar*	*ō-kar, un-kar*	*itthū-kāi,* etc.	*otthū-kāi,* etc.
Plur.									
Nom.	*hamman, ham^{e}han, ham^{e}nē*	*ham^{e}rē, ham^{e}ran*	*tũhan, tũhanē*	*tuh^{e}rē, tuh^{e}ran*	*rauran, rauan*	*inhan, inh^{e}nē, in-k^{e}rē, in-k^{e}ran*	*unhan, unh^{e}nē, un-k^{e}rē, un-k^{e}ran*	*ithuan*	*othuan*
Obl.	Ditto.	Ditto.	Ditto.	Ditto.	Ditto.	Ditto.	Ditto.	Ditto.	Ditto.

[1] or *on*, and so throughout.

	This	That	Self	Who	
Sing.					Like *jē* are declined *tē* or *sē*, he (correlative), and *kē*, who? The Nominative Singular of the first is *tē, sē. taun.* Its obl. plur. is *tinhan, sinhan,* or *taunan.*
Nom.	*haī*	*haū*	*āp, āpū, apuē, ap^{e}nā, ap^{e}nē*	*jē, jaun*	
Obl.	*hē, hin*	*hō, hun*	*āpan, ap^{e}nē*	*jē, jehi, jin, jaunē, jāhē*	
Gen.	*hē-kar, hin-kar*	*hō-kar, hun-kar*	*āpan*	*jē-kar, jin-kar, jaunē-kāi, jāhē-kāi*	
Plur.					
Nom.	*hinhan, hinh^{e}nē, hin-k^{e}rē, hin-k^{e}ran*	*hunhan, hunh^{e}nē, hun-k^{e}rē, hunh-k^{e}ran*	*apuan, ap^{e}nan*	*jinhan, jinh^{e}nē, jin-k^{e}rē, jin-k^{e}ran, jaunan, jaunhan, jāūn^{e}nē, jāūnh^{e}nē*	
Obl.	Ditto.	Ditto.	Ditto.	Ditto.	

In all the above, the Genitive Singular has a feminine in ī, as *mōrī bēṭī*, my daughter. The oblique form ends in *ē*, as *mōrē bāp-kē*, to my father. As usual, the oblique genitive can be used as a declensional base. Thus *mōrē-kē*, and so on. The oblique form of *hamār* is *ham^{e}rē*, of *tuhār*, *tuh^{e}rē*, of *ē-kar*, *e-k^{e}rē*, and so on.

The relative and correlative pronouns have neuter forms, viz., *jitthū* or *jithuā*, *sitthū* or *sithuā*, *titthū* or *tithuā*, which are declined exactly like *itthū*. The neuter Interrogative Pronoun is *kā*, *kitthū*, or *kithuā*, what? obl., *kāhē*, *kitthū* or *kithuā*. Any one is *kew*, *kehu*, or *kaunō*. Anything is *kichh*, *kichchhū*, or *kichhaū*. In both of these two last, the oblique form is the same as the nominative.

IV.—VERBS—

We find the first person singular much more generally used than in Standard Bhojpurī.

The Verb Substantive is as follows :—

Present, I am, etc.—

	Form I.				Form II.			
	Sing.		Plur.		Sing.		Plur.	
	Masc.	Fem.	Masc.	Fem.	Masc.	Fem.	Masc.	Fem.
(1)	*bāṭō̃*	*bāṭiū̃*	*bāṭī*	......	*hauō̃*	*hauiū̃*	*hauī*	......
(2)	*bāṭē*	*bāṭī, bāṭis*	*bāṭā*	*bāṭū, bāṭiū*	*hauē*	*hauī, hāī, hauis*	*hauā*	*hauū, hauiū*
(3)	*bā*							
	bāy	*bāi*	*bāṭaī̃*	*bāṭī̃*	*hau, hāw*	......	*hauaī̃*	*hauī̃, hāī̃*

In the first form *ṛ* may be substituted for *ṭ*. Thus *bāṛō̃*, and so on throughout. This is principally in the east of the District. Note that, in Western Bhojpurī the first person plural throughout ends in *ī*, not in *ī̃*.

The Past tense is *rah^{a}lō̃*, I was, which is conjugated regularly like the past tense of a neuter verb.

The following are the principal tenses of the Finite verb. Only Masculine forms are given. The Feminine forms are formed on the analogy of *bāṭō̃*, above.

	Simple Present and Present Conditional, I see; (if) I see.		*Present Indicative*, I see, etc.	
	Sing.	Plur.	Sing.	Plur.
(1)	*dēkhō̃*	*dēkhī*	*dēkhāī-lō̃*	*dēkhī-lā̃*
(2)	*dēkh*	*dēkhā*	*dēkhāī-lē*	*dēkhāi-lā*
(3)	*dēkhai, dēkhō*	*dēkhaī̃*	*dēkhāi-lā* (fem. *dēkhāi-lī*)	*dēkhāi-laī̃*
	Past, I saw, etc.		*Future*, I shall see, etc.	
	Sing.	Plur.	Sing.	Plur.
(1)	*dekh^{a}lō̃*	*dekh^{a}lī*	*dekh^{a}bō̃*	*dēkhab, dekh^{a}baī̃*
(2)	*dekh^{a}lē*	*dekh^{a}lā*	*dekh^{a}bē*	*dekh^{a}bā*
(3)	*dekh^{a}las, dekh^{a}les* (fem. *dekh^{a}lasi*)	*dekh^{a}laī̃, dekh^{a}lan*	*dēkhī*	*dekhihaī̃*

	Past Conditional, (if) I had seen.		
	Sing.	Plur.	*Imperative—Present*—Sing. *dēkh*, *dēkhu*; Plur. *dēkhá*, *Future*—Sing. *dekhihē*; Plur. *dekhihá*.
(1)	*dekh^{a}tẽ*	*dekh^{a}tī*, *dēkhit*	*Present Definite*—*dēkhat bāṭõ̃*, or *dekh^{a}lāṭõ̃*, or *dēkhat hauõ̃*.
(2)	*dekh^{a}tē*	*dekh^{a}tá*	*Imperfect*—*dēkhat rah^{a}lõ̃*.
(3)	*dēkhat*	*dekh^{a}taĩ*	*Perfect*—*dekh^{a}lē bāṭõ̃* (or *hauõ̃*). *Pluperfect*—*dekh^{a}tē rah^{a}lõ̃*.
	Past Tense of a Neuter verb, I fell, etc.		
	Sing.	Plur.	
(1)	*gir^{a}lẽ*	*gir^{a}lī*	*Perfect*—*giral bāṭõ̃*.
(2)	*gir^{a}lē*	*gir^{a}lá*	*Pluperfect*—*giral rah^{a}lõ̃*.
(3)	*giral* (Fem. *girali*)	*gir^{a}laĩ*, *gir^{a}lan*	

The rest of the Conjugation is as in Standard Bhojpurī, except that the oblique forms of the Verbal nouns are as follows :—

(1) *dēkh*, — oblique form, *dēkhe*, or *dēkhāī*.
(2) *dēkhal*,— oblique form, *dekh^{a}lē*.
(3) *dēkhab*,— oblique form, *dekh^{a}bāī*.

The Perfect sometimes has forms like *aīlaī-haī*, he (hon.) has come; *kaīlaī haī*, he (hon.) has done.

As regards the irregular verbs they are as in Standard Bhojpurī, except that beside the form *dih^{a}las*, he gave, I have noted *deh^{a}las*, as also used. The verb for 'to begin' is *lagal*, not *lāgal*. 'I will go' is *jāb*.

The two following specimens are in the dialect illustrated in the foregoing grammatical sketch. The only thing to note is the attempt made to represent the peculiar *á* sound by a long *ā*. Thus *dá*, give, is written दा *dā*. In transcribing such cases, I shall write *á* not *ā*. The specimens are printed in Kaithī type. The first is a version of the Parable of the Prodigal Son, and the second is a statement made by a person accused in a criminal case and recorded in his own language.

They were written in Azamgarh, and may be taken as specimens of the dialect of that District and of Fyzabad. The western boundary of Bhojpurī in the latter district may be taken to be a line drawn from Tanda to the trijunction point of the Districts of Fyzabad, Sultanpur, and Azamgarh.

[No. 49.]

INDO-ARYAN FAMILY. EASTERN GROUP.

BIHĀRĪ.

BHOJPURĪ DIALECT.

WESTERN SUB-DIALECT. (DISTRICT AZAMGARH.)

SPECIMEN I.

(Babu Rama Smaran Lal, 1898.)

𑂉𑂍 𑂃𑂠𑂧𑂲 𑂍𑂵 𑂠𑂴 𑂥𑂵𑂗𑂰 𑂩𑂯𑂪 𑃀 𑂋 𑂧𑂵𑂁 𑂮𑂵 𑂓𑂷𑂗𑂍𑂰 𑂃𑂣𑂢𑂵 𑂥𑂰𑂣 𑂮𑂵 𑂍𑂯𑂪𑂮 𑂍𑂲 𑂉 𑂥𑂰𑂣 𑂯𑂧𑂢𑂵 𑂥𑂎𑂩𑂰 𑂍𑂵 𑂔𑂫𑂢 𑂧𑂰𑂪 𑂃𑂮𑂥𑂰𑂥 𑂯𑂷 𑂞𑂫𑂢 𑂯𑂧 𑂍𑂵 𑂠𑂰, 𑂉𑂯𑂲 𑂣𑂩 𑂥𑂣𑂫𑂰 𑂠𑂴𑂢𑂷𑂁 𑂥𑂵𑂗𑂢 𑂍𑂵 𑂄𑂣𑂢 𑂡𑂢 𑂥𑂰𑂀𑂗 𑂠𑂵𑂯𑂪𑂮𑃀 𑂥𑂯𑂳𑂞 𑂠𑂱𑂢 𑂢𑂰 𑂥𑂲𑂞𑂶 𑂣𑂰𑂫𑂪 𑂍𑂲 𑂓𑂷𑂗𑂍𑂰 𑂥𑂵𑂗𑂰 𑂍𑂳𑂪 𑂄𑂣𑂢 𑂡𑂢 𑂥𑂗𑂷𑂩 𑂍𑂵 𑂍𑂇𑂢𑂷𑂁 𑂠𑂴𑂩 𑂠𑂵𑂮 𑂍𑂵 𑂢𑂱𑂍𑂪 𑂏𑂅𑂪 𑂌𑂩 𑂄𑂣𑂢 𑂡𑂢 𑂎𑂩𑂰𑂥 𑂒𑂰𑂪 𑂧𑂵𑂁 𑂇𑂚𑂰 𑂣𑂳𑂚𑂰 𑂇𑂚𑂫𑂪𑂮𑃀 𑂔𑂥 𑂍𑂳𑂪 𑂋𑂍𑂩 𑂡𑂢 𑂋𑂩𑂰 𑂏𑂅𑂪 𑂞𑂥 𑂋𑂯 𑂠𑂵𑂮 𑂧𑂵𑂁 𑂥𑂯𑂳𑂞 𑂍𑂰𑂪 𑂣𑂚𑂪, 𑂋 𑂇 𑂠𑂰𑂢𑂰 𑂍𑂵 𑂧𑂷𑂯𑂞𑂰𑂔 𑂯𑂷𑂫𑂵 𑂪𑂰𑂏𑂪𑃀 𑂞𑂥 𑂈 𑂔𑂰 𑂍𑂵 𑂋𑂯 𑂠𑂵𑂮 𑂍𑂵 𑂉𑂍 𑂮𑂯𑂩 𑂍𑂵 𑂩𑂯𑂫𑂅𑂨𑂰 𑂍𑂵 𑂣𑂰𑂮 𑂣𑂯𑂳𑂀𑂒𑂪𑃀 𑂈 𑂃𑂠𑂧𑂲 𑂋 𑂍𑂵 𑂃𑂣𑂢𑂵 𑂎𑂵𑂞 𑂧𑂵𑂁 𑂮𑂴𑂃𑂩 𑂒𑂩𑂰𑂫𑂵 𑂍𑂵 𑂫𑂰𑂮𑂞𑂵 𑂦𑂵𑂔 𑂠𑂵𑂯𑂪𑂮𑃀 𑂋𑂍𑂩 𑂆 𑂠𑂮𑂰 𑂯𑂷 𑂏𑂅𑂪 𑂍𑂲 𑂔𑂫𑂢 𑂮𑂳𑂃𑂩𑂱𑂨𑂰 𑂦𑂳𑂮𑂲 𑂎𑂰𑂞 𑂩𑂯𑂪𑂲𑂁 𑂈𑂯𑂲 𑂔𑂷 𑂋 𑂍𑂵 𑂧𑂱𑂪𑂞 𑂞𑂷 𑂈 𑂋𑂯𑂲 𑂮𑂵 𑂄𑂣𑂢 𑂣𑂵𑂗 𑂦𑂳𑂮𑂲 𑂮𑂵 𑂦𑂩𑂞, 𑂪𑂵𑂍𑂱𑂢 𑂍𑂵𑂯𑂷 𑂢𑂰 𑂋 𑂍𑂵 𑂍𑂵𑂫 𑂠𑂵𑂞 𑂩𑂯𑂪𑃀 𑂔𑂥 𑂋 𑂍𑂵 𑂒𑂵𑂞 𑂦𑂅𑂪 𑂞𑂷 𑂈 𑂃𑂣𑂢𑂵 𑂧𑂢 𑂧𑂵𑂁 𑂍𑂯𑂪𑂮 𑂍𑂲 𑂍𑂵𑂞𑂢𑂰 𑂢𑂷𑂍𑂩𑂱𑂯𑂰 𑂧𑂔𑂠𑂳𑂩𑂱𑂯𑂰 𑂯𑂧𑂢𑂵 𑂥𑂰𑂣 𑂍𑂵 𑂥𑂰𑂀𑂗𑂵𑂁 𑂔𑂵𑂍𑂢𑂵 𑂎𑂰𑂉 𑂍𑂵 𑂥𑂯𑂳𑂞 𑂛𑂵𑂩 𑂥𑂜𑂱𑂍𑂵 𑂥𑂒 𑂔𑂰𑂪𑂰 𑂋 𑂯𑂧 𑂦𑂴𑂎𑂢 𑂧𑂩𑂞 𑂯𑂆𑂁𑃀 𑂯𑂧 𑂇𑂘𑂥 𑂃𑂣𑂢𑂵 𑂥𑂰𑂣 𑂍𑂱𑂯𑂰𑂀 𑂔𑂰𑂥 𑂋 𑂍𑂯𑂥 𑂍𑂲 𑂉 𑂥𑂰𑂣 𑂯𑂧 𑂞𑂷𑂯𑂢𑂵 𑂄𑂏𑂵 𑂋 𑂠𑂅𑂇 𑂍𑂵 𑂣𑂰𑂣 𑂍𑂩𑂪𑂲, 𑂉𑂯 𑂪𑂰𑂉𑂍 𑂢𑂅𑂎𑂷 𑂍𑂲 𑂃𑂥 𑂯𑂧 𑂍𑂵 𑂍𑂵𑂯𑂴 𑂞𑂷𑂯𑂰𑂩 𑂥𑂵𑂗𑂰 𑂍𑂯𑂶𑃀 𑂃𑂣𑂢𑂵 𑂢𑂷𑂍𑂩𑂱𑂯𑂰 𑂧𑂔𑂠𑂳𑂩𑂱𑂯𑂰 𑂧𑂵𑂁 𑂮𑂵 𑂯𑂧 𑂍𑂵 𑂮𑂧𑂳𑂕 𑂍𑂵 𑂩𑂎𑂰𑃀 𑂆 𑂍𑂯 𑂍𑂵 𑂈 𑂇𑂘𑂪 𑂋 𑂃𑂣𑂢𑂵 𑂥𑂰𑂣 𑂍𑂱𑂯𑂰𑂀 𑂄𑂅𑂪𑃀 𑂔𑂥 𑂠𑂴𑂩𑂵 𑂩𑂯𑂪 𑂞𑂥𑂶 𑂋𑂍𑂩 𑂥𑂰𑂣 𑂋 𑂍𑂵 𑂠𑂵𑂎𑂪𑂮𑃀 𑂋 𑂍𑂵 𑂠𑂩𑂠 𑂦𑂅𑂪, 𑂠𑂇𑂚 𑂍𑂵 𑂏𑂅𑂪, 𑂋𑂍𑂢𑂵 𑂏𑂪𑂵 𑂪𑂰𑂏𑂪 𑂋 𑂋 𑂍𑂵 𑂒𑂴𑂧𑂪𑂮𑃀 𑂞𑂥 𑂥𑂵𑂗𑂸𑂄 𑂃𑂣𑂢𑂵 𑂥𑂰𑂣 𑂮𑂵 𑂍𑂯𑂪𑂮 𑂍𑂲 𑂉 𑂥𑂰𑂣 𑂯𑂧 𑂞𑂷𑂯𑂢𑂵 𑂯𑂔𑂴𑂩 𑂋 𑂠𑂅𑂇 𑂍𑂵 𑂣𑂰𑂣 𑂍𑂩𑂪𑂲, 𑂃𑂥 𑂞𑂷𑂯𑂰𑂩 𑂥𑂵𑂗𑂰 𑂍𑂯𑂰𑂫𑂵 𑂪𑂰𑂉𑂍 𑂢𑂅𑂎𑂷𑂁𑃀 𑂪𑂵𑂍𑂱𑂢 𑂥𑂣𑂫𑂰 𑂃𑂣𑂢𑂵 𑂢𑂷𑂍𑂩𑂢 𑂮𑂵 𑂍𑂯𑂪𑂮 𑂍𑂲 𑂔𑂫𑂢 𑂃𑂒𑂹𑂓𑂰 𑂮𑂵 𑂃𑂒𑂹𑂓𑂰 𑂍𑂣𑂚𑂰 𑂯𑂷 𑂞𑂫𑂢 𑂪𑂱𑂄 𑂍𑂵 𑂋𑂍𑂩 𑂍𑂵 𑂣𑂯𑂱𑂢𑂰𑂫𑂞 𑂔𑂰 𑂋 𑂇𑂮 𑂍𑂵 𑂯𑂰𑂟 𑂧𑂵𑂁 𑂃𑂁𑂏𑂴𑂘𑂲 𑂋 𑂣𑂶𑂩 𑂧𑂵𑂁 𑂔𑂴𑂞𑂰 𑂣𑂯𑂱𑂢𑂰𑂫𑂰 𑂋 𑂮𑂥 𑂍𑂵𑂯𑂳 𑂄𑂫𑂰 𑂎𑂰𑂞 𑂔𑂰𑂅 𑂋 𑂎𑂳𑂮𑂲 𑂍𑂩𑂲𑂁, 𑂍𑂰𑂯𑂵 𑂮𑂵 𑂍𑂲 𑂆 𑂯𑂧𑂰𑂩 𑂥𑂵𑂗𑂰 𑂧𑂩 𑂍𑂵 𑂤𑂵𑂩 𑂔𑂲𑂃𑂪 𑂯𑂶, 𑂯𑂵𑂩𑂰𑂉 𑂍𑂵 𑂤𑂵𑂩 𑂧𑂱𑂪𑂪 𑂯𑂶𑃀 𑂉𑂯𑂲 𑂣𑂩 𑂮𑂥 𑂍𑂵𑂯𑂳 𑂎𑂳𑂮𑂲 𑂍𑂩𑂵 𑂪𑂰𑂏𑂪𑃁

વડ઼ક્ા વેટા ઓરૂ ઘડ઼ા ધેતે નરૂમ। ળવ આરઠ ઘને કે નગોચે પહુંચઠ તો દેખ્ખઠસ કી વાળા વળત હ્લ નાચ હોત હ્લ। તવ એક નોકન કે વોઠા કે પુછ્છઠસ દ્ર કા હોત હ્લ। તવ નોકનક્ા કહ્ઠસ કા, તોહાન ભાઈ અએં હૈ ઓરો પન તોહાન વાપ સવ કન નેવ્ઠા કરલેં હૈં કી તોહને ભાઈ સે સહી સઠામત ભેંટ ભરઠ હૈ। એ પન વડ઼ક્ા વેટા કે રંળ ગરઠ, ઓ ઊ ઘન મેં ળરવે ના કૈને। તવ ઓકન વાપ આરઠ ઓ ચિનવ્નો મિનતો કને ઠગઠ। તવ વડ઼ક્ા વેટા અપને વાપ કે ળવાવ દેહઠસ, ભઠ દેખ્ખા એતના દિન કરઉ વનસ તક હન તોહાન ખિદમત કરઠી, કહ્નો તોહાન કહ્ના ના ટનઠો ઓ તૂં કબ્વૌ હમ કે એક ઠો વક્નો કૈ વચ્ચો ના દેહ્ઠ કી હમ અપને સંગિન કે ઠે કે ખુસી કનિત। અવ તોહાન દ્ર વેટા જૈસે આરઠ હૈ ળે તોહાન ધન દઉઠત કસ્વો પતુરિઆ મેં ખૂંક ઉઠઠસ, તરસે દ્રં દાવ્ત ઓકને વદે કરઠ હૈ। તવ વપક્ા વડ઼કે વેટૌઆ સે કહ્ઠસ કી એ વેટા તૂં તો હરદમે હમને સાથ વાઠા ઓન ળવ્ન કુછ્છ હમાન હ્લ, સવ તોહાન હ્લ। દ્ર તોહાન ભાઈ મન કે ળોઅઠ હૈ, હેનાએ કે ફેન મિઠઠ હૈ, તો નોનાસિવ રહૈ નરઠ કી હમ ઠગ ખુસી કનો ઓ ખુસ હોઈ॥

[No. 49.]

INDO-ARYAN FAMILY. EASTERN GROUP.

BIHARĪ.

BHOJPURĪ DIALECT.

WESTERN SUB-DIALECT. (DISTRICT AZAMGARH.)

SPECIMEN I.

TRANSLITERATION AND TRANSLATION.

(Babu Rama Smaran Lal, 1898.)

Ēk ad^{a}mī-kē dū bēṭā rahal. Ō-mẽ-sē chhoṭ^{a}kā ap^{a}nē bāp-sē
One man-of two sons were. Them-in-from the-younger his-own father-to

kah^{a}las kī, 'ē bāp, ham^{a}rē bakh^{a}rā-kāī jawan māl as^{a}bāb hō tawan ham-kē
said that, 'O father, my share-of what property goods may-be that me-to

dā.' Ehi-par bap^{a}wā dūnõ bēṭan-kē āpan dhan bā̃ṭ deh^{a}las.
give.' This-upon the-father both sons-to his-own property dividing gave.

Bahut din nā bītāī pāwal kī chhoṭ^{a}ka bēṭā kul āpan dhan
Many days not to-pass were-allowed that the-younger son all his-own property

baṭor-ke kaūnõ dūr dēs-kē nikal-gaïl, aur āpan dhan kharāb chāl-mẽ
collecting some far-off country-to went-out, and his-own fortune bad conduct-in

uṛā-puṛā-ḍal^{a}las. Jab kul ōkar dhan orā-gaïl tab oh dēs-mẽ bahut
squandered. When all his fortune was-exhausted then that country-in much

kāl paṛal, o ū dānā-kāī moh^{a}tāj hōwāī lagal. Tab ū jā-ke oh
famine fell, and he grain-of poor to-be began. Then he going that

dēs-kē ēk sahar-kē rah^{a}waïā-kē pās pahũchal. Ū ad^{a}mī ō-kē ap^{a}nē khēt-mẽ
country-of one city-of inhabitant-of near reached. That man him his-own field-in

sūar charāwāī-kē-wāstē bhēj-deh^{a}las. Ō-kar ī dasā hō-gaïl kī jawan suariā
swine to-feed sent-away. His this condition became that what swine

bhūsī khāt-rah^{a}lī ūh-ō jō ō-kē milat tō ū ōhī-sē āpan
husks used-to-eat that-even if him-to was-given then he that-very-with his-own

pēṭ khusī-sē bharat, lēkin ih-ō nā ō-kē kew dēt-rahal.
belly pleasure-with would-have-filled, but this-even not him-to anybody used-to-give.

Jab ō-kē chēt bhaïl, tō ū ap^{a}nē man-mẽ kah^{a}las kī, 'ket^{a}nā
When him-to senses became, then he his-own mind-in said that, 'how-many

nokarihā maj^{a}durihā ham^{a}rē bāp-kē bāṭaī, jek^{a}rē khāē-kē bahut
servants day-labourers my father-of are, with-whom (food) for-eating much

hâw, balik bach-jā-lā, o ham bhūkhan marat-bâī. Ham chalab,
is, and-also is-saved, and I by-hunger dying-am. I will-start,

ap^{a}nē bāp kihā̃ jāb o kahab kī, "ē bāp, ham toh^{a}rē āgē
my-own father near I-will-go and I-will-say that, "O father, I thee before

o Daïu-kăī pāp kailī; eh lāek naïkhī kī ab ham-kē kew
and God-of sin have-done; this-(for) fit not-am that now me any-body

tohār bēṭā kahaï. Ap^{a}nē nokarihā maj^{a}durihā-mē̃-sē ham-kē samujh-ke
thy son may-call. Thy-own servants day-labourers-in-from me knowing

rakkhâ."' Ihai kah-ke ū uṭhal o ap^{a}nē bāp kihā̃ āil. Jab
keep."' This (very) saying he arose and his-own father near came. When

dūrai rahal, tabai ō-kar bāp ō-kē dekh^{a}las. Ō-kē darad
far-off-even he-was, then-even his father him saw. Him-to compassion

bhaïl. Daūṛ-ke gaïl. Ok^{a}rē galē lagal, o ō-kē chum^{a}las. Tab
became. Running he-went. His neck-on applied,[1] and him kissed. Then

beṭauā ap^{a}nē bāp-sē kah^{a}las kī, 'ē bāp, ham toh^{a}rē hajūr o Daïu-
the-son his-own father-to said that, 'O father, I thy presence-in and God-

kăī pāp kaïlī. Ab tohār bēṭā kahāwăī lāek naïkhī.' Lēkin bap^{a}wā
of sin did. Now thy son to-be-called worthy I-not-am.' But the-father

ap^{a}nē nok^{a}ran-sē kah^{a}las kī, 'jawan achchhā-sē achchhā kap^{a}ṛā hō,
his-own servants-to said that, 'what good-than good clothes there-may-be,

tawan liā-ke on-kē pahirāwat-jā, o on-kē hāth-mē̃ ā̃guṭhī o
those having-brought him-to cause-to-be-clothed, and his hand-on a-ring and

pair-mē̃ jūtā pahirāwâ, o sab-kehu āwâ, khāt-jāī̃ o khusī karī̃.
feet-on shoes put-on, and every-one come, let-us-eat and merriment let-us-make.

Kāhē-sē-kī i hamār bēṭā mar-ke phēr jīal-hai; herāe-ke
Because this my son having-died again become-alive-is; having-been-lost

phēr milal hai.' Ēhi-par sab kehu khusī karăī lagal.
again found is.' This-upon all persons merriment to-make began.

Baṛ^{a}kā bētā oh ghaṛī khētē rahal. Jab āil gharē-kē
The-elder son (at)-that hour the-field-in was. When he-came the-house-of

nagīchē pahũchal, to dekh^{a}las kī bājā bajat-hâw,
near he-arrived, then he-saw that musical-instruments are-being-played-upon,

nāch hōt hâw. Tab ēk nōkar-kē bolā-ke puchh^{a}las, 'ī kā
dance being(-carried-on) is. Then one servant calling he-asked, 'this what

hōt hâw?' Tab nokar^{a}wā kah^{a}las kī, 'tohār bhāī āïlaī̃-haī̃. Ohī-par
being-(done) is?' Then the-servant said that, 'thy brother come-has. That-very-upon

tohār bāp sab-kar new^{a}tā kaïlaī̃-haī̃; kī toh^{a}rē bhāī-sē sahī-salāmat
thy father all-of invitation made-has; that thy brother-with with-safety

bhē̃ṭ bhaïl-hai. Ē-par baṛ^{a}kā bēṭā-kē raññj gaïl, o ū ghar-
meeting has-taken-place. This-upon the-elder son-to anger went, and he house-

[1] i.e., Pressed neck to neck, the equivalent of embracing. A custom common among women when welcoming their returned relatives.

mẽ jaïbāï na karai. Tab ō-kar bāp āil o chiraürī-min'tī kare
into going not would-do. Then his father came and entreaties to-make

lagal. Tab baṛ'kā bēṭā ap'nē bāp-kē jabāb deh'las, 'bhalā! dēkhā,
began. Then the-elder son his-own father-to answer gave, 'well! see,

et'nā din kaïu baras tak ham tohār khid'mat kaïlī, kaünō tohār
so-many days how-many years for I thy service did, any thy

kah'nā nā ṭar'lī, o tū kabb-ō̃ ham-kē ek-ṭhō bak'rī-kāï bachch-ō
saying not transgressed, and thou ever-even me-to one goat-of young-one-even

nā deh'lā, kī ham ap'nē saṅgin-kē lē-ke khusī karit. Ab
not gavest, that I my-own companions taking merriment might-make. Now

tohār ī bēṭā jaisē āil-hai, jē tohār dhan-daülat kas'bī paturiyā-mẽ
thy this son as-even he-come-is, who thy fortune harlots dancing-girls-in

phū̃k-ḍal'las, taïsē tū̃ dāwat ok'rē badē kaïlā-hai. Tab bap'wā baṛ'kē
burnt-down, so-even thou a-feast him for made-hast. Then the-father the-elder

beṭauā-sē kah'las kī, 'ē bēṭā, tū̃, to, har dam-ai ham'rē sāth
son-to said that, 'O son, thou, to-be-sure, every moment-even me with

bāṭā äür jawan-kuchh hamār hâw, sab tohār hâw. Ī tohār bhāī mar-
art and whatever mine is, all thine is. This thy brother having-

ke jīal-hai, herāe-ke phēr milal hai, tō monāsib ihai
been-dead has-become-alive, having-been-lost again found is, then proper this

rahal kī ham lōg khusī karī o khus hoī.'
was that we people merriment might-make and glad might-be.'

[No. 50.]

INDO-ARYAN FAMILY. EASTERN GROUP.

BIHĀRĪ.

BHOJPURĪ DIALECT.

WESTERN SUB-DIALECT. (DISTRICT AZAMGARH.)

SPECIMEN II.

(Babu Rama Smaran Lal, 1898.)

મૈં મહુઆને વનયા ઘનોહૈ ગરઠોં । તવ ઘેતાપટ્ટો ગરઠોં । મહુઆને વનયા ના મિઠઠ । ઘેતાપટ્ટો મેં વનયા ના મિઠઠ । ઠજટઠ આવત નહઠો । પઠયો મેં સાહ હો ગરઠ । વનિઆ કે દુકાન પર વળાન મેં ડહર ગરઠો । નામ વનિઅવા કૈ નાહીં ળાનિત । સવેરા મૈઠ તવ સવ ઠાગ સોર કરઠૈ કી નાળા કે રહીં ચોનો ળરઠ । સવેરા કે ળૂન હમ સડ઼ક ચરઠે ળાત નહઠો । નાળા કૈ તોન ચઠકીદાર હમ કે પકડ઼ લિહલેં । તોનોં અદમો ઠપઠ કે મરઠેં । વારસ રુપેયા હમને પાસ નહઠ ઔર અંગૌછા મોરળર દુપટ્ટા હમને પાસ નહઠ । સે છોર લિહલેં । એક ચોતી નહઠા ઉહો છિન લિહલેં । રુપેઆ જો છોર લિહલેં હમ અકેલે નહઠો । ઠાત મુક્ષા સે મરલેં ઔર ઉગ્ગ વેગ કે દે મરલેં । સગરો વદન મેં ચોટ ઠગઠ હૌ । ગઢ઼ નાહીં હો ળાત । મૈં ના ચોનો જને ગરઠ નહઠોં । છત પર સે હમ નાહીં ગિરઠો છત પર સે ગિરિત તો જપાન છૂટ ળાત । વોછે કે દિન ગાંવ સે ચઠઠ નહઠો । રુપેઆ હમ એક વનિઆ સે જરળા લિહલે નહઠો । નાહીં । વનિઆ સે હમ રુપેઆ ના લિહઠો, ઘર સે રુપેઆ લે કે ચઠઠ નહઠો । તોન વનયા હમને ઘને હા । એક હમ ઔર ઘનોહૈ ગરઠ નહઠો ।

[No. 50.]

INDO-ARYAN FAMILY. EASTERN GROUP.

BIHARĪ.

BHOJPURĪ DIALECT.

WESTERN SUB-DIALECT. (DISTRICT AZAMGARH.)

SPECIMEN II.

TRANSLITERATION AND TRANSLATION.

(Babu Rama Smaran Lal, 1898.)

Maĩ Mahuārē bar'dhā kharīdăĩ gaïlō̃. Tab Khētā-paṭṭī gaïlō̃.
I Mahuārā-to ox to-buy went. Then Khētā-paṭṭī-(to) I-went.

Mahuārē bar'dhā nā milal. Khēt-ō-paṭṭī-mẽ bar'dhā nā milal. Laüṭal
In-Mahuārā ox not was-found. Khētā-paṭṭī-also-in ox not was-found. Back

āwat rah'lī, Pal'thī-mẽ sā̃jh hō-gaïl. Baniā-kē dukān-par bajār-mẽ
coming I-was, Pal'thī-in evening became. A-shopkeeper-of shop-at market-in

ṭhahar-gaïlī. Nām baniawā-kăī nāhī̃ jānit. Sabērā bhail tab sab
I-stayed. The-name the-shopkeeper-of not I-know. The-dawn became then all

lōg sōr kaïlaĩ, ki Rājā-kē ihā̃ chōrī bhaïl. Sabērā-kē jūn
people a-noise made, that the-Rājā-of near a-theft has-occurred. Dawn-of time

ham saṛak dhaïlē jāt rah'lī. Rājā-kăī tīn chaükīdār ham-kē pakaṛ lih'laĩ.
I road holding going was. Rājā-of three watchmen me hold-of took.

Tīnō̃ ad'mī lapaṭ-ke mar'laĩ. Bāis rupeā ham'rē pās rahal, ăür
The-three men closing-with(-me) beat(-me). Twenty-two rupees me with were, and

ā̃gauchhā mir'jaī dupaṭṭā ham'rē pās rahal, sē chhōr-lih'laĩ. Ēk
body-cloth a-waist-coat double-wrapper me with were, those they-seized-by-force. One

dhōṭī rahal; uhō chhin-lih'laĩ. Rupeā bhī chhōr-lih'laĩ. Ham
loin-cloth was; that-too they-seized-by-force. Rupees too they-seized-by-force. I

akēlē rah'lī. Lāt mūkā-sē mar'laĩ, ăür uṭhā băĩṭhā-ke
alone was. Kicks fists-with they-beat(-me), and taking-(me)-up (and)-making-(me)-sit

dē-mar'laĩ. Sag'rō badan-mẽ chōṭ lagal-hau. Ṭhāṛh nāhī̃
threw-(me)-down. The-entire body-in wounds have-been-produced. To-stand not

hō-jāt. Maĩ nā chōrī-kare gaïl rah'lō̃. Chhat-par-sē ham nāhī̃ gir'lī.
I-am-able. I not to-do-theft gone had. The-roof-on-from I not fell.

Chhat-par-sē girit tō kapār phāṭ-jāt.
The-roof-on-from (if)-I-had-fallen then (my-)skull would-have-been-fractured.

Biphē-kē din gā̃w-sē chalal-rah^{a}lī. Rupeā ham ēk baniyā-sē
Thursday-of day the-village-from I-started-had. Rupees I one shopkeeper-from

kar^{a}jā lih^{a}lē-rah^{a}lī. Nāhī̃, baniyā-sē ham rupeā nā lih^{a}lī. Ghar-sē
loan had-taken. No, a-shopkeeper-from I rupees not took. House-from

rupeā lē-ke chalal-rah^{a}lī. Tīn bar^{a}dhā ham^{a}rē gharē hau. Ēk ham äūr
rupees taking I-had-started. Three oxen my house-at are. One I more

kharīde gaïl rah^{a}lī.
to-buy gone had.

FREE TRANSLATION OF THE FOREGOING.

I went to the village of Mahuārā to buy a bullock. Then I went on to Khēta-paṭṭī, as I could not find one at Mahuārā. Nor could I find one in Khēta-paṭṭī either. Evening fell when I was at Palthī, on the way home; so I stopped for the night in a shop in the *bāzār*. I do not know the name of the shopkeeper. As soon as it was morning the people raised a cry that a theft had been committed in the Rājā's palace. Just then I was going home along the road, and three watchmen of the Rājā's came and caught hold of me. They all closed upon me and beat me. I had twenty-two rupees upon me, and they forcibly took from me not only these, but also my body cloth, my waistcoat, and my double-wrapper. I was wearing a loin-cloth, too, and that also they seized by force. They even took my money from me. I was quite alone, and they kicked me and struck me with their clenched fists, and lifted me up and threw me down.[1] My whole body is covered with wounds, so that I cannot stand up. I never fell from the roof. If I had done that I should have fractured my skull.

I started from my village on Thursday last, after borrowing the money from a shopkeeper. No, I did not borrow it from a shopkeeper. I had the money with me in my house, and took it and started. I have three bullocks at home, and had set out to buy one more.

Western Bhojpurī is also spoken by some 80,000 people in the east of the District of Jaunpur, mainly in Taluka Dobhi of Pargana Chandwak. In the rest of the District a form of Eastern Hindī, locally known as Banaudhī, is spoken. The former dialect is practically the same as that of Azamgarh, as will be evident from the following specimen of the Parable of the Prodigal Son. The following peculiarities may be noticed. The broad Bhojpurī *á* is represented in writing by *ā*. Thus *dyā* for *dyá*, give. The oblique form of the pronoun of the third person is usually written *wahi* instead of *ohi*, and, in the conjugation of verbs, the two vowels *aï* are usually, but not always, written *aya*. Thus, *gayal, bhayal*, instead of *gaïl, bhaïl*, etc. These are all mere varieties of spelling. Among verbal forms, we may note *dyá*, above mentioned, which is the second person plural Imperative, instead of the more usual *dá*.

The specimen comes from Pargana Chandwak, Tahsil Keraket.

---

[1] This is a technical term for a kind of assault. The victim is first made to sit down, and the aggressor then lifts up his legs and throws him on his back.

[No. 51.]

INDO-ARYAN FAMILY. EASTERN GROUP.

BIHĀRĪ.

BHOJPURĪ DIALECT.

WESTERN SUB-DIALECT. (DISTRICT JAUNPUR.)

एक जने के दुइ बेटवा रहलैं। लहुरका बेटवा अपने बाप से कहलेस की बाप धन में से जवन हमार बखरा होय तवन हम्मैं देइ द्या। बाप बखरा देइ दिहलेस। किछु दिन पाछे लहुरका बेटवा जवन बखरा पउले रहल तवन लेइ के बिदेस गयल। उहाँ अपने चाल चलन के खराबी से कुल जहबुम कइ दिहलेस। और जब सब खरिच होय चुकल तब वहि देस में काल पड़ल। जब दाना बिना मरै लगलैं तब कौनेउ भला अदमी के इहाँ गयलैं। ऊ उन्हें खेतारी में सूअर चरावै के रखलेस। उहाँ ऊ चहलैं की जौन छिकुला सूअर खात रहलैं ऊहो हम्मैं मिलत तौ खाइत। बाकी ऊहो नाहीं मिलल। जब पेट जरै लागल तब घर कै चेत भयल की हमरे बाप के इहाँ नोकर चाकर खात पहिरत और बचावत हउऐं और हम इहाँ दाना बिना मरत हई। तब श्रोन के जिय में भयल की अब हम अपने घरे चलो और बाप से कही की हम से कसूर भयल और ईसर के इहाँ से हम बेजाँय कयल और चल के कहब की अब हम तोहार बेटवा बन के रहै लायक नाँहीं बाटी। जैसे और मजूर बाटैं तइसे हमहूँ से मजूरी करावा। उहाँ से अपने मन में ऐसन गुन के चलल और बाप के इहाँ आयल। जब बेटवा लामें रहल तब बाप देखलेस की हमार बेटवा उहै आवत हौ। देख-के मोह बढ़ल मारे छोह के आगे होइ के अँकवारी भर धइ के चूमै लगलैं। तब बेटवा कहलेस की बाप हम तोहार कसूर कइली और परमेसर के इहाँ से बेजाँय कइली। अब हम तोहार बेटवा कहावै लायक नाँहीं बाटी। नोकरन से बाप कहलेस की बढ़ियाँ कपड़ा ले आवा पहिरावा और अँगुरी में मुनरी और गोड़े में पनहीं पहिरावा और रजगज होए द्या काहे से की जनुक बेटवा हमार मर के जीअल और हेरायल रहल फेर मिलल है। और रजगज होए लागल॥

जेठ बेटवा कतहूँ खेतारी में रहलैं। ऊ जब घरे अइलैं तब ई सब खुसिहाली कै बात देख के एक नोकर से पुछलेस की का भयल है। नोकर कहलेस की तोहार लहुरका भाय आयल हौ और उन के कुसलकारी से लउटले के संती तोहार बाप खिआवत पिआवत हउऐं। ई सुन के जेठरे बेटवा के जिव में खुन्स आयल और बखरी में नाँहीं गयल। जब ई सुन के बाप बाहर आयल और मनावै लागल तब बेटवा कहलेस की तोहार धंधा ढेर दिन से कइली और तोहरे कहले मतिन चलली। आगे तोहार जी कबहूँ नाँहीं भयल की एक खसी मार के लेइ अउता की अपने संगिन के खिआइत पिआइत। और ई तोहार बेटा जवन तोहार धन और दौलत बाँट के रंडो मुंडी के दिहलेस जैसे लौट के आयल तइसे प्रतवत भोज दिहला। बाप कहलेस की बेटवा तू हमरे संगी सब दिन रहाला। जवन किछु धन और ईसरज हौ तवन तोहरे हौ। ई बेटवा हम जनली की मुइ गयल अब हम पउली तवने से ई जलसा करै के चाहत रहल॥

[No. 51.]

INDO-ARYAN FAMILY. EASTERN GROUP.

BIHĀRĪ.

BHOJPURĪ DIALECT.

WESTERN SUB-DIALECT. (DISTRICT JAUNPUR.)

TRANSLITERATION AND TRANSLATION.

Ēk janē-kē dui beṭᵃwā rahᵃlaĩ. Lahurᵃkā beṭᵃwā apᵃnē bāp-sē
One man-to two sons were. The-younger son his-own father-to
kahᵃles kī, 'bāp, dhan-mẽ-sē jawan hamār bakhᵃrā hōy tawan
said that, 'father, property-in-from what my share may-be that
hammaĩ dei-dyâ.' Bāp bakhᵃrā dei-dihᵃles. Kichhu din pāchhē
to-me give.' The-father share gave-away. Some days after
lahurᵃkā beṭᵃwā jawan bakhᵃrā paūlē-rahal tawan lei-ke bidēs
the-younger son what share had-got that taking (to-)a-foreign-land
gayal. Uhā̃ apᵃnē chāl-chalan-kē kharābī-sē kul jahannum kaĩ-dihᵃles.
went. There his-own conduct-of wickedness-with all (to-)hell he-made (sent).
Āūr jab sab kharich hōy-chukal tab wahi dēs-mẽ kāl paṛal. Jab
And when all spent had-been then that country-in famine fell. When
dānā binā marăī lagᵃlaĩ tab kauneu bhalā adᵃmī-kē ihā̃ gayᵃlaĩ. Ū
grain without to-die he-began then a-certain well-to-do man-of near he-went. He
unhaĩ khetārī-mẽ sūar charāwăī-kē rakhᵃles. Uhā̃ ū chahᵃlaĩ kī,
him fields-in swine to-feed kept. There he wished that,
jaun chhikulā sūar khāt-rahᵃlaĩ, 'ūhau hammaĩ milat,
what husks swine used-to-eat, 'those-also to-me (if)-they-had-been-given,
tau khāit.' Bākī ūhau nāhĩ milal. Jab pēṭ
then I-would-have-eaten (-them).' But those-even not were-given. When belly
jarăī lāgal tab ghar-kăī chēt bhayal kī, 'hamᵃrē bāp-kē ihā̃
to-burn began then house-of the-remembrance became that, 'my father-of near
nōkar-chākar khāt pahirat, ăūr bachāwat haūaĩ ăūr ham ihā̃
servants eating wearing (clothes) and saving (money) are and I here
dānā binā marat-hāĩ.' Tab onᵃkē jiy-mẽ bhayal kī, 'ab ham
grain without dying-am.' Then his heart-in became that, 'now (let)-me
apᵃnē gharē chalī, ăūr bāp-sē kahī kī, "ham-sē kasūr
my-own in-house go, and the-father-to let-me-say that, "me-by fault

bhayal, ăŭr Īsar-kē ihā̃-sē ham bejā̃y kayal," ăŭr chal-ke
has-come-to-pass, and God-of near-from I evil did," and going

kahab kī, "ab ham tohār beṭ*wa ban-ke rahăī lāyak nā̃hī̃ bāṭī.
will-say that, "now I thy son becoming to-live worthy not am.

Jaīsē ăŭr majūr bāṭaī̃ taïsē ham-hū̃-sē majūrī karāwȧ."' Ubā̃-sē
As other labourers are so me-also-by labour cause-to-be-done."' There-from

āp*nē man-mē̃ aisan gun-ke chalal, ăŭr bāp-kē ihā̃ āyal. Jab
his-own mind-in so thinking he-started, and father-of near came. When

beṭ*wā lāmē̃ rahal, tab bāp dekh*les kī, 'hamār beṭ*wā uhai
the-son far-off was, then the-father saw that, 'my son there-yonder

āwat hau.' Dēkh-ke mōh baṛhal. Mārē chhōh-kē āgē-hōi-ke ā̃k*wārī-
coming is.' Seeing pity arose. Goaded-by pity advancing the-lap-

bhar dhaï-ke chūmăī lag*laī. Tab beṭ*wā kah*les kī, 'bāp, ham tohār
in holding to-kiss began. Then the-son said that, 'father, I thy

kasūr kaīli aur Par*mēsar-kē ihā̃-sē bejā̃y kaīlī. Ab ham tohār beṭ*wā
fault did and God-of near-from evil did. Now I thy son

kahāwăī lāyak nā̃hī̃ bāṭī.' Nok*ran-sē bāp kah*les kī, 'baṛhiyā̃
to-be-called fit not am.' Servants-to the-father said that, 'good

kap*ṛā lē-āwȧ, pahirāwȧ, ăŭr ā̃gurī-mē̃ munarī ăŭr gōṛē-mē̃ pan*hī̃
clothes bring, put-on-(him), and finger-in a-ring and feet-on shoes

pahirāwȧ; ăŭr raj-gaj hōe-dyȧ, kāhē-sē-kī januk beṭ*wā hamār
put; and rejoicings be-made-let, because as-if son my

mar-ke jīal; ăŭr herāyal rahal, phēr milal-hai.' Ăŭr
having-been-dead came-to-life; and lost was, again found-is.' And

raj-gaj hōe lāgal.
rejoicings to-be-made began.

Jēṭh beṭ*wā kat*hū̃ khetārī-mē̃ rah*laī. Ū jab gharē
The-elder son somewhere fields-in was. He when into-house

aīlaī, tab ī sab khusihālī-kăī bāt dēkh-ke ēk nōkar-sē puchh*les kī,
came, then these all rejoicings-of matters seeing one servant-from asked that,

'kā bhayal-hai?' Nōkar kah*les kī, 'tohār lahur*kā bhāy āyal-hau,
'what has-occurred?' The-servant said that, 'thy younger brother come-is,

ăŭr un-kē kusal-kārī-sē lauṭ*le-kē santī tohār bāp khiāwat
and his safety-with returning for thy father feeding (his-people)

piāwat hauaī.' Ī sun-ke jeṭh*rē beṭ*wā-kē jiw-mē̃
causing-to-drink (his-people) is.' This hearing the-elder son-of heart-into

khuns āyal ăŭr bakh*rī-mē̃ nā̃hī̃ gayal. Jab ī sun-ke bāp
anger came and the-house-into not went. Then this hearing the-father

bāhar āya. ăŭr manāwăī lāgal, tab beṭ*wā kah*les kī, 'tohār
outside came and to-appease (him) began, then the-son said that, 'thy

dhandhā ḍhēr din lē kaïlī, ăūr toh^ə^rē kah^a^lē matin chal^a^lī. Āgē tohār jī
works many days for I-did, and thy saying according-to went. But thy heart
kab-hū̃ nāhī̃ bhayal kī ēk khasī mār-ke lei-aūtâ,
ever-even not became that one he-goat having-slaughtered thou-mightest-have-brought,
kī ap^a^nē saṅgin-kē khiāit-piāit. Ăūr ī tohār bēṭā jawan tohār
that my-own companions I-might-have-feasted. And this thy son who thy
dhan ăūr daulat bā̃ṭ-ke ranḍī-munḍī-kē dih^a^les, jaisē lauṭ-ke
fortune and property dividing harlots-etcetera-to gave, as-even returning
āyal taïsē et^a^wat bhōj dih^a^lâ.' Bāp kah^a^les kī, 'beṭ^a^wā tū
came so-even so-great feast thou-gavest.' The-father said that, 'son thou
ham^a^rē saṅgē sab din rahâ-lâ; jawan-kichhu dhan ăūr īswar^a^j hau
me with all days livest; what-even property and prosperity is
tawan toh^a^rai hau. Ī beṭ^a^wā ham jan^a^lī kī mui gayal, ab ham paūlī;
that thine-verily is. This son I thought that dead he-was, now I got;
taw^a^nē-sē ī jal^a^sā karāï-kē chāhat rahal.'
owing-to-that this rejoicing to-do proper was.'

The dialect spoken in the District of Benares is Western Bhojpurī, the same as that of Azamgarh. It is locally known as Banār^a^sī. The following specimens, which I owe to the kindness of Pandit Mahārāj Nārāyaṇ Śivapurī, Rai Bahádur, are admirable examples of the language spoken of the country portions of the district, as distinct from the dialect of the city. The first is a version of the Parable of the Prodigal Son, for which no interlinear translation is necessary, and the second is the statement made in a criminal court by a man accused of theft.

The only peculiarities which need be noticed are methods of spelling. The peculiar Bhojpurī *â* is represented by *visarga, ḥ.* Thus दः *dâ*; लः *lâ*, and many others. The two vowels *aï* are often spelt *aē*, or *aya*. Thus *kaïlan, gaël, bhayal.* Similarly *aü* are usually spelt *awa*. Thus, instead of *bachaüt-ō*, we have *bachaw^a^t-ō*, and instead of *lagaüles, lagaw^a^les.*

The same specimen will also do as an example of the dialect spoken in Western Ghazipur and Central Mirzapur. As already explained on p. 201, we may estimate half the 938,000 speakers of Bhojpurī in the former district as speaking Standard and half as speaking Western Bhojpurī.

As regards Mirzapur, 1,111,500 persons were originally estimated as speaking 'Purbī.' Subsequent enquiry has shown that this is not a correct statement of the case, and that this population must be further sub-divided. Mirzapur District consists of three distinct areas. There is a small portion on the north of the Ganges. There is then the main, central, portion of the District, south of the Ganges and north of the Sone, and finally there is the tract south of the Sone, known as the Sōnpār.

Taking the North-Gangetic area first, it lies immediately to the east of Benares District, and south of that of Jaunpur. It is mainly composed of Pargana Bhadohi, which is a portion of the Family Domains of the Mahārāja of Benares; but in its south-east corner, on the north bank of the Ganges and close to the Benares border, lie the small tracts of Tappa Kon, Taluka Majhwa, and Pargana Karyat Sikhar. In Bhadohi, the language is a form of Eastern Hindī, similar to that which we shall find in Western Jaunpur and Eastern Allahabad. In Kon, Majhwa, and Karyat Sikhar, it is the Western Bhojpurī which is spoken in Benares District. The same form of Bhojpurī is spoken in the portion of Mirzapur which lies between the Ganges and the Sone. In the Sonpar, on the contrary, it appears that the mixed population there settled speak a form of Eastern Hindī, which, for convenience sake may be called Sōnpārī.

Converting the revised local estimates to round numbers, we find the original 1,111,500 speakers of 'Purbī' sub-divided as follows :—

Eastern Hindī	252,000
Western Bhojpurī	810,000
Sōnpārī	49,500
TOTAL	1,111,500

[No. 52.]

INDO-ARYAN FAMILY. EASTERN GROUP.

BIHĀRĪ.

BHOJPURĪ DIALECT.

WESTERN, BANĀR'SI, SUB-DIALECT. (DISTRICT BENARES.)

SPECIMEN I.

(Paṇḍit Mahārāj Nārāyaṇ Śivapurī, Rai Bahādur, 1898.)

एक अदमी के दुइठे बेटवा रहलन। ओ में से छोटका अपनें बाप से कहलेस हे बाबू जौन कुछ माल असबाब हमरे बखरा में पड़े तौन हम के दे दः। तब ऊ आपन कमाई दूनों के बाँट दिहलेस। थोरिकै दिन के बितले लहुरका बेटवा सब माल समेट के बड़ो दूर परदेस चलल गएल और उहाँ सब धन लुचपन में फूँक दिहलेस। जब सब गवाँय चुकल तब ओहि देस में बड़ा काल पड़ल। और ऊ भूखन मरे लगल। तब ओहि देस के एक रहीस से जाय मिलल और ऊ ओ के अपने खेत में सूअर चरावै बदे पठै दिहलेस। और जौन छिकुला भूसी सूअर खात रहलन ओही से ऊ आपन पेट भरै बदे ललचत रहल। कोइ ओ के न दिहलेस। तब ओ के चेत भयल और मन में सोचलेस की हमरे बाप किहाँ केतना अदमी नोकर बाटन को ऊ लोग पेट भर खाय के कुछ बचवतो छोड़हें और हम भूखन मरत बाटी। हम उट्ठीं और अपने बाप के पास चलीं और ओन से कहीं को हे बाबू भगवान के सामने और तोहरे सामने हम बड़ा पाप कइली। तोहार बेटवा कहावे लायक नाहीं बाटी हमें अपनें मजूरन में रख लः। ई बिचार के ऊठल और अपने बाप के पास गयल। बाप बड़ो दूर से बेटवा के आवत देख के मया के मारे दऊर के अपने गरे लगवलेस और चुम्मे लगल। बेटवा बोलल बाबू भगवान के और तोहरे सामने हम अपराधी हई अब हम तोहार बेटवा कहावे लायक नाहीं बाटी। सुदा बाप अपने नोकरन से कहलेस की बढ़ियाँ से बढ़ियाँ कपड़ा निकाल के हमरे लड़िका के पहिरावः और हाथ में मुनरी और गोड़ में पनहीं पहिरावः और हम लोग खाय पी के खुसी मनाईं काहे से की ई लड़िका हमार मर के फिर जीअल है बिछुड़ के फिर मिलल है। तब सब लोग खुसी मनावे लगलन॥

बड़का बेटवा खेत में रहल जब उहाँ से लौटल और घर के नगीच पहुँचल तब गीत और नाच कै धूम सुनाई पड़ल। एक नोकर के बोलाय के पुछलेस की ई सब का होत बाय। ऊ जबाब दिहलेस की तोहार भाई अइलन हैं और सही सलामत उन के बहुरले के खुसी में तोहार बाप जेवनार कइलन हैं। ई सुन के ऊ गुस्सा भयल और भित्तर नाहीं गयल। तब बाप बाहर निकल अइलें और लड़िका के मनावे लगलें। लड़िका बाप के जबाब दिहलेस वाह एतना दिन से तोहार गुलामी करत हई कबहीं तोहार हुकुम नाहीं टरली तेहू पर तूं कबहूँ एक खस्सी के बच्चो नाहीं दिहलः की हम अपने संगी के संग खाए पी के चैन करित। सुदा अपने छोटका बेटवा के अवते जौन तोहार सगरो कमाई रंडी बाजी में फूंक दिहलेस तेकरे बदे भोज दिहलः है। बाप बोलल की बेटा तू हमरे लगे सदा रहःलः और जौन कुछ हमरे पास बाय तौन सब तोहरे हौ। हम लोगन के खुसी करे के उचित रहल काहे से ई तोहार भाई मर के फिर जीअल है और बिछुड़ के फिर मिलल है॥

[No. 52.]

INDO-ARYAN FAMILY. EASTERN GROUP.

BIHĀRĪ.

BHOJPURĪ DIALECT.

WESTERN, BANĀR'SĪ, SUB-DIALECT. (DISTRICT BENARES.)

SPECIMEN I.

TRANSLITERATION.

(Pandit Mahārāj Nārāyan Śivapurī, Rai Bahādur, 1898.)

Ēk adᵃmī-kē dui-ṭhē beṭᵃwā rahᵃlan. Ō-mẽ-sē chhoṭᵃkā apᵃnē bāp-sē kahᵃles, 'hē bābū, jaun kuchh māl asᵃbāb hamᵃrē bakhᵃrā-mẽ paṛai taun ham-kē dē-dâ.' Tab ū āpan kamāī dūnõ-kē bā̃ṭ dihᵃles. Thōrikai din-kē bitᵃlē lahurᵃkā beṭᵃwā sab māl samēṭ-ke baṛī dūr parᵃdēs chalal-gael, ăūr uhā̃ sab dhan luchᵃpan-mẽ phū̃k-dihᵃles. Jab sab gawā̃y chukal tab ohi dēs-mẽ baṛā kāl paṛal, ăūr ū bhūkhan marăĭ lagal. Tab ohi dēs-kē ēk rahīs-sē jāy milal, ăūr ū ō-kē apᵃnē khēt-mẽ sūar charāwăĭ badē paṭhai dihᵃles. Ăūr jaun chhikulā bhūsī sūar khāt rahᵃlan ōhī-sē ū āpan pēṭ bharăĭ badē lalᵃchat-rahal. Kēhū ō-kē na dihᵃles. Tab ō-kē chēt bhayal ăūr man-mẽ sochᵃles kī, 'hamᵃrē bāp kihā̃ ketᵃnā adᵃmī nōkar bāṭan kī ū lōg pēṭ bhar khāy-ke kuchh bachawᵃt-ō hōihaĩ, ăūr ham bhūkhan marat-bāṭī. Ham uṭṭhī̃ ăūr apᵃnē bāp-kē pās chalī̃ ăūr on-sē kahī̃ kī, "hē bābū, Bhagᵃwān-kē sāmᵃnē ăūr tohᵃrē sāmᵃnē ham baṛā pāp kaïlī. Tohār beṭᵃwā kahāwăĭ lāyak nāhī̃ bāṭī. Hamaĩ apᵃnē majūran-mẽ rakh-lâ."' Ī bichār-ke ūṭhal ăūr apᵃnē bāp-kē pās gayal. Bāp baṛī dūr-sē beṭᵃwā-kē āwat dēkh-ke mayā-kē mārē daūr-ke apᵃnē garē lagawᵃles ăūr chummăĭ lagal. Beṭᵃwā bōlal, 'Bābū, Bhagᵃwān-kē ăūr tohᵃrē sāmᵃnē ham apᵃrādhī hâī. Ab ham tohār beṭᵃwā kahāwăĭ lāyak nāhī̃ bāṭī.' Mudā bāp apᵃnē nokᵃran-sē kahᵃles kī, 'baṛhiyā̃-sē baṛhiyā̃ kapᵃṛā nikāl-ke hamᵃrē larikā-kē pahirāwâ ăūr hāth-mẽ munᵃrī ăūr gōṛ-mẽ panᵃhī̃ pahirāwâ, ăūr ham lōg khāy-pī-kē khusī manāī̃; kāhē-sē kī ī laṛikā hamār mar-ke phir jīal-hai; bichhuṛ-ke phir milal-hai.' Tab sab lōg khusī manāwăĭ lagᵃlan.

Baṛᵃkā beṭᵃwā khēt-mẽ rahal. Jab uhā̃-sē lauṭal ăūr ghar-kē nagīch pahū̃chal tab gīt ăūr nāch kăĭ dhūm sunăĭ-paṛal. Ēk nōkar-kē bolāy-ke puchhᵃles kī 'ī sab kâ hōt bāy?' Ū jabāb dihᵃles kī, 'tohār bhāī aïlan haĩ, ăūr sahī salāmat un-kē bahurᵃlē-kâ khusī-mẽ tohār bāp jewᵃnār kaïlan-haĩ.' Ī sun-ke ū gussā bhayal, ăūr bhittar nāhī̃ gayal. Tab bāp bāhar nikal aïlaĩ ăūr laṛikā-kē manāwăĭ lagᵃlaĩ. Laṛikā bāp-kē jabāb dihᵃles 'Bāh! etᵃnā din-sē tohār gulāmī karat-hâī, kabᵃhī̃ tohār hukum nāhī̃ ṭarᵃlī; tēhū-par tū̃ kabᵃhū̃ ēk khassī-kăĭ bachch-ō nāhī̃ dihᵃlâ kī ham apᵃnē saṅgī-kē saṅg khāe-pī-ke chain karit. Mudā apᵃnē chhoṭᵃkā beṭᵃwā-kē awᵃtai jaun tohār sagᵃr-ō kamāī raṇḍī-bājī-mẽ phū̃k dihᵃles, tekᵃrē badē bhōj dihᵃlâ-hai. Bāp bōlal kī, 'bēṭā, tū hamᵃrē lagē sadā rahâ-lâ, ăūr jaun kuchh hamᵃrē pallē bāy taun sab tohᵃr-ai hau. Ham lōgan-kē khusī karăĭ-kē uchit rahal, kāhē-sē, ī tohār bhāī mar-ke phir jīal-hai, ăūr bichhuṛ-ke phir milal-hai.'

[No. 53.]

INDO-ARYAN FAMILY. EASTERN GROUP.

BIHĀRĪ.

BHOJPURĪ DIALECT.

WESTERN, BANĀR'SĪ, SUB-DIALECT. (DISTRICT BENARES.)

SPECIMEN II.

(Pandit Mahārāj Nārāyan Śivapurī, Rai Bahādur, 1898.)

सवाल॥ अबको सोम्मार अउर मंगर जौन बीतल हौ ओकरे बीच के रात में तूं हरगोबिन्द तिवारी के खेत से रहिला उपरल:॥

जवाब॥ पेट जरत रहल पिर्थीनाथ एक मुट्ठी उपरली॥

स:॥ तौंह के रमेसर गोंड़इत आधी रात के चोरी कै रहिला ले जात धइलेस॥

ज:॥ बेर बिसौले हम रहिला खात घर जात रहली। राम जिआवन गवाह कोल्हू हाँकत रहलन। हमैं देख के पुछलन कहाँ से लिहले आवत हउअ:। हम कहली की दुसरे सिवान से ले अइली हैं। तब राम जिआवन हमैं धइ लिहलन॥

स:॥ राम जिआवन तौं के धइ के फिर का कइलन॥

ज:॥ धइ कें पिर्थीनाथ गोंड़इत बोलाय के अकस बस चलान कइ दिहलन॥

स:॥ तौं से अउर राम जिआवन से का अकस हौ॥

ज:॥ ई अकस हौ राम जिआवन से को हमरे खेते में से लिहले आवत होवैं॥

स:॥ तोहार पहिले कबहीं चोरी में सजाय भइल हौ॥

ज:॥ हाँ बाबू एक दाँइ पँदरह दिन के चोरी में कइद रहली॥

[No. 53.]

INDO-ARYAN FAMILY. EASTERN GROUP.

BIHARĪ.

BHOJPURĪ DIALECT.

WESTERN, BANĀR'SĪ, SUB-DIALECT. (DISTRICT BENARES.)

SPECIMEN II.

TRANSLITERATION AND TRANSLATION.

(Pandit Mahārāj Nārāyan Śivapurī, Rai Bahādur, 1898.)

Sawāl.— Ab'kī Sommār aūr Maṅgar jaun bītal-hau, ok'rē bich-kē
Question.—Of-now Monday and Tuesday which have-passed, of-them between

rāt-mē̃ tū̃ Har-gōbind Tiwārī-kē khēt-sē rahilā upar'lā?
the-night-in you Har-gōbind Tiwārī's field-from gram plucked?

Jawāb.— Pēṭ jarat-rahal, Pirthī-nāth! Ēk muṭṭhī upar'lī.
Answer.—Belly burning-was, Earth-lord! A handful I-plucked.

Sawāl.—Tōh-kē Ramēsar Gōṛaīt ādhī rāt-kē chōrī-kāī rahilā lē-jāt dhaīles?
Question.—You Ramēsar Gōṛait half night-at theft-of gram taking-away arrested?

Jawāb.—Bēr-bisaulē ham rahilā khāt ghar jāt-rah'lī. Rām-jiāwan gawāh kōlhū hā̃kat-rah'lan. Hamaī dēkh-ke puchh'lan,
Answer.—At-sunset I gram eating home going-was. Rām-jiāwan witness sugar-cane-press driving-was. Me having-seen he-asked,

'kahā̃-sē lih'lē-āwat-haūā?' Ham kah'lī ki, 'dus'rē siwān-sē lē-aīlī-haī.' Tab Rām-jiāwan hamaī dhaī-lih'lan.
'where-from are-you-bringing-it?' I said that, 'other side-from I-have-brought-(it).' Then Rām-jiāwan me caught-hold-of.

Sawāl.— Ram-jiāwan tō-kē dhaī-ke phir kā kaīlan?
Question.—Rām-jiāwan you having-seized again what did?

Jawāb.— Dhaī-ke, Pirthī-nāth! Gōṛaīt bolāy-ke akas has chalān kaī-dih'lan.
Answer.—Having-seized, Earth-lord! the-Gōṛait having-called enmity under-the-influence-of sent-up-for-trial he-made (me).

Sawāl.— Tō̃-sē aūr Rām-jiāwan-sē kā akas hau?
Question.—You-with and Rām-jiāwan-with what enmity is?

Jawāb.— Ī akas hau Rām-jiāwan-sē, ki ham'rē khētē-mẽ-sē lih'lē
Answer.—This enmity is Rām-jiāwan-with, that my field-in-from having-taken
āwat-hauwaĩ.
coming-he-is.

Sawāl.— Tohār pahilē kab'hĩ chōrī-mẽ sajāy bhaïl-hau?
Question.—Of-you before ever theft-in punishment has-occurred?

Jawāb.—Hā̃, bābū, ēk dā̃ĩ pā̃d'rah din-kē chōrī-mẽ kaid rah'lī.
Answer.—Yes, Sir, one time fifteen days-for theft-in imprisoned I-was.

FREE TRANSLATION OF THE FOREGOING.

Question.—Did you pluck gram from Har-gōbind Tiwārī's field on the night between last Monday and Tuesday?

Answer.—My Lord of the Earth, my belly was burning. I did pluck one handful.

Question.—Did Ramēsar Gōṛait arrest you on the midnight of the theft, as you were going off with the gram?

Answer.—At sunset I was going home, munching the gram I had plucked. The witness Rām-jiāwan was driving his sugarcane-mill. He asked me where I had taken it from, and I told him that I had taken it from the other side of the village-boundary.[1] He then caught hold of me.

Question.—What did Rām-jiāwan then do?

Answer.—My Lord of the Earth, he had a grudge against me. And so he called the Gōṛait and made me over to him.

Question.—What is the grudge between you and Rām-jiāwan?

Answer.—It is this. He comes and takes grain from my field.

Question.—Have you ever previously been punished for theft?

Answer.—Yes, Sir, I was once imprisoned for fifteen days for theft.

The language spoken by the natives of Benares City varies considerably according to the castes of the speakers. For instance, the use of the word *bāṭē* for 'he is' is said to be confined to the Kasērās, or brass-workers, instead of which the Baniyā and other Vaiśya castes use *hau*, while the original inhabitants say *hāwā*. The city is, of course, largely inhabited by people from other parts of India, who speak corrupted forms of their mother-tongues, Panjābī, Gujarātī, Marāṭhī, Bengali, or what not. The influence is felt by the native inhabitants, and the true Benares language is every year becoming more and more uniform. The following specimen, which I owe to the kindness of Babu Śyām Sundar Dās, is a version of the Parable of the Prodigal Son, in the dialect spoken by Kasērās, Ahīrs, and similar castes. I have not thought it worth while to give any analysis of the local peculiarities. Most of them depend on pronunciation, or are mere varieties of spelling. It will be sufficient to draw attention to the representation of the Bhojpurī vowel *á* by the addition of another *a*, thus *dá*, give, is written दअ *daa*.

[1] Such a theft would be venial compared with stealing crops grown in one's own village. No village is its brother's keeper.

[No. 54.]

INDO-ARYAN FAMILY. EASTERN GROUP.

BIHĀRĪ.

BHOJPURĪ DIALECT.

WESTERN, BANĀR'SĪ, SUB-DIALECT. (BENARES CITY.)

(Babu Śyām Sundar Dās, 1898.)

कउनउ मिला के दुइठे बेटवा रहलयँ। उनहन में से लहुरका अपने बाप से कहलेस की ए बाबू अपने कमाई में जउन हमार बखरा होय तउन हम्मैं दे दअ। तब ऊ उनहन के आपन लेई पूँजी बाँट देहलेस। थोरिकै दिन में (or थोरो दिन नाहीं बीतल को) लहुरका बेटवा आपन सब कुछ एकट्ठा कइ के (or जुटाय के) परदेस चल गयल अउर उहाँ लुचई में दिन बितावे लगल अउर आपन कुल धन फूँक देहलेस। जब ऊ सब किछु उड़ाय चुकल ओही दिन म देस में भारी अकाल पड़ि गयल अउर ऊ कँगाल होय गयल। अउर ऊ जाय के ओहि देस के रहेवालन में से एक के इहाँ रहइ लगल जउन ओ के अपने खेत में सूअर चरावे बदे रखलेस। अउर ऊ ओहि मोथा सोथा से जे के सूअर खात रहलिन आपन पेट भरै चहलेस काहे बदे की कत्तौं ओ के अउर कुछ नाहीं मिलत रहल। तब ओकर आँख खुलल अउर ऊ सोचलेस की हमरे बाप के घरे केतना मजूरन के खइले ओ पर अलेल रोटी परल रहइ-ले अउर हम भुक्खन मूअत बाटी। हम अपने बाप के लग्गे जाब अउर ओन से कहब को हे बाबू हम दइउ से फिर के तोहरे सोझइ कुपद कइली। हम फिन तोहरे बेटवा कहावइ जोग क नाहीं रहली। हम्मैं अपने मजूरन में से एक के मतिन रख लअ। तब ऊ अपने बाप के लग्गे चलल अउर लग्गौं नाहीं पहुँचल को ओकर बाप ओ के देख के छोहाय गयल अउर दउड़ के ओ के गरे लपट के भेटलेस। बेटवा ओहि से कहलेस को ए बाबू हम दइउ से बिमुख अउर तोहरे सोझइ कुपद कइले हुई से अब हम तोहार बेटवा कहावइ जोग नाहीं रहली। तब ओकर बाप अपने नोकरवन से कहलेस की सब से नीक कपड़ा काढ़ के ए के पहिरावअ अउर उकरे हाथे में मुँदरी अउर गोड़े में पनही पहिरावअ। अउर आवअ आजु हमन खूब भोज भात करीं, काहे की ई हमार मूअल बेटवा फिन से जीअल हइ, हेराय गयल रहल फिन से मिलल हइ। तब ओनहन खाए पीए चैन करे लगलेन॥

ओकर जेठरका बेटवा खेते में रहल अउर जब ऊ बखरी के नियरे पहुँचल तब बाजा अउर नाच कइ हउरा सुनलेस अउर नोकरवन में से एक के गोहराय के पुछलेस की ई का हउ। नोकरवा कहलेस की तोहार भाय आयल हइ अउर तोहार बाबू नीक नीक तीवन जेवनार जेववलइ हइँ; काहे से की ओ के जीयत पउलेन हैं। ई सुन के ऊ खुनसयलेस अउर भित्तर जाए कइ मन न कइलेस। एहि से ओकर बाप बहरे निकस के ओ के मनावइ लगल। ऊ बाप के जबाब देहलेस की देखअ हम एतने बरिस से तोहार टहल करत हुई अउर तोहार हुकुम कब्बउँ नाहीं टारित बाकी तूँ हम्मैं कब्बउँ एकठे छेड़ियउ नाहीं देहलअ की हम अपने संगिन के संगे चैन करित। ई तोहार ऊ बेटवा हइ जउन पतुरियन के संगे तोहार धन उड़ाय देहलेस। जैसही ई आयल तैसही एकरे बदे तू नीक नीक जेवनार बनववलअ हइ। बाप ओ से कहलेस की बचवा तैं तो नित्ते मोरे संगे बाटे अउर जउन कुछ मोर हउ तउन सब तोरअ हउ। पइ तो के आज खुसी अनन्द करै के चाहत रहल काहे से की तोर मूअल भाय बहुरल हइ॥

[No. 54.]

INDO-ARYAN FAMILY. EASTERN GROUP.

BIHĀRĪ.

BHOJPURĪ DIALECT.

WESTERN, BANĀR'SĪ, SUB-DIALECT. (BENARES CITY.)

TRANSLITERATION.

(Babu Śyām Sundar Dās, 1898.)

Kaünaü milā-kē duiṭhē beṭ'wā rah'laỹ. Un'han-mẽ-sē lahur'kā ap'nē bāp-sē kah'les kī, 'ē bābū, ap'nē kamāī-mẽ jaün hamār bakh'rā hōy taün hammaĩ dē-dā.' Tab ū un'han-kē āpan lēī pū̃jī bā̃ṭ deh'les. Thorikai din-mẽ (*or* thōrō din nāhī̃ bītal kī) lahur'kā beṭ'wa āpan sab kuchh ekaṭṭhā-kaï-ke (*or* juhāy-ke) par'dēs chal-gayal aür uhā̃ luchchaī-mẽ din bitāwăï-lagal aür āpan kul dhan phū̃k deh'les. Jab ū sab kichhu uṛāy chukal ōhī din-mẽ dēs-mẽ bhārī akāl paṛi-gayal aür ū kā̃gāl hōy-gayal. Aür ū jāy-ke ohi dēs-kē rahăï-wālan-mẽ-sē ēk-kē ihā̃ rahaĩ-lagal, jaün ō-kē ap'nē khēt-mẽ sūar charāwăï badē rakh'les. Aür ū ohi mōthā sōthā-sē jē-kē sūar khāt rah'lin āpan pēṭ bharăï chah'les kāhē badē kī kattō̃ ō-kē aür kuchh nāhī̃ milat-rahal. Tab ō-kar ā̃kh khulal aür ū soch'les kī, 'ham'rē bāp-kē gharē ket'nā majūran-kē khaïlē-ō par alēl rōṭī paral rahaĩ-lē aür ham bhukkhan mūat bāṭī. Ham āp'nē bāp-kē laggē jāb aür on-sē kahab kī, "hē bābū, ham Daïu-sē phir-ke toh'rē sōjhaĩ kupad kaïlī. Ham phin toh'rē beṭ'wā kahāwaï jōg ka nāhī̃ rah'lī. Hammaĩ ap'nē majūran-mẽ-sē ēk-kē matin rakh-lā." ' Tab ū ap'nē bāp-kē laggē chalal aür laggō̃ nāhī̃ pahū̃chal kī ō-kar bāp ō-kē dēkh-ke chhohāy gayal aür daüṛ-ke ō-kē garē lapaṭ-ke bheṭ'les. Beṭ'wā ohi-sē kah'les kī, 'ē bābū ham Daïu sē bimukh aür toh'rē sōjha-i kupad kaïlē hâĩ, sē ab ham tohār beṭ'wā kahāwaï jōg nāhī̃ rah'lī.' Tab ō-kar bāp ap'nē nokar'wan sē kah'les kī, 'sab-sē nīk kap'ṛā kāṛh-ke ē-kē pahirāwâ. Aür uk'rē hāth-mẽ mū̃d'rī aür gōṛē-mẽ pan'hī pahirāwâ. Aür āwâ āju haman khūb bhōj bhāt karī̃, kāhē kī ī hamār mūal beṭ'wā phin-sē jīal haĩ; herāy-gayal-rahal, phin-sē milal haĩ. Tab on'han khāe pīe chain-kare lagalen.

Ō-kar jeṭhar'kā beṭ'wā khētē-mẽ rahal aür jab ū bakh'rī-kē niyarē pahū̃chal tab bājā aür nāch kaï haürā sun'les aür nokar'wan-mẽ-sē ēk-kē goh'rāy-ke puchh'les kī 'ī kā haü?' Nokar'wā kah'les kī, 'tohār bhāy āyal-haï aür tohār bābū nīk nīk tīwan jew'nār jewaw'laĩ haĩ; kāhē-sē kī ō-kē jīyat paülen haĩ.' Ī sun-ke ū khun'say'les aür bhittar jāe-kaï man na kaïles. Ehi-sē ō-kar bāp bah'rē nikas-ke ō-kē manāwaï lagal. Ū bāp-kē jabāb deh'les kī, 'dēkhâ, ham et'nē baris-sē tohār ṭahal karat-haī, aür tohār hukum kabbaū̃ nāhī̃ ṭārit; bākī tū̃ hammaĩ kabbaū̃ ek-ṭhē chhēṛiyaü nāhī̃ deh'lā kī ham ap'nē sangin-kē sangē chain kariṭ. Ī tohār ū beṭ'wā haï jaün paturiyan-kē sangē tohār dhan uṛāy deh'les. Jăïs'hī ī āyal tăïs'hī ek'rē badē tū nīk nīk jew'nār ban'waw'lâ-haĩ. Bāp ō-sē kah'les kī, 'bach'wā, taĩ tō nittai mōrē sangē bāṭē, aür jaün kuchh mōr haü taün sab torā haü. Paĩ tō-kē āj khusī anand karăï-kē chāhat-rahal kāhē-sē kī tōr mūal bhāy bahural haĩ.'

The foregoing specimen may be taken as representing the speech of the middle-classes of the City of Benares. The dialect of the lowest dregs of the populace has many marked peculiarities, and has occupied more than one native scholar. The late Rājā Hariśchandra gives a description of it in his account of the Hindī Language, and a poet, named Tēgh 'Alī, has written a collection of verses in it, which is very popular. Unfortunately, few of them will bear translation. They present a striking instance of the depths to which religious poetry can sink. The book is entitled the *Badmāsh-darpan* or 'Mirror of Sturdy Rogues,' and gives a curious picture of the habits of these gentry. The poems are religious ones in praise of Kṛishṇa, and are couched in the slang, and illustrated with the ideas, of the lewdest of the low. The following is one of the least objectionable. It is really an adoration of the God, but, on the surface, is an address of a city thief to a well-beloved youth.

Two things may be pointed out with regard to the language. One is the mark ' which means that a final *a* is very lightly pronounced. Thus क' is pronounced *kᵃ*. The other is the frequency with which the Present Indicative is used in a future sense. Thus *tanāī-lā*, I will get (a tent) pitched.

[No. 55.]

INDO-ARYAN FAMILY. EASTERN GROUP.

BIHĀRĪ.

BHOJPURĪ DIALECT.

WESTERN, LOW BANĀRᵃSĪ, SUB-DIALECT. (BENARES CITY.)

(Tēgh 'Alī.)

का माल असर्फी हौ रुपैया तोरे बदे । हाजिर बा जिउ समेत करेजा तोरे बदे ॥
मंगर में अब की रेती पै रजवा तोरे बदे । जर-दोजी का तनाईला तमुवा तोरे बदे ॥
बनवा देईला अबकी देवारी में राम धै । जर-दोजी जूता टोपी डुपट्टा तोरे बदे ॥
चढ़ जालैँ कौनो दाँव पै सारे तो लेईला । कञ्चन कै गोप मोती कै माला तोरे बदे ॥
हम खर-मिटाव कैली है रहिला चबाय के । भेंवल धरल बा दूध में खाजा तोरे बदे ॥
मलिया से कह देली है ले आवल करी रजा । बेला चमेली जूही कै गजरा तोरे बदे ॥
झोला में लेहले पान तोरे सँग रहल करो । कह देली है रिखइया तमोलिया तोरे बदे ॥
अपने के लोई लेहली है कमरी भी आ धइल । किनली है, रजा, लाल दुसाला तोरे बदे ॥
पारस मिलल बा बीच में गंगा के राम धै । सजवा देईला सोने कै बँगला तोरे बदे ॥
संझा सबेरे घूमँ छलावा बदल बदल । काबुल से हम मँगौली है घोड़ा तोरे बदे ॥
अत्तर तू मल के रोज नहायल करँ, रजा । बीसन भरल धयल बा कराबा तोरे बदे ॥
जानीला आज काल में झनाझन चली, रजा । लाठी, लोहाँगी, खञ्जर औ बिछुआ तोरे बदे ॥
बुलबुल बटेर लाल लड़ावैलँ दुकड़हा । हम काबुली मँगौली है मेढ़ा तोरे बदे ॥
कुस्ती लड़ा के माल बना देब राम धै । बैठक में अब खोदीला अखाड़ा तोरे बदे ॥
कासी, पराग, द्वारिका, मथुरा और बृन्दावन । धावल करैलें तेग, कँधैया, तोरे बदे ॥

TRANSLITERATION AND TRANSLATION.

Kā māl asarfī hau rupaiyā tore badē;
What value gold-coin is rupees thee for;
Hājir bā jiu samēt karējā tore badē.
Present is life with liver thee for.

Maṅgar-mẽ ab-kī rētī-pai, rajᵃwā, tore badē
The-Mangal-festival-in this-year sands-on, my-king, thee for
Jar-dōjī-kā tanāī-lā tamuā tore badē.
Embroidery-of I-will-get-set-up tent thee for.
Banᵃwā-dēī-lā ab-kī Dewārī-mẽ Rām dhăī
I-will-get-made this-year Diwālī-festival-in Rām taking
Jar-dōjī jūtā, ṭōpī, ḍupaṭṭā, tore badē.
Embroidered shoes, cap, double-wrapper, thee for.

Charh-jā-laĩ kaunō dā̃w-pai sārē to lēī-lā;
(If)-there-rise any turn-on brother-in-law then I-will-take;
Kañchan-k' gōp, mōtī-k' mālā tore badē.
Gold-of neck-ornament, pearls-of rosary thee for.
Ham khar-miṭāw kailī-h' rahilā chabāy-ke;
I breakfast done-have gram eating;
Bhẽwal dharal-bā dūdh-mẽ khājā tore badē.
Soaked kept-is milk-in khājā-sweets thee for.
Maliyā-sē kah-dēlī-hai, 'le-āwal-karī,' rajā,
The-flower-seller-to I-said-have, 'bring-thou-regularly,' my-king,
'Bēlā, chamelī, jūhi-k' gaj'rā,' tore badē.
'Jasmine, Arabian-Jasmine, Indian-Jasmine-of garland,' thee for.
'Jhōlā-mẽ leh'lē pān tore saṅg rahal-karī,'
'Bag-in taking betel thee with regularly-remain,'
Kah-dēlī-hai Rikhaīyā tamoliyā tore badē.
Have-said-to Rikhaī betel-leaves-grower thee for.
Ap'nē-kē lōī leh'lī-hai kam'rī bhī bā dhaīl;
Myself-for a-blanket I-have-brought a-coarse-blanket also is kept;
Kin'lī-hai, rajā, lāl dusālā tore badē.
I-purchased-have, my-king, a-red shawl thee for.
Pāras milal-bā bīch-mẽ Gaṅgā-kē, Rām-dhăī;
A-philosopher's-stone found-is the-middle-in the-Ganges-of, Rām-taking;
Saj'wā-dēī-lā sōnē-kăī băg'lā tore badē.
I-will-get-furnished gold-of a-bungalow thee for.
Sañjhā sabērē ghūmâ chhalāwā badal badal;
In-the-evening in-the-morning walk-about fashion changing changing;
Kābul-sē ham mā̃gaulī-hai ghōṛā tore badē.
Kābul-from I sent-for-have a-horse thee for.
Attar tū mal-ke rōj nahāyal-karâ, rajā;
Otto-of-roses thou rubbing-on-the-body daily bathe-regularly, my-king;
Bīsan bharal dhayal-bā karābā tore badē.
Scores-of filled kept-are glass-pots thee for.
Jānī-lā āj kal-mẽ jhanā-jhan chalī, rajā,
I-know to-day to-morrow-in clashing will-go, my-king,
Lāṭhī, lohā̃gī, khañjar, au bichhuā tore badē.
Bludgeons, iron-bound-staves, poniards, and stilettos thee for.
Bulbul, baṭēr, lāl, laṛāwăī-lā̃ duk'ṛahā;
Bulbuls, quails, amaduvats, cause-to-fight men-of-straw;
Ham kābulī mā̃gaulī-hai mēṛhā tore badē.
I of-Kābul have-sent-for ram thee for.
Kustī-laṛā-ke māl banā-dēb, Rām-dhăī;
Getting-you-exercised-in-wrestling a-wrestler I-shall-make-thee, Rām-taking;

Baiṭhak-mẽ ab khōdī-lā akhāṛā tore badē.
The-sitting-room-in now will-I-get-dug wrestling-ground thee for.

15. Kāsī, Parāg, Dwārikā, Mathurā āūr Brindāban;
Benares, Allahabad, Dwārikā, Mathurā and Brindāban;

Dhāwal-karāī-lẽ Tēgh, kãdhaiā, tore badē.
Regularly-runs-to Tēgh, O-beloved, thee for.

FREE TRANSLATION OF THE FOREGOING.

What are gold *ashrafīs* and rupees that I should offer them to thee, when my heart and my life are thine.

At the next Maṅgal fair[1] will I have an embroidered tent set up for thee on the sand of the banks of the Ganges, O my Prince.

By Rām I swear that I will have made for thee for the next Diwālī festival embroidered shoes, and hat, and cape.

If by good luck any fool of a rich man falls into my clutches, I will take from him a necklace of gold and a rosary of pearls, all for thee.

5. For my own breakfast I munch a few grains of parched gram, but for thee I have kept sweetmeats soaked in milk.

O my Prince, I have told the florist to supply thee regularly with garlands of all kinds of jasmine.

For thee have I ordered Rikhaī, the betel seller, to be always at thy side with betel.

For myself have I bought a blanket, and I have another rough one at home, but for thee, O my Prince, have I purchased a scarlet shawl.

By Rām I swear that I have found a philosopher's stone in the midst of the Ganges, and now will I get furnished a bungalow of gold for thee.

10. Morning and evening saunter thou about with ever varying gait. Lo, I have sent to Kābul for a horse for thee.

My Prince, rub thou otto of roses daily on thy body. Scores of jars of it have I stored for thee in my house.

Well know I that to-day or to-morrow there will be the clash of arms for thee in the streets—the clash of bludgeons and of iron-bound staves, of poniards and stilettos.[2]

Common people[3] get up matches between fighting bulbuls, quails, or amadavats, but I have sent to Kābul for a fighting ram for thee.

By Rām I swear that I will have thee taught wrestling, and make thee a champion athlete, and in my sitting-room will I have dug for thee a wrestling-ground.

15. Tēgh 'Alī, the poet, is ever visiting the sacred shrines of Benares, Allahabad, Dwārikā, Mathurā and Bṛindāban, for thee, O Kṛishṇa.

---

[1] A well-known fair held at Benares, entitled the *Buṛh'wā Maṅgal.*

[2] The *bichhuā* may be described as a kind of curved stiletto.

[3] A *duk'rahā* is a man who is worth only a *duk'rā*, or the fourth part of a pice.

NAGPURIĀ OR SADĀN.

We have seen that on the extreme northern border of the Palamau District the language is Standard Bhojpurī, and that, on the north-east corner of the same district, where it abuts on Gaya, it is Magahī. In the rest of the Palamau District, and over nearly the whole of the Ranchi District, the language of the settled Aryans is a corrupt form of Bhojpurī, which has undergone modifications, partly by the influence of the Magahī dialect which surrounds it on three sides and of the Chattīsgaṛhī spoken to its west, and partly owing to the influx of words into its vocabulary which belong to the languages of the Non-Aryan population. The same language is spoken in the north and east of the Native State of Jashpur. (In the west of that State, the language is the form of Chattīsgaṛhī known as Sargujiā, and in the south, Oṛiyā.) It is generally known as Nagpuriā (strictly transliterated 'Nagᵃpuriā'), or the language of Chota Nagpur proper. It is also known as Sadān or Sadrī (Sadᵃrī), and is called by the Non-Aryan Muṇḍās 'Dikkū Kājī,' or the language of the *Dikkū* or Aryans. The word 'Sadᵃrī' in this part of the country is applied to the language of the settled, as distinct from the unsettled, population. Thus, the corrupt form of Chattīsgaṛhī, which is spoken by the semi-Aryanised Korwās who have abandoned their original Muṇḍā language, is known as 'Sadrī Korwā,' as compared with the true Korwā language, belonging to the Muṇḍā family, which is still spoken by their wilder brethren.

A reference to what has already been said under the head of Eastern Magahī on pp. 139 and ff. will remind the reader that the Division of Chota Nagpur contains two main plateaux, known, respectively, as the plateau of Hazaribagh, to the north, and the plateau of Ranchi, to the south,—the two being separated by the river-system of the Damuda. The Ranchi plateau includes nearly the whole of the present Ranchi District, and most of the Gurjat States. To the north-west, it gradually shades off into the lowlands of Palamau, while on the east and south it drops more abruptly into the plain countries of Manbhum and Singhbhum. On the east, a small portion of the sub-plateau tract belongs politically to the District of Ranchi, and here the language is not Nagpuriā, but is the form of Magahī known as Pā̃ch Parganiā. Again, across the south-east corner of Ranchi, a colony of Jains speak the variety of Western Bengali known as Sarākī, while the other Aryan inhabitants of the same tract speak either Nagpuriā or Pā̃ch Parganiā according to the locality. Finally, on the north of the District, a colony of some 20,000 immigrants from Hazaribagh still speak the language of their mother-country, in the midst of a Nagpuriā population.

We may roughly divide up the languages of the two Districts of Ranchi and Palamau, and of the State of Jashpur as follows:—

Name of Language.	Spoken by the undermentioned population in			
	Ranchi.	Palamau.	Jashpur.	Total.
Bengali,—				
Sarāki	48,127			48,127
Bihārī,—				
Standard Magahī	20,141	150,000		170,141
Pāc̃h Parganiā Magahī	8,000			8,000
Standard Bhojpurī		50,000		50,000
Nagpuriā Bhojpurī	297,585	250,000	46,672	594,257
Chhattīsgaṛhī,—				
Sargujiā			20,000	20,000
Sadrī Korwā			4,000	4,000
Oṛiyā			10,000	10,000
Muṇḍā Languages	406,086	35,200	11,100	452,386
Dravidian Languages	325,860	30,000	20,000	375,860
Other Languages	23,086	81,570	1,864	106,520
Total	1,128,885	596,770	113,636	1,839,291

It will be seen from the above that Nagpuriā is spoken by, altogether, 594,257 people. It is bounded on the north-west by the Standard Bhojpurī of North Palamau, on the north-east and north by the Magahī of Hazaribagh, on the east by the languages of the sub-plateau population of Eastern Rānchi speaking the Pāc̃h Parganiā variety of Magahī, and of the mixed population of Manbhum, some of whom speak Kuṛmālī Magahī, and others Western Bengali. On the south it is bordered by the Chakradharpur Thana, and by the two Native States, of Singhbhum, the main language of which is Oṛiyā, but in which a portion of the population speaks Magahī. Further to the west, the southern boundary is the northern frontier of the Gangpur State till it meets Jashpur, which State the language-pale crosses up to its western frontier. South of this line the language is here Oṛiyā without any admixture of Magahī. At the western boundary of Jashpur, the line turns north across the State, and then continues in the direction of the common frontier of Sarguja and Palamau up to the river Sone. East of this line, the language is Nagpuriā, and west of it the Sargujiā form of Chattīsgaṛhī. The above boundary line will be clearly seen on the map facing p. 1.

Nagpuriā has the advantage of having been well illustrated by the Reverend E. H. Whitley. In order to understand the title of his Grammar, it is necessary to explain that the old District of Lohardaga originally included Palamau. The latter district was separated off, and the remaining portion retained the name of Lohardaga. Finally, in the year 1899, the name of the newly formed District of Lohardaga was changed to that of Ranchi.

AUTHORITY—

Whitley, The Rev. E. H., S. P. G., Ranchi, assisted by Salkar, A.—*Notes on the Gánwári Dialect of Lohardaga, Chhota Nagpur.* Calcutta, 1896.

The following account of the grammar of the Nagpuriā Sub-dialect is based on Mr. Whitley's Grammar:—

NAGPURIĀ SKELETON GRAMMAR.

I.—PRONUNCIATION.—A final *i* is pronounced, and written in the preceding syllable. Thus *suarī*, a pig, becomes *suaīr*. This peculiarity runs right through the language. The influence of the neighbouring Bengali leads the letter *a* to be sometimes pronounced as *ŏ* or *o*. Thus *sab*, all, becomes *sŏb* or *sob*.

II.—NOUNS.—Nouns do not change in the singular. The plural is formed by adding *man*,—a termination borrowed from Chhattisgaṛhī. The plural termination is seldom used, except in the case of animate nouns.

The cases are formed by the following postpositions,—*kē*, to (also forms Accusative); *k*, *kēr*, or *kar*, of; *mē̃*, in; *le*, *lāi*, *lagin*, *lagē*, for; *sē̃*, from.

There is an Instrumental in *ē*. Thus *bhukhē*, by hunger.

To give the idea of definiteness, the Chhattisgaṛhī suffix *har* is sometimes added to nouns. Thus *bēṭā-har*, *the* son.

III.—PRONOUNS.

	I.		Thou.		Your Honour.	This.	That, he.	Who.	That.	Who?	What?
	Inferior.	Superior.	Inferior.	Superior.							
Sing.											
Nom.	*mō̃*	*ham,*	*tō̃*	*tōh*	*rāure, ap^{a}ne*	*ī, ihē*	*ū, ūhē*	*jē*	*sē*	*kē*	*kā*
Acc.	*mō-kē*	*ham-kē*	...	*tō-kē*	*rāur-kē, ap^{a}ne-kē*	*ī-kē*	*ū-kē*	*jē-kē*	*sē-kē*	*kē-kē*	*kā-kē*
Gen.	*mōr*	*hamar*	...	*tōr, tōhar*	*rāur-kar, ap^{a}ne-kar*	*ī-kar*	*ū-kar*	*jē-kar*	*sē-kar*	*kē-kar*	*kā-kar*
Plur.											
Nom.	...	*ham^{a}rē, ham^{a}rē-man, ham^{a}nī, ham^{a}nī-man, ham^{a}rin, hamī.*	...	*toh^{a}rē toh^{a}rē-man toh^{a}nī, toh^{a}nī-man*	*rāure-man, rāur-man, ap^{a}ne-man*	*ī-man*	*ū-man*	*jē-man*	*sē-man*	*kē-man*	*kā-man*

'Any one,' 'some one' is *koī* or *keū*. It is thus declined—

	Sing.	Plur.
Nom.	*koī, keū*	*koī koī*, or *koī koī-man*
Acc.	*kēkhō̃*	*koī koī-kē.*
Gen.	*kek^{a}rō*	*kek^{a}rō kek^{a}rō*, or *koī koī kēr.*
Loc.	*kek^{a}rō-mē̃*	*kek^{a}rō kek^{a}rō-mē̃*
	and so on.	and so on.

Except in the case of the Accusative of all the above, and in the case of *rāure* or *ap^{a}ne*, the postpositions forming cases are added, in the singular, to the Genitive. Thus, *mōr-mē̃*, in me. *Rāure* or *ap^{a}ne* forms the other cases of the singular like the accusative. Thus *rāur-mē̃* or *ap^{a}ne-mē̃*. In the plural, all postpositions are added to the Nominative form. Note that *rāure* always governs the verb in the first person plural.

Pronominal Adjectives are *jaun*, *taun*, *kaun*, as in Standard Bhojpurī.

'Anything' is *kōnō* which does not change in declension, except that the Plural is *kōnō kōnō*: *kuchh* (obl. *kuchhō*) also occurs. The Indefinite Pronominal Adjective is *kōnō*, any.

The Reflexive Pronoun is *apan*; Acc. *apan-kē* or *ap^{a}ne-kē*, and so throughout.

IV.—VERBS.

A.—Auxiliary Verbs and Verbs Substantive.

Present, I am.		*Past*, I was	
Sing.	Plur.	Sing.	Plur.
1. *ahō̃*, *hō̃*, or *haū̃*,	*ahī* or *hai*	*rahō̃*	*rahī* or *rah^{a}lī*
2. *ahais*, *hais* or *his*	*ahā* or *hā*	*rahis*	*rahā* or *rah^{a}lā*
3. *ahē* or *hai*	*ahaī̃* or *haī̃*	*rahē* or *rah^{a}lak*	*rahaī̃* or *rah^{a}laī̃*

Ahō̃, etc., are sometimes spelt *āhō̃*, and so throughout.

The following form of the Present is borrowed from Magahi:—

Sing.	Plur.
1. *hekō*	*hekī*
2. *hekis*	*hekī*
3. *hekē*	*hekaī̃*

Ahaū̃ and *haū̃* are used as copulas, as in 'the water is hot', when the predicate is an adjective. *Hekō̃* is used when the predicate is a substantive, as in 'this is water.'

The Negative Verb Substantive is *nakhī*, I am not.

B.—Finite Verb.

Infinitive, *dēkhek*, to see (dative); of seeing (genitive);
Verbal Nouns, *dēikh*, Obl. *dēkhe*; *dēkhal*, Obl. *dekhal*, the act of seeing.
Present Participle, *dēkhat*, seeing.
Past Participle, *dēkhal*, seen.

The *Present Conditional* is the same as the Future, except that the 3rd person is often, singular, *dēkhŏk*; plural, *dēkhõ*. The Tense, which in other dialects is used for the *Present Conditional*, is used, in *Nagpuriā*, as an optional form of the Perfect.

Present, I see, etc. — *Past*, I saw, etc. — *Imperative*.

Present Sing.	Present Plur.	Past Sing.	Past Plur.	Imperative Sing.	Imperative Plur.
1. *dēkhō-nā*	*dēkhi-lā*	*dekhᵃlō̃*	*dekhᵃlī*	2. *dēkh*, *dekhᵃbē*	*dēkhā*, *dekhᵃbā*
2. *dēkhisi-lā*, *dēkhis-lā*	*dēkha-lā*	*dekhᵃlis*	*dekhᵃlā*	Respectful, *dēkhū*	
3. *dēkhe-lā*	*dēkhai-nā*	*dekhᵃlak*	*dekhᵃlaĩ*	3. *dēkhŏk*	*dēkhõ*

Future, I shall see, etc. — *Past Conditional*, (if) I had seen.

Future Sing.	Future Plur.	Past Cond. Sing.	Past Cond. Plur.
1. *dekhᵃbō̃*	*dēkhab*, *dekhᵃbai*	*dekhᵃtō̃*	*dekhᵃtī*
2. *dekhᵃbē*	*dekhᵃbā*	*dekhᵃtis*	*dekhᵃtā*
3. *dēkhī*, *dekhᵃtai*	*dekhᵃbaĩ*	*dekhᵃtak*	*dekhᵃtaĩ*

The *Definite Present* is formed in the usual way. Thus *dēkhat-hō̃*, I am seeing. So also the *Imperfect*, *dēkhat-rahō̃*, I was seeing.
The Present is usually contracted to *dekhathō̃* or *dekhatthō̃*, I am seeing.

In the above, *dekhᵃtai* and *dekhᵃbai* are borrowed from Magahi.
The *Perfect*, I have seen, has two forms, as follows:—

Sing.	Plur.	Sing.	Plur.
1. *dekhᵃlō-hō̃*	*dekhᵃlī-haī*	*dēkhō̃*	*dēkhī*
2. *dekhᵃlē-hais*	*dekhᵃlā-hā*	*dēkhis*	*dēkhā*
3. *dekhᵃlak-hai*	*dekhᵃlaĩ-haĩ*	*dēkhē*	*dēkhaĩ*

It will be seen that the first form is only the Past Tense, with the Present Tense of the Auxiliary suffixed. This principle of formation is borrowed from Magahi. The second form is the tense which in other dialects is the Present Conditional, and represents the old Sanskrit Present Indicative.

The *Pluperfect*, I had seen, is formed as follows:—

	Sing.	Plural.
1	*dēkh rahō̃*	*dēkh rahī*
2	*dēkh rahis*	*dēkh rahā*
3	*dēkh rahē*	*dēkh rahaĩ*

Causals and Passives are formed as usual: thus, *dekhāek*, to cause to see, *dekhᵃwāek*, to cause to cause to see; *dēkhal jāek*, to be seen.

The only irregular verbs noted are *hōek*, to be; Present Participle, *hōat* or *hōᵃwat*; Past Participle, *hōal* or *hēl*: *jāek*, to go; Past Participle, *gēl*: *dēwek*, to give; Present Participle, *dēt* or *dēwat*; Past Participle, *dēl* or *dēwal*.

Note that the Conjunctive participle is *dēikh* or *dēikh-ke*. Comparison with other Bihārī dialects shows that the original form was *dēkhi*, but the final *i* is epenthetically pronounced in the preceding syllable. This *i* sometimes affects a preceding *ā*, so that it is pronounced something like *ē*. Thus *māir*, having struck, is pronounced, and sometimes written, *mēir*.

I am indebted to the Rev. E. H. Whitley for the two following specimens of Nagpuriā. They may be taken as illustrating the form of the dialect spoken in the Districts of Ranchi and Palamau.

[No. 56.]

INDO-ARYAN FAMILY. EASTERN GROUP.

BIHĀRĪ.

BHOJPURĪ DIALECT.

NAGPURIĀ SUB-DIALECT. (DISTRICT RANCHI.)

SPECIMEN I.

(Rev. E. H. Whitley, 1898.)

कोनो आदमी केर दूइझन बेटा रहैं। ऊ मन मधे छोटका बाप के कहलक ए बाप खुरजी मधे जे हमर बटवारा है से हम के दे। तब ऊ ऊ मन के अपन खुरजी बाँइट देलक। थोरको दिन नइ भेलक कि छोटका बेटा सोब कुछ जमा कइर के दूर देस चइल गेलक और उहाँ लुचपनई में दिन बिताते अपन खुरजी उड़ाए देलक। जब ऊ सोब उड़ाए चुकलक तब ऊ मुलुक में बड़ा अकाल भेलक और ऊ गरीब होए गेलक। और ऊ जाए के ऊ मुलुक केर आदमी मन मधे एक झन ठिन रहे लागलक; जे ऊ के अपन खेत में सुवइर चराएक भेजलक। और ऊ ऊ भुसा से जे के सुवइर मन खात रहैं अपन पेट भरे खोजत रहे और कोऊ ऊ के कोनो नइ देत रहैं। तब ऊ के चेत चढ़लक और ऊ कहलक कि हमर बाप केर केतइ केतइ धाँगर मन के खाएक से पुरे रोटी होए-ला और हम भुखे मोरथी। हम उइठ के अपन बाप ठिन जाब और ऊ के कहब ए बा हम सरग केर बिरुध और राउर आगु पाप करली हई। हम फेर राउर बेटा कहाएक लाएक नखी। हम के राउर धाँगर मन मधे एक झन नियर कइर देउ। तब ऊ उइठ के अपन बाप ठिन चललक। मगर ऊ दूरे रहे कि ऊ-कर बाप ऊ के देइख के ऊ कर ऊपर मया करलक और कुइद के ऊ के घेचा में लपइट के चुमा करलक। बेटा ऊ के कहलक ए बा हम सरग केर बिरुध और राउर आगु पाप करली हई और फेर राउर बेटा कहाएक लाएक नखी। मगर बाप अपन नोकर मन के कहलक; सोब से बेस लुगा निकलाए के ऊ के पिँधावा और ऊ कर हाथ में अंगूठी और गोड़ में जुता पिँधावा और मोटाल बछरू लाइन के मारा और लगे हमरे खाब और आनन्द करब, काहे कि ई हमर बेटा मोइर रहे फेर जिलक है। हेराए जाए रहे फेर मिललक है। तब ऊ मन आनन्द करे लागलैं॥

ऊ कर बड़का बेटा खेत में रहे। और आते आते जब ऊ घर पोहोंचलक तब बजना और नाच केर सबद सुनलक। और ऊ अपन नोकर मन मधे एक झन के अपन ठिन बोलाए के पुछलक ई का है। ऊ ऊ के कहलक, तोहर भाई आलक है और तोहर बाप मोटाल बछरू मारलक है, काहे कि ऊ ऊ के बेसे बेस पालक है। मगर ऊ खिसालक और भितरे नइ जाए खोजलक। से ले ऊ कर बाप बाहरे आए के ऊ के मनाए बुझाए लागलक। ऊ बाप के जबाब देलक कि देखू हम एतइ बछर से राउर सेवा करथी और कहियो राउर हुकुम नइ तोरली और राउरे हम के कहियो एकाठो पठरुओ नइ देली कि हम अपन संगी मन से आनन्द करती। मगर राउर ई बेटा जे छिनारिर मनक संग राउर खुरजी खाए गेलक है; जैसे आलक तैसे राउरे ऊ कर ले मोटाल बछरू मारली हई। बाप ऊ के कहलक ए बेटा तोएँ सोब दिन हमर संगी हइस और जे कुछ हमर है से सोब तोहर है। मगर आनन्द करेक और रिझेक उचित रहे काहे कि ई तोहर भाई मोइर रहे फेर जिलक है; हेराए रहे फेर मिललक है॥

[No. 56.]

INDO-ARYAN FAMILY. EASTERN GROUP.

BIHĀRĪ.

BHOJPURĪ DIALECT.

NAGPURIĀ SUB-DIALECT. (DISTRICT RANCHI.)

SPECIMEN I.

TRANSLITERATION AND TRANSLATION.

(Rev. E. H. Whitley, 1898.)

Kōnō ād^ami-kēr dū jhan bēṭā rahaī. Ū-man madhē chhoṭ^kā
A-certain man-of two persons sons were. Them among the-younger
bāp-kē kah^lak, 'ē bāp, khur^ji-madhē jē hamar baṭ^wārā
the-father-to said, 'O father, the-property-in what my share
hai, sē ham-kē dē.' Tab ū ū-man-kē apan khur^ji bā̃iṭ
is, that me-to give.' Then he them-to his-own goods dividing
dēlak. Thor^kō din naī bhēlak ki chhoṭ^kā bēṭā sōb kuchh
gave. A-few days not were that the-younger son all anything
jamā-kaīr-ke dūr dēs chaīl-gēlak, ā̆ūr uhā̃ luch^panaī-mē din
collecting a-far country-to went-away, and there riotous-living-in days
bitātē apan khur^ji uṛāe-dēlak. Jab ū sōb uṛāe
passing his-own goods squandered. When he all-things having-wasted
chuk^lak, tab ū muluk-mē̃ baḍḍā akāl bhēlak, ā̆ūr ū
finished, then that country-in a-great famine happened, and he
garīb hōe-gēlak. Aūr ū jāe-ke ū muluk-kēr ad^mī-man madhē ēk
poor became. And he going that country-of men amongst one
jhan ṭhin rahe lāg^lak; jē ū-kē apan khēt-mē̃ suwaīr
person near to-live began; who him his-own field-in swine
charāek bhej^lak. Aūr ū ū bhusā-sē jē-kē suwaīr-man khāt-
to-feed sent. And he that chaff-with which swine eating-
rahaī apan pēṭ bhare khōjat-rahē, ā̆ūr keū ū-kē kōnō naī
were his-own belly to-fill seeking-was, and any-one him-to anything not
dēt-rahaī. Tab ū-kē chēt chaṛh^lak, ā̆ūr ū kah^lak ki,
giving-was. Then him-to consciousness arose, and he said that,
'hamar bāp-kēr keṭaī ketaī dhā̃gar-man-kē khāek-sē purē
'my father-of how-many how-many hired-servants-to to-eat-than more

rōṭī hōe-lā, ăŭr ham bhukhē mōratthī. Ham uiṭh-ke apan
bread is(there), and I hunger-from am-dying. I arising my-own
bāp ṭhin jāb, ăŭr ū-kē kahab, "ē bā, ham Sarag-kēr
father near will-go, and him-to will-say, "O father, I Heaven-of
birudh ăŭr rāur āgu pāp kar'lī-haī; ham phēr rāur
against and Your-Honour-of before sin have-done; I again Your-Honour's
bēṭā kahāek lāek nakhī; ham-kē rāur dhãgar-man
son to-be-called worthy am-not; me Your-Honour's hired-servants
madhē ēk jhan niyar kaīr-dēū."' Tab ū uiṭh-ke apan bāp
among one person like make."' Then he arising his-own father
ṭhin chal'lak. Magar ū dūrē rahē ki ū-kar bāp ū-kē dēikh-ke
near went. But he afar was that his father him seeing
ū-kar ūpar mayā kar'lak, ăŭr kuid-ke ū-kē ghēchā-mẽ lapaīṭ-ke
him upon pity made, and running him-to neck-in enfolding
chumā kar'lak. Bēṭā ū-kē kah'lak, 'ē bā, ham Sarag-kēr
kissing did. The-son him-to said, 'O father, I Heaven-of
birudh ăŭr rāur āgu pāp kar'lī-haī, ăŭr phēr rāur
against and Your-Honour-of before sin done-have, and again Your-Honour's
bēṭā kahāek lāek nakhī.' Magar bāp apan nōkar-man-kē
son to-be-called worthy am-not.' But the-father his-own servants-to
kah'lak, 'sōb-sē bēs lugā nik'lāe-ke ū-kē pīdhāwā, ăŭr ū-kar
said, 'all-than good cloth taking-out him put-on, and his
hāth-mẽ ãg'ṭhī ăŭr gōṛ-mẽ jutā pīdhāwā, ăŭr moṭāl bachh'rū
hand-on ring and foot-on shoes put-on, and fatted calf
lāin-ke mārā ăŭr lagē, ham'rē khāb ăŭr ānand karab,
bringing slay and come, (let-)us eat and merriment (let-us-)make,
kāhē-ki ī hamar bēṭā mōir-rahē, phēr jilak hai; herāe-jāe-rahē
because this my son dead-was, again alive is; was-lost
phēr mil'lak-hai.' Tab ū-man ānand kare lāg'laī.
again has-been-found.' Then they merriment making began.

Ū-kar baṛ'kā bēṭā khēt-mẽ rahē. Ăŭr ātē-ātē jab ū ghar
His elder son field-in was. And coming when he house
pohŏch'lak tab baj'nā ăŭr nāch-kēr sabad sun'lak. Aŭr ū apan
reached then music and dancing-of sound heard. And he his-own
nōkar-man madhē ēk jhan-kē apan ṭhin bolāe-ke puchh'lak,
servants among one person-to himself-of near calling asked,
'ī kā hai?' Ū ū-kē kah'lak, 'tōhar bhāī ālak-hai, ăŭr
'This what is?' He him-to said, 'thy brother come-is, and
tōhar bāp moṭāl bachh'rū mār'lak-hai, kāhē-ki ū ū-kē bēsē-bēs
thy father the-fatted calf has-killed, because he him very-well

pālak-hai.' Magar ū khisālak, āūr bhit^arē naī jāe khoj^alak:
has-found.' But he was-angered, and inside not to-go sought;
sē-lē ū-kar bāp bāh^arē āe-ke ū-kē manāe bujhāe
therefore his father outside coming him to-appease and-to-explain-to
lāg^alak. Ū bāp-kē jabāb dēlak ki, 'dēkhū, ham etaī bachhar-
began. He the-father-to answer gave that, 'see, I so-many years-
sē rāur sēwā karatthī, āūr kahiyō rāur hukum
since Your-Honour's service am-doing, and ever Your-Honour's command
naī tor^alī, āūr rāure ham-kē kahiyō ēk-ṭhō paṭharū-ō naī dēlī ki ham
not broke, and Your-Honour me-to ever one kid-even not gave that I
apan saṅgī-man-sē ānand kar^atī. Magar rāur
my-own companions-with merry-making might-make. But Your-Honour's
ī bēṭā, jē chhināīr-manak saṅg rāur khur^ajī khāe-gēlak-
this son, who harlots with Your-Honour's fortune has-devoured,
hai, jaisē ālak taisē rāure ū-kar-lē moṭāl bachh^arū mār^alī-hai.'
as he-came so Your-Honour him-for the-fatted calf has-slain.'
Bāp ū-kē kah^alak, 'ē bēṭā, tōē sōb-din hamar-saṅgē hais, āūr jē-kuchh
The-father him-to said, 'O son, thou all-days me-with art, and whatever
hamar hai, sē sōb tōhar hai. Magar ānand karek, āūr rijhek uchit
mine is, that all thine is. But merriment to-make, and to-be-glad right
rahē, kāhē-ki ī tōhar bhāī mōir rahē, phēr jilak hai; herāe rahē phēr
was, because this thy brother dead was, again alive is; lost was again
mil^alak-hai.'
has-been-found.'

[No. 57.]

INDO-ARYAN FAMILY. EASTERN GROUP.

BIHĀRĪ.

BHOJPURĪ DIALECT.

NAGPURIĀ SUB-DIALECT. (DISTRICT RANCHI.)

SPECIMEN II.

AN AGRARIAN DISPUTE.

(Rev. E. H. Whitley, 1898.)

A. बैठू। कने कने आली?

B. हमहे भाई, राउर केर मुकदमा सुइन के हम आली हई। जे में जानब कि का भेलक।

A. ए भाई का कहब। दुनिया ऐसन अँधेर भेलक। भला देखू तो, हम जोतली कोड़ली बुनली और से में कुछ हमर होवल धान के जबर-जस्ती काइट लेलक।

B. राउरे सेखन कहाँ रही, जे ऊ आए के ऐसन जबर-जस्ती काटे लागलक।

A. ए भाई, का कहब; से दिना केर दिन में हम लाइ किनें ले बाजार जाए रही।

B. सेखन का घरे कोई नहीं रहैं।

A. छउआ मन तो रहैं। मगर का करबैं। बुझाव कि कुछ अपन संगे दस जवान लाठी ली के और पंद्रह बनिहार ली के आए रहे। घड़ बिरिया हम के बाजार में हाल मिललक।

B. अच्छा तो अब का करेक चाही। मटियाले रहब कि कोनो करब।

A. हाँ घो ऊ मन के हम नहीं छोड़ब। राँची जाए के हम दरखास देब, और जेखन ऊ मन केर समन होई, सेखन हुने हम कुछुआ केर धान के कटवाए देब।

B. ई बात बहुत बेस है। हम राउर केर मदद में आवब। राउरे राँची में रहब। हम हुने धान के कटवाए देब।

A. बेस तो॥

[No. 57.]

INDO-ARYAN FAMILY. EASTERN GROUP.

BIHĀRĪ.

BHOJPURĪ DIALECT.

NĀGPURIĀ SUB-DIALECT. (DISTRICT RANCHI.)

SPECIMEN II.

TRANSLITERATION AND TRANSLATION.

(Rev. E. H. Whitley, 1898.)

AN AGRARIAN DISPUTE.

B comes to see A, whose paddy has been fraudulently cut.

A. Baiṭhū; kanē-kanē ālī?
Sit-down; whither have-you-come?

B. In^ahē, bhāī. Rāur-kēr mukad^amā suin-ke ham ālī-haī, jē-mē̃
Hither, brother. Your-Honour's law-suit hearing I am-come, in-order-that
jānab ki kā bhēḷak.
I-shall-know that what happened.

A. Ē bhāī, kā kahab? Dūniyā aisan ādhēr bhēlak!
O brother, what shall (I) say? The-world so outrageous is-become!
Bhalā, dēkhū tō, ham jot^alī, koṛ^alī, bun^alī, āūr sē-mē̃ Budhu hamar hōal
Well, see now, I ploughed, dug, sowed, and thereupon Budhu my become
dhān-kē jabar-jastī kāiṭ-lēlak.
paddy by-force cut-and-took.

B. Rāure sē-khan kahā̃ rahī? jē ū āe-ke aisan jabar-jastī
Your-Honour then where was? that he coming thus by-force
kāṭe lāg^alak.
to-cut began.

A. Ē bhāī, kā kahab? sē dinā-kēr din-mē̃ ham lāh kine-le
O brother, what shall-I-say? that day-of days-in I lac buying-for
bājār jāe-rahī.
market-to had-gone.

B. Sē-khan, kā, gharē koī nahī̃ ṛahaī?
At-that-time, what, at-home any-one not was?

A. Chhaūā-man tō rahaĩ, magar kā kar^abaĩ? Bujhab ki Budhu
Children surely were, but what could-they-do? Know that Budhu
apan saṅgē das jawān lāṭhī lē-ke ǎūr pandrah banihār lē-ke
himself with ten young-men bludgeons taking and fifteen hired-servants taking
āe-rahē; aṛ-biriyā[1] ham-kē bājār-mẽ hāl mil^alak.
had-come; in-the-afternoon me-to market-in news came.

B. Achchā, tō, ab kā karek oh ui? Maṭiyālē rahab ki
Well, then, now what to-do is-proper? Silent will-you-remain or
kōnō karab?
something will-you-do?

A. Hā̃, bau, ū-man-kē ham nahĩ chhōṛab; Rā̃chī jāe-ke ham dar^akhās
Yes, brother, them I not will-let-go; Ranchi going I petition
dēb, ǎūr jē-khan ū-man-kēr saman hōī, sē-khan inē ham
will-present, and when them-of summons will-be, then here I
Budhuā-kēr dhān-kē kaṭ^awāe-dēb.
Budhu-of rice will-cause-to-be-cut.

B. Ī bāt bahut bēs hai, ham rāur-kēr madad-mẽ āwab;
This word very good is, I Your-Honour-of help-in will-come;
Rāure Rā̃chī-mẽ rahab, ham inē dhān-kē kaṭ^awāe-dēb.
Your-Honour Ranchi-in stay, I here the-paddy will-cause-to-be-cut.

A. Bēs tō.
Good then.

---

[1] This is a phrase borrowed from the Dravidian Orāon.

FREE TRANSLATION OF THE FOREGOING.

B comes to see A, whose paddy has been fraudulently cut.

A. Sit down. Why have you come?

B. I came here, brother, when I heard of your law-suit, that I might learn what has really happened.

A. O Brother, what can I say? So outrageous has the World become! Well, see now, I ploughed, I dug, I sowed, and then came Budhu and reaped my ripe paddy by force.

B. Where were you then, that he should come in this way and reap by force?

A. O Brother, what can I say? On that day of all days, I had gone to market to buy lac.

B. And was there no one in your house at the time?

A. Well, the children were there; but what could they do? You see, Budhu had come with ten young fellows armed with bludgeons and fifteen hired servants. I got the news the same afternoon in the market?

B. Well then, what do you think you should do? Are you going to grin and bear it, or are you going to take any active measures?

A. Yes, indeed, brother. I am not going to let them slip. I am off to Ranchi to file a petition against them, and will have them summoned. Then, while Budhu is away there, I'll have his paddy crop reaped in my turn.

B. That's a very good idea. I'll give you a helping hand. You just stay in Ranchi, and I'll bide here and have the paddy cut.

A. Good!

The following two specimens have been translated by Babu Manmatha-nath Chatterji, Manager of the Jashpur State, and are examples of the language of the 46,672 people inhabiting the eastern portion of that territory. In the western portion the language is the Sargujiā form of Chattīsgaṛhī, and hence it will be found that the specimens now given present more signs of the influence of that language than do the specimens from Ranchi. The most prominent peculiarity which is borrowed from Chhattīsgaṛhī is the use of the suffix *har* which is added to a noun to give the force of the definite article. Thus *bēṭā*, a son, but *bēṭā-har*. the son. In the second specimen, there occurs the curious form *kah"thēik*, he says, which seems to be a corruption of the Magahī *kahat-hakaï*.

[No. 58.]

INDO-ARYAN FAMILY. EASTERN GROUP.

BIHĀRĪ.

BHOJPURĪ DIALECT.

NAGPURIĀ SUB-DIALECT. (STATE JASHPUR.)

SPECIMEN I.

(Babu Manmatha-nath Chatterji, 1898.)

કોનો એક હન અદમિનકન દુગોડ઼ વેટા નહૈ । છોટ વેટા હન આપન વુઆ હન સે કહલક, એ વુઆ સોગનો માલ ઝાલ કર જે મોર વાંટા હોયલ સે મો કે દે । તવ ઊ આપન ઝોના કે ઊમન કે વાંટ દેલક । થોનકો દિન નો વોત નહે તિસને છોટે વેટા હન સોગનો કે કુનાલક આઉ ઢેરન દુનિહા મુલુક વટ ગેલક આઉ ઊહાં આપન ઝોના કે વરવાદ કરલક । ઝવ સોગનો કે સિરાલક તવ ઓહે મુલુક માંહ વડ઼ા અકાલ પરલક આઉ ઊ કે તકલીત હોવેક લાગલક । આઉ ઊ ઝાય કનિ કે એક હન નહવૈયા કર સંગે ઝોનાય મેલક આઉ ઊ ઊ કે સૂઅર ચરાએક લગિન ડાંડ઼ે મેઝલક । આઉ સૂઅર મન જે જૂસા કે ખાત નહૈં સેકહોં પાતક તો આપન પેટ કે ભનતક મગર કોનો નો દેહૈં । આઉ ઝખન ઊ કે હોંસ મેલક તખન કહલક મરને મોર વાપ કર એતેક એતેક કમિઆ મન ખાયકહોંલ પૂરે પાવત હૈં આઉ મોંય રહાં ભુખે મરથોં । મોંય ઉઠવોં આઉ વુઆ ઠન ઝાવોં આઉ ઊ કર સે કહવોં, એ વુઆ મોંય ભગવાન ડન આઉ તોરો ડન કસૂર કરન પારલોં આવ તોર વેટા હેકોં સે કા તિઅર કહવોં । સે તોર કમિઆ મન મવે એક હન તિઅર મોકહોં નાખ । આઉ ઊ ઉઠલક આઉ વુઆ હન ઝગ આલક । સેખન વુઆ હન ઊ કે ઢેરન તાવ લે દેખલક આઉ ઊ કે મયા લાગલક, આઉ કૂરદ ગેલક, આઉ ઊ કર ઢેંઢુ કે પોટારલક આઉ ઊ કે ચૂમા લેલક । આઉ વેટા હન વાપ હન સે કહલક, એ વુઆ મોંય ભગવાન ડન આઉ તોરો ડન કસૂર કરન પારલોં આઉ આવ તોર વેટા કહાવોં સે લાએક તિખોં । લેકિન વાપ હન કમિઆ મન ડન કહલક, સોગનો લે વેસ લુગા કે તિકલાલા આઉ ઇ કે પિંધાલા આઉ હાંથ માંહા મુંદરો દેલા આઉ ઊ કર ગોડ઼ મન માંહા ઝૂતા પિંધાલા । અઉ લેગે હમે મન ખાવ આઉ ખુસી કરવ । ઇ લેકિન કિ ઇ મોર વેટા મરન ઝાય રહલક આઉ સેન ઝો આહે । હેરાય ઝાય રહલક, આઉ મેટાલક । આઉ ઊ મન ખુસી કરેક લાગેં ॥

સેપ્યન જે ઓકર વડ઼ે વેટા હર ડાંડ઼ે નહળક । આનુ જખ્યન આળક આનુ ઘર ડન નિઅરાળક, તખ્યન વળા આનુ નાચ કે સુનળક । આનુ ઓનિઓ મન મધે એક હન કે વળાળક આનુ પુછળક કિ ઈ કા હોવથે । આનુ ઉ ઉ કે કહળક તોર ભાઈ આર હૈ આનુ ઉ કે વેસે વેસ પાળક સેઓને ઠેગિન વાપ તોર ભોજ દેર હૈ । આનુ ઉ નિસાળક આનુ ભીતર વટ નો જાયક ળાગળક । સેપ્યન વાપ હર ઉ ઓર નિકરળ આળક આનુ ઉ કે મનાવેક ળાગળક । સેપ્યન ઉ ઓહિ ઘુરાળક આપન વાપ હર કે કિ દેપ્યના, એતેક વછર તોર ડન કમાળોં આનુ કહિયો તોર હુકુમ કે ઉડાય નિખ્યોં । સેહોં મે જખ્યનો તોય મો કે ગોટેક પડનૂ અનુમાનહો ની દેર હિસ કિ મોંય મોર હોત મન સંગે ખુસી કરતોં । આવ ઈ વેટા હર તોર આવો કરળક કિ તોય ઉ ઓર ઠેગિન ભોજ દેવેક ળાગળે । તવ ઉ ઉ ઓર સે કહળક એ વેટા તોય સગર દિન મોર સંગે રહિસળા આનુ મોર જે કુછ હૈ સે સગરો તોરે હેકે । હમેં મન કે ચાહત રહે કિ ખુસી કરતોં આનુ ખુસ હોતોં ઈ ઠેગિન કિ તોર ભાઈ મરર જાય રહળક આનુ ફેર જો આહે । આનુ હેરાય જાય રહે આનુ ભેટાળક ॥

[No. 58.]

INDO-ARYAN FAMILY. EASTERN GROUP.

BIHĀRĪ.

BHOJPURĪ DIALECT.

NAGPURIĀ SUB-DIALECT. (STATE JASHPUR.)

SPECIMEN I.

TRANSLITERATION AND TRANSLATION.

(Babu Manmatha-nath Chatterji, 1898.)

Kōnō ēk-jhan ad^{a}min-kar dū-gōṛ bēṭā rahaī. Chhōṭ bēṭā-har āpan

Some one-person man-of two sons were. The-younger son his-own

buā-har-sē kah^{a}lak, 'Ē buā, sōg^{a}rō māl-jāl-kar jē mōr bā̃ṭā hōel sē mō-kē

father-to said, 'O father, all property-of which my share will-be that me-to

dē.' Tab ū āpan jīnā-kē ū-man-kē bā̃iṭ dēlak. Thor^{a}kō din nī

give.' Then he his-own living them-to dividing gave. A-few days not

bīt-rahē tis-nē chhōṭē bēṭā-har sog^{a}rō-kē ṭhurālak āru ḍhēir durihā muluk-

had-passed then the-younger son all collected and very distant country-

bat gēlak; āru uhā̃ āpan jīnā-kē bar^{a}bād kar^{a}lak. Jab sog^{a}rō-kē

towards went; and there his-own living wasting did. When all

sirālak tab ōhē muluk-mā̃h baṛā akāl par^{a}lak; āru ū-kē tak^{a}līt

was-spent then that-very country-in great famine fell; and him-to trouble

hōwek lāg^{a}lak. Āru ū jāy-kari-ke ēk-jhan rah^{a}waiyā-kar-sangē jorāy bhēlak;

to-be began. And he going one-person inhabitant-of-with joined became;

āru ū ū-kē sūar charāek-lagin ḍā̃ṛē bhej^{a}lak. Āru sūar-man jē bhūsā-kē

and he him swine feeding-for in-fields sent. And swine which husks

khāt-rah^{a}laī sē-k-hō̃ pātak tō āpan pēṭ-kē bhar^{a}tak;

were-eating that-too had-he-got then his-own belly he-would-have-filled;

magar kōnō nī dēlaī. Āru jakhan ū-kē hō̃s bhēlak

but any-one not used-to-give. And when him-to senses became

takhan kah^{a}lak, 'mar-rē! mōr bāp-kar etek etek kamiā-man khāyak-hō̃-lē

then he-said, 'alas! my father-of so-many so-many servants to-eat-even-than

pūrē pāwat-haī, āru mō̃y ihā̃ bhūkhē mar^{a}thō̃. Mō̃y uṭh^{a}bō̃ āru buā

more get, and I here hunger-from am-dying. I will-arise and father

ṭhan jābō̃, āru ū-kar-sē̃ kah^{a}bō̃, "ē buā, mō̃y Bhag^{a}wān ṭhan āru

near I-will-go, and him-to I-will-say, "O father, I God near and

tōr-ō ṭhan kasūr kaïr-pāralō̃ āb tōr bēṭā hēkō̃ se kā-niar kah^abō̃?
thee-too near sin have-done now thy son I-am that how shall-I-say?
Sē tōr kamiā-man-madhē ēk jhan niar mō-k-hō̃ rūkh."' Āru ū
Therefore thy servants-among one person near me-too keep."' And he
uṭh^alak āru buā-har jag ālak. Sē-khan buā-har ū-kē ḍhēir tān-lē
arose and the-father near came. Then the-father him much distance-from
dekh^alak, āru ū-kē mayā lāg^alak, āru kūid-gēlak, āru ū-kar
saw, and him pity took-possession-of, and running-he-went, and his
ḍhē̃ṭu-kē poṭār^alak, āru ū-kē chūmā lēlak. Āru bēṭā-har bāp-har-sō
neck embraced, and him kiss took. And the-son the-father-to
kah^alak, 'ē buā, mō̃y Bhag^awān ṭhan āru tōr-ō ṭhan kasūr
said, 'O father, I God near and thee-too near sin
kaïr-pār^alō̃, āru āb tōr bēṭā kahābō̃ sē lāek nikhō̃.'
have-done, and now thy son I-will-be-called that-of worthy I-am-not.'
Likin bāp-har kamiā-man-ṭhan kah^alak, 'sog^arō-lē bēs lugā-kē
But the-father servants-to said, 'all-than better cloth
nik^alāwā āru i-kē pĩdhāwā āru hā̃th-mā̃hā mū̃d^ari
cause-to-be-taken-out and this-(person)-to put-on and hand-in a-ring
dēwā, āru ū-kar gōṛ-man-mā̃hā jūtā pĩdhāwā. Āru legē, hamē-man
give, and his feet-on shoes put-on. And come, we
khāb āru khusī karab; ī-legin-ki ī mōr bēṭā maïr-jāy-rah^alak,
will-eat and merriment make; this-for-that this my son dead-was,
āru phēr jī-āhē; herāy-jāy rah^alak, āru bheṭālak.' Āru ū-man khusī
and again alive-is; lost was, and is-found.' And they merriment
karek lāg^alaĩ.
to-make began.

Sēkhan ū-kar baṛē bēṭā-har ḍā̃rē rah^alak. Āru jakhan ālak āru ghar
At-that-time his elder son field-in was. And when he-came and the-house
ṭhan niarālak takhan bajā āru nāch-kē sun^alak. Āru kamiā-man
near drew-nigh then music and dance heard. And servants
madhē ēk jhan-kē balālak āru puchh^alak ki, 'kā kā how^athē?'
among one person he-called and asked that, 'what what is-going-on?'
Āru ū ū-kē kah^alak, 'tōr bhāī āi-hai āru ū-kē bōsē-bēs
And he him-to said. 'thy brother come-is and him well-well
pālak sek^arē-legin bāp tōr bhōj dēi-hai.' Āru ū risālak
he-has-found that-for father thy feast has-given.' And he grew-angry
āru bhītar-baṭ nī jāek lāg^alak. Sē-khan bāp-har ū-kar nikaīl-ālak
and within-towards not to-go began. Then the-father his out-came
āru ū-kē manāwek lāg^alak. Sē-khan ū kahi ghurālak āpan
and him to-conciliate began. Then he saying returned his-own
bāp-har-kē ki, 'dēkh^anā, etek bachhar tōr than kamālō̃ āru
father-to that, 'see, so-many years thee near I have-served and

kahiyō tōr hukum-kē uṭhāy-nikhō̃. Sē-hō̃-mē kakhᵃnō tō̃y mō-kē
ever thy orders put-off-I-have-not. Nevertheless ever thou me-to

goṭek paṭhrū anᵃmān-hō nī dōi-his, ki mō̃y mōr hīt-man-saṅgē
one kid even not hast-given, that I my friends-with

khusī karᵃtō̃. Āb, ī bēṭā-har tōr āb-ō-karᵃlak, ki tō̃y
merriment might-have-made. Now, this son thy come-even-did, that thou

ū-kar legin bhōj dēwek lāgᵃlē.' Tab ū ū-kar-sē kahᵃlak, 'ē bēṭā,
him for feast to-give beganest.' Then he him-to said, 'O son,

tō̃y sagar din mōr saṅgē rahis-lā, āru mōr jē kuchh hai sē
thou all days me with livest, and mine what ever is that

sagᵃr-ō tōrē hekē. Hamē-man-kē chāhat-rahē ki khusī
all-also thine is. Us-for meet-was that merriment

karᵃtō̃ āru khus hōtō̃ ī-lagin-ki tōr
we-should-have-made and glad we-should-have-become? this-for-that thy

bhāī maïr-jāy rahᵃlak, āru phēr ji āhē; āru herāy-jāy-rahē, āru
brother dead was, and again alive is; and lost-was, and

bheṭālak.'
is-found.'

[No. 59.]

INDO-ARYAN FAMILY. EASTERN GROUP.

BIHĀRĪ.

BHOJPURĪ DIALECT.

NAGPURIĀ SUB-DIALECT. (STATE JASHPUR.)

SPECIMEN II.

(Babu Manmatha-nath Chatterji, 1898.)

𑂉𑂍 𑂮𑂯𑂩 𑂩𑂯𑂵𑃀 𑂩𑂰𑂔𑂰 𑂩𑂯𑂶𑂁𑃀 𑂣𑂯𑂰𑂩𑂵 𑂥𑂰𑂐 𑂩𑂯𑂞 𑂩𑂯𑂵𑃀 𑂄𑂠𑂧𑂱𑂢 𑂡𑂩 𑂡𑂩 𑂎𑂰𑂞 𑂩𑂯𑂵𑃀 𑂩𑂰𑂔𑂰 𑂯𑂳𑂍𑂳𑂧 𑂍𑂩𑂪𑂶𑂁𑃀 𑂥𑂰𑂐 𑂪𑂰𑂏𑂪𑂍 𑂦𑂰𑂏𑂵𑃀 𑂥𑂢𑂱𑂨𑂰 𑂏𑂷𑂗𑂵 𑂥𑂶𑂪 𑂪𑂰𑂠 𑂍𑂵 𑂔𑂰𑂞 𑂩𑂯𑂪𑂍𑃀 𑂥𑂰𑂐 𑂍𑂯𑂪𑂍 𑂉 𑂦𑂰𑂅 𑂧𑂷 𑂍𑂵 𑂥𑂁𑂒𑂰𑂫𑃀 𑂥𑂢𑂱𑂨𑂰 𑂍𑂯𑂪𑂍 𑂍𑂰 𑂢𑂱𑂨𑂩 𑂞𑂷 𑂍𑂵 𑂥𑂁𑂒𑂰𑂫𑃀 𑂥𑂰𑂐 𑂍𑂯𑂪𑂍 𑂍𑂱 𑂗𑂰𑂗 𑂧𑂵𑂁 𑂧𑂷 𑂍𑂵 𑂮𑂰𑂩𑂪 𑂠𑂵 𑂄𑂇 𑂥𑂶𑂪𑂰 𑂧𑂵𑂁 𑂪𑂰𑂠𑃀 𑂥𑂶𑂪 𑂧𑂵𑂁 𑂪𑂰𑂠 𑂍𑂵 𑂥𑂢𑂱𑂨𑂰𑂁 𑂔𑂰𑂉𑂍 𑂪𑂰𑂏𑂪𑂍, 𑂍𑂷𑂮𑂵𑂍 𑂦𑂳𑂁𑂅 𑂔𑂰𑂨 𑂩𑂯𑂶𑂁 𑂯𑂷𑂩 𑂍𑂱 𑂥𑂰𑂐 𑂥𑂢𑂱𑂨𑂰 𑂍𑂵 𑂍𑂯𑂪𑂍 𑂍𑂱 𑂧𑂷 𑂍𑂵 𑂢𑂱𑂍𑂰𑂩 𑂠𑂵𑃀 𑂥𑂢𑂱𑂨𑂰 𑂢𑂱𑂍𑂰𑂩𑂪 𑂠𑂵𑂪𑂍𑃀 𑂞𑂥 𑂞𑂷 𑂥𑂰𑂐 𑂔𑂰𑂩𑂞 𑂄𑂇 𑂣𑂮 𑂔𑂰𑂩𑂞 𑂍𑂯𑂪𑂍 𑂉 𑂥𑂢𑂱𑂨𑂰 𑂧𑂷𑂁𑂨 𑂞𑂷 𑂍𑂵 𑂡𑂩𑂥𑂷𑂁𑃀 𑂥𑂢𑂱𑂨𑂰 𑂍𑂯𑂪𑂍 𑂍𑂱 𑂍𑂰 𑂪𑂵𑂩 𑂧𑂷 𑂍𑂵 𑂡𑂩𑂥𑂵𑃀 𑂧𑂶𑂁 𑂞𑂷 𑂞𑂷 𑂍𑂵 𑂥𑂒𑂰𑂪𑂷𑂁𑃀 𑂥𑂰𑂐 𑂞𑂷 𑂢𑂯𑂲𑂨 𑂧𑂰𑂢𑂵 𑂍𑂯𑂪𑂍 𑂍𑂱 𑂡𑂩𑂥𑂵 𑂍𑂩𑂥𑂷𑂁𑃀 𑂪𑂵𑂏𑂵 𑂞𑂷 𑂍𑂵 𑂎𑂰𑂥 𑂍𑂱 𑂞𑂷𑂩 𑂥𑂩𑂡𑂰 𑂍𑂵 𑂎𑂰𑂫𑃀 𑂥𑂢𑂱𑂨𑂰 𑂍𑂯𑂪𑂍 𑂒𑂪 𑂣𑂁𑂒 𑂘𑂢 𑂔𑂰𑂫𑃀 𑂣𑂲𑂣𑂩 𑂠𑂵𑂫𑂞𑂰 𑂯𑂵𑂍𑂵 𑂋𑂯𑂵 𑂍𑂯𑂱 𑂠𑂵𑂆 𑂞𑂥 𑂞𑂷𑂁𑂨 𑂧𑂷 𑂍𑂵 𑂎𑂰𑂫𑂵𑃀 𑂞𑂪𑂵 𑂣𑂲𑂣𑂩 𑂮𑂳𑂎𑂹𑂎 𑂞𑂢𑂵 𑂏𑂵𑂪𑂶𑂁𑃀 𑂥𑂢𑂱𑂨𑂰 𑂍𑂯𑂟𑂵 𑂯𑂵 𑂣𑂲𑂣𑂩 𑂠𑂵𑂫𑂞𑂰 𑂢𑂵𑂍𑂲 𑂍𑂩𑂪 𑂍𑂩 𑂧𑂵𑂁 𑂥𑂠𑂲 𑂯𑂷𑂉𑂪𑃀 𑂣𑂲𑂣𑂩 𑂍𑂯𑂪𑂍 𑂯𑂷𑂉𑂪 𑂔𑂴𑂢𑃀 𑂧𑂷𑂁𑂨 𑂮𑂩𑂏𑂵 𑂩𑂯𑂟𑂷𑂁 𑂄𑂠𑂧𑂱𑂢 𑂧𑂢 𑂄𑂩𑂍𑂷𑂯𑂲𑂢 𑂧𑂷𑂩 𑂓𑂰𑂁𑂯 𑂞𑂩𑂲 𑂥𑂶𑂘𑂟𑂶𑂁 𑂮𑂟𑂰𑂨𑂵𑂁 𑂄𑂇 𑂔𑂎𑂢 𑂔𑂰𑂉𑂍 𑂪𑂰𑂏𑂟𑂶𑂁 𑂞𑂷 𑂧𑂷𑂩 𑂙𑂯𑂳𑂩𑂰 𑂍𑂰𑂗𑂟𑂶𑂁 𑂄𑂇 𑂣𑂞𑂆 𑂗𑂷𑂩𑂟𑂶𑂁𑃀 𑂞𑂥 𑂥𑂰𑂐 𑂍𑂯𑂟𑂶𑂍 𑂍𑂰 𑂢𑂵 𑂥𑂢𑂱𑂨𑂰 𑂪𑂵𑂏𑂵 𑂍𑂯 𑂞𑂷 𑂍𑂵 𑂎𑂰𑂥 𑂍𑂱 𑂞𑂷𑂩-𑂥𑂩𑂡𑂰 𑂍𑂵 𑂎𑂰𑂫𑃀 𑂥𑂢𑂱𑂨𑂰 𑂍𑂯𑂪𑂍 𑂒𑂪 𑂏𑂰𑂓 𑂥𑂢𑂰𑂧𑂳-𑂯𑂢 𑂯𑂵𑂍𑂵 𑂋𑂯𑂵 𑂍𑂯𑂪 𑂠𑂵𑂆 𑂞𑂪𑂵 𑂞𑂷𑂁𑂨 𑂎𑂰𑂫𑂵𑃀 𑂏𑂷𑂗𑂵𑂍 𑂥𑂳𑂜𑂱𑂨𑂰 𑂏𑂰𑂨 𑂎𑂣𑂍𑂢 𑂧𑂵𑂁 𑂎𑂣𑂩𑂍 𑂩𑂯𑂵 𑂔𑂵 𑂞𑂵𑂍𑂩 𑂘𑂢 𑂣𑂯𑂳𑂁𑂒𑂪𑃀 𑂍𑂰 𑂏𑂰𑂓 𑂧𑂰𑂞𑂰 𑂢𑂵𑂍𑂲 𑂍𑂩𑂞 𑂍𑂵 𑂥𑂠𑂲𑂋 𑂯𑂷𑂉𑂪𑃀 𑂍𑂯𑂪𑂍 𑂯𑂷𑂩𑂪 𑂔𑂴𑂢𑃁

[No. 59.]

INDO-ARYAN FAMILY. EASTERN GROUP.

BIHĀRĪ.

BHOJPURĪ DIALECT.

NAGPURIĀ SUB-DIALECT. (STATE JASHPUR.)

SPECIMEN II.

TRANSLITERATION AND TRANSLATION.

(*Babu Manmatha-nath Chatterji, 1898.*)

Ēk sahar rahē. Rājā rah^{a}laī. Pahārē bāgh rahat-rahē. Ad^{a}min
One city was. A-king was. On-a-mountain a-tiger used-to-live. Men

dhar-dhar khāt-rahē. Rājā hā̃k^{a}wā kar^{a}laī. Bāgh lāg^{a}lak bhāge.
catching used-to-eat. The-king driving did. The-tiger began to-run-away.

Baniyā goṭē bail lād-ke jāt-rah^{a}lak. Bāgh kah^{a}lak, 'ē
Shop-keeper one a-bullock having-loaded going-was. The-tiger said, 'O

bhāī, mō-kē bā̃chāo.' Baniyā kah^{a}lak, 'kā-niar tō-kē bā̃chā̃w?'
brother, me save.' The-shop-keeper said, 'how thee may-I-save?'

Bāgh kah^{a}lak ki, 'ṭāṭ-mē̃ mō-kē sāīj-dē āru bailā mē̃ lād.'
The-tiger said that, 'bag-in me shut-up and the-bullock on load.'

Bail mē̃ lād-ke baniyā jāek lāg^{a}lak. Kōsek bhũi
The-bullock on loading the-shop-keeper to-go began. About-a-kos ground

jāy-rah^{a}laī-hōi, ki bāgh baniyā-kē kah^{a}lak ki, 'mō-kē
he-gone-have-might, when the-tiger the-shop-keeper-to said that, 'me

nikāil-dē.' Baniyā nikāil-dēlak. Tab tō bāgh-jāit
let-out.' The-shop-keeper let-(him-)out. Then indeed the-tiger-kind

āru pas-jāit kah^{a}lak, 'ē baniyā, mō̃y tō tō-kē dhar^{a}bō.'
and animal-kind said, 'O shop-keeper, I indeed thee will-seize.'

Baniyā kah^{a}lak ki, 'kā-lei mō-kē dhar^{a}bē? Maĩ tō tō-kē
The-shop-keeper said that, 'why me will-you-seize? I indeed thee

bachālō̃.' Bāgh tō nahīch mānē. Kah^{a}lak ki, 'dhar^{a}bē
have-saved.' The-tiger indeed not-verily would-listen. He-said that, 'seizing-even

kar^{a}bō̃. Legē, tō-kē khā̃w ki tōr bar^{a}dhā-kē khā̃w?' Baniyā
I-will-do. Come-now, thee shall-I-eat or thy bullock shall-I-eat?' The-shop-keeper

kah^{a}lak, 'chal pañch than jāb. Pīpar deotā hekē. Ohē
said, 'come a-mediator near let-us-go. The-Pīpal-tree a-God is. He-even

kahi-dēī tab tõy mō-kē khābē.' Ta-lē Pīpar rūkh tarē
will-say then thou me will-eat.' Afterwards the-Pīpal tree under

gelaĩ. Baniyā kah^{a}thē, 'hē Pīpar deotā, nēkī karal-kar-mē̃
they-went. The-shop-keeper says, 'O Pīpal God, good doing-in

badī hōel?' Pīpar kah^{a}lak, 'hōel jūn. Mõy sar^{a}gē rah^{a}thõ;
evil becomes?' The-Pīpal said, 'it-becomes surely. I in-the-sky live;

ad^{a}min-man āi-kohon mōr chhāĩh-tarī baiṭh^{a}thaĩ, sathāthaĩ, āru jakhan
men coming my shade-under sit, take-rest, and when

jāek lāg^{a}thaĩ tō mōr ḍahurā kāṭ^{a}thaĩ āru pataī ṭor^{a}thaĩ.' Tab
to-go they-begin then my boughs they-cut-off and leaves they-pluck-off.' Then

bāgh kah^{a}thēik, 'kā! rē baniyā, lẹgē, kah tō-kē khā̃w ki
the-tiger says, 'what! O shop-keeper, come, say thee shall-I-eat or

tōr bar^{a}dhā-kē khā̃w?' Baniyā kah^{a}lak, 'chal gaū B^{a}rāmhan
thy bullock shall-I-eat?' The-shop-keeper said, 'come, the-cow Brahman

hekē; ōhē kaĩh dēī, talē tõy khābē.' Goṭek buṛhiyā gāy
is; she saying will-give, then thou mayst-eat.' One old cow

khap^{a}kan-mē̃ khapaĩk rahē, jē tē-kar-ṭhan pahũch^{a}laĩ. 'Kā! gaū
mud-in sunk was, that her-to they-approached. 'What! cow

mātā, nēkī karat-kē badi-ō hōel?' Kah^{a}lak, 'hōel
mother, good doing-for evil-also does-become?' Said-she, 'it-does-become

jūn.'
surely.'

FREE TRANSLATION OF THE FOREGOING.

There was once upon a time a city which had a king. On a mountain near by there dwelt a tiger who used to catch and eat the citizens. So the king got up a hunting-drive, and the tiger started off in flight. On his way he met a travelling grain-merchant trudging along with his loaded bullock.

Said the tiger, 'Brother, save me.'

Said the merchant, 'how can I do that?'

'Put me into one of your bags, and tie me on the bullock's back, like a load of grain.'

So the merchant loaded up the tiger on to the bullock's back as he had suggested. When they had gone on a couple of miles the tiger asked to be let out, and the merchant released him. Then, after his own wild-beast nature, said the tiger, 'now, merchant, I am going to kill and eat you.'

Said the other, 'Why should you do that? It is I who have saved your life.'

But the tiger would not listen to his prayers, and said, 'I am certainly going to seize you. Come now, choose whether I shall eat you or your bullock.'

The merchant asked that the matter should be decided by an arbitrator. 'The fig-tree,' said he, 'is a God. If he says that you are to eat me, well and good.' So they went under a fig-tree. 'O divine Fig-tree,' said the merchant, 'can evil be done in return for good?'

'Certainly,' said the fig-tree, 'I live high up in the sky, and men come and rest under my shade. Then when they are going away, they cut down my branches, and pluck off my leaves.'

'Now,' says the tiger, 'shall I eat you or your bullock?' But the merchant replied, 'Come, the cow is a Brāhman. If she says you are to eat me, well and good.' So they went on and found an old cow sunk in the mire, and went up to her. 'O Mother Cow,' said the merchant, 'can evil be done in return for good?'

'Certainly,' said the cow.

NOTE.—The story, as given above, abruptly ends here. The tale is an old one, and is current all over Northern India. The cow explains that she benefits mankind by her various products, and that in return her owner beats her, and, when she is old, turns her out to die. Then the merchant appeals to the road. The road replies that he makes travelling easy and in return men trample on him, and crush him under cartwheels. Finally the man appeals to a jackal. The latter pretends to be very stupid, and to be unable to understand what has happened. Finally he refuses to believe that the tiger could ever have got into the sack. The tiger gets in to show how it was done, and then the merchant ties him up in it, and goes his way rejoicing.

MADHESĪ.

Going to the east from the District of Gorakhpur, and crossing the river Gaṇḍak, we find ourselves in the District of Champaran. This District is to the north of, and separated by, the same river from Saran, with which it has historical and political connections. On the other hand, it forms part of the ancient country of Mithilā. The language spoken in it illustrates this state of affairs. Although it is based in the main on the same stock as that of the Bhojpurī spoken in Saran and East Gorakhpur, it has some peculiarities borrowed from the Maithilī spoken in the neighbouring District of Muzaffarpur. These will be pointed out in the proper place. The Maithilī influence is strongest in the east of the District on the Muzaffarpur border, where Maithilī, and not Bhojpurī, is spoken in a strip of land about two miles wide, and eighteen miles long in Ḍhākā Thānā. As we go west, the influence decreases, till, on the banks of the Gaṇḍak, the language is the same as that spoken in North-east Saran, and in Eastern Gorakhpur. This dialect is locally known as Madhēsī, a word formed from the Sanskrit *Madhya-dēśa*, meaning 'midland,' an appropriate name enough for the language of the country situated between the Maithilī-speaking country of Tirhut, and the Bhojpurī-speaking country of Gorakhpur. Some of the people actually name the form which the dialect takes in the western part of the District 'Gōrakhpurī,' but such minute distinctions are not necessary, and, excepting the small strip in which Maithilī is spoken, it is sufficiently accurate to say that the language spoken over the whole of Champaran is Madhēsī.

The figures originally supplied by the local authorities for Champaran, so far as regards Bihārī dialects, were as follows :—

Madhēsī	1,686,036
Gōrakhpurī	36,000
Maithilī	28,800
Ḍomṛā	4,000
TOTAL	1,754,836

Subsequent enquiries show that, under the head of Gōrakhpurī, were erroneously included some, 8,000 Ṭikulihārs, who spoke a form of Eastern Hindī. These will have to be discussed under the head of that language.

On the other hand, the Thārūs of Champaran, who were erroneously shown as speaking a Tibeto-Burman Language, really speak, like their brethren of Bahraich and Gonda, a corrupt form of Bhojpurī. No doubt, the Thārūs of Gorakhpur and Basti do the same, but no information on the subject is available. Farther west, beyond the Gogra, in the District of Kheri, they speak a corrupt form of the local dialect of Eastern Hindī.

After combining the figures for Madhēsī and Gōrakhpurī, and making the above corrections, we arrive at the following revised figures for the dialects of Bihārī spoken in Champaran :—

Madhēsī	1,714,036
Maithilī	28,800
Ḍomṛā	4,000
Thārū	27,620
TOTAL	1,774,456

Of the above, Maithilī has been already dealt with, *vide* p. 107 *ante*. Ḍomṛā and Thārū will be dealt with in their proper places. I now proceed to give specimens of Madhēsī.[1]

The first specimen is a version of the Parable of the Prodigal Son, and the second is a folk-tale. Both are given in the Kaithī character, in facsimile of the original manuscript. They are excellent specimens of the current style of Kaithī writing which obtains in Champaran. They are each accompanied by a transliteration and an interlinear translation. Among the peculiarities to be noted are the following.

The dialect shares with Maithilī a dislike to the cerebral *ṛ*, frequently substituting the dental *r* for it. Thus, we find *paral*, instead of *paṛal*, it fell: *baṛ*ᵃ*kā*, for *baṛ*ᵃ*kā*, great: *bārā*, for *bāṛā*, you are; *korhiā*, for *koṛhiā*, a leper. We have noticed the same peculiarity in Gorakhpur and Basti.

The Maithilī form *ok*ᵉ*nī*, current in Muzaffarpur, is used for 'to them.'

For the auxiliary verb, we have both *bārā*, you are, and *bāṭē*, he is. In the Finite verb, note the form *khās*, they used to eat. The third person singular of the Past tense of transitive verbs regularly ends in *ak*, as in Maithilī. Thus, we have *kah*ᵒ*lak*, he said; *dēlak*, he gave, and many others. The word for 'he came,' is the Maithilī *āel*, not the Bhojpurī *āil*. So also, the Maithilī *kahal*ᵉ*kaï*, she said.

[1] For most of the above information, the writer is indebted to a full and interesting note on the Dialects of Champaran drawn up by Pandit Rama-ballabh Misra, Assistant Settlement Officer, Champaran. Ḍomṛā will be discussed when dealing with Gipsy dialects. As for Thārū, see pp. 311 and ff.

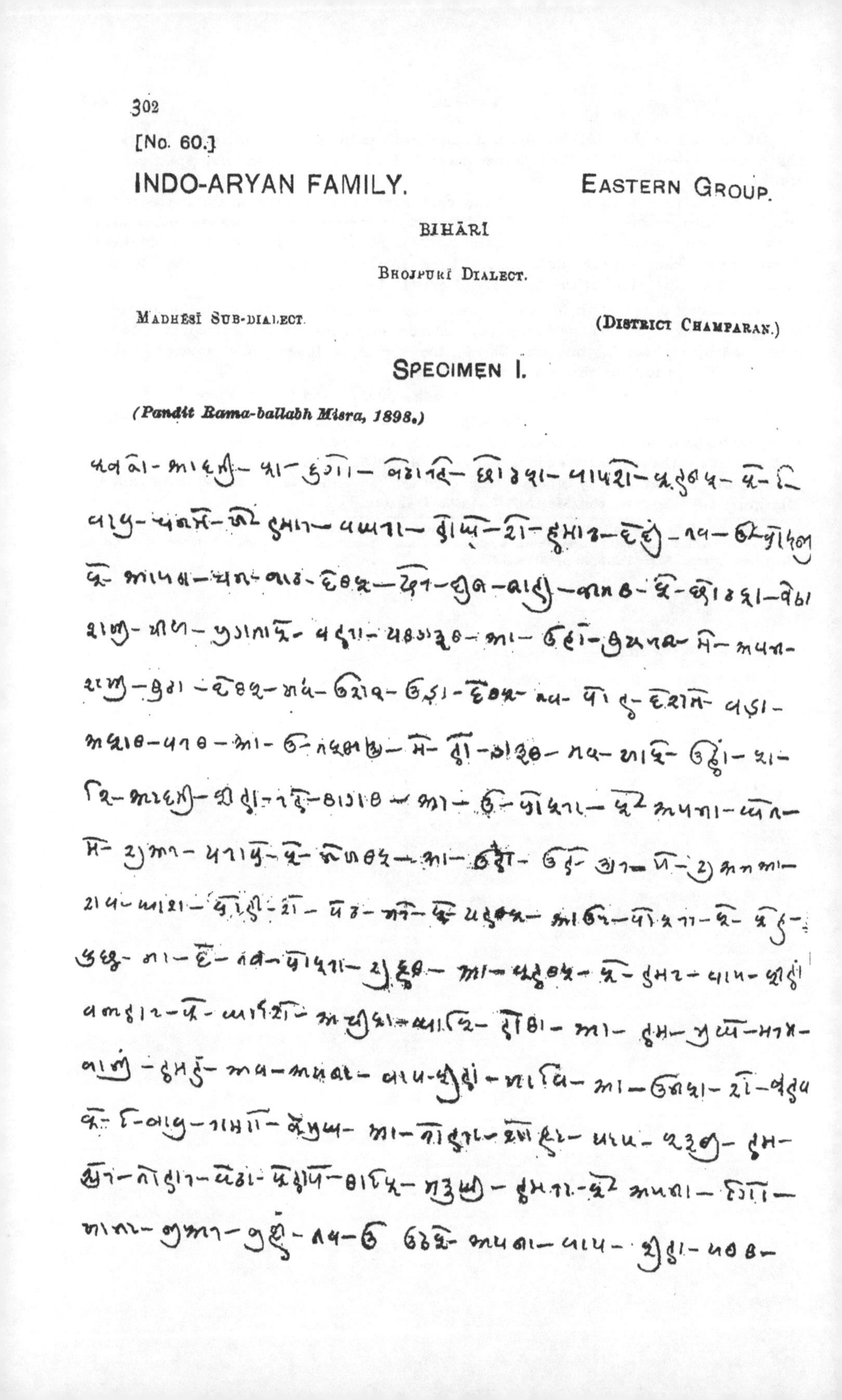

[No. 60.]

INDO-ARYAN FAMILY. EASTERN GROUP.

BIHĀRĪ

BHOJPURĪ DIALECT.

MADHESĪ SUB-DIALECT. (DISTRICT CHAMPARAN.)

SPECIMEN I.

(Pandit Rama-ballabh Misra, 1898.)

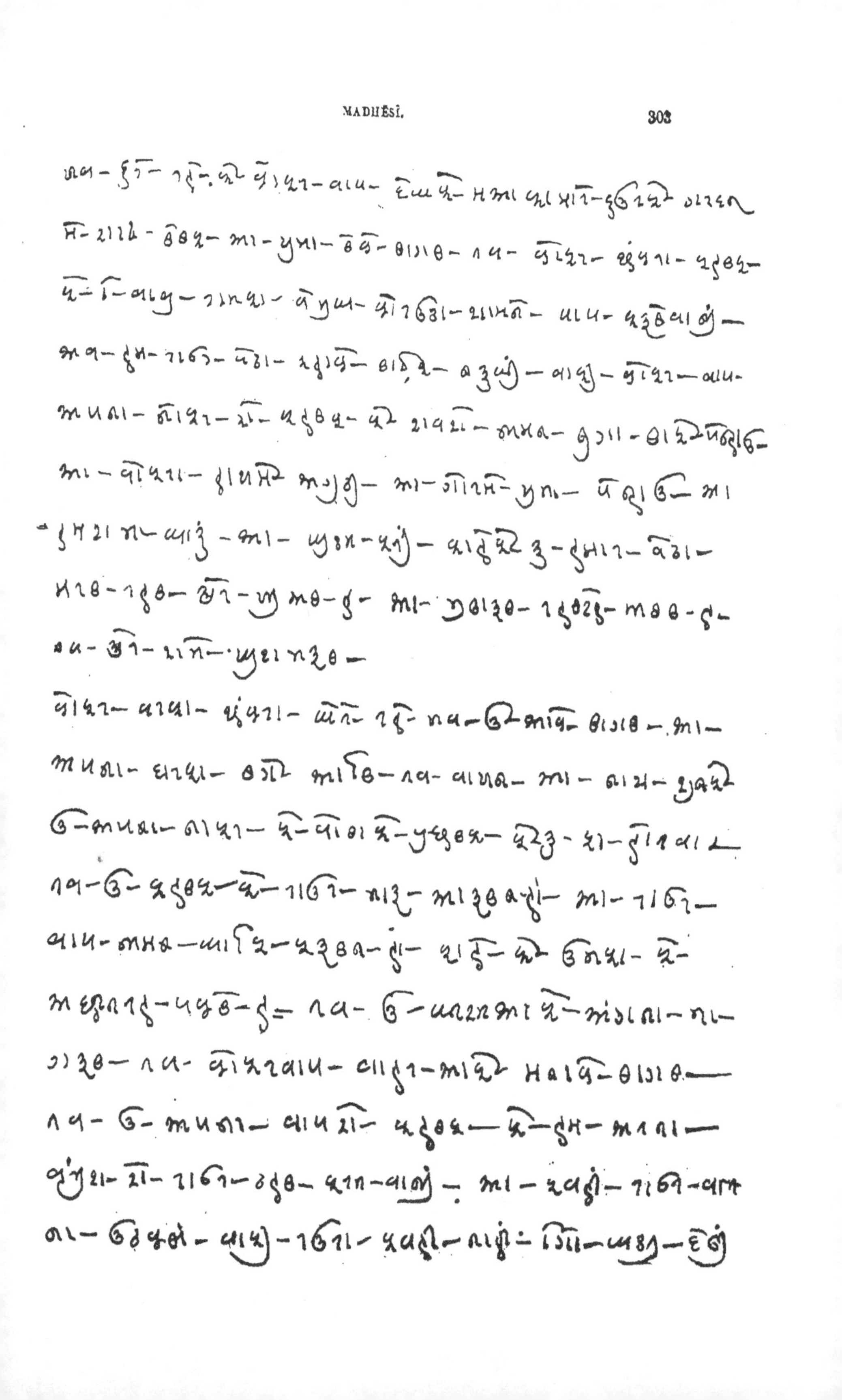

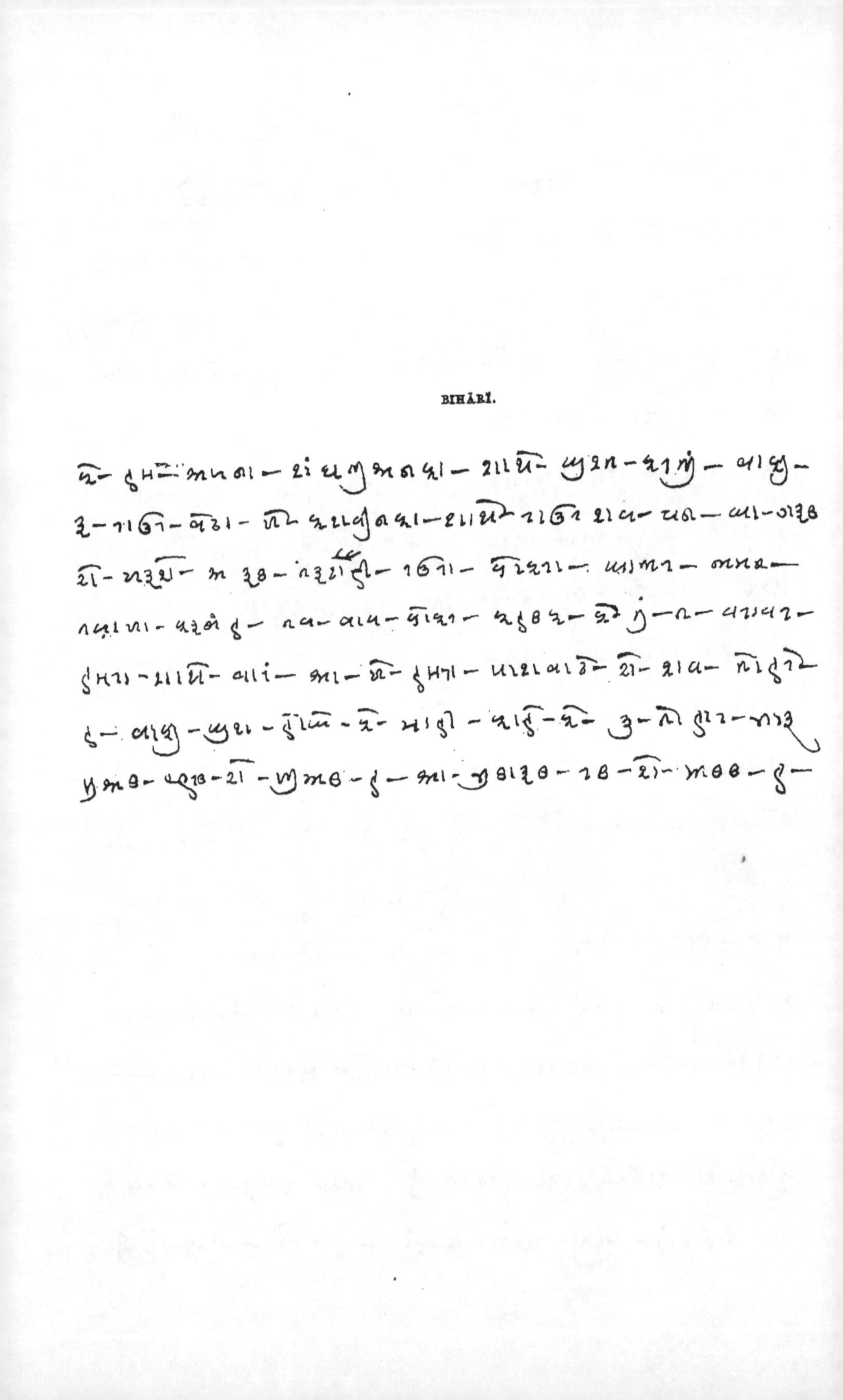

BIHĀRĪ.

[illegible]

[No. 60.]

INDO-ARYAN FAMILY. EASTERN GROUP.

BIHĀRĪ.

BHOJPURĪ DIALECT.

MADHĒSĪ SUB-DIALECT. (DISTRICT CHAMPARAN.)

TRANSLITERATION AND TRANSLATION.

(Pandit Rama-ballabh Misra, 1898.)

Kaw'nō ād'mī-kā du-gō bēṭā rahē. Chhoṭ'kā bāp-sē kah'lak
A-certain man-of two sons were. The-younger the-father-to said
ke, 'ē bābū, dhan-mē jē hamār bakh'rā hōkhē, sē hamār
that, 'O father, the-property-in which my share may-be, that mine
dē-dī.' Tab ū ok'nī-kē āpan dhan bā̃ṭ dēlak. Ḍhēr din
give-(me).' Then he them-to his-own property dividing gave. Many days
nāhī̃ bītal ke chhoṭ'kā bēṭā saji chīj jug'tā-ke bah'rā chal-gaīl,
not passed that the-younger son all things collecting out went-away,
ā uhā̃ luch'pan-mē apan sajī luṭā-dēlak. Jab ū sab uṛā-dēlak
and there riotous-living-in his-own all squandered. When he all had-squandered
tab oh dēs-mē baṛā akāl paral, ā ū tak'līph-mē hō-gaīl. Tab
then that country-in a-great famine fell, and he misery-in became. Then
jā-ke uhā̃-kā ēk ād'mī kihā̃ rahe lāgal, ā ū ok'rā-kē ap'nā khēt-
going there-of one man near to-live he-began, and he him his-own field-
mē sūar charāwe-kē bhej'lak. Ā uhā̃ uhē phar jē suariā sab
in swine feeding-for sent. And there that-very fruit which the-swine all
khās, ōhī-sē pēṭ bhare-kē chah'lak. Āur ok'rā-kē kēhu
used-to-eat, that-very-with belly for-filling he-wished. And him-to any-one
kuchh nā dē. Tab ok'rā sūjhal ā kah'lak ke, 'hamar
anything not used-to-give. Then him seeing-came and he-said that, 'my
bāp kihā̃ banihār-kē khāe-sē adhikā khāek hō-lā, ā ham
father near day-labourers-to eating-than more food is, and I
bhukhē marat-bānī. Ham-hū̃ ab ap'nā bāp kihā̃ jābi ā un-kā-sē
in-hunger am-dying. I-too now my-own father near will-go and him-to
kahab ke, "ē bābū, Rām-sē bemukh ā toh'rā sōjhā pāp kailī. Ham
will-say that, "O father, God-from opposed and thee before sin I-did. I
phēr tohār bēṭā kahāwe lāek naīkhī. Ham'rā-kē ap'nā ēgō jānā niar
again thy son to-be-called fit am-not. Me thine-own one servant like

būjhī̃." ' Tab ū uṭh-ke ap'nā bāp kihā̃ chalal. Jab dūrē rahē
consider." ' Then he arising his-own father near went. When far-off he-was

ke ō-kar bāp dēkh-ke mayā-kā-mārē daūr-ke gar'dan-mē sāṭ-lēlak ā
that his father seeing love-through running neck-in enfolded and

chūmā lēwe-lāgal. Tab ō-kar chhā̃w'rā kah'lak ke, 'ē bābū Rām-kā
kisses to-take-began. Then his son said that, 'O father, God-of

bemukh o raūrā sām'nē pāp kailē-bānī̃. Ab ham rāur bēṭā
opposed and Your-Honour before sin I-have-done. Now I Your-Honour's son

kahāwe lāek naïkhī̃.' Bākī ō-kar bāp ap'nā nōkar-sē kah'lak ke,
to-be-called worthy am-not.' But his father his-own servants-to said that,

'sab-sē nīman lūgā lā-ke penhāu ā ok'rā hāth-mē aguṭhī
'all-than good cloth bringing put-on and his hand-on ring

ā gōṛ-mē jūtā penhāu; ā ham sabh khāī̃ ā khusī karī̃; kāhe-ke
and feet-on shoes put; and (let)-us all eat and merriment make; what-for

ī hamār bēṭā maral rahal, pher jīal-hâ; ā bhulāil rahal, sē milal-hâ.'
this my son dead was, again alive-is; and lost was, he found-is.'

Tab phēr sabhē khus bhaïl.
Then again all merry became.

Ō-kar bar'kā chhā̃w'rā khētē rahē. Jab ū āwe lāgal ā ap'nā
His elder son in-the-field was. When he to-come began and his-own

ghar-kā lagē āel tab bājan ā nāch sun-ke ū ap'nā nōkar-kē bolā-ke
house-of near came then music and dancing hearing he his-own servant-to calling

puchh'lak ke, 'ī kā hōt-bā?' Tab ū kah'lak ke, 'rāur
he-asked that, 'this what is-going-on?' Then he said that, 'Your-Honour's

bhāī āïlan-hā̃, ā rāur bāp nīman khāek kaïlan-hā̃, kāhe-kē
brother is-come, and Your-Honour's father good feast has-done, because-for

un-kā-kē achchhī-tarah paw'lē-hâ.' Tab ū khisiā-ke āg'nā
him (in)-good-manner he-has-found.' Then he being-angry to-the-inner-courtyard

nā gaïl. Tab ō-kar bāp bāhar ā-ke manāwe lāgal. Tab ū ap'nā
not went. Then his father outside coming to-conciliate began. Then he his-own

bāp-sē kah'lak ke, 'ham at'nā baris-sē rāur ṭahal karat-bānī̃ ā
father-to said that, 'I so-many years-from Your-Honour's service am-doing and

kab-hī̃ rāur bāt nā uṭhaw'lī̃, bākī raūrā kab'hī̃ nāhī̃ ēgō
ever Your-Honour's orders not I-put-off, but Your-Honour ever not one

khasī delī̃ ke ham ap'nā sā̃ghatian-kā sāthē khusī kar'tī̃.' Bākī
he-goat gave that I my-own companions-of with merriment might-make.' But

ī rāur bēṭā jē kas'bin-kā sāthē rāur sab dhan khā-gaïl
this Your-Honour's son who harlots-of with Your-Honour's all fortune ate-up

sē jaïsē āil taïs'hī raūrā ok'rā khātir nīman tawājā kailī̃-hâ. Tab
that as came so-even Your-Honour him for good feast has-done. Then

bāp ō-kar kah'lak ke, 'tū̃, tâ, barābar ham'rā sāthē bārâ
the-father of-him said that, 'thou, to-be-sure, always me with art

ā jē ham'rā-pās bātē, sē sab tohrē hâ. Bākī khus hōkhe-kē
and whatever me-with is, that all thine-even is. But glad to-be
chāhī, kāhe-ke ī tohār bhāī mūal ra(ha)l, sē jīal hâ; ā bhulāil
ought, because-for this thy brother dead was, he alive is; and lost
ra(ha)l, sē mīlal hâ.'
was, he found is.'

[No. 61.]

INDO-ARYAN FAMILY.

EASTERN GROUP.

BIHĀRĪ.

BHOJPURĪ DIALECT.

MADHĒSĪ SUB-DIALECT.

(DISTRICT CHAMPARAN.)

SPECIMEN II.

A FOLK-TALE.

(Pandit Rama-ballabh Misra, 1898.)

[No. 61.]

INDO-ARYAN FAMILY. EASTERN GROUP.

BIHĀRĪ.

BHOJPURĪ DIALECT.

MADHĒSĪ SUB-DIALECT. (DISTRICT CHAMPARAN.)

SPECIMEN II.

TRANSLITERATION AND TRANSLATION.

(Pandit Rama-ballabh Misra, 1898.)

Ēgō Rājā-kā sāt bēṭī rahē. Ēk din Rājā ap'nā sātō
One King-of seven daughters were. One day the-king his-own the-seven

bēṭī-kē bolaūlē ā sātō-sē puchh'lan ke, 'tū̃ lōg'ni kek'rā karam-sē
daughters-to called and the-seven-from asked that, 'you people whose fate-from

khā-lū?' Tab chhaw-gō-sâ kah'lī̃ ke, 'ham toh'rē karam-sē khāī-lā.'
(do-you)-eat?' Then six said that, 'we thy fate-from eat.'

Tab Rājā sun-ke barā khus bhaīlē. Tab ap'nā chhoṭ'kī
Then the-king hearing very glad became. Then his-own the-youngest

bēṭī-sē puchh'lan ke, 'tū̃ tâ kuchhu-nā bol'lū.' Tab ū
daughter-from asked that, 'thou to-be-sure nothing saidst.' Then she

kah'lak ke, 'ham ap'nā karam-sē khāī-lā.' Tab ē-par Rājā barā
said that, 'I my-own fate-from eat.' Then her-at the-king great

jōr-sē khisiaīlē, ā ō-kar biāh ēgō kōṛhī-kā sāthē kar-dih'lan, ā
force-with became-angry, and her marriage one leper-of with did, and

dūnō-kē ban-mē̃ nikāl-dēlan. Tab ū bechārī ohi korhiā-ke māth
both a-forest-into sent-out. Then she poor-one that leper-of head

ap'nā jā̃gh-par dhâ-ke oh ban-mē̃ jār-bejār rōat rahē; ā ok'rā
her-own thigh-on putting that forest-in bitterly crying was; and her

rōalā-sē ban-ke pachhī saji rōat rahē. At'nē-mē̃ uhā̃ kahī̃
cry-from forest-of birds all crying were. In-the-meantime there somewhere

Siv-jī ā Pār'batī-jī jāt rahas. Pār'batī-jī Siv-jī-sē kah'lī ke,
Śiva-jī and Pārvatī-jī going were. Pārvatī-jī Śiva-jī-to said that,

'ab jab-lē raūrā̃ ē-kar dukh nā chhorāib tab-lē ham ihā̃-sē
'now as-long-as Your-Honour this-one's trouble not removes so-long I here-from

nā jāib.' Tab Siv-jī ok'rā-sē kah'lan ke, 'ē bēṭī, āpan ā̃kh
not will-go.' Then Śiva-jī her-to said that, 'O daughter, your eyes

mū̃dâ.' Ū ā̃kh mūd'lakh. Jab ā̃kh khulal tab dēkhē-tō
shut.' She eyes shut. When eyes opened then saw (to-her-wonder)

ū	korhiā	sun^{a}dar	sob^{a}ran	hō-gaïl.	Tab	Rājā-ke	bēṭī
that	*the-leper*	*beautiful*	*gold-(like)*	*became.*	*Then*	*the-king-of*	*daughter*

barā	as^{a}tut	kaïl,	ō	dūnō	bekat	khusī	sāth	rahe	lāgal.
great	*praises*	*did,*	*and*	*both*	*persons*	*pleasure*	*with*	*to-live*	*began.*

Dukh-dalidar	bhāg-gaïl.
Pain-(and)-misery	*ran-away.*

FREE TRANSLATION OF THE FOREGOING.

Once upon a time there was a king who had seven daughters. One day he called the whole seven and asked them by whose good fortune they got their food to eat. Then six of them replied, 'it is by thy good fortune that we eat our food,' whereat the king was much pleased. Then said he to his youngest daughter, 'thou hast not spoken.' She answered, 'I get my food by my own good fortune.' Thereon the king was mightily enraged against her, and married her to a leper, and banished the two into the forest. The poor Princess sat in the forest weeping with the leper's head in her lap, and so piteous were her tears that the birds of the forest all wept with her. It happened that just then the god Śiva and his wife Pārvatī were passing by, and Pārvatī said to Śiva, 'until thou remove the grief of this poor girl, I will not leave this place.' So Śiva said to the Princess, 'my daughter, shut thine eyes.' She did so, and when she opened them, lo-and-behold, the leper had become as beautiful as gold. So she uttered praises to the god, and both lived happy ever after; for pain and poverty had fled from them.

THE THĀRŪ BROKEN DIALECTS.

The Thārūs are an aboriginal tribe who inhabit the Sub-Himalayan-Tarāī, from Jalpaiguri on the east, to the Kumaun Bhābar on the west. Regarding the origin of this tribe much has been written by many authors from Dr. Buchanan-Hamilton's[1] time to the present day. It will here suffice to refer the reader to Mr. Nesfield's article in the Calcutta *Review* for January 1885, and to the articles in Mr. Risley's *Tribes and Castes of Bengal*, and Mr. Crooke's *Tribes and Castes of the North-Western Provinces and Oudh*, in which all that has been said by previous writers has been summed up. Mr. Crooke, the latest authority on the subject, says, 'The most probable explanation based on the available evidence seems to be that the Thārūs are originally a Dravidian race who, by alliances with Nepalese and other hill races, have acquired some degree of Mongolian physiognomy.'

Whatever doubts may exist concerning the origin of this curious race, there can be no doubt that the languages spoken by those members of the tribe who are accessible to students in India are Aryan. There is, however, no such thing as a Thārū language. Everywhere the Thārūs speak, more or less correctly, the language of the Aryan races with whom they are immediately in contact. For instance the Thārūs of the north of Purnea appear to speak a corrupt form of the Eastern Maithilī spoken in that District,[2] those of Champaran and Gorakhpur, a corrupt Bhojpurī, and those of the Naini Tal Tarāī the ordinary Western Hindī of the locality.

The following are the figures for the Thārū population of British India, according to the Census of 1891 :

Province.	District.	Number of Thārūs.	
Bengal	Bogra	3	
	Darjeeling	172	
	Jalpaiguri	65	
	Darbhanga	453	
	Muzaffarpur	1	
	Saran	26	
	Champaran	27,620	
	Total for Bengal .	...	28,340

[1] Alberuni, *Indica*, Chapter xviii, mentions a country called Tilwat, immediately to the south of, and bordering on, Nepal. The inhabitants are called '*Tarū*, a people of a very black colour, and flat nosed like the Turks.' See Sachau's Translation, vol. i, p. 201.

[2] *Vide ante*, p. 86.

Province.	District.	Number of Thārūs.	
	Brought forward .		28,340
United Provinces of Agra and Oudh	Bareilly	8	
	Pilibhit	46	
	Gorakhpur	3,072	
	Basti	208	
	Kumaun	65	
	Naini Tal Tarāī	15,332	
	Kheri	1,975	
	Gonda	2,475	
	Bahraich	2,311	
	Total for United Provinces of Agra and Oudh	...	25,492
	GRAND TOTAL .	...	53,832

No estimate can be made of the number of Thārūs in the Tarāī outside British India.

The figures returned for the Survey as the number of persons speaking what was reported to be the 'Thārū Language,' a thing which does not really exist, were as follows:

Province.	District.	Number of persons reported as speaking 'Thārū.'	
Bengal	Champaran	27,620	
	Purnea	3,300	
	Total for Bengal .	...	30,920
United Provinces of Agra and Oudh	Kheri	3,000	
	Gonda	3,500	
	Bahraich	2,000	
	Total for United Provinces of Agra and Oudh	...	8,500
	GRAND TOTAL .	...	39,420

This list, as compared with the preceding one, presents both deficiencies and an instance of redundance. With regard to the former, it is easily intelligible that where the Thārūs have adopted the language of their Aryan neighbours, there was nothing to induce the local authorities to show them as speaking a separate language. This accounts for the absence from the second list of the names of the Districts of Bogra, Darjeeling, Jalpaiguri, Darbhanga, Muzaffarpur, and Saran in Bengal. As to the United Provinces, subsequent inquiries have shown that this is certainly the case in the District of Pilibhit and in the Naini Tal Tarāī. It also appears that the Thārūs of Kheri speak the ordinary Awadhī of that district, although they were originally returned as speaking a separate language. In Bahraich, on the contrary, they speak a corrupted form of the Bhojpurī spoken to the east. No 'Thārū Language' was returned from Gorakhpur, but, here, there is no doubt that the 3,072 Thārūs of that district, speak a corrupt form of the Bhojpurī locally spoken, and differing considerably from it, though closely resembling the Thārū Bhojpurī of Champaran. I have no doubt that the same is the case with the 208 Thārūs of Basti, whose number was evidently too insignificant for the local authorities to return as speaking a separate dialect; for the members of the tribe who inhabit Gonda, the district immediately to the west of Basti, do speak a corrupt Bhojpurī. Returning to the Lower Provinces, the language of the large number of Thārūs who inhabit the north of Champaran is a corrupt form of the local Bhojpurī. As to Purnea, the local authorities have reported that the 'Thārū Language' is spoken by 3,300 people in that district, although, according to the Census, it does not contain a single member of the tribe. Here the Census is probably wrong, and the local authorities are probably right. Unfortunately, the Purnea Thārūs are a particularly wild section of their tribe, and every effort which has been made to obtain specimens of their language has proved unavailing. So far as I can ascertain it is there a corrupt form of the local Eastern Maithilī, and as such it has been dealt with on pp. 86 and ff.

In other districts the presence of Thārūs is more or less of an accident. The Districts of Darbhanga and Muzaffarpur do not, as is the case with Champaran and its districts to the west, run up into the Nepal Tarāī, and the few Thārūs found there at the time of the Census have become absorbed, so far as language goes, into the rest of the population. When I served in the former district, more than twenty years ago, I met several of these men, and though they had traditions and customs of their own, their language was even then the Maithilī of the lower orders of the country. So also, in Jalpaiguri, their language is the Bengali of the Aryan population of the district.

We may tabulate these results, so far as they concern the British districts adjoining the Himalayan Tarāī as follows, dividing the language spoken by Thārūs into three groups, according as it is the same as that of the surrounding population, or is a corrupted form of it. In the latter case, we must, for the sake of accuracy in statistics, and to avoid quoting the same men twice over, show separately when the corrupted form of the local language has been separately reported by the local officials or not.

Name of District.	Number of Thārūs speaking			Name of language.
	The local language without alteration.	A corrupted form of the local language.		
		Reported by local officials.	Not reported by local officials.	
Naini Tal Tarāī	15,332			Western Hindī.
Pilibhit	46			Ditto.
Kheri	3,000			Ditto.
Bahraich		2,000		Bhojpurī.
Gonda		3,500		Ditto.
Basti			208	Ditto.
Gorakhpur			3,072	Ditto.
Champaran		27,620		Ditto.
Muzaffarpur	1			Maithilī.
Darbhanga	453			Ditto.
Purnea		3,300		Eastern Maithilī.
Dinagepore				*Nil.*
Darjeeling	172			Probably Bengali.
Jalpaiguri	65			Bengali.
Other Districts . . .	76			……
Total .	19,145	36,420	3,280	

Total number of Thārūs speaking a corrupt language	39,700
Add those who speak the local language without alteration	19,145
Grand Total of all Thārūs .	58,845

This total differs from the Grand Total given on page 312 by about 5,000. The difference is due, partly to the inclusion of the Purnea figures, and partly to the fact that the figures reported from Kheri, Gonda, and Bahraich differ from those of the Census.

Omitting from consideration the figures in the first column commencing from those for Muzaffarpur, all of which are accidental, it will be observed that broadly speaking, so far as language goes, the Thārūs of the Western Tarāī have amalgamated much more completely with the rest of the population than those more to the east. There is another point to notice, which is not clearly brought out in the above table.

The language spoken by the Thārūs is not always the same as, or a corruption of the language of the people among whom they live, but is, in some instances, the language of a neighbouring district. Thus, we shall see that the language of the District of Kherī is on the main a form of Eastern Hindī, though it shows signs of shading off into the neighbouring Western Hindī, spoken in Shahjahanpur. But the language spoken by the Thārūs of Kheri is not this form of speech, but closely resembles the Western Hindī spoken in Pilibhit and the Naini Tal Tarāī. Similarly, the Thārūs of Bahraich and Gonda do not talk the Eastern Hindī of those districts, but speak a corrupt form of the Bhojpurī spoken in the neighbouring District of Basti. In fact, so far as I can gather from the specimens of their language, none of the frontier Thārūs speak any form of Eastern Hindī. They either speak the Western language of the Naini Tal Tarāī, or else Bhojpurī or Maithilī.

A vocabulary of the Thārū dialect will be found in Hodgson's Essay entitled *Continuation of the Comparative Vocabulary of the Languages of the broken Tribes of Nēpāl,* in the Journal of the Asiatic Society of Bengal, Vol. xxvi, 1857, pp. 317 and ff., which has been reprinted in his *Miscellaneous Essays relating to Indian Subjects,* Vol. i, sec. ii, pt. 2, London, 1880. Judging from the forms of the verb given by him, the particular dialect of Thārū there exemplified is a corrupt Bhojpurī.

With regard to the Thārūs of Purnea, see pp. 86 and ff. The language spoken by the Thārūs of Kheri and the districts to the west will be dealt with in their proper place. Here, I propose to give specimens of the corrupt Bhojpurī spoken by the Thārūs of Champaran, Gorakhpur, Basti, Gonda, and Bahraich.

The following specimens, for which I am indebted to Pandit Rama-ballabh Misra, Assistant Settlement Officer of Champaran, come from that district, and may be taken as examples of the language spoken by the Thārūs of the north of Champaran and Gorakhpur. As the Thārūs have no written character, the specimens are given in the Roman character only.

[No. 62.]

INDO-ARYAN FAMILY. EASTERN GROUP.

BIHĀRĪ.

BHOJPURĪ DIALECT.

THĀRŪ BROKEN DIALECT. (DISTRICT CHAMPARAN.)

SPECIMEN I.

(Pandit Rama-ballabh Misra, 1898.)

Ek manªsē-ke dui bēṭā rahªlaī. Ū-mā̃-sē chhuṭukā beṭªwā
One man-of two sons were. Them-in-from the-younger son
kahªlia āpan bābā-sē, 'arē bābā, dhan-bit jaūn baraī, taūn mōr bakhªrā
said his-own father-to, 'O father, riches-property which is, that my share
phā̃ṭ lagāi dē.' Tab ō-kar bābā dhan-bit chhoṭªkahªwā beṭªwā-kē bakhªrā
division making give.' Then his father property the-younger son-to share
bā̃ṭi delia. Bakhªrā lēl-par bahuṭ din haīnī bhelaī, tâ chhoṭªkahªwā
dividing gave. The-share taking-on many days not passed, then the-younger
beṭªwā āpan dhan bakhªrā lē-lē dōsar desªwā chali-gēlia. Tab uhªwā̃
son his-own property share taking another country went-away. Then there
lamēṭaī kām karªlia. Tab āpan dhan chhūṭi uṛāy-delia. Jab chhūṭi
evil deeds he-did. Then his-own fortune all he-squandered. When all
dhan uṛāi-delia āpan, tab ū desªwā-mā̃ [illegible] [illegible] parªlai.
fortune had-squandered his-own, then that country-in great famine fell.
Tab ū manªsawā barā kaṅgāl bhelia. Tab ū desªwā-ke ek manªsē-ke
Then that man very indigent became. Then that country-of one man-of
ghar rahe lagªlia. Tab okªrā-kē āpan khetªwā-mā̃ sūar charāwāī-kē
house to-live he-began. Then him his-own field-in swine to-feed
paṭhaülia. Tab jawªnē ṭhōṭhi sūar khātl.in tawªnē ṭhōṭhū ṭūri-ke
he-sent. Then what gram swine used-to-eat that-very gram breaking
manªsawā khaia chāhē, āpan peṭªwā bharia chāhē. Okªrā-kē kawªnō manªsē
the-man to-eat wished, his-own belly to-fill wished. Him any man
kathiō nāhī̃ khāi-kē dēthī. Tab ū manªsawā-kē hōs bhelaī.
anything not to-eat used-to-give. Then that man-to senses became.
Tab ū kahªlia, 'mōr bābā āpan gharªwā-mā̃ bahutē bahutē manªsē
Then he said, 'my father his-own house-in many many men
banihārā lagōsia; khāy-kē banihārani-kē bahutē bahutē rōṭi bhāt
labourers has-employed; to-eat labourers-to much much bread cooked-rice

khiōsia. Khāy-ke pēṭ-sē ub'rī jē, seiā mōi ih'wā̃
causes-to-eat. Food-of belly-(full)-than is-saved in-as-much-as, yet I here

bhūkhē maraik bar'hī. Āb ih'wā̃-sē uṭhi-ke mōhū āpan bābā-ke
by-hunger dying am. Now here-from arising I-too my-own father-of

laghī jeb'hī. Bābā-sē kah'babī, "Arē bābā, mōi Bhag'wan'wā̃-ke
near will-go. The-father-to I-will-say, "O father, I God-of

kah'nī hai-nō-lel'hī, tōr kah'nī phuni hai-nō-lel'hī. Tōr lagē pāp
saying have-not-taken, thy saying again I-have-not-taken. Thy near sin

kar'lahī; āb mōi tōr bēṭā kahāwāī jōkar hai-nō-bar'hī. Āb mōrā-kē
I-have-done; now I thy son to-be-called fit I-not-am. Now me

harohiyā-ke samān rakh'hī."' Tab chhoṭ'kah'wā beṭ'wā āpan bap'wā-ke
ploughman-of like keep."' Then the-younger son his-own father-of

lagē jāy lag'lia. Ghar'wā-sē thoriak dūri niaraūlia, tab
near to-go began. The-house-from a-little distance he-approached, then

ō-kar bap'wā dekh'lia chhoṭ'kā beṭ'wā-ke āwaik. Tab ō-kar bābā
his father saw the-younger son-of the-coming. Then his father

dekh'tē-mān māyā kaīlia. Dagurī-ke bhar-ak'wār dhaī-ke, garē
just-as-he-saw-him compassion made. Running full-embrace holding, on-neck

garē milāi-ke chūme lag'lia. Beṭ'wā āpan bap'wā-sē kah'lia, 'arē
on-neck joining to-kiss began. The-son his-own father-to said, 'O

bābā, mōi Bhag'wan'wā̃-ke kah'nī hai-nō-lel'hiā, tōrā-sē pāp kar'lahī,
father, I God-of saying not-have-taken, thee-from sin did,

āb mōi phuni tōr bēṭā kahāwāī lāyak hai-nō-bar'hī.' Tab ō-kar bap'wā
now I again thy son to-be-called fit I-not-am.' Then his father

āpan mar'hariā-sē kah'lia, 'arē mar'hariawā, ek'rā-kē sabh-sē ḍaūl
his-own servant-to said, 'O servant, this-one all-of good

luggā nikāri-ke pahir'wahiā. Ō-kar hath'wā-mā̃ aguṭhiā gor'wā-mā̃ jūtā
cloth taking-out put-on. His hand-on ring feet-on shoes

pehar'wahi; āb khaia, piia, sukh karia; kaisē-kī ī beṭ'wā
put; now let-us-eat, drink, pleasure let-us-do; because this son

maral rah'lia, phuni jialia; bhulāil rah'lia, bhē̃ṭ'lia.' Tab ū
dead was, again alive-became; lost was, is-found.' Then he

sukh kare lag'lia.
pleasure to-do began.

Ō-kar jeṭh'kā beṭ'wā khet'wā-mā̃ rah'lia. Jab ōi ghar'wā-ke nijīkihī
His elder son field-in was. When he house-of near

elia, tab bājā nāch-ke āwāj sun'lia. Tab ōi āpan mar'hariawā-kē
came, then music dance-of noise heard. Then he his-own servant-to

balolia, puchh'lia, 'arē mar'hariawā, ī kathī hōkhaï?' Tab
he-called, he-asked, 'O servant, this what is-happening?' Then

mar'hariawā kah'lia, 'tōr bhaewā āil baria, tōr bap'wā ḍaūl ḍaūl
the-servant said, 'thy brother come is, thy father good good

khāe-kē kailē baṛia; kaisē ki ō chhuṭ^{a}kā beṭ^{a}wā-kē
(preparations)-for-eating done has; because that he the-younger son

chik^{a}han paūlē.' Tab ō-kar jeṭh^{a}kā beṭ^{a}wā khisiailīa, ghar^{a}wā bhītar
well found.' Then his elder son grew-angry, the-house into

jāy-ke manē na paraī. Tab ōhī khātir ō-kar bābā bah^{a}rī ailīa,
going-of heart-in not chose. Then this-even for his father outside came,

kahe lag^{a}līa bujhāwāi lag^{a}līa jeṭh^{a}kā beṭ^{a}wā-kē. Tab jeṭh^{a}kā
to-say began to-remonstrate began the-elder son-to. Then the-elder

beṭ^{a}wā āpan bap^{a}wā-kē jabāb delīa, 'Dekhahī, utarā baris tōrā-ke
son his-own father-to answer gave, 'See, so-many years thy

sēwā kar^{a}lahī, tōr bachan kahu nāhī̃ tar^{a}lahī, tōi mōrā-kē ek
service I-did, thy words ever not I-transgressed, thou me-to one

khasī-ke chhōkan hai-nō-dēl^{a}hī. Mōi āpan saṅghatiyā-sē sawakh
goat-of young-one not-gavest. I my-own friends-with merriment

karaṭ-hī. Bākī, tōr chhoṭ^{a}kah^{a}wā beṭ^{a}wā, tō, paturiyā ke sā̃g^{a}wā
might-have-made. But, thy younger son, surely, harlots of with

tōr sajē dhan khōi-delīa, tab ōi jas-hi elīa tab tōi tas-hī
thy all fortune squandered, then he as-even came then thou so-even

ḍaūl ḍaūl khāe-kē kailīa.' Tab ō-kar bap^{a}wā
good good (preparations)-for-food made-hast.' Then his father

kah^{a}līa, 'arē babuā, tōi, tā, mōr saṅgē barōbarī barahī;
said, 'O son, thou, to-be-sure, me with always art;

jaūn mōr dhan baraī taūn dhan sab tōrē hokhaī.
what my fortune is that fortune all thine-even is.

Bākī, khusī karahī, anand karahī-kē chāhai ka-rahal-hī,
But, merriment to-make, joy to-celebrate proper was,

kāhē-ki tōr ī bhaewā maral rah^{a}līa, jī-gēlīa;
because-that thy this brother dead was, alive-became;

bhulāil rah^{a}līa, sē bheṭelīa.'
lost was, and is-found.'

[No. 63.]

INDO-ARYAN FAMILY. EASTERN GROUP.

BIHĀRĪ.

BHOJPURĪ DIALECT.

THĀRŪ BROKEN DIALECT. (DISTRICT CHAMPARAN.)

SPECIMEN II.

A FOLK-TALE.

(Pandit Rama-ballabh Misra, 1898.)

Eur̤ā aw^{a}niyā rahē barad char^{a}wait. Bhā̃j^{a}hariyā sab biyā
One herdsman was bullocks feeding. The-labourers all seedlings

kaṭait. Eur̤ā har^{a}nā baiṭhal rahalīa. Euniwā kah^{a}lās, 'tōr
transplanting. One deer sitting was. The-herdsman said, 'thee

āgē kathi bar̤aü?' Bhā̃j^{a}hariyā kah^{a}las, 'arē, ke jani kathi hōkhai
before what is-for-thee?' The-labourers said, 'O, who knows what is

kathi na. Dēkhahī-tâ.' Bhā̃j^{a}hariē gelīa, har^{a}nā dekh^{a}līa. Tab euniwā̃
what not. See.' The-labourers went, a-deer saw. Then the-herdsman

mār-delīa. Bhā̃j^{a}hariyā kah^{a}līa, 'arē sasur, tohi kihā̃-kē
killed (the-deer). The-labourers said, 'O father-in-law, thou why

māral-hī? Saran-mē̃ ãel-rah^{a}lai. Kah-dēwasu mah^{a}tauā-kē aghi.
hast-killed-(it)? Refuge-into it-come-had. I-will-say the-head-man-of before.

Ḍanḍ^{a}bihē. Tōr gunāwan par^{a}laü.'
He-will-punish (you). On-thee fault fell-for-thee.'

FREE TRANSLATION OF THE FOREGOING.

There was a herdsman tending his bullocks. The farm-labourers[1] were transplanting paddy. There was a deer crouching down. The herdsman said to the labourers 'what is that before you?' They replied, 'Who cares what is before us, and what is not? Go and see for yourself.' However, they went to see what it was and the herdsman killed the deer. Then said the labourers, 'O foul-one, why have you killed it? It had taken refuge with us. We shall tell the headman, and he will punish you. A great shame has fallen on you.'

The two following specimens of Thārū Bhojpurī come from the District of Gonda, and may be taken as specimens of the Thārū language of that District, as well as of that of the adjoining District of Basti. They are admirably idiomatic versions, and well illustrate the peculiar idioms of the tribe. The first is a translation of the Parable of the Prodigal Son, and the second a little song.

---

[1] A *bhā̃j^{a}hariyā* is a man who gives his labour in exchange for mutual obligation, such as the loan of a pair of bullocks.

[No. 64.]

INDO-ARYAN FAMILY. EASTERN GROUP.

BIHĀRĪ.

BHOJPURĪ DIALECT.

THĀRŪ BROKEN DIALECT. (DISTRICT GONDA.)

SPECIMEN I.

(Pandit Janardan Joshee, 1898.)

Ek manaī-kē dū-ṭhau lauṛā bāṭel. Chhoṭ^{a}kā kah^{a}lis ki,
One man-of two sons were. The-younger said that,

'bāpū rē, mōr bakh^{a}rā bā̃ṭ dē. Ab nāhī̃ nib^{a}hī.'
'father O, my share dividing give. Now not it-will-suffice (under

Tab bakh^{a}rā bā̃ṭ dih^{a}lis. Thōrik din chhoṭ^{a}kā
present arrangements).' Then share dividing he-gave. A-few days the-younger

lauṛā baṭōril ghar dwār sab jōr-ke bah-gaïl. Rupaïyā
son together house door all collecting flowed-(went)-away. The-rupees

païsā jawan sasur pāis-rahal, tawan jāy-ke nak^{a}ṭī-mā̃
pice which the-low-fellow had-got, that going evil-conduct-in

uṛāy-dih^{a}lis. Rupaiyā païsā nāin rahil. Parāē dēs
he-squandered. Rupees pice not remained. Foreign country-(in)

sukkhā paril. Tab sasur bhukkhan muat rahē. Tab sasur
famine fell. Then the-low-fellow of-hunger dying was. Then the-low-fellow

har^{a}wāhī jōte lāgil, sūar charāwāī lāgil, aur uk^{a}rē-mā̃
ploughing to-plough began, swine to-feed began, and heart-in

kah^{a}lis ki, 'chaiā pēṭ-bhar khāū̃.' Kahū̃ mā̃gai
said that, 'pork belly-full let-(me)-eat.' Anywhere he-asked

païbai-nā-karai. Jab chetaïl ki, 'mōr bhuṛ^{a}wā-ke kamāhī-mā̃
he-used-not-to-get. When he-remembered that, 'my old-one-of earnings-in

manaī khāy jāt āṭē̃, bur-chōdī maī̃ bhūkhan marat āṭū̃.
men eating going are, the-foul-one I by-hunger dying am.

Jāit āṭū̃ bāpū lagē. Bāpū-sē kah^{a}yū̃ ki, "bāpū rē,
Going I-am the-father near. The-father-to I-will-say that, "father O,

mōhi-sē kasūr bhaïl, twār put^{a}wā banē lāyak naī̃ hū̃. Jas
me-by fault has-occurred, thy son to-become fit not I-am. As

āūr kam^{a}waïyā āṭē̃, mōhū̃-kā rākh-lē."' Ap^{a}nē bāpū pās ram-gaïl.
other earners are, me-too keep."' His-own father near he-went-away.

Jab bāpū pās pahũchil bāpū-kē mōh lāgil. Daur-ke
When the-father near he-approached the-father pity seized. Running

pakar-lihis ăũr mile lāgil. Rōwāī lāgil bur-chōdī. Laurā
he-caught(-him) and to-embrace began. To-cry began the-foul-one. The-boy

kahil, 'mō-sē kasūr bhaïl.' Bāpū ṭahaluan-sē kah^{a}lis, 'bhaïā rē,
said, 'me-by fault has-occurred.' The-father servants-to said, 'brothers O,

lūgā dē-ḍār. Ăgochhā wãgochhā pahir-lē. Mũdarī bāth-mā̃ ăũr gōṛē-mā̃
cloth give-away. Kerchief etc. put-on. Ring hand-on and feet-on

pan^{a}hī pahir-lē. Khusī manāïl bāṭē, ki mōr lauṛā muat, jiat āïl.'
shoes put. Joy celebrated is, that my son dying, living came.'

Bahur khusi kar^{a}le lāgil.
Again merriment to-make they-began.

Ăũr baṛ^{a}kā lauṛā khētē rahil. Jab gharē āil, gāwe
And the-elder son field-in was. When house-to he-came, singing

nāche sunil. Tab ek ṭahaluā-sē pūchhis ki, 'āj kā
dancing he-heard. Then one servant-to he-asked that, 'to-day what

gharē bāṭē rē, ki baṛā gaunai hōitā?' Tab ṭahaluā
house-in is O, that great singing is-going-on?' Then the-servant

kah^{a}lis ki, 'bhaïwā āil ăũr tohār bāpū khiwāit piāitā,
said that, 'brother came and thy father is-feeding is-causing-to-drink,

ki lauṛā milē bāṭē.' Baṛ^{a}kā lauṛā bhusiāil ki, 'maĩ nāĩ
that the-son found is.' The-elder son grew-angry that, 'I not

jāũ bhit^{a}rē.' Bāpū bah^{a}rē āil manāil. Lauṛā
will-go inside.' The-father outside came (and) appeased-(him). The-son

bāp-sē kah^{a}lis ki, 'maĩ tōrē ag^{a}wā̃ rah^{a}lũ; ki jaun kahat
father-to said that, 'I thee before lived; that which saying

rah^{a}lis, taun karat rahilũ. Kabbaũ ek-ṭhē paṭh^{a}rū nāĩ dih^{a}lē
thou-wast, that doing I-was. Ever-even one-even kid not thou-gavest

ki maĩ ap^{a}nē gōchā-sē khusī kar^{a}nũ. Ăũr jab twār
that I my-own friends-with merriment might-be-made. And when thy

ī lauṛā āil, ū twār rupaïyā païsā jawan rah^{a}lis tawan bēṛin-kā
this son came, he thy rupees pice which was that harlots-to

dē-ghālis; tū uh-kē tān baṛā mōh karat āṭā.' Bāp kah^{a}lis,
gave-away; thou him for great love doing art.' The-father said,

'arē bhaiyā, tū mōrē ṭhīnā rah^{a}lis, jawan kuchh jōril-pailil
'O brother,[1] thou me near livedst, what ever was-got-(by-fate)

khailis kamailis. Jō-kuchh bāṭē, toh^{a}rē hōil. Bara khusi
thou-atest(-and) didst-earn. Whatever is, thine-very is. Great joy

karat chāhil, ki twār bhaiwā muat jiat āil.'
to-be-done ought, that thy brother dying living came.'

[1] This is the regular term by which a Thārū addresses his son.

[No. 65.]

INDO-ARYAN FAMILY. EASTERN GROUP.

BIHĀRĪ.

BHOJPURĪ DIALECT.

THĀRŪ BROKEN DIALECT. (DISTRICT GONDA.)

SPECIMEN II.

(Pandit Janardan Joshee, 1898.)

Rāmā o Lachhiman chal^a^nē shikār.
Rām and Lakshman started to-hunt.

Bel^a^waṭ hath^a^nī dārē palān.
Belwaṭ female-elephant-on was-put cot.

Hath^a^nī palānē as^a^nī-bas^a^nī gir^a^lē.
The-female-elephant ran-away the-howdah-etcetera fell-down.

Rām tā lag^a^lē piyās.
Rām indeed was-seized-by thirst.

Erī erī bahinī, kūĩā-panihariā, bundā ek, bahinī, paniyā piāu.
O O sister, well-water-drawer, drop one, sister, water make-(me)-drink.

Sōnē kerī jhariā, rup^a^nē kerī ṭōṭī, jehi bharī lāwai, rē, Gaṅgā-jal-pānī.
Gold of gugglet, silver of spout, which filling she-brings, O, Ganges-water.

Jō tōhi Rāmā Hari jatiyā nā puchh^a^thē, ham^a^rē bāp Śatal Siṅgh rāj.
If thee Rām God caste (expletive) asked, my father Śatal Singh king.

FREE TRANSLATION OF THE FOREGOING.

Rāma and Lakshmaṇa went forth to hunt. On Belwaṭ, the she-elephant, was placed the riding-seat, but (excited by the chase) the elephant ran away, and the howdah and all its fittings fell from her back.

Rāma felt thirsty. 'O sister,' said he, 'thou who drawest water from the well, give me one drop of water, sister, to drink.' A gugglet of gold, with a silver spout, did she bring, all full of Ganges water. (Then said she to herself), 'if the divine Rāma had asked my caste, I should have told him that my father was Rājā Śatal Singh.'

The last specimen of the Thārū dialect comes from the District of Bahraich. Here and there, words such as *rahis* and *kahis* show the influence of the Eastern Hindī spoken by the other inhabitants of the district, but in the main the language is Bhojpurī.

[No. 66.]

INDO-ARYAN FAMILY. EASTERN GROUP.

BIHĀRĪ.

BHOJPURĪ DIALECT.

THĀRŪ BROKEN DIALECT. (DISTRICT BAHRAICH.)

(Munshī Rāj Bahadur, 1898.)

Ek manaī dū chhāwā rahis. Duinõ-mā̃ chhoṭ'kawā kahis ki, 'bābā rē, mōr
One man-of two sons were. Both-in the-younger said that, 'father O, my
hīsā bā̃ṭ dē.' Bābā bā̃ṭ dihal. Halī bhaīl
share dividing give.' The-father dividing gave. Short-time had-passed
bāṭhā-baṭṭ'hā chhoṭ'kawā chhāwā āpan bāṭhā lāī-kāī chal-gal aurē muluk.
(after-) division the-younger son his-own share taking went-away (to)-another land.
Āūr paturiyā-bājī kaīlas, dhan-daulat luṭā-ḍal'las aū sakor āg'las. Ui
And wenching did, fortune squandered and all was-spent. That
muluk-mā̃ sukkhā par-gaīl, aū ū bhukkhan mao lāg. Tabbai ui
country-in famine fell, and he from-hunger to-die began. Then-even that
muluk ek manaī basal-rahil. Oṭṭhin ū gaīnū̃. Ū sūrī charāwāī khet'wā-mā̃
country one man lived. There he went. He swine to-feed fields-in
paṭhā-deh'las. Ū āpan man-sē kahit, 'ihē khar-pat'wār jaūn sūrī khāit
sent-away. He his-own mind-to was-saying, 'this dry-grass which swine eating
bā, taūnē khāt pēṭ bhar-lētõ.' Kaūnõ nā kachhū dihal. Tan
are, that-very eating belly may-I-fill.' Any-body not any-thing gave. Then
chēt-kaīlas, kaha lāgal, 'ham'rē bābā-kē manaī-tanaī rakh-rakh'las;
he-remembered, to-say he-began, 'my father-to servants-etcetera are-employed;
sab-kar nīk baṭī sāp. Mah bhūkhē mūtāṭū̃. Ab mah
all-of good is food-supply. I from-hunger am-dying. Now I
ghūm-ghumā āpan bābā ṭhin jāithõ. Ō-sē kahyõ ki, "hē
having-wandered-about my-own father near going-am. Him-to I-will-say that, "O
bābā, mah pāpī ṭhahar'nõ. Mah-sē chūk hō-gal. Mah
father, I sinner have-been-proved. Me-by guiltiness has-come-to-pass. I
kachhō lāik nē hõ, ki tōr chhāwā rahõ. Ek kamoiā̃
any-thing-for fit not am, that thy son I-may-remain. One day-labourer
na rākh, mohī rākh." Tō ī sam'jhanõ āpan bābā ṭhin aitõ.'
do-not keep, (but)-me keep." Then this I-understood my-own father near I-came.'
Ab-hī ū barā dūr hā, ō-he dēkh bābā sōg lag'las.
Now-even he very far-off was, him seeing (by)-the-father compassion was-felt.

Daur-kāī sēnā-lagal. Chhāwā kah^{a}las ki, 'hē bābā, rē, mah pāpī
Running he-embraced-(him). The-son said that, 'O father, O, I sinner
tahar^{a}nō̃. Mah-sē chūk hō-gal. Mah kachhō lāik nē hō̃,
have-been-proved. Me-by guiltiness has-come-to-pass. I any-thing fit not am,
ki tōr chhāwā rahō̃.' Bābā kah^{a}las kamoiā̃-nō̃, 'chumur chumur
that thy son I-may-remain.' The-father said servants-to, 'good good
lūgā lē-āinō̃, ihē orāh^{a}nō̃, pah^{a}rāh^{a}nō̃; ihē mūdarī ā̃gurī-mā̃ ghailā dēō,
cloth bring, this-one wrap, put-on; this-one-to ring finger-on putting give,
aū pan^{a}hī goarā-mā̃ ghailā dēō. Ihē khaībī, mahū̃ khāō̃, piō̃,
and shoes feet-on putting give. This-one will-eat, I will-eat, will-drink,
khusī kar-nō̃; ki mōr chhāwā maral rahē ab-lē jial āil; herāil
merriment I-will-make; that my son dead had-been now alive came; lost
rahē, ab-lē painō̃.' Sab-ke jui khusī hoilāh.
had-been, now I-have-found-(him).' All-of heart glad began-to-be.

Baṛ^{a}kawā laūṛā khet^{a}wan hā. Jō ghar lagehā gail, nāchat gāib
The-elder son fields-in was. As house near he-went, dancing singing
sunnānō̃. Kamoiā̃ goh^{a}rāwal, 'eh kā kar^{a}tāṭō?' Ū kah^{a}las, 'tōr bhaīwa
he-heard. A-servant he-called, 'this what is-being-done?' He said, 'thy brother
ā-rahalas. Tōr bābā khaile pīlā nāch kar^{a}tāṭa, ki ū nīka nika āil.'
come-is. Thy father eating drinking dancing doing-is, that he well well came.'
Ōhē ris lāgal. Kah lāgal, 'mah ghar-mā̃ nāhī̃ jaībō̃.' Bap^{a}wā duārō
To-him anger was-felt. To-say began, 'I house-in not will-go.' The-father door-to
āil. Kah lāgal aū phus^{a}lāil, 'ris jin karū.' Tō ū āpan
came. To-say he-began and propitiated-(him), 'anger do-not do.' Then he his-own
bābā-sē kahil, 'hēr-rarē! mah at^{a}rah baras toār dhandhā kar^{a}nō̃, hāth
father-to said, 'look-here! I so-many years thy work did, (thy)-hands
dab^{a}nō̃, goār dab^{a}nō̃; kabbō toār bātan char^{a}chā nē kīnhō̃; kabbō
I-shampooed, feet I-shampooed; ever-even thy words-(of) criticism not I-did; ever-even
mōhe chhag^{a}ri-k bachchā nahī̃ dih^{a}lē, ki sā̃ghutin khusī kar^{a}-
me-to goat-of young-one not thou-gavest, that friends-(with) merriment I-might-
tō̃. Aū jab toār ihō chhāwā āil, jaūn toār dhan paturiā-bājī-mā̃
have-made. And when thy this son is-came, who thy fortune wenching-in
uṛā-deh^{a}las, taī̃ mān-mar^{a}jāt kar^{a}tāṭē.' Tō ū kahil, 'hē chhāwā, taī̃
squandered, thou feasting-in-his-honour art-doing.' Then he said, 'O son, thou
sab din mōr ṭhin rahalē. Jaūn mōr bāt taūn tōr bāt. Khusiālī
all days me near livest. What-(is) my word that-(is) thy word. Merriment
kara-ga rahē. Tohār bhaiwā maral rahē, ab jial āil; herāil rahē, ab
to-be-done was. Thy brother dead was, now alive came; lost was, now
milal.'
found-(is).'

STANDARD LIST OF BIHĀRĪ WORDS AND SENTENCES.

These lists have been prepared independently of the translations of the Parable of the Prodigal Son in the corresponding dialects. Variations of spelling will, therefore, be observed. These have been deliberately left untouched, as they illustrate the pronunciation in doubtful cases.

SPECIMENS IN THE

English.	Maithilī (Darbhanga Brāhmaṇs).	Chhikā-chhikī (Bhagalpur).	Magahī (Gayā).
1. One	Ēk	Ēk	Ēk
2. Two	Dū	Dui	Dū
3. Three	Tīn^{i}	Tin	Tīn
4. Four	Chār^{i}	Chāir	Chār
5. Five	Pā̃ch	Pā̃ch	Pā̃ch
6. Six	Chhao	Chhau	Chhau
7. Seven	Sāt	Sāt	Sāt
8. Eight	Āṭh	Aṭh	Āṭh
9. Nine	Nao	Nau	Nau
10. Ten	Das	Das	Das
11. Twenty	Bīs	Bīs	Bīs
12. Fifty	Pachās	Pachās	Pachās
13. Hundred	Sai	Sai	Sau
14. I	Ham	Hamē̃	Ham
15. Of me	Hamar, hamâr	Hamar, ham^{a}ra	Mōrā, hammar, ham^{a}rā
16. Mine	Hamar, hamār	Hamar, ham^{a}ra	Mōr, hammar; ham^{a}rā
17. We	Ham^{a}rā lok^{a}ṇi	Ham^{a}rā ār, ham^{a}rā sabh	Ham^{a}nī, ham-sab, ham lōg, ham^{a}ranhī, ham^{a}nhī.
18. Of us	Ham^{a}rā sab^{a}hik; ham^{a}rā lok^{a}nik.	Ham^{a}rā ārak	Ham^{a}nī-ke, hām-sab-ke, ham-lōg-ke.
19. Our	Ham^{a}rā sab^{a}hik; ham^{a}rā lok^{a}nik.	Ham^{a}rā ārak	*Ditto.*
20. Thou	Tõ, ahā̃, ap^{a}ne	Tõ	Tū̃, tē̃
21. Of thee	Tōhar, tohār, ahā̃k, ap^{a}nek	Tōhar, toh^{a}ra, tōr	Tōrā-ke, tōhar, tōr
22. Thine	Tōbar, tohār, ahā̃k, ap^{a}nek	Tōhar, toh^{a}ra, tōr	Tōhar, tōr
23. You	Toh^{a}rā lok^{a}ni, ahā̃ lok^{a}ni, ap^{a}ne lok^{a}ni.	Tōrā ār, *etc.*	Āp, ap^{a}ne, tõ, toh^{a}nī
24 Of you	Toh^{a}rā lok^{a}nik, *etc.*	Tōrā ārak	Āp-ke, ap^{a}ne-ke, toh^{a}ranhī-ke, toh^{a}ni-ke.
25 Your	Toh^{a}rā lok^{a}nik, *etc.*	Tōrā ārak	Āp^{a}ne-ke, apan, toh^{a}ranhī-ke, toh^{a}nī-ke.

Kuṛmālī (Manbhum).	Pā̃ch Parganiā* (Ranchi).	Bhojpurī (Shahabad).
Ek-ṭā	Ēk	Ē-gō
Du-ṭā	Dui, dū	Dū-gō
Tin-ṭā	Tīn	Tīn-gō
Chār-ṭā	Chār	Chār-gō
Pā̃ch-ṭā	Pā̃ch	Pā̃ch-gō
Chha-ṭā	Chha	Chhau-gō
Sāt-ṭā	Sāt	Sāt-gō
Aṭ-ṭā	Āṭh	Āṭh-gō
La-ṭā	Na	Nau-gō
Das-ṭā	Das	Das-gō
Bis-ṭā	Bīs	Bis-gō
Pāchās-ṭā	Pachās	Pachās-gō
Sa	Sa	Sau-gō
Hāmi	Maĩ	Ham
Hāmar	Mōr	Mōr, hamār
Hāmar	Mōr	Mōr, hamār
Hāmni	Hām^a^rē	Ham^a^nī-kā, ham^a^nin-kā
Hāmrā-kar	Hām^a^rē, hām^a^rē-kēr	Ham^a^nī-ke
Hāmrā-kar	Hām^a^rē, hām^a^rē-kēr	Ham^a^nī-ke
Tū̃	Taĩ	Tū
Tōhar	Tōr	Tōr, tohār
Tōhar	Tōr	Tōr, tohār
Tohnī	Taĩ, toh^a^rē	Tū-lōg, toh^a^nī-kā
Tohrā-kar	Toh^a^rē-kēr	Toh^a^nī-ke
Tohrā-kar	Toh^a^rē-kēr	Toh^a^nī-ke

* This is Nagpuriā rather than Pā̃ch Parganiā. *Vide* remarks on page 167 *ante*.

Bhojpurī (North Centre of Saran).	Sarwariā (Basti).	Western Bhojpurī (Jaunpur).
Ēk	Ēk	Ēk
Dū, dui	Dō	Dui
Tīn	Tīn	Tīn
Chār	Chār	Chāri
Pā̃ch	Pā̃ch	Pā̃ch
Chhaw	Chha	Chha
Sāt	Sāt	Sāt
Āṭh	Āṭh	Āṭh
Naw	Nau	Nau
Das	Das	Das
Bīs	Bīs	Bīs
Pachās	Pachās	Pachās
Sau, saî	Sau	Sau
Ham	Maĩ	Ham
Hamār	Mōr	Hamār
Hamār	Mōr	Hamār
Ham^a^nī	Ham^a^rē	Ham
Ham^a^nī-ke	Haman-kāĩ	Ham^a^rē sab-kāĩ
Ham^a^nī-ke	Haman-kāĩ	Ham^a^rē sab-kāĩ
Tē̃	Taĩ, tū	Tū̃
Tōr	Tōr	Tōr
Tōr	Tōr	Tōr
Tū̃	Tū̃	Tōhan lōgan, tū̃
Toh^a^rā-ke, tohār	Tohār	Toh^a^rē-lōgan-kāĩ
Toh^a^rā-ke, tohār	Tohār	Toh^a^rē-lōgan-kāĩ

Nagpuriā (Bauchi).	Madhēsī (Champaran).	Thārū (Champaran).	English.
Ēk	Ēk	Ēk	1. One.
Dui	Dū	Dui	2. Two.
Tīn	Tīn	Tīn	3. Three.
Chāir	Chār	Chār	4. Four.
Pā̃ch	Pā̃ch	Pā̃ch	5. Five.
Chhaw	Chhaw	Chhā	6. Six.
Sāth	Sāt	Sāt	7. Seven.
Āṭh	Āṭh	Āṭh	8. Eight.
Nāo	Naw	Nau	9. Nine.
Das	Das	Das	10. Ten.
Bīs	Bīs	Bīs	11. Twenty.
Pachās	Pachās	Pachās	12. Fifty.
Sai	Sai	Sau	13. Hundred.
Mō̃ẽ	Ham	Moi, moẽ	14. I.
Mōr	Hamār, hamar	Mōr	15. Of me.
Mor	Hamār, hamar	Mōr	16. Mine.
Ham^{a}rē-man	Ham^{a}nī	Ham^{a}rā sab, moẽ	17. We.
Ham^{a}rē-kēr	Ham^{a}nī-ke	Ham^{a}rā sab-ke	18. Of us.
Ham^{a}rē-kēr	Ham^{a}nī-ke	Ham^{a}rā sab-ke	19. Our.
Tō̃ẽ	Tē, tū	Taĩ; toẽ	20. Thou.
Tōr, tōhar	Tōr	Tōr	21. Of thee.
Tōr, tōhar	Tōr	Tōr	22. Thine.
Toh^{a}rē-man	Tū	Tū̃; toẽ	23. You.
Toh^{a}rē-kēr	Tohār, tōhar	Toh^{a}rā-ke, tōrā	24. Of you.
Toh^{a}rē-kēr	Tohār, tōhar	Toh^{a}rā-ke, tōrā	25. Your.

English.	Maithilī (Darbhanga Brāhmaṇs).	Chhikā-chhikī (Bhagalpur).	Magahī (Gayā).
26. He	Ō, sē	Ū	Ū
27. Of him	Ō-kar, ta-kar	Ok^a^ra	Un-kar, ō-kar
28. His	Ō-kar, ta-kar	Ok^a^ra	Un-kar, ō-kar
29. They	Ō lok^a^ni, hun^a^kā lok^a^ni	Ū sabh, *etc.*	Un^a^khanī, un^a^hanī, ū-sab, ū-lōg.
30. Of them	Hunak	Hun^a^kā sabhak	Un^a^khani-ke, un^a^hani-ke, ū-sab-ke, ū-lōg-ke.
31. Their	Hunak	Hun^a^kā sabhak	*Ditto*
32. Hand	Tar^a^bā, hāth	Hāth	Hā̃th
33. Foot	Tabā	Pair	Pā̃ō, pair, gōṛ
34. Nose	Nā̃k	Nāk	Nāk
35. Eye	Ā̃kh^i^	Āikh	Akh
36. Mouth	Mukh, muh	Muh	Mū̃h
37. Tooth	Dant, dā̃t	Dā̃t	Dā̃t
38. Ear	Karn, kān	Kān	Kān
39. Hair	Kēs	Kēs	Bār, rōā̃, kēs
40. Head	Sir, māth	Māth	Māthā, mūṛh
41. Tongue	Jihwā, jībh	Jī	Jībh
42. Belly	Pēṭ	Pēṭ	Pēṭ
43. Back	Pīṭh^i^	Pīṭh	Pīṭh
44. Iron	Lōh	Lōh	Lōhā
45. Gold	Subarn, sōn	Sōn	Sōnā, kañchan
46. Silver	Chānī, rūp	Rūp, chānī	Chā̃dī, rūpā
47. Father	Pitā, bāp	Bāp	Bāp, bābū-jī, bapā
48. Mother	Mātā, māe	Māī, mai	Māi, maīā, māe
49. Brother	Bhrātā, bhāe	Bhāī, bhai	Bhāi, bhaīyā, bhaīwā
50. Sister	Bhagini, bahin^i^	Bahin	Bahin, didī, maīyā̃, māī̃
51. Man	Manukhya, jan	Manush, lōg	Ad^a^mī, manukh, jan, mard
52. Woman	Strī	Strī, maugi, jhoṭ^a^hā	Aurat, meh^a^rārū, janī, janiaurī.

Kuṛmālī (Manbhum).	Pā̃ch Parganiā (Ranchi).	Bhojpurī (Shahabad).
Ũo	Ũ	Ũ
Tē-kar	Ō-kar, a-kar	Ō-kar
Tē-kar	Ō-kar, a-kar	Ō-kar
Ũo-sab	Ũ-sab, ū-man	Unhᵃnī-kā. ū-sab. okanī-kā
Ũo-sab-kar	Ō-man-kēr	Un-kar, unhᵃnī-ke
Ũo-sab-kar	Ō-man-kēr	Un-kar, unhᵃnī-ke
Hāth	Hāth	Hāth
Gaṛtār	Gōṛ	Pā̃w, gōṛ
Nāk	Nāk	Nāk
Chakh	Ā̃kh	Ā̃kh
Muh, bā̃t	Mũh	Mũh
Dā̃t	Dā̃t	Dā̃t
Kān	Kān	Kān
Chul	Chūhar	Bār
Mur	Mū̃ṛ	Māth, kapār
Jībh	Jībh	Jībh
Pēṭ	Pēṭ	Pēṭ
Piṭh	Piṭh	Piṭh
Luhā	Lōhā	Lōhā
Sauā	Sōnā	Sōnā
Chā̃dī	Rūpā	Chā̃dī
Bāp	Bāp, bābā	Bāp, bābū
Māi	Mā	Māī, mahᵃtārī, īyā
Bhāi	Bhāī	Bhāī, bhaiyā
Bahin	Bahin	Bahin, bahinī, dīdī
Mānush	Adᵃmī	Adᵃmī
Mēyā-lak, mehrār	Mehᵃrārū	Maugī, mehᵃrārū

Bhojpurī (North Centre of Saran).	Sarwariā (Basti).	Western Bhojpurī (Jampur).
Ū	**Ū**	**Ū** . . . . .
Un-kar	**Ō-kar**	**Ō-kar** . . . .
Un-kar	**Ō-kar**	**Ō-kar** . . . .
Ū-lōg *or* **un** . . .	**Unh^{a}nē**	**Ū-lōg** . . . .
Ū-lōg-ke	**Un-kar**	**Un-kar sab-kāī** .
Ū-lōg-ke	**Un-kar**	**Un-kar sab-kāī** .
Hāth	**Hāth, pakhurā** . .	**Hāth** . . . .
Gōr	**Gōṛ**	**Gōṛ** . . . .
Nāk	**Nāk, nakurā** . . .	**Nekurā** . . . .
Ākh	**Ā̃kh**	**Ā̃khi** . . . .
Mũh	**Mũh**	**Mũh** . . . .
Dā̃t	**Dā̃t**	**Dā̃t** . . . .
Kān	**Kān**	**Kān** . . . .
Bār, kēs	**Bār**	**Bār** . . . .
Māth, kapār . . .	**Mūṛ, kapār** . . .	**Kapār** . . . .
Jībh	**Jībh**	**Jībhi** . . . .
Pēṭ	**Pēṭ**	**Pēṭ** . . . .
Pīṭh	**Pīṭh**	**Pīṭhi** . . . .
Lōhā	**Lōh**	**Lōh** . . . .
Sōnā	**Sōnā**	**Sōnā** . . . .
Chānī, chā̃dī . . .	**Chānī**	**Chānī** . . . .
Bap^{a}sī, bāp, pitā . .	**Bāp**	**Bāp, bābū, kakā, dadā** .
Māī	**Mah^{a}tārī** . . .	**Māī, mah^{a}tārī** . . .
Bhāī	**Bhāī**	**Bhāī** . . . .
Bahin	**Bahin**	**Bahiṇi** . . . .
Marad	**Manaī**	**Ad^{a}mī** . . . .
Meh^{a}rārū . . .	**Meh^{a}rārū**	**Meh^{a}rārū** . . .

Nagpuriā (Ranchi).	Madhēsi (Champaran).	Thārū (Champaran).	English.
Ū	Ū	Ū, unhī	26. He
Ū-kar	Un-kar, ō-kar	Ō-kar	27. Of him.
Ū-kar	Un-kar, ō-kar	Ō-kar	28. His.
Ū-man	Ū-sabh, ū-lōg	Ū, un	29. They.
Ū-man-kēr	Unhan-ke	Ō-kar	30. Of them.
Ū-man-kēr	Unhan-ke	Ō-kar	31. Their.
Hā̃th	Hāth	Hāth	32. Hand.
Gōṛ	Gō̃ṛ	Gōṛ	33. Foot.
Nākh	Nāk	Nāk	34. Nose.
Aĩkh	Ā̃kh	Ā̃khi	35. Eye.
Mũh	Mũh	Mũh	36. Mouth.
Dā̃t	Dā̃t	Dā̃t	37. Tooth.
Kān	Kān	Kān	38. Ear.
Kē̃s	Kēs, bār	Kēs	39. Hair.
Mũṛ	Mũṛ	Mũḍ	40. Head.
Jībh	Jībh	Jībhi	41. Tongue.
Odaⁿ, pēṭ	Pēṭ	Pēṭ	42. Belly.
Pīṭh	Pīṭh	Piṭhi	43. Back.
Lōhā	Lōhā	Lōh	44. Iron.
Sonā	Sōnā	Sōnā	45. Gold.
Rūpā	Chānī	Rūpā	46. Silver.
Bāp	Bāp	Bābā	47. Father.
Māy, āyō	Mahᵃtāri	Daīyō	48. Mother.
Bhāī	Bhāī	Dādā	49. Brother.
Bahin	Bahin	Dādī	50. Sister.
Adᵃmī	Adᵃmī	Mānisō	51. Man.
Janī	Mehᵃrārū	Janī	52. Woman.

English.	Maithilī (Darbhanga Brāhmaṇs).	Chhikā-chhikī (Bhagalpur).	Magahī (Gayā).
53. Wife	Strī ; patnī ; bahū	Bahū, ḍērāk lōg	Jōru, mäug, mangī, kanaïyā, ghar-ke lōg.
54. Child	Nēnā, bachchā	Santān, bedᵃrā, nānā	Laṛᵃkā ; bachchā
55. Son	Putra	Bēṭā	Bēṭā, laṛᵃkā, pūt, chẽgū, butᵃrū.
56. Daughter	Putrī, kanyā	Bēṭī	Bēṭī ; laṛᵃkī, dhīā
57. Slave	Bahiā	Bahiā, naphar	Gulām
58. Cultivator	Gṛihast	Girᵃhath	Girᵃhast, kasht-kār, kisān
59. Shepherd	Bheṛihar	Gaṛērī	Gaṛērī
60. God	Parmēswar	Bhagᵃwān, Issar	Bhagᵃwān; Nāräen ; Īshwar ; Parᵃmēsar.
61. Devil	Saitān	Bhūt, parēt	Shaitān
62. Sun	Sūrya	Sūrj	Śūraj, ṭhākur
63. Moon	Chandramā	Chān, chā̃d, chanarᵃmā̃	Chā̃d, chandarmā
64. Star	Tārā	Tārā	Sitārā ; tārā, tarēgan
65. Fire	Agnⁱ, āgⁱ	Āgi	Āg
66. Water	Jal, pāni	Pāni	Pānī, jal
67. House	Gṛih, ghar	Ghar	Ghar, girᵃhī, makān
68. Horse	Ghōṛ	Ghōṛā	Ghōṛā
69. Cow	Gō, gāy	Gāy	Gāy, gau, gaiyā
70. Dog	Kukur	Kukur	Kuttā, kukur
71. Cat	Bilāṛⁱ	Bilāri, bilāi	Billī, bilāi, bilaïyā
72. Cock	Murᵃgā	Murᵃgā	Murᵃgā
73. Duck	Battak	Batak	Batak, bakat, bat
74. Ass	Gardabh, gadᵃhā	Gadhā	Gadᵃhā
75. Camel	Uṭ	Ū̃ṭ	Ū̃ṭ
76. Bird	Pakshī, chaṭak, chiṛaī	Chaṛai, chiraī, pachchhī	Chiṛiyā̃, chiriyā̃, chiṛaī, chiraī.
77. Go	Jā, jāh	Jāū	Jō, jāo, jā
78. Eat	Khā	Khāū	Khō, khāo, khā
79. Sit	Bais	Baisū	Baiṭhō

Kuṛmālī (Manbhum).	Pãch Parganiā (Ranchi).	Bhojpurī (Shahabad).
Meyā	Janī	Māhar, maugī . . .
Chhā	Chhuwā	Larikā, chhauṛā, chhauṛ .
Bēṭā-chhā	Bēṭā-chhuwā . . .	Bēṭā, pūt, chhokᵃṛā . .
Biṭī-chhā	Bēṭī-chhuwā . . .	Bēṭī, chhokᵃrī . .
Munish	Kinal adᵃmī . . .	Gulām, gulammā, naphar .
Āidhar, kishān . . .	Chāshā	Kisān, girᵃhath . .
Bāgāl	Ḍhā̃gar	Bheṛīhar, gaṛērī . .
Ṭhākur	Bhagᵃwān . . .	Īsar . . . .
Dāna	Bhūt	Saitān, bhūt, prēt . .
Sujji	Sūruj	Sūruj . . . .
Chā̃da	Chā̃d	Chandarᵃmā, chā̃d . .
Tārā	Taīr-gan . . .	Jōdhī, tarēgan . .
Āgun	Āig	Āgi . . . .
Pāni	Pānī	Pānī, paniyā . . .
Ghar	Ghar	Ghar . . . .
Ghaṛā	Ghōṛā	Ghōṛā, ghoṛᵃwā . .
Gāi	Gāi	Gāy, gaū . . .
Kuttā	Kukur	Kūkur . . . .
Bilār, billī . . .	Bilāī	Bilāī . . . .
Kũkri	Khukhᵃri . . .	Murᵃgā . . . .
Hā̃s	Kōṛō	Batak . . . .
Gādhā	Gādhā	Gadᵃhā . . . .
Ū̃ṭ	Uṭh	Ū̃ṭ . . . . .
Pākh	Charaī	Chiraī . . . .
Jā	Jāhiṅg, jāwā, jāu . .	Jā, jō . . . .
Khā	Khāhiṅg, khāwā, khāu .	Khā, khō . . .
Baisā	Basiṅg, baisā, basu . .	Baisā, baiṭhā . . .

Bhojpurī (North Centre of Saran).	Sarwariā (Basti).	Western Bhojpurī (Jaunpur).
Mehar, gharᵃnī	Parānī, basᵃhī	Mĕhar, mehᵃrārū
Laṛikā, jātak	Larikā	Larikā, gadēlā
Bēṭā	Beṭᵃwā	Beṭᵃwā
Bēṭī	Larikanī	Biṭiyā, bhawānī
Chēr, gulām	Gulām, chākar	Gulām
Girᵃhast	Girᵃhast	Asāmī
Bheṛihar, bheṛīhār	Gaṛeriyā	Gaṛēr
Rām, Bhagᵃwān, Daib, Parmēsar.	Bhagᵃwān	Īsar, Bhagᵃwān, Rām
Bhūt, saitān	Bhūt, prēt	Bhūt, prē
Sūraj narāyan	Sūraj	Suruj
Chā̃d gosā̃ī; chān gosā̃ī	Chandarᵃmā	Chanarᵃmā
Jōnhī, tarengan, tārā	Jōnhī	Tarai
Āg	Āg	Āgi
Pānī	Pānī	Pānī
Ghar	Ghar	Ghar, bakhᵃrī
Ghōṛā	Ghōṛā	Ghōṛā
Gāy	Gāy	Gāy
Kuttā, pillā	Kūkur	Kukur
Bilāī	Bilār	Bilāri
Murᵃgā	Murᵃgā	Murᵃgā
Battak	Battak	Battak
Gadᵃhā	Gadᵃhā	Gadᵃhā
Ū̃ṭ	Ū̃ṭ	Ūṭ
Chirai	Chirai	Chirai
Jā	Jā	Jā
Khā	Khā	Khā
Baiṭh	Baiṭh	Baiṭh

Nagpuriā (Ranchi).	Madhēsī (Champaran).	Thārū (Champaran).	English.
Janānā ad^{a}mī	Kabilā, mēhar	Janī	53. Wife.
Chhauā	Laṛikā	Chhok^{a}nā, chhok^{a}nī	54. Child.
Bēṭā	Bēṭā	Bēṭā, chhok^{a}nā	55. Son.
Bēṭī	Bēṭī	Bēṭī, chhok^{a}nī	56. Daughter.
Dhā̃gar	Gulām, ṭah^{a}lū	Nafar	57. Slave.
Kisān	Gir^{a}hast	Gir^{a}hast	58. Cultivator.
Ahir	Bhē̃ṛihar	Bhēṛī char^{a}waiyā	59. Shepherd.
Bhag^{a}wān	Bhag^{a}wān	Bhag^{a}wān	60. God.
Bhūt	Bhūt	Rākas	61. Devil.
Bēir	Sūraj	Bariyā	62. Sun.
Chā̃d	Chandarmā	Jōnhā	63. Moon.
Tarigan	Jōnhī	Tar-gan	64. Star.
Āig	Āg	Āgi	65. Fire.
Pānī	Pānī	Pānī	66. Water.
Ghar	Ghar	Ghar	67. House.
Ghōṛā	Ghōṛā	Ghōṛā	68. Horse.
Gāy	Gāy	Gāī	69. Cow.
Kukur	Kūkur	Kukur	70. Dog.
Bilār, bilāo	Bilāī	Bilār	71. Cat.
Mur^{a}gā	Mur^{a}gā	Chī̃g^{a}nā	72. Cock.
Gēṛē	Batak	Hā̃s	73. Duck.
Gad^{a}hā	Gad^{a}hā	Gad^{a}hā	74. Ass.
Ū̃ṭh	Ū̃ṭ	Ū̃ṭ	75. Camel.
Charaī	Chiraī	Chiṛaī	76. Bird.
Jā	Jā	Jāō	77. Go.
Khā	Khā	Khōē	78. Eat.
Baiṭh	Baiṭh	Bais	79. Sit.

English.	Maithilī (Darbhanga Brāhmaṇs).	Chhikā-chhikī (Bhagalpur).	Magahī (Gayā).
80. Come	Āb	Āū	Āō, āwō, ō, ā
81. Beat	Mār	Mārū	Mārō, mār, pīṭō, pīṭ
82. Stand	Ṭhāṛh hō	Ṭhāṛh hōū	Khaṛā rahō, khaṛā rah, ṭhāṛh rahō.
83. Die	Mar	Marū	Mar jāo ; mū jō
84. Give	Dē	Diū	Dēo, dō, dā
85. Run	Daur	Daurū	Daurō, daur
86. Up	Ūpar	Ūpar	Upar
87. Near	Nikaṭ ; samīp ; lag	Lag	Najīk ; nagīch, niarē, bhirī
88. Down	Nīchā	Hēṭh	Nichē, tarē
89. Far	Dūrasth, dūr	Dūr	Dūr
90. Before	Pūrb	Āgū	Āgē, āgāṛī, āgu, sām^a^nē
91. Behind	Paśchāt	Pāchhū	Pīchhē, pichhāṛī
92. Who	Kē	Jè (*relative*), kē (*interrogative*).	Kaun, kē
93. What	Kī, kōn	Kī	Kā
94. Why	Kiaik	Kiai, kiaik	Kāhe ; kāhē-lā
95. And	Āor	Āro	Āūr, au
96. But	Parant[u]	Mahaj, mudā	Magar, par, lēkin
97. If	Jad[i]	Jyō	Agar
98. Yes	Hā̃	Hā̃	Hā̃, jī
99. No	Nahī̃	Naiī	Nahī̃, nah, nā
100. Alas	Hā, oh	Hāy	Hāē
101. A father	Ēk pitā	Bāp	Bāp
102. Of a father	Kōnō pitā-k	Bāpak	Bāp-ke
103. To a father	Kōnō pitā-kē̃	Bāp-kai	Bāp-kē
104. From a father	Kōnō pitā-sā̃	Bāp-sē̃	Bāp-sē
105. Two fathers	Dū pitā	Dui bāp	Dū bāp
106. Fathers	Pitā lok[a]ni	Bāp sabh	Bāp-lōg

Kuṛmālī (Manbhum).	Pā̃ch-Parganiā (Ranchi).	Bhojpurī (Shahabad).
Āo	Āiṅg, āwā, āu	Āwā
Piṭā	Mariṅg, mārā, māru	Mārā; piṭā
Dā̃rao	Thāṛh hō hiṅg, thāṛh bawā; thāṛh hau.	Kharā bōkhā; ūṭhā
Mar	Mariṅg	Mūā, mū jā, marā
Dihā	Dēhiṅg, dēwā	Dā
Dauṛ	Kūdiṅg, kūd	Dauṛā
Ū̃chā	Ūpar	Ūpar
Pās	Pās	Niarō, nagichē, lagē
Nāma	Hē̃ṭh	Nīchē
Dhur	Dhūr	Dūr
Āgō	Āgū	Pahilē, sām^a^nē, sōjhē
Pāchhē	Pēchhū	Pichhē, pāchhē
Kē	Kō	Kē, kō, kawan
Ki	Kā	Kā
Kis-kō	Kātōhē̃	Kāhō
Ār	Āur, ār	Āūr, awar
Kintu	Magar	Bāki
Jadi	Jadi	Jō
Hā̃	Hō̃	Hā̃
Nāi	Nāhī̃	Nē, nāhī̃
Hāy	Hāy hāy	Hā, hāy
Bāp	Ēk bābā	Bāp
Bāp-kar	Ēk bāp-kēr	Bāp-ko
Bāp-kē	Ēk bāp-kēr ṭhin	Bāp-kē
Bāp-kar-pās-tē	Ēk bāp-lēk	Bāp-sō
Du-ṭā bāp	Dū bābā	Dū-gō bāp
Bāp-gulā	Bāp-man	Bāpan, bāp-sab

Bhojpuri (North Centre of Saran).	Sarwariā (Basti).	Western Bhojpuri (Jaunpur).
Ā	Ā	Ā
Mār	Mār, piṭ	Mār
Khaṛā hō	Thāṛh rah	Ṭhāṛh hoi jā
Mar	Muā	Mui jā
Dē	Dē	Dē
Daur	Dauṛ	Daur
Ūpar	Ūpar	Ūpar
Nigᵃchā, niarā	Nagīch	Niarē, nagīchē
Nīchē	Nīchē	Nīchē, hōṭhē, khālē
Lamᵃhar	Lām	Dūri, lamē
Agᵃtē	Āgē	Āgē, sāmᵃnē
Pāchhē	Pāchhē	Pāchhē
Kē	Kē	Kē, kaun
Kā	Kāw	Kā
Kāhē	Kāhē	Kāhē
Āur	Awar	Awar
Bā	Lēkin	Hai, mūdā
Jō	Jō	Jau
Hā	Achchhā	Hā̃-tau
Nā	Nahī	Nāhī̃
Āh	Pachhᵃtāwā	Hāy, galān
Ēk bāp, bapᵃsī	Bāp	Kaunō kakā
Ēk bāp-ke	Bāp-kāī	Kaunō kakā-kāī
Ēk bāp-kē	Bāp-kē lagē	Kaunō kakā-kē
Ēk bāp-sē	Bāp-se	Kaunō kakā-sē
Dū bāp	Dui bāp	Dui kakā
Bāpan	Bāp lōg	Kaiu kakā

Nagpuriā (Rānchi).	Madhēsi (Champaran).	Thārū (Champaran).	English.
Ā	Āī	Āū	80. Come.
Mār	Mār	Mār	81. Beat.
Thāṛh hō	Khaṛā hō	Ṭhaḍhiya	82. Stand.
Mor	Mar-jā	Mar	83. Die.
Dēw	Dō	Dēn	84. Give.
Daur, kūd	Dauṛ	Dagar	85. Run.
Upᵃrē	Ūpar	Ūpar	86. Up.
Najik	Nagich	Eṭā-hū̃	87. Near.
Nīchē, tarē	Nīchē	Hēṭh	88. Down.
Dūr	Dūr	Tanāw	89. Far.
Āgū	Sōjhē	Sōjhi	90. Before.
Pichhū	Pāchhē	Pachhā	91. Behind.
Kē	Kē	Kawan	92. Who.
Kā	Kā	Kathi	93. What.
Kāhē	Kāhē	Kihā	94. Why.
Āūr	Āur	Ākō	95. And.
Magar	Bāki, lēkin	Bāki	96. But.
Hōlē (*enclitic after verb*)	Jō, agar	Jō	97. If.
Hōī	Hō, hā̃, hā	Hā̃	98. Yes.
Nāi	Nā, nāhi	Nāhī	99. No.
Hāe, hāy	Āh	Oh	100. Alas.
Bāp	Ēk bāp	Ēk bāp	101. A father.
Bāp-kēr	Ēk bāp-ke	Bābā-ko	102. Of a father.
Bāp-kē	Ēk bāp-kā	Bābā-kē	103. To a father.
Bāp-sē	Ēk bāp-sō	Bābā-ōri	104. From a father.
Dui bāp	Dū bāp	Dugudā bāp	105. Two fathers.
Bāp-man	Bāp	Bābā sab	106. Fathers.

English.	Maithili (Darbhanga Brāhmaṇ).	Chhikā-chhikī (Bhagalpur).	Magahī (Gayā).
107. Of fathers	Pitā lokᵃni-k	Bāp sabhak	Bāp lōg-ke
108. To fathers	Pitā lokᵃni-kẽ	Bāp sabh-kai	Bāp lōg-kē
109. From fathers	Pitā lokᵃni-sã	Bāp sabh-sẽ	Bāp lōg-sē
110. A daughter	Ēk kanyā, kōnō kanyā	Bēṭi	Bēṭi
111. Of a daughter	Kōnō kanyā-k	Bēṭik	Bēṭi-ke
112. To a daughter	Kōnō kanyā-kẽ	Bēṭi-kai	Bēṭi-kē
113. From a daughter	Kōnō kanyā-sã	Bēṭi-sẽ	Bēṭi-sē
114. Two daughters	Dū kanyā	Dui bēṭi	Dū bēṭi, dū bēṭin
115. Daughters	Kanyā lokᵃni	Bēṭi sabh	Bēṭin, bēṭan sab
116. Of daughters	Kanyā-lokᵃni-k	Bēṭi sabhak	Bēṭin-ke
117. To daughters	Kanyā lokᵃni-kẽ	Bēṭi sabh-kai	Bēṭin-kē
118. From daughters	Kanyā lokᵃni-sã	Bēṭi sabh-sẽ	Bēṭin-sē
119. A good man	Ēk nik byaktⁱ	Nik lōg	Nēk adᵃmi
120. Of a good man	Ēk nik byakti-k	Nik lōgak	Nēk adᵃmi-ke
121. To a good man	Ēk nik byaktⁱ-kẽ	Nik lōg-kai	Nēk adᵃmi-kē
122. From a good man	Ēk nik byaktⁱ-sã	Nik lōg-sẽ	Nēk adᵃmi-sē
123. Two good men	Dū nik byaktⁱ lokᵃni	Dui nik lōg	Dū nēk adᵃmi, dū achchhē adᵃmi.
124. Good men	Nik byaktⁱ lokᵃ ni	Nik lōg sabh	Āchhā lōg
125. Of good men	Nik byaktⁱ lokᵃni-k	Nik lōg sabhak	Āchhā lōg-ke
126. To good men	Nik byaktⁱ lokᵃni-kẽ	Nik lōg sabh-kai	Āchhā lōg-kē
127. From good men	Nik byaktⁱ lokᵃni-sã	Nik lōg sabh-sẽ	Āchhā lōg-sē
128. A good woman	Ēk nik strī	Nik maugī	Nēk mehᵃrārū
129. A bad boy	Ēk adhᵃlāh nēnā	Adhᵃlāh nēnā	Kharab laṛᵃkā
130. Good woman	Nik strī sabh	Nik maugī sabh	Nēk mehᵃrārun
131. A bad girl	Kōnō adhᵃlāhⁱ kanyā	Adhᵃlāh chauṛī	Kharāb laṛᵃkī
132. Good	Uttam	Nik	Āchhā, uttam, nēk, bēs, authaṛ, bhalā, baṛhiā.
133. Better	Ati uttam	Bahut nik	Āūr āchhā, behᵃtar, baṛhiā.

Kurmālī (Manbhum).	Pāch Pargania (Ranchi).	Bhojpurī (Shahabad).
Bāp-gulār . . .	Bāp man-kēr . . .	Bāpan-ke . . .
Bāp-gulā-kē . . .	Bāp-man-kēr-pās . .	Bāpan-kė . . .
Bāp-gulā-kar-pās-tē . .	Bāp-man-lēk . . .	Bāpan-sē . . .
Biṭi-chhā . . .	Ēk bēṭi	Bēṭī . . . .
Biṭi-chhā-kar . . .	Ēk bēṭi-kēr . . .	Bēṭī-ke . . . .
Biṭi-chhā-kē . . .	Ēk bēṭi-kēr-pās . .	Bēṭī-kē . . . .
Biṭi-chhā-kar-pās-tē . .	Ēk bēṭi-lēk . . .	Bēṭī-sē . . .
Du-ṭā biṭi-chhā . .	Dū bēṭī	Dū-gō bēṭin . . .
Biṭi-chhā-gulā . . .	Bēṭi-gulā . . .	Bēṭin . . . .
Biṭi-chhā-gulār . .	Bēṭi-gulā-kēr . . .	Bēṭin-ke . . . .
Biṭi-chhā-gulā-kē . .	Bēṭi-gulā-kēr-ṭhinē . .	Bēṭin-kē . . .
Biṭi-chhā-gulā-kar-pās-tē .	Bēṭi-gulā lēk . . .	Bēṭin-sē . . .
Bhālā lak . . .	Ēk bēs ad^a^mī . . .	Niman ad^a^mī . . .
Bhālā lakar . . .	Ēk bēs ad^a^mī-kēr . .	Niman ad^a^mī-ke . .
Bhālā lak-kē . . .	Ēk bēs ad^a^mī-kēr-ṭhinē .	Niman ad^a^mī-kē . .
Bhālā lakar-pās-tē . .	Ēk bēs ad^a^mī-lēk . .	Niman ad^a^mī-sē . .
Du-ṭā bhālā lak . .	Dū bēs ad^a^mī . . .	Dū-gō niman ad^a^mī . .
Bhālā lak-gulā . .	Bēs ad^a^mī-man . .	Niman ad^a^mī . . .
Bhālā lak-sab-kar . .	Bēs ad^a^mī-man-kēr . .	Niman ad^a^min-ke . .
Bhālā lak-sab-kē . .	Bēs ad^a^mī-man-kēr-ṭhinē	Niman ad^a^miyan-kē . .
Bhālā lak-sab-kar-pās-tē .	Bēs ad^a^mī-man-lēk . .	Niman ad^a^miyan-sē . .
Bhālā mēyā-lak . .	Ēk bēs meh^a^rārū . .	Niman meh^a^rārū . .
Khārāb chhõr . . .	Ēk khārāp chhuwā . .	Bāur larikā . . .
Bhālā mēyā-lak-sab . .	Bēs meh^a^rārū-man . .	Niman meh^a^rārū . .
Bad chhõri . . .	Ēk khārāp bēṭi-chhuwā .	Bāur larikī . . .
Bhālā	Bēs	Niman . . . .
Ō-kar-tē bhālā . .	Lēk bēs (*than good*) . .	Bahut niman . . .

Bhojpurī (North Centre of Saran).	Sarwariā (Basti).	Western Bhojpurī (Jaunpur).
Bāpan-ke . . .	Bāp lōgan-kāī . . .	Kaiu kakā-kāī . . .
Bāpan-kē . . .	Bāp lōgan-kē lagē . .	Kaiu kakā-kē . . .
Bāpan-sē . . .	Bāp lōgan-sē . . .	Kaiu kakā-sē . . .
Ēk bēṭi	Laṛikanī . . .	Ēk biṭiyā . . .
Ēk bēṭi-ke . . .	Laṛikanī-kāī . . .	Ēk biṭiyā kāī . . .
Ēk bēṭī-kē . . .	Laṛikanī-kē lagē . .	Ēk biṭiyā-kē . . .
Ēk bēṭī-sē . . .	Laṛikanī-sē . .	Ēk biṭiyā-sē . . .
Dū bēṭī	Dui laṛikī . . .	Dui biṭiyā . . .
Bēṭin	Laṛikī	Kaiu biṭiyā . . .
Bēṭin-ke . . .	Laṛikanin-kāī . . .	Biṭiyan kāī . . .
Bēṭin-kē . . .	Laṛikanin-kē lagē .	Biṭiyan-kē . . .
Bēṭin-sē . . .	Laṛikanin-sē . . .	Biṭiyan-sē . . .
Ēk nīman adᵃmī . .	Ēk nīk manaī . . .	Ēk nīk adᵃmī . . .
Ēk nīman adᵃmī-ke . .	Nīk manaī-kāī . . .	Ēk bhalē adᵃmī-kāī . .
Ēk nīman adᵃmī-kē . .	Nīk manaī-kē-lagē . .	Ēk bhalē adᵃmī-kē . .
Ēk nīman adᵃmī-sē . .	Nīk manaī-sē . . .	Kēhū bhal adᵃmī-sē . .
Dū nīman adᵃmī . .	Dui nīk manaī . .	Dui bhal adᵃmī . .
Nīman adᵃmin . . .	Nīk manaī . . .	Bhal manᵃsē . . .
Nīman adᵃmin-ke . .	Nīk manaīn-kāī . .	Bhal manᵃsē-kāī . .
Nīman adᵃmin-kē . .	Nīk manaīn-kē lagē . .	Bhal manᵃsan-kē . .
Nīman adᵃmin-sē . .	Nīk manaīn-sē . .	Nīk adᵃmin-sē . .
Ēk nīman mehᵃrārū . .	Ēk nīk mehᵃrārū . .	Ēk nīk mehᵃrārū . .
Ēk kharāb larikā . .	Ēk kharāb laṛikā . .	Ēk nikām larikā . .
Achchhī mehᵃrārun . .	Nīk mehᵃrārū . . .	Nīki mehᵃrārū . .
Ēk kharāb laṛᵃkī . .	Ēk kharāb laṛikī . .	Ēk nikām biṭiyā . .
Nīman	Nīk	Nīk, nagad . . .
Baṛā nīman . . .	Bahut nīk . . .	Bahut nīk . . .

Nagpuriā (Ranchi).	Madhēsi (Champaran).	Thārū (Champaran).	English.
Bāp-man-kēr	Bāpan-ke	Bābā-ke	107. Of fathers.
Bāp-man-kē	Bāpan-kā	Bābā-sab-kē	108. To fathers.
Bāp-man-sē	Bāpan-sē	Bābā sabhō-han-sē	109. From fathers.
Bēṭī	Egō bēṭī	Ēk chhok^a nī	110. A daughter.
Bēṭī-kēr	Egō bēṭī-ke	Ēk chhok^a nī-ke	111. Of a daughter.
Bēṭī-kē	Egō bēṭī-kā	Ēk chhok^a nī-kē	112. To a daughter.
Bēṭī-sē	Egō bēṭī-sē	Ēk chhok^a nī-sē	113. From a daughter.
Dui bēṭī-man	Dū bēṭī	Dugaḍā chhok^a nī	114. Two daughters.
Bēṭī-man	Bēṭī sabh	Chhok^a nī sabh	115. Daughters.
Bēṭī-man-kēr	Bēṭī-ke, beṭian-ke	Chhok^a nī sabh-ke	116. Of daughters.
Bēṭī-man-kē	Bēṭī-kā, beṭian-kā	Chhok^a nī sabh-kē	117. To daughters.
Bēṭī-man-sē	Beṭian-sē	Chhok^a nī sabh-sē	118. From daughters.
Bēs ād^a mī	Egō niman ad^a mī	Bhalā manisē	119. A good man.
Bēs ād^a mī-kēr	Egō niman ad^a mī-ke	Bhalā manisē-ke	120. Of a good man.
Bēs ād^a mī-kē	Egō nīman ad^a mī-kā	Bhalā manisē-kē	121. To a good man.
Bēs ād^a mī-sē	Egō niman ad^a mī-sē	Bhalā manisē-sē	122. From a good man.
Dui bēs ād^a mī-man	Dugō niman ad^a mī	Dū jan chik^a han manisē	123. Two good men.
Bēs ād^a mī-man	Niman ad^a mī	Chik^a han manisē	124. Good men.
Bēs ād^a mī-man-kēr	Nīman ad^a mī-ke	Chik^a han manisē-ke	125. Of good men.
Bēs ād^a mī-man-kē	Niman ad^a mī-kā	Chik^a han manisē-kē	126. To good men.
Bēs ād^a mī-man-sē	Niman ad^a mī-sē	Chik^a han manisē-sab-sē	127. From good men.
Bēs jani	Egō niman meh^a rārū	Ēk lagad jani	128. A good woman.
Kharāp chhok^a rā, kharāp chhōṛā.	Ego lāṛhēr laṛikā	Lab^a rahā chhok^a nā	129. A bad boy.
Bēs jani	Niman meh^a rārū	Lagad janī sab	130. Good women.
Kharāp chhōṛī	Egō baur laṛ^a kī	Lab^a rī chhok^a nī	131. A bad girl.
Bēs	Niman	Lagad	132. Good.
U-kar-sē bes (*than that good*).	Bhalā	Khub chik^a han	133. Better.

English.	Maithilī (Darbhanga Brāhmaṇa).	Chhikā-chhikī (Bhagalpur).	Magahī (Gayā).
134. Best . . .	Atyant uttam; uttamōttam.	Sabh-sẽ nīk . . .	Sab-sē ăchhā, sab-sē bĕs .
135. High . . .	Uchch	Ũch	Uchā, ũch . . .
136. Higher . . .	Uchch-tar . . .	Bahut ũch . . .	Ăūr ũchā . . .
137. Highest . . .	Atyant uchch . . .	Sabh-sẽ ũch . . .	Sab-sē ũchā . . .
138. A horse . . .	Kōnō ghōṛā . . .	Ghōṛā	Ghōṛā . . . .
139. A mare . . .	Kōnō ghōṛī . . .	Ghōṛī	Ghōṛī . . . .
140. Horses . . .	Ghōṛā sabh . . .	Ghōṛā sabh . . .	Ghōṛā sab, ghōṛan . .
141. Mares . . .	Ghōṛī sabh . . .	Ghōṛī sabh . . .	Ghōṛī sab, ghōṛin . .
142. A bull . . .	Ēk sā̃ṛh, kōnō sā̃ṛh .	Sā̃ṛh	Sā̃ṛh . . . .
143. A cow . . .	Ēk gāy, kōnō gāy .	Gāy	Gāy, gaiā, gaū . .
144. Bulls . . .	Sā̃ṛh sabh . . .	Sā̃ṛh sabh . . .	Sā̃ṛh sab, saṛhᵃwan . .
145. Cows . . .	Gāy sabh . . .	Gāy sabh . . .	Gāy sab, gaian . .
146. A dog . . .	Ēk kukur . . .	Kukur	Kuttā, kukur . . .
147. A bitch . . .	Ēk kuttī . . .	Pillī	Kuttī, kutiā . . .
148. Dogs . . .	Kukur sabh . . .	Kukur sabh . . .	Kuttā sab, kutᵃwan . .
149. Bitches . . .	Kuttī sabh . . .	Pillī sabh . . .	Kuttī sab, kutian . .
150. A he goat . .	Ēk khassī . . .	Bōtu	Khasī . . . .
151. A female goat . .	Ēk bakᵃrī . . .	Bakᵃrī	Bakᵃrī . . . .
152. Goats . . .	Khassī sabh; bakᵃrī sabh .	Bakᵃrī sabh . . .	Khasī sab, bakᵃrī sab; khasian, bakarian.
153. A male deer . .	Ēk harin . . .	Harinā	Harin, harᵃnā, mirig .
154. A female deer . .	Ēk harinī . . .	Harinī	Harinī, mirgī . . .
155. Deer . . .	Harin sabh . . .	Harin	Harin sab . . .
156. I am . . .	Ham thikāhū . . .	Hamẽ chhikaū . . .	Ham hī . . . .
157. Thou art . . .	Tõ thikẽ . . .	Tõ chhikaī . . .	Tū̃ baī, tū̃ bahī . .
158. He is . . .	Ō thik	Ū chhikai, chhai, achh .	Ū baī, ū bathī (*or* bathū) ū haū.
159. We are . . .	Hamᵃrā lokᵃni thikāhū .	Hamᵃrā sabh chhikaū .	Hamᵃnī hī . . .
160. You are . . .	Ahā̃ thikāhū . . .	Tōra sabh chhikā . .	Tõ hā; apᵃne hī . .

Kurmālī (Mānbhum).	Pāch Parganiā (Rānchi).	Bhojpurī (Shahabad).
Sab-tē bhālā . . .	Besāi bēs . . .	Sab-sē niman . . .
Ũchā	Ũch	Ũch . . . .
Ō-kar-tē ũchā . .	Ũch-lē ũch . . .	Bahut ũch . . .
Sab-tē-ũchā . . .	Sab-lē ũch . . .	Sab-sē ũch . . .
Ghaṛā	Ēk ghōṛā . . .	Ghōṛā . . . .
Ghōṛī	Ēk ghōṛī	Ghōṛī . . . .
Ghaṛā-gulā . . .	Ghōṛā-gulā . . .	Ghōṛan . . . .
Ghōṛi-gulā . . .	Ghōṛī-gulā . . .	Ghōṛin . . . .
Sā̃ṛ	Ēk sā̃ṛ, ēk ā̃ṛiyā . .	Sā̃ṛ . . . .
Gāi	Ēk gāī	Gaū . . .
Sā̃ṛ-gulā . . .	Ā̃ṛiyā-gulā . . .	Sā̃ṛ-sab . . .
Gāi-gulā	Gāi-gula . . .	Gāin . . .
Kuttā	Ēk kukur . . .	Kūkur . . .
Kuttī	Ēk kuti	Kuttī . . .
Kuttā-gulā . . .	Kukur-gulā . .	Kūkur-sab . .
Kutti-gulā . . .	Kuti-gulā . . .	Kuttī-sab . . .
Pā̃ṭhā	Ēk bokᵃrā . . .	Khasī . .
Pā̃ṭhī	Ēk ḍhāīṛ chhāgair, ēk pā̃ṭhiyā.	Chhēr . . .
Pā̃ṭhā-gulā . . .	Chhāgaïr-gulā . .	Chhēr-sab . .
Harin	Ēk sā̃ṛhā harin, ēk jhā̃k harin.	Harin . . .
Madwan harin . .	Ēk ḍhāīṛ harin . .	Harᵃnī . . .
Harin-gulā . .	Harin-gulā . . .	Harin-sab . .
Hāmi rahī . . .	Maī hekõ . . .	Ham hāī, ham bānī
Ṭū hua *or* rahā . .	Taī hekis . .	Tū hāwā, tū bāṛō .
Ūo huē *or* rahō . . .	Ū hekē	Ū bā . . . .
Hāmnī rahī . . .	Hāmᵃrē hokī . . .	Hamᵃnī-kā bānī . .
Tohnī rahā . . .	Tohᵃrē hekā . .	Tohᵃnī-kā bāṛā . .

Bhojpurī (North Centre of Saran).	Sarwariā (Basti).	Western Bhojpurī (Jaunpur).
Khūb niman	Sab-sē nik	Bahutai nik
Ũch	Ũch	Ũch
Bahut ũch	Bahut ũch	Bahut ũch
Khūb ũch	Sab-sē ũch	Bahutai ũch
Ēk ghōṛā	Ēk ghōṛā	Ēk ghōṛā
Ēk ghōṛī	Ēk ghōṛī	Ēk ghōṛī
Ghōṛan	Ghōṛē	Ḍhēr ghōṛā
Ghōṛin	Bahut ghōṛī	Ghōṛin
Ēk sā̃ṛh	Ēk sā̃ṛ	Ēk barad
Ēk gāy	Ēk gāy	Ēk gāy
Sā̃ṛhan	Kaī sā̃ṛ	Ḍhēr bar^{a}dā
Gāin	Kaī gāy	Gaiyan
Ēk kuttā, ēk pillā	Ēk kuttā	Ēk kukur
Ēk kuttī, ēk pillī	Ēk kuttī	Ēk kukurī
Kuttan, pillan	Bahut kuttā	Kukuran
Kuttin, pillin	Kuttī	Kukurin
Ēk khassī	Khassī	Ēk khāsī
Ēk bak^{a}rī	Chhag^{a}ṛī	Ēk chhēṛī
Chhēran	Kaī chhag^{a}ṛī	Bahutai chhēṛī
Ēk har^{a}nā	Har^{a}nā	Ēk harinā
Ēk har^{a}nī	Har^{a}nī	Ēk harinī
Harin	Kaī har^{a}nā	Bahutai harinā
Ham hāĩ	Maĩ hõ	Ham haĩ, ham bāṭī̃
Tē̃ hāwas	Tū hō	Tū̃ hauā
Ū hāwas	Ū hai	Ū hau
Ham^{a}nī hāĩ	Ham^{a}rē bāṭī	Ham haĩ
Tū̃ hāwā	Tū̃ hō	Tū̃ hayē

Nagpuriā (Ranchi).	Madhēsi (Champaran).	Thārū (Champaran).	English.
Sob-sē bēs	Baṛhiā̃	Khūb jōr chik^ahan	134. Best.
Ū̃ch	Ū̃ch	Ḍhēg	135. High.
Ū-kar-sē ū̃ch	Bahut ū̃ch	Barā ḍhēg	136. Higher.
Sob-sē ū̃ch	Sabh-sē ū̃ch	Barā jabaḍh ḍhēg	137. Highest.
Ghōṛā	Egō ghōrā	Ghōṛā	138. A horse.
Ghōṛi	Egō ghōrī	Ghōṛi	139. A mare.
Ghōṛā-man	Ghōrā-sabh	Pog^arāhī̃ ghōṛā	140. Horses.
Ghōṛi-man	Ghōrī sabh	Pog^arāhī̃ ghōṛī	141. Mares.
Sā̃ṛh	Egō sā̃ṛh	Dhakūr	142. A bull.
Gāy	Egō gāy	Gāi	143. A cow.
Sā̃ṛh-man	Bail sabh	Baradh	144. Bulls.
Gāy-man, garu-man (*com. gen.*)	Gāy sabh	Pog^arāhī̃ gāy	145. Cows.
Kukur	Egō kūkur	Kukur	146. A dog.
Kuṭī kukur	Egō kutti	Pillī	147. A bitch.
Kukur-man	Kut^awan	Pog^arāhī̃ kukur	148. Dogs.
Kuṭī kukur-man *or* kuṭī-man.	Kutian	Pog^arāhī̃ pillī	149. Bitches.
Bak^arī, *also* khasī *and* chhag^arī.	Egō khasī	Khasī	150. A he goat.
Bak^arī	Egō bak^arī	Chhēr	151. A female goat.
Chhag^arī-man	Bōkā sabh	Pog^arāhī̃ chhēr	152. Goats.
Harin	Egō har^anā	Harin	153. A male deer.
Harinī	Egō har^anī	Har^anī	154. A female deer.
Harin-man	Harin sabh	Har^anā har^anī	155. Deer.
Mōẽ hekō̃ *or* ahō̃	Ham bānī	Moi bar^ahī̃	156. I am.
Tōẽ hekis *or* ahis	Tū bāṛā	Toẽ bārē	157. Thou art.
Ū hekē *or* ahē	Ū bāṛan	Ū bariyā	158. He is.
Ham^arē-man hekī, ahī, *or* hai.	Ham^anī haiī̃	Ham^arā bārī	159. We are.
Toh^arē-man hekā, ahā, *or* hā.	Rauā̃-sabhan bānī	Tū̃ bārē	160. You are.

English.	Maithilī (Darbhanga Brāhmaṇs).	Chhikā-chhikī (Bhagalpur).	Magahī (Gayā).
161. They are . . .	Ō lok^ani thikāh . .	Ū sabh chhikath, chhikainh	Ū sab hathin, ū sab hathun
162. I was . . .	Ham chhaláh^ū, ham rahī .	Hamẽ chhalā̃ . . .	Ham hali . .
163. Thou wast . .	Tō̃ chhalẽ . . .	Tō̃ chhalaĩ . . .	Tū̃ halẽ *or* halē . .
164. He was . . .	Ō chhal, ō rahai . .	Ū chhala	Ū halaī . . . .
165. We were . . .	Ham^arā sabah^ī rahī . .	Ham^arā sabh chhaliai .	Ham^ani halī . . .
166. You were . . .	Ahā̃ rahī	Tōrā sabh chhalâ . .	Tō̃ halâ, toh^ani halâ, ap^ane halī.
167. They were . .	Ō lok^ani rahathⁱ . .	Ū sabh chhalāt . .	Ū sab hal^athī, hal^athin .
168. Be	Hōâh	Hō	Hō, hōe, hōwe . .
169. To be . . .	Hōeb	Haib	Hōeb . . . .
170 Being . . .	Hōit	Hōta . . .	Hoait, hōt . .
171. Having been . .	Hōi-kay-kā̃ . . .	Bhai-ke	Hō, hō-ke . . .
172. I may be . . .	Ham hōī	Hamẽ hōaū̃ . . .	Ham hōī . . .
173. I shall be . . .	Ham hōeb . . .	Hamẽ haib . . .	Ham hōeb . . .
174. I should be . .	Ham^arā hōmak chāhī .	Ham^arā hōla chāhī . .	Ham^arā hōwe-kē chāhī .
175. Beat . . .	Mārâh	Mārū	Piṭō, piṭ . . . .
176. To beat . . .	Mārab	Mārab	Piṭab . . . .
177. Beating . . .	Mārait	Mār^ata . . .	Piṭait . . . .
178. Having beaten . .	Māri-kay-kā̃ . . .	Māri-ke, māir-ke . .	Piṭ-ke, piṭ-kar-ke . .
179. I beat . . .	Ham mārai-chhī . .	Hamẽ māraichhī . .	Ham piṭa-hī . . .
180. Thou beatest . .	Tō̃ mārai-chhẽ . .	Tō̃ māraichhaī . .	Tū̃ piṭa-hẽ *or* piṭa-hā̃ .
181. He beats . . .	Ō mārai achhⁱ . . .	Ū māraichhai . . .	Ū piṭa-haī . . .
182. We beat . . .	Ham^arā sabah^ī mārai-chhī .	Ham^arā sabh māraichhī .	Ham^anī piṭa-hī . .
183. You beat . . .	Ahā̃ mārai-chhī . .	Tōrā sabh māraichhâ . .	Tō̃ piṭa-hâ; toh^anī piṭa-hī .
184. They beat . . .	Ō lok^ani mārai-chhathinhⁱ .	Ū sabh māraichhainh .	Un^akhanī piṭa-hathī *or* piṭa-hathin.
185. I beat (*Past Tense*) .	Ham māral . . .	Hamẽ mār^alā̃ . . .	Ham piṭ^alī . . .
186. Thou beatest (*Past Tense*).	Tō̃ mār^alẽ . . .	Tō̃ mār^alaī . . .	Tū̃ piṭ^alē . . .
187. He beat (*Past Tense*) .	Ō mār^alak . . .	Ū mār^alak . . .	Ū piṭ^alak . . .

Kuṛmālī (Manbhum).	Pāch Pargaṛiā (Ranchi).	Bhojpurī (Shahabad).
Ūo-sab rahat	Ū-man hekaĭ	Ok^{a}ni-kā bāṛan
Hāmi rah-haliõ	Maĭ rahõ	Ham rah^{a}lĩ
Tũ rah-hali	Taĭ rahis	Tū rah^{a}lā
Ūo rah-halĕik	Ū rahā	Ū rah^{a}lē
Hāmnī rah-haliõ	Hām^{a}rē rahi	Ham^{a}ni-kā rah^{a}lĩ
Tohnī rah-halē	Ṭoh^{a}rē rahā	Toh^{a}ni-kā rah^{a}lā-sā
Ūo-sab rah-halĕik	Ū-man rahaĭ	Ok^{a}ni-kā rah^{a}lan-sā
Huō	Hōu	Hōkhā
Huōt	Haĭ-kaĭ	Hōkhal
Hayal	Hōt	Hōkhat
Raha hayal	Haĭ-kaīr-kan	Hō-kar-ke, hōkh-ke, hō-ke
Hāmi huē pāri	Maĭ hai pārõ	Ham hōkhĩ, ham hōĩ
Hāmi huab	Maĭ hamũ	Ham hōib, ham hōkhab
Hāmi hue-kē chāhī	Maĭ hatõ	Ham^{a}rā hōkhe-kē chāhī
Piṭā	Māru	Mār
Piṭa khātir	Māre-kaĭ	Māral
Piṭuni	Mārat	Mārat
Piṭlā sē	Māīr-kaīr-kan	Mār-ke
Hāmi piṭa-hī	Maĭ mārõ-lā	Ham māri-lā
Tũ piṭ	Taĭ māris-lā	Tū mārā-lā
Ūo piṭa-hat	Ū māre-lā	Ū māre-lā
Hāmnī piṭa-hī	Hām^{a}rē māri-lā	Ham^{a}ni-kā māri-lā
Tohnī piṭa-hā	Toh^{a}rē mārā-lā	Toh^{a}ni-kā mārā-lā
Ūo-sab piṭa-hat	Ū-man maraï-lā	Ok^{a}ni māre-lē
Hāmi piṭliõ	Maĭ māir rahõ	Ham mar^{a}lĩ
Tũ piṭlē	Taĭ māir rahis	Tū mar^{a}lā
Ūo piṭlak	Ū māir rahē	Ū mar^{a}las

Bhojpurī (North Centre of Saran).	Sarwariā (Basti).	Western Bhojpurī (Jaunpur).
Ū lōg hâ, hâwan . .	Unh^{a}nē haĩ . . .	Ū lōg hauan . . .
Ham rahī̃ . . .	Maĩ rah^{a}lō̃ . . .	Ham rah^{a}lī̃ . . .
Tẽ ṛahas . . .	Taĩ rah^{a}lē . . .	Tū̃ rah^{a}lâ . . .
Ū rahas . . .	Ū rahal . . .	Ū rah^{a}lan . . .
Ham^{a}nī rahī̃ . .	Ham^{a}rē rah^{a}lī . .	Ham sabhẽ rah^{a}lī̃ . .
Tū̃ rahâ . . .	Tū̃ rah^{a}lâ . . .	Tū̃ sabhẽ rah^{a}lâ . .
Ū lōg rahā̃ . .	Unh^{a}nē rah^{a}laĩ . .	Ū lōg rah^{a}lan . . .
Hō	Hō	Hō . . . .
Hōkhal	Hōb	Hōib . . . .
Hōt	Hōt	Hōt . . . .
Hō-ke	Hō-kar	Hoi kăī . . . .
Ham hōĩ . . .	Maĩ hō sakăī-lō̃ . .	Ham hōī . .
Ham hōkhab . . .	Maĩ hōbō̃ . . .	Ham rah^{a}bai . .
Ham^{a}rā hōkho-kē chāhī .	Mō-kē hōăī-kē chāhī . .	Hamaĩ rahăī-kē chāhī .
Mār	Mār, piṭ	Mār . . . .
Māral	Mār^{a}nā, piṭ^{a}nā . . .	Mārab . . . .
Mārat	Mārat	Mārat . . . .
Mār-ke	Mār-ke	Mari kăī . . .
Ham māri-lā . . .	Maĩ marăī-lō̃ . . .	Ham māri-lā . . .
Tẽ māro-las . . .	Taĩ mārăī-lē . . .	Tū̃ mārăī-lâ . . .
Ū māro-lā . . .	Ū mārăī-lā . . .	Ū mārăī-lā . . .
Ham^{a}ni mārī-lā . .	Ham^{a}rē mārī-lā . .	Ham sabhẽ mārī-lā . .
Tū̃ māro-lâ . . .	Tū̃ mārăī-lâ . . .	Tū̃ sabhē mārăī-lâ . .
Ū-lōg māro-lā . . .	Unh^{a}nē mārăī-laĩ . .	Ū lōg mārăī-leni . .
Ham mar^{a}lī̃, ham marnī̃ .	Maĩ maṛ^{a}lō̃ . . .	Ham mar^{a}lī . . .
Tē̃ mar^{a}las, tẽ marnas .	Taĩ mar^{a}lō . . .	Tū̃ mar^{a}lâ . . .
Ū mar^{a}lan, ū marnan .	Ū mar^{a}lis . . .	U mar^{a}les . . .

Nagpuriā (Ranchi).	Madhēsī (Champaran).	Thārū (Champaran).	English.
Ū-man hekaī, ahaī, *or* haī .	Ū-lōg bā . . .	Un bāriyā . . .	161. They are.
Mōẽ rahẽ . . .	Ham rahᵃli-hā . .	Moi rahᵃlī . . .	162. I was.
Tōẽ rahis . . .	Tū rahᵃlā-hā . .	Tū̃ rahᵃlē . . .	163. Thou wast.
Ū rahē	Ū rahᵃlan-hā . .	Unhi rahᵃliyā . . .	164. He was.
Hamᵃrē rahī . . .	Hamᵃni rahᵃli-hā . .	Moi rahᵃlī . . .	165. We were.
Tohᵃrē rahā . . .	Tohᵃnī rahᵃlā-hā . .	Tū̃ rahᵃlē . . .	166. You were.
Ū-man rahẽ . . .	Ū lōg rahal . . .	Ū rahᵃlē . . .	167. They were.
Hō, hohī . . .	Hōy	Hā̃	168. Be.
Hōek	Honā	Hōnī-hārī . . .	169. To be.
Hōe-ke	Hōat	Sẽ	170. Being.
Hōe-kair-kē *or* hōe-ke .	Hō-ke	Sẽ	171. Having been.
Mōẽ hōek parbõ . .	Ham hōī . . .	Moi hokhᵃhī . . .	172. I may be.
Mōẽ hōbõ . . .	Ham hōkhab . . .	Moi hokhᵃbahī . .	173. I shall be.
Mōẽ hōtõ-tō . . .	Hamᵃrā hokhe-kē chāhī .	Mōrā hokhe-kē chāhī . .	174. I should be.
Mār	Mār	Mārᵃbi	175. Beat.
Mārek	Māral	Māre-kē	176. To beat.
Mārat	Mārat	Mārat	177. Beating.
Mār-ke	Mār-ke	Mār-ke	178. Having beaten.
Mōẽ marõ-nā . . .	Ham mārī-lā . . .	Moi mārat badhᵃhī . .	179. I beat.
Tōẽ mārisi-lā . . .	Tū mārā-lā . . .	Tū̃ mārat badhᵃhī . .	180. Thou beatest.
Ū māre-lā . . .	Ū māre-lā . . .	Ū mārat badhᵃhī . .	181. He beats.
Hamᵃrē mārī-lā . .	Hamᵃni mārī-lā . .	Moi mārat badhᵃhī . .	182. We beat.
Tohᵃrē māra-lā . .	Tohᵃni mārā-lā . .	Tū̃ mārat badhᵃhī . .	183. You beat.
Ū-man mārai-na . .	Ū lōg māre-lā . . .	Ū mārat badhᵃhī . .	184. They beat.
Mōẽ mārᵃlõ, ham mārᵃlī .	Ham mārᵃlī . . .	.....	185. I beat (*Past Tense*).
Tōẽ mārᵃlis . . .	Tū marᵃlā . . .	.....	186. Thou beatest (*Past Tense*).
Ū mārᵃlak . . .	Ū marᵃlē . . .	.....	187. He beat (*Past Tense*).

English.	Maithilī (Darbhanga Brāhmaṇs).	Chhikā-chhikī (Bhagalpur).	Magahī (Gayā).
188. We beat (*Past Tense*) .	Ham^{a}rā sabah^{i} māral .	Ham^{a}rā sabh mār^{a}liai .	Ham^{a}nī piṭ^{a}lī . . .
189. You beat (*Past Tense*)	Ap^{a}ne māral . . .	Tōrā sabh mār^{a}lā . .	Tō̃ piṭ^{a}lā . .
190. They beat (*Past Tense*)	Ō lok^{a}ni mār^{a}lainh^{i} . .	Ū sabh māral^{a}kāt . .	Ū sab piṭ^{a}lan . . .
191. I am beating . .	Ham mārai-chhī . .	Hamē̃ māraichhī . .	Ham piṭaitiaī . . .
192. I was beating . .	Ham mārait rahī . .	Hamē̃ māraichhalā̃ . .	Ham piṭait baliaī, *or* piṭait halī.
193. I had beaten . .	Ham māral achhī . .	Hamē̃ mār^{a}lē chhalā̃ . .	Ham piṭ^{a}lē-hī . . .
194. I may beat . .	Ham mārī . . .	Hamē̃ mārañ . .	Ham piṭiaī . . .
195. I shall beat . .	Ham mārab . . .	Hamē̃ mār^{a}bañ . .	Ham piṭ^{a}baī, *or* ham piṭab .
196. Thou wilt beat . .	Tō̃ mār^{a}bāh . . .	Tō̃ mār^{a}baĩ . .	Tū̃ piṭ^{a}bā . . .
197. He will beat . .	Ō mārat . . .	Ū mār^{a}ta . . .	Ū piṭ^{a}tañ . . .
198. We shall beat . .	Ham^{a}rā sabah^{i} mārab .	Ham^{a}rā sabh mār^{a}bai .	Ham^{a}nī piṭ^{a}bau, ham sab piṭab.
199. You will beat . .	Ap^{a}ne mārab . . .	Tōrā sabh mār^{a}bā . .	Tō̃ piṭabā . . .
200. They will beat . .	Ō lok^{a}ni mār^{a}thīnh^{i} . .	Ū sabh mār^{a}tāt . .	Ū sabh piṭ^{a}tin . . .
201. I should beat . .	Ham^{a}rā mārak chāhī .	Ham^{a}rā mār^{a}la chāhī .	Ham^{a}rā piṭe-kē chāhī .
202. I am beaten . .	Ham māral jāichhī . .	Hamē̃ mār^{a}la jāichhī .	Ham piṭailā-hī . .
203. I was beaten . .	Ham māral geláh^{ū} .	Hamē̃ mār^{a}la jāichhalā̃ .	Ham piṭailā-hal, *or* piṭailā-halī.
204. I shall be beaten .	Ham māral jāeb . .	Hamē̃ mār^{a}la jaibañ . .	Ham piṭāeb . . .
205. I go . . .	Ham jāichhī . . .	Hamē̃ jāichhī . . .	Ham jā-hī . . .
206. Thou goest . .	Tō̃ jāichhē̃ . . .	Tō̃ jāichhaĩ . . .	Tū̃ jā-hē̃, jā-hā̃ . .
207. He goes . . .	Ō jāit-achhī . . .	Ū jāichhai . . .	Ū jā-hai, jā-hathī, jā-hathin
208. We go . . .	Ham^{a}rā sabah^{i} jāi-chhī .	Ha[illegible] sabh jāichhī .	Ham^{a}nī jā-hī . . .
209. You go . . .	Ap^{a}ne jāi-chhī . . .	Tōrā sabh jāichhā . .	Tō̃ jāh, ap^{a}ne jāñ . .
210. They go . . .	Ō lok^{a}ni jāi-chhath^{i} . .	Ū sabh jāichhainh . .	Ū sab jā-hathī . .
211. I went . . .	Ham geláh^{ū} . . .	Hamē̃ gēlā̃ . . .	Ham gēlī . . .
212. Thou wentest . .	Tō̃ gēlē̃ . . .	Tō̃ gēlaĩ . . .	Tū̃ gēlē̃, *or* gēlā̃ . .
213. He went . . .	Ō gēl	Ū gēla	Ū gēl . . .
214. We went . . .	Ham^{a}rā sabah^{i} geláh^{ū} .	Ham^{a}rā sabh geliai . .	Ham^{a}nī gēlī . . .

Kurmālī (Mānbhum).	Pāñch Parganiā (Ranchi).	Bhojpurī (Shahabad).
Hāmnī piṭliō	Hām^{a}rē māir rahī	Ham^{a}nī-kā mar^{a}lī
Tohnī piṭe-halə	Toh^{a}rē māir rahā	Toh^{a}nī-kā mar^{a}lā
Ūo-sab piṭe-halēik	Ū-man māir rahaĩ	Ok^{a}nī mar^{a}lan
Hāmi piṭa-hiō	Maĩ mār^{a}tō-hõ	Ham mārat-bānī, ham mar^{a}tānī.
Hāmi piṭa-haliō	Maĩ mārat-rahõ	Ham mārat rah^{a}lĩ
Hāmi piṭe-haliō	Maĩ māir āhõ	Ham mar^{a}lī-hã
Hāmi piṭe-pāri	Maĩ māre pārõ	Ham mārĩ
Hāmi piṭab	Maĩ mār^{a}mū	Ham mārab
Tũ piṭbhĩ	Taĩ mār^{a}bē	Tū mar^{a}bā
Ūo piṭṭa	Ū mārī	Ū mārī
Hāmnī piṭab	Hām^{a}rē mārab	Ham^{a}nī-kā mārab
Tohnī piṭbē	Toh^{a}rē mār^{a}bā	Toh^{a}nī-kā mar^{a}bā
Ūo-sab piṭṭa	Ū-man mār^{a}baĩ	Ok^{a}nī marihẽ
Hāmar piṭe-kē chāhī	Maĩ mār^{a}tõ	Ham^{a}rā māre-kē chāhī
Hāmrā-kē piṭal	Maĩ māir khāy āhõ	Ham mār khātānī
Hāmrā-kē piṭal-halēi	Maĩ māir khāy rahõ	Ham mār khāt rah^{a}lĩ hã
Hāmrā-kē piṭṭa	Maĩ māir khāmū	Ham mār khāib
Hāmi jā-hī	Maĩ jãwa-lā, maĩ jãw	Ham jāl-lā
Tũ jāo	Taĩ jāis-lā	Tū jā-lā
Ūo jāo-hat	Ū jāy^{a}lā	Ū jā-lā
Hāmnī jā-hī	Hām^{a}rē jāi-lā	Ham^{a}nī-kā jāi-lā
Tohnī jāo	Toh^{a}rē jāwā	Toh^{a}nī-kā jā-lā
Ūo-sab jā-hat	Ū-man jāt-haĩ	Ok^{a}nī jā-lan
Hāmi geliō	Maĩ jāy-rahõ	Ham gailĩ
Tũ gēl-hali	Taĩ jāy-rahis	Tū gailā
Ūo gēl-halēi	Ū jāy-rahē	Ū gail
Hāmnī gēl-hali	Hām^{a}rē jāy-rahī	Ham^{a}nī-kā gailĩ

Bhojpurī (North Centre of Saran).	Sarwariā (Basti).	Western Bhojpurī (Jaunpur).
Ham^{a}nī mar^{a}lī̃, ham^{a}nī maruī̃.	Ham mar^{a}lī	Ham sabhē mar^{a}lī
Tū̃ mar^{a}lā, tū̃ maruā	Tū mar^{a}lā	Tū sabhe mar^{a}lā
Ū̃-lōg mar^{a}lan	Unh^{a}nē mar^{a}laĩ	Ū̃ lōg mar^{a}les
Ham mar^{a}tānī	Maĩ mārat-bāṭō̃	Ham mārat-haī
Ham mārat rah^{a}lī̃	Maĩ mārat-rah^{a}lō̃	Ham mārat-rah^{a}lī
Ham mar^{a}lī̃ hā	Maĩ mar^{a}lē rah^{a}lō̃	Ham mar^{a}lē rah^{a}lī
Ham mārī̃	Mō-kē mārāī-kō chāhī	Ham mārilā
Ham mārab	Maĩ mar^{a}bō̃	Ham mar^{a}bai
Tē̃ mar^{a}bē	Taĩ mar^{a}bē	Tū̃ mar^{a}bai
Ū̃ mārī	Ū̃ mārī	Ū̃ mārī
Ham^{a}nī mārab	Ham mārab	Ham sabhē mārab
Tū̃ mar^{a}bā	Tū̃ mar^{a}bā	Tū sabhē mar^{a}bā
Ū̃-lōg maribē̃	Unh^{a}nē maribaĩ	U-lōg mārī
Ham^{a}rā māre-kē chāhī	Maĩ nij mar^{a}bō̃	Hamai mārāī-kē hau
Ham māral jāī-lā	Maĩ māral jāt-bāṭō̃	Ham māral jāī-lā
Ham māral gaīlī	Maĩ māral gaīlō̃	Ham māral gailī
Ham māral jāib	Maĩ māral jābō̃	Ham māral jābai
Ham jāī-lā	Maĩ jā-lō̃	Ham jāī-lā
Tē̃ jā-las	Taĩ jā-lē	Tū̃ jā-lā
Ū̃ jā-lā	Ū̃ jā-lā	Ū̃ jā-lē
Ham^{a}nī jāī-lā	Ham jāt-bāṭī̃	Ham sabhē jāī-lā
Tū̃ jā-lā	Tū̃ jāt-bāṭā	Tū sabhē jā-lā
Ū̃ lōg jā-lan	Unh^{a}nē jāt-bāṭaĩ	Ū̃ lōg jā-leni
Ham gaīlī̃	Maĩ gaīlō̃	Ham gaīlī
Tē̃ gaīlē	Taĩ gaīlē	Tū̃ gaīlā
Ū̃ gaīlē	Ū̃ gaīl	Ū̃ gailaĩ
Ham^{a}nī gaīlī̃	Ham gaīlī	Ham sabhē gaīlī

English.	Maithilī (Darbhanga Brāhmaṇs).	Chhikā-chhikī (Bhagalpur).	Magahī (Gayā).
215. You went . . .	Ap^{a}nē geláh$^{\bar{u}}$	Tōrā sabh gēlâ . . .	Tō̃ gēlâ . . . . .
216. They went . . .	Ō lokan^{i} gēlāh	Ū sabh gēlāt	Ū sab gēlau . . .
217. Go	Jāh, jō	Jāū	Jō . . . . . .
218. Going . . .	Jāit	Jāita	Jāit . . . . .
219. Gone	Gēl bhāl	Gēla	Gēl . . . . .
220. What is your name? .	Ahā̃-k nām ki thīk? .	Ap^{a}nek nām kī chhikau? .	Tōhar kā nām hau? . .
221. How old is this horse?	Ī ghōṛā kat^{a}bā dinak thīk?	Hai ghōṛā kataik dinak chhikai?	Yah ghōṛā kit^{a}nā bachhar-ke haï.
222. How far is it from here to Kashmir?	Ehi ṭhām-sā̃ Kaśmīr kat^{a}bā dūr achh^{i}?	Āīṭhiyā̃-sē̃ Kaśmīr kataik dūr chhikai?	Hiā̃-sē Kashmīr kit^{a}nā dūr haï?
223. How many sons are there in your father's house?	Ap^{a}ne-k pitā-k ghar madhya kai gōṭ putra chhath^{i}?	Toh^{a}rā bāpak ghar-mē̃ kataik bēṭā chhikau?	Tōhar bāp-ke ghar-mē̃ kit^{a}nā bēṭā hau; (*or to a woman*) tōhar naihar-mē̃ kit^{a}nā bēṭā hau?
224. I have walked a long way to-day.	Ham āj bahut dūr dhari ṭahal^{a}lāh$^{\bar{u}}$ achh^{i}.	Hamē̃ āij bahut har^{a}laū bul^{a}laū achh.	Āj baṛī dūr chal^{a}lī . .
225. The son of my uncle is married to his sister.	Ham^{a}rā pittī-k putra ok^{a}rā bahin^{i}-sā̃ bibāhal gēlāh achh^{i}.	Ham^{a}rā pitik bēṭāk biāh bhēl achh ok^{a}rā bahin-sē̃.	Hamnar chachā-ke bēṭā ō-kar bahin-sē biāhal-haï.
226. In the house is the saddle of the white horse.	Ghar madhya uj^{a}rā ghōṛā-k jīn achh^{i}.	Uj^{a}rā ghōṛak jīn ai ghar-mē̃ dhaila chhikaik.	Ujar ghōṛā-ke jīn ghar-mē̃ haï.
227. Put the saddle upon his back.	Sē jīn ok^{a}rā pīṭh par kasū .	Jīn ok^{a}rā pīṭh^{i}-par rāikh dahōk.	Ō-kar pīṭh-par jīn rakhâ .
228. I have beaten his son with many stripes.	Ham hun^{a}kā putra par anēk chābuk prahār kaïl achh^{i}.	Hamē̃ ok^{a}rā bēṭā-kai bahut bēt mār^{a}liaik.	Ham ō-kar bēṭā-kē kaï-ēk bēt mār^{a}lī-haï.
229. He is grazing cattle on the top of the hill.	Ō parbat śikhar-par māl charāy rahal chhath^{i}.	Ū māl-jāl-kai pahāṛ-upar charai-rahal-achh.	Ū pahāṛ-ke ūpar (*or* phungī par) mawēshī charāwait-haï
230. He is sitting on a horse under that tree.	Ō oh^{i} bṛikah tar ghōṛā-par baisal chhath^{i}.	Ū gāchh-tar ghōṛā par baisal achh.	Gāchh talē ghōṛā par baiṭhal-haï.
231. His brother is taller than his sister.	Hunak bhrātā ok^{a}rā bahini-k prat^{i} adhik nāmh chhath^{i}.	Ō-kar bhāī ok^{a}rā bahin-sē̃ lām chhaik.	Ō-kar bhāī ō-kar bahin-sē lambā haï.
232. The price of that is two rupees and a half.	Ō-kar mulya aṛhāi rupaiā thīk.	Ō-kar dām aḍhāi ṭakā chhaik.	Ō-kar aṛhāī rupaiā dām haï.
233. My father lives in that small house.	Hamār pitā oh^{i} chhoṭ^{a}kā ghar madhya rahai chhath^{i}.	Hamar bāp oi chhōṭ ghar-mē̃ rahai-chhath.	Hamār bāp ū chhoṭ^{a}kā ghar-mē̃ raha-haï.
234. Give this rupee to him	Ī rupaiā hun^{a}kā diauh^{i} .	Ī ṭakā ok^{a}rā diōk . .	Ī rupaiā ok^{a}rā-kē dē dâ .
235. Take those rupees from him.	Ō rupaiā sabh hun^{a}kā-sā̃ lā liā.	Ū ṭakā-sabh ok^{a}rā-sē̃ lē liā .	Ū rupaiā ok^{a}rā-sē lē-lâ .
236. Beat him well and bind him with ropes.	Ok^{a}rā nīkē̃ mārū āor rassā-sā̃ bādhū.	Ok^{a}rā khub piṭā āor ḍōri-sē̃ bānhā.	Ok^{a}rā-kē khūb mār-ke rassī-sē bā̃dhâ.

Kuṛmālī (Manbhum).	Pāch Parganiā (Ranchi).	Bhojpurī (Shahabad).
Tohnī gēl-halē . . .	Tohᵃrē jāy rahā . .	Tohᵃni-kā gaī . . .
Ūo-sab gēl-halēi . .	Ū-man jāy rahaĩ . .	Okᵃni gailan . . .
Jāo	Jāwā	Jā, jō . . . . .
Jao-hat	Jāt	Jāit . . . .
Gēl	Jāwal, gēl	Gail . . . .
Tōhar nām ki ? . .	Tōr kā nām hekē ? . .	Tohār kā nā̃w bā ? .
Ē gharā-kē katē umar ? .	Ēhē ghoṛāṭā-kēr umar katik hekē ?	Ī ghōṛā kai baris-ke bā ? .
Ēkhān-lē Kāshmīr katē dhur ?	Ihā̃-lēk Kashmir katik dhūr hekē ?	Ehi jā-sē Kaśmīr katek dūr bā ?
Kay-gō gidrā hōkēi tōhar bāp-gharē ?	Tōr bāpek gharē kayᵃṭā bēṭā-chhuwā āhē ?	Tohᵃrā bāp-ke ghar-mē̃ kai-gō bēṭā bāṛā ?
Hāmi āj bohut dhur bullio .	Maĩ āij bahut dhūr buil-āhō̃	Āj ham dhēr dūr chal gail rahᵃlī hā̃.
Hāmar khuṛār bēṭār bihā ō-kar bāhin-sē bhelai.	Mōr kākā-kēr bēṭā saṅg ō-kar bahin-kēr bihā hay-āhā.	Hamār kākā-kā larikā-ke biyāh okᵃrā bahin-sē bhail bā.
Dhaba gharā-ke khagir gharē hatēi.	Chāiᵃkā ghoṛāṭā-kēr jīn ghar bhītᵃrē āhē.	Ō ghar-mē̃ ujarᵃkā ghōṛā-ke khōgīr bā.
Ō-kar piṭhē khagir dihā .	Ō-kar piṭh upᵃrē jīn-ṭā rāikh dēhiṅg.	Okᵃrā piṭh-par khōgir kasā .
Hāmi ō-kar bēṭā-kē bahut karā piṭliō.	Maĩ ō-kar bēṭā-kē bahut saiṭ āhō̃.	Ham okᵃrā bēṭā-kā kai ēk chābuk marᵃlī hā̃.
Ūo pāhār-par paś charāo-hat.	Pāhāṛ upᵃrē ū gōrū chārātē hē.	Ū pasuan-kē pahāṛī-ke ūpar charā rahal-bā.
Ūo ū gāchh-tar gharā-par baisal hat.	Ahē gāchh tarē ghōṛā upᵃrē ū baīste-hē.	Ū oh phēṛ-tar ghōṛā-par baiṭhal bā.
Ō-kar bhāi ō-kar bahin-lē ḍhēṅgā baṭē.	A-kar bhāī akar bahin-lēkē ḍhā̃gā āhē.	Ō-kar bhāī okᵃrā bahin-sē baṛ bā.
Ō-kar dām aṛhāi ṭākā .	A-kar dām dū ṭakā āṭh ānā hekē.	Ō-kar dām aṛhāi rupᵃyā bā.
Hāmar bāp ū chhuṭā gharē rahat.	Ahē chhōṭ ghar-ṭāy mōr bābā rahe-lā.	Hamār bāp oh chhoṭᵃkā ghar-mē̃ rahe-lē.
Okrē yah ṭākā dihā . .	Ō-kē ēhē rupiyā-ṭā dēwā .	Ī rupaiyā okᵃrā-kē dē dā .
Ō-kar-pās-lō ū ṭākā-sab lihā	A-kar ṭhinē ōhē rupiyā-gulā lēhiṅg.	Ū rupaiyā okᵃrā-sē lē lā .
Okrē khub piṭ[illegible] ār pāg[illegible] dēi-ke bā̃dhā. .	Bēs nihār ō-kē piṭiṅg āūr ḍorāy bā̃dhiṅg.	Okᵃrā-kē khūb mārā āūr rasī-sē bā̃dh-dā.

Bhojpurī (North Centre of Saran).	Sarwariā (Basti).	Western Bhojpurī (Jaunpur).
Tũ gailâ	Tũ gailâ . . .	Tũ sabhē gaïlâ . .
U-lōg gailan . . .	Unh^a^nē gailaĩ . . .	U-lōg gaïlan . . .
Jā	Jā	Jā . . . .
Jāib	Jāt	Jāt . . . .
Gail	Gaïl	Gaïl . . . .
Tohār kā nā̃w bâ? . .	Tohār kā nā̃w hai? . .	Tohār kā nā̃w hau? . .
Ī ghōṛā-ke kā umir hâ? .	Ket^a^nē din kāī i ghōṛā hai?	Ghōṛā ket^a^nē din-kāī hauwai?
Ih^a^wā̃-sē Kaśmīr kit^a^nā dūr bā?	Ihā̃-sē Kaśmīr két^a^nā lām bai?	Ihā̃-sē Kaśmīr ket^a^nī dūri bā?
Toh^a^rā bāp-kā ghar-mē̃ kit^a^nā bēṭā bāṛan?	Toh^a^rē bāp-kē ghar-mē̃ ket^a^nē beṭ^a^wā haĩ?	Toh^a^rē bāp-kē gharē ket^a^nā laṛikā hauwan?
Āj ham bahut dūr chal^a^lī̃ hā̃.	Āju ham bahut ghum^a^lī .	Āju ham bahut dauṛē .
Ham^a^rā chachā-kā bēṭā-ke biyāh un-kā bahin-sē bhaïl-bā.	Ham^a^rē piti-kāī beṭ^a^wā ham^a^rē bahin-sē biahal bāy.	Ham^a^rē kakā-kāī beṭ^a^wā on-kē bahin-sē biahal-hau.
Ujar^a^kā ghōṛā-ke chār-jāmā ghar-mē̃ bā.	Ujar^a^kē ghōṛā-kāī char^a^jāmā ghar-mē̃ hai.	Ghar-mē̃ ujar^a^kē ghōṛā-kāī charijāmā hauwai.
Ghōṛā-kā pīṭh par chār-jāmā kas dâ.	Char^a^jāmā ok^a^rē pīṭh-par dharâ.	Ok^a^rē pīṭhī-par charijāmā dharâ.
Ham un-kā bēṭā-kē ba-maūr ukhār ukhār-ke mar^a^lī̃ hā.	Maĩ ok^a^rē beṭ^a^wā-kē kōṛā-sē mar^a^lō̃-hai.	Ham on-kē beṭ^a^wā-kē kaïu kōṛā mar^a^lī.
Ū pahāṛ-kā math^a^nī par chanan-kē charāwatāran.	Ū pahāṛ-kē chōṭī-par chanan-kē charāwat hai.	Ū pahāṛ-kē chōṭī-par gōrū charāwat hauwai.
Ū oh gāchh tar ēk ghōṛā par baïṭhal bāran.	Ū ghoṛā-par pēṛ-kē nīchē baïṭhal bāy.	Wahi pēṛē tarē ū ad^a^mī ghōṛā-par chaṛhal-hau.
Un-kar bhāī un-kā bahin-sē lam^a^har bāran.	Ō-kar bhāī ok^a^rē bahin-sē baṛā hai.	Ō-kar bhāy o-k^a^rī bahinī-sē baṛā bā.
Ō-kar dām aṛhāī rupaiā hâ	Ō-kar dām aṛhāī rupaiā hai	Ō-kar dām aṛhāī rupiā hauwai.
Hamār bāp woh chhoṭ^a^kā ghar-mē̃ rahe-lan.	Mōr bāp obe chhoṭ^a^kē ghar-mā̃ rahat-hai.	Hamār bābū chhoṭ^a^kī bakh^a^rī-mē̃ rahāī-leni.
Ī rupaiā un-kā-kē dē-dâ .	Eh rupaiā ō-kē dēo . .	Ī rupiā un-kē dyâ . .
Ū rupaiā un-kā-sē lē-lâ .	Ū rupaiā ō-sē lēw . .	Ī rupiā on-sē lyâ . .
Ok^a^rā-kē banā-ke mārâ ā rassā-sē bā̃dh lâ.	Ō-kē bhalē mārâ ō rassī-sē bā̃dhâ.	On-kē khūb māri-kāī ras^a^rī-sē bānhi dyâ.

Nagpuriā (Ranchi).	Madhēsī (Champaran).	Thārū (Champaran).	English.
Tohᵃrē *or* tohᵃrē-man gēlā	Tū gailā	......	215. You went.
Ū-man gēlaĩ	Ū lōg gailan	......	216. They went.
Jāhē̃ *or* jāu	Jā	Jō	217. Go.
Jāt	Jāt	Jāit	218. Going.
Gāl	Gaīl	Geliā	219. Gone.
Tōr kā nām hekē?	Tohār kā nām bāṭē?	Tōr kihā nām?	220. What is your name?
Ī ghōṛā katai din-kēr hekē?	Ī ghorᵃwā ketᵃnā din-ke bhaīl?	Ī ghōṛā-ke kihā umer?	221. How old is this horse?
Ihā̃-sē Kaśmīr katai dūrē hai?	Ihā̃-sē Kasmīr ketᵃnā dūr bāṭē?	Ihᵃwā̃-sē Kaśmīr katᵃhar dūr?	222. How far is it from here to Kashmir?
Tōr bāp-kēr ghar-mē̃ katai chhauā-man haĩ?	Tohᵃrā bāp-ke ghar-mē̃ kaiṭhō bēṭā-lōg bāṭan?	Tōr bāp-ke kē̃-goḍā chhokᵃnā?	223. How many sons are there in your father's house?
Āj moē̃ ḍhēr dūr hithᵃlō̃	Ham āj bahut ṭahalᵃli hā	Āj moi dūr-lē ghumᵃla-hi	224. I have walked a long way to-day.
Mō̃r kākā-kēr bēṭā ū-kar bahin-sē sādī karᵃlak-hai.	Hamᵃrā chachā-ke bēṭā okᵃrā bahin-sē biāhal bāṭē.	Mōr buṛhā bābā-ke chhokᵃnā-ke biyāh ō-kar bahui-sē hokhait hā.	225. The son of my uncle is married to his sister.
Ghar-mē̃ charᵃkā ghōṛā-kēr khugīr hai.	Ujarᵃkā ghōṛā-ke khogīr ghar-mē̃ bāṭē.	Gorᵃhar ghōḍā khogīr ghar-ke bhitar bariyā.	226. In the house is the saddle of the white horse.
Ū-kar piṭh-mē̃ khugīr-kē rakhā.	Khogīr-kē okᵃrā piṭh par rakkhā (*or* dharā).	Ō-kar piṭh-mē̃ khogīr bā̃dh dēhī.	227. Put the saddle upon his back.
Mō̃ē̃ ū-kar bēṭā-kē bahut (*or* khūb) chābhuk-sē marᵃlī.	Ham okᵃrā bēṭā-kē baṛā kōṛā marᵃli-hā.	Moē̃ ō-kar chhokanᵃwā-kē kē kōrā marᵃla-hi.	228. I have beaten his son with many stripes.
Ū tō̃ṛī upᵃrē garū-man charūthē.	Ū gōrū-kē pahāṛ-ke chōṭī-par charūwᵃtā.	Ū bathāniyā pahāṛ-ke upar charᵃwait-bā.	229. He is grazing cattle on the top of the hill.
Ū gāchh hē̃ṭhē ghōṛā-mē̃ chaṛhal-hai.	Ū gāchh-tar ghōrā-par baiṭhal bāṭē.	Ū ū gachhiyā-ke tar ghoṛᵃwā-mē̃ bēṭhal barᵃhi.	230. He is sitting on a horse under that tree.
Ū-kar bhāī apan bahin-sē ū̃ch hai.	Un-kar bhāi un-kā bahin-sē lāmā bā.	Ō-kar bhaiawā āpan babuiyā-sē ḍhē̃gā barᵃhī.	231. His brother is taller than his sister.
Ū-kar dām aṛhāī rupaiā hai.	Ō-kar dām aṛhāī rupaiyā hā.	Ō-kar dām aḍhāī rupēā	232. The price of that is two rupees and a half.
Mō̃r bāp ū chhoṭᵃkā ghar-mē̃ rāhe-lā.	Hamar bāp ōhī chhoṭᵃkā ghar-mē̃ rahā-lan.	Mōr bapᵃwā ū chhōṭ gharᵃwā-mē̃-rahat barᵃhī.	233. My father lives in that small house.
Ī rupaiā-kē ū-kē dē dēhī	I rupaiyā un-kā dē-dā	Ū rupēawā okᵃrā-kē dēhī	234. Give this rupee to him.
Ū rupaiā-kē ū-kar-sē lē lēhī.	Ū sabh rupaiyā un-kā-sē lē-lā.	Ū rupēā okᵃrā-sē la-lēhī	235. Take those rupees from him.
Ū-kē bēs-sē piṭhī̃ āūr ḍōrā-sē bā̃dhī̃.	Un-kā-kē banā-ke mārā, āur rasā-sē bānhā.	Ōkᵃrā-kē khūb mārah wō rassā-sē bā̃dhah.	236. Beat him well and bind him with ropes.

English.	Maithilī (Darbhanga Brāhmaṇs).	Chhikā-chhikī (Bhagalpur).	Magahī (Gayā).
237. Draw water from the well.	Kūp-sã jal bharū . .	Kūp-sẽ pāni bharâ . .	Kūã-sə̃ pānī bhar-lâ . .
238. Walk before me . .	Ham^a^rā āgū chalū . .	Ham^a^rā āgū chalâ . .	Hamar āgə̄ chalâ . .
239. Whose boy comes behind you?	Ap^a^nek pāchhā̃ ka-kar bālak âbai-achh^i^?	Ka-kar bēṭā toh^a^rā pāchhū awai-chhau?	Tōhar pīchhē kē-kar laṛ^a^kā âwait?
240. From whom did you buy that?	Ō ap^a^ne kak^a^rā-sã kinal? .	Kak^a^rā-sẽ ū mōl lēlâ achh?	Ū kek^a^rā-sə̄ kin^a^lâ-hâ? .
241. From a shopkeeper of the village.	Oh^i^ grāmak banik-sã .	Ōi gāmak baniā-sẽ . .	Gā̃w-ke dukāndār-sē .

Kuṛmālī (Manbhum).	Pāch Parganiā (Ranchi).	Bhojpurī (Shahabad).
Kuā̃-lē pānī lānā . .	Kuā̃-lēk pānī uṭhāiṅg .	Inᵃrā-sē pānī bharā . .
Hāmar chhāmulē bulā .	Mōr āgū chalā . . .	Hamᵃrā sōjhā ghūmā phirā
Kā-kar bēṭā āo-hat tōhar pīchhē ?	Kē-kar chhuwā tōr pēchhū āwatē-hē ?	Tohᵃrā pīchhē kē-kar larikā āwat-bā ?
Kā-kar-pās ū-ṭā kharīd kār-lē ?	Kē-kar ṭhinē ū-ṭā kin rāhā ?	Ū kekᵃrā-sē kinᵃlā-hā ? .
Yah gā̃yēr ēk dōkānī-pās-lē.	Gā̃w-kēr ēk dōkāndār ṭhinē	Gā̃wē-kē mōdī-sē . .

Bhojpurī (North Centre of Saran).	Sarwariā (Basti).	Western Bhojpurī (Jaunpur).
In^{a}rā-sē pānī bharā . .	Kũā-sē pānī bharā . .	Inārē-sē pānī nikāri li-āwā .
Ham^{a}rā sām^{a}nē chalā .	Ham^{a}rē āgē chalā . .	Ham^{a}rē āgē ghūmā . .
Toh^{a}rā pāchhē kē-kar laṛikā āwat bā?	Kē-kar laṛikā toh^{a}rē pīchhē āwat-hai?	Toh^{a}rē pāchhē kē-kar laṛikā āwat-hau?
Tũ ū kek^{a}rā-sē kin^{a}lē rahā?	Kē-sē tū ū mōl lih^{a}lā-hai? .	Ō-kē kē-sē mōl lih^{a}lyā? .
Gā̃w-kā ēk baniyā̃-sē .	Gā̃w-kē ēk dukāndār-sē .	Gā̃waī-kē bech^{a}waiyā-sē .

Nagpuriā (Ranchi).	Madhēsī (Champaran).	Thārū (Champaran).	English.
Kū̃ā-sē pānī ghīch *or* ghīū̃chhī̃.	In^{a}rā-sē pānī bharā . .	Inār-mē̃ pānī bhar . .	237. Draw water from the well.
Hamar āgū chalhī̃ . .	Ham^{a}rā sām^{a}nē ṭah^{a}lā .	Mōr āgē chal . . .	238. Walk before me.
Kē-kar bēṭā tōr pīchhū pīchhū āwathē ?	Kē-kar laṛikā toh^{a}rā pīchhē āw^{a}tā ?	Kā-kar chhok^{a}nā tōr pāchhē āwat baṛh^{a}hi ?	239. Whose boy comes behind you ?
Tōé kē-kar-sē ū-kē kin^{a}lē ? .	Ū kek^{a}rā-sē kin^{a}lā-hā ? .	Ok^{a}rā-kē tū kek^{a}rā-sē kin^{a}lahi ?	240. From whom did you buy that ?
Gāõ-kēr ēk ghur dokāndār-sē.	Ehī gā̃wā̃-ke egō dōkāndār-sē.	Gā̃w māh-ke ēk dokān-sē .	241. From a shopkeeper of the village.

ORIYĀ.

Oṛiyā is the language of Orissa proper, and of the surrounding country. The area over which it is spoken is, roughly speaking, 82,000 square miles, and the number of people who speak it is, in round numbers, nine millions.

Name of the Language.

It is called Oṛiyā, Ōḍrī, or Utkalī, that is to say the language of Ōḍra or Utkala, both of which are ancient names of the country now known as Orissa. It is sometimes incorrectly called Uriya by Europeans, but this name is merely a misspelling of the more correct 'Oṛiyā.' The earliest example of the language which is at present known consists of some Oṛiyā words in an inscription of king Narasiṁha Dēva II, dated 1296 A.D. An inscription of Narasiṁha Dēva IV, dated 1395 A.D., contains several Oṛiyā sentences, which show that the language was then fully developed, and was little different from the modern form of speech either in spelling or in grammar.

Area in which spoken.

The Orissa country is not confined to the Division which now bears that name. It includes a portion of the district of Midnapore in the north, which, together with part of Balasore, was the 'Orissa' of the phrase 'Bengal, Bihar, and Orissa,' met in the regulations framed by the Government in the last decades of the 18th century. Oṛiyā is also the language of most of the district of Singhbhum, belonging to the Division of Chota Nagpur, and of several neighbouring Native States which fall politically within the same division. On the west it is the language of the greater part of the district of Sambalpur and of a small portion of the district of Raipur in the Central Provinces, and also of the number of Native States which lie between these districts and Orissa proper. On the south, it is the language of the north of the Madras district of Ganjam, with its connected Native States, and of the Jeypore Agency of Vizagapatam. It is thus spoken in three Governments of British India, *viz.*, in the Lower Provinces of Bengal, in the Central Provinces, and in the Madras Presidency.

Political Boundaries.

On the east Oṛiyā is bounded by the Bay of Bengal. On the north, its boundary, to the east, coincides with the River Haldi, which here forms at the same time the northern boundary of the Contai sub-division of Midnapore. It then turns north-west along the river Kalighai, as far as the district of Bankura, so as to include in the Oṛiyā-speaking area the four Midnapore police circles of Dantan, Gopiballabhpur, Jhargaon, and Binpur.[1] It next turns back along the eastern boundary of the Singhbhum district, leaving the side of that district which is known as Dhalbhum in possession of Bengali. Thereafter it follows the common boundary of Singhbhum and the Native State of Mayurbhanja as far as the State of Sarai Kala, where it again turns north and crosses the Singhbhum district up to its northern boundary, being stopped by the elevated plateau of Ranchi. It skirts this plateau along the southern boundary of Ranchi district till it meets the State of Jashpur, which it crosses so as to include the southern portion of that State in the Oṛiyā area. It thence turns south, along the boundary between that State and the State of Udaipur, across the States of Raigarh and Sarangarh and the districts of Sambalpur and Raipur.

---

[1] See the map illustrating the meeting ground of Bengali, Oṛiyā, and Bihārī, Vol. V, Pt. I, facing p. 106.

and along the boundary between the Jeypore Agency of Vizagapatam and the State of Bastar to near Tindiki, where it turns east, across Vizagapatam and Ganjam, and joins the sea coast near Barwa, a small port in the latter district.

Linguistic Boundaries.

Oṛiyā is bounded on the north by Bengali and, where the political boundary runs along the south of the Ranchi Plateau, by the form of Bihārī spoken in that district. On the west it is bounded by Chhattīsgaṛhī, and on the south by Telugu.

Oṛiyā not the only vernacular of its area.

Oṛiyā is not the only vernacular spoken in the above area. It is the only Aryan one, but over the whole tract, except the settled portions of Orissa, there are a number of tribes who know no Oṛiyā, and whose only form of speech is some Dravidian or Muṇḍā language. Of these, the speakers of Kandhī are probably the most numerous.

Place of Oṛiyā in reference to other Indo-Aryan languages.

Oṛiyā, with Bengali, Bihārī, and Assamese, forms one of the four speeches which together make up the Eastern Group of the Indo-Aryan languages. Its grammatical construction closely resembles that of Bengali. It has the same weak sense of number, and, as in Bengali, when the plural has to be signified, it must be done with the aid of some noun of multitude. In the case of living rational beings, this noun of multitude is the word *mānē*, which is said to mean literally 'men.' In the case of other nouns it is usually some word meaning 'all.' In the verb, as is also the case in Bengali, the singular of the first and second persons are only used by the uneducated, or when respect is not intended. It has one great advantage over Bengali in the fact that, as a rule, it is pronounced as it is spelt. There are few of those slurred consonants and broken vowels which make Bengali so difficult to the foreigner. Each letter in each word is clearly sounded, and it has been well described as 'comprehensive and poetical, with a pleasant sounding and musical intonation, and by no means difficult to acquire and master.' The Oṛiyā verbal system is at once simple and complete. It has a long array of tenses, but the whole is so logically arranged, and built on so regular a model, that its principles are easily impressed upon the memory. It is particularly noticeable for the very complete set of verbal nouns, present, past, and future, which take the place of the incomplete series of infinitive and gerund which we meet in Bengali, and for want of which that language is sometimes driven to strange straits in order to express the simplest idea. When Bengali wishes to express the idea embodied in what in Latin would be called the Infinitive, it has to borrow the present participle for the occasion, and then has to use it for all tenses, so that the word is used, in the first place, not as a participle, and, in the second place, often not in the present tense. Oṛiyā, on the other hand, simply takes the appropriate Verbal Noun, and declines it in the case which the meaning necessarily requires. As every Infinitive must be some oblique case of a Verbal Noun, it follows that Oṛiyā grammar does not know the so-called 'Infinitive-mood' at all. The veriest beginner does not miss it, and instinctively makes up his 'Infinitive' or his 'Gerund' as he requires it. In this respect Oṛiyā is in an older stage of grammatical development than even Classical Sanskrit, and, among Indo-Aryan Languages, can only be compared with the ancient Sanskrit spoken in Vedic times. This archaic character, both of form and vocabulary, runs through the whole language, and is no doubt accounted for by geographical position. Orissa has ever been an isolated country bounded on the east by the ocean, and on the west by the hilly tracts, inhabited by wild aboriginal tribes and bearing an evil reputation for air and water. On the south, the language is Dravidian, and belongs to an altogether different family, while, on the north, it has seldom had political ties with Bengal.

On the other hand, Orissa has been a conquered nation. For eight centuries it was subject to the kings of Tilinga, and, in modern times, it was for fifty years under the sway of the Bhōslās of Nagpur,[1] both of whom left deep impressions of their rule upon the country. On the language they imposed a number of Telugu and of Marāṭhī words and idioms, respectively, which still survive. These are, so far as we know, the only foreign elements which have intruded themselves into Oṛiyā, except the small vocabulary of English court terms, and a few other English expressions, which English domination and education have brought into vogue.[2]

Dialects.

Oṛiyā is remarkably free from dialectic variation. The well-known saying, which is true all over the north of India, that the language changes every ten *kōs*, does not hold in Orissa. In Orissa proper, *i.e.*, in what is known as the Mughalbandī, which consists of the regulation districts of Cuttack, Puri, and of the southern half of Balasore, the language is one and the same. Purists discover deflections from the recognised standard in Balasore and Cuttack, but these are very slight, and are merely local peculiarities, which are not worthy of the name of dialects. Three localities each claim to be the places where Oṛiyā is spoken in its greatest purity, *viz.*, Cuttack, Khurda in Puri, and Gumsar in the north of Ganjam. Probably Khurda has the greatest claim to being considered the well of Oṛiyā undefiled. Cuttack, especially the town, is to a certain extent affected by Bengalisms, owing to the residence there of a number of Bengalis who have settled in the district for some generations,[3] and the language of Gumsar is said to be affected by the neighbouring Telugu. Further south in Ganjam, the language becomes more and more subject to the influence of the last named language, so that not only is the vocabulary infected, but even the typical Telugu termination *u* is added by the uneducated to the genuine Oṛiyā nouns, and the Telugu pronunciation of *ch* and *j* as if they were *ts* and *z* respectively is adopted universally. On the other hand, the Oṛiyā of North Balasore shows signs of being Bengalised, and, as we cross the boundary between that district and Midnapore, we find at length almost a new dialect. It is not, however, a true dialect. It is a mechanical mixture of corrupt Bengali and of corrupt Oṛiyā. A man will begin a sentence in Oṛiyā, drop into Bengali in its middle, and go back to Oṛiyā at its end. The vocabulary freely borrows from Bengali, and, in North-West Midnapore, even from the Santali which is spoken by the aborigines who there live among their Oṛiyā-speaking neighbours. All this time, however, the language is Oṛiyā in its essence. It has put on strange clothes, like Peter in the 'Tale of a Tub,' but the heart that beats under the strangely embroidered waistcoat is the same. Nevertheless a person speaking this Midnapore Oṛiyā is often unintelligible to a man from Puri, and *vice versâ*. According to Babu Monmohan Chakravarti, this mutual unintelligibility is due, not so much to actual change in the language as to differences of pronunciation. In Bengali, the accent is thrown back as

---

[1] See Beames' *Comparative Grammar*, i, 110.

[2] In the north of Orissa, there is a tendency to use Bengali words and idioms which we do not notice in the South. The influence of the Muhammadan languages of Upper India has been very small in Oṛiyā.

[3] These Bengali settlers in Cuttack and Balasore have developed a curious jargon of their own, their ancestral language being interlarded with Oṛiyā and Hindī expressions. Owing to their frequent use of the word *kerā*, a corruption of the Oṛiyā *kari*, their speech is vulgarly known as *kērā* Bengali. In former times sales of Orissa estates for arrears of land-revenue were held in Calcutta, and the purchasers were frequently Calcutta Bengalis, who became the ancestors of the present-day speakers of this mongrel language, which has in its turn re-acted on the local Oṛiyā.

far as possible, and, to assist this, the succeeding syllables are contracted or slurred over in pronunciation. The same method of pronunciation is affected by the speakers of Midnapore Oṛiyā. In true Oṛiyā, on the other hand, every syllable is distinctly pronounced, and the accent is put on the penultimate syllable if it is a long one, and never further back than the antepenultimate. Thus the pure Oṛiyā *ṭaṅkā'ē* which has the accent on the penultimate syllable, has that accent transferred to the first syllable in Midnapore, all the following syllables being consequently shortened, and the word is pronounced as if it were *ṭáṅke*. In Midnapore, too, the written characters are changed. Sometimes the Oṛiyā character is frankly abandoned, and the language is written in the Bengali character. At other times, when the Oṛiyā character is used, it is changed by an angular shape being given to the curved tops which are so indicative of Oṛiyā writing.

In the west, in Sambalpur, and the Chhattisgarh Feudatory States, there are also slight changes of pronunciation, but not to the same extent as in Midnapore. The pronunciation is said to be 'sharper,' by which it is probably meant that the round sound of *a*, which, in pure Oṛiyā, is something like that of the *o* in *hot*, is gradually approaching the flatter sound of the *a* in *America*, which is the sound that the vowel has in the adjoining Chhattīsgaṛhī. On this point, I have, however, no certain information.

In the extreme north-west, in the Native State of Jashpur, where the Oṛiyā language is spoken it is mixed with the Bihārī spoken in the same State, much as it is mixed with Bengali in Midnapore.

Finally, we come upon a genuine dialect of Oṛiyā in the north-east of the Native State of Bastar. The main language of that State is Halbī, which is a dialect of Marāṭhī. Immediately to its east, the language is Oṛiyā, but in the north-east of the State the Bhatrī dialect, which is a true dialect of Oṛiyā, forms the connecting link between that language and the Marāṭhī Halbī. It is reported to be spoken by 17,387 people. It is written, not in the Oṛiyā character, but in the Dēva-nāgarī used for Marāṭhī.

Oṛiyā literature.

The following account of Oṛiyā literature is taken from Volume I of Mr. Beames' Comparative Grammar, pages 88 and 89:—

'Oṛiyā literature begins with Upēndra-Bhanja, who was a brother of the Rājā of Gumsar, a petty hill-state in the south of Orissa, which even to the present day is celebrated as the home of the purest form of the language. This voluminous poet composed a great number of religious works, many of which are still highly esteemed. His date is not exactly known, but he is supposed to have lived about three hundred years ago. I have a list of thirty of his productions, two of which are rhyming dictionaries, the Śabdamālā and Gītābhidāna; the rest are episodes from the ancient Pauranic legends, erotic poems, and panegyrics on various gods. They are stated to be generally disfigured by gross indecency and childish quibblings about words, endless repetitions, and all sorts of far-fetched rhetorical puzzles. Dīna-kṛushna Dāsa, a poet of the same age, is the author of the Rasakallōḷa, the most celebrated poem in the language; the versification of which is its chief merit, being fluent and graceful. The subject-matter, however, is obscene, and contains very little that is new or original. There are also numerous paraphrases of well-known Sanskrit works, such as Bhagavadgītā, Rāmāyaṇa, Padma Purāṇa, and Lakshmī Purāṇa.

'In modern times a few prose works have been composed of considerable merit, but no originality, being either translations or adaptations from the English or Bengali,

The Oriyās are beginning to wake up, but none of them have yet received sufficient cultivation to make them really good authors. Nor is there much demand for vernacular literature—the Oriyā seldom reads, and not one man in a hundred can write his native language without falling into the grossest errors of spelling and grammar at every turn.'

Population speaking Oriyā in the Oriyā area.

Having completed a rapid survey of the various forms taken by the Oriyā language, we may take stock and see how many people speak it in its proper home. This is shown in the following table:—

PROVINCE.	Name of District or State.		Number of speakers.	REMARKS.
Lower Provinces of Bengal.	Midnapore (mixed dialect) . . .		572,798	
	Cuttack		1,859,623	
	Balasore		950,335	
	Puri		921,180	
	Angul and Khondmals		121,938	
	Orissa Tributary States, *viz.*,—			
	Athgarh	36,429		
	Athmallik . . .	30,805		
	Baramba . . .	32,447		
	Bod	87,867		
	Daspalla	36,975		
	Dhenkanal . . .	228,870		
	Hindol	37,658		
	Keonjhar . . .	201,410		
	Khondpara . . .	62,554		
	Mayurbhanja . . .	242,857		
	Narsingpur . . .	33,648		
	Nayagarh . . .	111,322		
	Nilgiri	48,090		
	Pal Lahara . . .	17,978		
	Ranpur . . .	39,666		
	Talcher	52,535		
	Tigaria	20,179	1,322,190	Revised figures.
	Singhbhum		114,402	
	Carried over		5,862,466	

Province.	Name of District or State.		Number of speakers.	Remarks.
	Brought forward		5,862,466	
	Chota Nagpur Tributary States, *viz.*,—			
	Jashpur (mixed dialect)	10,000		
	Sarai Kala	21,219		
	Kharsawan	8,867		
	Gangpur	133,915		
	Bonai	26,341	200,342	
TOTAL for the Lower Provinces of Bengal			6,062,808	
Central Provinces	Raipur		89,200	
	Sambalpur		595,000	
	Chhattisgarh Feudatory States, *viz.*,—			
	Raigarh	29,000		
	Sarangarh	23,271		
	Bamra	78,653		
	Rairakhol	19,367		
	Bastar (Bhatri Dialect)	17,387		
	Sonpur	187,000		
	Patna	313,000		
	Kalahandi	249,000	916,678	
TOTAL for the Central Provinces			1,600,878	
Madras	Ganjam		797,132	Madras figures are taken from the Census report. As regards the Oṛiyā of Vizagapatam proper, as distinct from the Agency, it is a corrupt mixture of Oṛiyā and Telugu spoken by Chachādis and Pakis scavengers and market-gardeners, all over the district.
	Ganjam Agency		80,994	
	Vizagapatam		27,916	
	Vizagapatam Agency		382,685	
TOTAL for Madras			1,288,727	
GRAND TOTAL for Oṛiyā spoken in the Oṛiyā-speaking area			8,952,413	

We have counted up the number of people who speak Oṛiyā at home, and it now remains to see how many people speak it abroad. As the returns of this Survey do not take cognisance of the languages spoken by small groups of people who are away from their homes, we shall not follow them, but shall, unless it is otherwise stated, take instead the figures of the Census of 1891.

Table showing the number of Speakers of Oṛiyā in places in India other than the area in which that language is a local vernacular.

Province.		Number of speakers.	Remarks.
Assam—			
Sylhet	1,399		
Cachar	5,698		
Sibsagar	1,591		
Lakhimpur	1,715		
Elsewhere	1,468	11,867	Most of these are employed on tea-gardens.
Lower Provinces of Bengal and Feudatories—			
Hooghly	1,711		
Howrah	3,979		
24-Parganas	23,219		The speakers of Oṛiyā in the 24-Parganas are mostly immigrants from Hijlī. The figures for the States of Sarguja and Udaipur are those reported for the Survey, and are not Census ones.
Calcutta	23,899		
Ranchi	3,816		
Manbhum	1,244		
Sarguja	107		
Udaipur	293		
Elsewhere	7,531	65,799	
Berar		...	
Bombay		...	
Burma		3,377	
Central Provinces—			
Bilaspur	568		
Other British Districts . .	1,734		
Bastar	2,138		
Other Feudatory States . .	156	4,596	
Madras—			
Godavari	1,710		
Godavari Agency	249		
Elsewhere	1,477	3,436	
Carried over .		89,075	

Province.	Number of speakers.	Remarks.
Brought forward .	89,075	
North-Western Provinces, Oudh and Native States .	270	
Punjab and Feudatories	4	
Nizam's Dominions	180	
Baroda	...	
Mysore	573	
Rajputana	?	No information available.
Central India	?	Ditto.
Ajmere-Merwara	1	
Coorg	...	
Kashmir	?	No information available.
Total .	90,112	

We thus arrive at the following result—

Total number of people speaking Oṛiyā at home	8,952,413
" " " " " elsewhere in India	90,112
Grand Total of people who speak Oṛiyā in India	9,042,525

AUTHORITIES.

I am not aware of any very old reference to the Oṛiyā Language. The *Sprachmeister*[1] and the *Alphabetum bramhanicum*[1] are both silent concerning it. Yule and Burnell, in *Hobson-Jobson*, give two references to the country of 'Orisa' in works dating 1516 and 1568 respectively, but no similar reference for the name of the language. The earliest account of the language with which I am acquainted is in H. T. Colebrooke's Essay *On the Sanscrit and Prácrit Languages*, in Vol. vii, 1799, of the Asiatic Researches, p. 225.[2] Here there is a brief description of Oṛiyā and its peculiar written character. The following are the more modern works dealing with the language. I know of nothing published on the subject between Colebrooke's essay, and Sutton's grammar published in 1831.

A.—Grammars, Dictionaries, etc.

Sutton, Rev. A.—*An introductory Grammar of the Oriya Language.* Calcutta, 1831.

Sutton, Rev. A.—*An Oriya Dictionary in three Volumes.* Cuttack, 1841. Contains a Grammar, and an Oṛiyā-English and English-Oṛiyā Dictionary.

Lacey, W. C., *Oriya Grammar.* Third Edition, Calcutta, 1861.

Campbell, Sir G.—*The Ethnology of India. Journal* of the Asiatic Society of Bengal, Vol. xxxv. Pt. II. Special Number, 1866. Appendix C. contains a list of words in the Ooryah Language.

Campbell, Sir G.—*Specimens of the Languages of India, including those of the aboriginal Tribes of Bengal, the Central Provinces, and the Eastern Frontier.* Calcutta, 1874. List of Oorya words on pp. 2 and ff.

Miller, Rev. W., and Rughunath Mesra,—*Oriya Dictionary with Oriya Synonyms.* Cuttack, 1868.

[1] *Vide* Vol. V, Pt. I, p. 23.

[2] Reprinted in his *Essays.* Ed. Cowell, Vol. ii, p. 26.

LINGAM LAKSHMIJI,—*A practical Grammar of the Odhra Language.* Calcutta, 1869.

MILLER, W.,—*An English-Oriya Dictionary.* Cuttack, 1873.

BROOKS, W.—*An Oriya and English Dictionary, designed for the use of European and Native Students and Schools.* Cuttack, 1874.

MALTBY, T. J.,—*A practical Handbook of the Uriya or Ōḍiyā Language.* Calcutta, 1874.

HALLAM, E. C. B.,—*Oriya Grammar for English Students.* Calcutta, 1874.

HUTCHINSON, C. W.,—*Specimens of various vernacular Characters passing through the Post Office in India.* Calcutta, 1877. Contains specimens of Uria handwriting.

BROWNE, J. F.,—*An Uriyā Primer in Roman character.* London, 1882.

ARTATRĀṆA SATAPATHI,—*Apabhraṁśabōdhinī.* A Dictionary of *Dēśī* words not derived from Sanskrit. Cuttack, 1891.

PRABHĀKARA BIDYĀRATNA,—*Bhāshādarśa.* An Oṛiyā Grammār in Oṛiyā. Cuttack, 1893.

JAGANNĀTH RĀŌ,—*Saṁkhyipta Utkala Abhidhāna.* An abridged Uriya Dictionary. Cuttack, 1895.

ŚRĪKṚISHṆA MAHĀPĀTRA and AKSHAYA KUMĀRA GHŌSHA,—*Dvibhāshī.* A vocabulary in English and Oṛiyā.

B.—MISCELLANEOUS.

BEAMES, J.,—*On the Relationship of Uriyā to the modern Aryan Languages. Proceedings* of the Asiatic Society of Bengal for 1870, p. 192. Remarks on the above by Rājēndra Lāla Mitra on pp. 201 and ff.

BEAMES, J.,—*The indigenous Literature of Orissa. Indian Antiquary*, Vol. I, 1872, p. 79.

BEAMES, J.,—*Folklore of Orissa. Ib. ib.*, pp. 168, 211.

BEAMES, J.,—*Notes on the Rasa-kallōḷa, an ancient Oṛiyā Poem. Ib. ib.*, pp. 215, 292.

BEAMES, J.,—*A Comparative Grammar of the Modern Aryan Languages of India.* Three Vols. London, 1872-79.

HUNTER, SIR W. W., LL.D.,—*Orissa.* London, 1872. Appendix ix, Vol. ii, pp. 199 and ff. contains an account of the Literature of Orissa.

HOERNLE, F. R.,—*Essays in aid of a comparative Grammar of the Gaurian Languages. Journal* of the Asiatic Society of Bengal, Vol. xli, Pt. I, 1872, p. 120; xlii, Pt. I, 1873, p. 59; xliii, Pt. I, 1874, p. 22.

HOERNLE, F. R.,—*A Grammar of the Eastern Hindī compared with the other Gauḍian Languages.* London, 1880.

CUST, R. N.,—*A sketch of the modern Languages of the East Indies.* London, 1878.

MONMOHAN CHAKRAVARTI,—*Notes on the Language and Literature of Orissa. Journal* of the Asiatic Society of Bengal, Vol. lxvi, Pt. I, 1897, p. 317; lxvii, Pt. I, p. 332.

Written character.

Oṛiyā is encumbered with the drawback of an excessively awkward and cumbrous written character. This character is, in its basis, the same as Dēva-nāgarī, but is written by the local scribes with a stylus on a talipot palm-leaf. These scratches are, in themselves, legible, but in order to make them more plain, ink is rubbed over the surface of leaf and fills up the furrows which form the letters. The palm-leaf is excessively fragile, and any scratch in the direction of the grain tends to make it split. As a line of writing on the long, narrow, leaf is necessarily in the direction of the grain, this peculiarity prohibits the use of the straight top line, or mātrā, which is a distinguishing characteristic of the Dēva-nāgarī character. For this, the Orissa scribe is compelled to substitute a series of curves, which almost surround each letter. It requires remarkably good eyes to read an Oṛiyā printed book, for the exigencies of the printing press compel the type to be small, and the greater part of each letter is this curve, which is the same in nearly all, while the real soul of the character, by which one is distinguished from another, is hidden in the centre, and is so minute, that it is often difficult to see. At first glance, an Oṛiyā book seems to be all curves, and it takes a second look to notice that there is something inside each.[1]

[1] See Beames' *Comparative Grammar*, Vol. i, pp. 62 and ff., and *Notes on the Language and Literature of Orissa* by M. M. Chakravarti, in the *Journal* of the Asiatic Society of Bengal, Vol. lxvi, Pt I, 1897, p. 323.

Alphabet.—The order and number of the vowels and consonants are the same in Oṛiyā as in the other Aryan languages of India. The following is the system of transliteration adopted for this language:—

VOWELS.

ଅ *a* ଆ *ā* ଇ *i* ଈ *ī* ଉ *u* ଊ *ū*
ଋ *ṛu* ୠ *ṛū* ଌ *ḷu* ୡ *ḷū* ଏ *ē* ଐ *ai*
ଓ *ō* ଔ *au* ଅଂ *aṅg* ଅଃ *aḥ*.

CONSONANTS.

କ *ka*	ଖ *kha*	ଗ *ga*	ଘ *gha*	ଙ *ṅa*	
ଚ *cha*	ଛ *chha*	ଜ *ja*	ଝ *jha*	ଞ *ña*	
ଟ *ṭa*	ଠ *ṭha*	ଡ *ḍa*	ଢ *ḍha*	ଣ *ṇa*	
ତ *ta*	ଥ *tha*	ଦ *da*	ଧ *dha*	ନ *na*	
ପ *pa*	ଫ *pha*	ବ *ba*	ଭ *bha*	ମ *ma*	
ଯ *ya*	ୟ *ja*	ର *ra*	ଲ *la*	ଳ *ḷa*	ଵ *wa*
ଶ *śa*	ଷ *sha*	ସ *sa*	ହ *ha*	କ୍ଷ *khya*.	

Although, for the sake of completeness, the vowel signs ୠ *ṛū*, ଌ *ḷu*, and ୡ *ḷū* are included in the list of characters, they are not used at all in ordinary Oṛiyā. They are, however, required in transcribing Sanskrit grammatical works into the Oṛiyā character, and in Sanskrit grammars written for the use of Oṛiyā students.

The forms of the vowels given above are the initials, and are used only at the beginning of a word or syllable; when subjoined to a consonant they take the following forms:—

a (not expressed) *ā* ା, *i* ି, *ī* ୀ, *u* ୁ, *ū* ୂ, *ṛu* ୃ, *ē* େ, *ai* ୈ, *o* ୋ, *au* ୌ.

Thus କ *ka*, କା *kā*, କି or କି *ki*, କୀ *kī*, କୁ *ku*, କୂ *kū*, କୃ *kṛu*, କେ *kē*, କୈ *kai*, କୋ *kō*, କୌ *kau*.

In using these non-initial vowels, there are a few irregularities.

ା *ā* is often combined with the curve of the consonant into one letter, thus ଭା or ଭା *bhā*. When this occurs the form of the consonant is sometimes altered slightly, so as to prevent confusion with other letters. Thus *cha* is ଚ, but *chā* is ଚା or ଚା, the ୍ being added in the second form to prevent confusion with ଗ *ga*. So ର *ra* becomes ରା or ରା *rā*, the tail of ର being transferred to the body of the letter. Similarly ଲ *la* becomes ଲା or ଲା *lā*.

As seen above, the sign, ି for *i* is often combined with the top curve as in କି or କି *ki*. Moreover, this letter sometimes takes the form ି as in ଧି or ଧି *dhi* and ଥି or ଥି *thi*. So the sign ୀ for *ī* is sometimes combined with the consonant, as in ଲୀ or ଲୀ *lī*.

The sign ୁ for *u* is often written ୁ, as in the first specimen.

When the consonant follows another with no vowel between, the two are, as in the Bengali and Dēva-nāgarī alphabets, combined into one compound letter. In most cases the elements of the compound are easily distinguishable କ୍ଲ *kla* ଗ୍ଧ *gdha*; but there are some in which the elements are so altered as to be with difficulty recognised.

The most commonly met with are the following :—

(1) Nasals preceding other consonants :—

ଙ *ṅ* usually takes the forms of two small circles written respectively at the top right-hand corner and at the bottom left-hand corner of the letter with which it is combined.

Thus	with	କ *ka*	it becomes	ଙ୍କ *ṅka*
	,,	ଖ *kha*	,,	ଙ୍ଖ *ṅkha*
	,,	ଗ *ga*	,,	ଙ୍ଗ *ṅga*
But	,,	ଘ *gha*	,,	ଙ୍ଘ *ṅgha*
ଞ *ñ*	,,	ଚ *cha*	becomes	ଞ୍ଚ *ñcha*
	,,	ଛ *chha*	,,	ଞ୍ଛ *ñchha*
	,,	ଜ *ja*	,,	ଞ୍ଜ *ñja*
	,,	ଝ *jha*	,,	ଞ୍ଝ *ñjha*
ଣ *ṇ*	,,	ଟ *ṭa*	,,	ଣ୍ଟ *ṇṭa*
	,,	ଠ *ṭha*	,,	ଣ୍ଠ *ṇṭha*
	,,	ଡ *ḍa*	,,	ଣ୍ଡ *ṇḍa*
	,,	ଢ *ḍha*	,,	ଣ୍ଢ *ṇḍha*
	,,	ଣ *ṇa*	,,	ଣ୍ଣ *ṇṇa*
ନ *n*	,,	ତ *ta*	,,	ନ୍ତ *nta*
	,,	ଥ *tha*	,,	ନ୍ଥ *ntha*
	,,	ଦ *da*	,,	ନ୍ଦ *nda*
	,,	ଧ *dha*	,,	ନ୍ଧ *ndha*
	,,	ନ *na*	,,	ନ୍ନ *nna*
ମ *m*	,,	ପ *pa*	,,	ମ୍ପ *mp*
	,,	ଫ *pha*	,,	ମ୍ଫ *mpha*
	,,	ବ *ba*	,,	ମ୍ବ *mba*
	,,	ଭ *bha*	,,	ମ୍ଭ *mbha*
	,,	ମ *ma*	,,	ମ୍ମ *mma*

(2) Sibilants preceding other consonants :—

ଷ *sh*	with	ଟ *ṭa*	becomes	ଷ୍ଟ *shṭa*
	,,	ଣ *ṇa*	,,	ଷ୍ଣ *shṇa*
ସ *s*	,,	ତ *ta*	,,	ସ୍ତ *sta*
	,,	ଥ *tha*	,,	ସ୍ଥ *stha*
	,,	ପ *pa*	,,	ସ୍ପ or ସ୍ପ *spa*
	,,	ଫ *pha*	,,	ସ୍ଫ or ସ୍ଫ *spha*

(3) Miscellaneous :—

The letter ଯ *ya* when following another consonant is written ୍ୟ *by the side* of the letter with which it is combined. Thus ତ୍ୟ *tya*.

When the letter ୱ *wa* follows another letter it is always pronounced *wa* (elsewhere it is always pronounced *ba*), and is written *under* the letter with which it is combined. Thus ସ୍ୱ *swa*.

When the letter ର *ra* precedes a consonant it is written *above* the letter with which it is combined. Thus ର୍ଜ *rja*. When it follows a consonant, it takes the form and is written below, as in ଦ୍ର *dra*. For *kra* and *tra*, see below.

The compound *stu* takes the altogether anomalous form of ସ୍ତୁ.

କ୍ *k*	with ମ *ma*	becomes	କ୍ମ *kma*	
	,, ର *ra*	,,	କ୍ର or କ୍ର *kra*	
ଚ୍ *ch*	,, ଚ *cha*	,,	ଚ୍ଚ *chcha*	
	,, ଛ *chha*	,,	ଚ୍ଛ *chchha*	
ଜ୍ *j*	,, ଞ *ña*	,,	ଜ୍ଞ *jña* (which is pronounced and transliterated *gyã*).	
ତ୍ *t*	,, ତ *ta*	,,	ତ୍ତ *tta*	
	,, ଥ *tha*	,,	ତ୍ଥ *ttha*	
	,, ପ *pa*	,,	ତ୍ପ *tpa*	
	,, ର *ra*	,,	ତ୍ର or ତ୍ର *tra*	
	,, ସ *sa*	,,	ତ୍ସ *tsa*	
ଦ୍	,, ଦ *da*	,,	ଦ୍ଦ *dda*	
	,, ଧ *dha*	,,	ଦ୍ଧ *ddha*	
	,, ଭ *bha*	,,	ଦ୍ଭ *dbha*	
ପ୍ *p*	,, ତ *ta*	,,	ପ୍ତ *pta*	
ବ୍ *b*	,, ଦ *da*	,,	ବ୍ଦ *bda*	
ମ୍ *m*	,, ହ *ha*	,,	ମ୍ହ *mha* (which is pronounced and transliterated *mbha*).	
ହ୍ *h*	,, ମ *ma*	,,	ହ୍ମ *hma*	

As in Sanskrit and Bengali, the short vowel ଅ *a* when it follows a consonant is not expressed, but is held to be inherent in every consonant unless its absence is specially indicated; for instance କ is *ko*, not *k*. When the absence of ଅ *a* has to be noted, the mark ୍ (called in Oṛiyā *hasanta*) is used; thus କ୍ *k*, as shown in the above list of compound consonants.

The sign ଁ, called *chandra-bindu* (*i.e.*, moon and drop), indicates that a nasal sound is given to the vowel over which it stands as in ଅଛୁଁ *achhũ*, we are. It is represented, in transliteration, by the sign ~ over the nasalized vowel.

The characters for the numerals are these—

୧	୨	୩	୪	୫	୬	୭	୮	୯	୦
1	2	3	4	5	6	7	8	9	0

Pronunciation.—The pronunciation of the vowels is much the same as in Bengali. The short *a* is usually pronounced like the *o* in *hot* or *hod* (not, however, so positively as in Bengali), and at the end of a word, like the second *o* in promote. According to purists, it is pronounced, as in Hindī, like the *u* in *nut*, but even those who teach this admit that it is a counsel of perfection. The main difference in this respect between Oṛiyā and Bengali consists in the pronunciation of the vowel ଋ, corresponding to the Bengali ঋ, and the Sanskrit ऋ. This is pronounced *ru*, not *ṛi*, and will be transliterated *ṛu*. The diphthongs *ai* and *au* are, as in Bengali, pronounced as the *oi* in *oil*, and the *ou* in *house* respectively.[1] I have found no record in Oṛiyā of the broken vowels, *ă*, *ĕ*, and *ŏ* which are so common in Bengali.

There is one most important difference between Oṛiyā and Bengali, which affects nearly every word in the language. In pure Oṛiyā the final *a* at the end of a word is

[1] Mr. Beames compares the sound of the vowels in 'Ould Oirland.'

always pronounced. Thus in Oṛiyā ଘର a house is pronounced *ghara*, or rather *ghŏrō*, but in Bengali ঘর is pronounced *ghar* (*ghŏr*).

As a rule the pronunciation of the consonants is much clearer in Oṛiyā than in Bengali. There is not that elision of a *y* or *v* at the end of a compound consonant, which is so prominent a feature in the latter language.

There is a tendency to pronounce the letters ଚ *cha* and ଛ *chha*, as if they were *tsa* and *tsha* respectively. This is not so marked in Orissa proper, as in the country south of Puri. In Southern Oṛiyā, they are regularly pronounced *tsa* and *tsha* except when the vowel *e*, *ē*, *i*, or *ī* follows, when they have their proper sound. Thus ଚାଲ, go on, is pronounced *tsāla*, but ଚିଠାଉ a letter *chiṭāu*. So ଛତା *tshatā*, an umbrella, but ଛିଡ଼ା *chhiḍā*, standing. Similarly there is a tendency, which becomes more and more accentuated as we go south to pronounce ଜ *ja* and ଝ *jha* as if they were *dza* and *dzha*, but not before *e*, *ē*, *i*, or *ī*. Thus in the south ଜାଲ *dzāla*, a net, ଝାଳ *dzhāḷa*, perspiration; but ଜିଣିବାର *jiṇibāra*, to conquer, and ଝିଅ *jhia*, a daughter.

The pronunciation of the cerebral letters is much more pure than in Bengali or Hindī. ଡ and ଢ are pronounced both as *ḍa* and *ḍha* respectively and as *ṛa* and *ṛha* respectively. In the latter case, a dot is put under them. As we go south the *ṛ* sound disappears. Thus 'it will fall,' is *paṛiba* in Cuttack, but *paḍiba* (something like *pŏrddibō*) in Puri.

In Bengali, the cerebral ণ *ṇa* has altogether lost its true sound, and is pronounced exactly as the dental ন *na*. In Oṛiyā ଣ *ṇa* has preserved its true sound, as a strongly burred *ṇ*, almost like *ṇṛ* pronounced through the nose, as we hear it in Western India, and in correctly pronounced Sanskrit. The best way of giving an idea of its pronunciation is to say that the pronunciation of the Oṛiyā word କଣ *kaṇa* is what would be represented in Bengali by কঁড়ো *kā̃ṛō*.

ଯ, as in other Eastern Indo-Aryan languages, has two sounds that of *ya* and that of *ja*. The second is derivative, just as the English have corrupted 'Yehovah' to 'Jehovah.' When it is pronounced as *ja*, I shall henceforth transliterate it as *ǰa*, so as to distinguish it from ଜ *ja*. When ଯ is pronounced as *ya*, the Oṛiyās affix to it the sign ˛, so that there are practically two letters, *viz.*, ଯ *ǰa* and ୟ *ya*.

The letter ଳ *ḷ*, which is found in the middle or at the end of certain words, is pronounced with the tongue inverted against the palate. We hear it in London in the morning cry of '*milk*,' pronounced '*mulk*' (*u* as in *nut*).

The letter ବ is pronounced as *b* except when in combination with other letters, when it is a clear *w*, as on ସ୍ୱର *swara*, a voice.

Of the three sibilants, ଶ *ś*, and ଷ *sh* are both properly pronounced as the *sh* in 'shell,' and ସ *s* as the *s* in 'sin'; but in practice, they are all three pronounced alike, as the *s* in 'sin,'—thus exactly reversing the Bengali practice.

The letter କ୍ଷ which is properly *ksha*, is pronounced, and transliterated, *khya*.

The compound ଜ୍ଞ *jña* is pronounced *gyā̃*, and is so transliterated.

So also the compound ମ୍ହ *mha* is pronounced *mbha*, and is so transliterated.

It is believed that the following grammatical sketch will enable the reader to understand the interlinear translations of the Oṛiyā specimens which follow.

ORIYĀ SKELETON GRAMMAR.

I.—NOUNS—

(1) Rational beings, and places.—

	Full forms.		*Colloquial forms.*	
	Sing.	Plur.	Sing.	Plur.
Nom.	*purusha*, a man	*purusha-mānē*		*purushē*
Acc.	*purusha-ku*	*purusha-mānaṅku*		*purushaṅku*
Instr.	*purusha-dwārā*,	*purusha-mānaṅka-dwārā*		*purushaṅka-dwārā*
Dat.	*purusha-ku*	*purusha-mānaṅku*		*purushaṅku*
Abl.	*purusha-ṭhāru*	*purusha-mānaṅka-ṭhāru*	*purusha-ṭhū*	*purushaṅka-ṭhū*
Gen.	*purusha-ra*	*purusha-mānaṅka-ra*		*purusha-mānaṅka* / *purushaṅka*
Loc.	*purusha-ṭhārē*	*purusha-mānaṅka-ṭhārē*		*purushaṅka-ṭhārē*
Voc.	*hē purusha*	*hē purusha-mānē*		

In the Instrumental *dēi* or *karttṛuka* may be substituted for *dwārā*.

Instead of *mānē*, nouns of multitude like *dala* or *lōka* may be used to form the plural. When these are added, the noun is declined as if in the Singular.

Nouns ending in *ī*, shorten it in the other cases; as *swāmī*, a husband; Acc. Sing. *swāmi-ku*, Nom. Plur. *swāmi-mānē*.

(2) Irrational beings, and common nouns without life.

ghara, a house.

	Sing.	Plur.	
Nom.	*ghara*	Usually found by adding noun of multitude, such as *sabu*, or *sakaḷa*, all. If *māna* is used, the nom. plur. is *māna*, not *mānē*.	If a noun ends in *ā*, *i*, or *u*, the locative ends only in *rē*; thus *ghōṛā-rē*, on a horse; *pasu-rē*, in a beast. **Expletive additions,**—*ṭa* is added to give emphasis, as in *bāpa-ṭa sē-ṭhārē thilē*, it was *father* who was there. The suffix *ṭā* or *ṭi* has the force of a definite article. The first is used with irrational beings and things, the second with rational beings: thus *ghōṛā-ṭā*, *the* horse, *pilā-ṭi*, *the* child.
Acc.	*ghara*		
Instr.	*ghara-rē*		
Dat.	*ghara-ku*		
Abl.	*ghara-ru* or *gharu*		
Gen.	*ghara-ra*		
Loc.	*gharē*, *ghara-rē*		

Adjectives rarely change for gender. *Tatsamas* in *a* sometimes change the *a* to *ā* or *ī* for the feminine; those in *i* to *inī*; those in *mān* to *matī*; and those in *vān* to *batī*.

II.—PRONOUNS—

	I.		Thou.		He, she.		It.
	Inferior.	Superior.	Inferior.	Superior.	Inferior.	Superior.	
Sing.							
Nom.	*mu*, *mũ*	*āmbhē* [1]	*tu*, *tũ*	*tumbhē* [2]	*sē*	*sē*,	*se*,
Acc. Dat.	*mō-tē*,	*āmbha-ku*	*tō-tē*	*tumbha-ku*	*tāhā-ku*, *tā-ku*	*tāhāṅku*	*tāhā(-ku)* *tā(-ku)*;
Gen.	*mō-ra*, *mōha-ra*	*āmbha-ra*	*tō-ra*	*tumbha-ra*	*tāhā-ra*, *tā-ra*	*tāhāṅka-ra*	*tāhā-ra*, *tā-ra*, / *tahī-ra*
Obl.	*mō*, *mōhō*	*āmbha*	*tō*	*tumbha*	*tāhā*, *tā*	*tāhāṅka*	*tāhā*, *tahī*
Plur.							
Nom.	*mō-mānē* [1]	*āmbhē-mānē*	*tō-mānē* [1]	*tumbhē-mānē*	*sē-mānē*	*sē-mānē*	*sē-sakaḷa*
Obl.	*mō-mānaṅka* [1]	*āmbha-mānaṅka*	*tō-mānaṅka* [1]	*tumbha-mānaṅka*	*sē-mānaṅka*	*sē-mānaṅka*	and so on.

[1] Rare except in the north. [2] Spelt *āmhē*, *tumhē*.

	This.		That.		His (Your) Honour.	Self.
	Thing or Inferior person.	Superior person.	Thing or Inferior person.	Superior person.		
Sing.						
Nom.	*ēhi*, *ēhā*, *ē*	*ēhi*, *ē*	*sēhi*, *sēi*	*sēhi*, *sēi*	*āpaṇa*	*āpē*
Obl.	*ēhā*, *ēhi*	*ēhāṅka*	*sēihi*	*tāhāṅka*	*āpaṇaṅka*	*āpaṇā*
Plur.						
Nom.	*ēhi-sakaḷa*	*ēhi-mānē* / *ē-mānē*	*sēhi-sakaḷa*	*sēhi-mānē* / *sēi-mānē*	*āpaṇa-mānē*	*āpaṇā-mānē*

	Who (Relative)		What (Relative)	Who?		What?
	Inferior.	Superior.		Inferior.	Superior.	
Sing.						
Nom.	*jē*, *jēũ*	*jē*, *jēũ*	*jē*	*kē*, *kiē*, *kēũ*	*kē*, *kiē*, *kēũ*	*ki*, *kaṇa*, *kaüṇa*, *kisa*
Acc. Dat.	*jāhā-ku*	*jāhāṅku*	*jāhā(-ku)*, *jā (-ku)*	*kāhā-ku*	*kāhāṅku*	*kāhā (-ku)*
Gen.	*jāhā-ra*, *jā-ra*	*jāhāṅkara*	*jahī-ra*	*kāhā-ra*, *kā-ra*	*kāhāṅkara*	*kāhī-ra*
Obl.	*jāhā*	*jāhāṅka*	*jahī*	*kāhā*	*kāhāṅka*	*kāhī*
Plur.						
Nom.	*jē-mānē*	*jē-mānē*	*jē-sakaḷa*	*kēũ-mānē*	*kēũ-mānē*	

Kēhi, *kēsē*, Gen., *kāhāri-ra*, or *kāhā-ra*, Obl., *kāhāri*, means 'some one,' 'any one.' Its plural is *kēhi kēhi*, Obl. *kāhāri kāhāri*. *Kichhi*, anything, is regularly declined. So are *amuka* and *thōkāe*, both meaning 'a certain person.' Adjectival pronouns are *ē*, *ēhi*, this; *sē*, *sēhi*, that; *jēũ*, which; and *kēũ*, which?

The same expletive additions are used as in the case of nouns. Thus *tā-ṭa*, that exactly. *Muhī* means 'even I.' *Jē* is often added expletively at the end of a sentence, as in *ārē Baidā*, *chāli āsa*, *bhāta khāiba jē*, Baidā, come along, you will have to eat your rice. The cases are liable to contraction, as in the case of nouns, *e.g.*, *mō-ṭhũ*, from me. The syllable *hā* is often omitted, *e.g.*, *tā-ra* for *tāhā-ra*.

II.—VERBS

General Remarks.—When respect is intended, the plural is used instead of the singular. Colloquially *l* is frequently substituted for *n* and *vice versâ*. Thus *lẽli* for *nẽli*, I took; *luhẽ* for *nuhẽ*, it is not; *paḍhinẽ* for *paḍhilẽ*, they read. Verbs are usually quoted in the genitive of the present verbal noun.

A. Verbs Substantive only. These are not used as Auxiliary Verbs.

1. I am, etc.		2. I become, etc.		I became, etc.		I shall become, etc.		I usually became, etc.	
Sing.	Plur.	Sing.	Plur.	Sing.	Plur.	Sing.	Plur.	Sing.	Plur.
1. *aṭẽ*	*aṭũ*	*hõẽ*	*heũ*	*hẽli*	*hõilũ, hẽlũ*	*hẽbi*	{ *hõibũ* / *hẽbũ* }	*huanti*	*huantu*
2. *aṭu*	*aṭa*	*hõ*	*hua*	*hẽlu*	*hõila, hẽla*	*hẽbu*	{ *hõiba* / *hẽba* }	*huantu*	*huanta*
3. *aṭẽ, aṭaĩ*	*aṭanti*	*huẽ*	*huanti*	*hẽlã*	*hõilẽ, hẽlẽ*	*hẽba*	{ *hoibẽ* / *hẽbẽ* }	*huantã*	*huantẽ*

Imperative, *hõ*, become, *hẽu*, let him become; *hua*, become ye; *hẽuniu*, let them become.

Verbal noun, *hõibã* or *hẽbã*. **Participles**, Present, *hẽu*; Continuative, *huantẽ*; Past, *hõi*; Conditional Past, *hõilẽ, hẽlẽ*.

3. **Negative Verb Substantive**; Pres. Sing. 1, *nuhẽ*; 2, *nuhu*; 3, *nuhẽ*. Plur. 1, *nãhũ*; 2, *nãha*; 3, *nãhãnti*. Past Sing. 1, *nõhili*, and so on. Future, *nõhibi*.

B. Verbs both Substantive and Auxiliary.

1. I am, etc.		2. I remain, etc.		I remained, I was, etc.		I shall remain, etc.		I usually remained, etc.	
Sing.	Plur.	Sing.	Plur.	Sing.	Plur.	Sing.	Plur.	Sing.	Plur.
1. { *achhĩ* / *achhi* }	*achhũ*	*thãẽ*	*thãũ*	*thili*	*thilũ*	*thibi*	{ *thibũ* / *thibã* }	*thãnti*	*thãntu*
2. *achhu*	*achha*	{ *thã* / *thãu* }	*thãa*	*thilu*	*thila*	*thibu*	*thiba*	*thãntu*	*thãnta*
3. { *achhaĩ,* / *achhẽ* / *achhi* }	*achhanti*	*thãẽ*	*thãnti*	*thilã*	*thilẽ*	*thiba*	*thibẽ*	*thãntã*	*thãntẽ*

Imperative, *thã*, remain thou; *thãu*, let him remain; *thãa*, remain ye; *thãuntu*, let them remain.

Verbal noun; *thibã*. **Participles**, Present, *thãu*; Continuative, *thãntẽ*; Past, *thãi*; Conditional Past, *thilẽ*.

C. Finite Verb, *dẽkhibã-ra*, to remain.

Verbal nouns; Present, *dẽkhibã*, seeing (in the future); Past, *dẽkhilã*, seeing (in the past); Present, *dẽkhã*, *dẽkhan*, seeing (in the present).

Participles; Present, *dẽkhu* or *dẽkhũ*, seeing; Continuative, *dẽkhantẽ*, whilst seeing, on seeing, about to see; Past, *dẽkhi*, having seen; Conditional Past, *dẽkhilẽ*, if (I) had seen; Imperfect Past, *dẽkhu-thilẽ*, though (I) was seeing; *dẽkhi-thilẽ*, though (I) had seen; Relative Present, *dẽkhibã*, which is seen, or will be seen; Relative Present Definite, *dẽkhu-thibẽ*, which is being seen; Relative Past, *dẽkhilẽ*, which was seen; Relative Perfect, *dẽkhi-thibẽ*, which has been seen.

Adverbial forms; *dẽkhibã-mãtra*, immediately on seeing; *dẽkhibã-sakãẽ*, in consequence of seeing.

(*a*) Simple Tenses—

Present, I see, etc.		*Past*, I saw, etc.		*Future*, I shall see, etc.		*Habitual Past*, I used to see, or *Present Cond.* (if) I see.		*Imperative*, let me see, etc.	
Sing.	Plur.	Sing.	Plur.	Sing.	Plur.	Sing.	Plur.	Sing.	Plur.
1. { *dẽkhẽ* / *dẽkhi* }	*dẽkhũ*	*dẽkhili*	*dẽkhilũ*	{ *dẽkhibi* / *dẽkhimi* }	{ *dẽkhibũ* / *dẽkhibã* }	*dẽkhanti*	*dẽkhantu*	*dẽkhẽ*	*dẽkhũ*
2. *dẽkhu*	*dẽkha*	*dẽkhilu*	*dẽkhila*	*dẽkhibu*	*dẽkhiba*	*dẽkhantu*	*dẽkhanta*	*dẽkh*	*dẽkha*
3. { *dẽkhẽ* / *dẽkhaĩ* }	*dẽkhanti*	*dẽkhilã*	*dẽkhilẽ*	*dẽkhiba*	*dẽkhibẽ*	*dẽkhantã*	*dẽkhantẽ*	*dẽkhu*	{ *dẽkhantu* / *dẽkhuntu* }

(*b*) Periphrastic tenses—

1. Present Definite; *dẽkhu-achhĩ* or *dẽkhu chhĩ*, I am seeing, and so on; negative, *dẽkhu-nuhẽ*, I am not seeing; Imperfect, *dẽkhu-thili*, I was seeing, and so on; Habitual Imperfect, *dẽkhu-thãẽ*, I usually was seeing, I *then* was seeing; Future Conditional, *dẽkhu-thibi*, I may be seeing, I shall be seeing; Imperfect Conditional, *dẽkhu-thãnti*, (if) I were seeing.
2. Perfect, *dẽkhi-achhĩ* or *dẽkhi-chhĩ*, I have seen; Pluperfect, *dẽkhi-thili*, I had seen; Habitual Pluperfect, *dẽkhi-thãẽ*, I usually had seen, I *then* had seen; Past-Future Conditional, *dẽkhi-thibi*, I may have seen, I shall have seen; Pluperfect Conditional, *dẽkhi-thãnti*, (if) I had seen.

D. Irregular Verbs, *jibã-ra*, to go. Pres., *jãẽ*, etc., like *thãẽ*: Past, *gali*; Future, *jimi* or *jibi*. Verb. noun, *jibã*; Pres. part., *jãu*; Past Part., *jãi*; Contin. part., *jãntẽ*; Cond. part., *galẽ*.

Hẽbã-ra and *thibã-ra* are given above.

Dẽbã-ra, to give, has Present Sing. 1, *dẽaĩ*; 2, *dẽu*; 3, *diẽ, dia*; Plur. 1, *dẽũ*; 2, *diya*; 3, *diyanti*; Past, *dẽli*; Fut., *dẽbi*; Habit. past, *diyanti*. *Nẽbã-ra*, to take, is declined in the same way.

Piibã-ra, to drink, has Present Sing. 1, *piyi*; 2, *piyu*; 3, *piyẽ*; Plur., 1, *piyũ*; 2, *piya*; 3, *piyanti*.

The verbs *karibã-ra*, to do, *māribã-ra*, to strike, and *āsibã-ra*, to come, usually drop the last consonant of the root in the Past Tense and the Conditional Participle. Thus *kali* or *karili*, I did, *kalẽ*, if (I) had done; *māili* or *mārili*, I struck, *māilẽ* or *mārilẽ*, if (I) had struck; *aili* (not *ãili*) or *ãsili*, I came; *ailẽ* or *ãrilẽ*, if (I) had come.

E. Causal Verbs, add *ã* to the root, as *dẽkhãẽ*, I cause to see. Roots ending in *ã* change that *ã* to *u*. Thus *khãi*, I eat, *khuãi*, I cause to at. The causal of *dẽbã-ra*, to give, is *diyãibã-ra*; of *nẽbã-ra*, to take, *niyãibã-ra*; and of *piibã-ra*, to drink, *piyãibã-ra*.

F. Passive Voice. Formed by conjugating the present Verbal noun in *ã*, with *jibã-ra*, to go. Thus, *dẽkhã jãi*, I am seen.

G. Expletive additions. The letter *ta* added gives emphasis, *e.g.*, *achhi-ta*, I am indeed. *ṭi* [illegible] and *ṇi* are added without affecting the meaning much, as in *tu jibu-ṭi*, will you go; *sẽ galẽ-ṇi*, he has gone already.

H. Examples of the use of the Relative Participles—

1. *mu-dẽbã dhãna*, the corn which I give.
2. *ghushuri-khãu-thibẽ tashu*, the husks which the swine are eating.
3. *mu-dẽlã ṭaṅkã*, the rupee which I gave.
4. *mu-dẽi-thibẽ ṭaṅkã*, the rupee which I have given.

The form of Oṛiyā spoken in the neighbourhood of Cuttack is usually considered to be the standard dialect of the language, though its claim is not universally admitted. Probably the purest Oṛiyā is spoken more to the south-west near Khurda.

The following two specimens come from Cuttack. The first is given in facsimile as well as in type, as a good example of clear Oṛiyā current hand-writing. The second is given in Oṛiyā type. Each is accompanied by a transliteration and a translation. The language is that shown in the preceding grammar. The only form in it which is not explained therein, nor, so far as I am aware, in any Oṛiyā Grammar is the word *jāuṇu*, having gone. We may also note *naïlā*, he did not come, in the second specimen. A good example of the Relative Participle is *ghushuri khāu-thibā tashu*, literally, the swine-being-eaten husks, *i.e.*, the husks which the swine are eating.

The second specimen is one of the most popular songs of Orissa, entitled the *kēśaba-kōili*, of Markaṇḍa-dāsa, which, according to Babu Monmohan Chakravartti, is probably more than three hundred years old, and is still taught to children in the schools.

III.—VERBS

General Remarks.—When respect is intended, the plural is used instead of the singular. Colloquially *l* is frequently substituted for *n* and *vice versâ*. Thus *lēli* for *nēli*, I took ; *luhẽ* for *nuhẽ*, it is not ; *paḍhinē* for *paḍhilē*, they read. Verbs are usually quoted in the genitive of the present verbal noun.

A. Verbs Substantive only. These are not used as Auxiliary Verbs.

1. I am, etc.		2. I become, etc.		I became, etc.		I shall become, etc.		I usually became, etc.	
Sing.	Plur.	Sing.	Plur.	Sing.	Plur.	Sing.	Plur.	Sing.	Plur.
1. *aṭē*	*aṭũ*	*hōē*	*hēũ*	*hēli*	*hōilũ, hēlũ*	*hēbi*	{ *hōībũ* / *hēbũ*	*huanti*	*huantu*
2. *aṭu*	*aṭa*	*hō*	*hua*	*hēlu*	*hōila, hēla*	*hēbu*	{ *hōība* / *hēba*	*huantu*	*huanta*
3. *aṭē, aṭaī*	*aṭanti*	*huē*	*huanti*	*hēlā*	*hōilē, hēlē*	*hēba*	{ *hoibē* / *hēbē*	*huantā*	*huantē*

Imperative, *hō*, become, *hēu*, let him become ; *hua*, become ye ; *hēuntu* let them become.

Verbal noun, *hōibā* or *hēbā*. **Participles,** Present, *hēu* ; Continuative, *huantē* ; Past, *hōi* ; Conditional Past, *hōilē, hēlē*.

3. **Negative Verb Substantive** ; Pres. Sing. 1, *nuhē* ; 2, *nuhu* ; 3, *nuhẽ*. Plur. 1, *nāhũ* ; 2, *nāha* ; 3, *nāhānti*. Past Sing. 1, *nōhēli*, and so on. Future, *nōhibi*.

B. Verbs both Substantive and Auxiliary.

1. I am, etc.		2. I remain, etc.		I remained, I was, etc.		I shall remain, etc.		I usually remained, etc.	
Sing.	Plur.	Sing.	Plur.	Sing.	Plur.	Sing.	Plur.	Sing.	Plur.
1. { *achhī* / *achhi* }	*achhũ*	*thāē*	*thāũ*	*thili*	*thilũ*	*thibi*	{ *thibũ* / *thibē* }	*thānti*	*thāntu*
2. *achhu.*	*achha*	{ *thā* / *thāu* }	*thāa*	*thilu*	*thila*	*thibu*	*thiba*	*thāntu*	*thānta*
3. { *achhaī,* / *achhē* / *achhi* }	*achhanti*	*thāē*	*thānti*	*thilā*	*thilē*	*thiba*	*thibē*	*thāntā*	*thāntē*

Imperative, *thā*, remain thou ; *thāu*, let him remain ; *thāa*, remain ye ; *thāuntu*, let them remain.

Verbal noun ; *thibā*. **Participles,** Present, *thāu* ; Continuative, *thāntē* ; Past, *thāi* ; Conditional Past, *thilē*.

C. Finite Verb, *dēkhibā-ra*, to remain.

Verbal nouns ; Present, *dēkhibā*, seeing (in the future) ; Past, *dēkhilā*, seeing (in the past) ; Present, *dēkhā*, *dēkhan*, seeing (in the present).

Participles ; Present, *dēkhu* or *dēkhũ*, seeing ; Continuative, *dēkhantē*, whilst seeing, on seeing, about to see ; Past, *dēkhi*, having seen ; Conditional Past, *dēkhilē*, if (I) had seen ; Imperfect Past, *dēkhu-thilē*, though (I) was seeing ; *dēkhi-thilē*, though (I) had seen ; Relative Present, *dēkhibā*, which is seen, or will be seen ; Relative Present Definite, *dēkhu-thibā*, which is being seen ; Relative Past, *dēkhilā*, which was seen ; Relative Perfect, *dēkhi-thibā*, which has been seen.

Adverbial forms ; *dēkhibā-mātre*, immediately on seeing ; *dēkhibā-sakāē*, in consequence of seeing.

(*a*) Simple Tenses—

Present, I see, etc.		*Past*, I saw, etc.		*Future*, I shall see, etc.		*Habitual Past*, I used to see, or *Present Cond.* (if) I see.		*Imperative*, let me see, etc.	
Sing.	Plur.	Sing.	Plur.	Sing.	Plur.	Sing.	Plur.	Sing.	Plur.
1. { *dēkhī* / *dēkhi* }	*dēkhũ*	*dēkhili*	*dēkhilũ*	{ *dēkhibi* / *dēkhimi*	{ *dēkhibũ* / *dēkhibā*	*dēkhanti*	*dēkhantu*	*dēkhē*	*dēkhũ*
2. *dēkhu*	*dēkha*	*dēkhilu*	*dēkhila*	*dēkhibu*	*dēkhiba*	*dēkhantu*	*dēkhanta*	*dēkh*	*dēkha*
3. { *dēkhē* / *dēkhaī* }	*dēkhanti*	*dēkhilā*	*dēkhilē*	*dēkhiba*	*dēkhibē*	*dēkhantā*	*dēkhantē*	*dēkhu*	{ *dēkhantu* / *dēkhuntu*

(*b*) Periphrastic tenses—

1. Present Definite ; *dēkhu-achhī* or *dēkhu chhī*, I am seeing, and so on ; negative, *dēkhu-nuhē*, I am not seeing ; Imperfect, *dēkhu-thili*, I was seeing, and so on ; Habitual Imperfect, *dēkhu-thāē*, I usually was seeing, I *then* was seeing ; Future Conditional, *dēkhu-thibi*, I may be seeing, I shall be seeing ; Imperfect Conditional, *dēkhu-thānti*, (if) I were seeing.
2. Perfect, *dēkhi-achhī* or *dēkhi-chhī*, I have seen ; Pluperfect, *dēkhi-thili*, I had seen ; Habitual Pluperfect, *dēkhi-thāē*, I usually had seen, I *then* had seen ; Past-Future Conditional, *dēkhi-thibi*, I may have seen, I shall have seen ; Pluperfect Conditional, *dēkhi-thānti*, (if) I had seen.

D. Irregular Verbs, *jibā-ra*, to go. Pres., *jāē*, etc., like *thāē* : Past, *gali* ; Future, *jimi* or *jibi*. Verb. noun, *jibā* ; Pres. part., *jāu* ; Past Part., *jāi* ; Contin. part., *jāntē* ; Cond. part., *galē*.

Hēbā-ra and *thibā-ra* are given above.

Dēbā-ra, to give, has Present Sing. 1, *dēuī* ; 2, *dēu* ; 3, *diē, dia* ; Plur. 1, *dēũ* ; 2, *diya* ; 3, *diyanti* ; Past, *dēli* ; Fut., *dēbi* ; Habit. past, *diyanti*. *Nēbā-ra*, to take, is declined in the same way.

Piibā-ra, to drink, has Present Sing. 1, *piyi* ; 2, *piyu* ; 3, *piyē* ; Plur., 1, *piyũ* ; 2, *piya* ; 3, *piyanti*.

The verbs *karibā-ra*, to do, *māribā-ra*, to strike, and *āsibā-ra*, to come, usually drop the last consonant of the root in the Past Tense and the Conditional Participle. Thus *kali* or *karilē*, I did, *kalē*, if (I) had done ; *māili* or *mārili*, I struck, *māilē* or *mārilē*, if (I) had struck ; *aīli* (not *āili*) or *āsili*, I came ; *ailē* or *āsilē*, if (I) had come.

E. Causal Verbs, add *ā* to the root, as *dēkhāē*, I cause to see. Roots ending in *ā* change that *ā* to *u*. Thus *khāi*, I eat, *khuāi*, I cause to eat. The causal of *dēbā-ra*, to give, is *diyāibā-ra* ; of *nēbā-ra*, to take, *niyāibā-ra* ; and of *piibā-ra*, to drink, *piyāibā-ra*.

F. Passive Voice. Formed by conjugating the present Verbal noun in *ā*, with *jibā-ra*, to go. Thus, *dēkhā jāi*, I am seen.

G. Expletive additions. The letter *ta* added gives emphasis, *e.g.*, *achhi-ta*, I am indeed. *Ṭi* and *ṇi* are added without affecting the meaning much, as in *tu jibu-ṭi*, will you go ; *sē galā-ṇi*, he has gone already.

H. Examples of the use of the Relative Participle—

1. *mu-dēbā dhāna*, the corn which I give.
2. *ghushuri-khāu-thibā tasha*, the husks which the swine are eating.
3. *mu-dēlā ṭankā*, the rupee which I gave.
4. *mu-dēi-thibā ṭankā*, the rupee which I have given.

The form of Oṛiyā spoken in the neighbourhood of Cuttack is usually considered to be the standard dialect of the language, though its claim is not universally admitted. Probably the purest Oṛiyā is spoken more to the south-west near Khurda.

The following two specimens come from Cuttack. The first is given in facsimile as well as in type, as a good example of clear Oṛiyā current hand-writing. The second is given in Oṛiyā type. Each is accompanied by a transliteration and a translation. The language is that shown in the preceding grammar. The only form in it which is not explained therein, nor, so far as I am aware, in any Oṛiyā Grammar is the word *jāuṇu*, having gone. We may also note *naïlā*, he did not come, in the second specimen. A good example of the Relative Participle is *ghushuri khāu-thibā tashu*, literally, the swine-being-eaten husks, *i.e.*, the husks which the swine are eating.

The second specimen is one of the most popular songs of Orissa, entitled the *kēśaba-kōili*, of Markaṇḍa-dāsa, which, according to Babu Monmohan Chakravartti, is probably more than three hundred years old, and is still taught to children in the schools.

[No. I.]

INDO-ARYAN FAMILY. EASTERN GROUP.

ORIYĀ.

STANDARD DIALECT. (CUTTACK DISTRICT.)

SPECIMEN I.

ଜଣାକର ଦୁଇ ପୁଅ ଥିଲେ । ତାଙ୍କ ମଧ୍ୟରେ ଯେ ସନ୍ତାନରେ ସାନ ଥିଲା ଆପଣା ବାପକୁ କହିଲା ବାପା, ମୋ ଭାଗରେ ଯେଉଁ ସମ୍ପତ୍ତି ପଡ଼ିବ ତାହା ମୋତେ ଦିଅ । ବାପ ଆପଣା ବିଷୟକୁ ସେମାନଙ୍କ ଭିତରେ ବାଣ୍ଟି ଦେଲା । କେତେ ଦିନ ନ ଯାଉଣୁ ସାନ ପୁଅ ନିଜର ସର୍ବସ୍ୱ ଘେନି କୌଣସି ଦୂର ଦେଶକୁ ଗଲା ସେଠାରେ ବଦଖେୟାଲରେ ସେ ସବୁ ଉଡ଼ାଇ ଦେଲା । ତାହାର ସବୁ ସରିଗଲାରୁ ସେ ଦେଶରେ ବଡ଼ ଅକାଳ ପଡ଼ିଲା, ତେଣୁ ତାହାର ବଡ଼ କଷ୍ଟ ହେଲା । ତହିଁରେ ସେ ସେଠାର ଜଣେ ନଗରବାସୀର ଆଶ୍ରା ନେଲା । ନଗରବାସୀ ତାକୁ ଘୁଷୁରିମାନ ଚରାଇବା ପାଇଁ ବିଲକୁ ପଠାଇଲା । ସେ ସେଠାରେ ଘୁଷୁରିମାନ ଖାଉଥିବା ଚୋପାରେ ପେଟ ପୁରାଇବାକୁ ଇଚ୍ଛା କରୁଥିଲା, ମାତ୍ର ତାହା ତାକୁ କେହି ଦେଉ ନାହିଁ । ଯେତେବେଳେ ତାହାର ଚେତା ହେଲା ସେ ଭାବିଲା ମୋହୋ ବାପର କେତେ ମୂଲିଆ ଖାଇ ପିଇ ବାଣ୍ଟି ଦେଇ ଅଛନ୍ତି ମୁଁ ଭୋକରେ ମରୁଅଛି । ମୁଁ ଉଠି ବାପ ପାଖକୁ ଯିବି ଓ ତାଙ୍କୁ କହିବି, ବାପା, ମୁଁ ତୁମ୍ଭ ଆଗରେ ଈଶ୍ୱରଙ୍କ ଠାରେ ଦ୍ରୋହ କରିଅଛି ଓ ତୁମ୍ଭର ପୁଅ ନାମ ଯୋଗ୍ୟ ନୁହେଁ । ମୋତେ ମୂଲିଆ କରି ରଖ । ସେଥି ଉତ୍ତାରୁ ସେ ଉଠି ବାପ ପାଖକୁ ଗଲା । ବାପ ତାକୁ ଦୂରରୁ ଦେଖି ଦୟା କଲେ । ଦୌଡ଼ି ଯାଇଁ ତାହାର

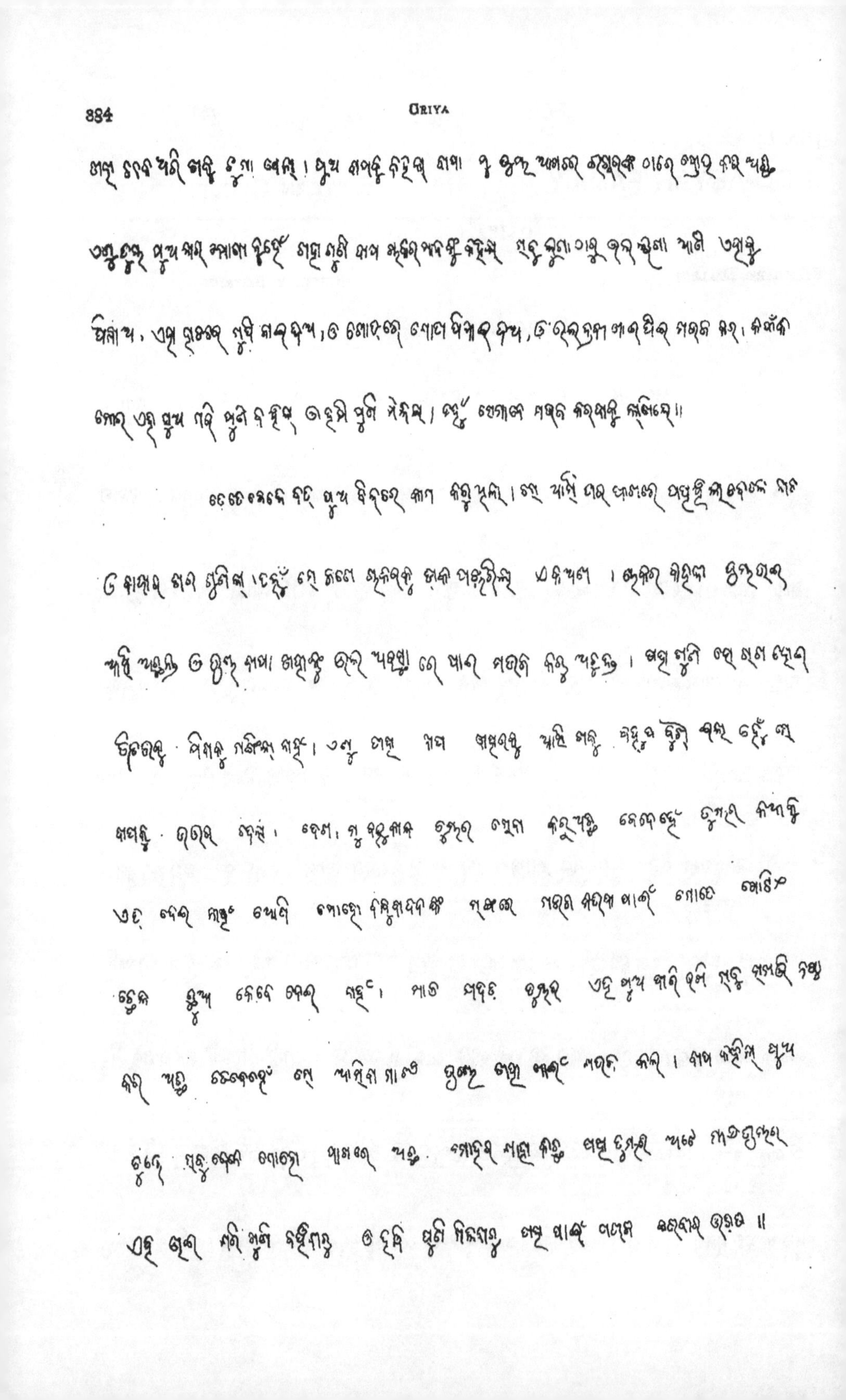

[illegible]

[illegible]

[No. 1.]

INDO-ARYAN FAMILY. EASTERN GROUP.

ORIYĀ.

STĀNDARD DIALECT. (CUTTACK DISTRICT.)

SPECIMEN I.

ଜଣକର ଦୁଇ ପୁଅ ଥିଲେ । ତାଙ୍କ ମଧ୍ୟରେ ଯେ ବୟସରେ ସାନ ସେ ଆପଣା ବାପକୁ କହିଲା, ବାପା, ମୋ ବାଣ୍ଟରେ ଯେଉଁ ସମ୍ପତ୍ତି ପଡ଼ିବ ତାହା ମୋତେ ଦିଅ । ବାପ ଆପଣା ବିଷୟକୁ ସେମାନଙ୍କ ଭିତରେ ବାଣ୍ଟି ଦେଲା । ବେଶି ଦିନ ନ ଯାଉଣୁ ସାନ ପୁଅ ନିଜର ସର୍ବସ୍ୱ ନେଇ କୌଣସି ଦୂରଦେଶକୁ ଚାଲି ଯାଇ ବଦଖେୟାଲିରେ ସେ ସବୁ ଉଡ଼ାଇ ଦେଲା । ତାହାର ବିଷୟ ଯାକ ସରଗଲାରୁ ସେ ଦେଶରେ ବଡ଼ ଅକାଳ ପଡ଼ିଲା, ତହୁଁ ତାହାର ବଡ଼ କଷ୍ଟ ହେଲା । ତହୁଁରେ ସେ ଯାଇ ସେଠାର ଜଣେ ନଗରବାସୀର ଆଶ୍ରା ନେଲା । ନଗରବାସୀ ତାକୁ ଘୁସୁରିପଲ ଚରାଇବାପାଇଁ ବିଲକୁ ପଠାଇଲା । ସେ ଭୋକରେ ଘୁସୁରି ଖାଉଥିବା ଚଷୁ ଖାଇ ପେଟ ପୂରାଇବାକୁ ଇଚ୍ଛା କରି ଥିଲା, ମାତ୍ର ତାହା ତାକୁ କେହି ଦେଲେ ନାହିଁ । ଯେତେବେଳେ ତାହାର ଚେତା ହେଲା ସେ ଭାବିଲା ମୋହୋ ବାପର କେତେ ମୂଲିଆ ଖାଇକରି ବାଣ୍ଟି ଦେଉ ଅଛନ୍ତି ମୁ ଭୋକରେ ମରୁ ଅଛି, ମୁ ଉଠି ବାପ ପାଖକୁ ଯିବି ଓ ତାଙ୍କୁ କହିବି, ବାପା, ମୁ ତୁମ୍ଭ ଆଗରେ ଈଶ୍ୱରଙ୍କଠାରେ ଦ୍ରୋହ କରି ଅଛି, ଓ ତୁମ୍ଭର ପୁଅନାଉ ଯୋଗ୍ୟ ନୁହେଁ । ମୋତେ ମୂଲିଆ କରି ରଖ । ସେଥି ଉତ୍ତାରୁ ସେ ଉଠି ବାପ ପାଖକୁ ଗଲା । ବାପ ତାକୁ ଦୂରରୁ ଦେଖି ଦୟା କଲା, ପୁଣି ଧାଁଇ ଯାଇ ତାହା ବେକ ଧରି ତାକୁ ଚୁମ୍ବା ଦେଲା । ପୁଅ ବାପକୁ କହିଲା ବାପା ମୁ ତୁମ୍ଭ ଆଗରେ ଈଶ୍ୱରଙ୍କଠାରେ ଦ୍ରୋହ କରି ଅଛି, ଏଣୁ ତୁମ୍ଭ ପୁଅନାଉ ଯୋଗ୍ୟ ନୁହେଁ । ତାହା ଶୁଣି ବାପ ଚାକରମାନଙ୍କୁ କହିଲା ସବୁ ଲୁଗା ଠାରୁ ଭଲ ଲୁଗା ଆଣି ଏହାକୁ ପିନ୍ଧାଅ, ଏହା ହାତରେ ମୁଦି ନାଇ ଦିଅ ଓ ଗୋଡ଼ରେ ଯୋତା ପିନ୍ଧାଇ ଦିଅ, ଓ ଭଲ ଦ୍ରବ୍ୟ ଖାଇ ପିଇ ମଉଜ କର, କଅଁାକି ମୋର ଏହି ପୁଅ ମରି ପୁଣି ବଞ୍ଚିଲା ଓ ହଜି ପୁଣି ମିଳିଲା । ତହୁଁ ସେମାନେ ମଉଜ କରିବାକୁ ଲାଗିଲେ ॥

ସେତେବେଳେ ବଡ଼ ପୁଅ ବିଲରେ କାମ କରୁଥିଲା । ସେ ଆସି ଘର ପାଖରେ ପହଞ୍ଚିଲା ବେଳେ ନାଚ ଓ ବାଜଣାର ଶବ୍ଦ ଶୁଣିଲା । ତହୁଁ ସେ ଜଣେ ଚାକରକୁ ଡାକି ପଚାରିଲା ଏ କଅଣ । ଚାକର କହିଲା ତୁମ୍ଭ ଭାଇ ଆସି ଅଛନ୍ତି ଓ ତୁମ୍ଭ ବାପା ତାହାଙ୍କୁ ଭଲ ଅବସ୍ଥାରେ ପାଇ ମଉଜ କରୁ ଅଛନ୍ତି । ତାହା ଶୁଣି ସେ ରାଗ ହୋଇ ଭିତରକୁ ଯିବାକୁ ମନିଲା ନାହିଁ । ଏଣୁ ତାହା ବାପ ବାହାରକୁ ଆସି ତାକୁ ବହୁତ ବୁଝାଇଲା । ତହୁଁ ସେ ବାପକୁ ଉତ୍ତର ଦେଲା । ଦେଖ, ମୁ ବହୁକାଳ ତୁମ୍ଭର ସେବା କରୁ ଅଛି, କେବେହେଁ ତୁମ୍ଭର କଥାକୁ ଏଡ଼ି ଦେଇ ନାହିଁ, ତଥାପି ମୋହୋ ବନ୍ଧୁବାନ୍ଧବଙ୍କ ସଙ୍ଗରେ ମଉଜ କରିବା ପାଇଁ ମୋତେ ଗୋଟିଏ ଛେଳି ଛୁଆ କେବେ ଦେଇ ନାହିଁ । ମାତ୍ର ଯେତେ ତୁମ୍ଭର ଏହି ପୁଅ ଦାରି ରଖି ସବୁ ସମ୍ପତ୍ତି ନଷ୍ଟ କରି ଅଛି ସେତେବେଳେ ସେ ଆସିବା ମାତ୍ରେ ତୁମ୍ଭେ ତାହା ପାଇଁ ମଉଜ କଲ । ବାପ କହିଲା, ପୁଅ ତୁମ୍ଭେ ସବୁବେଳେ ମୋହୋ ପାଖରେ ଅଛ, ମୋହର ଯାହା ଅଛି ତାହା ତୁମ୍ଭର ଅଟେ, ମାତ୍ର ତୁମ୍ଭର ଏହି ଭାଇ ମରି ପୁଣି ବଞ୍ଚିବାରୁ ଓ ହଜି ପୁଣି ମିଳିବାରୁ ତାହା ପାଇଁ ମଉଜ କରିବାର ଉଚିତ ॥

INDO-ARYAN FAMILY. EASTERN GROUP.

OṚIYĀ.

STANDARD DIALECT. (CUTTACK DISTRICT.)

SPECIMEN I.

TRANSLITERATION AND TRANSLATION.

Jaṇa-ka-ra dui pua thilā. Tāṅka madhya-rē jē bayasa-rē
Man-one-of two sons were. Them midst-in that age-in

sāna sē āpaṇā bāpa-ku kahilā, 'bāpā, mō bāṇṭa-rē jēū
young-one he his-own father-to said, 'father, my share-in what

sampatti paṛiba, tāhā mōtē dia.' Bāpa āpaṇā bishaya-ku
property will-fall, that to-me give.' The-father his-own property

sē-mānaṅka-bhitarē bāṇṭi dēlā. Bēsi dina na jā-uṇu sāna
them-amongst dividing gave. Many days not having-gone the-younger

pua nija-ra sarbbasva ghēni kauṇasi dūra-dēśa-ku chāli-jāi,
son himself-of all-things taking a-certain distant-land-to going-going,

bada-khēyāli-rē sē sabu uṛāi dēlā. Tāhā-ra bishaya-jāka
bad-mind-in that all wasting gave. His property-all

sari-galā-ru, sē dēśa-rē baṛa akāḷa paṛilā; tahū
spent-on-having-gone, that land-in a-great famine fell; therefrom

tāhā-ra baṛa kashṭa hēlā. Tahī-rē sē jāi sē-ṭhā-ra
his great want became. Thereupon he going that-place-of

jaṇē nagara-bāsī-ra āśrā nēlā. Nagara-bāsī tā-ku
one-person town-resident-of shelter took. The-town-resident him

ghushuri-pala charāibā pāĩ bila-ku paṭhāilā. Sē bhōka-rē
swine-flock grazing for the-field-to sent. He hunger-in

ghushuri khāu-thibā tashu khāi pēṭa purāibā-ku ichchhā
(by-the)-swine being-eaten husks eating belly to-fill wish

kari-thilā, mātra tāhā tā-ku kēhi dēlā nāhĩ. Jētēbēḷē tāhā-ra
made, but that him-to any-one gave not. When his

chētā hēlā, sē pāñchilā, 'mōhō bāpa-ra kētē muliā
senses happened, he thought, 'my father's how-many labourers

khāi-kari bāṇṭi dēu-achhanti, mu bhōka-rē maru-achhi. Mu
eating-doing dividing giving-are, I hunger-in dying-am. I

uṭhi bāpa-pākha-ku jibi, ō tāṅku kahibi, "bāpā, mu
rising father-side-to will-go, and to-him will-say, "father, I

tumbha āga-rē Īśvaraṅka-ṭhārē drōha kari-achhi, ō tumbha-ra
your presence-in God-of-before sin done-have, and your

pua-nā-ra jōgya nuhẽ, mōtē muliā kari rakha." ' Sēthi-uttāru
son-name-of fit am-not, me labourer making keep." ' That-after

sē uṭhi bāpa-pākha-ku galā. Bāpa tā-ku dūra-ru dēkhi
he rising father-side-to went. Father him distance-from seeing

dayā kalā, puṇi dhā̃i jāi tāhā bēka dhari tā-ku chumā
pity did, and running going his neck holding him-to kiss

dēlā. Pua bāpa-ku kahilā, 'bāpā, mu tumbha āga-rē
gave. The-son the-father-to said, 'father, I your presence-in

Īśvaraṅka-ṭhārē drōha kari-achhi, ēṇu tumbha pua-nā-ra jōgya
God-of-before sin done-have, hence your son-name-of fit

nuhẽ.' Tāhā śuṇi bāpa chākara-mānaṅku kahilā, 'sabu
I-am-not.' That hearing the-father the-servants-to said, 'all

lugā-ṭhāru bhala lugā āṇi ēhā-ku pindhāa; ēhā
cloth-from good cloth bringing this(-person)-to put-on; this-(person's)

hāta-rē mudi nāi dia, ō gōṛā-rē jōtā pindhāi dia,
hand-on ring putting give, and feet-on shoes putting-on give,

ō bhala drabya khāi pii maüja kara; kipā̃ki
and good thing eating drinking merry-making do; because

mōra ēhi pua mari, puṇi bañchilā; ō haji, puṇi miḷilā.'
my this son having-died, again survived; and being-lost, again was-got.'

Tahũ sē-mānē maüja karibā-ku lāgilē.
Thereupon they merry-making doing-to began.

Tētēbēḷē baṛa pua bila-rē kāma karu-thilā. Sē āsi
At-that-time the-elder son in-the-field work doing-was. He coming

ghara-pākha-rē pahañchilā-bēḷē, nācha ō bājā-ra śabda śuṇilā.
house-side-to arriving-time-at, dancing and music-of sound heard.

Tahũ sē janē chākara-ku ḍāki pachārilā, 'ē kaāṇa?'
Thereupon he a-person servant calling asked, 'this what?'

Chākara kahilā, 'tumbha bhāi āsi-achhanti, ō tumbha bāpā
The-servant said, 'your brother come-has, and your father

tāhāṅ-ku bhala abasthā-rē pāi maüja karu-achhanti.' Tāhā
him good state-in getting merry-making doing-is.' That

śuṇi sē rāga hōi, bhitara-ku jibā-ku maṅgilā
hearing he (in-)anger having-become, inside-to going-for desired

nāhĩ. Ēṇu tāhā bāpa bāhāra-ku āsi tā-ku bahuta bujhāilā.
not. Therefore his father outside-to coming him much entreated.

Tahũ sē bāpa-ku uttara dēlā, 'dēkha, mu bahu-kāḷa
Thereupon he the-father-to reply gave, 'see, I (for)-long-time

tumbha-ra sēbā karu-achhi; kēbēhẽ tumbha-ra kathā-ku ēṛi
your service doing-am; ever your word transgressing

dēi nāhĩ; tathāpi mōhō bandhu-bāndhabaṅka saṅga-rē
I-gave not; nevertheless my friend-relatives company-in

maũja karibā-pāĩ mōtē gōṭi-ē chhēḷi-chhuā kēbē
merry-making make-for me a-single goat-young-one ever
dēi-nāhã. Mātra jadi-cha tumbha-ra ēhi pua dāri rakhi
you-have-not-given. But though your this son harlot keeping
sabu sampatti nashṭa kari-achhi, tēbēhẽ sē āsibā-mātrē
all property destroyed made-has, yet he immediately-on-coming
tumbhē tāhā pāĩ maũja kala.' Bāpa kahilā, 'pua, tumbhē
you him for merry-making did.' The-father said, 'son, you
sabu-bēḷē mōhō pākha-rē achha, mōha-ra jāhā kichhi, tāhā
at-all-times my side-by are, my what anything, that
tumbha-ra aṭē; mātra tumbha-ra ēhi bhāi mari, puṇi
yours is; but your this brother having-died, again
bañchibā-ru; ō haji, puṇi miḷibā-ru;
surviving-on-account-of; and being-lost, again being-found-on-account-of;
tāhā pāĩ maũja karibā-ra uchita.'
that for merry-making doing (is)-fit.'

[No. 2.]

INDO-ARYAN FAMILY.

EASTERN GROUP.

ORIYĀ.

STANDARD DIALECT.

(CUTTACK DISTRICT.)

SPECIMEN II.

A. FOLKSONG—THE KESABA-KOILI.

କୋଇଲି କେଶବ ଯେ ମଥୁରାକୁ ଗଲା ।
କାହା ବୋଲେ ଗଲା ପୁଣି ବାହୁଡ଼ି ନଇଲା ଲୋ କୋଇଲି । ୧ ।
କୋଇଲି ଖଣ୍ଡ କ୍ଷୀର ଦେବ ମୁଁ କାହାକୁ ।
ଖାଇବାର ପୁଣି ଗଲା ମଥୁରା ପୁରକୁ ଲୋ କୋଇଲି । ୨ ।
କୋଇଲି ଗଲା ପୁଣି ବାହୁଡ଼ି ନଇଲା ।
ଗହନର ବୃନ୍ଦାବନ ଶୋଭା ନପାଇଲା ଲୋ କୋଇଲି । ୩ ।
କୋଇଲି ଘର ମୋର ନ ମଣନ୍ତି ନନ୍ଦ ।
ଘଣ୍ଟଣି ନ ହଣେ ପୁର ନଥିଲେ ଗୋବନ୍ଦ ଲୋ କୋଇଲି । ୪ ।
କୋଇଲି ନନ୍ଦ ଦେହ ପାଷାଣେ ଗଢ଼ିଲା ।
ନସ୍ନେ କଷ୍ଟଲ ଦେଇ ରଥେ ବସାଇଲା ଲୋ କୋଇଲି । ୫ ।
କୋଇଲି ଚଳୁ ଥାଇ କଟିସୁ ମେଖଳୀ ।
ଛକଛ ହୋଇଲେ ଶୁଣି ଗୋପପୁର ବାଳୀ ଲୋ କୋଇଲି । ୬ ।

କୋଇଲି ଝଟକେ ମୁଁ ମାଇଲି ପୁରୁବେ ।
ଝଡ଼ି ଅବା ଗଲେ କୃଷ୍ଣ ସେହି ପଥଇବେ ଲୋ କୋଇଲି । ୭ ।
କୋଇଲି ଞଭପଣେ ଅଇଲା ଅକ୍ରୁର ।
ଯାଏ ବୋଲି ଭଣ୍ଡି ନେଲା ବସାଇ ରଥରେ ଲୋ କୋଇଲି । ୮ ।
କୋଇଲି ଟୁଲୁଟୁଲୁ ଲୁହ ନ ଛନ୍ଦୁଲା ।
ଟଗଡ଼ା ସାରଣ କୃଷ୍ଣ ମଥୁରା ରହିଲା ଲୋ କୋଇଲି । ୯ ।
କୋଇଲି କଣାବାଟେ ହୁଇ ମାଗେ ଗୁଢ ।
ନନ୍ଦନ ଟେକେଅ ଡାଙ୍କୁ ସଦଥାନ୍ତି ନନ୍ଦ ଲୋ କୋଇଲି । ୧୦ ।
କୋଇଲି ଠହ ଠହ ହସୁଥାନ୍ତି କୋଳେ ।
ଠନଠନ ହେଉଥାନ୍ତି ଝୁଲିବାର ବେଳେ ଲୋ କୋଇଲି । ୧୧ ।
କୋଇଲି ଠଣ ଯେ ସୁନ୍ଦର ଦେଢ ଯୋଧ ।
ଠେ ଭଣ୍ଡି ଗଲେ କୃଷ୍ଣ ନଇଲେ କେବାଧ ଲୋ କୋଇଲି । ୧୨ ।

[No. 2.]

INDO-ARYAN FAMILY. EASTERN GROUP.

ORIYĀ.

STANDARD DIALECT. (CUTTACK DISTRICT.)

SPECIMEN II.

(A Folksong. The Kēśaba-kōili.)

TRANSLITERATION AND TRANSLATION.

Kōili,	Kēśaba	jē	Mathurā-ku	galā,
Cuckoo,	*Krishṇa*	*who*	*Mathurā-to*	*went,*

Kāhā-bōlē	galā	putra	bāhuṛi	naïlā?
On-whose-words	*went*	*son*	*returning*	*not-came?*

lō kōili.
O Cuckoo. (1)

Kōili,	khaṇḍa	khyīra	dēbi	mũ	kāhā-ku;
Cuckoo,	*sugar*	*thickened-milk*	*will-give*	*I*	*whom-to;*

Khāibā-ra	putra	galā	Mathurā-pura-ku.
The-eating-of	*son*	*went*	*Mathura-town-to.*

lō kōili.
O Cuckoo. (2)

Kōili,	galā	putra,	bāhuṛi	naïlā;
Cuckoo,	*went*	*the-son,*	*returning*	*not-came;*

Gahana-ta	Bṛundābana	śōbhā	na	pāilā.
The-groves (of)	*Vṛindāvana*	*charm*	*not*	*got.*

lō kōili.
O Cuckoo. (3)

Kōili,	ghara	mō-ra	na	maṇanti	Nanda,
Cuckoo,	*home*	*my*	*not*	*likes*	*Nanda,*

Ghaṭaṇa	na	diśē	pura	na	thilē	Gōbinda.
Fair	*not*	*looks*	*house*	*not*	*remaining*	*Gōvinda.*

lō kōili.
O Cuckoo. (4)

Kōili,	Nanda-dēha	pāshāṇē	gaṛhilā.
Cuckoo,	*Nanda's-body*	*of-stone*	*made.*

Nayanē	kajjvaḷa	dēi	rathē	basāilā
In-the-eyes	*collyrium*	*giving*	*on-the-chariot*	*he-seated*

lō kōili.
O Cuckoo. (5)

Kōili chalu-thāi kaṭi-stha mēkhaḷī,
Cuckoo moved on-the-waist-situated ornament,

Chakita hōilē śuṇi Gōpa-pura-bāḷī,
Startled became hearing Gōpa-pura-girls,

lō kōili.
O Cuckoo. (6)

Kōili, chhāṭēka[1] mũ māili pūrubē;
Cuckoo, one-cane-(blow) I struck before;

Chhāṛi abā galē Kṛushṇa sēhi parābhabē,
Leaving methinks went Kṛishṇa that on-castigation,

lō kōili.
O Cuckoo. (7)

Kōili, jūta-paṇē aïlā Akrūra;
Cuckoo, messenger-in-the-guise-of came Akrūra;

Jātrā bōli bhaṇḍi nēlā basāi ratha-rē;
Festival saying deceitfully took seating on-the-chariot;

lō kōili.
O Cuckoo. (8)

Kōili, jhuru jhuru luha na rahilā;
Cuckoo, mourning mourning tears not remained;

Jhagaṛā sāri-ṇa Kṛushṇa Mathurā rahilā,
Quarrels having-ended Kṛishṇa at-Mathurā stayed,

lō kōili.
O Cuckoo. (9)

Kōili, niśā-kāḷē Hari māgē chānda;
Cuckoo, night-at-time-of Hari would-ask-for the-moon;

Nayana ṭēki ā tāṅ-ku rāu-thānti Nanda,
Eyes raising come him would-call Nanda,

lō kōili.
O Cuckoo. (10)

Kōili, ṭaha-ṭaha hasu-thānti kōḷē;
Cuckoo, loudly (Kṛishṇa) would-laugh in-the-arms;

Ṭaḷa-ṭaḷa hēu-thānti jhulibā-ra-bēḷē,
Staggered would-become rocking-of-at-the-time,

lō kōili.
O Cuckoo. (11)

Kōili, ṭhaṇa jē sundara bēni pōē,
Cuckoo, symmetrically that graceful both sons,

Ṭhaki bhaṇḍi galē Kṛushṇa nailē-bēṛhāē,
Fraudulently deceiving went Kṛishṇa not-came-back,

lō kōili.
O Cuckoo. (12)

[1] Written *chhāṭakā* in original.

FREE TRANSLATION OF THE FOREGOING.

The song is supposed to be sung by Yaśōdā, the foster-mother of Kṛishṇa, after he had left Vṛindā-vana, in company with Akrūra, and had remained in Mathurā whither he had gone to kill the demon Kaṁsa. Nanda, Yaśōdā's husband, was Kṛishṇa's foster-father, and he had consented to Akrūra taking the child away. He and his wife, as well as all the inhabitants of Vṛindā-vana, where the God had spent his infancy and boyhood, were Gowālās by caste, and hence she calls the country round her home 'Gōpa-pura,' or the 'City of Cowherds.' One of Kṛishṇa's many names was Kēśava, and another was Gōvinda. He was the incarnation of the God Hari or Vishṇu. His brother was Bala-rāma.

1. O Cuckoo, cuckoo. At whose words did Kṛishṇa go to Mathurā? For my son has not returned.

2. O Cuckoo, cuckoo. To whom shall I now give sweets and thickened milk? For my son who used to eat it has gone to Mathurā-town.

3. O Cuckoo, cuckoo. My son went and returned not; and the groves of Vṛindāvana have lost their charm.

4. O Cuckoo, cuckoo. Nanda no more loves my home: for no longer fair appears the dwelling without Gōvinda.

5. O Cuckoo, cuckoo. Surely Nanda's body was of stone, when he anointed Kṛishṇa's eyes with collyrium[1] and put him sitting in the chariot.

6. O Cuckoo, cuckoo. When the maidens of Gōpa-pura heard of his departure, they started, and the (bells of) their girdles shook.

7. O Cuckoo, cuckoo. I once struck him a single cane-blow (for some fault), and I fear that it was on account of that punishment that Kṛishṇa left me.

8. O Cuckoo, cuckoo. Akrūra came in the guise of a messenger. He seated Kṛishṇa in the chariot deceitfully, and took him away on the excuse of some festival.

9. O Cuckoo, cuckoo. Mourning, mourning. I have no tears left. Kṛishṇa had ended his quarrels (with the demon), and has stayed in Mathurā.

10. O Cuckoo, cuckoo. At night-time (in his baby way) Hari used to ask for the moon, and raising his eyes, Nanda would call out to him 'Come.'

11. O Cuckoo, cuckoo. Loudly used he to crow in my arms, and (gleefully) used he to shake as I rocked him.

12. O Cuckoo, cuckoo. A graceful pair were the two brothers; but Kṛishṇa has deceived me and has not come back.

Standard Oṛiyā is also spoken in the district of Balasore. Here, however, we may note a few provincialisms, though not sufficient to entitle the form of speech to be classed as a separate dialect. Some of the points of differences are of pronunciation. Others are of grammatical inflection due to the influence of the neighbouring Bengali of Midnapore.

As regards pronunciation, there is a tendency to drop the aspiration in the definite present and perfect tenses, so that *achhi* is spelt *achi*. Examples are *nēi jāi-chi*, he has carried off; *palāi-chi*, he has fled; *hēi-chi*, it has taken place; *kāndu-chu*, thou art weeping; *karu-chu*, thou art making. Note the way in which *n* is substituted for *l*, as in *thinē* for *thilē*, if it had been.

---

[1] To protect them from the dust of the journey.

In the declension of nouns, the letter *ē* added to the nominative gives the force of the indefinite article. Thus, *muṇḍ-ē*, a lump : *din-ē*, one day : *khaṇḍ-ē*, a piece. In one instance, we have the accusative ending in *ka* instead of *ku*, *viz.*, in *sunā-muṇḍā-ka*, (he carried off) the lump of gold.

In the declension of pronouns we find *tuma-ra*, instead of *tumbha-ra*, your.

It is unnecessary to give the Parable of the Prodigal Son in the Balasore dialect. The following short folk-tale shows the peculiarities to which attention has been drawn above. It is given in facsimile of the original writing, and is accompanied by a transliteration and a translation.

[No. 3.]

INDO-ARYAN FAMILY. EASTERN GROUP.

ORIYĀ.

STANDARD DIALECT. (DISTRICT BALASORE.)

[illegible]

[illegible]

[illegible]

[illegible]

5. [illegible]

[illegible]

[illegible]

[illegible]

[illegible]

10. [illegible]

[No. 3.]

INDO-ARYAN FAMILY. EASTERN GROUP.

OṚIYĀ.

STANDARD DIALECT. (DISTRICT BALASORE.)

TRANSLITERATION AND TRANSLATION.

Eka kirapaṇa-ra kichhi daulatā thilā. Sē
A miser-of some wealth was. He

sabu bēḷē ēi bhābanā karē pachhē chura sandhāna pāi
all times-at this thought makes lest a-thief a-trace having-got

churi karē. Anēka bhābi chinti sē sarbaswa
theft may-do. Much having-thought having-considered he (his)-entire-property

bikiri kalā, āu muṇḍē sunā kiṇi māṭi-rē
sale made, and a-lump gold having-bought the-earth-in

putā rakhilā. Sēhi dina-ru sē rōja tharē lēkhā̃ sē jāgā-ku
buried put. That day-from he day once at-the-rate that place-to

jāi dēkhi āsē, 'kēhi sandhāna pāi nēi jāi-chi
having-gone having-seen returns-home, 'anyone a-trace having-got having-taken has-gone

kinā.' Kirapaṇa rōja-rōja i mati karibā-ru tā-ra
or-not.' The-miser every-day this manner doing-by his

chākara mana-rē ēi sandē hēlā, 'haē-ta
servant the-mind-in this suspicion arose, 'perhaps

ēi jāgā-rē luchā dhana achhi; na-hēlē sē
this place-in hidden wealth is; otherwise he

rōja tharē tharē sōṭi-ku jāāntā kēnē?' Dinē
daily once once there-to is-in-the-habit-of-going why?' One-day

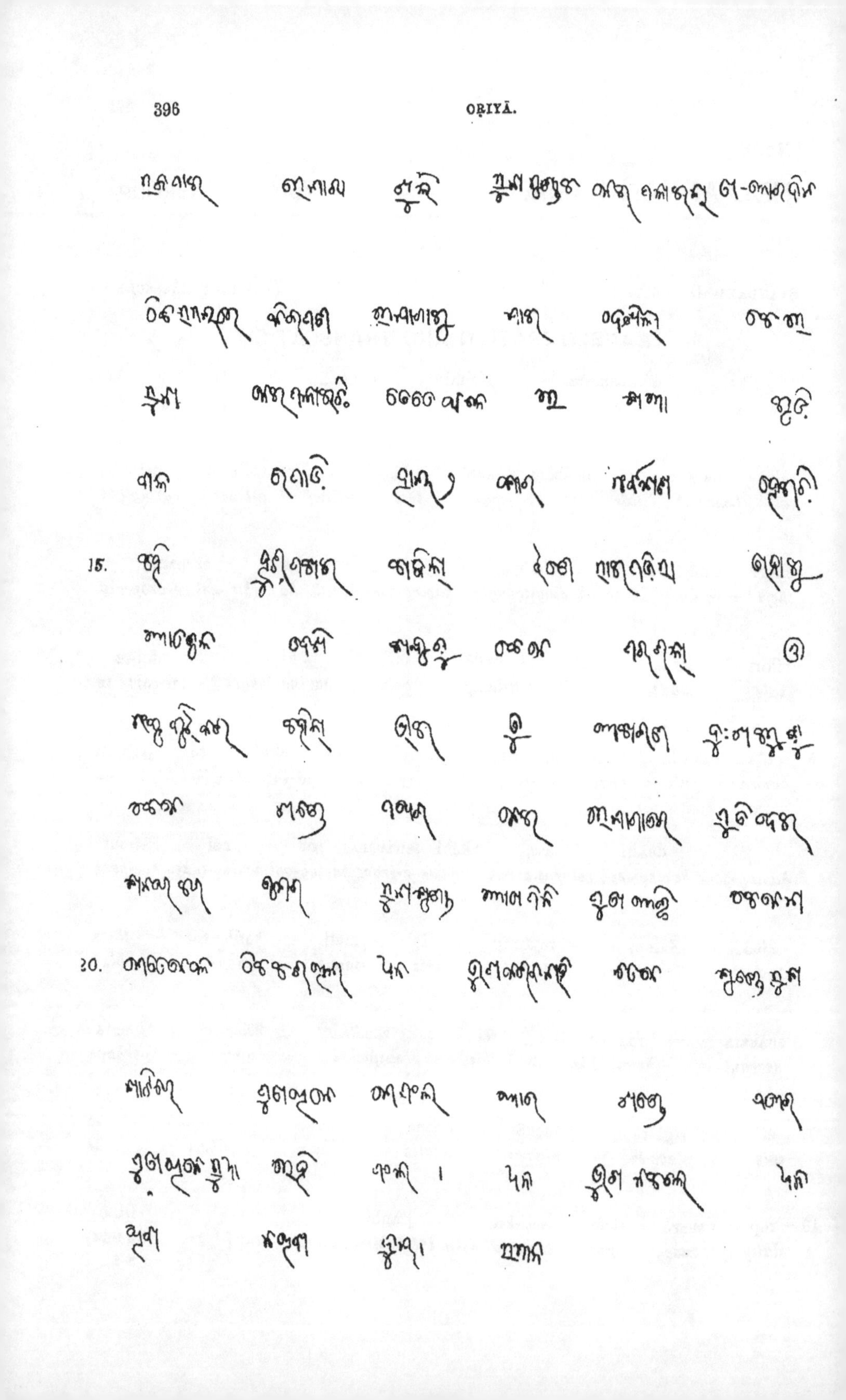

saja pāi sē jāgā khuli sunā-muṇḍā-ka nēi paḷāiḷā. Tā āra dina
opportunity having-got that place having-opened the-gold-lump having-taken he-absconded. That next day

ṭhika samaya-rē kirapaṇa sē jāgā-ku jāi dēkhilā kēsē
fixed time-at the-miser that place-to having-gone saw someone

sunā nēi paḷāi-chi. Tētē-bēḷē sē mathā kuṛi,
the-gold having-taken absconded-has. At-that-time he (his)-head having-struck,

bāḷa upāṛi, 'hāya hāya mō-ra sarbanāśa hēi-chi'
(his)-hair having-torn-out, 'alack, alack, my entire-destruction has-taken-place,'

kahi huri pakāi kāndilā. Jhaṇē sāipaṛisā tāhā-ku
saying cry having-raised he-wept. A-person neighbour him

ātaguḷa dēkhi, 'kāndu-chu kēnē?' pachārilā, ō
distressed having-seen, 'thou-art-weeping why?' asked, and

sabu bujhi-kari kahilā, 'bhāi, tu ākāraṇa duḥkha karu-chu
all having-understood said, 'brother, thou without-a-cause sorrow art-doing

kēnē? Khaṇḍē pathara nēi sē jāgā-rē puti-dēi
why? A-piece stone having-taken that place-in having-buried

mana-rē kara tuma-ra sunā-muṇḍā āga-pini putā achhi. Kēnēnā
mind-in make your gold-lump as-before buried is. For

jētē-bēḷē ṭhika kari-thila dhana bhuga kariba-nāhi, tētē muṇḍē sunā
at-what-time fixed made-you-had the-wealth enjoyment you-will-make-not, then a-lump gold

māṭi-rē putā-thinē jē phala, āu khaṇḍē pathara
the-earth-in if-it-had-been-buried what profit, and a-piece stone

putā-thinē sudhā sēhi phala.' Dhana bhuga na kalē, dhana
if-it-had-been-buried even that profit.' Wealth enjoyment not if-you-make, wealth

thibā na-thibā duyā samāna.
being not-being both equal.

FREE TRANSLATION OF THE FOREGOING.

A miser had some property, and was continually in fear that some thief would find it out and one fine day steal it. So, after much consideration, he sold all that he had, and having bought a lump of gold with the proceeds, buried it in the earth. Thereafter, he used to visit the spot regularly once a day, to see if anyone had taken it away. His servant observed his conduct, and smelt a rat. 'Perhaps,' thought he, 'he has something of value buried there. Otherwise, why should he make a point of going to the place every day?' So, one day, he found an opportunity, dug up the lump of gold, and ran off with it. Next day, up came the miser at the regular time, and saw that someone had made away with his gold. He beat his head and he tore his hair, and he wept crying, 'alack, alack, I'm altogether ruined.' A neighbour who saw him in this pickle asked him why he was weeping, and when he had understood the whole affair he said, 'brother, why are you weeping without a cause? Bury a stone in the same place, and make up your mind that it's your lump of gold. For, once you had made up your mind that you would not enjoy your wealth, what greater advantage had you from burying a lump of gold than from burying a stone?'

The Moral of this is that a buried talent is as good as no talent at all.

It is unnecessary to give any examples of the dialect spoken in the District of Puri. The language is exactly the same as that of Cuttack. The specimens received from it only differ from the Cuttack ones in that the language is more Sanskritised, a matter which depends a good deal on the idiosyncrasies of the writer. For instance *putrá* is used instead of *pua*, a son, and *pitā*, instead of *bāpa*, a father. We should however remember that the letter ଡ is more commonly pronounced as a strongly cerebral *ḍ*, in Puri, while, in Cuttack, its sound is more nearly that of *ṛ*. This, at least, is the evidence borne by the specimens. In the transliteration received from Cuttack the word for 'he fell' is transliterated *'paṛilā,'* while in the specimens which come from Puri, it is spelt *'parḍilā.'*

Similar remarks apply to the Oṛiyā spoken in the District of Angul and in the various Native States of Orissa. The Aryan language of the whole of this area is Standard Oṛiyā. The only difference is that of pronunciation. As already stated, the farther south we go, the greater is the tendency to pronounce *ch* as *ts*, and *j* as *dz*. So also while we find that the sound *ṛ* is more common in the north, *ḍ* is more common in the south. We may thus say that the Oṛiyā spoken over the whole of Orissa proper, including its Native States, is Standard Oṛiyā. It will of course be understood that other aboriginal languages especially Kandhī are also vernaculars of the area. But they do not appear to have affected Oṛiyā at all.

Oṛiyā is also spoken south of Orissa in the north of the districts of Ganjam and Vizagapatam, which belong to the Madras Presidency. This tract of country does not fall within the operations of the Linguistic Survey, but it may be stated that the Southern limit of Oṛiyā may be taken roughly as commencing at the small seaport town of Barwa in the District of Ganjam, and running first nearly due west and then south-west up to Tindiki on the border between Vizagapatam and Bastar. South of this line a corrupt Oṛiyā which is much mixed with Telugu is spoken by some of the lowest castes, but the language of the bulk of the population is Telugu. Thence it turns north so as to include the Jeypore Agency of Vizagapatam and the eastern half of the Chhattisgarh Division of the Central Provinces. The Oṛiyā of Ganjam and Jeypore is still the standard dialect. It is well illustrated in Mr. Maltby's *Handbook*. The characteristic southern pronunciation is here prominent. The four first palatal letters are here clearly *ts*, *tsh*, *dz*, and *dzh*. The *ch*- and *j*- sounds are unknown. So also, we have always *ḍ* and *ḍh*, and never *ṛ* and *ṛh*. The common folk sometimes add the Telugu termination *u* to nouns, but this is not done by the educated.

Standard Oṛiyā is also the form of the language which is spoken in the Districts and Native States of the Central Provinces, in which Oṛiyā is the vernácular. From Raigarh in the north, to Kalahandi in the south, and from Raipur in the west to Bamra in the east, the language is exactly the same in its grammar. There is only a slight difference in pronunciation which we may notice, though it is not necessary to give specimens to illustrate the peculiarity. It is that in the extreme west of the Oṛiyā-speaking area, the influence of the neighbouring Chhattīsgaṛhī has led to the letter *a* not being pronounced at the end of a word. Thus, in Raipur, and the State of Sarangaṛh, the word for 'of a man' is *jaṇaka-r*, not *jaṇaka-ra*, and the word for 'younger' is *sān*, not *sāna*. Apparently also, the sound of the vowel *a* gradually loses the tone of the *ŏ* in *hot*, as we go westwards, and approaches the sound of the *a* in *America*, which it has in the neighbouring Chhattīsgaṛhi.

It is hence hardly necessary to give specimens of the forms of speech spoken in this area. I shall content myself with giving the version of the Parable of the Prodigal Son which has been received from the Native State of Kalahandi, which is nearly in the extreme south-west of the Oṛiyā-speaking area. Here, it will be observed, a final *a* *is* pronounced.

[No. 4.]

INDO-ARYAN FAMILY. EASTERN GROUP.

ORIYĀ.

STANDARD DIALECT. (KALAHANDI STATE.)

ଜଣକର ଦୁଇ ପୁଅ ଥିଲେ । ସେମାନଙ୍କ ମଧ୍ୟରୁ ସାନ ପୁଅ ପିତାକୁ କହିଲା, ହେ ପିତା, ତୁମ୍ଭ ସମ୍ପତ୍ତିର ଯେଉଁ ଭାଗ ଆମ୍ଭେ ପାଇବୁଁ ତାହା ଦିଅ । ତହିଁରେ ସେ ଆପଣା ସମ୍ପତ୍ତି ଭାଗ କରି ସେମାନଙ୍କୁ ଦେଲା । ଅଳ୍ପ ଦିନ ଉତ୍ତାରେ ସେହି ସାନ ପୁଅ ସବୁ ଯାକ ଏକା କରି ନେଇ ଦୂର ଦେଶକୁ ଯାଇ ଦୁଷ୍ଟ ଆଚରଣରେ ସବୁ ସମ୍ପତ୍ତି ଉଡ଼ାଇ ଦେଲା । ସବୁ ଖର୍ଚ୍ଚ କଲା ଉତ୍ତାରେ ସେହି ଦେଶରେ ମହା ଦୁର୍ଭିକ୍ଷ ପଡ଼ନ୍ତେ ତାହାର ଦୁଃଖାବସ୍ଥା ଘଟିଲା । ଏଥିରେ ସେ ଯାଇ ସେହି ଦେଶର ଏକ ଗୃହି ଲୋକର ଆଶ୍ରା ନେବାରୁ ସେହି ଲୋକ ତାହାକୁ ଘୁଷୁରି ଗୋଠ ଚରାଇବାକୁ କ୍ଷେତକୁ ପଠାଇଲା । ସେଠାରେ ତାହାକୁ କେହି କିଛି ଖାଇବାକୁ ନ ଦେବାରୁ, ସେ ଘୁଷୁରିର ଖାଦ୍ୟ ଚୋପାରେ ପେଟ ପୁରାଇବାକୁ ଇଚ୍ଛା କଲା । ପଛେ ସେ ମନେମନେ ଚେତା ପାଇ କହିଲା, ହାୟ, ଆମ୍ଭ ପିତାଙ୍କ ପାଖରେ କେତେ ଭୁତିଆର ଲୋକ କେତେ ଅଧିକ ଖାଇ ଯାଉଅଛନ୍ତି, ମାତ୍ର ଆମ୍ଭେ ଭୋକେ ମରୁଅଛୁଁ । ଆମ୍ଭେ ଉଠି ପିତାଙ୍କ ନିକଟରେ ଯାଇ ବୋଲିବା, ହେ ପିତା, ଆମ୍ଭେ ଈଶ୍ୱରଙ୍କର ପୁଣି ତୁମ୍ଭର ବିରୁଦ୍ଧରେ ପାପ କଲୁଁ, ତୁମ୍ଭର ପୁଅ ବୋଲି ବିଖ୍ୟାତ ହେବାର ଯୋଗ୍ୟ ଆଉ ନୋହୁଁ, ତୁମ୍ଭର ଏକ ଭୁତିଆର ପରି ଆମ୍ଭଙ୍କୁ ରଖ । ତାହାପରେ ସେ ଉଠି ପିତା ନିକଟକୁ ଗଲା । ମାତ୍ର ତାହାର ପିତା ବହୁତ ଦୂରରୁ ତାହାକୁ ଦେଖି ଦୟା କଲା, ପୁଣି ଧାଇଁ ଯାଇ ତାହାର ବେକ ଧରି ତାହାକୁ ଚୁମ୍ବନ କଲା । ଏଥିରେ ପୁଅ ତାହାକୁ କହିଲା, ହେ ପିତା, ଈଶ୍ୱରଙ୍କର ଓ ତୁମ୍ଭ ବିରୁଦ୍ଧରେ ପାପ କଲୁଁ, ଏଣୁ ତୁମ୍ଭର ପୁଅ ବୋଲି ବିଖ୍ୟାତ ହେବାର ଆଉ ଯୋଗ୍ୟ ନୋହୁଁ । ମାତ୍ର ତାହାର ପିତା ଆପଣା ନୌକରମାନଙ୍କୁ କହିଲା, ଅତି ଉତ୍ତମ ବସ୍ତ୍ର ଆଣି ଏହାକୁ ପିନ୍ଧାଅ, ଏହାର ହାତରେ ମୁଦି ପିନ୍ଧାଅ, ଏହାର ପାଦରେ ପାଣ୍ଡୋଇ ଲଗାଅ । ପୁଣି ଆମ୍ଭେମାନେ ଭୋଜନ କରି ଆନନ୍ଦ କରୁଁ, ଯେହେତୁ ଆମ୍ଭର ଏହି ପୁଅ ମରି ଯାଇ ପୁନଶ୍ଚ ଜୀବନ ପାଇଲା, ସେ ହଜି ଥିଲା ପୁଣି ମିଳିଲା । ତହିଁରେ ସେମାନେ ଆନନ୍ଦ କରିବାକୁ ଲାଗିଲେ ।।

ସେତେବେଳେ ତାହାର ବଡ଼ ପୁଅ କ୍ଷେତରେ ଥିଲା । ପୁଣି ଆସୁ ଆସୁ ଘର କଟରେ ପ୍ରବେଶ ହୋଇ ନାଟ ଓ ବାଦ୍ୟର ଶବ୍ଦ ଶୁଣି ପାରି ନୌକର ଏକ ଜଣକୁ ଡାକି ପଚାରିଲା ଏହାର କାରଣ କି? ସେ କହିଲା ତୁମ୍ଭର ଭାଇ ଆଇଲେ, ପୁଣି ତୁମ୍ଭର ପିତା ତାଙ୍କୁ କୁଶଳରେ ଆସିବାର ଦେଖି ବହୁତ ଭୋଜନ ଦେଇ ଅଛନ୍ତି । ତହିଁରେ ସେ ରାଗ ହୋଇ ଭିତରକୁ ଯିବାକୁ ରାଜି ନ ହେଲା । ଏଣୁ ତାହାର ପିତା ବାହାରେ ଆସି ତାହାକୁ ବହୁତ ବୁଝାଇ କହିଲା । ମାତ୍ର ସେ ଆପଣା ପିତାକୁ ଉତ୍ତର ଦେଲା, ଦେଖ, ତୁମ୍ଭର କୌଣସି ହୁକୁମ ଅମାନ୍ୟ ନ କରି ବହୁତ ବର୍ଷରୁ ତୁମ୍ଭର ସେବା କରି ଆସୁ ଅଛୁଁ । ତଥାପି ମିତ୍ରମାନଙ୍କ ସଙ୍ଗରେ ଉତ୍ସବ କରିବାକୁ କେବେହେଁ ଗୋଟିଏ ଛେଳି ଆମ୍ଭଙ୍କୁ ଦେଇ ନାହିଁ ; ମାତ୍ର ତୁମ୍ଭର ଯେଉଁ ପୁଅ ବେଶ୍ୟା ଆଦିଙ୍କ ସଙ୍ଗରେ ତୁମ୍ଭର ସମ୍ପତ୍ତି ବୃଥାରେ ଖର୍ଚ୍ଚ କରିଅଛି ସେ ଆସିବାମାତ୍ରକେ ତାହାପାଇଁ ବଡ଼ ଭୋଜ ଦେଲ । ତାହାର ପିତା କହିଲା ହେ ପୁଅ, ତୁମ୍ଭେ ସର୍ବ୍ବଦା ଆମ୍ଭର ସଙ୍ଗେ ଅଛ ଆଉ ଆମ୍ଭର ଯେ କିଛି ଅଛି ସେହି ସବୁ ତୁମ୍ଭର, ପୁଣି ଏହି ଯେ ତୁମ୍ଭର ଭାଇ ମରି ଯାଇ ପୁନର୍ବ୍ବାର ବଞ୍ଚିଲା, ସେ ହଜି ଥିଲା ମିଳିଲା, ଏ ହେତୁରୁ ଉତ୍ସବ ଆନନ୍ଦ କରିବା ଆମ୍ଭମାନଙ୍କର ଉଚିତ ।।

[No. 4.]

INDO-ARYAN FAMILY. EASTERN GROUP.

OṚIYĀ.

STANDARD DIALECT. (KALAHANDI STATE.)

TRANSLITERATION AND TRANSLATION.

Janak'a-ra dui pua thilē. Sēmānaṅka madhya-ru sāna
A-man-of two sons were. Them among-from the-younger

pua pitā-ku kahilā, 'hē pitā, tumbha sampatti-ra j̈ēũ bhāga
son the-father-to said, 'O father, your goods-of what portion

āmbhē pāibũ, tāhā diya.' Tahĩ-rē sē āpaṇā sampatti bhāga-kari
I will-get, that give.' That-on he his goods having-divided

sēmānaṅ-ku dēlā. Alpa dina uttārē sēhi sāna pua sabujāka
them-to gave. A-few days after that younger son every-thing

ēkā kari nēi dūra dēśa-ku j̈āi dushṭa ācharaṇa-rē
together having-made having-taken a-far country-to having-gone riotous living-in

sabu sampatti uḍāi-delā. Sabu kharchcha kalā uttārē sēhi dēśa-rē
all the-substance squandered. All spending having-done after that land-in

mahā durbhikhya paḍantē tāhā-ra duḥkhābasthā ghaṭilā. Ēthi-rē
a-mighty famine arising his want-condition happened. This-on

sē j̈āi sēhi dēśa-ra ēka gṛuhi-lōka-ra āśrā nēbā-ru, sēhi lōka
he going that country-of a citizen-person-of shelter taking-on, that man

tāhā-ku ghushurā-gōṭha charāibā-ku khyēta-ku paṭhāilā. Sē-ṭhārē tāhā-ku
him swine-flock feeding-for the-field-to sent. There him-to

kēhi kichhi khāibā-ku na dēbā-ru sē ghushurā-ra khādya
any-body any-thing eating-for not giving-on he the-swine-of food

chōpā-rē pēṭa purāibā-ku ichchhā kalā. Pachhē sē manē-manē
husks-with belly filling-for desire made. Afterwards he on-his-mind

chētā pāi kahilā, 'hāya, āmbha pitāṅka-pākha-rē kētē bhutiāra-lōka
sense having-got said, 'alas, my father-with how-many hired-servants

kētē adhika khāi j̈āu-achhanti, mātra āmbhē bhōkhē maru-achhũ.
how-much more having-eaten going-are, but I with-hunger dying-am.

Āmbhē uṭhi pitāṅka nikaṭa-rē j̈āi bōlibā, "hē pitā, āmbhē
I having-arisen father near-in having-gone will-say, "O father, I

Īśwaraṅka-ra puṇi tumbha-ra biruddha-rē pāpa kalũ, tumbha-ra pua
God-of and you-of opposition-on sin did, your son

bōli-bikhyāta-hēbā-ra j̈ōgya āu nōhũ; tumbha-ra ēka bhutiāra
called-(and)-noted-being-of worthy more I-am-not; your one hired-servant-of

pari āmbhaṅku rakha."' Tatparē sē uthi pitā nikaṭa-ku galā. Mātra
as me kept."' Then he having-arisen father near-to went. But

tāhā-ra pitā bahuta dūra-ru tāhā-ku dēkhi dayā kalā, puṇi
his father great distance-from him having-seen compassion made, and

dhā̃i jāi tāhā-ra bēka dhari tāhā-ku chumbana kalā.
having-run having-gone his neck having-seized him-to kiss made.

Ēthi-rē pua tāhā-ku kahilā, 'hē pitā, Īśwaraṅka-ra ō tumbha
This-on the-son him-to said, 'O father, heaven-of and you(-of)

biruddha-rē pāpa kalũ, ēṇu tumbha-ra pua bōli-bikhyāta-hēbā-ra āu
opposition-in sin I-did, so your son called-(and)-noted-being-of more

jōgya nōhũ.' Mātra tāhā-ra pitā āpaṇā naukaramānaṅ-ku kahilā,
worthy I-am-not.' But his father his-own servants-to said,

'ati-uttama bastra āṇi ēhā-ku pindhāa; ēhā-ra
'very-excellent robe having-brought this-(person)-to put-on; this-one's

hāta-rē mudi pindhāa, ēhā-ra pāda-rē pāṇḍhōi lagāa; puṇi
hand-on ring put-on, this-one's feet-on shoes put; and

āmbhē-mānē bhōjana-kari ānanda karũ; jē-hētu āmbha-ra ēhi pua
(let)-us eating-having-done rejoicing do; because my this son

mari-jāi, punaścha jībana pāilā; sē haji thilā, puṇi miḷilā.' Tahĩ-rē
having-died, again life got; he lost was, and was-found.' That-on

sē-mānē ānanda karibā-ku lāgilē.
they rejoicing making began.

Tētiki-bēḷē tāhā-ra baḍa pua khyēta-rē thilā. Puṇi āsu-āsu
At-that-time his elder son the-field-in was. And while-coming

ghara-kati-rē prabēśa hōi nāṭa ō bādya-ra śabda
the-house-near-in entering having-become dancing and music-of sound

śuṇi-pāri naukara ēka-jaṇa-ku ḍāki pachārilā, 'ēhā-ra
having-got-to-hear servant one-person having-called he-asked, 'this-of

kāraṇa ki?' Sē kahilā, 'tumbha-ra bhāi āilē, puṇi tumbha-ra pitā
the-cause what?' He said, 'your brother came, and your father

tāṅ-ku kuśaḷa-rē āsibā-ra dēkhi bahuta bhōjana dēi-achhanti.'
him good-health-on come-being having-seen great feast given-has.'

Tahĩ-rē sē rāga hōi bhitara-ku jibā-ku rāji na hēlā.
That-on he angry having-become inside-to going-for willing not became.

Ēṇu tāhā-ra pitā bāhārē āsi tāhā-ku bahuta bujhāi kahilā.
Hence his father outside having-come him-to much having-entreated spoke.

Mātra sē āpaṇā pitā-ku uttara dēlā, 'dēkha, tumbha-ra kauṇasi
But he his-own father-to answer gave, 'see, your any

hukuma amānya na kari bahuta barsha-ru tumbha-ra
commandment neglected not having-made many years-from your

sēbā kari āsu-achhũ. Tathāpi mitramānaṅka-saṅga-rē utsaba
service having-done coming-I-am. Yet friends-company-on feasting

karibā-ku kēbēhẽ gōṭiē chhēḷi āmbhaṅ-ku dēi-nāhã. Mātra
making-for ever one-single kid me-to give-you-did-not. But

tumbha-ra jēũ pua bēśya-ādiṅka saṅga-rē tumbha-ra sampatti
your which son harlots-et-cetera company-in your property

bṛuthā-rē kharchcha kari-achhi, sē āsibā-mātra-kē tāhā pāĩ baḍa
vainness-in spending done-has, he immediately-on-coming him for great

bhōji dēla.' Tāhā-ra pitā kahilā, 'hē pua, tumbhē sarbadā āmbha-ra
feast you-gave.' His father said, 'O son, you always my

saṅgē achha, āu āmbha-ra jē-kichhi achhi, sēhi sabu tumbha-ra;
company-in are, and mine whatever is, that all yours (is);

puṇi ēhi jē tumbha-ra bhāi mari-jāi punarbāra jiīlā; sē
and this who your brother having-died again become-alive; he

haji-thilā, miḷilā; ē-hētu-ru, utsaba ānanda karibā āmbhamānaṅka-ra
lost-was, was-found; hence, feasting rejoicing doing us-of

uchita.'
proper (is).'

Turning north to the Chota Nagpur Division and its Tributary States, we find that Oṛiyā is spoken in the District of Singhbhum, and in the States of Jashpur, Sarai Kalā, Kharsāwān, Gangpur, and Bonai. In the last two, it is the only Aryan language spoken in the States, but, in the others, the case is different. In Singhbhum, Oṛiyā is the Aryan language which is spoken over the whole District except Dhalbhum. But in the north, in the Chakradharpur Thānā, immediately under the Chota Nagpur Plateau, the Magahī dialect of Bihārī is spoken by that portion of the population, which traces its original home to Chota Nagpur in the north. This part of the country is therefore bilingual. Next door neighbours may talk different home languages. The same is the case in the small States of Sarai Kalā and Kharsāwān, which are enclaves in the north of the Singhbhum District. As regards Jashpur, Oṛiyā is the language of the south of the State, where it borders on Gangpur. The northern portion of the State speaks, on the east, Nagpuriā, a form of the Bhojpurī dialect of Bihārī, and on the west, the Sargujiā form of Chhattīsgaṛhī. The Oṛiyā of Jashpur, being subject to the influence of both these languages is somewhat impure, and presents peculiarities which require illustration. In Singhbhum and the other Tributary States, the Oṛiyā spoken is the standard form of the language. In Singhbhum, the Bengali character is sometimes used for writing it, and all over this tract the only trace of the influence of the Bihārī language which lies to its north is the tendency to drop a final *a*, which we have already noticed in the most western form of Oṛiyā spoken in Chhattīsgaṛh. Thus, in Singhbhum, the word for 'of a man' is pronounced *lōkar*, and not *lōka-ra*, as it is pronounced in Orissa.

It is thus necessary to give specimens only of the form of Oṛiyā spoken in Jashpur. It is spoken by an estimated number of 10,000 people.

The following specimens have been prepared by Babu Manmatha Nath Chatterji, Manager of the Jashpur State. The first is a translation of the Parable of the Prodigal Son, and the second a folktale. The character in which they are written differs slightly from that of standard Oṛiyā. Both are therefore given in facsimile of the original manuscript and each is accompanied by a transliteration and translation.

The following are the main points in which the language of the specimens differs from the standard form of speech.

The letter *a* is sometimes written instead of *ō*. Thus, *matē* instead of *mōtē*, to me. The letter *n* is substituted for *l*, as in *pāunē* for *pāulē*, if he had got; *kanĩ*, I did. The letter ଡ in the middle of a word is pronounced *ṛ* not *ḍ*. Thus *baṛa*, instead of *baḍa*, great. Moreover, the two letters *ṛ* and *ḷ* are interconvertible, as in *baṛuka* or *baḷuka*, but. This last is a corruption of the Bhojpurī *baluk*.

In the declension of nouns there are several irregularities. The nominative plural of *pua*, a son, is, in the second specimen, *puē*, thus recalling Hindī. Beside *ku*, the suffix of the dative is sometimes *ki*, as in *kāhĩ-ki*, for what; *bhāi-ki*, to the brother. The locative termination is often *ra* instead of *rē*, thus resembling the genitive. Examples are *sē-mulukha-ra*, in that country; *jabāba-ra*, in answer; *baṇa-ra*, in the forest. In the word *padā-ru*, in the field, the ablative is used in the sense of the locative. In pronouns, note the form *tōhōr*, instead of *tō-ra*, thine.

In verbs, we meet *haïlā*, as well as *hēlā*, it became. *Nuhõya*, is 'I am not.' In the past tense, we have *kanĩ*, for *kali*, I did. The tendency of the Standard dialect to drop a medial consonant in this tense is extended to the case of *baïle*, they said, for *balilē*. Instead of *ailē*, we have *āilē*, they came, with the first *a* lengthened, or, rather, with the original long *ā* preserved.

The Habitual Past, which is also used as a Past, not a Present, Conditional, in this agreeing with Bihārī, differs widely from the Standard, and agrees more nearly with Bihārī. Examples are *karati*, I might have made (merry); *karitũ*, we should have made (merriment): *haïtũ*, we should have become (merry); *jānt*, they used to go; *balā̃t*, they used to say. The following forms of the Present Definite are irregular, *pāu-chhẽi*, I am getting; *karu-chhẽi*, I am doing. The Conjunctive Past Participle with *kari*, which is common in Bihārī, also frequently occurs. Thus, *jāi-kari*, having gone; *uṭhi-kari*, having arisen, and many others.

The Potential Passive, formed by adding *ā* to the root, which is common in Bihārī, also occurs. Instances are *suṇāy*, it can be heard; and perhaps *kahēbā lāekar*, worthy of being called.

[No. 5.]

INDO-ARYAN FAMILY. EASTERN GROUP.

ORIYĀ.

NORTH-WESTERN MIXED DIALECT. (JASHPUR STATE.)

SPECIMEN I.

(Babu Manmatha Nath Chatterji, 1898.)

କୋଣସୀ ମନୁଷର ଦୋଇଟି ପୁଅ ଥିଲା । ସାନ ପୁଅ ବାପଙ୍କୁ କହିଲା : ଏ ବୁଆ ଯାହା ଧନ ମାଲ୍ ଘର ଅଛି ତାହା ମତେ ବାଣ୍ଟି ଦେ । ଆଉ ସେ ଆପଣ ଜିନା ସେମାନଙ୍କୁ ବାଣ୍ଟି ଦେଲା । ଆଉ ଭଉତ ଦିନ ନାହିଁ ହୋଇ କି ସେ ସାନ ପୁଅ ସବୁ ଠୁଳିଇଲା ବଡେ ଦୂର ପଳାଇଲା ଆଉ ସେଠାରେ ସବୁ ଧନ ମାଲ୍ ବୁଡ଼ାଇ ଦେଲା । ଆଉ ଯେବେ ତାର ସବୁ ସର ଗଲା ସେ ମୁଲୁକର ବଡ଼ା ମହଙ୍ଗୀ ପଡ଼ିଲା । ଆଉ ସେ ଦୁଖ ପାଇଲା । ଆଉ ସେ ଯାଇକରି . ସେ ମୁଲୁକର ଏକ ମାନୁଷର ପାଂଗରେ ଭିଡ଼ କଲା ଆଉ ସେ ତାକୁ ଘୁଷୁରି ଚରାଇବାକୁ ଛାଁଡ଼ଲୁ ପଠାଇଲା । ଆଉ ଯାହା ଘୁଷୁରୀ ଚୁଷ ଖାଉଥିଲା ତାହା ଖାଇକରି ସେ ଖୁସୀରେ ପେଟ ଭରନ୍ତା । ତାହାଭି କେହି ନାହିଁ ଦେନେ । ଆଉ

[No. 5.]

INDO-ARYAN FAMILY. EASTERN GROUP.

ORIYA.

NORTH-WESTERN MIXED DIALECT. (JASHPUR STATE.)

SPECIMEN I.

TRANSLITERATION AND TRANSLATION.

(Babu Manmatha Nath Chatterji, 1898.)

Kauṇaśī manusa-ra jōṛiē pua thilā. Sāna pua bāpa-ku kahilā, 'ē buā,
A-certain man-of two sons were. The-younger son the-father-to said, 'O father,

jāhā dhana-māla ghara achhi tāhā matē baṇṭā dē.' Āu sē
what property (in)house is that me-to share give.' And he

āpaṇa jinā sē-mānaṅ-ka bā̃ṭi-dēlā. Āu bhaüt dini nāhī̃
his living them-to dividing-gave. And many days not

hōi ki sē sāna pua sabu ṭhuṛaïlā baṛē dhura paṛāilā. Āu
passed that that younger son all gathered a-great distance(to) fled. And

sē-ṭhārē sabu dhana-māla buṛāi-dēlā. Āu jēbē tā-ra sabu
there all the-property caused-to-sink. And when his all

sarī-galā sē mulukha-ra baṛā mahā̃gī paṛilā, āu sē dukha
was-spent-entirely that country-in great famine fell, and he distress

pāilā. Āu sē jāi-kari sē mulukha-ra jhaṇē mānusa-ra
got. And he having-gone that country-of one man-of

sāṅgga-rē bhāva kalā, āu sē tā-ku ghusarā charāibā-ku ḍā̃ṛa-ku
company-in acquaintance made, and he him swine feeding-for the-field-to

paṭhāilā. Āu jāhā ghusarā tusa khāu-thilā tāhā pāunē-i
sent. And what swine husks eating-were that if-he-had-got-even

sē khūsī-rē khāi-jāitā; tāhā-bhi kēhi nāhī̃ dēlā. Āu
he gladness-with would-have-eaten-up; that-even any-one not gave. And

ସେତେବେ ତାକୁ ସୁରତ ହେଲା ସେ କହିଲା ଆମ୍ଭର ବାପ ଘରେ ଏତେ ଗୁଡ଼ି ଧାଙ୍ଗଡ଼ା ଭଉତ୍ ଖାଉଛନ୍ତି ଆଉ ଏଠି ଏତକି ମାନ ଭୁଖ ଭୁଖ ମାଉରେଛେଁରେ । ମୁଁ ଏଠୁଁ ଉଠି ମୋ ଲୋଗବି ମୋର ବାପ କତକେ ଯିବି ଆଉ ତଠି କହିବି ଏ ବୁଆ ମୁ ଦେବ ଠାରେ ଆଉ ତୋଠାରେ ଦୋଷ କଲି । ଅଥର ମୁ ତୋର ପୁଅ କହେବା ଲାଏକର ନୁହେଁଇ । ମୁ ସେ ସବୁ ଗୁଡ଼ି ଧାଙ୍ଗଡ଼ ରଖିଛୁ ସେ ପୋକର ସରି ମତେ ରଖ । ଆଉ ସେ ହେଠୁଁ ଉଠିକରି ତାର ବାପ କତକେ ଗଲା । ତାକୁ ବଡ଼ ଦୂରଁ ବାପ ଦେଖିଲା । ଆଉ ବାପକୁ ଦୁଃଖ ହେଲା । ବାପ କୁଦି ଗଲା ଆଉ ପୁଅର ବେକକୁ ପୁଟାଟି ଧରିଲା ଆଉ ତାକୁ ଚୁକ ଦେଲା । ଆଉ ପୁଅ ତାକୁ କହିଲା ଏ ବୁଆ ମୁ ଦେବ ଠାରେ ଆଉ ତୋର ଦେଖିବାକୁ ଦୋଷ କଲିଁ । ଆଉ ତୋର ପୁଅ ଲାଏକର ମୁ ନୁହେଁଇ । ସେଠୁଁ ବାପ ଗୁଡ଼ି ହାଉଡ଼ିଠି କହିଲା ସବୁଠୁଁ ସେ ନୂଆ ବେଶ ଅଛି ତାକୁ ବାହାରା ଆଉ ତାକୁ ପିନ୍ଧାଇ ଦିଅ । ଆଉ ତାର ଅଂଗୁଳିରେ

jēbē tā-ku surtā hēlā sē kahilā, 'āmbha-ra bāpa gharē
when him-to sense became he said, 'my father's house-in

ētē guti-dhāṉggaṛa bhaüt khāu-chhanti, āu ēṭhi ētki mān-ḍukha
so-many servants much are-eating, and here so-much distress

bhūkha pāu-chhē̃i. Mu ēṭhū uṭhi palāibi, mō-ra bāpa-katkī
hunger I-am-getting. I here-from having-arisen will-run-away, my father-toward

jibi āu tā-ṭhi kahibi, "ē buā, mu daiba-ṭhārē āu tō-ṭhārē
I-will-go and him-to I-will-say, "O father, I God-near and thee-near

dōsha kanī, athara mu tō-ra pua kahēbā lāekar nuhōya.
sin did, after-this I thy son to-be-called worthy am-not.

Tu jē pari guti-dhāṉggaṛa rakhi-chhu sē jhaṇa-ka-ra pari matē rakha."'
Thou what like servants hast-kept that one-person-of like me keep."'

Āu sē hē-ṭhū uṭhi-kari tā-ra bāpa-katkī galā. Tā-ku baṛa dharī
And he there-from having-arisen his father-toward went. Him great distance-from

bāpa dēkhilā; āu bāpa-ku suga haïlā. Bāpa kudi gali
the-father saw; and the-father-to sorrow became. The-father having-run went

āu pua-ra bēk-ku puṭāṛi-pakāilā, āu tā-ku buka dēlā.
and the-son's neck having-embraced-clasped, and him-to kiss gave.

Āu pua tā-ku kahilā, 'ē buā, mu daiba-ṭhārē āu tō-ra
And the-son him-to said, 'O father, I God-near and thy

dēkhibā-ku dōsha kanī. Āu tō-ra pua lāyakar mu nuhōya.'
seeing-to sin did. And thy son worth-of I am-not.'

Sē-ṭhū bāpa guti-hāṛi-ṭhi kahilā, sabu-ṭhū jē nugā bēs achhi,
That-on the-father the-servants-to said, all-than what cloth best is,

tā-ku bāhārā, āu tā-ku pīdhaï-dia; āu tā-ra āṉggu|aria
that bring-out, and him-to clothe; and his finger-on

ମୁଦି ଦେଇଁଦିଅ. ଆଉ ଗୋଡ଼ରେ ପାହେଲ ଘଞ୍ଚେଇ ଦିଅ । ଏବେ ଆଉଁ ସେଉଁ ଆନନ୍ଦ କରୁଁ । କାହିଁକି ଏ ମୋର ପୁଅ ମରି ଯାଇଥିଲା ଅଥର ଜୀଇଲା ଆଉ ହଜି ଯାଇଥିଲା ସେ ଅଥର ମିଳିଲା । ଆଉ ସେ ମାନେ ଖୁସି ହୋଇ ଲାଗିଲେ ।

ସେ ସମୟରେ ବଡ଼ ପୁଅ ପଦାରେ ଥିଲା । ଆଉ ସେ ଗୁଡ଼ି ଲୋକକୁ ଡାକିଲା ଆଉ ତାକୁ ପଚାରିଲା କି ଏଠି କିସ ହିସ ହୋଇଛି । ସେ ତାକୁ କହିଲା ତୋର ଭାଇ ଆସିଛି । ଆଉ ତୋର ବାପ ଖିଆଉଛି ପିଆଉଛି । କାହିଁକି ତାକୁ ଦେହେ ଦେହେ ପାଇଲା । ଆଉ ତାକୁ ରିସା ହେଲା ଆଉ ସେ ଭିତରକୁ ନାହିଁ ଯାଉଥିଲା । ଏଠି ତାହିଁକି ବାପ ତାର ବାହାର ଆଇଲା ଆଉ ତାକୁ ସମଝାଇଲା ବୁଝାଇଲା । ତେତେବେଳେ ସେ ଜବାବର ବାପକୁ କହିଲା : ଦେଖତ ମୁ ଏତେ ବରଷରୁଁ ତୋର କାମ କରୁଛେଁଇ କେବେହେଁ ମୁ ତୋର କଥାରୁଁ ବାହାର ନାହିଁ ହେଇ ତେବେଭି ମତେ ଛେଳି ଛୁଆଟେ ଅନ୍ମାନ୍ ଲାଇ .

mudi pĩdhaï-dia ; āu guṛa-rē pāṇhaï maṇḍēi-dia. Ebē
ring put ; and feet-on shoes put. Now

khāũ piũ ānanda karũ. Kāhĩki ê mō-ra pua mari
let-us-eat drink rejoicing make. Because this my son dead

jāi-thilā, athara jiïlā ; āu haji jāi-thilā, sē athara
gone-had, and-now lived ; and lost gone-had, he now

miḷilā.' Āu sē-mānē khusi hōï lāgilē.
was-found.' And they merry to-be began.

Sē pahariyā baṛa pua padā-ru thilā. Āu
(At)that time the-elder son field-in was. And

sē guti-jhaṇa-ku ḍākilā, āu tā-ku pachārilā ki, 'ēṭhi kisa kisa
he a-servant-person-to called, and him-to asked that, 'here what what

hōi-chhi ?' Sē tā-ku kahilā, 'tō-ra bhāi āsi-chhi. Āu tō-ra
is-going-on ?' He him-to said, 'thy brother is-come. And thy

bāpa khiaü-chhi piaü-chhi ; kāhĩki tā-ku besēbēs pāilā.'
father feeding-is giving-drink-is ; because him safe-and-sound got.'

Āu tā-ku risā haïlā āu sē bhitara-ku nāhĩ jāu-thilā. Eṭhi
And him-to anger became and he within-to not going-was. This-for

pāhĩki bāpa tā-ra bahiri āilā, āu tā-ku samajhāilā bujhāilā.
reason the-father him-of out came, and him-to entreated (and)explained.

Tētēbēṛē sē jabāba-ra bāpa-ku kahilā : 'dēkha-ta, mu ētē
Then he answer-in the-father-to said : 'see-now, I so-many

barasa-rũ tō-ra kāma karu-chhẽi ; kēbēhẽ mu tō-ra kathā-rũ bāhār
years-from thy work doing-am ; at-any-time I thy word-from beyond

nāhĩ haï ; tēbē-bhi matē chhēṛi-chhuā-ṭhē anmān nāi
not am ; nevertheless to-me she-goat-kid-one even not

ଦେଲୁ କି ପୁ ମୋର ସଙ୍ଗେ ମାନଙ୍କ ସାଂଗରେ ଖୁସି କରନ୍ତି । ଏବେ
ତୋର ଏ ପୁଅ ଆସି ହେଲା ଯେ ତୋର ଜୀଉନାକୁ ଦାଣ୍ଡ-ଘାଟରେ ଆଳି
ମାନଙ୍କ ସୁଖରେ ଦେଲା ତା ଲାଗି ତୁ ଭୋଜି ଦେଉଛୁ । ତେବେ
40. ସେ ତାଙ୍କି କହିଲା ଏ ପୁଅ ତୁ ସବୁ ଦିନେ ମୋ ସାଂଗରେ ଅଛୁ ;
ଆଉ ଯାହା ମୋର ଅଛି ସେ ସବୁ ତୋହୋର । ଆମ୍ଭେ ଏ ଅବେ ରହୁଥିଲା
କି ଖୁସି କରନ୍ତୁଁ ଆଉ ଖୁସି ହବନ୍ତୁଁ : କାହିଁକି ଏ ତୋର ଭାଇ ମରି
ଯାଇଥିଲା ଆଉ ଫେର ଏବେ ଜୀଇଲା । ହଜି ଯାଇଥିଲା ଆଉ
ଅଧର ମିଳିଲା ।

dēlu ki mu mō-ra sakhi-mānaka sāṅgga-rē khusi karati. Jēbē
thou-gavest that I my friends with merriment might-have-made. When

tō-ra ē pua āsi-hēlā jē tō-ra jiunā-ku dāri-pātariāṇi-
thy this son had-come who thy living harlots-to

māna-ka khuaï dēlā, tā lāgi tu bhōja dēu-chhu.' Tēbē
having-fed has-given, him for thou feast art-giving.' Then

sē tā-ṭhi kahilā, 'ē pua, tu sabu dinē mo sāṅgga-rē achhu;
he him-to said, 'O son, thou all days me with art;

āu jāhā mō-ra achhi, sē sabu tōhōr-i. Āmbha-tē ē pari chāhu-thilā
and what mine is, that all thine-even. To-us this like was-meet

ki khusi karitũ, āu khusi haïtũ, kāhĩki ē tō-ra
that merriment we-should-have-made, and glad should-have-become, because this thy

bhāi mari jāi-thilā, āu phēra ēbhē jiilā; haji jāi-thilā, au
brother dead gone-had, and again now lived; lost gone-had, and

athara miḷilā.'
now was-found.'

[No. 6.]

INDO-ARYAN FAMILY. EASTERN GROUP.

ORIYĀ.

NORTH-WESTERN MIXED DIALECT. (JASHPUR STATE.)

SPECIMEN II.

(Babu Manmatha Nath Chatterji, 1898.)

ଗୁଟେ ରଜା ଥଲା । ତାର୍ ଘରେ । ସୁଆ ଥଲା । ତାର୍
ଛିଅଟେ । ସୁଅର ବହୁ ଆନି ଥଲା । ଗୁଟେ ସୁଅର ବହି ନାଇ
ଆନି ଥଲା । ସେ ଛିଅଟେ । ତାର୍ କିଆ କହ୍ର ସାଙ୍ଗୁ
ଯାନ ତାର୍ କୋଟେ କାମ କର୍ ନାଇ ସାଙ୍ଗୁ
ସେ ଛି ତାର୍ ସାଙ୍ଗି ବିଆହିଁ ପାନି ତାରକି ତାଟି
ଜେଲ ଦେବୁ କାଳକୁ ସେ କୋଟେ ନାଇ ନେଇ ଦିଏ ।
ବଡକୁ ଦିନେ ଛି ତାର୍ ବିପେର ଗଲେ । ବଇଲେ
ଆଜି ବଜାର ଜେଇ କର ସୁଦି ଦିଅ । ତାକୁ ବଜାର
ନେଇ କହ୍ର ଘୁଷି ଦେଲେ । ଘରକୁ ଫେର ଆଇଲେ ।
ଛି ତାର୍ ଆଜି ଘରକୁ ଫେର ଆଇଲେ ବାପକୁ ତାର୍

[No. 6.]

INDO-ARYAN FAMILY. EASTERN GROUP.

OṚIYA.

NORTH-WESTERN MIXED DIALECT. (JASHPUR STATE.)

SPECIMEN II.

TRANSLITERATION AND TRANSLATION.

(Babu Manmatha Nath Chatterji, 1898.)

Guṭī rajā thilā. Tā-ra sāt-ṭā pua thilā. Tā-ra
One king was. Him-of seven sons were. Him-of

chhaya-ṭā pua-ra bahu āni-thilā. Guṭē pua-ra bahu nāi
six sons-of wives he-had-brought. One son-of wife not

āni-thilā. Sē chha-ṭā bhāi kama kari jānt;
he-had-brought. Those six brothers work to-do would-go;

sāna bhāi kēbhē kama kari nāi jāya.
the-youngest brother ever work to-do not goes.

Sē chha bhāi jāka balāt sāna bhāi-ki, 'bhāta
Those six brothers when would-say youngest brother-to, 'boiled-rice

nēi dēbu,' baḷaku sē kēbhē nāi nēi diē.
having-taken (to-us) give,' but he ever not having-taken (to them)gives.

Baṛaku dinē chha bhāi khisēi galē. Bailē,
Many days-after six brothers angry became. They-said,

'āku baṇa-ra nēi-kari puji-dia.' Tā-ku baṇa-ra
'him the-wood-in having-taken let-us-out-down.' Him a-wood-in

nēi-kari puji-dēlē. Ghara-ku phēri āilē.
having-taken they-out-down. Home-to back they-came.

Chha bhāi jāka ghara-ku phēri āilā, baṛaku tā-ra
Six brothers when home-to back they-came, then their

ମା ପଚାରିଲା ମୋର ଧାନ ଗୁଆ କାହିଁ ଗଲା। ଚଢ଼େଇକୁ ଛ ଭାଇ ଆସି କହିଲେ କି ତୋର ଧାନ ଗୁଆକୁ ମାରି ଦେଇ ଜାଇ ସଙ୍ଗରେ ଆଣିନୁ । ତାର ମା କହିଲା କିସ ଲାଗି ଯାଇଲା ରେ ଗୁଏ କୋଠି ମାରୁଛି ଗୁଲି କରି ଦିଅ କଡ଼ିକୁ ମାକୁ । ଦାଗରେ କାଟି ନେଇ ଦେଲେ । ଦେଖିଲା ଯେ ଗୁଣ୍ଡ ଛିଡି ଜାଇ ପଡିଛି । କାହିଁକି ମୋର ଗୁଆକୁ ମାରିଲ ରେ ଗୁଏ । କହିଲା କି କାଳୀଗ୍ରହ କରି ଯାଇଲା । କହୁଛି କ୍ରନ୍ଦନ କଲା । ମହାଦେବ ପାର୍ବତି ଆକାଶରେ ଯାଉଥିଲେ ପାର୍ବତି ପୁଛିଲେ କହିଲେ କି ମହାଦେବ ଅପେକ୍ଷ ଦେଖ କାହିଁର ଡର ଶୁଣୁ ପୁଲାଞ୍ଚ । ସେ ନାରୀ ଗୁଆକୁ କିଛି କିଅଛି ପଡଛି । ଗଲା ତାକୁ ଦେଖି ଜୀବ ଦାନ କରି ମହାଦେବ ପାର୍ବତି ଉଠିଗଲେ । ପାର୍ବତି ପଚାରିଲେ

mā	pachārilā,	'mō-ra	sāna	pua	kāĩ	galā?'
mother	*asked,*	*'my*	*youngest*	*son*	*where*	*went?'*

Baṛaku	chha	bhāi	jā-ka	baïlē	ki,	'tō-ra	sāna	pua-ku
Then	*six*	*brothers*	*to-her*	*said*	*that,*	*'thy*	*youngest*	*son*

māri-dēi-kari	paḷāi	āinu.'	Tā-ra	mā
having-killed	*running*	*we-came.'*	*Their*	*mother*

baïlā,	'kisa	lāgi	māilā,	rē	puē?	Kēṭhi	māri-chha?
said,	*'what*	*for*	*did-you-kill,*	*O*	*sons?*	*Where*	*have-you-slain?*

chāla	kaï-dia.'	Baṛaku	mā-ku	ḍagaraï-kari
come	*tell (me).'*	*After*	*the-mother*	*having-led*

nēi-dēlē.	Dēkhilā	jē	muṇḍa	chhiṛi-kari
they-took.	*She-saw*	*that*	*head*	*having-been-severed*

paṛi-chhi.	'Kāhiki	mō-ra	pua-kū	māila,	re	puē?'
has-fallen.	*'Why*	*my*	*son*	*did-you-kill,*	*O*	*sons?'*

Baïlā	ki,	'kaḷāgrat	kari-dhaïlā.'	Bahuta
They-said	*that,*	*'fate*	*seized (him).'*	*Much*

rudana	kalā.	Mahādēba	Pārbati	ākāsa-rē	jāu-thilē.
lamentation	*she-made.*	*Mahādēva*	*Pārvatī*	*the-sky-in*	*going-were.*

Pārbati	suṇilē;	baïle	ki,	'Mahādēba,	asēkha	baṇa-ra
Pārvatī	*heard;*	*said*	*that,*	*'(O) Mahādēva,*	*fathomless*	*jungle-in*

kāhira	tiri	ṭuṇḍa	suṇāy?	Sē	nāi,	tā-ku	kichhi
what	*woman's*	*voice*	*is-heard?*	*That*	*not,*	*her-to*	*some*

bipati	paṛi-chhi.'	'Chāla,	tā-ku	dēkhi	jibā,'	bali-kari
calamity	*fallen-has.'*	*'Come,*	*her*	*to-see*	*we-will-go,'*	*having-said*

Mahādēba	Pārbati	utirilē.	Pārbati	pachārilē
Mahādēva	*Pārvatī*	*came-down.*	*Pārvatī*	*asked*

କି ବୁଢ଼ି କାହିଁକି କାନ୍ଦୁଛୁ । ବୁଢ଼ି କହିଲା କି ମୋର

ପୁଅକୁ ମୋର ସାପ ଖାଇ ଦେଲେ । ତେଣୁ କରି

କାନ୍ଦୁଛେଁ । ଯେବେ ମୋର ପୁଅ ନ ଜୀଇବ ତେବେ

ଏହି ପୁଅ ସାଂଗର ମୁ ମରିବି । ପାର୍ବତି କହିଲେ

ହେ ମହାଦେବ ଏହାକୁ ଜିଂଆଇ ଦିଅ । ମହାଦେବ

ଅମୃତ ପାଣି ପୁଅ ମୁହଁକର ଛିଂଚି ଦେଲେ ।

ତିନି ଥର ପାଣି ଛିଂଚିଲେ । ପିଲା ଜିଇ ଉଠି ବସିଲା ।

ki, 'buṛhi kā̃hiki kā̃du-chhu?' Buṛhi baïlā ki, 'mō-ra
that, 'O-old-woman why crying-art-thou?' The-old-woman said that, 'my

putra-ku mō-ra puē māri-dēlē. Tēṇu kari
son my sons killed. That for

kā̃du-chhē. Jēbē mō-ra putra na jiïba hēnē
I-crying-am. When my son not will-live then

ēi putra sāṅggara mu maribi.' Pārbati baïlē,
this son with I will-die.' Pārvatī said,

'hē Mahādēba, ēhā-ku jīāi-dia.' Mahādēba
'O Mahādēva, him bring-to-life.' Mahādēva

amṛuta pāṇi muṇḍa juṛi-kari chhīṭi-dēlē.
nectar water head having-rejoined sprinkled.

Tini muṭhi pāṇi chhīṭilē. Jiï-kari uṭhi basilā.
Three handfuls water he-sprinkled. Having-become-alive having-arisen he-sat.

The language of the Contai Sub-division of the Midnapore District is certainly Oṛiyā, but it is strongly corrupted by the Bengali spoken to the north across the river Haldi. It is not that a new dialect has been formed, partaking of some of the characteristics of each, and intermediate between each language. On the contrary, the language of the sub-division is a curious mixture of fairly pure Bengali and fairly pure Oṛiyā, the speakers using words of each language apparently at haphazard, and mixing them up into a kind of bilingual sentence. The basis of the language is Oṛiyā, that is to say, the majority of words and grammatical forms belong to it, while the rest are Bengali.

It is unnecessary to give full examples of this jargon, and the first few lines of the Parable of the Prodigal Son will be sufficient to show its character.

Judging from the local transliteration, which, in this respect, is reproduced in the transliteration annexed, the language hesitates between the Bengali custom of not pronouncing a final *a*, and the Oṛiyā one of pronouncing it. Thus, take the very first word *jhan-kara*. Here the final *a* of the Oṛiyā *jhana* is omitted, but it is retained at the end of *kara*. On the other hand, in the word *tākara-man-kar*, it is retained in *tākara*, which is itself hardly Oṛiyā, but is omitted at the end of *kar*. In this, too, the Oṛiyā has reverted to what was the original plural form *man-kar*, for *mana-kara*, instead of *maṅkara*. The suffix *rē* of the locative has, as we also notice in Jashpur, become *ra*; and in *madhyēra*, we have a double locative, *viz.*, first the Bengali locative *madhyē* to which has been added the Oṛiyā locative termination *ra*. *Tākar* is Bengalised from *tā-kara*, which is bad Oṛiyā for *tā-ra*. In *bāp-ku*, we have the proper Oṛiyā declension, but the final *a* of *bāpa* has been dropped. Next *bisayēr* is the Oṛiyā pronunciation of the pure Bengali *bishayēr*, instead of the Oṛiyā *bishaya-ra*. On the other hand, *hĩśyā* is the Bengali attempt at representing the sound of *hĩssā*, i.e., *hissā*, and *āmē* is a compromise between the Bengali *āmi*, and the Oṛiyā *āmbhē*. Similarly *ām-ku* is shortened from *āmbha-ku*. *Dina-ra* and *dēśa-ku* are pure Oṛiyā, while *ār*, and, is pure Bengali. In *kari-kiṛi* and *jāi-kiri* we have a true dialectic development, the suffix *kiri*, a corruption itself of the Bihārī *kari*, being used to form a conjunctive participle. *Dabār* is a compromise between the Bengali *dibār* and the Oṛiyā *dēbā-ra*, in which the vowel of the first syllable, being unaccented, has been allowed to go to the wall. In the phrase *hēibē-lāgilā*, the speaker has mixed up the Bengali *haïtē-lāgila* with the Oṛiyā *hēbā-ku*, or *hōibā-ku-lāgilā*. These examples serve to show the nature of this mongrel jargon. I have omitted from consideration most of the pure Oṛiyā forms.

The specimen received from Contai was written in the Bengali character, which is another instance of the composite nature of the language. This character is not suited for writing Oṛiyā, as is shown by the way in which it has been found necessary to spell the word *hissā*.

[No. 7.]

INDO-ARYAN FAMILY.

EASTERN GROUP.

ORIYĀ.

MIXED BENGALI AND ORIYĀ OF CONTAI. (DISTRICT MIDNAPORE.)

ঝনকর দুই পো থিলা, তাকরমন্‌কর মধ্যের সান পো-তাকর বাপকু কহিলা, বাপ ! বিসয়ের জে হিঁশ্যা আমে পাইবা, তা আম্‌কু দিয়া। সে তাঁইর তাকরমন্‌কর মধ্যের বিশয় হিঁশ্যা করি দেলা। অল্প দিনর বাদে সান পো সবু একঠাঁই করি কিরি দূর দেশকু চালি গলা, আর সেঠি সে বেসি খরচ করি কিরি তাকর বিশয় উড়াই দেলা। সে সবু খরচ করিদবার পর সেই মুলুক্‌র ভারি দুর্ভিক্ষ্য পড়িলা, ও তাকর কষ্ট হেইবে লাগিলা। তেতে বেলে সে জাইকিরি সেই দেসর ঝনে দেসবাসির শরন নেলা। সে লোক তাকু নিজর বিলরে ঘুসরি চরাইবাকু পাঠাই দেলা॥

TRANSLITERATION AND TRANSLATION.

Jhan-kara dui pō thilā. Tākara-man-kar madhyēra sāna pō tākar
A-man-of two sons were. Them-of among the-younger son his
bāp-ku kahilā, 'bāpa, bisayēr jē hĩśyā āmē pāibā, tā ām-ku
father-to said, 'father, of-the-property what share I will-get, that me-to
diyā.' Sē tā̃i-ra tākara-man-kar madhyēra biśaya hĩśyā kari
give.' He there-on them-of among the-property share having-made
dēlā. Alpa dina-ra bādē sāna pō sabu ēk-ṭhā̃i kari-kiri dūra
gave. A-few day-of after the-younger son all together having-made a-far
dēśa-ku chāli-galā, ār sē-ṭhī sē bēsi kharach kari-kiri tā-kar
country-to went-away, and there he excessive expenditure having-done his
biśaya uṛāi-dēlā. Sē sabu kharach kari-dabār par sēi muluk-ra
property squandered. He all expenditure making-of after that country-in
bhāri durbhikhya paṛilā, ō tā-kar kashṭa hēibē lāgilā. Tētē-bēlē sē
a-severe famine fell, and him-of trouble to-be began. Then he
jāi-kiri sēi dēsa-ra jhanē dēsa-bāsir śaran nēlā. Sē
having-gone that country-in a-man country-dweller-of refuge took. That
lōk tā-ku nija-r bila-rē ghusari charāibā-ku pāṭhāi-dēlā.
person him his field-in swine grazing-for sent.

Besides the sub-division of Contai, Oṛiyā is also spoken in the south of Midnapore District, *i.e.*, in the southern half of Thana Narayangarh, and in Thana Dantan.

It is also spoken in the west of the district by the Aryan population of Thanas Gopiballabhpur, Jhargaon, and Binpur. The non-Aryan population of these last Thanas and also of Thana Dantan, speaks Santali. The Oṛiyā of the south of the district is infected by Bengali peculiarities, and that of the west is infected by the language of the non-Aryan inhabitants, and has incorporated a certain number of Santali words into its vocabulary.

It will be sufficient to give one specimen, *viz.*, a version of the Parable of the Prodigal Son in the dialect of Dantan. It will be observed that though affected by Bengali, this has not occurred to nearly the same extent that we have observed in Contai. The form of the Oṛiyā character used in this part of Midnapore differs somewhat from the alphabet used in Balasore and Cuttack. The specimen is therefore given in the vernacular character in facsimile, as it was written down by a Dantan man. Besides variations in the actual shapes of the letters, it will be noticed that there is a strong tendency to give an angular shape to the top curve which is so characteristic of the Oṛiyā alphabet. The dialect of South Midnapore is sufficiently distinct from that of Orissa proper, to prevent the respective speakers of these dialects from being always mutually intelligible, and a similar want of mutual legibility exists between the written characters of the two tracts. There are numerous stories current whose points depend on the mistakes made by a speaker of one dialect when listening to a speaker of the other.

In the vernacular character a short *i* is often written as if it were a long *ī*. I have silently corrected this in the transliteration. As regards pronunciation, it will be seen that the Bengali influence is sufficiently strong to prevent the sounding of the vowel *a* when it occurs at the end of a word. In order to illustrate this, I have followed the local transliteration in every case in which a final *a* is written or omitted.

The following Bengalisms may be noted :—

1. The use of the present tense of the verb in a past sense, when accompanied by a negative. Thus, *kari nāhĩ*, I did not make; *diya nāhĩ*, you did not give.
2. The use of the Bengali infinitive, as in *charāitē paṭhāi-dēlē*, he sent him to feed; *karitē lāgilē*, they began to make; *dēitē lāgilē*, he began to give.
3. Miscellaneous idioms, such as *pāoyā jāi-chhi*, he has been found; *harā hōi thilā*, he had been lost; and others.

The following are dialectic forms.—*Habā-ru* for *hēbā-ru*, from becoming; *nahũ* for *nāhũ*, I am not; *kari-achhanta*, he has made; *pāi-achhanta*, he has got; and others.

[No. 8.]

INDO-ARYAN FAMILY. EASTERN GROUP.

ORIYA.

MIXED DIALECT OF DANTAN THANA. MIDNAPORE DISTRICT.

(Babu Krishna Kishor Acharji, 1898.)

ଏକ ଲୋକର ଦୁଇଟା ପୁଅ ଥିଲୁ ସେମାନଙ୍କର ମଧ୍ୟରେ ସାନ ଆପଣାର ବାପକୁ କହିଲା ବାପା। ସମ୍ପତ୍ତିର ଯେଉଁଭାଗ ଆମ୍ଭେ ପାଇବୁ ତାହା ଆମ୍ଭଙ୍କୁ ଦିଅ। ତହୁଁ ସେ ସେମାନଙ୍କ ମଧ୍ୟରେ ବିଷୟ ଭାଗ କରି ଦେଲେ। ଅଳପ ଦିନ ମଧ୍ୟରେ ସାନ ପୁଅ ସମସ୍ତ ଏକତ୍ର କରି ଦୂର ଦେଶକୁ ଚାଲିଗଲା। ଆଉ ସେଠାରେ ବହୁତ ଖରଚ କରି ବିଷୟ ଉଡ଼ାଇଦେଲା ସେ ସବୁ ଖରଚ କରିବାର ପର ସେ ଦେଶରେ ଅତ୍ୟନ୍ତ ଅକାଳ ହବାରୁ ସେ କଷ୍ଟରେ ପଡ଼ିଲା ସେ ସମୟରେ ସେ ଯାଇ ସେଠାର ଏକ ନଗର ବାସୀର ଆଶ୍ରୟ ନେଲା ସେ ତାହାକୁ ଆପଣାର ବିଲରେ ଘୁଷୁରୀ ଚରାଇବାକୁ ପଠାଇ

[No. 8.]

INDO-ARYAN FAMILY.

EASTERN GROUP.

OṚIYĀ.

MIXED DIALECT OF DANTAN THANA. (MIDNAPORE DISTRICT.)

TRANSLITERATION AND TRANSLATION.

(Babu Krishna Kishor Acharji, 1898.)

Ēk	jaṇa-ra	dui-ṭi	puya	thilā.	Sē-mānaṅka-ra	madhya-rē
One	*person-of*	*two*	*sons*	*were.*	*Them-of*	*among*

sāna	āpaṇā-ra	pitā-ku	kahilā,	'bāpa,	sampatti-ra	jē	bhāg
the-younger	*his-own*	*father-to*	*said,*	*'father,*	*the-property-of*	*what*	*share*

āmbhē	pāibu,	tāhā	āmbha-ku	diya.'	Tahī-rē	sē-mānaṅka
I	*will-get,*	*that*	*me-to*	*give.'*	*There-on*	*them*

madhya-rē	bishaya	bhāg	kari	dēlē.	Alpa	din	madhya-rē
among	*wealth*	*division*	*having-made*	*he-gave.*	*A-few*	*days*	*in*

sāna	puya	samasta	ēkatra	kari	dūra	dēśa-ku	paḷāi	galā.
the-younger	*son*	*everything*	*together*	*having-made*	*a-far*	*country-to*	*having-run-away*	*went.*

Ār	sē-ṭhārē	bahut	kharach	kari	bishaya	uṛāi-dēlā.
And	*there*	*much*	*expenditure*	*having-made*	*wealth*	*squandered.*

Sē	sabu	kharach	karibā-r	par	sē	dēśa-rē	atyanta
That	*all*	*expenditure*	*making-of*	*after*	*that*	*country-in*	*an-excessive*

akāḷ	habā-ru	sē	kashṭa-rē	paṛilā.	Sē	samaya-rē
famine	*occurring-from*	*he*	*distress-in*	*fell.*	*That*	*time-at*

sē	jāi	sē-ṭhāra-r	ēk	nagar-bāsi-r	āśraya	nēlā.
he	*having-gone*	*that-place-of*	*a*	*city-dweller-of*	*refuge*	*took.*

Sē	tāhā-ku	āpaṇā-r	bila-rē	ghusarī	charāitē	paṭhāi-
He	*him-to*	*his-own*	*field-in*	*swine*	*to-feed*	*despatched.*

ଦେଲେ ଘୁଷୁରୀ ଯେ ଖୋସା ଖାଏ ତହିଁରେ ପେଟ ଭରଣ ଯାକୁ ଇଚ୍ଛା କଲା କିନ୍ତୁ କେହି ତାହାକୁ ଦେଲା ନାହିଁ ପରେ ଚେତିଲା ପାରେ ସେ କହିଲା ଆମ୍ଭ ବାପର କେତେ ବେତନ-ଭୋଗୀ ଲୋକର ଦରକାରୁ ଅଧିକ ଖାଇବାକୁ ଅଛି; ଆଉ ଆମ୍ଭେ ଏଠାରେ କ୍ଷୁଧାରେ ମରୁଅଛୁଁ । ଆମ୍ଭେ ଉଠି ଆମ୍ଭର ବାପାଙ୍କୁ ଯିବୁ ତାହାଙ୍କୁ କହିବୁ ଆମ୍ଭେ-ତୁମ୍ଭର ସାକ୍ଷାତରେ ଓ ଭଗବାନଙ୍କ ବିରୁଦ୍ଧରେ ପାପ କରିଅଛୁଁ । ଆମ୍ଭେ ଆଉ ତୁମ୍ଭର ପୁତ୍ର ବୋଲି ଗଣିବାକୁ ଯୋଗ୍ୟ ନହୁଁ । ଆମ୍ଭକୁ ତୁମ୍ଭର ଗୋଟିଏ ବେତନଭୋଗୀ ଲୋକ ପରି ରଖ । ପରେ ସେ ଉଠି ଆପଣାର ବାପାଙ୍କୁ ଗଲା ଦୂରରୁ ତାହାର ବାପ ତାହାକୁ ଦେଖିବାକୁ ପାଇ ଦୟାର୍ଦ୍ର ଚିତ୍ତ ହୋଇ ଦଉଡ଼ି ଯାଇ ତାହାର ବେକ ଧରି ଚୁମ୍ବନ କରିଲେ । ପୁତ୍ର ତାହାଙ୍କୁ

dēlē.	Ghusarī	jē	khaśā	khāya,	tahī-rē	sē	pēṭ	bharāī-
	The-swine	*what*	*husks*	*eat,*	*that-on*	*he*	*the-belly*	*filling-*

bā-ku	ichchhā	kalā;	kintu	kēhi	tāhā-ku	dēlā	nāhī.	Parē
for	*wish*	*made;*	*but*	*anyone*	*him-to*	*gave*	*not.*	*Afterwards*

akkēl	pāi	sē	kahilē,	'āmbha	bāpa-r	kētē	bētan-
senses	*having-got*	*he*	*said,*	*'my*	*father-of*	*how-many*	*wages-*

bhōgī	chākar	darakār	adhik	khāibā-ku	pāya,	ār
enjoying	*servants*	(*than*) *what-is-necessary*	*more*	*eating-for*	*get,*	*and*

āmbhē	ē-ṭhārē	khyudhā-rē	maru-achhū.	Āmbhē	uṭhi
I	*here*	*hunger-in*	*dying-am.*	*I*	*having-arisen*

āmbha-r	bāpa-ṭhāku	jibu;	tāhāṅ-ku	kahibu,	"āmbhē
my	*father-near*	*will-go;*	*him-to*	*I-will-say,*	"*I*

tumbha-r	sākhyāta-rē	ō	bhagabānaṅka	biruddha-rē	pāp
you-of	*sight-in*	*and*	*God-of*	*opposition-in*	*sin*

kari-achhū.	Āmbhē	āu	tumbha-r	putra	bōli
done-have.	*I*	*any-more*	*your*	*son*	*being-called*

parichaya	dēbā-r	jōgya	nahū.	Āmbha-ku	tumbha-r
recognition	*giving-of*	*fit*	*am-not.*	*Me*	*your*

janē	bētan-bhōgī	chākar	pari	rakha."'	Parē	sē
a-person	*wages-enjoying*	*servant*	*like*	*keep."'*	*Afterwards*	*he*

uṭhi	āpaṇār	bāpa-ṭhāku	galā.	Dūra-ru	tāhā-r	pitā
having-arisen	*his-own*	*father-near*	*went.*	*A-distance-from*	*his*	*father*

tāhā-ku	dēkhibā-ku	pāi,	dayārdra-chitta	hōi,	dauṛi
him	*seeing-to*	*having-got,*	*compassion-moistened-minded*	*having-become,*	*having-run*

jāi,	tāhā-r	gaḷā	dhari,	chumban	karilē.	Putra	tāhā-ku
having-gone,	*his*	*neck*	*having-seized,*	*kissing*	*did.*	*The-son*	*him-to*

କହିଲା ବାପ ଆମ୍ଭେ ତୁମ୍ଭର ସାକ୍ଷାତରେ ଓ ଭଗବାନଙ୍କ ବିରୁଦ୍ଧରେ ପାପ କରିଅଛୁ ଆମ୍ଭେ ତୁମ୍ଭର ପୁତ୍ର ବୋଲି ପରିଚିତ ହୋଇବାର ଯୋଗ୍ୟ ନହୁଁ। ଆମ୍ଭକୁ ତୁମ୍ଭର ଜଣେ ବେତନ ଭୋଗୀ ଭୃତ୍ୟ ପରି ରଖ କିନ୍ତୁ ତାହାଙ୍କର ବାପ ଆପଣା ଭୃତ୍ୟ ମାନଙ୍କୁ କହିଲେ ଶୀଘ୍ର ଭଲ ଲୁଗା ଆଣି ଏହାଙ୍କୁ ପରିଧାଅ ଓ ଏହାଙ୍କ ହାତରେ ଅଙ୍ଗୁଠି ଓ ଗୋଡ଼ରେ ଯୋତା ପରିଧାଅ ଓ ଆସ ଆମ୍ଭେ ଖାଇପିଇ ଆନନ୍ଦ କରୁଁ। କାରଣ ଆମ୍ଭର ପୁତ୍ର ମରି ଯାଇଥିଲା ବଞ୍ଚି ଅଛି ହଜି ଯାଇଥିଲା ପାଓ୍ୱା। ପାଇଅଛୁଁ। ପରେ ସେମାନେ ଆନନ୍ଦ କରିବାକୁ ଲାଗିଲେ ॥

ଆଉ ତାହାଙ୍କର ବଡ଼ ପୁଅ କିଲରେ ଥିଲା। ସେ ଆସି ଘର ପାଖରେ ପହଞ୍ଚି ଗୀତ ବାଦ୍ୟ ଶୁଣିବାକୁ ପାଇଲା ସେ

kahilā, 'bāp, āmbhē tumbha-r sākhyāta-rē ō
said, 'father, I you-of sight-in and

bhagabānaṅka biruddha-rē pāp kari-achhũ. Āmbhē
God-of opposition-in sin done-of. I

tumbha-r putra bōli parichita hōibā-r jōgya nahũ.
your son being-called recognised being-of fit am-not.

Āmbha-ku tumbha-r janē bētan-bhōgī chākar pari
Me your a-person wages-enjoying servant like

rakha.' Kintu tāhāṅka-r bāp āpaṇ chākar-mānaṅku
keep.' But his father his-own servants-to

kahilē, 'śīghra bhala lugā āṇi-kari ihāṅku
said, 'quickly good cloth having-brought this-person-to

paharāo; ō ihāṅku hāta-rē aṅguri ō gōṛa-rē
clothe; and this-person-to the-hand-on a-ring and the-foot-on

jutā paharāo; ō āmbha-mānē āhāra kari ānanda
shoe put-on; and (let) us feeding having-done rejoicing

karũ. Kāraṇ āmbha-r putra mari jāi-thilā, bañchi-
make. Because my son having-died gone-was, survived-

achhi; harā hōi-thilā, pāoyā-(pāwā) jāi-chhi.' Parē
has; lost been-had, found gone-is.' Afterwards

sē-māna ānanda karitē lāgilē.
they rejoicing to-do began.

Āu tāhāṅka-r baṛa puya bila-rē thilā. Sē āsi ghara
And his elder son the-field-in was. He having-come the-house

pākha-rē pahañchi gāṇ-bādya śunibā-ku pāilā.
neighbourhood-in having-arrived singing-music hearing-to got. He

ଏଣେ ଗୋଟିଏ ଚାକରକୁ ଡାକି ପଚାରିଲା ଏ ସବୁ କି? ସେ ତାହାକୁ କହିଲା ତୁମ୍ଭର ଭାଇ ଆସିଅଛି । ଆଉ ତୁମ୍ଭର ବାପ ଉତ୍ତମ ଖାଦ୍ୟ ଭୋଜି କରିଅଛନ୍ତି ଯେହେତୁ ସେ ତାହାକୁ ସୁସ୍ଥ ଅବସ୍ଥାରେ ପାଇଅଛନ୍ତି କିନ୍ତୁ ସେ କ୍ରୋଧ ଭିତରକୁ ଗଲା ନାହିଁ ଏଣେ ତାହାଙ୍କର ବାପ ବାହାରକୁ ଆସି ତାହାକୁ ପ୍ରବୋଧ ଦେଇ ଡେକାଇଲେ । କିନ୍ତୁ ସେ ଜବାବ ଦେଇ ଆପଣ ବାପକୁ କହିଲା, ଦେଖ ଏତେ ବରଷ ଧରି ତୁମ୍ଭର ସେବା କରିଅଛି, ତୁମ୍ଭର କୌଣସି ଆଜ୍ଞା ଲଙ୍ଘନ କରି ନାହିଁ ତଥାପି ତୁମ୍ଭେ କୌଣସି ଦିନ ଆମ୍ଭକୁ ଗୋଟିଏ ଛେଳି ଛୁଆ ଟିଏ ଦେଇ ନାହିଁ ଯେ ଆମ୍ଭେ ବନ୍ଧୁ ମାନଙ୍କ ସଙ୍ଗେ ଆନନ୍ଦ କରୁ । କିନ୍ତୁ ତୁମ୍ଭର ଏ ସନ୍ତାନ କସବା ମାନଙ୍କ ସଙ୍ଗରେ

janē	chākara-ku	ḍāki	pacharilā,	'ē	sabu	ki?'	Sĕ	tāhāku
a-person	*servant-to*	*having-called*	*asked,*	*'this*	*all*	*what?'*	*He*	*him-to*

kahilā,	tumbha-r	bhāi	āsi-achhi,	āu	tumbha-r
said,	*your*	*brother*	*come-has,*	*and*	*your*

bāp	uttama	khādya	tayāri	kari-achhanta,	kēnēnā
father	*excellent*	*food*	*preparation*	*made-has,*	*because*

sē	tāhāṅku	sustha	abasthā-rē	pāi-achhanta.'	Kintu
he	*him*	*healthy*	*condition-in*	*found-has.'*	*But*

sē	rāgi	bhitar-ku	galā	nāhĩ.	Parē	tāhāṅka-r
he	*having-become-angry*	*inside-to*	*went*	*not.*	*Afterwards*	*his*

bāp	bāhār-ku	āsi	tāhā-ku	prabōdh	dēitē
father	*outside-to*	*having-come*	*him-to*	*remonstrance*	*to-give*

lāgilē.	Kintu	sē	jabāb	dēi	âpaṇ	bāpa-ku
began.	*But*	*he*	*answer*	*having-given*	*his-own*	*father-to*

kahilā,	'dēkha,	ētē	barash	dhari	mu	tumbha-r	sēbā
said,	*'see,*	*so-many*	*years*	*during*	*I*	*your*	*service*

kari-achhi;	tumbha-r	kōna	ājñā	kēbhē	laṅghan
done-have;	*your*	*any*	*order*	*at-any-time*	*infringement*

kari	nāhĩ;	tathāpi	tumbhē	kōṇaśi	dina	āmbha-ku
I-made	*not;*	*nevertheless*	*you*	*any*	*day*	*me-to*

guṭiyē	chhēḷi-chhuyā	madhya	diya	nāhĩ,	jē
a-single	*goat-young-one*	*even*	*gave*	*not,*	*that*

āmbhē	bandhu-mānaṅku	nēi	ānanda	karĩ.	Kintu
I	*friends*	*having-taken*	*rejoicing*	*may-make.*	*But*

tumbha-r	ē	santān	kaśabī-mānaṅka	saṅga-rē
your	*his*	*offspring*	*harlots-of*	*company-in*

ତୁମ୍ଭର ସମ୍ପତ୍ତି ଖାଇ ପକାଇ ଅଛି ତୁମ୍ଭେ ତାହା ଲାଗି ଉତ୍ତମ ଖାଦ୍ୟ ପ୍ରସ୍ତୁତ କରିଅଛ। ତହିଁରେ ସେ କହିଲା ବାପ ତୁମ୍ଭେ ସବୁ ସମୟରେ ଆମ୍ଭ ସଙ୍ଗରେ ଅଛ ଆଉ ଆମ୍ଭର ଯାହା କିଛି ଅଛି ସମସ୍ତ ତୁମ୍ଭର କିନ୍ତୁ ଆନନ୍ଦ କରି ଓ ଉଲ୍ଲାସିତ ହେବା ଉଚିତ ହୋଇଅଛି। କାରଣ ତୁମ୍ଭର ଏହି ଭାଇ ମରି ଯାଇଥିଲା ବଞ୍ଚିଅଛି ହଜିଯାଇଥିଲା ପାଇଲୁ। ପାଇଅଛି।—

tumbha-r	sampatti	khāi	pakāi-achhi,	tumbhē
your	*wealth*	*having-eaten*	*has-wasted,*	*you*

tāhā-lāgi	uttama	khādya	prastut	kari-achha.'
him-for	*excellent*	*food*	*ready*	*made-have.'*

Tahī̃-rē	sē	kahilā,	'bāp,	tumbhē	sabu
Thereon	*he*	*said,*	*'my-dear-son,*	*you*	*all*

samaya-rē	āmbha	saṅga-rē	achha,	ār
time-in	*my*	*company-in*	*are,*	*and*

āmbha-r	ǰāhā	kichhi	achhi,	samasta	tumbha-ra;
mine	*what*	*anything*	*is,*	*all*	*yours (is);*

kintu	ānanda	karā,	ō	ullaśita	huyā	saṅgat
but	*rejoicing*	*making,*	*and*	*merry*	*being*	*proper*

hēu-achhi,	kāraṇ	tumbha-r	ēi	bhāi	mari
being-is,	*because*	*your*	*this*	*brother*	*having-died*

ǰāi-thilā,	bañchi-achhi;	haji	ǰāi-thilā,	pāoyā
gone-was,	*survived-has;*	*having-been-lost*	*gone-was,*	*found*

ǰāi-achhi.'
gone-is.'

BHATRĪ.

The Bhatrās or Bhat'rās are an aboriginal tribe found almost solely in the north-east of the State of Bastar, between the Raipur and the Jagdalpur Zamindaries. They are cultivators, and a good many of them have the privilege of wearing the sacred thread. The number of Bhat'rās here found is 32,990. Ninety-seven more of them are found in British territory, so that the total number of the tribe according to the Census of 1891 was 33,087. They are said to be a sept of the Bastar Gōṇḍs, and Bhatrī, or more properly Bhat'rī, their language, has hitherto been classed as a form of Gōṇḍī. I have been able to obtain very little information about the tribe. Sherring in his *Hindu Tribes and Castes* (Vol. ii., p. 148) devotes three or four lines to it. Mr. Hislop, in the vocabulary printed in *Papers relating to the Aboriginal Tribes of the Central Provinces* gives a few words of what he names Bhatráin, and more full particulars are given on p. 41 of Part II of the *Report* of the Ethnological Committee of the Jubbulpore Exhibition of 1866-67. On pages 1, 10, and 12 of Part III of the same *Report* there are vocabularies of Parji and Bhatri, which are treated as one and the same language. On p. 141 of the Census Report of the Central Provinces for 1891, Mr. Robertson with some hesitation classes Bhatrī as a Gōṇḍ dialect, but points out that Colonel Glasfurd considers it to be a form of Haḷabī. The latter officer's *Report on the dependency of Bastar*[1] contains a Bhuttra or Purja Vocabulary.

The following specimen will show quite clearly that Bhatrī is really a corrupt form of Oṛiyā, with a few Marāṭhī and Chattīsgaṛhī forms intermingled. It may be taken as the connecting link between that language and Halabi, which is a mixture of Marāṭhī and Chhattīsgaṛhī. The specimens given in the Report of the Ethnological Committee are apparently nearly all Dravidian words, and this is probably due to Bhatrī having been confounded by the Committee with Parjī, which latter, as the specimens which I have received show, is a Dravidian form of speech.

According to the Census of 1891, the total number of speakers of Bhatrī is 29,396, all of whom inhabit the Bastar State. For the purposes of this Survey, the Bastar State has returned 17,387 speakers of the dialect. It must be explained that 8,000 speakers of Bhatrī were also returned from the district of Chhindwara, but subsequent enquiry has shown that this is a mistake. There are no Bhat'rās in the district. The following specimen, which comes from Bastar, is a version of the Parable of the Prodigal Son.

It will be observed that it is written in the Dēva-Nāgarī, and not in the Oṛiyā character. A comparison with the list of words on pp. 441 and ff. will show that Marāṭhī forms can be used much more freely than appears from the specimen. Note how this dialect omits aspirates. For instance *ūkum*, not *hūkum*, is 'an order,' and *āchē*, not *achhē*, is 'is.' Compare *hōelā*, *haulā*, and *ōelā*, all meaning 'he' or 'I became.'

[1] Selections from the Records of the Government of India, Foreign Department, No. 39, Calcutta, 1863.

[No. 9.]

INDO-ARYAN FAMILY.

EASTERN GROUP.

ORIYĀ.

BHATRĪ DIALECT. (STATE BASTAR.)

कोनी मनुखर दुइ गोटा बेटा रला। हँय भीतर सान पीला बूबा-की बलला ये बूबा धन भीतर जे मोर भाग रले ता-कि मो-कि देस। तेबे हँय हँय-मन-की धन बाँट देला। खूब दिन ना होइ रला सान बेटा सब-की गोटकी थाने बनाइ-करि दूरि देश उठि-गला और हँय ठाने फंदी होइ-करि दिन सारते आपनार धन-की उड़ाइ-देला। जेबे हँय सब-के सारला तेबे हँय राज-में बहुत भूख पड़ला और हँय गरीब होइला। और हँय पुरथी कहारी घरे जाइ-करि गोटकोर घरे थेबला। हँय मनुख आपनार बेड़ा-में बर्या चरायकि पठाइला। और हँय जे गोटा-की बर्या खायतो-रला ता-के खाइ-करि पेट भरबा काजे खोजते-रला। और कोई ता-की काई ना देते-रला। तेबे ता-की चेत पड़ला और हँय बलला मोर बूबा घर कतेक भूती लोगर खाइबार ठाने बाचसी आसे और मैं भूखि मरबी आचे। मैं उठि करि मोर बूबा लगे जीबी और ता-की बलबी ये बूबा भगवानर हुकुम ना मानलु और तमर पूरे पाप करली। फेर तमर बेटा बलबार डौल ना होइला। मो-की आपनार भुतिआर संग-में गोट-की समान बनाइ-दीयास। तेबे हँय उठि-करि आपनार बाप लगे गला। तेबे हँय खूबे दूर रला तेबे तार बाप ता-की देख-करि मया करला औरि पराइ-करि तार टोडरा पोटारि-करि चुमला। बेटा ता-की बलला बूबा मुये भगवानर हुकुम ना मानली और तुम्हर पूरे पाप करली औरि मैं तुम्हर बेटा बोलाइबार डौल ना होला। बूबा आपनार कबाड़ी-की बलला सब-ले नगद फटई हिटाइ-करि ता-की पिंधाहा औरि तार हाथे मुन्दी और गोड़े पन्हई पिंधाहा। और चमीं खाई-करि हरिख करबू। मोर बेटा मरि-रला फेर जीव पड़ला। हजि-जाइ-रला फेर मिलला। तेबे हँय हरिख करबा-धाचत॥

तार बड़े बेटा बेड़ा में रला। औरि जेबे हँय आसबा बेरा घर कठा धमरला बाजार नाचर गजर सुनला। और हँय कबाड़ी भीतर गोटक-

माने बुलाइ-करि पचारला ए काए-गोटा घाय है। हकी बलला तुम्हर भाई आसला-आचे और तुम्हर बाप नंगद राँधा बनाइला अतक थाने की हकी नीको पाइला। हतोले हँय रौस करला भीतरी जीबार मन ना करला। तार बूबा बाहर आसि-करि ता-की मनाएला। हँय तार बूबा बलला देखो मैँ अतक बरस-ले तुम्हर सेवा करबी-आचे आउरि तुम्हर ऊकुम-की केबे ना पेलली। आउरि तुम्ही मो-की केबे गोटक मेड़ा पीला बले ना देलीस की मैँ मोहरी मैँतर संगे हरिख करती। हतोले तुम्हर ए बेटा किसबिन संगे तुम्हर धन खाइ-पकाएला जड़क दाँई आसला अड़क दाँई तुम्ही तार काजे नगद राँधा बनाइलास। बूबा ता-की बलला ए बेटा तुय मोर संगे संग आचिस। जे मोर आए हँय तोहरी आए। तेबे आनन्द और हरिख होएबार आए कमतार तोर भाई मरि रला फेर जीवला हजि रला फेर मिलला ॥

[No. 9.]

INDO-ARYAN FAMILY. EASTERN GROUP.

OṚIYĀ.

BHATRĪ DIALECT. (STATE BASTAR.)

TRANSLITERATION AND TRANSLATION.

Kōnī manukhar dui gōṭā bēṭā ralā. Hãy bhītar sān
A-certain man-of two individuals sons were. Them among the-younger

pilā būbā-kē ballā, 'yē būbā, dhan bhītar jē mōr bhāg
child the-father-to said, 'O father, the-wealth amidst what my share

ralē tā-kē mō-kē dēs.' Tēbē hãy hãy-man-kē dhan bā̃ṭi
may-be that me-to give.' Then he them-to the-wealth having-divided

dēlā. Khūb din nā hōi ralā sān bēṭā sab-kē goṭkī
gave. Many days not having-been were the-younger son everything one

thānē banāi-kari dūr dēś uṭhi galā, aur hãy
place-in having-made a-far country(-to) having-arisen went, and that

ṭhānē phandī hōi-kari, din sārtē, āpnār dhan-kē uṛāi-dēlā.
place-in debauched having-become, days spending, his-own wealth squandered.

Jēbē hãy sab-kē sārlā, tēbē hãy rāj-mē̃ bahut bhūkh paṛlā, aur
When he everything spent, then that kingdom-in much hunger fell, and

hãy garib hōelā. Aur hãy purthī kahāṛī gharē jāi-kari
he poor became. And that country some house-in having-gone

goṭkōr gharē theblā. Hãy manukh āpnār bēṛā-mē̃
of-a-certain-man the-house-in joined-himself. That man his-own field-in

baryā charāy-kē paṭhāelā. Aur hãy jē gōṭā-kē baryā khāytō-ralā,
swine feeding-for sent(-him). And he what things the-swine eating-were,

tā-kē khāi-kari pēṭ bharbā kājē khojtē-ralā. Aur kōī
those having-eaten his-belly filling for wishing-was. And any-one

tā-kē kāī nā dētē-ralā. Tēbē tā-kē chēt paṛlā, aur hãy
him-to anything not giving-was. Then him-to sense fell, and he

ballā, 'mōr būbā ghar katek bhūtī lōgar khāibār ṭhānē
said, 'my father('s) house(-in) how-many hired persons-of eating-of than

bāchsī āsē, aur maĩ bhūkhē marbī-āchē. Maĩ uṭhi-kari mōr
excess comes, and I hunger-by perishing-am. I having-arisen my

būbā lagē jībī, aur tā-kē balbī, "Yē būbā, Bhagawānar
father near will-go, and him-to I-will-say, "O father, God-of

ūkum nā mānlu, aur tamar pūrē pāp karlī. Phēr tamar
the-command not obeyed, and thee-of before sin I-did. Any-more thy

bēṭā balbār ḍaul nā ōelā. Mō-kē āpnār bhutiār
son being-called-of worthy not I-became. Me thine-own hired-servants-of

saṅg-mẽ gōṭ-kē samān banāi-diyās."' Tēbē hãy uṭhi-kari āp^{a}nār
company-in one like make."' Then he having-arisen his-own

bāp lagē galā. Tēbē hãy khūbē dūr ralā tēbē tār bāp tā-kē
father near went. Then he very distant was then his father him

dēkhi-kari mayā kar^{a}lā, auri parāi-kari tār ṭoḍ^{a}rā poṭāri-kari
having-seen compassion made, and having-run his neck having-embraced

chum^{a}lā. Bēṭā tā-kē bal^{a}lā, 'būbā, muyē Bhagawānar ūkum nā
kissed. The-son him-to said, 'father, I God-of the-command not

mān^{a}lī, aur tumhar pūrē pāp kar^{a}lī, auri maĩ tumhar bēṭā bolāebār
obeyed, and thee-of before sin did, and I thy son being-called-of

ḍaul nā haulā.' Būbā āp^{a}nār kabāṛī-kē bal^{a}lā, 'sab-lē nagad
worthy not became.' The-father his-own servants-to said, 'all-than good

phaṭaī hiṭāi-kari tā-kē pĩdhāhā; auri tār hāthē mundī aur
robe having-brought-forth him-to put-on; and his hand-on a-ring and

gōṛē panhaī pĩdhāhā. Auri amĩ khāi-kari harikh kar^{a}bũ. Mōr
feet-on shoes put-on. And we having-eaten rejoicing will-do. My

bēṭā mari-ralā, phēr jīw-paṛ^{a}lā; haji-jāi-ralā, phēr mil^{a}lā.' Tēbē
son dead-was, again alive-has-become; lost-gone-was, again was-found.' Then

hãy harikh kar^{a}bā āchat.
they rejoicing doing were.

Tār baṛē bēṭā bēṛā-mẽ ralā. Auri jēbē hãy ās^{a}bā
His elder son the-field-in was. And when he coming(-of)

bērā ghar kaṭhā amar^{a}lā, bājār nāchar gajar
time(-at) the-house near approached, music-of dancing-of noise

sun^{a}la. Aur hãy kabāṛī bhītar gōṭak mānē bulāi-kari
he-heard. And he the-servants among a-certain man having-called

pachār^{a}lā, 'Ē kāē gōṭā āy-hai?' Hakē bal^{a}lā, 'tumhar bhāi
enquired, 'This what thing is-being?' Him-to he-said, 'thy brother

ās^{a}lā-āchē, aur tumhar bāp naṅgad rā̃dhā banāilā, atak ānē
has-come, and thy father excellent feast made, this because

kī hakē nīkō pāilā.' Hatī-le hãy rīs kar^{a}lā; bhitarī
that him safe he-found.' But he anger made; within

jībār man nā kar^{a}lā. Tār būbā bāhar āsi-kari tā-kē
going-of mind not he-made. His father outside having-come him

manāelā. Hãy tār būbā bal^{a}lā, 'dēkhō, maĩ atak baras-lē
entreated. He his father said, 'see, I so-many years-from

tumhar sēwā kar^{a}bī-āchē, āuri tumhar ūkum-kē kēbē nā pel^{a}lī.
thy service am-doing, and thy command ever not disobeyed.

Āuri tumhī mō-kē kēbē gōṭak mēṛā-pilā balē nā dēlis kī
And thou me-to ever a-single goat-young-one even not gavest that

maĩ moh^{a}rī maītar saṅgē harikh kar^{a}tī. Hatī-lē tumhar
I my friends with rejoicing might-have-made. But thy

ē bēṭā kisᵃbin saṅgē tumhar dhan khāi-pakāelā, jaṛak-dā̃ī āsᵃla,
this son harlots with thy wealth has-devoured, as-soon-as he-came,
aṛak-dā̃ī tumhī tār kājē nagad rā̃dhā banāilās.' Būbā
so-soon thou his sake-for an-excellent feast madest.' The-father
tā-kē balᵃlā, 'ē bēṭā, tuy mōr saṅgē-saṅg āchis; jē mōr
him-to said, 'O son, thou me-of with art; what mine
āē, hā̃y tohᵃrī āē. Tēbē ānand aur harikh hōebār
is, that thine-even is. Then merriment and rejoicing being-of (propriety)
āē, kamᵃtār tōr bhāī mari-ralā, phēr jīwᵃlā; haji-ralā, phēr
is, because thy brother dead-was, again lived; lost-was, again
milᵃlā.'
was-found.'

LIST OF STANDARD WORDS AND SENTENCES IN ORIYĀ.

English.	Oṛiyā (Standard of Puri).	Bhatri.
1. One	Eka	Gōṭōk.
2. Two	Dui	Dui gōṭā.
3. Three	Tini	Tin.
4. Four	Chāri	Chār.
5. Five	Pā̃cha	Pā̃ts.
6. Six	Chha	Chhō.
7. Seven	Sāta	Sāt.
8. Eight	Āṭha	Āṭh.
9. Nine	Naa	Nau.
10. Ten	Daśa	Das.
11. Twenty	Kōḍiē	Bis.
12. Fifty	Pachāś	Pachās.
13. Hundred	Śaē	San.
14. I	Mũ	Mui.
15. Of me	Mōra	Mōtsō (*Marāṭhī genitive*)
16. Mine	Mōra	Mōtsō.
17. We	Āmbhēmānē	Hamī.
18. Of us	Āmbhamānaṅkara	Hamar.
19. Our	Āmbhamānaṅkara	Hamar.
20. Thou	Tũ	Tui.
21. Of thee	Tōra	Tutsō (*Marāṭhī genitive*)
22. Thine	Tōra	Tōr (*Oṛiyā genitive*).
23. You	Tumbhē	Tui, tumī.
24. Of you	Tumbhar	Tutsō (*Marāṭhī genitive*).
25. Your	Tumbhar	Tumhar (*Oṛiyā genitive*).

English.	Oṛiyā (Standard of Purī).	Bhatri.
26. He	Sē	Hun, hāy.
27. Of him	Tāhāra	Hun-kē (*Chhattīsgaṛhī genitive*).
28. His	Tāhāra	Hun-kē.
29. They	Sēmāne	Hun-man, hāy-man.
30. Of them	Sēmānaṅkara	Hun-man-kē.
31. Their	Sēmānaṅkara	Hun-man-kē.
32. Hand	Hāta	Hā̃th.
33. Foot	Pāda	Pā̃y.
34. Nose	Nāka	Nāk.
35. Eye	Ākhi	Ā̃khī.
36. Mouth	Pāṭi	Mū.
37. Tooth	Dānta	Dā̃t.
38. Ear	Kāna	Kān.
39. Hair	Bāla *or* kēśa	Kē̃s.
40. Head	Muṇḍa	Mūṇḍ.
41. Tongue	Jibha	Jībh.
42. Belly	Pēṭa	Peṭ.
43. Back	Piṭhi	Pīṭh.
44. Iron	Luhā	Lōhā.
45. Gold	Suna	Sōn.
46. Silver	Rūpā	Rūp.
47. Father	Bāpa	Bābā.
48. Mother	Mā	Āyā.
49. Brother	Bhāi	Bhāī.
50. Sister	Bhauṇi	Bahin.
51. Man	Manushya	Manukh.
52. Woman	Māikinia	Bāilī.

English.	Oṛiyā (Standard of Puri).	Bhatri.
53. Wife . . .	Māipa	Bāīh.
54. Child . . .	Pilā	Lōkā.
55. Son . . .	Puā	Pilā.
56. Daughter . . .	Jhia	Lōkī.
57. Slave . . .	Dāsa	Kabāḍī.
58. Cultivator . .	Chashā	Kisān.
59. Shepherd . . .	Mēṇḍha-rākhuāla . .	Dhōrai.
60. God . . .	Paramēśwar *or* Īśwar .	Bhagᵃwān.
61. Devil . . .	Asura *or* Saitān . .	Ḍūmā.
62. Sun . . .	Sūrjya	Sūruj.
63. Moon . .	Chandra . . .	Chāndā.
64. Star . . .	Tārā *or* tarā . . .	Tārā.
65. Fire . . .	Niā	Jōy.
66. Water . . .	Pāṇi	Pāni.
67. House . . .	Ghara	Ghar.
68. Horse . . .	Ghōḍā	Ghōḍā.
69. Cow . .	Gāi	Gāy.
70. Dog . . .	Kukkura . . .	Kukūr.
71. Cat . . .	Bilāi	Bilai.
72. Cock . . .	Kukuḍā . . .	Gānjā.
73. Duck . . .	Pāti-hangsa . .	Hãsa.
74. Ass . . .	Gadha	Gadᵃhā.
75. Camel . . .	Ōṭa	Hũṭ.
76. Bird . . .	Chaḍhāi . . .	Chirai.
77. Go	Jāa	Jānā (? *infinitive*).
78. Eat	Khāa	Khānā.
79. Sit	Basa	Bas.

English.	Oṛiyā (Standard of Puri).	Bhatrī.
80. Come	Āsa	Āwᵃtā.
81. Beat	Māra	Pōṭᵃnā.
82. Stand	Ṭhiā hua	Thiyā.
83. Die	Mara	Marūn-gēlā (*Marāṭhī past tense*).
84. Give	Dia	Dēun-dēs.
85. Run	Daüḍa	Parā.
86. Up	Uparē	Upᵃrē.
87. Near	Nikūṭarē	Lagē.
88. Down	Talē	Khālē.
89. Far	Dūra	Khubē dūr.
90. Before	Āgē	Āgē.
91. Behind	Pachhē	Pāṭᵃbāṭē.
92. Who	Kiē	Kaun.
93. What	Kaaṇa	Kaun.
94. Why	Kāhũki	Kāy-kājē.
95. And	Ebang	Aur.
96. But	Kintu	...
97. If	Jadi	...
98. Yes	Hã	Hōy.
99. No	Nāhĩ	Nāhī.
100. Alas	Hāya	Āhā.
101. A father	Eka bāpa	Bābā.
102. Of a father	Eka bāpara	Bāp-tsō.[1]
103. To a father	Eka bāpa-ku	Bāp-tsō.
104. From a father	Eka bāpa-ṭhāru	Bāp-lagēlē.
105. Two fathers	Dui bāpa	Duīg ṭhā bāp.
106. Fathers	Pitṛu-lōka	Bābā-man.

[1] Here, and elsewhere in the list, Marāṭhī forms are given, but Oṛiyā ones are also used. See, for instance, the specimen.

English.	Oṛiyā (Standard of Purī).	Bhatrī.
107. Of fathers	Pitṛu-lōkaṅkaru	Bābā-man-taō.
108. To fathers	Pitṛu-lōkaṅku	Bābā-man-taō.
109. From fathers	Pitṛu-lōkaṅka-ṭhāru	Bābā-man-lagēlē.
110. A daughter	Gōṭiē jhia	Lēkī.
111. Of a daughter	Gōṭiē jhiara	Lēkī-taō.
112. To a daughter	Gōṭiē jhia-ku	Lēkī-taō.
113. From a daughter	Gōṭiē jhia-ṭhāru	Lēkī-lagēlē.
114. Two daughters	Jōḍiē jhia	Duī gōṭā lēkī.
115. Daughters	Jhia-mānē	Lēkī-man.
116. Of daughters	Jhia-mānaṅkara	Lēkī-man-kē.
117. To daughters	Jhia-mānaṅku	Lēkī-man-kē.
118. From daughters	Jhia-mānaṅka-ṭhāru	Lēki-man-lagēlē.
119. A good man	Jaṇē bhala lōka	Nīkō manukh.
120. Of a good man	Jaṇē bhala lōkara	Nīkō manukh taō.
121. To a good man	Jaṇē bhala lōka-ku	Nīkō manukh-taō.
122. From a good man	Jaṇē bhala lōka-ṭhāru	Nīkō manukh-lagēlē.
123. Two good men	Dui jaṇa bhala lōka	Duī gōṭā nikō manukh.
124. Good men	Bhala lōka-mānē	Nīkō manukh-man.
125. Of good men	Bhala lōka-mānaṅkara	Nīkō manukh-man-taō.
126. To good men	Bhala lōka-mānaṅku	Nīkō manukh-man-taō.
127. From good men	Bhala lōka-mānaṅka-ṭhāru	Nīkō manukh-man-lagēlē.
128. A good woman	Bhala māi piṭiē *or* jaṇē bhala strī.	Nīkō bāilī.
129. A bad boy	Jaṇē manda bālaka	Aḍᵃrā pīlā.
130. Good women	Bhala māikiniā-mānē *or* bhala strī-mānē.	Nīkō bāilī-man.
131. A bad girl	Gōṭiē manda bālikā	Aḍᵃrā lēkī.
132. Good	Bhala	Nīkō.
133. Better	Apekhyā kṛuta bhala	Khubē nīkō.

English.	Oṛiyā (Standard of Puri).	Bhatrī.
134. Best . . .	Sabu-ṭhāru bhala . .	Jugē nīkō.
135. High . . .	Uchcha	Ū̃ch.
136. Higher . . .	Uchchatara . . .	Khubē ū̃ch.
137. Highest . . .	Uchchatama . . .	Jugē ū̃ch.
138. A horse . . .	Gōṭiē ghōḍā . . .	Ghōḍā.
139. A mare . . .	Gōṭiē ghōḍī . . .	Ghōḍī.
140. Horses . .	Ghōḍā-mānē . . .	Khubē ghōḍā.
141. Mares . . .	Ghōḍī-mānē . . .	Khubē ghōḍī.
142. A bull . . .	Gōṭāē saṇḍha . . .	Buyal.
143. A cow . . .	Gōṭāē gāi . . .	Gāy.
144. Bulls . . .	Saṇḍha-mānē . . .	Khubē buyāl.
145. Cows . . .	Gāi-sabu *or* gāi-mānē .	Khubē gāy.
146. A dog . . .	Gōṭiē kukkura . .	Kukūr.
147. A bitch . . .	Gōṭiē māi kukkura . .	Kutᵃrī.
148. Dogs . . .	Kukkura-sabu *or* kukkura-mānē.	Jugē kukūr.
149. Bitches . . .	Māi kukkura-sabu . .	Jugē kutᵃrī.
150. A he goat . .	Gōṭiē aṇḍirā chhēli . .	Bōkᵃrā.
151. A female goat . .	Gōṭiē māi chhēli . .	Chhērī.
152. Goats . . .	Chhēli-sabu . . .	Jugē bōkᵃrā.
153. A male deer . .	Gōṭāē aṇḍirā hariṇa .	Kōḍᵃrā.
154. A female deer . .	Gōṭāē māi hariṇa . .	Kōḍᵃrī.
155. Deer . . .	Hariṇa	Jugē kōḍᵃrā.
156. I am . . .	Mũ huē, mũ achhi, āmbhē hēũ *or* āmbhē achhũ.	Mui āsē.
157. Thou art . . .	Tũ hua, achhu; tumbhē hua, achha.	Tui āsis.
158. He is . . .	Sē huē, achhi, huanti, achhanti.	Hun āsē.
159. We are . . .	Āmbhēmānē hēũ, achhũ .	Hamī āchhũ.
160. You are . . .	Tumbhēmānē hua, achha .	Tumī āchhat.

English.	Oṛiyā (Standard of Puri).	Bhatri.
161. They are	Sēmānē huanti, achhanti	Hun āsē.
162. I was	Mũ thili	Mui ralā.
163. Thou wast	Tũ thilu	Tui ralā.
164. He was	Sē thilā	Hun ralā.
165. We were	Āmbhēmānē thilũ	Hamī ralō.
166. You were	Tumbhēmānē thila	Tumī ralā.
167. They were	Sēmānē thilē	Hun-man ralō.
168. Be	Hua	Hōun.
169. To be	Hēbā-ku	
170. Being	Hēu	
171. Having been	Hōi	
172. I may be	Mũ hōi pāri	Mui hōy-dē.
173. I shall be	Mũ hēbi	Mui hōībī.
174. I should be	Mōra ḥēbā uchita	Mui hỗy-dē.
175. Beat	Māra	Mārªbī.
176. To beat	Māribā-ku	Mārªbī.
177. Beating	Māru	Mārªtōr.
178. Having beaten	Māri	Mārun bhātī.
179. I beat	Mũ mārẽ, māri	Mui mārªbī.
180. Thou beatest	Tũ māru	Tui mārªbī.
181. He beats	Sē mārē	Hun mārªsī.
182. We beat	Āmbhēmānē mārũ	Hamī mārªbī.
183. You beat	Tumbhēmānē māra	Tumī mārªbis.
184. They beat	Sēmānē māranti	Hun-man mārªsī
185. I beat (*Past Tense*)	Mũ mārili	Mui mārªlī.
186. Thou beatest (*Past Tense*).	Tũ mārilu	Tui mārªlī.
187. He beat (*Past Tense*)	Sē mārilā	Hāy mārªlī.

English.	Oṛiyā (Standard of Puri).	Bhatrī.
188. We beat (*Past Tense*) .	Āmbhēmānē mārilū̃ .	Hamī mār^{a}lū̃.
189. You beat (*Past Tense*)	Tumbhēmānē mārila .	Tumī mār^{a}lū̃.
190. They beat (*Past Tense*)	Sēmānē mārilē . .	Hāy mār^{a}las.
191. I am beating . .	Mū̃ māṛuachhi . .	Mui mār^{a}bī.
192. I was beating . .	Mū̃ māruthili . . .	Mui mār^{a}tē ralī.
193. I had beaten . .	Mū̃ mārithili . . .	Mui mār^{a}li āyē.
194. I may beat . .	Mū̃ māri pāri . . .	Mui mārendē.
195. I shall beat . .	Mū̃ māribi . . .	Mui mār^{a}bī.
196. Thou wilt beat . .	Tū̃ māribu . . .	Tui mār^{a}bis.
197. He will beat . .	Sē māriba . . .	Hāy mār^{a}bis.
198. We shall beat . .	Āmbhēmānē māribū̃ . .	Hamī mār^{a}bū̃.
199. You will beat . .	Tumbhēmānē māriba .	Tumī mār^{a}bās.
200. They will beat . .	Sēmānē māribē . .	Hāy man mār^{a}bās.
201. I should beat .	Mōra māribā uchita . .	Mū̃i mārendē.
202. I am beaten . .	Mū̃ māra khāi . . .	Mō-kē mār^{a}lāsat.
203. I was beaten . .	Mū̃ māra khāithili .	Mō-kē mārun-ralā.
204. I shall be beaten .	Mū̃ māra khāibi . .	Mō-kē mār-dē.
205. I go . . .	Mū̃ jāi	Mui jāy-sē.
206. Thou goest . .	Tū̃ jāu	Tui jāy-sē.
207. He goes . . .	Sē jāē	Hun jāy-sē.
208. We go	Āmbhēmānē jāū̃ . .	Hamī jibū̃ āchhē.
209. You go . . .	Tumbhēmānē jāa . .	Tumī jibā ās.
210. They go . . .	Sēmānē jānti . . .	Hāy-man jibā āchhē.
211. I went . . .	Mū̃ jāithili, gali . .	Mui gēlō.
212. Thou wentest . .	Tū̃ jāithilu, galu . .	Tui gēlō.
213. He went . . .	Sē jāithilā, galā . .	Hun gēlō.
214. We went	Āmbhēmānē jāithilū̃, galū̃	Hamī gēlū̃.

English.	Oṛiyā (Standard of Puri).	Bhatri.
215. You went	Tumbhēmānē jāithila, gala	Tumi gēlās.
216. They went	Sēmānē jāithilā, galē	Hày-man gēlāy.
217. Go	Jāa	Jāa.
218. Going	Jāu	Jāsla.
219. Gone	Jāi	Gēlō.
220. What is your name?	Tumbhara nã̄ kaaṇa?	Tu-tsō nā̃v kāy?
221. How old is this horse?	E ghōḍāra bayasa kētē?	Yē ghōḍā kitᵃlō baraksh-tsō āsē?
222. How far is it from here to Kashmir?	Kāśmir ē-ṭhāru kētē dūra?	Yahā̃lē Kāśmir kitᵃlō dūr āsē?
223. How many sons are there in your father's house?	Tumbha-bāpa-gharē kētēli pua achhanti?	Tutsō bāp-gharē kitᵃrō lēkā āsat?
224. I have walked a long way to-day.	Mū̃ āji bēsi bāṭa chālichhi	Mui āj lāpē dūr chalē̃u.
225. The son of my uncle is married to his sister.	Mōra khuḍutā-puā bhāi tāra bhaüṇi-ku bibhā hōi-achhi.	Mōtsō kakātsō lēkātsō bibāv huntsō bahin saṅgē hali.
226. In the house is the saddle of the white horse.	Dhalā ghōḍāra jin gharē achhi.	Ghar-bhitᵃrē paṇḍrā ghōḍā-tsō khāṭhi āsē.
227. Put the saddle upon his back.	Tā piṭhi-rē jin kaaha.	Hun-tsō pāṭ-ūpᵃrē kāṭhi-kē rākhā.
228. I have beaten his son with many stripes.	Mū̃ tā pua-ku bahut māṛa mārichhi.	Mui hū̃n-tsō lēkā-kē khūbē mārᵃli.
229. He is grazing cattle on the top of the hill.	Sē pāhāḍa upari gōru charāu-achhi.	Huni gōhᵃḍikē hun ṭikᵃrā upᵃrē charāy-si āchhē.
230. He is sitting on a horse under that tree.	Sē gachha-mūlē gōṭiē ghōḍā uparē basi-achhi.	Huni hun rūkh-khālē ghōḍā-upᵃrē basᵃlā āsē.
231. His brother is taller than his sister.	Tāhāra bhāi tāhāra bhaüṇi-ṭhāru ḍēṅga.	Hun-tsō bhāi hun-tsō bahin-lē ḍēṅg āsē.
232. The price of that is two rupees and a half.	Tāhāra dām aḍhēi ṭaṅkā	Hun-tsō mōl dui rupayā āṭh ānā āsē.
233. My father lives in that small house.	Mōra bāpa sēbi sāna ghara-ṭi-rē rahē.	Mōtsō bābā huni nāni ghar-mē rah-si āchhē.
234. Give this rupee to him	Tā-ku ē ṭaṅkā dia	Yē rupayā hun-kē diyās
235. Take those rupees from him.	Tā-ṭhāru sē ṭaṅkā-sabu nia	Hun rupayā-kē hun-sē māṅgā.
236. Beat him well and bind him with ropes.	Tā-ku khub māra ō daüḍi-rē bāndha.	Hun-kē khūb mārā aur ḍōri-saṅgē bāndhā.
237. Draw water from the well.	Kua-ru pāṇi kāḍha	Chūālē pāni nikᵃrāwā.
238. Walk before me	Mō āga-rē chāla	Mōtsō parālē jāo.
239. Whose boy comes behind you?	Tumbha pachha-rē kāhā pua āsu-achhi?	Kōtsō lēkā tumtsō pāṭhᵃlē jāy-si āchhē.
240. From whom did you buy that?	Kāhā-ṭhāru tā-ku kinila?	Tumhi hunkē kā-tsō-lagālē gēnᵃlās?
241. From a shopkeeper of the village.	Gā̃ra jaṇē dōkāni-ṭhāru	Gā̃o-tsō gōṭōk rōjᵃgāri-ṭhān-lē.

VOLUME V—PART II.

Page 18, line 11.—I find that Father Antonio's translation was not into Chhikā-chhikī Bōlī, but was into ordinary Western Hindī. For further particulars, see the Addenda Minora to page 96.

Page 19, Heading IV.—GENERAL LITERATURE. *Add* the following works dealing with Vidyāpati :—

NAGENDRA NATH GUPTA.—*Vidyāpati Ṭhākur.* *Journal* of the Asiatic Society of Bengal, Vol. lxxiii, 1904, Part I, Extra Number, pp. 20ff.

" " —*Vidyāpati Ṭhākurer Padāvalī.*—No. 24 of the series entitled the *Baṅgīya-sāhitya-parishad Granthāvalī.* Calcutta B. S. 1316 (=1909 A. D.). This is a very complete edition of Vidyāpati's songs, in the Bengali character, and with a full Introduction in the Bengali language. An edition in the Nāgari character was published at Allahabad by the Indian Press in 1910.

GRIERSON, G. A.—*Vidyāpati Ṭhākur.* *Journal* of the Asiatic Society of Bengal, New Series, Vol. I, p. 228. Remarks on Nagendra Nath Gupta's article in Vol. lxxiii, mentioned above.

Page 19, line 20 from below.—*For* 'Vol. xxviii', *read* 'Vol. lxxviii'.

Page 19, line 2 from below.—*For* 'vers.' *read* 'verse.'

Page 25, line 11 from below.—*For* 'this cart,' *read* 'his cart'.

Page 26, Pronouns.—The honorific oblique singular of *ī*, this, is *his*', and of *ō*, that, is *hun*'.

Page 41, line 15.—Since this was written, I have ascertained that the language of the western part of Mirzapur, including the Sadr Tahsil, and a part of Chunar Tahsil, is not Bhojpurī, but is the Awadhī dialect of Eastern Hindī. *See* Addenda Minora to Vol. VI, p. 1. The number of speakers of Awadhī in this tract is roughly estimated at about 350,000, and this amount should be deducted from the number of speakers of Bhojpurī in this volume.

Page 44.—In the table on this page, as explained in the Addenda to p. 41, alter the figures for Western Dialect from 3,939,500 to 3,589,500, and alter the Total from 16,776,937 to 16,426,937.

Page 47.—The following example of the use of the word 'Bhojpurī' may be added to those of 'Poorbeea' on this page :—

1789. Two days after, as a regiment of Sepoys on its way to Chunar-ghur, was marching through the City at daybreak, I went out, and was standing to see it pass by, the Regiment halted ; and a few men from the centre ran into a dark lane, and laid hold of a hen and some roots : the people screamed. " Do not make so much noise," said one of the men in his Bodjpooria Idiom ; "we go to-day with the Frenghees, but we are all servants (tenants) to Chëyt-Sing, and may come back to-morrow with him ; and then the question will be not about your roots, but about your wives and daughters." *Raymond*, Translation of the *Sëir Mutaqherin*, 2nd Ed., Translator's Preface, p. 8.

Page 96, line 8.—Up to the time of writing this passage, I had failed in identifying the Father Antonio here referred to. Since then, Father H. Hosten, S. J. has very kindly communicated to me the following particulars :—He was Father Antonio Pezzoni, a Capuchin, who came to India in 1806. His translation was not into the Chhikā-chhikī dialect of Maithilī, but into ordinary Western Hindī, written in the Nāgarī character. It consisted of the Pentateuch, the Psalms, the Gospels, the Acts and the Epistles. He also wrote many works of Catholic devotion, and was engaged on a Latin-Hindōstānī dictionary when he died at Lugano in 1844. According to Dr. Long in the Calcutta Review[1], the Rev. Dr. John, who wrote in 1809, mentioned the translations of the Gospels and the Acts, so that they must have been made within three years of Father Antonio's landing in India. He lived for many years in Bettiah, in the north of the Champaran District of Bihar, and there does not appear to be any record of his having made any lengthy stay in Bhagalpur. A copy of his Gospels and Acts (made in 1837) is still in Bettiah. Another copy is to be found in the Convent of the Native Nuns of Agra, and is dated 1844. Father Felix O. C., in a letter to 'The Examiner' (Bombay) published in the issue of December 13, 1913 (p. 495), states that he found a copy of the whole work in the Jesus and Mary Convent at Lahore, and that he had presented it to the Provincial of the Capuchins of the Swiss Province, Lucerne, where, at the time of his writing, it was kept. He had, moreover, in his own possession a copy of the manuscript of the New Testament only. Father Felix, in this letter, gives as a sample Father Antonio's version of the Magnificat. For further information, *see* also a letter from Father H. Hosten S. J. on pp. 435ff. of the 'Examiner' of November 1, 1913.

[1] Vol. V, p. 272. 1846. Not p. 722, as misprinted in the Text.

Page 238.—The following book gives specimens of the Sarwariā dialect :—

MANAN DWIVEDI GAJPURI, PAṆDIT.—*Sarwaria (A collection of folk tales and folk songs in Sarwaria dialect of Gorakhpur District).* Printed at the Jārj (George) Printing Works, Benares, 1913.

Page 326, Nos. 14, 15, and 16, Maithilī column.—Older forms, now not used are *mẽ*, I, and *mōr*, of me, mine.

Page 328, Nos. 14, 15, and 16, Bhojpurī column.—Older forms, not now in use, are *mẽ*, I, and *mōr*, of me, mine.

Page 330, No. 35, Magahī column.—Read 'ãkh'.

Page 332, No. 35, Bhojpurī column.—Read 'ãkh'.

Page 333, No. 51, Nagpuriā column.—Read 'ād^{a}mī'.

Page 334, No. 75, Maithilī column.—Read 'ड़'.

Page 338, No. 86, Magahī column.—Read 'uppar'.

Page 338, No. 94, Magahī column.—For 'kābe', *read* 'kābē'.

Page 341, No. 82, Nagpuriā column.—For 'thãṛh', *read* 'thāṛh'.

Page 342, No. 115, Magahī column.—For 'bĕtin', *read* 'bĕṭin'.

Page 344, No. 131, Bhojpurī column.—For 'laṛᵃkā', *read* 'laṛikī'.

Page 345, No. 129, Nagpuriā column.—For 'chŏṛā,' *read* 'chhŏṛā'.

Page 350, No. 161, Maithilī column.—For 'thikăh', *read* 'thikāh'.

Page 350, Nos. 179 and 181, Magahī column.—For 'pita', *read* 'piṭa'.

Page 353, Nagpuriā column, No. 179, read 'mārŏ-nā': *No. 184, read* 'mārai-nā'.

Page 358, No. 216, Maithilī column.—Read 'lokᵃni'.

Page 359, No. 215, Bhojpurī column.—For 'gaï', *read* 'gaïlā'.

ORIYĀ.

Pages 367ff.—I am indebted for the following corrected information regarding Oṛiya to the kindness of Babu Monmohan Chakravarti, a gentleman who served as Deputy Magistrate and Deputy Collector for several years in Orissa and in the adjoining District of Midnapore.

Page 367, lines 10ff of text from below.—The number of speakers of Oṛiyā in Binpur Thana of Midnapore is small. On the other hand there are many speakers of the language in Thana Narayangarh of that District. In the map facing p. 106 of Vol. V, Pt. I, the main language of the latter Thana is shown as South-Western Bengali. While this is correct, it must be understood that many speakers of Oṛiyā are to be found in the same tract.

Page 368, line 2.—I have fixed the point at which the southern limit of Oṛiyā touches the sea as near Barwa. This is so shown in the map facing page 367. Babu Monmohan Chakravarti is of opinion that it does not extend farther south than the station of Ichchapuram on the East Coast section of the Bengal-Nagpur Railway. Ichchapuram is marked 'Echapur' in the map facing page 367, and this would move the southern boundary of Oṛiyā about fifty miles to the north. My own statements on page 368 were based on reports received from Ganjam, and it is probable that between Barwa and Ichchapuram there is a debatable tract, in which both languages are spoken.

Page 369, line 20.—Regarding the Oṛiyā spoken in Cuttack Town, Babu Monmohan Chakravarti informs me that it has not been affected by Bengaliams. On the contrary, the speech of the Bengali settlers has been much changed by the surrounding Oṛiyā. The speech of the lower classes of the town has to some extent been affected by the bastard Urdū of the local Musalmāns, who represent settlers from up-country.

Page 369, line 30.—Babu Monmohan Chakravarti has given me the following additional notes on the Midnapore pronunciation :—'I think the speech of Contai Thana is in its skeleton Oṛiyā, but is otherwise so modified by the adjoining Bengali, as to be called a Bengalized dialect of Oṛiyā. The speech in Narayangarh and in Dantan Thanas closely approaches the dialect of North Balasore. In Thanas Gopiballabhpur and Jhargaon the pronunciation and apparently some of the grammatical terminations and words approach the hill dialect prevalent in Mayurbhanj and Keunjhar Tributary States.' Regarding the Oṛiyā of the south, he says, 'The Oṛiyā speech of Berhampore [in Ganjam] and downwards looks also like a separate dialect, differing to some extent from the Standard'.

Page 375.—*Add* to Authorities, List A.

McPherson, Sir Hugh, K.C.I.E., C.S.I.—*The Oṛiyā Alphabet. Journal* of the Bihar and Orissa Research Society, Vol. X (1924), pp. 168ff. Contains a full account of the Alphabet, with specimens of all conjunct consonants.

Page 378.—Section on pronunciation. Babu Monmohan Chakravarti gives me the following additional information :—In ordinary talk no distinction is made between long and short *i* and *ī*, or between *u* and *ū*.

Page 379, line 17.—The statement about the southern pronunciation of ଡ and ଢ is incorrect. When between vowels in the same word, these letters are everywhere pronounced as *ṛa* and *ṛha* not as *ḍa* and *ḍha*, respectively. The omission of a dot under them is purely a matter of writing, and does not indicate any variation of pronunciation. All that can be said about the southern pronunciation of these letters is that the further south we go, the stronger is the cerebralization. So also as regards the letter ଳ *ḷa*.

Page 380.—**Pronouns.** In the colloquial language, *āmmāne* is commonly used for *āmbhē-mānē*, and *tumē* for *tumbhē-mānē*.

Page 383.—It should be noted that the specimen from Cuttack on this page is from the pen of Babu Monmohan Chakravarti, and is hence of special value.

Page 398, line 22.—Regarding the pronunciation of the cerebral ଡ *ṛa* in Puri, *see* the remarks on page 379. So also in regard to what is said about this letter in line 32, lower down. The Puri spelling *pardila* is merely an attempt to represent the sound of *paṛila* in a new way.

Page 425.—Babu Monmohan Chakravarti informs me that this specimen from Dantan Thana of Midnapore is here and there Sanskritized, and is not in all places colloquial.

Page 441.—In the Addenda Majora will be found a Standard List of Words and Sentences in Oṛiyā which has been prepared by Babu Monmohan Chakravarti. It is more correct and is in a more colloquial style than that given on pp. 441ff.

You may also enjoy ...

Wandering Between Two Worlds: Essays on Faith and Art
Anita Mathias
Benediction Books, 2007
152 pages
ISBN: 0955373700

Available from www.amazon.com, www.amazon.co.uk
www.wanderingbetweentwoworlds.com

In these wide-ranging lyrical essays, Anita Mathias writes, in lush, lovely prose, of her naughty Catholic childhood in Jamshedpur, India; her large, eccentric family in Mangalore, a sea-coast town converted by the Portuguese in the sixteenth century; her rebellion and atheism as a teenager in her Himalayan boarding school, run by German missionary nuns, St. Mary's Convent, Nainital; and her abrupt religious conversion after which she entered Mother Teresa's convent in Calcutta as a novice. Later rich, elegant essays explore the dualities of her life as a writer, mother, and Christian in the United States--Domesticity and Art, Writing and Prayer, and the experience of being "an alien and stranger" as an immigrant in America, sensing the need for roots.

About the Author

Anita Mathias was born in India, has a B.A. and M.A. in English from Somerville College, Oxford University and an M.A. in Creative Writing from the Ohio State University. Her essays have been published in The Washington Post, The London Magazine, The Virginia Quarterly Review, Commonweal, Notre Dame Magazine, America, The Christian Century, Religion Online, The Southwest Review, Contemporary Literary Criticism, New Letters, The Journal, and two of HarperSanFrancisco's The Best Spiritual Writing anthologies. Her non-fiction has won fellowships from The National Endowment for the Arts; The Minnesota State Arts Board; The Jerome Foundation, The Vermont Studio Center; The Virginia Centre for the Creative Arts, and the First Prize for the Best General Interest Article from the Catholic Press Association of the United States and Canada. Anita has taught Creative Writing at the College of William and Mary, and now lives and writes in Oxford, England.
Website: www.anitamathias.com/
Blog: wanderingbetweentwoworlds.blogspot.com/

www.ingramcontent.com/pod-product-compliance
Lightning Source LLC
Chambersburg PA
CBHW020904100426
42737CB00043B/126

* 9 7 8 1 8 4 9 0 2 6 1 7 8 *